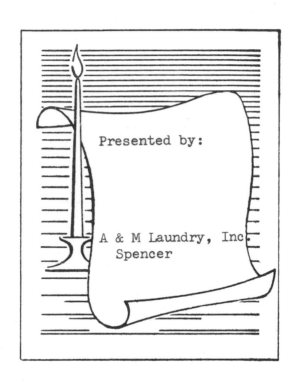

Presented by:

A & M Laundry, Inc.
Spencer

HAZLITT

Other Books by Ralph M. Wardle

Mary Wollstonecraft: A Critical Biography (1951)

Oliver Goldsmith (1957)

Edited:

Godwin and Mary: Letters of William Godwin and Mary Wollstonecraft (1966)

HAZLITT

by

Ralph M. Wardle

UNIVERSITY OF NEBRASKA PRESS · LINCOLN

Publishers on the Plains

UNP

Copyright © 1971 by the University of Nebraska Press

All rights reserved

International Standard Book Number 0–8032–0790–5

Library of Congress Catalog Card Number 75–130870

Manufactured in the United States of America

For Mary,
Again

Contents

A picture section follows page 242.

vii

Preface

"It has been made an objection to the biography of literary men," wrote William Hazlitt, himself a biographer and a literary man, in 1820, "that the principal events of their lives are their works; and that there is little else to be known of them, either interesting to others, or perhaps creditable to themselves. We do not feel the full force of this objection" (16:153). Five years later he remarked: "An author . . . may be full of inconsistencies elsewhere, but he is himself in his books" (12:370–71).

In writing his biography I have been guided by both statements. I have chronicled his life, from birth to death, in detail and have considered the impressions he made on contemporary critics and acquaintances. I have drawn more freely than earlier biographers on his surviving letters, especially those he wrote to Peter George Patmore when driven close to distraction by his hapless love for Sally Walker. And I have examined all his published works—which total some four million words—and have quoted generously from them.

Hazlitt has already been the subject of seven full-length biographies, two of which are outstanding. One of these, P. P. Howe's *Life of William Hazlitt*, is an excellent objective account, correcting and supplementing the findings of earlier biographers, but attempting little in the way of analysis or interpretation. The other, Herschel Baker's *William Hazlitt*, is a brilliant study of Hazlitt as thinker, concentrating on his productive years and viewing him against the intellectual background of his era.

My own aim is more modest. Because the character of Hazlitt has fascinated me ever since I first read his essays, I have focused my attention on his development as man and as writer, paying attention to the historical background or to his associates only when it seemed essential to my primary purpose of understanding the man himself. Although I cannot claim to have unearthed any startling new facts, I have had the advantage of materials not available to Howe and not within the concern of Baker.

I expected, when I began my work, to have access to Herschel M. Sikes's proposed edition of Hazlitt's letters. Because of Professor Sikes's unfortunate death, publication of that volume has been indefinitely postponed, and I have been obliged to quote from the various sources where Hazlitt's letters have appeared over the past century. I have drawn also on manuscript letters in the Yale University Library and the Lockwood Memorial Library of the State University of New York at Buffalo and am indebted to the officers of those libraries for granting me permission to quote from their papers. I am obliged also, for assistance and hospitality, to the staffs of the libraries at Cambridge and Harvard universities, the University of Nebraska at Lincoln and at Omaha, the British Museum, and the Royal Academy of Arts.

Inevitably I owe much to my predecessors in the field, notably P. P. Howe, Professor Baker, and Professor Ernest J. Moyne, editor of *The Journal of Margaret Hazlitt*. For replies to various queries I am grateful to Professor Willard H. Bonner, Mr. Alan Grove of the Maidstone Museum, Mr. David Piper of the National Portrait Gallery, Mr. D. S. Porter of the Bodleian Library, Mrs. J. Keeling Roberts of Wem, Shropshire, and the late Professor Sikes.

Most of all though I wish to thank the Senate Research Committee of the University of Nebraska at Omaha and the University of Nebraska Foundation for a grant to aid in the preparation and publication of my manuscript, Mrs. Orville D. Menard for her exemplary care in typing it, and my wife, Mary Elizabeth Wardle, for her unfailing assistance and encouragement.

R. M. W.

University of Nebraska at Omaha

List of Short Titles Used in the Notes

When two arabic numbers are enclosed in parentheses within the body of the text (e.g., 12:234), they refer to the volume and page of the definitive edition of Hazlitt's works: *Complete Works of William Hazlitt*, ed. P. P. Howe, centenary ed., 21 vols. (London and Toronto: J. M. Dent and Sons, Ltd., 1930–34).

Baker	Herschel Baker. *William Hazlitt.* Cambridge, Mass.: Harvard University Press, 1962.
Blunden	Edmund Blunden. *Keats's Publisher: A Memoir of John Taylor (1781–1864).* London: Jonathan Cape, 1936.
BNYPL	*Bulletin of the New York Public Library.*
Coleridge Letters	*Collected Letters of Samuel Taylor Coleridge.* Edited by Earl Leslie Griggs. 4 vols. Oxford: Clarendon Press, 1956–59.
Cornwall Recollections	*Literary Recollections of Barry Cornwall.* Edited by R. W. Armour. Boston: Meador Publishing Co., 1936.
ELH	[*Journal of English Literary History*].
Elwin	*Autobiography and Journals of Benjamin Robert Haydon.* Edited by Malcolm Elwin. New York: Coward-McCann; London: Macdonald, 1950.
Four Generations	W. Carew Hazlitt. *Four Generations of a Literary Family.* 2 vols. London, 1897.
Haydon Diary	*Diary of Benjamin Robert Haydon.* Edited by Willard Bissell Pope. 5 vols. Cambridge, Mass.: Harvard University Press, 1960–63.
The Hazlitts	W. Carew Hazlitt. *The Hazlitts: An Account of Their Origin and Descent.* Edinburgh: Ballantyne, Hanson and Co., 1911.
Howe	P. P. Howe. *Life of William Hazlitt.* New edition with an introduction by Frank Swinnerton. London: Hamish Hamilton, 1947.

Journals   *Journals of Sarah and William Hazlitt, 1822–31.* Edited by Willard Hallam Bonner. University of Buffalo Studies, vol. 24, no. 3. 1959.

Keats Circle   *The Keats Circle: Letters and Papers 1816–1878.* Edited by Hyder Edward Rollins. 2 vols. Cambridge, Mass.: Harvard University Press, 1948.

Keats Letters   *Letters of John Keats 1814–1821.* Edited by Hyder Edward Rollins. 2 vols. Cambridge, Mass.: Harvard University Press, 1958.

Keynes   Geoffrey Keynes. *Bibliography of William Hazlitt.* London: Nonesuch Press, 1931.

Lamb Letters   *Letters of Charles Lamb, to Which are Added Those of His Sister Mary Lamb.* Edited by E. V. Lucas. 3 vols. London: J. M. Dent and Sons, Ltd.; Methuen and Co., Ltd., 1935.

Landseer   Thomas Landseer. *Life and Letters of William Bewick.* 2 vols. London, 1871.

L'Estrange   *Life of Mary Russell Mitford.* Edited by Alfred Guy L'Estrange. 3 vols. London, 1870.

Memoirs   W. Carew Hazlitt. *Memoirs of William Hazlitt.* 2 vols. London, 1867.

MLN   *Modern Language Notes.*

MLQ   *Modern Language Quarterly.*

Moyne   *Journal of Margaret Hazlitt.* Edited by Ernest J. Moyne. Lawrence: University of Kansas Press, 1967.

NQ   *Notes and Queries.*

Patmore   Peter George Patmore. *My Friends and Acquaintance.* 3 vols. London, 1854.

PMLA   [*Publications of the Modern Language Association of America*].

PQ   *Philological Quarterly.*

Robinson   *Henry Crabb Robinson on Books and Their Writers.* Edited by Edith J. Morley. 3 vols. London: J. M. Dent and Sons, Ltd., 1938.

Sadler   *Diary, Reminiscences, and Correspondence of Henry Crabb Robinson.* Edited by Thomas Sadler. 3 vols. Boston and New York, 1898.

Shelley and His Circle	*Shelley and His Circle 1773–1822.* Edited by Kenneth Neill Cameron. 4 vols. Cambridge, Mass.: Harvard University Press; London: Oxford University Press, 1961–70.
Stephenson	H. W. Stephenson. *William Hazlitt and Hackney College.* London: The Lindsey Press, 1930.
Stoddard	*Life, Letters, and Table Talk of Benjamin Robert Haydon.* Edited by R. H. Stoddard. New York, 1876.
Talfourd	Thomas Noon Talfourd. *Final Memorials of Charles Lamb.* 2 vols. London, 1848.
TLS	*Times Literary Supplement* (London).

HAZLITT

CHAPTER I

Like Father?

The Irish Hazlitts were an independent breed; dissent was imbedded in their very bones. In an era when men were advised to accept the situation in which God had placed them, the Hazlitts had a penchant for striking out in unexpected directions. During the early eighteenth century several members of the clan left their native Ulster to emigrate to the New World. But John Hazlitt took an even more unorthodox course: by the time he was twenty-five years old he had left his home at Coleraine, in county Derry, and was settled as a merchant in Shrone Hill, or Shronell, in the alien territory of Tipperary.[1] And his three sons, each in his own way, continued the family tradition. John, the youngest, emigrated to America; James, the second son, prepared for the Dissenting ministry at the University of Glasgow, but later took orders in the Church of Ireland and, after serving several years as a curate, managed eventually to amass a considerable fortune as a tanner and miller. Meanwhile his elder brother William, father of the

1. Biographical material in this chapter is drawn largely from Ernest J. Moyne's edition of *The Journal of Margaret Hazlitt* (Lawrence: University of Kansas Press, 1967) (hereafter cited as Moyne). Moyne has presented the complete text of the *Journal* for the first time and has supplemented it with thorough notes drawing on and verifying the earlier investigations of W. Carew Hazlitt in *The Hazlitts: An Account of Their Origin and Descent* (Edinburgh: Ballantyne, Hanson and Co., 1911), chaps. 1–5 (hereafter cited as *The Hazlitts*). In an appendix Moyne reprints "An Account of the State of Rational Religion in America; by an Unitarian Minister, Who Travelled in That Country," the Reverend William Hazlitt's record of his stay in the United States, first published in the *Monthly Repository* for June, 1808. Except when otherwise specified, all quotations in this chapter and the next are drawn from Margaret Hazlitt's *Journal* (Moyne, pp. 31–110). Since the material included in Moyne's notes and appendix are most easily available in his volume, I have referred to it rather than to the original sources in my notes.

essayist, had also studied for the ministry at Glasgow, where he received his master's degree in 1760 at the age of twenty-three. And he too broke with the past: he became a convert to Unitarian doctrines and went down to England to follow his vocation.

There was little demand in England for Irish Unitarian clergymen—or for Unitarians of any stamp. Because the Toleration Act of 1689 banned public worship by all faiths which denied the Trinity, a clergyman of Hazlitt's convictions had no recourse but to seek shelter among dissenters of liberal beliefs. He appeared for examination before a tolerant committee which included the Reverend Richard Price, one of the most distinguished rational Dissenters of the time, and was given a "testimonial of approbation."[2] Then, after serving his apprenticeship as an occasional preacher for several congregations and as chaplain in the household of Sir Conyers Jocelyn of Hyde Hall, Hertfordshire, he was called in 1764 to minister to a dissenting congregation at Wisbech in the Isle of Ely. On January 19, 1766, he was married to Grace Loftus, the pretty nineteen-year-old daughter of a local ironmonger, recently deceased, and settled with her in Marshfield, Gloucestershire, where he had accepted a new pastorate. During their four years at Marshfield, Grace Hazlitt bore two sons, John (born May 13, 1767) and Loftus.

The Reverend William Hazlitt soon proved himself an able preacher and a dedicated pastor. When a vacancy occurred in the larger congregation of Lewin's Mead in Bristol, twelve miles from Marshfield, he was invited to preach there as a candidate for the pulpit. Here, however, he encountered his first rebuff; as his daughter Margaret explained years later, "a few bigots raised an outcry of heresy against him. In other words, he did not think exactly as they did. This alarm put an effectual stop to his being chosen there." It was an augury of the future.

Soon, however, there came another call, this one from a congregation of liberal Presbyterians at the Earl Street Meeting House in Maidstone, Kent. This time Hazlitt won approval, and in June of 1770 the family moved from Marshfield into a house in Mitre Close, Maidstone, a short distance from the chapel.

Life was good to the Hazlitts during the ten years which they spent at Maidstone. The town itself, as center of the hop-growing trade, was flourishing, and the congregation at the Earl Street Meeting House included several of the most prosperous and enlightened citizens. The Reverend Mr. Hazlitt found time to write periodically for the *Theological Repository*, the

2. See Price's letter of March 3, 1783, in *The Hazlitts*, p. 375.

liberal magazine edited by Dr. Joseph Priestley,[3] and was soon on friendly terms with several of the most prominent rational Dissenters of the nation—men like Priestley, Price, and the Reverend Dr. Andrew Kippis. His sympathy with republican causes won him friends among laymen too—men like Thomas Viny of Tenterden, twenty miles from Maidstone, at whose house he met the great Benjamin Franklin. The future looked promising. Sorrow struck the family when the boy Loftus died soon after their arrival in Maidstone, but it was balanced by joy in the birth of their first daughter, Margaret (usually known as Peggy), on December 10, 1770. And seven years later, on April 10, 1778, a third son, William, was born. He was baptized by his father on the following June 21.

In 1780 the pleasant life at Maidstone ended abruptly. There was a split in the congregation—so sharp that neither of the two parties would come to meeting if the other were to be present. In describing the trouble fifty years later Peggy Hazlitt claimed that the dispute was due to "money matters," that both factions "professed the highest regard" for their pastor, but that he "did not chuse to interfere."[4] Probably, however, her father's liberal principles, especially his ardent sympathy with the revolting American colonists, lay at the root of the trouble. At least, when a congregation at Bandon, in county Cork, invited him to come over as their pastor, he insisted that he could not accept until he had visited and preached to them.

In March of 1780 the five Hazlitts set off from Maidstone for their new home in Ireland. However the parents felt about the move, it must have seemed like a lark to the older children. They had a week in London as guests of David Lewis, son of a member of the Maidstone congregation; then they traveled north to Chester and across Wales, where Peggy was charmed at "the first sight of the Welsh peasants with their flat beaver hats and blue coats," but frightened by the trip over Penmaenmawr, "the grand and terrific appearance of the cliff that overhung the road, and the dreadful depth of the sea beneath." Then came two days of drenching rain at Holyhead and a stormy crossing to Dublin, where they arrived at six o'clock in the morning. "It was wet and cold," Peggy later recalled, "and we were obliged to wait at a little dirty ale-house until a customhouse officer had

3. W. C. Hazlitt claims (*The Hazlitts*, p. 17) that Rev. William Hazlitt signed his contributions "Philolethes" and "Rationalis." Articles so signed appeared in vol. 2 (1770), 186–88; 3 (1771), 434–44, 444–51; 4 (1784), 234–44; 5 (1786), 295–98; and 6 (1788), 216–17, 415–24, 425–27. All of these are either corrections of points made in earlier articles or discussions of fine points in interpretation of Scripture.

4. As Moyne points out (p. 25), Peggy was prone to find pretexts, other than his liberal principles, for her father's failure to find a permanent situation.

seen to our baggage." They spent a month as guests of the Reverend Samuel
Thomas in Dublin, then went south to Bandon to begin their new life—in
a house on Gallow-hill Street!—among people of strange accents and
strange manners. It was an arduous trip for all involved—especially for
Grace Hazlitt, who was now pregnant again. As for little William, who
celebrated his second birthday en route, it must have been confusing from
first to last. It was only a taste of what lay ahead.

In Bandon they found "a very large and respectable congregation,"
as Peggy described it, though she added presently: "But I do not mean to
say there were no *Black Sheep* among the flock. In truth, there were some
who gave trouble, but their names are better passed over in silence." There
were domestic problems too: soon after their arrival Mrs. Hazlitt was delivered of a fifth child, Thomas, who lived only a few weeks. And within a
matter of months she was again pregnant. But much more serious: her husband became embroiled in a full-scale conflict with the British army, or at
least with that segment of it quartered in Kinsale, at the mouth of the
Bandon River. Officers lounging in their messroom at the White Hart Inn
in Bandon had been amusing themselves by hurling turf at passing countrymen—or forcing local Catholics at sword's point to eat meat on Friday.
They were said also to be brutal in their treatment of American prisoners of
war interned at Kinsale—even to have slashed with their swords at the
hammocks of patients in the prison hospital.

The Reverend Mr. Hazlitt was outraged—and he spoke out emphatically. He wrote letters to Cork newspapers.[5] He visited the prison and did
what he could to relieve the inmates. And when three of them escaped,
he helped hide them from the authorities.

Inevitably the officers at Kinsale resented his interference. One Sunday
three of them, meeting him on the street, taunted him as a rebel and threatened to be revenged on him. But he refused to be cowed. "I will report you
to the War Office," he told them. And so he did.

To add weight to his protest, he wrote also to his influential friends Dr.
Price and the Reverend John Palmer asking them to intercede. The
Reverend John Wiche, Baptist preacher back in Maidstone, hearing of his
plight, wrote on February 18, 1782, sympathizing with him and tactfully
advising that he give up *"parsoning"* in favor of "the study of Physic." "In
that profession," he explained, "you would be less obnoxious to censure;

5. Hazlitt's letters to the Cork newspapers are reprinted by E. J. Moyne in "The
Reverend William Hazlitt: A Friend of Liberty in Ireland during the American Revolution," *William and Mary Quarterly*, 3d ser. 21 (1964): 288–97.

and, possibly, besides great usefulness as a physician, you might be able, with more ease, to forward with greater advantage the best purposes and wishes of an honest Christian divine." [6] Of course Hazlitt would not consider abandoning his true vocation, yet he was seriously concerned about his safety, as he told his friend Samuel Perrot of Cork. Perrot wrote back on May 18:

> Your letter this morning has affected me much, not from any thing you have to apprehend from the evidence of these men, but on account of that vexation which has been increasing upon you and rendered your situation a most unfortunate one. I would not have you entertain any idea of their proceeding to what you mention: the law will protect you, and they are too much afraid of a gallows to proceed to extremity: that fear, probably is all the virtue they are possessed of; but it may be sufficient for your protection, and will be so. Unless anything should happen which I am not acquainted with, it would not be advisable to fly. Try to keep your spirits and weather the storm; and when malice cannot prove any thing against you . . . then, indeed the sooner the better you employ your friends to find you a place of refuge, where you will not be subject again to so many causes of distress.[7]

Soon the crisis passed. Dr. Price relayed Hazlitt's complaint to Lord Shelburne, the prime minister, who forwarded Price's letter to Colonel Fitzpatrick, commandant of the prison at Kinsale. A court of inquiry was held, the guilty officers were censured, and the regiment was transferred.[8] By this time, however, the Reverend Mr. Hazlitt had had his fill of Bandon. His liberal principles had shocked many of the townspeople, some of whom cautioned their friends, when they met him on the street, to beware of the black rebel. Even members of his congregation were turning against him; one of them stalked out of the chapel in the middle of his sermon one Sunday, shouting, "I didn't come here to listen to treason."

For some time Hazlitt had considered following those of his family who had emigrated to America. Now more than ever the new nation appealed to him as his natural haven. Friends warned him against taking such a move. Dr. Price wrote on June 28: "I heartily wish you may be extricated out of your troubles and find a provision for yourself and family. You mention going over to America, but I cannot advise you to this. I am afraid you would only find your difficulties increased." [9] But Hazlitt was not convinced. Because the peace treaty between England and the new nation

6. *Christian Reformer* 5 (1838): 698.

7. Ibid., p. 701.

8. According to Peggy Hazlitt, the officers were spared severer punishment by her father's appeal in their behalf. She remarks, too, that when her father's letter was read in court, "they said who could have thought a Presbyterian parson could have written such a letter."

9. *The Hazlitts*, p. 374.

was still pending, he could not yet secure passage; but he was eager to leave Bandon, wait out the winter, in Bristol perhaps, and then set out for the New World. His friend the Reverend Samuel Thomas of Dublin cautioned him in August: "I am full of apprehension that your relinquishing your present situation, without any certain prospect of another settlement, may be injurious beyond your expectations. It is always easier to negociate a removal from one place to another than to secure a settlement when a person has been any time unemployed in his profession." He suggested that "the appointment of an afternoon preacher at Cork might answer for you as well as any thing that can be expected, in the way of a temporary expedient at least, especially if you would engage in the education of a few young gentlemen, for which useful employment there is a good opening." He concluded: "At all events would it not be better to winter at Cork, and have something to receive, than at Bristol? And could you not remove more advantageously from thence to your favourite country, if you will go? I can only warn you that it is the last part of God's creation to which a man of your sentiments in your profession ought to think of." 10

Hazlitt heeded the warning, at least in part. He stayed on in Bandon through the fall and early winter, but he refused to be deflected from his ultimate purpose. On February 4 the Reverend John Palmer wrote him with some exasperation:

> I can say no more, that is material, in addition to what I have so repeatedly urged, and which continues to be the best dictate of my judgment, to dissuade from carrying your purpose into execution. Dr. Price forms the same idea with myself of the great discouragements which attend your removal to A[merica] in the character of your profession. . . . I will just hint that Mr. Gordon, a Dissenting minister, who quitted a place in London to go to A[merica] some few years ago, is now returning with his family to England.11

But Hazlitt had made up his mind: as soon as the peace was confirmed, he uprooted his family once again and, after a two-week stay at Cork, they embarked on the *Henry* for New York on April 3.

No doubt he set off on the voyage with eyes sparkling and mind crammed with visions of a glorious future: he was escaping from the Old World of prejudice to the New World of justice and toleration where he belonged by birthright. And he carried with him a testimonial letter from Dr. Price describing him as "a zealous friend to civil and religious liberty, and the

10. *Christian Reformer* 5 (1838): 757.
11. Ibid.

cause of America," citing his recent efforts "in favour of some American prisoners," and assuring the reader that he was "a man of integrity and ability."[12] In a postscript Dr. Andrew Kippis, the Reverend John Palmer, and Dr. Abraham Rees declared that they concurred in the testimonial. Surely a document signed by these distinguished friends of liberty would open innumerable doors in the New World.

But how did Grace Hazlitt react to this latest move? Like most eighteenth-century women, she remains a shadowy figure. She is scarcely mentioned in the writing of her husband or even her son, who is said to have been devoted to her. Her daughter Peggy later remarked that she had been as eager to emigrate as her husband. Yet she must have had some misgivings. She had followed him from Wisbech to Marshfield to Maidstone, then across to Ireland. She had borne him six children and lost two. She was, presumably, leaving her mother, her only brother, and all her friends forever. And she was asked now to undergo a hazardous ocean voyage of several weeks with four children, one of whom celebrated his fifth birthday at sea, another, the baby Harriet, little more than a year old. And—the *coup de grâce*—she was in the same uncomfortable condition as when she had moved from Marshfield to Maidstone and from Maidstone to Bandon, for she was five months along in her seventh pregnancy. As a philosopher the Reverend William Hazlitt may have believed in universal benevolence, but as a husband he could be at times singularly exasperating.

Even for the children this trip was no lark. Although the weather was "pretty good, on the whole," as Peggy remembered it later, there were bound to be some heavy seas in a voyage which lasted nearly eight weeks in early spring. Young John "suffered much from seasickness," according to Peggy; she herself "felt no inconvenience from the motion of the ship"— "except the first few days, or in stormy weather"; but their "poor mother [was] worn out with seasickness and the fear of the rough and boisterous ocean and the still more rough and brutish captain," a man named Jefferson who "longed to throw us all overboard because we were the friends of liberty, which he cordially hated."[13] Only the father and the two little ones seem to have enjoyed the voyage; he, happily, "was never sick at sea," while little William and Harriet, "who did not know, or think of, any danger," were only amused when "the deadlights were put up and everything rolled about

12. *The Hazlitts*, p. 375.

13. Peggy's statement seems to invalidate W. C. Hazlitt's claim (*The Hazlitts*, p. 23) that the Reverend Mr. Hazlitt took offense at the attentions paid his wife by the captain of the *Henry*.

the cabin." There were calm days too, of course—days when all aboard turned to and fished for mackerel, which they presently ate "with the greater relish after our salt fare." But most of the time during their fifty-four days at sea there were no diversions, no new sights to please or startle—nothing to relieve the boredom of close confinement on the ship and the endless stretch of sea and sky.

At long last, on May 26, the *Henry* sailed into port at New York. As they approached land, all aboard happily breathed in the odor of fresh air and pine trees; "even the goats kept their heads to windward to snuff up the grateful odor." And suddenly all the discomfort of the past weeks was forgotten. Captain Jefferson apologized for his behavior and was quickly pardoned. The British officers who boarded the ship were told that the peace treaty had been concluded and that they must immediately "put a stop to their ravaging with fire and sword their brothers' land."

It was six o'clock in the evening before they could go ashore. The Reverend Mr. Hazlitt called on Tench Coxe, for whom he had a letter of introduction, and Coxe offered to help the family find lodgings. But they wandered the streets in vain; no one had a room to spare. At length poor Mrs. Hazlitt threw herself down exhausted on a doorstep "to wait, with no very pleasant feeling," while her husband and Coxe continued the search. And finally they got to the root of their difficulty: Coxe was a known Loyalist, and the Hazlitts had been taken to be Loyalist refugees. Only when they had cleared up the error were they able to find rooms at the house of a Mrs. Gregory. Nor did their troubles end then. The next morning their maidservant, a girl named Honour whom they had brought from Ireland, "decamped with what few things she could lay her hands on," and Peggy, aged twelve, was obliged to take over as cook and housekeeper. Her mother, by this time, was "too ill to do anything but direct."

They remained in New York only two days—just long enough for their belongings to be unloaded from the *Henry*. Then they set out once more by ship to Perth Amboy, then across country to Burlington, where Hazlitt was invited to stop over the week end and preach to the members of the New Jersey assembly. It was "a very pretty township by the side of a river" (the Delaware), and to Mrs. Hazlitt it seemed like an ideal place to settle. When she learned that they could rent the fine house belonging to Benjamin Franklin's natural son William, who had been the last royal governor of New Jersey, she urged her husband to open a school there. But he was determined to push on to Philadelphia.

They had two more days of travel "by stage-waggon," then put up at temporary lodgings on Strawberry Alley in Philadelphia before moving into a house on Union Street that they could call their own. It had some advantages from the housewife's point of view: "two bedrooms, two attics, cupboards in every room, and a good cellar." But "our only pantry [was] a shelf on the cellar stairs, where a colony of ants devoured everything that did not stand in a pail of water." And worse: the rent was fifty pounds per year in American currency, or about thirty in English. Living in the New World was not going to be cheap: at Maidstone the Hazlitts had paid a rent of twelve pounds per year. The head of the household needed to bestir himself at once to provide a steady income.

Unfortunately the New World proved less hospitable—and tolerant—than he had anticipated. "He . . . preached Unitarianism with acceptance, at Philadelphia, to some orthodox churches," he wrote in 1808, "and might have done so to this day, had not some cunning ones and busy bodies circulated the report that the worship of the great goddess Diana was in danger." [14] He had better luck in July in New London, Pennsylvania, "where no exceptions were made to his doctrines, but handsome compliments paid to him by his principal auditors." [15] New London would have been a congenial place for the family to settle down because some of their Hazlitt cousins were living there. But there was evidently no vacant pulpit.

There was, however, a very promising vacancy at Carlisle with "an expectancy of 400 guineas a-year to the preacher who should be chosen to fill it up." [16] Dr. John Ewing, provost of the University of the State of Pennsylvania, recommended Hazlitt for the position, and he was invited to preach there. But again he met with opposition: Dr. George Duffield of Philadelphia, the militant author of the hymn "Stand Up, Stand Up for Jesus," had sent word ahead that Hazlitt was a heretic. And although he managed, in his first two sermons, to counter the charge, General John Armstrong, a member of the congregation at Carlisle, incited the Reverend William Linn to take up the cudgels against him. "Lynn [sic] was punctually obedient to the commands of his master," Hazlitt later reported.

> He ascended the pulpit with rancour in his countenance. He bitterly declaimed against all heresy, and warned a thousand people who stood before him to be armed against the greatest danger which then threatened them, a greater danger than all the evils of the late war, the introduction of heresy by foreigners. Such was his modesty, forbearance, and charity, and such his rude treatment of a stranger, who, to his own hurt, had released some hundreds of his countrymen from a loathsome prison, and from famine.[17]

14. Moyne, pp. 116–17.   15. Ibid., p. 117.   16. Ibid.   17. Ibid.

The congregation at Carlisle was willing, nonetheless, to accept Hazlitt as their minister on one condition: that he subscribe to "the confession of faith, *as far as it was agreeable to the word of God*." [18] But he refused, affirming characteristically, that "he came there a free man, that he would continue such as long as he lived, that he would give way to nothing which had the most distant resemblance to trimming, and that he would not even subscribe those things which he most firmly believed, lest he might throw a stumbling block in his brother's way." So back to Philadelphia and his family he went, empty-handed—and "rather too hastily, it was afterwards said, as Dr. Ewing was informed, that, if he had remained there a fortnight longer, he would have been accepted upon his own terms, and been appointed a Principal of [Dickinson] College." [19]

By this time the Reverend Mr. Hazlitt's serene confidence in his prospects must have been shaken. And his wife would have had to be a philosopher extraordinary not to feel downright despondent. The ants in the house on Union Street were the least of her troubles; there were rent and food bills to harass her, since her husband's fees for occasional sermons could hardly have sufficed to meet their expenses. For Grace Hazlitt the New World had proved to be not a land of promise but a vale of tears. On June 25, just a month after their arrival in New York, the baby Harriet died of an attack of croup. Six weeks later, on August first Mrs. Hazlitt bore another daughter, who was named Esther. And six weeks after that this baby, too, died, after she had fallen from the arms of a negligent nurse. Of the seven children born to the couple, one lay buried in Maidstone, one in Bandon, and two in Philadelphia—a poignant record of the family's nomadic existence.

She had made a few friends, who offered what aid and consolation they

18. Ibid., pp. 117–18.

19. Ibid., p. 118. Although Hazlitt did not so specify in his "Account of the State of Rational Religion in America," Dr. Benjamin Rush of Philadelphia actively opposed his candidacy for the presidency of Dickinson College. Hazlitt seems, in fact, to have been the victim of a long-standing grudge between Rush and Ewing. Moyne (p. 6) says that Rush opposed Hazlitt's appointments to both the church at Carlisle and the presidency of the college. In a letter to Dr. Price dated November 15, 1785, Hazlitt expressed his bitterness toward Rush. (See E. J. Moyne, "The Reverend William Hazlitt and Dickinson College," *Pennsylvania Magazine of History and Biography* 85 [1961]: 289–302.) Cf. Hazlitt's statement in his article of 1808: "There was only one man (in Philadelphia) of whom he complained, who, upon his first introduction to him, paid him some fulsome flattery, and expressed his anxious wish that they could have many such men in that country. This was the celebrated Dr. Rush, who afterwards told him that he was satisfied with the religion of his ancestors, and abused Dr. Ewing for the friendly regards he had shewn him" (Moyne, p. 120).

could. Her well-to-do Jewish neighbors Moses and Esther Gomez were unfailingly kind, as were the Atkinsons, who lived next door with their widowed daughter, Mrs. Brewer, whose son George was young William's playmate. Mrs. Atkinson was "a cheerful old lady . . . fond of seeing young folks enjoy themselves," and on one occasion she took Peggy and John on a memorable all-day excursion up the Schuylkill River. Samuel Vaughan and his two sons, also men of means, tried, now and later, to give the Hazlitts a helping hand. They suggested that the Reverend Mr. Hazlitt open a school at Germantown, five miles from Philadelphia, and even offered to lend him whatever funds he might need to establish it. But again he refused to be distracted from his true vocation: preaching the word of God.

In the autumn he received an encouraging invitation from Centreville, Maryland, where the members of St. Paul's Church, formerly Episcopalians, were hoping to attract a clergyman of Unitarian leanings. This again would have been a congenial place for the family to settle; some of their American cousins lived there—had, in fact, probably suggested Hazlitt as a candidate for the vacancy. He went to Centreville to preach, "using his own prayers, and declaring to a numerous audience what he believed to be the doctrines of the New Testament."[20] But again there were difficulties.[21] And on his second Sunday in Centreville, before the problems could be resolved, he collapsed in the pulpit, a victim of the dreaded yellow fever.

A family named Earle took him in and gave him the most considerate care. Their son-in-law, a physician, took charge of the case, and two Negro servants were assigned to watch over the patient every night. When news of his illness reached Philadelphia, Dr. Ewing and Professor James Davidson of the University of the State of Pennsylvania went to Union Street to inform Mrs. Hazlitt. At first the poor woman was convinced, despite their assurances, that her husband must be dead. By this time, obviously, she was prepared for the worst.

The following morning she sent her son John, now sixteen, on horseback to Centreville. He rode hard, covering the 160 miles in fifty-six hours, and

20. Moyne, p. 118.

21. Moyne (p. 145) cites vestry records of St. Paul's parish for October 4, 1783, to the effect that "on application of the Rev. Mr. William Hazlitt to be admitted into St. Paul's parish as a minister and preacher of the gospel, the vestry was unanimously of opinion, he being a dissenter, that they have no authority for admitting him." Hazlitt himself wrote that "he might probably have settled there, had not some difficulties arisen concerning an Unitarian liturgy." There may, of course, be no conflict here: the question of the liturgy may have still been pending when Hazlitt fell ill, and he may never have known the vestrymen had decided he was ineligible for the position.

tended his father for several weeks until he was strong enough to make the trip back to Philadelphia. When they finally reached home one snowy day in November, the poor man was so exhausted that he had to be helped down from his horse. And for the rest of the winter he was confined to the house; still "very yellow," he huddled close to the fire, "wrapped in a great coat" and dosing himself with columbo root. He was, as he later told Dr. Price, "useless, whilst I was groaning under a great expence almost six months." [22] —Oh brave New World!

As soon as he was strong enough, he delivered a series of sermons, "Evidences of the the Truth of the Christian Religion," at the University of the State of Pennsylvania. And once again he met with opposition: "At first the place was well filled. But afterwards, through the artifices of those who never attended, the audience was greatly diminished, though Dr. Ewing from his pulpit had strenuously recommended the lecture to his hearers." [23] Dr. John Carson, a trustee of the university, urged him to publish the sermons; he was confident that he himself could find five hundred subscribers. But Hazlitt could not afford to linger in Philadelphia long enough to see the volume through the press. Instead he brought out an edition of Joseph Priestley's *Appeal to the Serious and Candid Professors of Christianity*, prefaced by three short sermons of his own. And for once he enjoyed a minor triumph. Despite organized opposition—or perhaps, as he believed, because of it[24]—the volume sold well, much to the distress of his orthodox foes.

22. *Proceedings of the Massachusetts Historical Society*, 2d ser. 17 (1903): 323.

23. Moyne, pp. 118–19.

24. "It was purposely contrived that this piece should be ready for sale on the first day of the meeting of the Synod. Some alarmists accordingly, having heard the awful tidings, introduced the subject into their venerable body, which was considered of such high importance, that it occupied their whole attention during two days of their sitting. At last, Dr. Sprout [James Sproat] made a motion, to address a printed circular letter to their respective flocks, to introduce into the letter extracts of all the heresies contained in the book, and solemnly to guard their hearers against the reading of it. The Dr. was seconded by a learned auctioneer belonging to his Church. But Mr. Lynn ... seeing farther into the consequences of such a measure than Dr. Sprout, opposed the motion, shrewdly observing, that such a letter would awaken general curiosity, and instead of suppressing the heresy would spread it far and near, and be the occasion of driving those very persons into heresy whom they intended to guard against it. But, though Mr. Lynn carried his point, his arguments did not seem conclusive to all his brethren. For, one clergyman, who lived 150 miles from Philadelphia, returned home so full of the subject, that he preached the whole of the following Sunday against the heresy, and earnestly cautioned his hearers never to look into so poisonous a book. This proceeding so whetted their curiosity, that the very week after they had 57 copies of it imported into their township" (Moyne, pp. 119–20).

What next? Hazlitt heard of an opening in Charleston, South Carolina, but ruled it out because of the heat and danger of fever there. Another in Pittsburgh was vetoed because it seemed "so far back in the wilderness." Then came a very tempting invitation to preach as a candidate for the pulpit at the Brattle Street Meeting House in Boston. Since churches in the North were said to be more liberal than those in Pennsylvania, he could anticipate a fairer hearing there, and he set out for Boston at once.

He arrived there on May 15, 1784, and was so well received—and so sure he would be appointed to the vacancy—that he sent for his family, and in August Mrs. Hazlitt pulled up roots once again and set out on another arduous journey. She and the three children traveled by stagecoach back to Perth Amboy, then by sloop to New York. Their vessel ran aground off Sandy Hook and "stuck fast on a sandbank for five hours." There were "many women and children on board," Peggy wrote afterwards, "and great was their fear and lamentation." Little William, now old enough to know fear, "wept in concert" with the others "on hearing some of the people say we shall be all drowned." But the rising tide set them afloat again, and they sailed into New York at sunset. After two days there they proceeded by packet to Newport, Rhode Island, where they spent another two days before boarding a vessel which carried them up the bay to Providence. The next day they traveled on to Boston by coach.

Here another disappointment awaited them: the Reverend Mr. Hazlitt had not been offered the vacancy at the Brattle Street Meeting House after all. This time it was apparently his character rather than his convictions that stood in his way.[25] And his character now sustained him; something, he was sure, would turn up. He settled his family first at a lodginghouse on State Street in Boston, then for several weeks at a farm in Lower Dorchester. And he himself kept busy.

25. In her diary Peggy maintained that "the persecuting zeal of the orthodox sent one of their chosen brethren after him, and thus put a stop to his settling there." But Samuel Vaughan wrote to Hazlitt on May 17, 1785: "I was informed that an indiscreet act of your own prevented your being chosen at Brattle Street" (*Christian Reformer* 5 [1838]: 698). And the Reverend John Eliot wrote about Hazlitt to the Reverend Jeremy Belknap on August 26, 1784: "Poor fellow, I am afraid he is in trouble. His wife and family are now come, and put themselves upon him, understanding, as I learn, that he was to be settled at Dr. Cooper's [Brattle Street Church]. He was buoyed up with such an idea, and flattered himself that there were no difficulties at all in the way. It was only to hear him, and they would be too much captivated to let him go. In short, he is the most conceited and most imprudent man I ever met with, and yet hath many good qualities both of head and heart" (Moyne, pp. 146–47).

He could console himself always with the knowledge that he was no mere rolling stone. Although he was gathering little for himself or his family, he was leaving his mark in history. In Boston he played a prominent part in converting the old King's Chapel, the first Episcopal church in New England, into the first Unitarian church in the United States.

It began on the very day of his arrival in Boston, when the Reverend John Eliot took him to a meeting of the Boston Association of Ministers at the home of the Reverend Charles Chauncy. During a discussion of ordination Hazlitt declared that "the people, or the congregation, who choose any man to be their minister, were his proper ordainers." Immediately James Freeman, lay reader at King's Chapel, "jumped from his seat in a kind of transport, saying, 'I wish you could prove that, Sir.'"[26] Freeman had good reason to be interested: although he had served as clergyman at King's Chapel for the past two years, his bishop refused to ordain him because he would not subscribe to the Thirty-nine Articles of the Anglican communion.

The two men saw a good deal of each other in the months ahead. Hazlitt soon persuaded Freeman that his interpretation of ordination was valid, and to convince others he published several pseudonymous letters in support of Freeman[27] and also "a scriptural confutation of the 39 Articles." The latter was so well advertised in advance of publication that the printer "threw off above a hundred papers beyond his usual number, and had not one paper remaining upon his hands at noon."[28] As a result the congregation at King's Chapel decided in 1787 to ordain their own pastor and to abandon their orthodox dogma.

Thus Hazlitt was busy, he was making his influence felt, and he was sustained by his indomitable optimism. On October 19 he wrote to Dr. Price: "I am very acceptable as a preacher in this part of America, and I have some dark prospect of a settlement. Dr. Chauncy, and many others, treat me with great civility and friendship. Your favorable mention of me to the Doctor, in your next letter, would do me an essential service. I am afraid that busy bigot Dr. Gordon [of Roxbury] endeavours to injure me."[29]

But what of the rest of the family? Early in November they moved from their lodgings in Lower Dorchester to part of a sizable house, the family

26. Moyne, p. 115.
27. See ibid., pp. 10–11, for a list of the letters.
28. Ibid., p. 116.
29. *Proceedings of the Massachusetts Historical Society*, 2d ser. 17 (1903): 323.

home of Mrs. John Adams, in Weymouth.[30] Peggy was delighted with the place and, years later, described it fondly: the spacious wainscoted rooms, the painting of Jacob and Esau said to be an early work of John Singleton Copley, the garden outside with fruit trees which attracted the humming birds, the meadows beyond, and the lovely situation—"in a most romantic spot, surrounded on three sides by very steep hills that sloped down just in sight of the windows, and were covered with locust trees."

The place was much less desirable in bad weather, and the Hazlitts' first winter in Weymouth was a bitter one. "There was no market or butcher's shop, or any baker, in the parish," Peggy wrote in her journal, "and only one shop, containing some remnants of linen, a few tapes and thread, with a small assortment of grocery. Hard sea biscuits, butter, cheese, some salt beef and pork were our winter's fare." In February a temporary thaw gave way to a freeze, and the wash-house was filled with a six-inch coat of ice which John and his father had to chop away. And the Reverend Mr. Hazlitt was obliged to make weekly trips through heavy snow to Boston, fifteen miles away, where he had arranged to repeat his sermons on the evidences of Christianity.[31]

When spring came, the old house proved a convenient headquarters for Hazlitt, who was asked to preach in several churches south of Boston—at Dorchester, Jamaica Plain, Marshfield, Scituate, and Providence. He spoke only rarely at the church in Weymouth; the congregation there found him too radical for their tastes. But he served virtually as assistant to the Reverend

30. The house had been inherited by Abigail Adams's elder sister, Mary (Smith) Cranch. In a letter to Mrs. Adams dated November 6, 1784, Mrs. Cranch offered some revealing remarks about her tenants: "He is a very sensible fine preacher but alass is not orthodox, & takes no pains to secrete it—He wishes to be settled in this State but unless he will be more prudent (I call it) he says tis cuning he will never get a Parish. He has a Family, a wife a very pretty sensible well Bred woman & three very likely children. . . . He has been preaching at Hingham & Situate. The people like him much. The people at Weymouth I hear wish to hear him but however they might like him as a preacher, I fear his freedom of speech would prevent there ever settling him let his Heart & his Head be ever so good" (Moyne, p. 148). Concerning the claims of both Peggy Hazlitt and W. Carew Hazlitt that their family had a connection with the Quincys of Boston, see ibid., pp. 148–49.

31. Hazlitt's first request to deliver the sermons in Faneuil Hall was rejected by the selectmen of the city. He was permitted to deliver them at the Second Church, but apparently they were much less successful than they had been in Philadelphia. On February 24, 1785, the Reverend John Eliot wrote to the Reverend Jeremy Belknap: "We have not set up Paddy for a lecturer, but he hath set himself up. He plagued Brother Lathrop till he obtained consent for his meetinghouse. His lectures are poorly attended. No wonder: he spins out the subject, proposes to have 30 lectures. They are good solid discourses, but not adequate to the expectations of them who wish to serve him. I wish he was in Ireland" (Moyne, pp. 151–52).

Ebenezer Gay at nearby Hingham, preaching at his "Old Ship Church" more than forty times. Gay was over ninety years old and had ministered to his congregation of twelve hundred for nearly seventy years. Some of the members of his parish hoped he would resign in Hazlitt's favor. But not so.

Hazlitt kept himself occupied with projects of one sort or other. When he learned from James Freeman that the parishioners at King's Chapel wished to retain a liturgical service despite their conversion to Unitarianism, he helped the committee in charge adapt to their needs the revision of the Anglican *Book of Common Prayer* made by the Reverend Dr. Theophilus Lindsey of the Essex Street Chapel in London. And when James Lewis, son of a Maidstone friend, stirred up a controversy in Boston by proposing to market goods imported from London "cheaper than ever before in this place," Hazlitt wrote for the *American Herald* a warm defense of Lewis and his family.[32]

Yet such activities produced no fixed income. A less sanguine man would have been despondent. There were occasional remittances from well-wishers in England to help make ends meet. In a letter from London dated January 21, 1785, Dr. Lindsey referred to "some little addition . . . made last year to a very small sum which your Maidstone friends sent you, by a lady of our congregation and one or two more of your friends in it."[33] Samuel Vaughan urged again that Hazlitt "undertake the tuition of a few youth." And he suggested, as diplomatically as he could, that his friend exercise more tact in dealing with congregations. "It is necessary," he wrote, "to be exceedingly attentive to the prejudices of those who, by education and long habit, have adopted erroneous opinions, more especially in religion, where *mystery* is admitted; their principles should be treated with the utmost delicacy and tenderness."[34] But Hazlitt was interested in neither teaching nor tact.

He was interested, rather, in rational religion, and he continued, with some success, to propagate it, regardless of the consequences. During the summer of 1785 he substituted several times in three churches in Salem. At the North Church he shocked his audience by publicly denying the doctrine of the Trinity. At the East Church he influenced the young minister, William Bentley, to abandon the Westminster Catechism in favor of Joseph Priestley's revision. Presently the congregation adopted Unitarian doctrines, and the Reverend Mr. Bentley gave a series of sermons attacking belief in the Trinity.[35]

Before the summer ended, Hazlitt was called to preach at Truro on Cape

32. See Moyne, pp. 155–56.   33. *Christian Reformer* 5 (1838): 507.
34. Ibid., pp. 698–99.   35. Moyne, p. 127.

Cod, and he spent three weeks there. However, "he could not," according to Peggy, "make up his mind to settle in so desolate a place." The boy William, now seven years old, went along with his father—and was similarly unimpressed. Were there no robins or Bob Lincolns there, he asked the natives. And when told that there were not, he declared baldly: "I suppose they do not like such an ugly place."

William was much happier at the big house in Weymouth. He probably had few playmates, but he loved the fields and the woods, even as he was to do in adult life. As the youngest of the surviving children—John was eleven years older and Peggy, nearly eight—he was petted and sheltered at home—obliged to stay in the shade on hot summer afternoons until four o'clock, when the sun went behind the hills. Peggy was devoted to him; in her journal she affectionately recalled standing at the window of the house at Weymouth watching her father walking up the road toward Hingham "with William, in his nankeen dress, marching at his side like one that could never be tired." He often went along on his father's trips and even sat in the pulpit while he preached. He was a favorite of Captain Abiah Whitman, one of their neighbors, and, according to Peggy, "spent half his time in going with him to the woods or to the fields to see them plough, or attending the milking of the cows." Old Mrs. Derby of Hingham "quite doated" on him "and would have him indulged in every whim." He was a docile little fellow, eager to please his elders. When he brought home a dead black snake on a stick one day, he innocently explained that "he thought mama would like to see it." Both family and friends had high hopes for his future.

In the autumn of 1785 his father left Weymouth and traveled to Hallowell, "in the Province of Maine," leaving the family behind. Samuel Vaughan, who owned a good deal of property in the area, was interested in building up the settlement, and he not only recommended Hazlitt to the townspeople as their minister but also promised to supplement the salary which they could afford to pay him. Hazlitt must have had some doubts about the situation: Hallowell, on the banks of the Kennebec River, was hardly an ideal location for a man of his intellectual interests. Yet he could ill afford to reject the chance of a steady income, especially when offered by his generous friend.

On his journey to Hallowell he met George Thatcher of Biddeford, soon to become a member of Congress, who asked permission to publish his "Discourse on the Apostle Paul's Mystery of Godliness Being Made Manifest in the Flesh." It appeared presently in Falmouth (later Portland) and enjoyed a minor success: four hundred copies were sold within a week. Meanwhile Hazlitt had set sail for Hallowell on a vessel which encountered a severe storm at the mouth of the Kennebec and narrowly escaped being completely wrecked.[36]

Hazlitt's stay at Hallowell proved more disastrous than any he had had to date. Life there was downright primitive: at night wolves prowled and howled around the house where he was staying, and since his door had no lock, he fastened the latch with his knife for protection. And he had other troubles, not so easily managed: he discovered, when he arrived, that members of the congregation at Hallowell already had a minister in residence; they had appointed the Reverend Seth Noble to fill their pulpit until the following March. Several orthodox members, led by Captain Henry Sewall, had objected to Noble's sermons and were holding separate meetings. Because Hazlitt had been sent to them (and partially subsidized) by Samuel Vaughan, the congregation voted on November 29 to retain him for two months. But when Captain Sewall went to hear him preach, he found him, if anything, more objectionable than Noble, and meetings of the orthodox group continued. A general "ferment" followed, which resulted in another meeting on December 20, when Hazlitt was officially hired "upon probation." But it was an awkward situation at best, and he was probably relieved when the congregation voted, on April 1, 1786, to appoint neither of the two candidates for their pulpit.[37] Hazlitt must have read with a rather ironic interest the letter which the Reverend John Palmer had written him on March 15 assuring him that "the income, from Mr. V[aughan]'s generosity and the contributions of the people, amounting to above 400 dollars per annum . . . is a pretty beginning, and, indeed, as you need not be told, much better a provision than is made for most ministers in country situations here." He added a cautionary note, now all too familiar:

> My friend will forgive me if I take this opportunity of reminding him, that *weak eyes are not able at once to bear a strong light*. By which I never would be understood to mean in the designed application, the suppression of any truth immediately concerning the duty or happiness or mankind; but merely such a degree of caution in

36. In her journal Peggy remarked that her father "narrowly escaped being lost in the Bay of Fundy" on his return trip. As Moyne (p. 159) observes, she "here defines the Bay of Fundy rather liberally." Probably she meant Sheepscot Bay, into which the Kennebec River flows. Hazlitt himself, in a letter to the Reverend Dr. Howard of Boston dated November 4, 1785 (*The Hazlitts*, p. 375), says that his ship was nearly wrecked at the mouth of the Kennebec on his way *to* Hallowell.

37. Moyne (pp. 157–59) has unearthed the true facts about Hazlitt's stay in Hallowell. In her journal Peggy wrote that her father left the place because life there was so primitive and it offered too little opportunity for his sons, especially John, who was already launched on a career as an artist.

the communication of your liberal ideas, on points hitherto much controverted, as is, in some degree, every where necessary to our acceptance and usefulness.[38]

Back in Weymouth Grace Hazlitt had contended all winter with innumerable hardships: a fatherless household, an inadequate income, isolation, an earthquake, and the generally harsh climate—which, as late as April 1, produced "a most tremendous gale . . . with a heavy fall of snow." And in the months ahead, though the weather improved, the family continued its meager existence, with Hazlitt again depending for support on what he could eke out from his preaching, his writing, or his friends' benevolence. Then in July, 1786, after nearly two years in Weymouth, they moved to a house in Upper Dorchester, five miles from Boston. Young John's developing career as an artist[39] kept him, like his father, away from home a good deal of the time, and Mrs. Hazlitt and the two younger children were often left alone. A house nearer the city would be safer and more convenient for all.[40]

The Dorchester house was smaller than the one in Weymouth—and, though "pleasantly situated" with a fine view of Boston Harbor, the city, and the Blue Hills, it was, in Peggy's estimation, "not to be compared to the one we had left." There were compensations though: the neighbors proved to be friendly, and the family could get back and forth to the city easily. But the move did not solve their most pressing problem, and Hazlitt finally admitted to himself that he was unlikely ever to find a "permanent settlement" in America. Experience had convinced him at last that liberal religion did not have so universal an appeal as liberal politics in the new nation.

He made plans then to sail back to England in the autumn, leaving his family to follow as soon as he could find a place for them. For his wife this meant another winter without her husband's support, another difficult voyage across the ocean. But she could console herself with the thought that, at long last, God willing, she could return to a more stable life. She may well have had a good deal to do with her husband's decision; for before he left Boston he took Peggy aside and "charged me, above all things, to

38. *Christian Reformer* 5 (1838): 759.

39. In his Introduction Moyne (pp. 15–20) discusses the quite remarkable achievements of John Hazlitt, still only nineteen years old, before he returned to England.

40. So Peggy explained the move. But a letter which Mrs. Cranch, owner of the house, wrote to her sister Abigail Adams on October 8 suggests that the Hazlitts may have been asked to move out of the house so that she could rent it to a Mr. Evans, the new minister at Weymouth. If so, she was the loser because Evans decided not to settle in Weymouth, and she was left without a tenant (see Moyne, p. 159).

be careful of and attentive to my mother, and endeavour by every means in my power to keep up her spirits and soften every care."

Hazlitt embarked from Boston aboard the *Rebecca* on October 23, but after sailing a mile, the captain of the ship was forced to return to port for the night. The next day they put out again, but the ship sprang a dangerous leak, and after several days of hovering near the coast in heavy seas they put back into Boston on November 2. Hazlitt had a few more days with his family in Dorchester, then sailed again on the seventh. But his ship encountered "squalls, tempests, and hurricanes in succession," and he was tortured by fears for his own life and for the welfare of his family.[41] At last they reached port in Dover on or about December 14, and he went to stay in London with his friend David Lewis until he could locate a place to settle.

He made little progress. At one point he thought he might be called to a congregation in Norwich, but they chose instead a man named Houghton, pastor of a little church in Wem in Shropshire. When he appealed to influential friends for aid, they only countered with more suggestions that he open a school or teach; he later complained bitterly that "some, even of his *quondam* Unitarian friends, whilst they congratulated him upon his successful transatlantic services, gave him but a cool reception."[42] And while he was still searching about, he received from America the chilling news that the death of old Ebenezer Gay of Hingham and the resignation of Dr. William Gordon of Roxbury had left vacant two pulpits which might well have been offered to him. His consolation, as always, was that he had made his presence felt, that he had paved the way for a more rational religion in America. In later years he proudly claimed that his "labours . . . laid the foundation of Unitarianism in that country, he having left behind him some warm friends to the cause wherever he went."[43] And he was not alone in thinking so; in June, 1789, the Reverend James Freeman wrote to the Reverend Theophilus Lindsey: "Before Mr. Hazlitt came to Boston, the Trinitarian doxology was almost universally used. That honest, good man prevailed upon several respectable ministers to omit it. Since his departure the number of those who repeat only scriptural doxologies has greatly increased, so that there are now many churches in which the worship is strictly Unitarian."[44]

---

41. Peggy copied into her journal (Moyne, pp. 82–88) several pages from the diary which her father kept when he was able to sit up and hold a pen.

42. Moyne, p. 122.   43. Ibid., p. 120.

44. Thomas Belsham, *Memoirs of the Late Rev. Theophilus Lindsey* (London and Edinburgh, 1873), p. 154 n. For other accounts of Hazlitt's share in the development of Uni-

In Dorchester the family was looking forward to their return to England in the spring. John spared time from his painting to teach young William the elements of Latin grammar, but the boy proved a rather reluctant pupil. He was still, however, as eager as ever to please his elders. On November 12, five days after his father's second departure, he wrote[45] dutifully:

> My dear Papa,—I shall never forget that we came to america. If we had not came to america, we should not have been away from one and other, though now it can not be helped. I think for my part that it would have been a great deal better if the white people had not found it out. Let the [Indians] have it to themselves, for it was made for them. I have got a little of my grammar; sometimes I get three pages and some-times but one. I do not sifer at all. Mama Peggy and Jacky are all very well, and I am to. I still remain
>
> Your most affectionate son
William, Hazlitt

Later in life he was to draw again and again in his essays on his recollections of his childhood—but not of his years in America. It was Peggy who was to recall William's trips about the countryside with his father, his days in the field with Captain Whitman, his dislike of barren Cape Cod, where no birds sang, the great fire at Boston which the family watched in horror on April 18, 1787, their absent father's fiftieth birthday. William himself referred in his writing only to "the taste of barberries, which have hung out in the snow during the severity of a North American winter" (8:259).[46] Apparently his family's venture into the New World was an unfortunate mistake which he would gladly have forgotten.

And no wonder; for certainly the frequent moves, the worries about finances, his little sisters' deaths, his mother's illnesses, the inevitable strain

---

tarianism, see George Willis Cooke, *Unitarianism in America* (Boston: American Unitarian Assn., 1902), pp. 71 and 76–79; Earl Morse Wilbur, *A History of Unitarianism* (Cambridge, Mass.: Harvard University Press, 1952), p. 391 n; and Conrad Wright, *The Beginnings of Unitarianism in America* (Boston: Star King Press, 1955), pp. 213–15. Hazlitt himself went so far as to prophesy that "there is every reason to expect, that in thirty or forty years more the whole of Massachusetts will be Unitarian" (Moyne, p. 122).

45. *The Hazlitts*, p. 377. Although several of William's early letters to his family were first printed in W. Carew Hazlitt, *Memoirs of William Hazlitt*, 2 vols. (London, 1867) (hereafter cited as *Memoirs*), I have followed the later transcripts in *The Hazlitts* because they are more inclusive. I have not, however, accepted W. C. Hazlitt's dating of the letters, which is often manifestly inaccurate.

46. Here and elsewhere two arabic numbers separated by a colon indicate the volume and page of the definitive edition of Hazlitt's works: *Complete Works of William Hazlitt*, ed. P. P. Howe, centenary ed., 21 vols. (London and Toronto: J. M. Dent and Sons, Ltd., 1930–34).

between his parents, the constant uncertainty and insecurity made their mark on him. Though pampered in the family, he had at the same time felt severe pressures as a child. If he seemed too eager to please, it was because he longed for a sense of security which he had never gained. Later in life he was to strike his readers as remarkably sensitive and his friends as abnormally irritable; he was never to mature emotionally, never to know any lasting serenity or even self-confidence; he was forever begging for acceptance, recognition—forever lamenting that he was unappreciated and unloved. By the time he was nine years old he had seen far more of the world than all but a few of his contemporaries would ever see. But his experiences had tended not to enrich his mind and character but to warp them.

At last, on Independence Day, 1787, the family sailed for England on the *Nonpareil*. They had a pleasant crossing; the weather was good, both crew and passengers were congenial, and they were able to spend most of their time on deck. There was one sad event, when a young crewman fell from the topmast and was drowned. But there was also much to delight a growing boy: fishing off the Grand Banks, watching the strange sea creatures—dolphins and porpoises, whales and sharks—and the even stranger menagerie aboard, consisting of several mocking birds, half a dozen foxes, some hens, and a rattlesnake. The high point of the trip came at the "half way house," when the boatswain dressed up as Neptune and claimed a fee from the passengers.

Yet no part of the trip could compare with the bright Sunday morning, August 12, when they reached Portsmouth at last and set their feet on good solid English earth. The next day they went by stagecoach to London, where the Reverend Mr. Hazlitt met them and took them to stay at the Lewises' house. In their joy at being reunited they could overlook for the time being their concern that he still had no prospect of a settlement.

After "some weeks" with the Lewises the family went to Walworth for two weeks so that Mrs. Hazlitt, whose health was, as Peggy put it, "very indifferent," might benefit from the bracing air. Back in London they took a part of a house on Percy Street, and Grandmother Loftus, still spry at eighty-four, came up to spend a month with the family.

Young William was delighted with the bustling city. His sister Peggy was kept constantly on the alert to prevent him from running out to explore the streets—though, she later recalled proudly, "he never lost his way." While his mother was recuperating, young William and his father spent a good deal of time together. One of their haunts was the Montpelier Tea Gardens at Walworth, which, twenty-five years later, stuck in William's memory as the "'first garden of my innocence,'" the ideal by which he judged all the gardens that he had seen afterwards (8:257).

The Reverend Mr. Hazlitt had high hopes for the boy: with Loftus and Thomas dead and John committed to a career as a painter, William was, as he interpreted the phrase, his "only begotten son." [47] If all went well, the boy who had sat in the pulpit while his father preached would one day be himself a preacher.

But always there must be an *if*. This time it hinged on the unformed character of young William. At Weymouth his brother John had painted his portrait in miniature, a portrait which could almost pass as that of a pretty, mild-mannered little girl. He seemed to be made all of soft, malleable clay which could be shaped at will. Yet who could tell? If this young Hazlitt proved to have the hard vein of independence which ran through his family —nowhere more prominently than in "that honest, good man" his father— he might turn out to be no more malleable than a slab of granite.

47. In a letter to the *Monthly Repository* for June, 1814, the Reverend Mr. Hazlitt argued that the phrase should be interpreted to mean *favorite*.

CHAPTER II

Man Proposes
(1787–1798)

Sometime during the autumn of 1787 the Reverend Mr. Hazlitt was at last offered a pastorate. The little congregation at Wem in Shropshire, ten miles from Shrewsbury, invited him to succeed the Reverend Mr. Houghton, the man who had been named to the vacancy at Norwich for which Hazlitt had applied. It was hardly the sort of situation he had hoped for; Wem was a little market town—"an obscure inland town," Peggy later called it— which offered small scope for a man of Hazlitt's bustling talents. There was a tradition in the place that Oliver Cromwell had looked down on it from a hill and decided that it was not worth taking. Hazlitt could not, however, afford to be so discriminating, and he reluctantly accepted the offer. At least it provided him with an income of sorts. And his Unitarian friends, the Lewises and David Williams, assured him that they would be on the alert for a better post.

Late in November Mr. and Mrs. Hazlitt, Peggy, and William moved down to Wem, leaving John behind in London to study under Sir Joshua Reynolds—and to embark, almost immediately, on a career as a miniaturist.[1] They felt very little enthusiasm for the place. As usual Mrs. Hazlitt's impressions went unrecorded; they were doubtless a mixture of resignation and relief. Young Peggy, however, was more vocal: so far as she was concerned, Wem was "a dismal place to sit down in after all that we had seen." And her

1. John Hazlitt exhibited his first painting at the Royal Academy in the following year. During that same year he painted portraits of Dr. Price and Dr. Kippis as well as several of his family's Maidstone friends. Apparently his father's friends were making an effort to aid him—and perhaps, through him, his parents.

father felt much the same way. He was fifty years old now and little better off than when he had started his career. His salary was thirty pounds a year, supplemented by such grants as his influential friends might secure for him from time to time. Dr. Kippis regularly sent him five pounds or more from the Presbyterian Fund and another five pounds from Dr. Williams's Trust,[2] and he received occasional gifts from William Tayleur, a prosperous Unitarian living in Shrewsbury. He had some additional income, too, from the day school which he took over from his predecessor, the Reverend Mr. Houghton. But it all added up to a meager income for a man in middle life with three people still dependent on him—one of them a boy who was to be educated for the ministry.

Hazlitt was a devout man who accepted his lot without bitterness. Yet he was a rationalist too, and he found it difficult to understand why his talents and his zeal had not been better rewarded. For years he persevered in his attempts to better his lot. And in 1808, after reviewing his contributions to the Unitarian cause, he commented ruefully in the *Monthly Repository:* "Our fashion is to expend large sums of money in training up young men for the ministry, and to desert those who have spent their best days in our service, or to suffer them to sink unpitied under the burden of age and infirmities, whilst we follow our pleasures, or act only upon the spur of caprice."[3] His articulate children were more outspoken; in her journal Peggy deplored his fate, "so very different from his former life . . . shut out from the society of men of learning and talents." And William, in 1823, wrote feelingly of his father's long banishment, "repining but resigned," spending "the last thirty years of his life, far from the only converse that he loved, the talk about disputed texts of Scripture and the cause of civil and religious liberty" (17:110).

However, young William had no complaints in 1787. According to his sister, "he liked Wem better than any of us"; he even liked the "ugly" old Tudor cottage which served as parsonage. And he especially relished the opportunity to attend school for the first time.

One Saturday morning in March, 1788, the boy sat down to reply to a letter which he had just received from his brother. "We were all glad to hear that you were well," he wrote, "and that you have so much business to do. We cannot be happy without being employed. I want you to tell me whether you go to the Academy or not, and what pictures you intend for

2. See H. W. Stephenson, *William Hazlitt and Hackney College* (London: The Lindsey Press, 1930), pp. 55–58 (hereafter cited as Stephenson).
3. Moyne, p. 122.

the exhibition. Tell the exhibitioners to finish the exhibition soon, that you may come and see us. You must send your picture to us directly." As for himself, he too was busy; he had decided, for the moment, that he would be a painter like his brother. "I am a busy body, and do many silly things," he continued; "I drew eyes and noses till about a fortnight ago. I have drawn a little boy since, a man's face, and a little boy's front face taken from a bust." But he was not neglecting his school work:

> Next Monday I shall begin to read Ovid's *Metamorphoses* and Eutropius. I shall like to know all the Latin and Greek I can. I want to learn how to measure the stars. I shall not, I suppose, paint the worse for knowing everything else. I begun to cypher a fortnight after Christmas, and shall go into the rule of three next week. I can teach a boy of sixteen already who was cyphering eight months before me; is he not a great dunce? I shall go through the whole cyphering book this summer, and then I am to learn Euclid.

He then reviewed his daily routine: "We go to school at nine every morning. Three boys begin with reading the Bible. Then I and two others show our exercises. We then read [Enfield's] *Speaker*. Then we all set about our lessons, and those who are first ready say first. At eleven we write and cypher. In the afternoon we stand for places at spelling, and I am almost always first. We also read, and do a great deal of business besides." He gave his schoolmates short shrift: ". . . some are so sulky they wont play; others are quarrelsome because they cannot learn, and are only fit for fighting like stupid dogs and cats." And presently he was indulging himself in a bit of brag: "I can jump four yards at a running jump, and two at a standing jump. I intend to try you at this when you come down." Then: "You spelled Mr. Vaughan's name wrong, for you spelled it Vaughn."[4]

John was fond of his little brother and doubtless pleased with the precocity which the letter displayed. He had been raised in the same household and would hardly have been annoyed by the preachy truism "We cannot be happy without being employed," or the boy's condescending attitude toward his fellows—even toward the brother whom he obviously longed to emulate. John probably took in his stride, too, the brusque statement later in the letter: "I don't want your old clothes." Certainly their father would have approved of the letter, and so would Peggy, who thought William a jewel of a child. Looking back on this period of his life years afterward, she wrote in her journal: "He was at this time the most active, lively, and happiest of boys; his time, divided between his studies and his childish sports, passed smoothly on. Beloved by all for his amiable temper and manners, pleasing

4. *The Hazlitts*, pp. 378–79.

above his years, [he was] the delight and pride of his own family." And the
Reverend Joseph Hunter reported that a neighbor at Wem remembered
him as "one of the most entertaining and prepossessing children ever seen." 5
But a less sympathetic reader of the boy's letter to his brother might have
deduced from it that there was another arrogant William Hazlitt in the
making.

He was probably not a great favorite among his schoolmates. To be sure,
a friend named William Cottam was well enough disposed toward him to
rescue him once when he was in danger of drowning. But he probably
shared (and made apparent) his sister's conviction that "there was but one
boy in the school who had more than common abilities or could give a spur
to his exertions." And they probably left him pretty much to himself. Later
in life, when he looked back nostalgically on his boyhood at Wem, he had
nothing to say about his companions; rather, he recalled watering the kitchen
garden, flying a kite, hearing the manager of a strolling company of players
knock on the door (18:294), listening to the curfew-bell (17:242) or to the
tunes which "our old fantastic dancing master used to scrape up on his kit"
(18:215); he told of looking at a series of prints of John Gilpin's Ride "while
the old ladies were playing at whist, and the young ones at forfeits" (18:222);
he remembered watching the distant blue hills of Wales at sunset like
"glimmering air woven into fantastic shapes"—and then finding them, at
close range, to be only "huge lumpish heaps of discolored earth" (8:256).
There were times when he even longed to be back in America.6

The year 1789 brought no changes to the family at the parsonage.
William continued to apply himself to his studies, honoring his father and
mother, though probably extending little charity toward his neighbors in the
classroom. His father continued to tend his flock and to hope for more
fertile pastures. He must have been cheered by the progress of freedom
across the Channel in France and shared the emotions which his friend Dr.
Price expressed so resonantly in the "Nunc Dimittis" concluding his sermon
on the hundredth anniversary of the "Bloodless Revolution": "Lord,
lettest thou thy servant depart in peace, for mine eyes have seen the salvation:
I have seen two glorious revolutions." It was indeed bliss to be alive at such

5. P. P. Howe, *Life of William Hazlitt*, new ed. (London: Hamish Hamilton, 1947),
pp. 11–12 (hereafter cited as Howe).

6. The Reverend James Freeman of Boston wrote to the Reverend Mr. Hazlitt in
June, 1789: "Your son Billy must not like America better than England, because this is
certainly not so fine a country as yours. Bid him remember that we have here many such
places as Cape Cod, where we are obliged to walk up to our knees in sand, and have little
else except fish to eat" (*Christian Reformer* 6 [1839]: 19).

a time—provided one was not buried alive in a place like Wem. The boy William, who reached his eleventh birthday in April, caught some of the fervor; he too was a lover of liberty. "I set out in life with the French Revolution," he wrote in 1827, "and that event had considerable influence on my early feelings, as on those of others. Youth was then doubly such. It was the dawn of a new era, a new impulse had been given to men's minds" (17:196–97).

In this same year the Reverend Mr. Hazlitt decided to bid for a wider audience—and, with luck, a better situation—by preparing ten "discourses" for publication. As usual he called on an influential friend, this time Dr. Theophilus Lindsey, to aid him, and Lindsey broached the project to the liberal bookseller Joseph Johnson. At first Johnson shied away; Lindsey reported to Hazlitt in August that "his advice is to desist for the present, as he has several publications of the kind for next winter, and they go on very heavily." [7] But by the following January 2, Lindsey was engaged in negotiations with Johnson: " . . . he desired me to acquaint you, that the expense of printing 250 copies will be defrayed by the sale of 150," he wrote to Hazlitt, "and leave some small matter for the author; but he does not undertake for his indemnification if he prints a greater number of copies." [8] The publisher must have been startled when Hazlitt presented him with a list of 141 subscribers—later printed in the published volume—who had agreed to buy a total of 183 copies of the discourses. It included all Hazlitt's distinguished friends in the clergy, several ministers from towns near Wem, plus numerous admirers from London, Dublin, Cork, New York, Halifax, Nova Scotia, Shrewsbury, Maidstone, Bandon, and Wem, among other places. Someone had done a very thorough job of salesmanship.

That summer, while his father's book was going through the press, William and another clergyman's son, George Dicken, were invited to spend a few weeks in Liverpool as guests of Mrs. Tracey, a widow from Jamaica who had been living at Wem while her daughters were in school. While he was away from home he reported faithfully—and sententiously— to his parents. "Dear Mother," he began, on Friday, July 9, "It is with pleasure I now sit down to write to you, and it is with pleasure that I do anything, which I know, will please you." And presently he was edifying her with a capsule sermon. He had dined with a Mr. Fisher,

a very rich man, but—The man who is a well-wisher to slavery, is always a slave himself. The King, who wishes to enslave all mankind, is a slave to ambition; The man who wishes to enslave all mankind for his King, is himself a slave to his King.

7. *Christian Reformer* 5 (1838): 756.　　　8. Ibid., p. 510.

He like others of his brethren, I suppose, wished that Mr. Beaufoy was out, or with the Devil, he did not care which. You see that he wished to have him out, merely because "*he would do to others as he would be done to.*" The man who is a well-wisher to liberty, wishes to have men good, and himself to be one of them, and knows that men are not good unless they are so willingly, and does not attempt to force them to it, but tries to put them in such a situation as will induce them to be good. Slavery is not a state for men to improve in, therefore he does not wish them to be in that condition.

Then, after remarking that he is "concerned to hear you have so little money, . . . but I hope that your portion is not in this world, you have trouble for a few days, but have joy for many. The RICH take their fill in a few years, are cut short in the midst of their career, and fall into ruin; Never to rise again. But the good shall have joy for evermore.—Be sure to tell me if I may sell my old Buckles."

On the following Tuesday he continued his letter in a curious mélange of childish treble and manly bass: he wants it known that he now understands "the 2nd problem," that he has translated eleven fables from French and learned to conjugate eleven verbs; he asks to be remembered to "Mrs. and Miss Cottons, and to every inquirer"; and, mindful of his father's interests, he reports that their friend Isaac Kingston has "attempted to get Papa to Cork, but found it was useless to attempt it." Kingston, he explained, "said that he was sorry that Papa had not a better place, and wished that he would set up a school, that is a boarding school; and that there was no man in the world to whom he would sooner send his children. He has 3 Boys, the eldest of which is 5 years old, within a few months." And again he was moved to philosophize, this time because he had seen men impressed for military service: "The world is not quite perfect yet; nor will it ever be so whilst such practices are reckoned lawful." [9]

The following Monday and Tuesday he wrote again, this time to his father. He was not, he made clear, frittering away his holiday in frivolous pursuits. He was translating the New Testament and had advanced "39 verses from the place I was in before." He was sharing the Tracey girls' geography lessons under a Mr. Clegg, had been "as attentive as I could be," and had mastered the maps of Asia and Africa. He was planning to resume his study of Latin and to that end had written to a local clergyman: "Mr. Hazlitt sends his compliments to Mr. Yates, and would be much obliged to him if he would send him a dictionary and an *Horace*. P.S. papa desired me to remember him to you." He had been almost letter perfect in his

9. *The Hazlitts,* pp. 383–86.

French lesson for "Mr. Dolounghpryee" (as he spelled De Lemprière), but had lagged in his study of music and to date had mastered only "God Save the King" on the harpsichord.

Yet he had occasional diversions: he was about to go to a concert, and he had already been to the theater with a Mr. Corbett to see John Philip Kemble's *Love in Many Masks*, a dramatic adaptation of Aphra Behn's *Rover*, and, as a companion piece, Prince Hoare's operatic farce, *No Song, No Supper*. The occasion inspired his first essay in dramatic criticism: "Suett, who acted in the character of Ned Blunt, was enough to make any one laugh, though he stood still; and Kemble acted admirably as an officer. Mr. Dignum sang beautifully, and Miss Hagley acted the country-girl with much exactness." [10]

He had been less pleased with his first Church of England service. "I do not care if I should never go into one again," he told his father. "The Clergyman, after he had gabbled over half a dozen prayers, began his sermon, the text of which was as follows: Zachariah, 3rd chapter, 2nd verse, latter part—'Is not this a brand plucked out of the fire?' If a person had come in five minutes after he began, he would have thought that he had taken his text out of Joshua. In short, his sermon had neither head nor tail. I was sorry that so much time should be thrown away upon nonsense." The youthful critic then closed his letter with a brief sermon of his own:

> How ineffectual are all pleasures, except those which arise from a knowledge of having done, as far as one knew, that which was right, to make their possessors happy. The people who possess them, at night, lie down upon their beds, and after having spent a wearisome night, rise up in the morning to pursue the same "pleasures," or, more properly, vain shadows of pleasures, which, like Jacks with lanthorns, as they are called, under a fair outside at last bring those people who are so foolish as to confide in them into destruction, which they cannot then escape. *How* different from them is a man who *wisely "in a time of peace, lays up arms, and such like necessaries in case of a war."* [11]

The following Saturday he was in an even more admonitory mood. "Dear Father," he began,

10. He never forgot that evening, although, characteristically, he confused the date. Thirty-six years later, in 1826, he wrote: "I met Dignum (the singer) in the street the other day: he was humming a tune; and his eye, though quenched, was smiling. I could scarcely forbear going up to speak to him. Why so? I had seen him in the year 1792 (the first time I ever was at a play), with Suett and Miss Romanzini and some others, in NO SONG NO SUPPER; and ever since, that bright vision of my childhood has played round my fancy with unabated, vivid delight" (12:193).

11. *The Hazlitts*, pp. 386–89.

I now sit down to spend a little time in an employment, the productions of which I know will give you pleasure, though I know that every minute that I am employed in doing anything which will be advantageous to me, will give you pleasure. Happy, indeed unspeakably happy, are those people who, when at the point of death, are able to say, with a satisfaction which none but themselves can have any idea of—"I have done with this world, I shall now have no more of its temptations to struggle with, and praise be to God I have overcome them; now no more sorrow, now no more grief, but happiness for evermore!" But how unspeakably miserable is that man who, when his pleasures are going to end, when his lamp begins to grow dim, is compelled to say—"Oh that I had done my duty to God and man! oh that I had been wise, and spent that time which was kindly given me by Providence, for a purpose quite contrary to that which I employed it to, as I should have done; but it is now gone; I cannot recal time, nor can I undo all my wicked actions. I cannot seek that mercy which I have so often despised. I have no hope remaining. I must do as well as I can—but who can endure everlasting fire?" Thus does the wicked man breathe his last, and without being able to rely upon his good, with his last breath, in the anguish of his soul, says, "Have mercy upon me a sinner, O God!"

He turned his attention then to more controversial matters:

After I had sealed up my last letter to you, George [Dicken] asked me if I were glad the Test Act was not repealed? I told him, No. Then he asked me why? and I told him because I thought that all the people who are the inhabitants of a country, of whatever sect or denomination, should have the same rights with others.—But, says he, then they would try to get their religion established, or something to that purpose.—Well, what if it should be so?—He said that the Church religion was an old one.—Well, said I, Popery is older than that.—But then, said he, the Church religion is better than Popery.—And the Presbyterian is better than that, said I. I told him I thought so for certain reasons, not because I went to chapel. But at last, when I had overpowered him with my arguments, he said he wished he understood it as well as I did, for I was too high learned for him.

He continued his letter on Monday morning, reporting on his progress in his studies during the past week: he had been, he declared, "very attentive" to "Mr. Dolounghpryeé," but he had "not yet learned the gamut perfectly." He had accomplished nothing in Latin because Mr. Yates had failed to send him the needed dictionary and Horace; however, he was devoting "an hour or two every other day" to "accompts," and he "spent a very agreeable day yesterday, as I read 160 pages of Priestley, and heard two good sermons." His sweet reasonableness abandoned him, though, when he described the "ceremonial unsociality" of some English ladies he had met. It had even made him wish himself, momentarily, back in America.[12]

12. Ibid., pp. 380–83.

On Sunday, July 31, his father replied to the letter, point by point, his his heart swelling with pride:

> The piety displayed in the first part of it was a great refreshment to me. Continue to cherish those thoughts which then occupied your mind, continue to be virtuous, and you will finally be that happy being whom you describe, and to this purpose you will have nothing more to do than to pursue that conduct, which will always yield you the highest pleasures even in this present life. But he who once gives way to any known vice, in the very instant hazards his total depravity and total ruin. You must, therefore, fixedly resolve never, through any possible motives, to do any thing which you believe to be wrong. This will be only resolving never to be miserable, and this I rejoycingly expect will be the unwavering resolution of my William.[13]

He was equally gratified by William's triumph over George Dicken, observing: "Your conversation upon the Test Act did you honour. If we only think justly we shall always easily foil all the advocates of tyranny." He could not, however, wholly approve of William's strictures on the English ladies:

> The inhospitable ladies whom you mention were, perhaps, treated by you with too great severity. We know not how people may be circumstanced at a particular moment, whose disposition is generally friendly. They may happen to pass under a cloud, which unfits them for social intercourse. . . . I do not say, however, that the English ladies whom you mentioned are not exactly as you described them. I only wish to caution you against forming too hasty a judgment of characters, who can seldom be known at a single interview.

But otherwise he offered nothing but praise for the boy's lofty sentiments and his diligence. "I am glad," he wrote, "that you have made so great a progress in French, and that you are so very anxious to hear Mr. Clegg's lectures. It is a pity that you cannot have another month at the French, &c. But, as matters are, I hope you will soon be able to master that language. I am glad that you employed the last Sunday so well, and that the employment afforded you so much satisfaction. Nothing else can truly satisfy us but the acquisition of knowledge and virtue. May these blessings be yours more and more every day." And he added the comments of Kirk Boot, one of their Boston friends, on a recent letter from William: "The letter does Billy much credit. He has uncommon powers of mind, and if nothing happens to prevent his receiving a liberal education, he must make a great

13. As Patricia Dale has pointed out (*NQ* 208 [1963]: 146), Joseph Conrad clearly echoes the third and fourth sentences of this passage in a letter written to "Lord Jim" by his father.

man." [14] "This compliment, I know," Hazlitt observed confidently, "will not make you proud or conceited, but more diligent."

He concluded his letter with detailed, solicitous directions for William's return home: he was to travel by boat from Liverpool to Eastham unless "the weather be blowing, or if it be not very fine," in which case he should "wait until it be just what you could wish." At Eastham a horse would be waiting to carry him to Wem "if you be not afraid to ride him, and if you do not dislike this mode of travelling." He must not fail "to call upon all persons who have shewn you any particular civilities" and to thank Mrs. Tracey for her hospitality, his teachers "for their attention," and Mr. Yates for the loan of his books. [15]

A week later, on Saturday, August 6, the Reverend Mr. Hazlitt wrote again, showing the same concern about his son's safe return and reminding him that he must take proper leave of all who had been kind to him. William's last letter, he wrote, "gave us much satisfaction, though you disappointed us in not being more particular in answer to my inquiries." [16]

It was clear, however, that the boy rarely disappointed him. He was well pleased with this, his "only begotten son"; he accepted complacently the boy's docile adherence to the pattern of the model child, his facile parroting of his elders. Young William seemed born to teach God's word. With such a son, a man could endure even Wem, if it were so ordained.

Still, he continued to hope for advancement for himself—and, no doubt, to pin his hopes on the publication of his discourses—with some justification. For this volume, which arrived from London soon after William's return from Liverpool, was addressed to simple, hardheaded people, the very sort who might be asked to serve on a committee to choose a Dissenting parson. The title itself, *Discourses for the Use of Families, on the Advantages of a Free Inquiry, and on the Study of the Scripture*, said what needed to be said, and no more. The advertisement went directly to the point:

> The author of the following plain Discourses hopes they will be useful. Plain discourses, in his opinion, are best calculated for general benefit. He must remark, also, that most clergymen seem to suppose their audiences wiser than they really are, and that, on this ground, they frequently address to them such profound disquisitions, as can be of no use because above their comprehension. It will be allowed, that the best mode of diffusing a knowledge of the scriptures, and of practically enforcing all its doctrines, is the great business of preaching. He does not, therefore, give in to

14. Peggy Hazlitt states in her *Journal* that Boot "wished to have my brother William and bring him up as a merchant."

15. *The Hazlitts*, pp. 389–93.   16. Ibid., pp. 393–95.

the fashion of amusing the reader, or the hearer, with a sentimental *ignis fatuus*, or with a trim philosophical essay, which seems to have almost any other object more in view than christian edification. Others will continue to think differently from him. Let every one be fully persuaded in his own mind.[17]

And the ten sermons themselves were similarly free of oratorical flourishes; in fact, Hazlitt was so eager to drive his points home that he had no mercy on his readers. For example:

> An indolent habit, and a precipitate conduct are equally prejudicial to our best interests.
>
> The mind, as well as the body, was, it is obvious, originally intended for labour.
>
> But, that we might not labour in vain, it has pleased God, in his goodness, to give us reason to *examine*, and an understanding to *know*, *the things that are true*.
>
> And, as he is the absolutely perfect being, who does nothing in vain, it must, therefore, be his sovereign will, that we exert, and improve those great talents which he has committed to our trust. Certainly, therefore, it must be our highest honour and happiness to comply with the divine appointment.[18]

In content the discourses fused Calvinism and Unitarianism, duty and reason; they stressed obedience to the Scriptures as the basis for a rational life. Their only shortcoming was that they might suggest, even to the simple, hard-headed members of a selection committee, that the author might be a rather prickly creature to handle. And no selection committee called on him, although he continued to hope for aid from his influential friends. In December, 1790, Dr. Kippis wrote, with a hint of impatience: "I am truly concerned for your disadvantageous situation, but I have had no opportunity of recommending you to a better. All the vacancies go to young men." Hazlitt seems to have expressed some concern about young William's education, for Kippis asked, "What is it that you design or wish with regard to your younger son?"[19]

The years 1790 and 1791 were disheartening in other ways to a man of the Reverend Mr. Hazlitt's sympathies. The excesses of the French Revolution had brought about a general revulsion in England: there was a surge of reactionary feeling, of ugly outbursts directed at all forms of liberal principles and their adherents. On July 14, 1791, a mob in Birmingham celebrated the second anniversary of the storming of the Bastille by marching on the

17. William Hazlitt, *Discourses for the Use of Families*, . . . (London, 1790), no page number or signature.

18. Ibid., pp. 1–2.

19. Stephenson, p. 57.

house of Dr. Joseph Priestley and burning it to the ground. In the aftermath Priestley became a symbol of the liberal cause—and the scapegoat of all antirevolutionists, several of whom poured out their spleen in letters to the Shrewsbury *Chronicle*. And it was in reply to them and in impassioned defense of religious freedom that young William Hazlitt, writing under the pseudonym *EΛIAΣON* ("Have mercy"), made his first appearance in print. "'Tis really surprising," he wrote, "that men—men, too, that aspire to the character of Christians—should seem to take such pleasure in endeavouring to load with infamy one of the best, one of the wisest, and one of the greatest of men." And presently: "Ah! Christianity, how art thou debased! How am I grieved to see that universal benevolence, that love to all mankind, that love even to our enemies, and that compassion for the failings of our fellow-men that thou art contracted to promote, contracted and shrunk up within the narrow limits that prejudice and bigotry mark out."[20]

There was a good deal more in a similar strain, impassioned if not profound, sincere if not original—and certainly remarkable as the production of a thirteen-year-old boy. The Reverend Mr. Hazlitt had been blessed indeed. Given a few more years and a suitable education, his son would surely prove to be one of the brightest ornaments of rational religion, a jewel in his father's crown.

Nor was this all. In the following year William took a much more decisive step. Writing about it thirty-six years later, he concluded that it was his first venture in independent thinking:

> When I was about fourteen (as long ago as 1792), in consequence of a dispute, one day after coming out of meeting, between my father and an old lady of the congregation, respecting the repeal of the Corporation and Test Acts and the limits of religious toleration, I set about forming in my head (the first time I ever attempted to think) [a] system of political rights and general jurisprudence.
>
> It was this circumstance that decided the fate of my future life. . . . (19:302)

The result was an ambitious essay eventually to be known as "Project for a New Theory of Civil and Criminal Legislation."

It was hard going. "I began," he recalled in 1828, "with trying to define what a *right* meant. . . . The next question I asked myself was, what is law and the real and necessary ground of civil government" (19:303–5). They were knotty questions for a boy of fourteen to master. But he was no quitter; having taken up the challenge, he grappled with the problem. When the

20. *The Hazlitts*, pp. 395–96. W. C. Hazlitt suspected that the Reverend Mr. Hazlitt might have had a hand in the letter; however, it is closer in style to the hortatory passages of young William's letters from Liverpool than to his father's published sermons.

Church of England rector at Wem made a practice of lighting a fire of weeds and rubbish whenever the wind was blowing toward a neighbor's garden, William asked himself, "Was this an action of assault and battery, or not? I think it was" (19:312–13). He applied himself so wholeheartedly to the subject that in time he quite literally collapsed.

It was not solely his work on the essay that brought on the trouble; it was overwork in general—the result of that relentless compulsion which drove him to cram his head full of mathematics and geography and French and Latin and music, to read sermons for his own edification and compose them for his parents'—all while he was supposedly in Liverpool on holiday. There must have been warning signs which his father ignored in his delight at the boy's precocity and which his mother was powerless to counter. And they were doubtless stunned when the crisis struck.

The nature of the crisis is vague. William himself referred to it only once in after years: in an essay addressed to his son when the boy was eleven years old he cautioned him against overwork at school, saying: "I applied too close to my studies, soon after I was of your age, and hurt myself irreparably by it" (17:91). His sister Peggy wrote in her journal that "he attended so closely to his studies [that] his overexertion (when about fifteen) brought on a fit. And although he had no return of it, it was long before he recovered [from] the effects of it." Was it a fit of nerves or did he suffer a physical breakdown as well? Peggy does not say.

But one point is clear: that coupled with it, or as a result of it, came a sudden, violent access of adolescent rebellion. So much is apparent from the report of the Reverend Joseph Hunter, a close friend of the Hazlitt family many years later. Hunter's facts were not always accurate;[21] he was repeating accounts, possibly exaggerated over the years, which he had heard from friends who had known the Hazlitts at Wem. But the symptoms which he records are typical:

> he became sullen: and this sullenness continued ever after, and formed the predominant feature in his character during the remainder of his schoolboy days. He now showed his talent for satire, mimicry, and caricature. By the time he was twelve or thirteen, he would not attend the devotions of the family. He would not go to chapel. He would shut himself up from the rest of the family: be seen by no one during the

21. Hunter claimed that the change in William's character took place when he was nine years old as a result of his stay at Mrs. Tracey's in Liverpool, where he felt slighted because his hostess left him so much to himself. The boy was twelve when he visited Mrs. Tracey, and his letters, though often critical, offer no hint that he felt neglected; moreover, they offer the clearest illustration that survives of his docility before the crisis.

day: but at night he would ramble forth no one knew where: and in the moonlight
nights he used to scamper about the fields like, as my informant says, any wild
thing.[22]

He was following a familiar pattern: the sullenness, the satire, the abrupt
rejection of religion and family, the solitary moonlight romps. William had
discovered that there were more things in heaven and earth than were
dreamt of in his father's philosophy.

He had always been an avid reader. He had been brought up among
readers: his father was a born bookworm, though of very limited tastes. His
library contained some "little duodecimo volumes of the Tatler," but they
were "overwhelmed and surrounded" by "tomes of casuistry and ecclesias-
tical history" (6:99). The shelves were dominated by the eight-volume
Biblioteca Fratrum Polonorum, a collection of Unitarian commentaries, in
Latin, on the New Testament—"learned lumber" (4:82), William later
called them. He sharpened his wits on the six-volume *Tracts and Posthumous
Works* of Thomas Chubb and "took a particular satisfaction from them"
(12:223). In school he encountered Mrs. Barbauld's poetry in Enfield's
Speaker and was "much divided in my opinion at that time, between her
Ode to Spring and Collins's Ode to Evening" (5:147). He dutifully mem-
orized a speech from John Home's *Douglas* "with good emphasis and discretion" and "entered, about the same age, into the wild sweetness of the
sentiments in Mrs. Radcliffe's Romance of the Forest, I am sure," he wrote
later, "quite as much as I should do now" (8:294). But he had never regarded poetry or fiction as a revelation of human life and feeling.

Then in 1792 his father, rather surprisingly, subscribed to John Cooke's
Select Editions of British Novels, which came out in installments. He probably thought they might brighten the dull days at Wem—for the ladies of
the family, at least. Instead, they stole the heart of his only begotten son.

"Tom Jones, I remember, was the first work that broke the spell . . . ,"
William recalled in 1821. "It smacked of the world I lived in, and in which
I was to live. . . . My heart had palpitated at the thoughts of a boarding-
school ball, or a gala-day at Midsummer or Christmas: but the world I had
found in Cooke's edition of the British Novelists was to me a dance through
life, a perpetual gala-day" (12:222–23). He had discovered the subject
which was to be his real love: not theology but human nature. And he
proceeded to indulge it.

At the same time his father was proceeding with arrangements to enter

22. Howe, p. 12. Some of these symptoms may, of course, have developed somewhat
later, when William returned to Wem after leaving the Hackney theological college.

him in theological school. For some time he had let it be known in proper circles that he had a talented son who was destined for the ministry. In July, 1791, he had received encouragement from the Reverend John Ralph, who asked in a letter, "What is your eldest son doing? and what have you done with your scholar?" In a postscript he added: "If you educate your son for the ministry, . . . let me know, and I will endeavour to procure you an exhibition which I got a few years since for a young man at Daventry, and which I find is now granted, upon my second application, to one at Hoxton."[23] Hazlitt finally decided to send his son to the New Unitarian College at Hackney founded by such prominent rational Dissenters as Priestley, Price, and Theophilus Lindsey. As a divinity student William was doubtless exempt from most, if not all, charges; for the fees at the college amounted to sixty guineas per year—twice his father's income as minister at Wem.

Not everyone—or even every Dissenting clergyman of liberal sympathies —would have chosen to send his son to the college. Many people looked upon it as a breeding ground of sedition and heresy; presently it was denounced as "the slaughterhouse of Christianity." Tom Paine had been an honored guest there shortly before he eluded arrest by fleeing to France; students had been accused of writing an anonymous handbill which helped precipitate the Birmingham riots. Even men who sympathized with the liberal objectives of the college deplored many of the policies of its "managers"; they charged that too much money had been invested in buildings and too little in faculty, that its financial structure was unsound, that it overreached itself in its attempt to provide a broad education for its students. In the spring of 1793 there had even been rumors that the college would close during the summer.

The Reverend Mr. Hazlitt was not the man to be alarmed by rumors of radical thought or fiscal insecurity. He had good reason to believe that the education provided at Hackney was as fine as any available in England. And he made his plans accordingly, doubtless ignoring the change that had recently come over his son.

Certainly the boy went off to Hackney reluctantly. The old ambition to preach God's word was dead in him; he was interested now in man, not God; in this world rather than the next. But he lacked the strength to defy his father completely; he yielded resentfully to his demands and—once away from home—was filled with remorse at his own conduct. "With respect to my past behaviour," he wrote to his father soon after he arrived at Hackney,

23. *Christian Reformer* 5 (1838): 703. There were liberal theological schools at both Daventry and Hoxton.

"I have often said, and I now assure you, that it did not proceed from any real disaffection, but merely from the nervous disorders to which, you well know, I was so much subject. This was really the case; however improbable it may appear." [24]

Hackney College proved, however, to be a surprisingly pleasant place. "The house," as described in the annual report of 1787, was "a large and noble building, and in the most substantial repair. The land belonging to it, and in which it stands, is computed to consist of about eighteen acres, enclosed within a brick wall. The walks, garden, ground, offices and other conveniences, correspond in every respect to the house itself. The situation is in a healthful and gravelly soil, well-watered, and affording agreeable and extensive prospects." [25] Since it was only five miles from London, William could choose, in his leisure hours, between walks in the country or visits to London with his brother John as guide.

The curriculum at Hackney was remarkably broad for the times. Dr. Price had announced earlier that

> the course of education will be comprehensive and liberal, and adapted to youth in general, whether they are intended for civil or commercial life, or for any of the learned professions. This course will include the Latin, Greek, and Hebrew Languages, Greek and Roman Antiquities, Ancient and Modern Geography, Universal Grammar, Rhetoric and Composition, Chronology, History, Civil and Ecclesiastical, the Principles of Law and Government, the several Branches of Mathematics, Astronomy, Natural and Experimental Physics and Chemistry, Logic, Metaphysics, and Ethics, the Evidences of Religion, Natural and Revealed, Theology, Jewish Antiquities, and Critical Lectures on the Scriptures, . . . and Elocution . . . ; French, other Modern Languages, Drawing, &c. at a separate expence. [26]

As for the aims of the college, they were beyond reproach. Price had declared that

> the best education is that which . . . impresses the heart with the love of virtue, and communicates the most expanded and ardent benevolence; which gives the deepest consciousness of the fallibility of the human understanding, and preserves from that vile dogmatism so prevalent in the world; which makes men diffident and modest, attentive to evidence, capable of proportioning their assent to the degree of it, quick in discerning it, and determined to follow it; which, in short, instead of producing acute casuists, conceited pedants, or furious polemics, produces fair enquirers.[27]

24. *The Hazlitts*, p. 404.
25. Stephenson, p. 1.
26. J. W. Ashley Smith, *The Birth of Modern Education* (London: Independent Press, Ltd., 1954), p. 172.
27. Ibid., p. 175.

No parent could have asked more of any college—though he might question, as some critics did, whether a faculty of six was adequate to the task expected of them.

William soon discovered that there was room at the college even for independent thinkers like himself. Shortly after his arrival his tutor, John Corrie, had assigned him a theme; but, he wrote to his parents, "as it was not a topic suited to my genius, and from other causes, I had not written anything on it." When the assignment fell due on the following Saturday, Corrie "asked me whether I had prepared my theme. I told him I had not. You should have a very good reason, indeed, sir, says he, for neglecting it. Why really, sir, says I, I could not write it. Did you never write anything, then? says he. Yes, sir, I said, I have written some things. Very well, then, go along and write your theme immediately, said he." But at the end of an hour, when it was time for the next lecture, William had made no progress. "My eyes were much swollen," he told his parents, "and I assumed as sullen a countenance as I could, intimating that he had not treated me well." But Corrie proved to be very patient:

> After the lecture, as I was going away, he called me back, and asked me very mildly if I had never written anything. I answered, I had written several things. On which he desired me to let him see one of my compositions, if I had no objection. I immediately took him my essay on laws [i.e., the essay which he had begun at Wem], and gave it to him. When he had read it, he asked me a few questions on the subject, which I answered very satisfactorily, I believe. Well, sir, says he, I wish you'd write some more such things as this. Why, sir, said I, I intended to write several things, which I have planned, but that I could not write any of them in a week, or two or three weeks. What did you intend to write? says he. Among other things I told him that I intended to inlarge and improve the essay he had been reading. Aye, says he, I wish you would. Well! I will do it then, sir, said I. Do so, said he; take your own time now; I shall not ask you for it; only write it as soon as you can, for I shall often be thinking about it, and very desirous of it. This he repeated once or twice. On this I wished him a good morning, and came away, very well pleased with the reception I had met.

On the whole life at the college was proving highly satisfactory. The schedule was heavy: ". . . on Monday at eleven," he wrote,

> I attend Dr. Rees on mathematics and algebra. This lecture lasts till twelve. At two I have a lecture, with several others, in shorthand, and one in Hebrew. . . . These detain us till dinnertime, and we have another lecture in shorthand, and another in Hebrew at eight at night. On Tuesday we have a lecture with Corrie at eleven, in the classics, one week Greek, another Latin, which continues till twelve; and another lecture with Corrie, on Greek antiquities, from one to two. On Wednesday we have the same business as on Monday, on Thursday as on Tuesday, and so on.

He had enjoyed an occasional triumph of the sort which he cherished. In his Greek class, composed of himself and two upperclassmen, a student had laughed at him "on account of my way of speaking." But Corrie had silenced him with: "Mr. Mason, you should be sure you can translate yours as well as Mr. Hazlitt does his, before you laugh at your neighbours." Moreover, he believed he was "liked very well by the students in general."[28]

In a letter written one Sunday evening later in the year he told his father that he had finished "the introduction to my essay on the political state of man" and shown it to Corrie, who "seemed very well pleased with it, and desired me to proceed with my essay as quickly as I could." He appended a "sketch of my plan" for his father's edification, adding that he hoped to finish the essay by Christmas.[29] When his father wrote approving the sketch, he replied gratefully and gave a detailed account of a typical day in his life as a student, from seven in the morning until eleven at night. He likes "Hebrew very well, the mathematics very much. They are very much suited to my genius." He is "glad to hear of the increase of my yearly allowance, and of what Corrie told Rowmann."[30] For the moment, at least, all seemed to be serene.

But at Wem the Reverend Mr. Hazlitt was perturbed. According to William's own account he was spending nine hours each week on his essay on laws. To be sure, Corrie had shown interest in it and had accepted it in place of regular assignments; still it hardly pertained to William's other studies. In two successive letters Hazlitt urged his son to put aside the essay for the time being. But William was determined to go on with it; it was progressing rapidly, he would finish it soon, and "I think it almost necessary to do so." "My chief reason for wishing to continue my observations," he explained,

is, that, by having a particular system of politics I shall be better able to judge of the truth or falsehood of any prevarication which I hear, or read, and of the justice, or the contrary, of any political transactions. Moreover, by comparing my own system with those of others, and with particular facts, I shall have it in my power to correct and improve it continually. But I can have neither of these advantages unless I have some standard by which to judge of and of which to judge by, any ideas, or proceedings, which I may meet with. Besides, so far is my studying this subject from making me gloomy or low-spirited, that I am never so perfectly easy as when I am, or have been, studying it.[31]

There was no question about it: William was showing more interest in

28. *The Hazlitts*, pp. 404–6.   29. Ibid., pp. 400-2.   30. Ibid., pp. 398–400.
31. Ibid., pp. 402–3.

political affairs than he was in theology and the classics. He came naturally by his interest in politics: he had grown up in a household where politics was a matter of intense concern, with a father who had made personal sacrifices for his liberal principles. He had read Joseph Priestley and inveighed against slavery and the Test Acts while he was still a boy visiting in Liverpool; had presumed to defend Priestley, now one of his teachers, when he was thirteen; and had begun his speculations on civil law soon afterwards. But at Wem politics had always been secondary to religion, while at Hackney it was the foremost concern of most of his fellow students. Only a few of them were preparing for the ministry, but all were deeply committed to the cause of human freedom. With France wallowing in the Reign of Terror and England daily reacting toward more conservative policies—and hounding all who still clung to revolutionary beliefs—the young men at Hackney College fastened their attention on this world rather than the old world or the next world. They found more relevance in the lectures of the humanist Priestley than in those of the theologian Thomas Belsham. And when critics from outside the college bore down on Priestley and his doctrines, the students responded by flaunting theories of government and religion which shocked even their liberal tutors.

"I shall certainly make it my study to acquire as much politeness as I can," William assured his father. "However, this is not the best place possible for acquiring it. I do not at all say that the fellows who are here do not know how to behave extremely well; but the behaviour which suits a set of young fellows, or boys, does not suit any other society." [32] They were, in fact, considered an unruly lot. William stood a much better chance of developing "politeness" (or *polish*) in the sophisticated company which he met at his brother John's house at 139 Long Acre in London. As a promising young artist of liberal connections John entertained many of the liveliest thinkers in the city. He and his new wife Mary were on friendly terms with William Godwin, whose family had known the Loftuses, Grace Hazlitt's people, at Wisbech. On September 17, 1794, near the beginning of William's second year at Hackney, he met Godwin,[33] whose *Enquiry Concerning Political Justice*, published during the preceding year, had outdistanced earlier radical thinkers with its doctrine of philosophical anarchism. William read it "with great avidity, and hoped, from its title and its vast reputation,

32. Ibid., p. 403.

33. See *Shelley and His Circle 1773–1822*, ed. Kenneth Neill Cameron, 4 vols. (Cambridge, Mass.: Harvard University Press; London: Oxford University Press, 1961–70), 1: 220–21 (hereafter cited as *Shelley and His Circle*).

to get entire satisfaction from it" (19:304). He was disappointed, however, perhaps because already he found Godwin's pure rationalism disturbing. He was disappointed in Godwin's conversation too: "flat as a pancake," as he later described it. At one gathering he attended the talk centered on the subject of prayer, with two of those present insisting that it was merely an attempt to dictate to the Almighty. But another asked if they would so label the Samaritan's prayer, "Lord, be merciful to me a sinner." "This did not appear to me at that time quite the thing," William commented, recalling the remark many years later (8:152 n.). Inevitably there were heated discussions of current events too—not only the developments in Paris or in Parliament but matters of immediate concern like Joseph Priestley's departure for America or the trials of Thomas Holcroft, John Horne Tooke, John Thelwall, and nine other liberals on charges of treason. Such topics were more absorbing than Greek or Hebrew declensions, and they pulled William ever closer to this world.

London offered other worldly distractions. From time to time he went to the theater, and there he found a quite different sort of stimulus. He admitted in after years that he "wept outright during the whole time" when he saw the incomparable Mrs. Siddons play the title role in Garrick's *Isabella* (5:199). And of *The School for Scandal* he wrote, after he had become a dramatic critic: "What would we not give to see it once more, as it was then acted, and with the same feelings with which we saw it then" (5:250). He read Schiller's romantic *The Robbers*, and it "stunned [him] like a blow" (6:362). His imagination, as well as his mind, was being stretched.

Eventually the pull of these new interests proved too strong, and at the end of his second year at Hackney he withdrew from the college. Crabb Robinson claimed, rightly or wrongly, that William was "one of the first students who left that college an avowed infidel." [34] If so, it was hardly surprising: he had been brought up to accept unorthodox beliefs, had read Thomas Chubb's deistic writings at about the same time that he had first encountered the English novelists (12:223), had given up regular church attendance at Wem; and his reading of modern philosophy at Hackney may well have dissolved whatever faith he had retained. At least he was sure now that he had no vocation for the ministry. He had become involved, as never before, in human affairs, human welfare. Henceforth he would be concerned about what could happen on this earth rather than what might happen in

34. *Henry Crabb Robinson on Books and Their Writers*, ed. Edith J. Morley, 3 vols. (London: J. M. Dent & Sons, Ltd., 1938, 1:6 (hereafter cited as Robinson).

heaven; in the present and the future rather than the past; in living languages and literatures rather than dead.

He was not alone; the kind of intellectual inquiry encouraged at the college had proved destructive, and morale was low. Dr. Belsham sadly acknowledged that "the studious and virtuous part of our family have generally given up Christianity." [35] And a year after William left Hackney, Belsham himself resigned, the college was closed, and the buildings were put up for sale.

Of course the Reverend Mr. Hazlitt was disconsolate when he learned of his son's defection. When he reported the sad news to Dr. Kippis, he evidently used terms which he might have chosen if the young man had died, for Kippis replied on August 14, 1795:

> what can I say to you? I can only say that I sincerely sympathize with you in your
> affliction. I deeply feel for your distress and disappointment, and wish that I could
> impart to you any sufficient thoughts or words of consolation. At any rate, you have
> the consciousness of your own integrity to support you. You have done everything
> in your power to make your son a wise and useful man, and may we not hope that
> he will be a wise and useful man in some other sphere of life? [36]

William himself, unfortunately, had no such consolation. Beneath all his superficial independence and his rebelliousness, he retained that longing for approval which had made him strive so hard, as a child, to please his parents. Now he had failed them miserably—failed all the people who had invested in his future. He needed to reinstate himself. He knew beyond a doubt what he wanted to do with his life: he wanted to be a philosopher—not one who grappled with the problems of man in his relationship to God or the universe, but man in his relationship with his fellows and himself—a sociologist or political scientist, in twentieth-century terms—above all a psychologist, essentially a *humanist*. But there was no university or academy which prepared a young man for such a career; he must acquire it for himself.

He set himself the task of reading the works of recent philosophers: Berkeley and Hume and Hartley. He divided his time between Wem, where he could find quiet for study, and his brother's house in London, where he could continue to profit from the stimulating conversation. He met Thomas Holcroft and was frustrated by his constant interruptions (17:112); he saw the feminist Mary Wollstonecraft and was struck by the "playful, easy air" with which she dismissed an objection from the great Godwin (17:111).

35. Stephenson, p. 48.
36. Ibid., p. 55.

Then one day while he was going through Baron Holbach's *Système de la Nature*, he hit upon an idea which differed sharply from the assumptions of recent philosophers. They had argued, again and again, that man was motivated primarily by self-love. Young William Hazlitt thought otherwise.

He had a theory to work on now, and he settled down to develop it in an essay "On the Natural Disinterestedness of the Human Mind," which might win him the recognition which he craved. It was slow going. He put his work aside and returned to it time after time, but still he failed to shape it into a coherent essay. In 1819, when a critic branded his writing as facile, he retorted: "As to the facility of which you, Sir, and others accuse me, it has not been acquired at once nor without pains. I was eight years in writing eight pages, under circumstances of inconceivable and ridiculous disparagement" (9:30).

In the midst of his frustration, on Sunday, October 23, 1796, he wrote, probably from his brother's house in London, to his father. He was still painfully aware of how he had failed his family, almost childishly eager to win their approval. "I write," he told his father,

> not so much because I have anything particular to communicate, as because I know that you, and my mother, and Peggy will be glad to hear from me. I know well the pleasure with which you will recognize the characters of my hand, characters calling back to the mind with strong impression the idea of the person by whom they were traced, & in vivid & thick succession, all the ready associations clinging to that idea & impattience with which you will receive any news which I can give you of myself. I know these things; & I feel them. Amidst that repeated disappointment, & that long dejection, which have served to overcast & throw into deep obscurity some of the best years of my life, years which the idle & illusive dreams of boyish expectation had presented glittering, & gay, & prosperous, decked out in all the fairness and all the brightness of colouring, & crowded with fantastic forms of numerous hues of ever-varying pleasure,—amidst much dissatisfaction and much sorrow, the reflection that there are one or two persons in the world who are [not] quite indifferent towards me, nor altogether unanxious for my welfare, is that which is, perhaps, the most "soothing to my wounded spirit."

He abandoned the letter then until the next day, when he added: "As to my essay, it goes on, or rather it moves backwards & forwards; however it does not stand still." [37]

37. *The Hazlitts*, pp. 406–7. The letter is dated Sunday, October 23, and W. C. Hazlitt assumes that it was written in 1793. Howe (p. 18) dates it 1795. But as Herschel Baker (*William Hazlitt* [Cambridge, Mass.: Harvard University Press, 1962], p. 28 n. [hereafter cited as Baker]) has pointed out, October 23 did not fall on a Sunday in either of these years, as it did in 1796.

Then one day in 1796 he happened on an excerpt from Burke's *Letter to a Noble Lord* in the *St. James's Chronicle*. He was interested immediately—not in Burke's ideas but in the clarity and force of his style. "I said to myself, 'This is true eloquence,'" he recalled afterwards; "this is a man pouring out his mind on paper" (16:222). And again, after a passage in praise of Burke's style: "If such is still my admiration of this man's misapplied powers, what must it have been at a time when I myself was in vain trying, year after year, to write a single Essay, nay, a single page or sentence; when I regarded the wonders of his pen with the longing eyes of one who was dumb and a changeling; and when, to be able to convey the slightest conception of my meaning to others in words, was the height of an almost hopeless ambition!" (12:229).

At about the same time he discovered Rousseau's *Nouvelle Héloise* and thrilled to its impassioned prose—"the description of the kiss; the excursion on the water; the letter of St. Preux, recalling the time of their first loves; and the account of Julia's death" (12:224). He went on to the *Social Contract* and *Émile* with the same delight. Yet when he turned back to his own writing, he was helpless as ever: he could not clothe his abstruse thoughts in the vivid colors of a Burke or a Rousseau, could not even patch them together into a decent fabric. He was plunged in a "gulph of abstraction" (17:114).

Then while traveling through Hertfordshire, he fell in with the Reverend Joseph Fawcett, a retired clergyman living at Edgegrove. Though a rational Dissenter, Fawcett was a man of catholic tastes: he supposedly had Burke's *Reflections on the Revolution in France* and Tom Paine's *Rights of Man* bound together in a single volume, arguing that together they made a very good book (17:65); he read widely too and dabbled in poetry. And he had a sensitivity which appealed to William. They chuckled together over a story that Fawcett told about Godwin. He had called Godwin's attention to Chatham's remark, after repeating the axiom "An Englishman's house is his castle," that though the wind and the rain might enter in, the king could not. And Godwin had treasured the thought and made use of it in his *Life of Chatham*. But when he came to the last line, he twisted it into "All the winds of Heaven may whistle round it, but the king cannot." This, said Fawcett, revealed "a defect of *natural imagination*" (11:26–27).

Unlike most of the men whom William had been taught to admire, Fawcett had imagination, and he felt no need to stifle it. "He had a masterly perception of all styles and every kind and degree of excellence, sublime or beautiful, from Milton's Paradise Lost to Shenstone's Pastoral Ballad, from

that Mackintosh was "a clever scholastic man—a master of the topics,—
or . . . the ready warehouseman of letters, who knew exactly where to lay
his hand on what he wanted, though the goods were not his own." But he
was "no match for Burke, either in style or matter. Burke was an orator
(almost a poet) who reasoned in figures, because he had an eye for nature:
Mackintosh, on the other hand, was a rhetorician, who had only an eye to
common-places."

At this point young William spoke up. He had, he declared, "always
entertained a great opinion of Burke" and was convinced that "the speaking
of him with contempt might be made the test of a vulgar democratical
mind." Coleridge pronounced this "a very just and striking" observation.

On and on he talked. He recalled that when Mackintosh and Tom
Wedgwood had spoken slightingly of his friend William Wordsworth, he
had told them flatly: "He strides on so far before you, that he dwindles in
the distance!" He repeated another crushing rebuke delivered to Godwin
after a three-hour argument with Mackintosh which had reached no conclusion: "If there had been a man of genius in the room, he would have
settled the question in five minutes."

He asked William if he had ever met Mary Wollstonecraft, and William
replied that he had once, briefly, recalling "that she seemed to me to turn
off Godwin's objections to something she advanced with quite a playful,
easy air." "This," said Coleridge, "was only one instance of the ascendancy
which people of imagination exercised over those of mere intellect." And
he went on, faulting Godwin for writing about immortality without understanding either life or death, praising Mary Wollstonecraft's "powers of
conversation," but deploring her "talent for book-making."

Holcroft's turn came next. Someone had asked Coleridge if he had not
been struck with him. No, he had replied; he had, rather, been afraid of
being struck *by* him. William complained that, when he had met Holcroft
in London, he had been unable to converse with him because Holcroft
kept interrupting him with questions: "What do you mean by a *sensation*,
Sir? What do you mean by an *idea?*" Coleridge sympathized. This, he said,
was "barricadoing the road to truth:—it was setting up a turnpike-gate at
every step we took."

"I forget a great number of things, many more than I remember,"
William wrote when he described the meeting in 1823. What he remembered, however, is telling; for a common theme underlay most of the snatches
of Coleridge's conversation that he retained: "the ascendancy which people
of imagination exercised over those of mere intellect." And William in-

Butler's Analogy down to Humphry Clinker. If you had a favourite author,
he had read him too, and knew all the best morsels, the subtle *traits*, the
capital touches. 'Do you like Sterne?'—'Yes, to be sure,' he would say, 'I
should deserve to be hanged, if I didn't'" (8:224). William spent "some of the
pleasantest days of my life" with him (3:171 n.). They discussed the English
novelists, Cervantes, Rousseau, Goethe, and Godwin, and the pleasure that
William had found while reading them "seemed more than doubled."
Here was a man who shared his love of good fiction and impassioned writing,
a man of keen intelligence who did not scorn the products of the imagination
or apologize for his tastes. It gave one pause.

Back in Wem in January, 1798, William heard that a man named Samuel
Taylor Coleridge was coming to Shrewsbury to succeed the Reverend Mr.
Rowe as minister to a congregation of rational Dissenters. Coleridge had no
experience as a preacher; what little fame he enjoyed rose from his efforts
as poet and philosopher.

Was this another Joseph Fawcett? "A poet and a philosopher getting up
into a Unitarian pulpit to preach the Gospel, was a romance in these degenerate days, a sort of revival of the primitive spirit of Christianity, which was
not to be resisted" (17:108). William determined to hear the man's first
sermon.

On Sunday, January 14, he climbed out of bed before dawn and tramped
the ten "cold, raw, comfortless" miles to Shrewsbury. The organ was playing
the Hundredth Psalm as he entered the chapel. Then a round-faced man
rose in the pulpit and, in resounding tones, announced his text: "And he
went up into the mountain to pray—HIMSELF—ALONE."

There was magic in his very intonation. Young Hazlitt sprang to
attention.

CHAPTER III

Lives of Great Men
(1798–1802)

"HIMSELF—ALONE." The words reverberated through the chapel. To William it seemed "as if the sounds had echoed from the bottom of the human heart, and as if that prayer might have floated in solemn silence through the universe" (17:108).[1] The man in the pulpit seemed to him like a latter-day Saint John crying out in the wilderness—the precursor of a new way of life.

Then Coleridge launched into his sermon, "like an eagle dallying with the wind":

> The sermon was upon peace and war; upon church and state—not their alliance, but their separation—on the spirit of the world and the spirit of Christianity, not as the same, but as opposed to one another. He talked of those who had "inscribed the cross of Christ on banners dripping with human gore." He made a poetical and pastoral excursion,—and to shew the fatal effects of war, drew a striking contrast between the simple shepherd boy, driving his team afield, or sitting under the hawthorn, piping to his flock, "as though he should never be old," and the same poor country-lad, crimped, kidnapped, brought into town, made drunk at an alehouse, turned into a wretched drummer-boy, with his hair sticking on end with powder and pomatum, a long cue at his back, and tricked out in the loathsome finery of the profession of blood.

William "could not have been more delighted if I had heard the music of the spheres." This was a new kind of sermon: it was grounded in reason, yet heightened by the speaker's imagination. "Poetry and Philosophy had

1. Except when otherwise indicated, all material and all quotations concerned with the meetings of Hazlitt and Coleridge in 1798 are taken from the essay "My First Acquaintance with Poets" (17:106–22).

met together. Truth and Genius had embraced, under the eye and with the sanction of Religion."

After the service had ended, William walked the ten miles back to Wem, now seeing the frozen countryside with a new eye. "The sun that was still labouring pale and wan through the sky, obscured by thick mists, seemed an emblem of the *good cause*; and the cold dank drops of dew that hung half melted on the beard of the thistle, had something genial and refreshing in them; for there was a spirit of hope and youth in all nature, that turned every thing into good."

On the following Tuesday the great man himself came to Wem to spend the night and get acquainted with the Reverend Mr. Hazlitt. William waited upstairs until his father called him; then he went down to the wainscoted parlor, "half-hoping, half-afraid," to meet their visitor. Coleridge "received [him] very graciously" and went on talking.

William sat with his head bowed, too awed to raise his eyes. For two hours, Coleridge later said, "he was conversing with W.H.'s forehead." But Coleridge always welcomed a good listener; twenty-five years afterwards William was to maintain that he did not stop talking throughout the three weeks he spent in and near Shrewsbury—"nor," he added, "has he since, that I know of."

The young man did, however, catch occasional glimpses of the talker and was surprised to find that he detected none of the "strange wildness" that had struck him when he had seen Coleridge in the pulpit. He was of medium size, "inclining to the corpulent," with hair "black and glossy as the raven's" falling down over a forehead "broad and high, light as if built of ivory, with large projecting eyebrows, and his eyes rolling beneath them like a sea with darkened lustre. . . . His mouth was gross, voluptuous, open, eloquent; his chin good-humoured and round; but his nose, the rudder of the face, the index of the will, was small, feeble, nothing."

The Reverend Mr. Hazlitt was enchanted by his strange guest. "He could hardly have been more surprised or pleased if our visitor had worn wings"; yet "whatever added grace to the Unitarian cause was to him welcome." And he "threw back his spectacles over his forehead, his white hairs mixing with its sanguine hue; and a smile of delight beamed across his rugged cordial face, to think that Truth had found a new ally in Fancy!"

While they dined on Welsh mutton and turnips, Coleridge talked about Mary Wollstonecraft and James Mackintosh, both of whom had written replies to Burke's *Reflections on the Revolution in France*. When his host praised Mackintosh's reply, *Vindiciae Gallicae*, Coleridge acknowledged

stinctively agreed; he too admired people of sensitivity, those who could grasp not only facts but overtones as well, who could understand not only abstract ideas but human feelings—people who could share the emotions of a character in a novel—even weep for the anguish of a Rousseau. "Coleridge in truth met me half-way on the ground of philosophy," he wrote later, "or I should not have been won over to his imaginative creed."

The next morning when William came down to breakfast Coleridge "had just received a letter" from Thomas Wedgwood offering him an annuity of one hundred fifty pounds.[2] He decided then and there to accept. Without bothering his head with a systematic analysis of advantages and disadvantages, he acted quickly, intuitively—he "seemed to make up his mind to close with this proposal in the act of tying on one of his shoes."

William was disappointed. He had looked forward to seeing more of this remarkable friend, but now he was off "to inhabit the Hill of Parnassus," and William "knew not the way thither, and felt very little gratitude for Mr. Wedgwood's bounty." However, Coleridge asked for pen and ink, wrote his address on a card, and gave it to the young man, inviting him to visit him at his house in Nether Stowey, Somersetshire, in a few weeks' time. He even offered to walk half the hundred fifty miles' distance to meet him.

Flattered and embarrassed, William "stammered out my acknowledgments and acceptance," and shortly the two set out on the road to Shrewsbury. It was a fine winter morning, and William, looking through the bare branches or the red oak leaves at the distant blue mountains, listened, still enchanted, to the "Siren's song" of Coleridge's monologue. "In digressing, in dilating, in passing from subject to subject, he appeared to me to float in air, to slide on ice." He had, however, an odd habit of shifting from one side of the footpath to the other. "He seemed unable to keep on in a strait line."

His talk too rambled. He confided that he would not have accepted the pastorate at Shrewsbury until he had preached once on Infant Baptism and once on the Lord's Supper, explaining why he could administer neither. He denounced Hume as a plagiarist and found fault with his style. He praised Bishop Berkeley and damned Dr. Johnson for his silly attempt to refute

2. As Baker (p. 125 n.) points out, Hazlitt's account of the arrival of the letter hardly squares with references to it in Coleridge's correspondence. If, as Hazlitt wrote, Coleridge went to Wem on Tuesday (January 16), his letter to Rev. John P. Estlin announcing the offer must have been written before he left Shrewsbury. See *Collected Letters of Samuel Taylor Coleridge*, ed. Earl Leslie Griggs, 4 vols. (Oxford: Clarendon Press, 1956–59), 1:370 (hereafter cited as *Coleridge Letters*).

Berkeley's theory of idealism by kicking a stone. He said Berkeley was a subtle thinker, but Tom Paine an acute thinker. He branded William Paley a casuist, but spoke highly of Bishop Joseph Butler—not his *Analogy of Religion* but a volume of sermons which William had never read. "Coleridge," he noticed, "somehow always contrived to prefer the *unknown* to the *known*."

Before they parted, William told Coleridge about his unfinished essay, timidly suggesting that he had made a discovery about the natural disinterestedness of the human mind. Coleridge listened patiently while he tried to explain his theory, but the young man could not seem to make it clear.

Nonetheless William walked home "pensive but much pleased." He "had met with unexpected notice" from this extraordinary man. "I had a sound in my ears," he wrote in 1823, "it was the voice of Fancy: I had a light before me, it was the face of Poetry." He had indeed been won over to Coleridge's imaginative creed. And, just as important: he had found a man whom he heartily admired, whom he longed to emulate—and, wonder of wonders, that man approved of him, liked him, wanted to see him again.

In the weeks that followed William tried to resume work on his unfinished essay, in which imagination was to play a significant role. "I sat down to the task . . . for the twentieth time, got new pens and paper, determined to make clear work of it, wrote a few meagre sentences in the skeleton-style of a mathematical demonstration, stopped half-way down the second page; and after trying in vain to pump up any words, images, notions, apprehensions, facts, or observations, from that gulph of abstraction in which I had plunged myself for four or five years preceding, gave up the attempt as labour in vain, and shed tears of helpless despondency on the blank unfinished paper." Meanwhile he kept reading—not Berkeley and Hume and Hartley now but "people of the imagination." He bought *Paradise Lost* and Burke's *Reflections* in Shrewsbury, "regarded the wonders of [Burke's] pen with the longing eyes of one who was dumb and a changeling" (12:227–29), and discovered that he had gained new "insight into the mysteries of poetry" from Coleridge. He read Rousseau's *Confessions* and again was moved to tears (4:91). Yet despite his frustration he felt "an uneasy, pleasurable sensation. . . . *I was to visit Coleridge in the spring.* This circumstance was never absent from my thoughts, and mingled with all my feelings."

Happily, Coleridge did not forget his invitation. On March 9, in a letter to John Wicksteed of Wem, he asked Wicksteed to "tell young Mr. Haseloed that I remember him with respect due his talents and that the wish which I expressed of seeing him at Stowey still lives within me."[3] And

3. *Coleridge Letters*, 1:394.

when William wrote to set a date, Coleridge asked him to postpone his visit a week or two, but urged him not to fail.

Early in April, William walked the forty miles from Wem to Llangollen Vale in Wales to initiate himself "in the mysteries of natural scenery" before going to visit Coleridge. He luxuriated in the role of young enthusiast, thrilling at his first sight of the valley, "which opens like an amphitheatre, broad, barren hills rising in majestic state on either side, with 'green upland swells that echo to the bleat of flocks' below, and the river Dee babbling over its stony bed in the midst of them." He spent April 10, his twentieth birthday, exploring the valley, observing how it " 'glittered green with sunny showers' and a budding ash-tree dipped its tender branches in the chiding stream." That evening at an inn he treated himself to a cold chicken, a bottle of sherry, and the *Nouvelle Héloise* which he had "brought along . . . as a *bonne bouche* to crown the evening with" (8 : 186). It was a perfect day for a young enthusiast, one that he never forgot. Later in life he regarded Llangollen Vale as "(in a manner) the cradle of a new existence: in the river that winds through it, my spirit was baptized in the waters of Helicon." "How proud, how glad I was," he wrote in his essay "On Going a Journey," "to walk along the high road that commands the delicious prospect repeating the lines [from Coleridge's 'Ode to the Departing Year']! But besides the prospect which opened beneath my feet, another also opened to my inward sight, a heavenly vision, on which were written, in letters large as Hope could make them, these four words, LIBERTY, GENIUS, LOVE, VIRTUE" (8 : 186).

A month later he set out from Wem southward across the plains of Worcestershire and Gloucestershire toward Nether Stowey. He had a delightful encounter with a strolling player who sang "blithe and clear, advancing with light step and a loud voice" (18 : 296) along the banks of the Severn River. At an inn at Witham Common he had a rewarding experience of a different sort when he "found out the proof that likeness is not a case of the association of ideas" (8 : 185). Yet he made better time than he expected and arrived two days ahead of schedule after walking all one day in a drenching rain. He put up at an inn, where he again played the enthusiast: staying up late to read a copy of *Paul and Virginia* that he had happened on, then sauntering along the river bank and reading two volumes of Fanny Burney's *Camilla* to while away the time until he was due at Nether Stowey.[4]

4. In "On Going a Journey" Hazlitt located the inn at Bridgwater and said he stayed up half the night reading *Paul and Virginia;* in "My First Acquaintance with Poets" he said he thought the inn was at Tewkesbury—and claimed he stayed up *all* night reading the novel.

On or about Monday, June 4,[5] he walked across the "beautiful, green and hilly" country to Nether Stowey, where he was "well received" by Coleridge. That afternoon the two walked the six miles over to Alfoxden, "a romantic old family mansion of the St. Aubins," which Coleridge's friends William and Dorothy Wordsworth had been able to rent cheap because it was owned by a minor. Wordsworth, they found, had gone to Bristol, but his sister prepared "a frugal repast" for them and let them look over the manuscripts of her brother's latest poems, soon to be published as *Lyrical Ballads*. William "dipped into a few of these with great satisfaction and with the faith of a novice."

He slept in "an old room with blue hangings, and covered with the round-faced family-portraits of the age of George I and II" and was roused at dawn by the call of a stag from the park outside. After breakfast he and Coleridge sat on the trunk of a fallen ash tree in the park, overlooking the Bristol Channel, while Coleridge read several of Wordsworth's poems in "a sonorous and musical voice" and William felt "the sense of a new style and a new spirit in poetry." It was an unforgettable experience.

That evening they walked back to Nether Stowey—and still Coleridge talked. He "could go on in the most delightful explanatory way over hill and dale, a summer's day, and convert a landscape into a didactic poem or a Pindaric ode. 'He talked far above singing.'" Their path seemed to William to wind "through echoing grove, by fairy stream or waterfall, gleaming in the summer moonlight." Coleridge lamented that, because Wordsworth rejected the traditional superstitions of the country, his descriptive poetry had "something corporeal, a *matter-of-fact-ness*, a clinging to the palpable, or often to the petty" about it. "His genius was not a spirit that descended to him through the air; it sprung out of the ground like a flower, or unfolded itself from a green spray, on which the gold-finch sang." Yet "his philosophic poetry had a grand and comprehensive spirit in it, so that his soul seemed to inhabit the universe like a palace, and to discover truth by intuition, rather than by deduction." Coleridge's theme was still the same: intuition over deduction, imagination over mere intellect.

The next day Wordsworth stopped in at Nether Stowey on his way home from Bristol. To William he looked "gaunt and Don Quixote-like. He was quaintly dressed . . . in a brown fustian jacket and striped pantaloons" and had "something of a roll, a lounge in his gait." He had "a severe, worn pressure of thought about his temples, a fire in his eye. . . , an intense high

5. See H. M. Margoliouth, "Wordsworth and Coleridge: Dates in May and June, 1798," *NQ* 198 (1953):352–54.

narrow forehead, a Roman nose, cheeks furrowed by strong purpose and feeling, and a convulsive inclination to laughter about the mouth, a good deal at variance with the solemn, stately expression of the rest of his face." He "talked very naturally and freely, with a mixture of clear gushing accents in his voice, a deep guttural intonation, and a strong tincture of the northern *burr*, like the crust on wine." As he discussed a performance of Monk Lewis's *The Castle Spectre* that he had seen at Bristol, he gorged himself on half a Cheshire cheese. To William he seemed no match for Coleridge as a talker. "I never got any ideas at all from him," he wrote in 1818, "for the reason that he had none to give" (9:5). Yet he was remarkably sensitive to natural beauty, as William sensed when the poet, glancing out the window, cried: "How beautifully the sun sets on that yellow bank!" Afterwards, whenever William saw the light of the setting sun fall on a landscape, he recalled those words.

Wordsworth was apparently not much impressed with his friend's young protegé. When William tried to explain his theory of human disinterestedness to him, he observed that, though there might be something to it, "it was what every shoemaker must have thought of" (9:4). The young man seemed to take himself and his books much too seriously; he needed to open his eyes and look about him. William was probably the "friend who was somewhat unreasonably attached to modern books of moral philosophy" whom the poet addressed as Matthew in "The Tables Turned":

> Up! up! my Friend, and quit your books;
> Or surely you'll grow double:
> Up! up! my Friend, and clear your looks;
> Why all this toil and trouble?
>
> The sun, above the mountain's head,
> A freshening lustre mellow
> Through all the long green fields has spread,
> Her first sweet evening yellow.
>
> . . . .
>
> Enough of Science and of Art;
> Close up those barren leaves;
> Come forth, and bring with you a heart
> That watches and receives.[6]

William stayed three weeks at Nether Stowey. Afternoons he and Coler-

6. *Poetical Works of William Wordsworth*, ed. E. de Selincourt and Helen Darbishire, 5 vols. (Oxford: Clarendon Press, 1940–49), 4:56–57. Ques: Did Wordsworth know that Hazlitt had been struck by his comment on the yellow light of the setting sun?

idge sat in an arbor beneath the trees drinking flip, listening to the humming of the bees, and of course talking. At least Coleridge talked; William listened and learned. If the conversation touched on politics—and it could hardly have avoided the subject—he might have learned that, since France's invasion of Switzerland, Coleridge was having second thoughts about the Revolution across the Channel. Yet there was evidently no rift in their friendship: William was not looking to Coleridge for political guidance.

A few days before it was time for him to return to Wem the two set out on a walking trip along the rugged coast of the Bristol Channel to Linton— the trip which Wordsworth, his sister Dorothy, and Coleridge had taken a year before, when they began work on the *Lyrical Ballads*. With them went John Chester, a stocky little native of Nether Stowey who trotted quietly beside Coleridge, drinking in his every word. They went past Dunster and through Minehead—with William relishing each picturesque detail: Dunster looked "as clear, as pure, as *embrowned* and ideal" as a painted landscape; a vessel off on the horizon at sunset recalled the specter ship in Coleridge's poem "The Ancient Mariner." It was almost midnight when they reached Linton, and they had some difficulty in rousing the inn- keeper. But eventually he took them in, and they topped off the evening with a supper of bacon and eggs.

The next morning they ate breakfast in the inn parlor overlooking a garden of thyme and wildflowers, then walked on the beach. Coleridge discussed Virgil's *Georgics*, "but not well." "I do not think," William re- marked later, "he had much feeling for the classical or elegant." When they found a thumb-worn copy of James Thomson's *The Seasons* on a window seat at the inn, Coleridge cried, "*That* is true fame!" And he described Thomson as "a great poet, rather than a good one." William Cowper, he added, was the best modern poet. He compared Shakespeare and Milton (to the advantage of the latter); damned Thomas Gray, Pope, Dr. Johnson, and "couplet-writers" in general; praised Burke and Jeremy Taylor; and so on—and on. He seemed "profound and discriminating with respect to those authors whom he liked . . . ; capricious, perverse, and prejudiced in his antipathies." Moreover, he "had no idea of pictures."

When a thunderstorm threatened, Coleridge ran out to a neighboring landmark, the Valley of Rocks,[7] to enjoy the full force of the elements. He told William that he and Wordsworth had planned to make this the setting for a prose tale in the manner of Salomon Gessner's *Death of Abel*. He ex-

7. So Hazlitt remembered the name. Actually the place was known as the Valley of Stones.

plained, too, the experiment that he and Wordsworth were making in their recent poems: "to see how far the public taste would endure poetry written in a more natural and simple style than had hitherto been attempted."

On the beach they chatted with a fisherman who told them about the drowning of a boy the day before. They had tried to save him, even risking their own lives, because, he said, "we have a *nature* towards one another." Here, Coleridge declared, was a striking example of the natural disinterestedness of the human mind, which William was seeking to prove in his essay. William then told him of his latest "metaphysical discovery": "that *likeness* was not a mere association of ideas." A footprint in the sand, he said, "put one in mind of a man's foot, not because it was part of a former impression of a man's foot (for it was quite new) but because it was like the shape of a man's foot." Coleridge agreed that he had a valid point. John Chester was stunned; he could not believe that anyone could tell his idol something which he did not already know. But this young man had a mind of his own, and it was gradually asserting itself.

The next day the three men headed back toward Nether Stowey, and on the following Sunday, William set out for home. Coleridge was going to Taunton to preach at a Dissenting chapel, but the two agreed to meet that evening in Bridgwater and continue on to Bristol the next day.[8] When William asked whether he had prepared his sermon, Coleridge replied that he had not even chosen a text—but would do so on the road. As usual he was depending on impulse to direct him.

William had a good deal to mull over in his mind when he reached home. Although he was shrewd enough to discern Coleridge's shortcomings,[9] he had been profoundly affected by his three weeks of close contact with this man who had so much to offer him. Coleridge's mind and conversation were brimming with new and fresh ideas; later in life William declared that Coleridge was the only person from whom he ever learned anything (5:167). But more important: Coleridge had shown confidence in him. "He used to say of me . . .," William wrote in 1818, "that 'I had the most metaphysical head he ever met with,' . . . that 'if ever I got language for

8. In "My First Acquaintance with Poets" Hazlitt said Coleridge was leaving for Germany, but Elisabeth Schneider (*Coleridge, Opium, and Kubla Khan* [Chicago: University of Chicago Press, 1953] p. 338) points out that he was probably going to visit the Wedgwoods and make the necessary arrangements about his annuity.

9. Hazlitt's account of his "First Acquaintance with Poets" was written twenty-five years after the meetings took place, and much of his incidental criticism of both Coleridge and Wordsworth may have been colored by his later, often bitter, relations with the two men.

my ideas, the world would hear of it, for that I had guts in my brains'"
(9:3–4).

He did not, however, return to his essay; instead he quitted his books—
at least his philosophical books—for the time being and cast about for an
outlet which would involve his imagination. Painting was a natural choice:
artistic talent ran in the family, and for a time, as a boy, he had planned to
be an artist like his brother.

At first he could not persuade himself that painting pictures, large or
small, would give him any lasting satisfaction. Twice in later life he observed
that, until he was twenty years old, he "thought there was nothing in the
world but books" (11:320, 269). One afternoon, as he sat reading Sir
John Vanbrugh's *Provoked Husband* before a Flemish landscape painting,
he glanced up at the picture from time to time "and wondered what there
could be in that sort of work to satisfy or delight the mind" (8:15). Writing
—even writing frivolous plays like Vanbrugh's or Colley Cibber's—seemed
a more dignified career. But in December, 1798, the Orleans Gallery—a
collection of old masters largely from the gallery of the Regent Orléans in
Paris—went on sale in London, and William contrived to visit it. For the
first time in his life he saw what a great artist could do with paints, and he
was "staggered." He went back again and again. "A mist passed away from
my sight; the scales fell off," he declared. "A new sense came upon me, a
new heaven and earth stood before me" (8:14). There was a Titian landscape with "a brown, mellow, autumnal look" that fascinated him. "The
sky was of the colour of stone. The winds seemed to sing through the rustling
branches of the trees" (4:78). And there was Carracci's *Susannah and the
Elders;* he "used to go and look at it by the hour together, till our hearts
thrilled with its beauty, and our eyes were filled with tears" (10:9). Soon
he was living "in a world of pictures. Battles, sieges, speeches in parliament
seemed mere idle noise and fury, 'signifying nothing,' compared with those
mighty works and dreaded names that spoke to me in the eternal silence of
thought" (8:14). He tried his own hand at painting and was amazed to
discover how much challenge and satisfaction it offered: "finding the difficulties and beauties it unfolded, opened a new field to me, and I began to
conclude that there might be a number of 'other things between heaven
and earth that were never dreamt of in my philosophy'" (9:320).

He settled down now at his brother's house at 12 Rathbone Place in
London, and John gave him regular lessons in painting. This meant, of
course, that he spent endless hours copying the work of successful painters.
He later recalled sitting in the back painting room at his brother's house

painstakingly copying a Rembrandt or a Vangoyen landscape by firelight—
and "how delighted I was when I had made the tremulous, undulating
reflection in the water, and saw the dull canvas become a lucid mirror of
the commonest features of nature!" (17:379). One could gain a sense of
achievement even from copying—if one were successful. It was an exhilarating experience for one who had so often failed.

He was eager to see as many fine paintings as he could, and "neither the
surliness of porters, nor the impertinence of footmen" (8:112 n.) would
discourage him. He went north to Stamford, where he managed to gain
admittance to the gallery at Burleigh House. Again he was ecstatic; he
went away "richer than he came, richer than the possessor" (8:14). At a
little inn at Saint Neot's in Huntingdonshire he happened on a series of
prints of Raphael's cartoons and was similarly enthralled. When he visited
his mother's old home at Wisbech, he stopped off at the cathedral in Peter-
borough, to see the monument to Mary Queen of Scots, and "the events
of the period, all that had happened since, passed in review before me"
(17:195). At last his life had meaning and direction.

Presently he attempted his first original portrait—of an aged country-
woman from near Manchester. It was in the manner of Rembrandt, one
of whose portraits he had seen at Burleigh House. "I certainly laboured it
with great perseverance," he wrote in 1820.

> I spared no pains to do my best. If art was long, I thought that life was so too at
> that moment. I got in the general effect the first day; and pleased and surprised
> enough I was at my success. The rest was a work of time—of weeks and months (if
> need were) of patient toil and careful finishing. . . . I did not then, nor do I now
> believe with Sir Joshua, that the perfection of art consists in giving general appear-
> ances without individual details, but in giving general appearances with individual
> details. Otherwise, I had done my work the first day. But I saw something more in
> nature than general effect, and I thought it worth my while to give it in the picture.
> There was a gorgeous effect of light and shade: but there was a delicacy as well as
> depth in the *chiaroscuro*, which I was bound to follow into all its dim and scarce
> perceptible variety of tone and shadow. Then I had to make the transition from a
> strong light to as dark a shade, preserving the masses, but gradually softening off
> the intermediate parts. It was so in nature: the difficulty was to make it so in the
> copy. I tried, and failed again and again; I strove harder, and succeeded, as I thought.
> The wrinkles in Rembrandt were not hard lines; but broken and irregular. I saw
> the same appearance in nature, and strained every nerve to get it. If I could hit off
> this crumbling appearance, and insert the reflected light in the furrows of old age in
> half a morning, I did not think I had lost a day. Beneath the shrivelled yellow parch-
> ment look of the skin, there was here and there a streak of blood-colour tingling the
> face; this I made a point of conveying, and did not cease to compare what I saw

with what I did (with jealous, lynx-eyed watchfulness) till I succeeded to the best of my ability and judgment. How many revisions were there! How many attempts to catch an expression which I had seen the day before! How often did we strive to get the old position, and wait for the return of the same light! There was a puckering up of the lips, a cautious introversion of the eye under the shadow of the bonnet, indicative of the feebleness and suspicion of old age, which at last we managed, after many trials and some quarrels, to a tolerable nicety. The picture was never finished, and I might have gone on with it to the present hour. I used to set it on the ground when my day's work was done, and saw revealed to me with swimming eyes the birth of new hopes, and of a new world of objects. (8:8–9)

As a first attempt, the portrait was truly remarkable. William confessed to the artist William Bewick that he "had the vanity to feel, or mistakingly judge, that my insignificant endeavour put me in mind of some of Rembrandt's heads." [10] And he was not alone in thinking so. When Benjamin Haydon first saw the painting, he is said to have cried, "Hallo! where did you get that Rembrandt? It looks like an early performance." [11]

Back in London he painted a portrait of young James Sheridan Knowles, who at fifteen was already a published poet. At times he despaired of catching the proper expression. "Hang your fat cheeks—frown, James," he burst out on one occasion. He painted Knowles's sister Charlotte too—"in white muslin, lamenting over a dead bird which she held in her lap." He was, apparently, already cultivating the melancholy effect which later sitters were to find annoying. But his kindness made a lasting impression on young Knowles, who later recalled that "he loved me, . . . taught me as a friend endearingly praising and condemning, as he saw cause, every little poem which I wrote. There was ore in him, and rich, but his mature friends were blind to it." [12]

He could, in fact, be painfully clumsy, even boorish, in older company. Henry Crabb Robinson, whom he met at Bury St. Edmunds in 1799, remarked that he was "struggling against a great difficulty of expression. . . . His bashfulness, want of words, slovenliness in dress, etc., made him the object of ridicule." He "was excessively shy, and in company the girls always made game of him. . . . he had a horror of the society of ladies, especially of smart and handsome and modest young women. The prettiest

10. Thomas Landseer, *Life and Letters of William Bewick*, 2 vols. (London, 1871), 1:131 (hereafter cited as Landseer).

11. W. Carew Hazlitt, *Four Generations of a Literary Family*, 2 vols. (London, 1897), 1:235–36 (hereafter cited as *Four Generations*). The painting, still preserved in the Maidstone Museum in Maidstone, Kent, is now almost indistinguishable.

12. Richard S. Knowles, *Life of James Sheridan Knowles* (London, 1872), pp. 10–12.

girl of our parties about this time was Miss Kitchener. She used to drive him mad by teasing him." Robinson himself, however, recognized that "he was an extraordinary man. He had few friends and was flattered by my attentions." They ate breakfast frequently together, William introduced him to the work of Wordsworth and Coleridge, and, when Robinson traveled to Wales in the summer of 1799, he stopped off at Wem to meet William's parents and sister.[13]

William still lacked confidence in himself—as a man and, inevitably, as an artist too. He was haunted by fears of failure; he suffered "the horrors" when he walked past "the old battered portraits at the doors of brokers' shops, with the morning-sun flaring full upon them." It was enough to keep him from painting all day—unless he happened to catch sight of a fine picture; then he "went back and set to work with redoubled ardour" (11:254–55). When he saw the rope dancer Richer perform at Sadler's Wells, he happened to be copying a portrait by Reynolds, and Richer seemed so much more adept than he that he was "put . . . out of conceit" (8:79–80). He persuaded Sheridan Knowles to take up rope dancing with him— in the hope that he might eventually compete with Richer if not with Reynolds.

He had not lost his interest in philosophy. He continued to mingle with the liberals: Godwin's diary records thirteen meetings with him during the first nine months of the year 1799,[14] and he saw Coleridge at least once (7:133), and met Robert Southey for the first time (7:183 n.). Now or later he attended James Mackintosh's lectures, the "Laws of Nature and Nations," at Lincoln's Inn Hall.[15] But he did not much care for what he heard: Mackintosh proved to be a disciple of Hume and Hartley, and in the course of the lectures he announced that he could no longer approve of the revolution in France. For the present William kept silence; yet he noted Mackintosh's points and eventually replied to them. His considered opinion was that Mackintosh was "no doubt a man of a very clear understanding, of an imposing elocution, a very able disputant, and a very metaphysical lawyer, but by no means a profound metaphysician, not quite a Berkeley in subtlety of distinction" (1:64). William had ranged himself firmly on the side of the men of imagination whom Coleridge commended.

13. Robinson, 1:6–7. In her *Life and Times of Henry Crabb Robinson* (London: J. M. Dent and Sons, Ltd., 1935), p. 10, Edith Morley points out that Robinson elsewhere says Catherine Buck introduced him to the work of Wordsworth and Coleridge.

14. Baker, pp. 130 n., 131 n.

15. Hazlitt might have heard the lectures when they were first given in January– June, 1799, or when they were repeated in the following year.

Late in the year he visited his family at Wem, traveling as economically as he could. By December 16 he was back in London reporting to his father that, by walking part way, riding outside a coach part way, and rationing the food that he had brought from home, he had managed to keep the expenses of his return trip down to forty-three shillings. He had been "too cold and uncomfortable" to stop long enough at Oxford to see any of the buildings; moreover, he had been "very much shook on the coach box & wore out my gloves; & bruised my hands by the rubbing of the iron rail, which I was obliged to keep fast hold of, to prevent my being thrown from my seat." Yet he was, he wrote, "in pretty good spirits" and planned to resume his painting as soon as he received his box of paints and brushes from home. He had noticed "two or three little views on the road, which I shall endeavour to sketch out in some way, or other from memory." And he closed affectionately: "When I looked back on the road to Lea Hills, & saw how dim, & low they grew, & how small the objects upon them appeared, & recollected, that you were still farther off, I wondered at the distinct Idea I had of you all: and yet I still recollect you as I saw you last in the parlour at breakfast."[16]

On the surface all seemed to be well with William. He was on reasonably good terms with his family, was applying himself to his task, and seemed to be making the best of his lot in life. Yet the letter has telling overtones: his careful accounting of his expenses and his almost-too-tender conclusion suggest that he was still dependent on his family, financially and emotionally. Although he had reached his twenty-first birthday seven months earlier, he was by no means an adult. The portrait which his brother painted of him at about this time shows a young man who is obviously intelligent, sensitive—perhaps intense—but hardly resolute.

He remained in London during the first half of the following year; Godwin's diary lists eight meetings with him between December 28, 1799, and June 15, 1800.[17] Undoubtedly he was still living at his brother's house and trying to improve his skills as a painter. After June 15, however, he disappears completely from view for over a year; no letter of the period seems to have survived, and none of his later reminiscences can be specifically assigned to those months. He might possibly have spent part of the time traveling from town to town in the provinces, supporting himself by painting portraits of local dignitaries.

Late in 1801 he was at home in Wem working on a portrait of his father.

16. *Shelley and His Circle*, 1:219–20.
17. Baker, p. 131 n.

The old man had, as he put it later, "as fine an old Nonconformist head as one could hope to see in these degenerate times" (12:108). It offered a real challenge to an artist interested in depicting character. But more important: painting this portrait helped close the breach between father and son.

Inevitably relations between the two had been strained in recent years; as William once admitted, when a son "brought up to the church . . . imbibes a taste for the Fine Arts, . . . there is an end of any thing like the same unreserved communication between them" (8:312). His father, he knew, "would rather I should have written a sermon than painted like Rembrandt or like Raphael" (8:12). Yet the sittings went surprisingly well; the old man developed an interest in the process in spite of himself—he actually enjoyed posing, and he and his son were drawn closer together than they had been in years. In 1820, after his father's death, William tenderly recalled the affection which had been revived by those sittings:

> One of my first attempts was a picture of my father, who was then in green old age, with strong-marked features, and scarred with the small-pox. I drew it with a broad light crossing the face, looking down, with spectacles on, reading. The book was Shaftesbury's Characteristics, in a fine old binding, with Gribelin's etchings. . . . The sketch promised well; and I set to work to finish it, determined to spare no time nor pains. My father was willing to sit as long as I pleased; for there is a natural desire in the mind of man to sit for one's picture, to·be the object of continued attention, to have one's likeness multiplied; and besides his satisfaction in the picture, he had some pride in the artist. . . . Those winter days, with the gleams of sunshine coming through the chapel-windows, and cheered by the notes of the robin-redbreast in our garden (that "ever in the haunch of winter sings")—as my afternoon's work drew to a close,—were among the happiest of my life. (8:12–13)

Well pleased with his work, William sent it off "with throbbing heart" to the Royal Academy, and to his great joy it was accepted for the exhibition of 1802. At last he could savor the sweet taste of success—of recognition.

Now certainly, if not earlier, he tried to set himself up as an itinerant portrait-painter. In March of 1802 he was in Manchester—and penniless.[18] "I once lived on coffee (as an experiment)," he wrote in 1827, "for a fortnight together, while I was finishing the copy of a half-length portrait of a Manchester manufacturer, who had died worth a plumb. I rather slurred over the coat . . . to receive my five guineas, with which I . . . dined on sausages and mashed potatoes. . . . Gentle reader, do not smile! Neither Monsieur de Very, nor Louis XVIII, over an oyster-paté, nor Apicius

18. See *Christian Reformer* 5 (1838): 562.

himself, ever understood the meaning of the word *luxury* better than I did
at that moment!" (17:180). He found some consolation in reading. "I
first read [Elizabeth Inchbald's] *Simple Story* (of all places in the world)
at M——," he wrote. "No matter where it was; for it transported me out
of myself. I recollect walking out to escape from one of the tenderest parts,
in order to return to it again with double relish. An old crazy hand-organ was
playing Robin Adair, a summer-shower dropped manna on my head, and
slaked my feverish thirst of happiness" (12:303–4). But there was little
in Manchester to slake the thirst or nourish the body of a sensitive young
artist. He probably tried his luck at Liverpool too, and attracted only the
Reverend Samuel Shepherd of Gateacre, a friend of his father, to sit for
him. He did not care to linger in a place where "they would persuade you
that your merchant and manufacturer is your only gentleman and scholar"
(8:103).[19] Even a visit to the artist Daniel Stringer, near Liverpool,
proved disillusioning. William had admired Stringer's work, had tried in
vain to copy one of his portraits—but he found to his distress that the aging
artist had now sacrificed "all his skill and love of art . . . to his delight in
Cheshire ale and the company of country-squires" (11:200).

By May 12 William was back in London, where he stopped overnight
at Godwin's.[20] A week later, on the nineteenth, he was attending a memorable performance of *The Winter's Tale* with Kemble as Leontes and Mrs.
Siddons playing Hermione "with true monumental dignity and noble passion." "Nothing could go off with more *éclat*, with more spirit, and grandeur
of effect," he wrote fifteen years later. "We shall never see these parts so
acted again" (4:325–26).

But he now had a specific project in mind. His stay in Liverpool had not
been fruitless after all, for he had fallen in with a prosperous manufacturer
named Railton who wanted some copies of old masters to adorn his parlor
walls.[21] And across the Channel in Paris there were old masters in abundance,
waiting to be copied: by systematically pillaging the finest art collections
in Europe Napoleon had managed to bring to the Louvre the most extraordinary gathering of paintings ever assembled. Moreover, since England

19. Of the two cities he preferred Manchester: "There you were oppressed only by
the aristocracy of wealth; in [Liverpool] by the aristocracy of wealth and letters by turns.
. . . The Manchester cotton-spinners, on the contrary, set up no pretensions beyond their
looms, were hearty good fellows, and took any information or display of ingenuity on
other subjects in good part" (8:204 n.).
20. Baker, p. 131 n.
21. W. C. Hazlitt (*The Hazlitts*, p. 205) records a tradition that William fell in love
with "Miss R."—that is, Railton's daughter—but he presents no confirming evidence.

and France had concluded the Peace of Amiens on March 27, Englishmen were free, for the first time in nine years, to travel to France.

It was too good an opportunity to let slide. After three years of uphill struggle William had gained his first foothold when the Royal Academy accepted his portrait of his father. Now he needed a lift—an upward jolt such as he had received earlier from Joseph Fawcett and Coleridge and the Orleans Gallery. He needed to be shown new goals, to have finer models to emulate. With them he might be inspired to the kind of achievement which would bring him a lasting sense of satisfaction.

Time was passing. On April 10 he had reached his twenty-fourth birthday. It behooved him to act promptly.

CHAPTER IV

Try, Try Again
(1802–1806)

By late summer of 1802 William was busy preparing for his trip to Paris. Railton had commissioned him to copy five of the old masters in the Louvre,[1] and Thomas Holcroft and the artist Robert Freebairn had agreed to write letters of introduction to the French painter J. F. L. Merimée (father of the poet Prosper) to ease his admission to the collection at the Louvre. To whet his appetite for the feast ahead he borrowed a descriptive catalogue of the paintings from a friend and studied it earnestly. "The pictures, the names of the painters, seemed to relish in the mouth," he wrote in 1820. "There were two portraits by the same hand [Titian's]—'A young Nobleman with a glove'—Another, 'a companion to it'—I read the description over and over with fond expectancy, and filled up the imaginary outline with whatever I could conceive of grace and dignity, and an antique *gusto*—all but equal to the original" (8:15).

Shortly before mid-October he set off across the Channel, carrying with him two of his own portraits—one of them that of the old woman in the bonnet—for purposes of comparison. In 1822 he was to write feelingly of his joy on first seeing the "laughing shores of France": he felt no loneliness, he declared; "Calais was peopled with novelty and delight. The confused, busy murmur of the place was like oil and wine poured into my ears. . . . I breathed the air of general humanity. I walked over 'the vine-covered hills and gay regions of France,' erect and satisfied; for the image of man was not

---

1. Margaret Hazlitt wrote in her journal (Moyne, p. 108) that Railton offered her brother one hundred guineas to copy ten paintings. But Hazlitt's letters make it clear that he copied only five for Railton.

cast down and chained to the foot of arbitrary thrones" (8:188–89). At the time, however, his reaction was somewhat different. "Calais is a miserable place in itself," he wrote to his father on October 16, "but the remains of the fortifications about it are very beautiful. . . . The country till within a few miles of Paris was barren and miserable. There were great numbers of beggars at all the towns we passed through."

His letter was dated from the Hôtel Coq Heron, Rue Coq Heron, in Paris, where he had arrived the day before. He found the city "very dirty and disagreeable, except along the river side."[2] At the Louvre he had been plagued by "Republican door-keepers, with their rough voices and affectation of equality" (10:108) who refused to admit him to the exhibition of old masters. It was tantalizing to catch only "a peep at them through the door (vile hindrance!) like looking out of purgatory into paradise—from Poussin's noble mellow-looking landscapes to where Rubens hung out his gaudy banner, and down the glimmering vista to the rich jewels of Titian and the Italian school." But once he learned that the doorkeepers could be bribed, he was admitted and "marched delighted through a quarter of a mile of the proudest efforts of the mind of man, a whole creation of genius, a universe of art!" (8:15).

At first he was especially taken with the historical paintings of Rubens. "They are superior to anything I saw," he told his father, "except one picture by Raphael. The portraits are not so good as I expected. Titian's best portraits I did not see, as they were put by to be copied. The landscapes are for the most part exquisite." He had found the stimulation he was seeking at the Louvre and was eager to settle down to work. He had already called on Merimée, who had promised to go with him the next day "to obtain permission for me to copy any pictures which I like, and to assist me in procuring paints, canvas, &c." He concluded reassuringly: "I hope my mother is quite easy, as I hope to do very well."[3]

Four days later he wrote that he was busy copying one of Titian's portraits. "I made a very complete sketch of the head in about three hours," he reported, "and have been working upon it longer this morning." He planned to copy two other Titians, two Vandykes, and a Raphael—all portraits— or, if he could not have them removed to the copying room "either through the influence of Mr. Merimée or by bribing the keepers," another Titian, a Guercino, or possibly a couple of landscapes. He could work at the Louvre only four days each week because it was closed on Friday for cleaning, and Saturday and Sunday were visiting days. But he was planning to spend his

2. *The Hazlitts*, pp. 411–12.   3. Ibid., p. 412.

week ends making duplicates of his copies for his own use and painting a portrait of himself "in the same view as that of Hippolito de Medici, by Titian." "There are great numbers of people in the rooms (most of them *English*) every day," he wrote, "and I was afraid at first that this would confuse and hinder me; but I found on beginning to copy that I was too occupied in my work to attend much to, or to care at all about what was passing around me; or if this had any effect upon me indirectly, it was to make me more attentive to what I was about." He was obviously absorbed in his job and could declare with satisfaction: "I find myself very comfortable here." He added in a postscript: "I saw Bonaparte."

While he was copying, he was constantly observing, appraising, criticizing. "The finest picture in the collection is the *Transfiguration*, by Raphael," he told his father; it is, in fact, "the finest picture I ever saw; I mean the human part of it, because the figure of Christ, and the angels, or whatever they are, that are flying to meet him in the air, are to the last degree contemptible." The modern French paintings he considered "many of them excellent in many particulars, though not the most material";[4] they were, generally, too artificial, too academic, too *perfect*. Baron Guérin's new *Phaedra and Hippolytus*, which had created "a prodigious sensation," seemed to him "too much cast in the mould of the antique"; "there was a *mannerism* about it that did not augur favorably for his future progress, but denoted a premature perfection" (10:122). When Merimée asked his opinion of one landscape, he complained that it seemed to him "too clear . . . that the leaves of the trees in shadow were as distinct as those in light, the branches of the trees at a distance as plain as those near. . . . I said, one could not see the leaves of a tree a mile off, but this, I added, appertained to a question in metaphysics"—to which Merimée only "shook his head, thinking that a young Englishman could know as little of abstruse philosophy as of fine art" (12:333). Hazlitt was shocked to learn that French artists sometimes "rouged" the casts which they used as models "with a beautiful rose colour" or dressed them in "a flesh-coloured Nankin, like that which adorns the bodies of their opera dancers." Did this account for the admired flesh tints of David? "It is thus," he wrote scornfully, "that these accomplished persons think to rival the hues of Titian and Correggio!" (18:88 n.).

To his delight he discovered that the original paintings which he had brought over with him did not suffer as much as he had expected from comparison with the masterpieces he was seeing. "Without vanity be it spoken," he wrote to his father, "they are very much in the style of the Flemish and

4. Ibid., pp. 413–14.

Italian painters. I like them better, instead of worse, from comparing them with the pictures that are here." 5

Gradually his taste in paintings underwent a change: he lost some of his enthusiasm for Flemish painting, gained more for the Italian masters. At first, he said later, he used to look at the work of Weenix, Wouwerman, and Ruysdael after "a hard day's work, and having taxed my faculties to the utmost . . . and to take leave of them with a *non equidem invideo, miror magis*" (10:111). Or he looked at Reynolds's *Marquis of Granby* and Vandyke's *Charles I,* which hung side by side, and observed that "the portrait of the nobleman looked heavy and muddled, from the mode of heaping on the colours, and the determination to produce effects alone, without attention to the subordinate details defeated itself. The portrait of the unfortunate monarch, on the contrary, displayed the utmost delicacy and facility of execution. Every part would bear the nicest inspection, and yet the whole composition . . . had all the distinctness, lightness, and transparency of objects seen in the open air" (18:61). Yet before long he had decided not to copy Vandyke's *Cardinal Bentivoglio* because "after Titian's portraits, there was a want of interest in Vandyke's which I could not get over" (10:111). By contrast Titian's *Ippolito de' Medici,* which he had promised to copy for his brother's friend James Northcote, "seemed 'a thing of life,' with supernatural force and grandeur" as he "turned and saw it with the boar-spear in its hand, and its keen glance bent upon me" (10:225). And eventually "nothing would serve my turn but heads like Titian—Titian expression, Titian complexions, Titian dresses" (17:139). Similarly the figures in two allegorical pictures by Rubens seemed but "of wool or cotton" when compared with those in Veronese's *Marriage of Cana* (8:319). The latter seemed to him "in all likelihood the completest piece of workmanship extant in the art." He marveled at its size: twenty by forty feet, covering almost all of one wall of a large room in the museum; "it seemed as if that side of the apartment was thrown open, and you looked out at the open sky, at buildings, marble pillars, galleries with people in them, emperors, female slaves, Turks, negroes, musicians, all the famous painters of the time, the tables loaded with viands, goblets, and dogs under them—a sparkling, overwhelming confusion, a bright, unexpected reality—the only fault you could find was that no miracle was going on in the faces of the spectators: the only miracle there was the picture itself!" (8:319).

By Sunday, November 14, when he wrote again to his father, he was busy copying Ludovico Lana's *Death of Clorinda,* which he considered "the

5. Ibid., p. 414.

sweetest picture in the place." He had been working on it for "forty hours, that is seven mornings" and hoped to have it finished by the end of the week. "I generally go to the Museum about half-past nine or ten o'clock," he explained, "and continue there untill half-past three or four."

In the same letter he announced that he had "not yet seen Bonaparte near." But he had seen another of his heroes, Charles James Fox, who had spent two or three mornings at the Louvre, "talked a great deal, and was full of admiration." 6 Hazlitt was overjoyed at this chance to observe the liberal leader "with hairs grown grey in the service of the public, with a face pale and furrowed with thought, doing honour to the English character as its best representative" (1:171). He listened carefully while Fox, "rapidly, but very unaffectedly," discussed the paintings with the artist John Opie and another friend, calling their attention to "all those blues and greens and reds" which distinguished Guercino's work and praising the "truth and good sense" of Domenichino's *St. Jerome* (12:274). Hazlitt was less favorably impressed by the fabulous collector William Beckford of Fonthill Abbey, who came in one day "very plainly dressed in a loose great coat, and looked somewhat pale and thin." He hardly looked like one who might, as it was rumored, have offered Napoleon two thousand guineas for Titian's *St. Peter Martyr* (18:176–77).

On Friday, November 29, he wrote again, reporting that his copy of *The Death of Clorinda* was "as good as finished" and he was busy copying Titian's *Portrait of His Mistress*. He expected to finish eight pictures in eight weeks and to "have a month left to do the other two heads, which will make up the whole number." He was working also on a copy of Raphael's *Holy Family*, "one of the most beautiful things in the world," and was hoping to have prints made of both it and *The Death of Clorinda*. He seemed anxious to convince his parents that he was, not wasting a minute of his time in Paris; in fact he added in a postscript: "I would have written a longer letter if I had had time." 7

By December 10 Hazlitt could report that he had finished the *Clorinda*, which "will certainly make as great a figure in Railton's parlour as the original does in the Louvre." And he added proudly:

> They [the French painters] have begun of late to compliment me on my style of getting on; though at first, they were disposed to be impertinent. This is the way of the world; you are always sure of getting encouragement when you do not want it. After I had done my picture yesterday, I took a small canvas, which I had in the place, and began a sketch of a head in one of the large historical pictures, being very

6. Ibid., pp. 414–15.   7. Ibid., pp. 416–17.

doubtful if I could; not at all expecting to finish it, but merely to pass away the time: however, in a couple of hours, I made a very fair copy, which I intend to let remain as it is. It is a side face, a good deal like yours, which was one reason of my doing it so rapidly. I got on in such a rapid style, that an Englishman, who had a party with him, came up, and told me, in French, that I was doing very well. Upon my answering him in English he seemed surprised, and said, "Upon my word, sir, you get on with great spirit and boldness: you do us great credit, I am sure." He afterwards returned; and after asking how long I had been about it, said he was the more satisfied with his judgment, as he did not know I was a countryman. Another wanted to know if I taught painting in oil. I told him that I stood more in need of instruction myself; that that sort of rapid sketching was what I did better than anything else; and that, after the first hour or two, I generally made my pictures worse and worse, the more pains I took with them. However, seriously, I was much pleased with this kind of notice, as however confident I may be of the real merit of my work, it is not always so clear that it is done in a way to please most other people. This same sketch is certainly a very singular thing, as I do not believe there are ten people in the world who could do it in the same way. [8]

He concluded his letter with a detailed account of his work to date and that projected for the remaining seven weeks of his stay. And four weeks later, on January 7, 1803, he wrote again, still confining himself to specific information about his work at the Louvre.[9] He could feel, at last, that he was truly making progress.

He was not, however, spending all his waking hours at the easel. He was seeing the sights of Paris: walking in the Bois de Boulogne and the Jardin des Tuilleries, attending the theater, reading French—puzzling over Racine and then, for relief, turning to *Antony and Cleopatra* and crying aloud, "Our Shakspeare was also a poet!" (10:27). He met several members of the English colony: the artist Richard Duppa, his brother John's friend the eccentric statistician John Rickman, and the Italian artist Domenico Pellegrini, who had spent some time in England. Through him he was introduced to the extraordinary artist and collector Richard Cosway and was taken to see his "fairy palace . . . of specimens of art, antiquarianism, and *virtù*, jumbled all together in the richest disorder, dusty, shadowy, obscure, with much left to the imagination . . . and with copies of the Old Masters, cracked and damaged, which he touched and retouched with his own hand, and yet swore they were the genuine, the pure originals." Cosway gravely displayed "the crucifix that Abelard prayed to—a lock of Eloisa's hair—the dagger with which Felton stabbed the Duke of Buckingham—the first finished sketch of the Jocunda—Titian's large colossal profile of Peter

8. Ibid., pp. 417–19.   9. See ibid., p. 419.

Aretine—a mummy of an Egyptian king—a feather of a phoenix—a piece of Noah's Ark." But the most fantastic exhibit of all was Cosway himself, who professed to having "conversed with more than one person of the Trinity" (12:95–96). Hazlitt was delighted with him and with his wife Maria, herself an artist and "the most lady-like of Englishwomen" (18:180). One day, after having taken tea with them the afternoon before, he encountered Mrs. Cosway strolling arm in arm down the street with Lucien Bonaparte, no less (10:254). He did not, of course, spend all his time in such cosmopolitan company; he was living, perforce, economically—and later in life would recall knowingly the "easy cavalier airs" that "an impudent waiter at a French table-d'hôte" could assume (5:365).

Wherever he went, he studied people as well as paintings; he had lost none of his consuming interest in human nature. The French, he decided, were lively and entertaining to chat with, but wanting in depth of feeling (1:24 n.). The students working with him in the Louvre were typical: they seemed blind to the beauty which surrounded them ."You see a solitary French artist in the Louvre copying a Raphael or a Rubens, standing on one leg, not quite sure of what he is about" (17:218). One who was copying Titian's *Portrait of His Mistress* began by filling in a square in a right-hand corner which represented a piece of board and a bottle. "He set to work like a cabinet-maker or an engraver, and appeared to have no sympathy with the soul of the picture" (17:217). Another spent eleven weeks making a pencil sketch of Leonardo's *Virgin of the Rocks:*

> He would first retouch an eyebrow or an eyelash, then do something to one of the fingers, then mark in a bit of the drapery, and then return to the face again. All this he did, sometimes leaning over the railing before the picture, sometimes sitting on a stool, mechanically screwed on to it, sometimes standing on one leg. He also relieved the monotony of his undertaking, by retiring to a small distance to compare his copy with the original, or shewed it to some one near him, or went round to look over others who were copying, or stood at the fire for an hour together, or loitered in the sculpture room, or walked round the gallery, and generally observed at his return that Poussin was excellent "pour la composition," Raphael "pour l'expression," Titian "pour les beaux coloris," but that David and his pupils united all these qualities to the fine forms of the antique. At the end of eleven weeks, we left him perfecting his copy. For anything we know, he may be at it still. (18:87 n.)

He was still observing and analyzing when, early in February, he left Paris by diligence on his way back to London. One of the passengers told of a man who had courted a woman thirteen years before marrying her. "Then, at least," said an Englishman in the coach, "he would be acquainted with her character." But a French mountebank retorted: "No, not at all; for that the very next day she might turn out the very reverse of the character that she had appeared in during all the preceding time"—and Hazlitt "could not help admiring the superior sagacity of the French juggler" (8: 303).

He carried back with him a certificate signed by Monsieur Derron, director general of the Louvre, on "12 Pluviose" (January 3, 1803) listing the paintings which he had copied. But more important: he carried with him a new knowledge of the art of painting and a new conception of what he, as an artist, should aim to achieve: the verve of a Titian rather than the stern realism of a Rembrandt. Paris and the Louvre had given him more than he anticipated. Seventeen years afterward he wrote: ". . . long after I returned, and even still, I sometimes dream of being there again—of asking for the old pictures—and not finding them, or finding them changed or faded from what they were, I cry myself awake." And in the same essay: "Reader, 'if thou hast not seen the Louvre, thou art damned!'" (8: 16–17).

Moreover, his three months away from England had given him his first real taste of self-reliance. Although he was by this time almost twenty-five years old, he had never before been so completely left to his own resources; hitherto there had always been his parents, his teachers, his elder brother—someone in the background to oversee and direct his affairs. Now for the first time he had been free of such surveillance, and he had proved himself perfectly capable of governing his own affairs. He had found a place for himself in a strange country, had made friends of his own, had carried out his self-imposed assignments on schedule, had found reason to be well pleased with his accomplishment to date as a painter, and had even won high praise from others—recognition!

He may have gone first to Liverpool to deliver Railton's paintings, but he was in London by March 22,[10] when he dined at Godwin's with a lively group which included Coleridge, Thomas Holcroft and his wife, and an odd pair of Lambs, Charles and Mary by name. The conversation, as usual, was highly serious, but Charles Lamb tended to take serious conversation with a grain of salt. While the group was "disputing fiercely which was the best—*Man as he was, or man as he is to be*," he observed wryly, "give me man as he is *not* to be" (17: 122). Hazlitt, no humorist himself, was delighted; he would like to see more of this man.

Coleridge was still interested enough in Hazlitt to make an effort to aid him in his career. On June 4 he wrote to Godwin asking if he could locate

10. Baker, p. 153 n.

a publisher for an abridgment of *The Light of Nature Pursued* by "Edward Search" [Abraham Tucker], explaining that "a friend of mine, every way calculated by his Taste, & prior Studies for such a work is willing to abridge & systematize that work from 8 to 2 Vols. . . . I would prefix to it an Essay containing the whole substance of the first Volume of Hartley, entirely defecated from all the corpuscular hypotheses—with new illustrations—& give my name to the Essay. Likewise, I will revise every sheet of the Abridgement." He concluded: ". . . you would essentially serve a young man of profound Genius and original mind, who wishes to get his *Sabine* Subsistence by some Employment from the Booksellers, while he is employing the remainder of his Time in nursing up his Genius for the destiny, which he believes appurtenant to it."[11]

For the time being nothing came of the proposal, but Coleridge's wealthy friend Sir George Beaumont came to the rescue by commissioning Hazlitt to paint portraits of Coleridge and his son Hartley. Soon Hazlitt was settled in the Lake District, where Coleridge and Wordsworth now lived, working on portraits of both men. By July 23 he had finished the two paintings and had left Coleridge's house at Keswick to visit Wordsworth at Grasmere. "You would be as much astonished at Hazlitt's coming, as I at his going," Coleridge wrote to Wordsworth that day. And he reported that the two portraits had disappointed practically everyone involved. Sir George and Lady Beaumont thought Hazlitt had made Wordsworth look like a philosopher rather than a poet; "Mrs. Wilkinson *swears* that your Portrait is 20 years too old for you—& mine equally too old, & too lank—," Coleridge wrote. "Every single person without one exception cries out!—What a likeness!—but the face is too long! you have a round face!—Hazlitt knows this: but he will not alter it. Why?—because the Likeness with him is a secondary Consideration—he wants it to be a fine Picture."[12] And although Coleridge assured Robert Southey in a letter of August 1 that "young Hazlitt has taken masterly Portraits of me & Wordsworth, very much in the manner of Titian's Portraits—he wishes to take Lamb—& you,"[13] Southey himself wrote to Richard Duppa on December 14, after he had seen the pictures, that Hazlitt had painted Wordsworth "so dismally . . . that one of his friends, on seeing it, exclaimed, 'At the gallows—deeply affected by his deserved fate—yet determined to die like a man.'"[14] And to Coleridge he wrote on the following June 11: "Hazlitt's [portrait] does look as if you

11. *Coleridge Letters*, 2:949–50.   12. Ibid., 957–58.   13. Ibid., 960.
14. Charles Cuthbert Southey, *Life and Correspondence of Robert Southey*, 6 vols. (London, 1850), 2:238.

were on your trial, and certainly had stolen the horse; but then you did it cleverly."[15]

All concerned must have been relieved when Hazlitt left the Lake District—for Manchester, Coleridge thought—taking the two portraits with him.[16] His second acquaintance with poets had been disappointing, quite apart from the affair of the portraits. Hazlitt was convinced that Coleridge had lost him a potential patron by attacking Junius so furiously that Hazlitt felt obliged to defend him. Beaumont had been irked by Hazlitt's defense and at his presumption in arguing with Coleridge, who admitted the next day that he agreed with Hazlitt but had not wanted to offend Beaumont.[17] Hazlitt had annoyed Wordsworth, too, when he had presumed to ask the poet if he had not borrowed the idea of his "Poems on the Naming of Places" from *Paul and Virginia* (17:115–16).

Coleridge, for his part, had been distinctly disappointed in Hazlitt. When Thomas Wedgwood asked whether he would recommend Hazlitt as a traveling companion on a trip to the Continent, he replied on September 16 that Hazlitt was

> a thinking, observant, original man, of great power as a Painter of Character Portraits, & far more in the manner of the old Painters, than any living Artist, but the Object must be *before* him / he has no imaginative memory . . . is disinterested, an enthusiastic Lover of the great men, who have been before us—he says things that are his own in a way of his own—& tho' from habitual Shyness & the Outside & bearskin at least of misanthropy, he is strangely confused & dark in his conversation & delivers himself of almost all of his conceptions with a Forceps, yet he says more than any man, I ever knew, yourself only excepted, that is his own in a way of his own—& oftentimes when he has warmed his mind & the synovial juice has come out & spread over his joints, he will gallop for half an hour together with real Eloquence. He sends well-headed & well-feathered Thoughts straight forwards to the mark with a Twang of the Bow-string.

15. Ibid., p. 291. Cf. Wordsworth's comment in a letter to Beaumont dated June 3, 1805, that Coleridge's expression in the portrait is "quite dolorous and funereal" (*Letters of William and Dorothy Wordsworth, 1787–1805*, ed. E. de Selincourt, 2nd ed., revised by Chester L. Shaver [Oxford: Clarendon Press, 1967], p. 594). It should be said in Hazlitt's defense that Wordsworth told Beaumont that Hazlitt's painting of Coleridge was superior to one recently painted by James Northcote, who failed to catch as true a likeness. Southey also preferred Hazlitt's portrait of Coleridge to Northcote's (see Southey, *Life and Correspondence of Robert Southey*, 2:291).

16. *Coleridge Letters*, 2:1004. The portraits have not survived.

17. See Robinson, 1:24. Hazlitt's later account (8:204 n.) of meeting a "distinguished patron of art and rising merit at a little distance from Liverpool" who received him "with every mark of attention and politeness" until they disagreed on the merits of Pope's "Ode on St. Cecilia's Day" may well be a disguised retelling of this incident.

"If you could recommend him, as a Portrait-painter," he told Wedgwood, "I should be glad." But not as a traveling companion: "His manners are 99 in 100 singularly repulsive—: brow-hanging, shoe-contemplative, *strange* . . . he is, I verily believe, kindly-natured—is very fond of, attentive to, & patient with, children / but he is jealous, gloomy, & of irritable Pride —& addicted to women, as objects of sexual Indulgence." [18]

What had happened to prompt that final charge? Crabb Robinson had remarked earlier that Hazlitt "suffered in the company of young ladies," and Charles Lamb presently described his terror when confronted with "Girlery"; for that matter, Coleridge himself had cited his "habitual Shyness." Yet a normal man of twenty-five—even a shy one—is bound to feel sexual compulsions which, if stifled, may erupt in strange ways. Thomas De Quincey later claimed that Hazlitt had proposed to Dorothy Wordsworth, who was seven years older than he.[19] Had he been too avid in his pursuit? Or, more likely, especially if he suffered again the familiar pangs of rejection, had he sought consolation impulsively elsewhere? In his calmer moments he regarded his sex as a burden; "there is but one instance," he wrote presently, "in which appetite hangs about a man as a perpetual clog and dead-weight upon the reason, namely the sexual appetite, and . . . here the selfish habit produced by this constant state of animal sensibility seems to have a direct counterpoise given it by nature in the mutual sympathy of the sexes" (1:46).[20] But what if the other sex proved unsympathetic?

By October 24 he was back in Keswick. That day he walked with Coleridge and Southey "thro' Borrodale into Watendlath, & so home to a late dinner."[21] Two days later there was friction again: he, Coleridge, and Wordsworth were involved in "a most unpleasant Dispute." "I spoke, I fear too contemptuously—," Coleridge confided to his notebook, "but they spoke

18. *Coleridge Letters*, 2:990–91.

19. See Thomas De Quincey, *Collected Writings*, ed. David Masson, 14 vols. (London, 1896), 2:294. De Quincey's testimony is at least suspect; he first visited the Lake District in 1807, four years after Hazlitt's visits. Moreover, as Barry Cornwall reported, he and Hazlitt always "thought poorly of each other. Hazlitt pronounced verbally that the other would be good only 'whilst the opium was trickling from his mouth,' but he never published anything derogatory to the other's genius. De Quincey, on the other hand, seems to have forced opportunities for sneering at Hazlitt" (*Literary Recollections of Barry Cornwall*, ed. Richard W. Armour [Boston: Meador Publishing Co., 1936], p. 117 [hereafter cited as *Cornwall Recollections*]).

20. Cf. Hazlitt's later explanation of why "excessive refinement" in a person's nature "tends to produce equal grossness" (4:136).

21. *Notebooks of Samuel Taylor Coleridge*, ed. Kathleen Coburn, 4 vols. (New York: Pantheon Books, 1957–61), 1:par. 1610.

so irreverently so malignantly of the Divine Wisdom, that it overset me. Hazlitt how easily roused to Rage & Hatred, self-projected / but who shall find the Force that can drag him up out of the Depth into one expression of Kindness, into the shewing of one Gleam of the Light of Love on his Countenance.—Peace be with *him!*—But *thou*, dearest Wordsworth." Presently he added the strange, contorted comment: "Hazlitt to feelings of Anger & Hatred Phosphorus—it is but to open the Cork & it flames—but to Love & serviceable Friendship, let them, like Nebuchadnezzer, heat the Furnace with a 7 fold Heat, this Triune Shadrach, Meshach, Abednego, will shiver in the midst of it." And the following day he reported that he sat for his portrait by Hazlitt and argued metaphysics with him: "I made out . . . the whole business of the Origin of Evil satisfactorily to my own mind, & forced H. to confess, that the metaphysical argument reduced itself to this: Why did not infinite Power *always* & exclusively produce such Beings as in each moment of their Duration were infinite / why, in short, did not the Almighty create an absolutely infinite number of Almighties?" [22] It was time for Hazlitt to move on.

And presently, suddenly, he did; in fact, he fled. His "addiction to women as objects of sexual Indulgence" had brought him into serious trouble. Wordsworth and Coleridge revealed the incident years later when both had been outraged by Hazlitt's personal attacks on them. Wordsworth told the artist Benjamin Haydon "with great horror" about Hazlitt's "licentious conduct to the girls of the Lake," insisting that "no woman could walk after dark, for 'his Satyr and *beastly* appetites.'" [23] He repeated the story to both Crabb Robinson and Lamb. Robinson, who was estranged from Hazlitt at the time, was scandalized and wrote in his diary that Hazlitt "even whipped one woman, *more puerum*, for not yielding to his wishes." [24] Lamb, however, took it all as a great joke and so treated it in a letter which he wrote to Wordsworth shortly afterwards. [25] Haydon too was amused— at Wordworth's righteous indignation as well as Hazlitt's conduct. His is the most specific and probably the least prejudiced account of the affair: "Some girl called him a black-faced rascal, when Hazlitt enraged pushed her down, '& because, Sir,' said Wordworth, 'she refused to gratify his abominable & devilish propensities,' he lifted up her petticoats & *smote* her on the *bottom*." [26]

22. Ibid., par. 1616–19.

23. *Diary of Benjamin Robert Haydon*, ed. Willard B. Pope, 5 vols. (Cambridge, Mass.: Harvard University Press, 1960–63), 2:470 (hereafter cited as *Haydon Diary*).

24. Robinson, 1:169.   25. See below, pp. 89–90.   26. *Haydon Diary*, 2:470.

The villagers of Keswick, however, were not amused; they vowed revenge. Wordsworth seems to have told Lamb and Robinson only that they wanted to submit Hazlitt to a humiliating "ducking" or possibly imprisonment. But Coleridge—and here his imagination undoubtedly ran away with him—declared that "not less than 200" men were on horseback in search of him and that he might have been transported or hanged if they had found him.[27]

With the aid of Coleridge and Southey, Hazlitt managed to escape from his pursuers. In his haste he left his clothes and paint box behind. Coleridge later claimed that he gave him "all the money, I had in the world, and the very Shoes off my feet."[28] He reached Wordsworth's house in Grasmere at midnight, spent the rest of the night there, and set off next day, having received from Wordsworth some clothing and "from three to five pounds."[29]

Where next? Well, "home is the place where, when you have to go there, they have to take you in." And presently Hazlitt turned up at Wem with little money, no paints, and not even a change of clothing. His parents must have been baffled at his appearance—he would hardly have told them the true story. And he himself, surely, suffered a grinding humiliation—he who a few months before had dreamed of rivaling Rembrandt or Titian. A pretty picture he made now!

He wrote presently to ask Coleridge to send him the portraits and sketches which he had left behind, and Coleridge sent word to his wife in January "to have the word of his Letter exactly obeyed," although he insisted on keeping sketches of himself and his son Hartley as payment for the money which he had given Hazlitt. He was clearly trying to be scrupulously fair, but he implied that Southey had lost all patience with Hazlitt.[30]

Wordsworth, too, seemed determined to be tolerant. On March 5, 1804, he wrote to Hazlitt at Wem apologizing for not having answered his letter sooner and objecting to Hazlitt's suggestion that he reduce his portrait of Hartley Coleridge by "taking away the legs, &c." He assured him that "no body durst venture to seize your clothes or box" (which Mrs. Coleridge had apparently not sent to him) and promised to look for them next time he went to Keswick. "I should have liked," he added, "to shew you 200 yards or so of mountain Brook scenery which I found out yesterday above Rydale. They are some of the finest old stumpified staring trees I ever saw, with a small waterfall, rocks of all shapes &c &c. I pass'd also under Nab scar at

27. *Coleridge Letters*, 4:692–93, 669–70, 735.
28. Ibid., p. 735.   29. Robinson, 1:169.
30. *Coleridge Letters*, 2:1024–25.

Rydale which you sketched a part of: it is infinitely finer in winter than summer time; and indeed is a noble place." And he concluded with "best remembrances" from all his family and signed himself "very affectionately yours." [31] He offered no hint of the horror which he later expressed at Hazlitt's "abominable and devilish propensities."

Meanwhile Hazlitt had lived through another dreary autumn and winter at Wem, with ample time to brood on his folly. It was an anxious period for all Englishmen because the war with France had been resumed in May, and Napoleon, growing ever bolder, was threatening to invade England. Hazlitt passed the time as best he could, perhaps painting another portrait of his father, then writing hopefully to a friend, probably Godwin, on December 29 to inquire whether "you could procure me 3, or 4 pictures to do at 5 guineas each among any of your friends, or acquaintances in London." He would like, he explained, to secure enough such commissions to pay his expenses for a month or six weeks in London, adding: "If you think there is any chance of this, & would let me know, I would send a picture of my father which I was to send to my brother to town immediately, which you might either see there, or it could be left at your house." [32]

Sooner or later he resurrected his thumb-worn essay on natural disinterestedness and struggled with it once more. He worked too on a related critique of the philosophical systems of Hartley and Helvétius, and eventually he managed to shape his thoughts into a form which he believed publishable. But his parents must have been apprehensive. This only begotten son, in whom they had once been so well pleased, reached his twenty-sixth birthday on April 10, and he was still dependent on them for the very food he ate. They had borne with him while he had supposedly prepared himself for three separate careers—as clergyman, philosopher, and painter. But his only true vocation seemed to be that of idler.

In July he turned up in London with his manuscript. He called on Godwin on the twenty-fifth and twenty-eighth, and on the thirty-first Godwin wrote in his diary: "Call on Johnson (Hazlit)," [33] presumably to indicate that he had made overtures to Joseph Johnson, the liberal bookseller who had published the Reverend Mr. Hazlitt's *Discourses* back in 1790. Hazlitt certainly welcomed the chance to mix with stimulating company again—people like Horne Tooke, who "sat like a king at his own table" at

---

31. *Letters of William and Dorothy Wordsworth: The Later Years*, ed. E. de Selincourt, 3 vols. (Oxford: Clarendon Press, 1939), 3:1349–50.
32. Baker, p. 140.
33. Ibid., p. 140 n.

his Sunday parties "and gave laws to his guests—and to the world" (11:49). By October his sister Peggy had come up to visit her brother John, and they were seeing a good deal of Hazlitt's new friends, Charles and Mary Lamb. Hazlitt persuaded Charles to pose for a portrait—in the costume of a Venetian senator, to add a Titianesque fillip.[34] Mary Lamb wrote to Sarah Coleridge on October 13: "William Hazlitt is painting my brother's picture, which has brought us acquainted with the whole family. I like William Hazlitt and his sister very much indeed."[35] Hazlitt especially relished Lamb's sense of humor, so unlike anything in his own nature: Lamb's jokes, he told a friend, "would be the sharpest in the world, but that they are blunted by good-nature. He wants malice—which is a pity."[36] As for Mary, he pronounced her the only thoroughly reasonable woman he had ever known.[37]

His prospects were brightening now: Joseph Johnson soon agreed to publish his essay, and in the following July it appeared anonymously as *An Essay on the Principles of Human Action: Being an Argument in Favour of the Natural Disinterestedness of the Human Mind*. For Hazlitt this was a momentous event: at long last he had managed to formulate his cherished original theory. If the world accepted it, his years of anguished labor would be vindicated.

To most readers, however, it was bound to seem a piece of special pleading. "It is the design of the following Essay," it began, "to shew that the human mind is naturally disinterested, or that it is naturally interested in the welfare of others in the same way, and from the same direct motives, by which we are impelled to the pursuit of our own interest" (1:1). By natural inclination and training Hazlitt recoiled at Hobbes's theory that self-interest determines man's actions. And he thought he had detected a flaw in it: he agreed with Bishop Butler that the very nature of man's "personal

34. This may have been the *Portrait of a Gentleman* which Hazlitt exhibited at the Royal Academy in 1805. It hangs now in the National Portrait Gallery in London.

35. *Letters of Charles Lamb, to Which are Added Those of His Sister Mary Lamb*, ed. E. V. Lucas, 3 vols. (London: J. M. Dent and Sons, Ltd.; Methuen and Co., Ltd., 1935), 1:380 (hereafter cited as *Lamb Letters*).

36. *New Monthly Magazine* 29 (1830), pt. 2, p. 480.

37. Thomas Noon Talfourd, *Final Memories of Charles Lamb*, 2 vols. (London, 1848), 2:227 (hereafter cited as Talfourd). Elsewhere Hazlitt remarked that he had met only one reasonable woman (20:42) and, in a discussion at the Lambs' rooms of women one would wish to have seen, he declared that there was one woman present "as good, as sensible, and in all respects as exemplary, as the best of them could be for their lives" (17:133). Hazlitt may have dwelt on Mary's good sense and reasonableness to compensate for her recurrent madness.

identity" militates against Hobbes's assumption. Man's identity, Hazlitt argued, exists only through sensation, operating in the present, or memory, recalling the past. Neither of these can operate in the future: before he decides on any future action, man must use his imagination, which inevitably depends on knowledge. Hazlitt admitted that men have a greater knowledge of their own experiences than they do of others', and that they can imagine what may happen to themselves in the future more easily than what will happen to others. As he expressed it: "I naturally desire and pursue my own good (in whatever this consists) simply from my having an idea of it sufficiently warm and vivid to excite in me an emotion of interest, or passion; and I love and pursue the good of others, of a relative, of a friend, of a family, or a community, or of mankind for just the same reason" (1:12).

He developed his thesis slowly and painstakingly, and inevitably he sought to fortify it with specific evidence. Since he was writing before scientific methods had been applied to the behavioral sciences, his evidence was generally hypothetical. When, for example, he hit on the case of the burnt child who dreads the fire, he launched into pages of diagnosis, often with surprising results:

> when I say that the child *does not* feel, that he *is not* interested in his future sensations, and consider this as equivalent to his *having* no real or personal interest in them, I mean that he *never* feels or can be affected by them before-hand; that he is always necessarily cut off from every kind of communication with them, that they cannot possibly act upon his mind as motives to action, or excite in him any kind of impulse in any circumstances or any manner: and I conceive that it is no great stretch of speculative refinement to insist that without some such original faculty of being immediately affected by his future sensations more than by those of others, his relation to his future self, whatever that may be, cannot be made the foundation of his having a real positive interest in his future welfare which he has not in that of others. (1:30–31)

More relevantly, he argued that, if children seem self-centered, it is because they have so little knowledge of the interests or feelings of others. Or if a man seems preoccupied with his own interests, it is because he has narrowed his mind, ignoring the interests and feelings of others. But too often he reiterated, apologized, abandoned an argument midway, then started all over again. At one point he burst out exasperatedly: "But I am tired of repeating the same thing so often; for 'as to those that will not be at the pains of a little thought, no multiplication of words will ever suffice to make them understand the truth or rightly conceive my meaning'" (1:31).[38]

38. In a footnote Hazlitt named Berkeley's *Essay on Vision* as the source of the quotation.

A harassed reader might have retorted that judicious writers rely more on the processes of subtraction or division than on those of addition or multiplication.

Hazlitt published, along with the essay, "Some Remarks on the Systems of Hartley and Helvétius." "It was my first intention," he explained in his opening paragraph,

> to have given at the end of the preceding essay a general account of the nature of the will, and to have tried at least to dig down a little deeper into the foundations of human thoughts and actions than I have hitherto done. At present I have laid aside all thoughts of this kind as I have neither time nor strength for such an undertaking; and the most that I shall attempt is to point out such contradictions and difficulties in both systems as may lessen the weight of any objections drawn from them against the one I have stated, and leave the argument as above explained in all it's original force. (1:50)

He proceeded to criticize Hartley's theory of association because his arbitrary theory of the operation of the brain is too mechanical: "Even where [Hartley] is greatest, he is always the physiologist rather than the metaphysician" (1:59). Hazlitt objected especially to Hartley's conception of ideas in chains vibrating one against another; ideas, he declared, should be compared to a nest of adders rather than to a line of pictures in a gallery. And he called attention to Hartley's neglect of the human will, which, Hazlitt believed, can determine the direction of man's ideas. In any event, he concluded, "My quarrel with [Hartley's theory of association] is not that it proves any thing against the notion of disinterestedness, but that it proves nothing" (1:77).

Hazlitt disposed of Helvétius in short order. Helvétius, he argued, maintains that men relieve others only because doing so relieves them of uneasiness—and that, in itself, proves the existence of sympathy, the concern for others. "It is absurd to say that in compassionating the distress of others we are only affected by our own pain or uneasiness, since this very pain arises from our compassion. It is putting the effect before the cause" (1:86).

Hazlitt later said that he made his *Essay* "as dry and meagre as I could, so that it fell still-born from the press. . . . Yet, let me say," he added, "that that work contains an important metaphysical discovery, supported by a continuous and severe train of reasoning, nearly as subtle and original as anything in Hume or Berkeley" (17:312). Again and again he declared that he was prouder of this essay than of anything else he had ever written.[39] And

39. See 8:237; 9:3 and 51.

although his claims were extravagant—probably, in part, defensive—the essay was to serve him well; for, as John M. Bullitt first pointed out, Hazlitt's principle of the sympathetic imagination underlies his later criticism.[40] It is, in fact, the keystone of most of his thinking, political and aesthetic as well as philosophical. For he recognized his own sympathetic imagination as the noblest of his faculties: thanks to it he could *feel with* other human beings, real or fictional; he could share the joys or sorrows of characters in novels or plays, could respond to a truly lifelike detail or expression in a fine painting, or could suffer with men in bondage and long to set them free. He believed that the imagination "stamps the character of genius on productions of art more than any other circumstance" (6:109), and he admired most highly the author who could, by exercise of his imagination, identify with his creations.

However, the *Essay* was by no means the original contribution to metaphysical thinking that he liked to think it,[41] and reviewers were in no hurry to notice it. When they did, they agreed to a man that the author's obscure presentation made his argument virtually impossible to follow. The *British Critic* delayed its review until November, 1806, then quarreled with all the principles presented, complained that "the author's language is often exceedingly involved and consequently obscure," referred three times to his "raving," and even accused him of "tapping the foundation of all religion."[42] The *Critical Review* for the following month was disposed to be indulgent and urged readers not to damn the book because of its obscurity. "The writer, we really think," the reviewer observed, "is one of more than ordinary merit and promise, and therefore we feel more than ordinarily interested to bespeak for him, what is not always easy to be had by anonymous publications, a fair opportunity to be heard." The *Anti-Jacobin Review and Magazine*, in its January, 1807, issue, suggested momentarily that the *Essay*

40. John M. Bullitt, "Hazlitt and the Romantic Conception of the Imagination," *PQ* 24 (1945): 343–61.

41. See Leonard M. Trawick, III, "Sources of Hazlitt's 'Metaphysical Discovery,'" *PQ* 42 (1963): 277–82, and Roy E. Cain, "David Hume and Adam Smith as Sources of the Concept of Sympathy in Hazlitt," *Papers on Language and Literature* 1 (1965): 133–40.

42. In a letter to *TLS* (19 September, 1968, p. 1062) the late Douglas Grant maintained that Wordsworth's brother Christopher wrote this review, that Hazlitt was aware of its authorship, and that it intensified Hazlitt's resentment toward Wordsworth. Grant claimed also that Hazlitt's frank remarks about female charms in his *Reply to the Essay on Population* confirmed Wordsworth's worst suspicions about Hazlitt's character. Grant promised to develop his points more fully in a study which, I understand, is being completed by his wife.

might be "a highly-finished burlesque," then finally dismissed it as "a little innocent, absurd essay, which a philosopher may be induced to read from seeing its title, and which he will lay aside with a smile of contempt." The April *Monthly Review* tried to keep an open mind. "He writes with candour," their critic declared, "and he states perspicuously the notions which he combats: but the reasoning which he opposes to them we are wholly unable to apprehend. Let the curious reader peruse the tract, and decide whether it is on the author's or on our part that capacity is wanting for metaphysical researches." But the *Eclectic Review* for the following August found fault with both Hazlitt's argument and "the extreme ambiguity and involution" of his style. "The author has intimated . . . ," the reviewer concluded, "that the present work developes but a small part of a plan which he has in contemplation. We hope he will take more care in simplifying his style, and endeavour to preserve such a strict logical relation between his sentences, as may enable him to detect and exclude any fallacious argument or erroneous principle. He would find it an advantage to compel himself to draw up an analysis of his performance." The reviews, when they came, were hardly encouraging; yet Hazlitt must have concluded, well before they appeared, that his *Essay* was doomed, like most of his other efforts, to failure.

It found an occasional appreciative reader. Coleridge's opinion, which Hazlitt would have valued, seems to have gone unrecorded, although Lamb sent him a copy of the *Essay* in February, 1806.[43] But Sir James Scarlett, later the first Lord Abinger, supposedly approved so highly of it that he even suggested that he might find employment for Hazlitt.[44] And James Mackintosh, who had gone out to India, was favorably impressed with the *Essay*, even though Hazlitt had handled him rather harshly in it.[45] It has received its most serious consideration, however, from a twentieth-century scholar, James Noxon, who has praised Hazlitt's reasoning, if not his style.[46]

Long before the reviews began appearing Hazlitt returned to Wem. On

---

43. See *Lamb Letters*, 1:420.

44. *Four Generations*, 1:92–93. W. C. Hazlitt states that the Reverend Mr. Hazlitt urged his son to refuse the offer because he distrusted Scarlett, a Whig turned Tory.

45. Hazlitt himself wrote in *The Spirit of the Age* that Mackintosh, while in India, "languished after the friends and the society he had left behind; and wrote over incessantly for books from England. One that was sent to him at this time was an *Essay on the Principles of Human Action;* and the way in which he spoke of that dry, tough, metaphysical *choke-pear*, showed the dearth of intellectual intercourse in which he lived, and the craving in his mind after those studies which had once been his pride and to which he still turned for consolation in his remote solitude" (11:102). For Hazlitt's judgment on Mackintosh in the *Essay*, see above, pp. 63–64.

46. James Noxon, "Hazlitt as a Moral Philosopher," *Ethics* 73 (1963): 279–83.

November 10, 1805, Charles Lamb wrote him a long letter from London. He had been glad, he said, to learn that Hazlitt's "journey was so *picturesque*" (he had stopped off at Oxford to see the paintings there). The Lambs miss him, "as we foretold we should." And he rattled on about the farce he was writing, the doings of Mrs. Rickman, "MONKEY" [little Louisa Martin], a new painting by their friend George Dawe, the death of Lord Nelson, and the like—concluding with the words: "Luck to Ned Search. . . ." [47] For Hazlitt had started work on the abridgment of *The Light of Nature Pursued* by "Edward Search" [Abraham Tucker] which Coleridge had earlier mentioned to Godwin. If nothing more, Hazlitt's *Essay* had brought him a connection with the publisher Johnson which could prove advantageous.

He was also painting another portrait of his father—as much, perhaps, to win the good man's favor as to exercise his own talent. He finished it in December, on or about the day that news of the battle of Austerlitz reached Wem. Although to most Englishmen Napoleon's triumph over his Russian and Austrian enemies was frightening, Hazlitt was overjoyed; he still regarded Bonaparte as a champion of liberty and the hope of Europe. "I walked out in the afternoon," he wrote years later, "and, as I returned, saw the evening star set over a poor man's cottage with other thoughts and feelings than I shall ever have again" (8:13).[48]

Now that life was looking brighter, Hazlitt was able to apply himself to his work. On January 5, 1806, he sent the completed manuscript of his abridgment to Godwin, asking him to deliver it to Joseph Johnson. "I have done my job quicker, & with less trouble, than I expected," he wrote, "& indeed I have done it better than I expected." He had written separately to Johnson, he explained, but feared that Johnson might not reply promptly. Accordingly, would Godwin remind him of the matter "'at some convenient & leisure hour,' by the time that you suppose Johnson has quite forgot the subject"? He even suggested that Godwin raise the question of payment —and whether half or all the amount could be advanced before publication. He would, he promised, be back in London in time to "overlook the press" or to delegate someone else for the task. And he added in a postscript: "If you see Lamb, will you tell him that I expected to have heard from him before this?" (1:370–71).

By the time Hazlitt's letter reached London, Lamb had already written,

47. *Lamb Letters*, 1:409–11.

48. In an article for the *Morning Chronicle* of January 27, 1814, Hazlitt defined "*true Jacobin*" as "he who has seen the evening star set over a poor man's cottage" (7:370).

on January 7, a gossipy letter describing the elaborate preparations for Lord Nelson's funeral and acknowledging receipt of St. John Crèvecoeur's *Letters of an American Farmer* ("a very stupid, uninteresting Book").[49] But he wrote again on the fifteenth "at Godwin's request," announcing that Johnson had promised to reach a decision about the abridgment in one month and expressing interest in a new project that Hazlitt had in mind: a biography of the Reverend Joseph Fawcett, who had just died.[50] The two were now fast friends.

On February 19 Lamb wrote again, saying that he had finished his farce and was sending it off the next day to be read by the manager at Drury Lane. But he could report no progress on Hazlitt's abridgment; in fact Joseph Johnson had had a fire in his house and would be unable to decide about publication for another month.[51] There were further letters from Lamb on March 8 and 15, relaying the gossip, telling Hazlitt about the unusual number of art exhibits scheduled in London, and asking, "What do you in Shropshire when so many fine pictures are a-going, a going every day in London?"[52]

On or about June 2 Hazlitt had arrived in London, and Mary Lamb was writing to her friend Sarah Stoddart: "William Hazlitt, the brother of him you know, is in town. I believe you have heard us say we like him? He came in good time; for the loss of Manning [who had gone to China] made Charles very dull, and he likes Hazlitt better than any body except Manning."[53]

Sarah Stoddart and Mary Lamb had been friends and correspondents for some time. Sarah, the daughter of a retired lieutenant in the Royal Navy who had lived at Winterslow, near Salisbury, was an unconventional sort of woman. Although she seems never to have agitated for the rights of women, she was keenly interested in her own rights as a human being—her rights to do and say what she pleased. A century later she would have fitted very well into society as an emancipated woman; in the early nineteenth century she fitted nowhere—except into the household of the easygoing Lambs. Charles had written of her in his January 15 letter to Hazlitt: "We have Miss Stoddart in our house, she has been with us a fortnight, and will stay a week or so longer. She is one of the few people who are not in the way when they are with you."[54]

49. *Spectator* 161 (Aug. 5, 1938): 237–38.
50. *Lamb Letters*, 1:416–18.   51. Ibid., pp. 423–24.
52. Ibid., 2:5.   53. Ibid., p. 10.
54. Ibid., 1:417.

Sarah was thirty-one, Mary forty-one; yet they had much in common: both, for example, enjoyed strenuous walks—or lively conversations over a glass of brandy (three parts) and water (one part).[55] Like Mary, Sarah had a brother to whom she was devoted, but he was a quite different sort of person from Charles Lamb. Ever since childhood Sarah and her brother John had been poles apart: when their father had offered them a taste of grog of an evening, John had always said, "No, thank-you, father," but Sarah had said, "Yes, please, father."[56] And much as Sarah admired her brother, she had no intention of reforming herself in his image.

However, a woman needed a male protector in the year 1806, and Sarah was keenly interested in finding one. Ever since 1802 she and Mary Lamb had been corresponding—often on the subject of possible husbands for Sarah. Mary, who could not think of marriage for herself, was an eager matchmaker, sympathetic to every turn of fortune: now confident that Sarah was about to marry brilliantly, now suggesting that spinsterhood was perhaps preferable. In 1803 she had followed with interest Sarah's elaborate preparations for a trip to Malta, where her brother John had gone to serve a term as King's Advocate—then shared her disappointment when all her finery had failed to attract a suitor. Then one by one a man named William (certainly *not* Hazlitt), a Mr. Turner, and a Mr. White came up for discussion, but sooner or later each slipped away. In fact, in the very letter which announced Hazlitt's arrival in London, Mary had written: "I am very sorry you still hear nothing from Mr. White. I am afraid that is all at an end. What do you intend to do about Mr. Turner?"[57]

And what, if anything, did Mary intend to do about Mr. Hazlitt? To be sure, he did not seem a very likely prospect as a husband: he had never made a decent living, his personality was far from endearing, and he was notoriously boorish in the company of young ladies. It was in this very month of June that Charles Lamb wrote to Wordsworth:

> W. Hazlitt is in Town. I took him to see a very pretty girl professedly, where there were two young girls—the very head and sum of the Girlery was two young girls—they neither laughed nor sneered nor giggled nor whispered—but they were young girls—and he sat and frowned blacker and blacker, indignant that there should be such

55. Ibid., p. 428.

56. *Memoirs*, 1:166.

57. *Lamb Letters*, 2:9. See also John R. Barker, "Some Early Correspondence of Sarah Stoddart and the Lambs," *Huntington Library Quarterly* 24 (1960–61): 59–69, for evidence of the string of candidates whom Sarah had considered before her correspondence with Mary Lamb began. They included a Mr. Read, a Mr. Warren, "Mr. Parsons' nephew," and a Mr. Barwis. She considered herself to be at a disadvantage because her father would allow her only five hundred pounds as a dowry.

a thing as Youth and Beauty, till he tore me away before supper in perfect misery and owned he could not bear young girls. They drove him mad. So I took him home to my old Nurse, where he recover'd perfect tranquillity. Independent of all this, and as I am not a young girl myself, he is a great acquisition to us.[58]

Hazlitt may have had good reason to feel uncomfortable in the presence of young ladies just now. For it was at about this time that he fell in love, perhaps with a girl named Sally Shepherd—and was once more rejected.[59] She in no way resembled Sarah Stoddart. "I never fell in love but once," Hazlitt wrote in his reply to Malthus in 1807; "and then it was with a girl who always wore her handkerchief pinned tight round her neck, with a fair face, gentle eyes, a soft smile, and cool auburn locks. . . . It was not a raging heat, a fever in the veins: but it was like a vision, a dream, like thoughts of childhood, an everlasting hope, a distant joy, a heaven, a world that might be. The dream is still left, and sometimes comes confusedly over me in solitude and silence, and mingles with the softness of the sky, and veils my eyes from mortal grossness" (1:283).

The young man who wrote those lines did not seem like a promising candidate for Miss Sarah Stoddart's list. However, Sarah had certain merits: at thirty-one she had long since outgrown Girlery, for years she had contemplated marriage with no apparent emotional involvement, and she had a small private income. For a young man of William Hazlitt's temperament who could not bear young girls—one who had been often jobless, penniless, and rejected—she might seem to be just the right answer—at least for the time being.

58. *Lamb Letters*, 2:15.

59. The name survives only in a chance remark made by Sarah Hazlitt in her journal in 1822: "I told him [his infatuation for Sally Walker] was like his frenzy about Sally Shepherd. he said *that* was but a flea-bite, nothing at all to this, for she had never pretended to love him; but all along declared she did not" (*Journals of Sarah and William Hazlitt, 1822–31*, ed. Willard H. Bonner, University of Buffalo Studies, vol. 24, no. 3 (Buffalo: University of Buffalo Press, 1959), pp. 247–48 [hereafter cited as *Journals*]). The Hazlitts had friends named Shepherd both at Gateacre, near Liverpool, and at Wem. As P. P. Howe has pointed out (p. 99), Sally Shepherd could hardly have been the daughter of the Reverend Samuel Shepherd of Gateacre, whose portrait Hazlitt painted in 1803. Nor would she be likely to be the Miss Shepherd of Wem listed as a subscriber to the Reverend William Hazlitt's *Discourses for the Use of Families* when it was published in 1790. Yet the spelling of the name (as opposed to *Shepard* or *Sheppard*) suggests some relationship.

CHAPTER V

Marry in Haste
(1806–1811)

One Friday evening in late June or early July, 1806, Mary Lamb wrote again to Sarah Stoddart. Hazlitt and Charles had gone off to Sadler's Wells for the evening, she reported, and she was at home reading a manuscript of Hazlitt's. As usual she sent Sarah all the available news: Charles's farce *Mr. H——* has been accepted and should be presented at Drury Lane before Christmas; Mrs. Rickman and Mrs. Wordsworth are ill; Charles and Mary themselves are working on their *Tales from Shakespeare*. Presently Charles and Hazlitt came back "dismal and dreary dull," and she "gave them both a good scolding—*quite a setting to rights.* . . ." She concluded her letter: "Write directly, for I am uneasy about your *Lovers;* I wish something was settled." The following Sunday she added playfully: "I am cooking a shoulder of Lamb (Hazlitt dines with us); it will be ready at two o'Clock, if you can pop in and eat a bit with us."[1]

If Mary was nourishing hopes of bringing Sarah and Hazlitt together, she soon abandoned them. By October 23 Sarah's brother had written that she was about to marry a young farmer named Dowling, and he had suggested that Mary go down to Salisbury to pass judgment on him and help draw up the marriage settlement. She did not relish the assignment, and she was inclined to be skeptical about the proposed marriage. "If you fancy a very young man," she wrote to Sarah, "and he likes an elderly gentlewoman; if he likes a learned and accomplished lady, and you like a not very learned youth, who may need a little polishing, which probably he will never acquire; it is all very well, and God bless you both together and may you be both very long in the same mind."[2]

1. *Lamb Letters*, 2:16–18.   2. Ibid., p. 23.

Hazlitt meanwhile kept busy writing and painting. Nothing came of his proposed biography of Joseph Fawcett; instead he dashed off (and, incredibly, printed at his own expense) an anonymous pamphlet *Free Thoughts on Public Affairs; or, Advice to a Patriot, in a Letter Addressed to a Member of the Old Opposition.* Lamb, who had little interest in public affairs, was nonplussed. On June 26 he wrote to Wordsworth: "He is, rather imprudently, I think, printing a political pamphlet on his own account, and will have to pay for the paper, &c. The first duty of an author, I take it, is never to pay for anything. But non cuivis attigit adire Corinthum." [3] Hazlitt, however, took his civic responsibilities seriously: he believed that Charles James Fox, who had become foreign secretary after the death of the Younger Pitt earlier in the year, could and should end the war with France at once. As a friend of human liberty he felt that he must speak his mind—even though he had to draw on his own meager supply of cash to make himself heard.

What he had to say was in no way startling. The war was, he declared, a futile effort. It could no longer pass as a war of defense—or at best it was a war in defense of England's colonial possessions and, like all such wars, costly, indecisive, and debilitating. The most arresting passage in the essay was a withering "character" of William Pitt, whose ineptitude he blamed for the present state of affairs:

> With few talents, and fewer virtues, he acquired and preserved in one of the most trying situations, and in spite of all opposition, the highest reputation for the possession of every moral excellence, and as having carried the attainments of eloquence and wisdom as far as human abilities could go. This he did (strange as it appears) by a negation (together with the common virtues) of the common vices of human nature, and by the complete negation of every other talent that might interfere with the only one which he possessed in a supreme degree, and which indeed includes the appearance of all others—an artful use of words, and a certain dexterity of logical arrangement. (1:108)[4]

Free Thoughts was remarkable, though, not so much for what Hazlitt had to say as for the way in which he said it. The essay was no masterpiece of organization; it was, in fact, difficult to follow, often obscured by a welter of words and by interminable paragraphs. However, Hazlitt had been reading Burke closely (he quoted or alluded to him eight times in the forty-six pages of his essay) and had learned the value of parallel sentence structure.

3. Ibid., p. 15.
4. Hazlitt acknowledged his debt to Coleridge's conversation and to a series of articles by him in the *Morning Post* in February, 1800, for much of his analysis of Pitt's character (1:112 n.).

For example, the essay began:

> Sir, If the opposition of character between individuals of different nations is that which attaches every one the most strongly to his own country; if the love of liberty instilled from our very cradle is any security for the hatred of oppression; if a spirit of independence, and a constitutional stubbornness of temper are not forward to crouch under the yoke of unjust ambition; if to look up with heart-felt admiration to the great names, whether heroes or sages, which England has produced, and to be unwilling that the country which gave birth to Shakespear and Milton should ever be enslaved by a mean and servile foe; if to love its glory—that virtue, that integrity, that genius, which have distinguished it from all others, and in which its true greatness consists,—is to love one's country, there are few persons who have a better right than myself (on the score of sincerity) to offer that kind of advice which is the subject of the following letter, however weak or defective it may be found. (1:95)

He had learned, too, that a well-chosen quotation may enrich an author's prose, and he drew on Bacon, Milton, Shakespeare, the Bible, Gray, Pope, and Goldsmith as well as Burke to heighten his argument. And although he sometimes depended on obvious rhetorical devices, he managed to convey an impression of ease and sincerity. He who had stammered his way through *The Principles of Human Action* had suddenly found his voice. But it was scarcely heard: *Free Thoughts* seems never to have been reviewed and certainly sold few copies. Yet it was not all wasted effort, for Hazlitt managed to reprint his character of Pitt on three subsequent occasions.[5]

As time passed he and the Lambs saw more and more of each other, and his social life centered around their rooms at 16 Mitre Court Buildings. When they established their "Wednesdays," a "new institution" late in 1806, he attended faithfully, along with the musician William Ayrton, "Jem" White, Captain James Burney (brother of Fanny) and his son Martin, John Rickman, "Ned" Phillips, and Mrs. Reynolds. The conversation was spirited, and everyone took part. Twenty years later Hazlitt described the unforgettable evening when Lamb led off with the question: who are the persons in history whom you most wish you had seen? "I suppose," said A———,[6] "the two first persons you would choose to see would be the two greatest names in English literature, Sir Isaac Newton and Mr. Locke?" Lamb's face was a study. "Yes, the greatest names," he agreed,

---

5. It appears in the introduction to *The Eloquence of the British Senate (Four Generations,* 1:98), *The Round Table* (4:125–28), and *Political Essays* (7:322–26).

6. Probably Ayrton. This is one of the few initials not altered in the essay as it was published in the *New Monthly Magazine* for January, 1826, where the "L———" of the original manuscript appears as "B———," etc. In the essay as published in Howe's edition of the *Complete Works*, the original initials have been restored.

"but they were not persons—not persons. . . . That is . . . not characters, you know. By Mr. Locke and Sir Isaac Newton, you mean the Essay on Human Understanding, and the *Principia*, which we have to this day. Beyond their contents there is nothing personally interesting in the men. . . . I dare say Locke and Newton were very like Kneller's portraits of them. But who could paint Shakespear?" ". . . then I suppose," said A———, "you would prefer seeing him and Milton instead?" "No," said Lamb, "neither. I have seen so much of Shakespear on the stage and on book-stalls, in frontis-pieces and on mantle-pieces, that I am quite tired of the everlasting repeti-tion: and as to Milton's face, the impressions that have come down to us of it I do not like; it is too starched and puritanical." And at last he came out with it: the two persons whom he wished he might have seen were Sir Thomas Browne and Fulke Greville—because "their writings are riddles, and they themselves the most mysterious of personages."

Others then joined in with suggestions: Chaucer (whom Hazlitt wished he might have seen conversing with Boccaccio), Spenser (suggested by Lamb), John Donne and Dante (Hazlitt again), Pope with Patty Blount (chosen by Mary Lamb—who could not resist adding, "and I *have* seen Goldsmith").[7] The conversation then veered around to the literary merits of Pope and Dryden. And eventually it touched upon English history, the theater (Hazlitt regretted that he would never see Garrick), criminals, philosophers, painters, good women, Frenchmen, and "heroes"—until one of the company said, "There is only one other person I can ever think of after this. . . . If Shakespear was to come into the room, we should all rise up to meet him; but if that person was to come into it, we should all fall down and try to kiss the hem of his garment!" The guests then left as "the morning broke with that dim, dubious light by which Giotto, Cimabue, and Ghirlandaio must have seen to paint their earliest works"—and, Hazlitt added nostalgically, "we parted to meet again and renew similar topics at night, the next night, and the night after that" (17:122–34).[8]

For Lamb and his friends the gala night of the year 1806 was December 10, when his farce *Mr. H———* was to be presented at Drury Lane. Hazlitt sat with Lamb and Crabb Robinson in the first row of the pit. He was sure the play would succeed—and he suffered more than Lamb himself did when

7. For a discussion of the identity of the speakers in this essay, see *TLS*, 27 February, 1953, p. 137; 6 March, 1953, p. 153; 13 March, 1953, p. 169; 8 May, 1953, p. 301; 5 June, 1953, p. 365; and 12 June, 1953, p. 381.

8. Cf. Hazlitt's more generalized account of the kind of conversation which prevailed at the Lambs' "Thursdays" (as they later became) in his essay "On the Conversation of Authors" (12:35–38).

it was hissed. "Bright shone the morning on the play-bills that announced thy appearance," he wrote ten years later, "and the streets were filled with the buzz of persons asking one another if they would go to see Mr. H———, and answering that they would certainly: but before night the gaiety, not of the author, but of his friends and the town, was eclipsed, for thou wert damned!" (18:210–11).

Lamb himself took the disappointment philosophically. "I had many fears," he wrote to Wordsworth the following morning;

> the subject was not substantial enough. John Bull must have solider fare than a *Letter.* We are pretty stout about it, have had plenty of condoling friends, but after all, we had rather it should have succeeded. You will see the Prologue in most of the Morning Papers. It was received with such shouts as I never witness'd to a Prologue. It was attempted to be encored. How hard! a thing I did merely as a task, because it was wanted—and set no great store by; and Mr. H———!
>
> The quantity of friends we had in the house, my brother and I being in Public Offices, &c. was astonishing—but they yielded at length to a few hisses. A hundred hisses . . . outweigh a 1000 Claps. The former come more directly from the Heart— Well, 'tis withdrawn and there is an end.⁹

That same day he sent the bad news to Sarah Stoddart, since Mary was, as he said, "a little cut" at the failure. "We are determined not to be cast down," he assured her.¹⁰ Hazlitt, however, was disconsolate. "I remember when L———'s farce was damned (for damned it was, that's certain)," he wrote in 1822,

> I used to dream every night for a month after (and then I vowed I would plague myself no more about it) that it was revived at one of the Minor or provincial theatres with great success, that such and such retrenchments and alterations had been made in it, and that it was thought *it might do at the other House.* . . . How often did I conjure up in recollection the full diapason of applause at the end of the *Prologue,* and hear my ingenious friend in the first row of the pit roar with laughter at his own wit! Then I dwelt with forced complacency on some part in which it had been doing well: then we would consider (in concert) whether the long, tedious opera of the *Travellers,* which preceded it, had not tired people beforehand, so that they had no spirits left for the quaint and sparkling "wit skirmishes" of the dialogue, and we all agreed it might have gone down after a Tragedy, except L——— himself, who swore he had no hopes of it from the beginning, and that he knew the name of the hero when it came to be discovered could not be got over.—Mr. H———, thou wert damned. (8:232)¹¹

9. *Lamb Letters,* 2:31.
10. Ibid., p. 32.
11. The plot of the farce hinged on the revelation of the hero's surname: *Hogsflesh.*

Feeling so acutely a friend's misfortune was a new experience for Hazlitt. So was the feeling of being so completely accepted as a friend.

On the whole, though, the year 1806 had been good to Hazlitt, and soon after the first of January, 1807, he moved from his brother's house on Great Russell Street to rooms of his own at 34 Southampton Buildings. He was supporting himself at last—as a writer rather than a painter—and enjoying a new measure of self-respect. It was glowingly reflected in a letter which he wrote to his father at about this time reporting that his cousin Tom Loftus had just arrived in London after a visit at Wem and had delivered the Welsh mutton and other meat sent him by his parents. "I have just finished the cheeks which I had dressed last Friday for my dinner after I had taken a walk round Hampstead and Highgate," he wrote. "I never made a better dinner in my life. T. Loftus came to help me off with them on Saturday, and we attacked them again at night, after going to the Opera, where I went for the first time and probably for the last. The fowls I took to Lamb's the night I received them, and the pickled pork. They were very good."

He announced that the preface to his abridgment of *Light of Nature Pursued* was in print "to my great comfort" and that he was "going on with my criticisms"—that is, a series of introductory notes for an anthology of English oratory that he was preparing for the publisher Thomas Ostell. He had "very nearly done Burke," he continued, adding: "I do not think I have done it so well as Chatham's. I showed the one I did of him to Anth. Robinson [liberal author and philanthropist], who I understand since was quite delighted with it, and thinks it a very fine piece of composition. I have only Fox's to do of any consequence. Pitt's I shall take out of my pamphlet [*Free Thoughts on Public Affairs*], which will be no trouble." He even allowed himself a bit of brag: "These four viz. Burke, Chatham, Fox, Pitt, with Sir R. Walpole's, will be the chief articles of the work, and if I am not mistaken confounded good ones. I am only afraid they will be too good, that is, that they will contain more good things, than are exactly proper for the occasion."

He was spending a good deal of time in company. He "supped at Godwin's on New Year's day and at Holcroft's on Sunday." He was going to his new friend Joseph Hume's the following day, "where I also was on Christmas day. . . . It was much such a day as it was two years ago, when I was painting your picture. *Tempus preterlabitur*. I am afraid I shall never do such another." Yet he was not disheartened. "I have done what I wanted in writing," he told his father cheerfully, "and I hope I may in painting." [12]

12. *The Hazlitts*, pp. 421–23.

In March, Johnson published his abridgment of *The Light of Nature Pursued*, a job of work which had offered little challenge to Hazlitt's talents. Yet deciding what to select and what to reject of the original text was a good exercise for one who was inclined to be prolix, and he took advantage of it. "Edward Search" could prose along for pages; in fact he prosed along for seven substantial volumes. Hazlitt cut down his tiresome exposition and made it sharper and clearer. Take, for example, a passage from the introduction to the book. In the original it runs:

> Wherefore, the worst kind of disputing is that which proceeds solely in the spirit of opposition, tending to overthrow but not to establish: for there is scarce any system so bad as not to be better than none at all. He that pulls down his neighbour's house does him a diskindness, how inconvenient a building soever it were, unless he furnishes him with a plan and materials for building one more commodious. Let every man by my consent offer whatever he thinks beneficial to the public; we stand obliged to him for his good intentions, however ineffectual they may prove, or how much soever we may perceive him mistaken; provided he does not meddle with the opinions of others until he finds them standing directly athwart his way; then indeed disputation becomes necessary, but it is never desirable, nor perhaps ever excusable, unless when absolutely necessary.
>
> In order to avoid this disagreeable necessity as long as possible, it seems advisable to begin with building upon ground that nobody claims or that we all possess in common: I mean, by working upon principles universally agreed to, and gathering all the conclusions they will afford that may be serviceable to the world, and wherin every body may acquiesce without prejudice to his favourite tenets. For there are many inducements to prudence, to honesty, to benevolence, to industry, acknowledged by persons of all persuasions; and if these were improved to the utmost, much good might be done to mankind, both towards advancing their knowledge and regulating their behaviour, before we need touch upon any controversial matters.[13]

Two hundred sixty-two words! Hazlitt sliced away the surplus fat and reduced the passage to eighty-six:

> The worst kind of disputing is, that which tends merely to overturn, without establishing any thing. For I can have no right to pull down my neighbour's house till I have furnished him with materials for building a more convenient one. I shall therefore take the contrary method by beginning with principles, universally agreed to. There are many inducements to prudence, honesty, benevolence, &c. acknowledged by persons of all persuasions, and these should be improved to the utmost, before we need touch upon any doubtful points.[14]

13. Abraham Tucker, *The Light of Nature Pursued*, 2nd ed., revised and corrected, 7 vols. (London, 1805), 1:xxxvii–viii.

14. *An Abridgment of the Light of Nature Pursued by Abraham Tucker, Esq.* (London, 1807), p. xl.

This sample would seem almost to bear out Hazlitt's statement in the preface that Tucker's seven volumes could be reduced to one without harm to the content. He was working from the discursive, repetitious second edition of the book, published without revision after Tucker's death, and he could discard whole chapters—even series of chapters—without real harm to the thesis of the original. He was learning the values of subtraction and division, and his wholesale omissions won the approval of reviewers. The *Critical Review* for November, 1807, commented: "The plan which the author . . . has followed is we think judicious, and the manner in which he has executed it is entitled to considerable praise. . . . We have in several instances compared the abridgment with the original, and have found nothing omitted which we could wish to retain, or retained which we could wish to omit." The *British Critic* accorded the book a lengthy three-part review in its issues for March, May, and June, 1808. At first the reviewer was dubious: ". . . though, tedious as Tucker's style is," he wrote, "we hardly think it possible to condense *all* that is of importance in his seven volumes into one of equal size. The doubts excited in our minds by this circumstance were not, we confess, removed, when, on perusing the preface, we found that this Abridgment had been made by the author of *An Essay on the Principles of Human Action*." However, after a long summary of the abridgment he concluded that "on the whole he appears to have performed the task which he prescribed to himself with great fidelity." And he made it clear that he objected to an abridgment of *The Light of Nature Pursued* by the author of *Principles of Human Action* only because he feared the latter's views might prevent him from treating Tucker's book fairly.[15] A glance at Hazlitt's enthusiastic preface should have reassured him on that score, for Hazlitt had changed his mind as a result of reading Tucker. As Bullitt points out,[16] he had questioned, in his "Remarks on the System of Hartley and Helvétius," the theory of associationism; now he adopted, in its place, Tucker's theory of "coalescence" with its stress on instinctive rather than consecutive thinking. It made better sense to him because he was an impulsive man himself: as long ago as 1798, when he first met Coleridge, he had been struck by the poet's ability to leap to conclusions. In Tucker he found a

---

15. The *Monthly Review* postponed its notice of the *Abridgment* until November, 1810. The critic acknowledged that some of Tucker's charm might be lost, but that his "views . . . are fairly and fully given, his peculiarities are retained, and the spirit of the original is preserved" and hailed the volume as "a valuable present to the public" (63 [1810]: 326–28).

16. *PQ* 24 (1945): 351.

rationale for such leaps; in the future it was to influence his critical judgments and his literary style.

In July Hazlitt's other major project appeared as *The Eloquence of the British Senate; or, Select Specimens from the Speeches of the Most Distinguished Parliamentary Speakers, From the Beginning of the Reign of Charles I to the Present Time*, which Ostell published anonymously in two volumes. It was largely a piece of bookmaking: Hazlitt chose the excerpts and wrote critical or biographical notes (varying from a line or two to a dozen pages) for each speaker represented. Of these introductory notes, four stand out: the character of the Younger Pitt, which he reprinted from *Free Thoughts*, and similar sketches of Chatham, Burke, and Fox. In his advertisement he remarked that these four were "the most laboured" of the introductions, by which he meant only that he had taken most pains with them. He was, in fact, carried away, and when he later reprinted the characters of Burke and Fox, he added a note to each confessing that he no longer subscribed to them wholeheartedly. Yet superficial and prejudiced as his judgments might be, they were expressed with a new force and clarity. His comparisons were especially telling:

> Fox in his opinions was governed by facts—Chatham was more influenced by the feelings of others respecting those facts. Fox endeavoured to find out what the consequences of any measure would be; Chatham attended more to what people would think of it. Fox appealed to the practical reason of mankind; Chatham to popular prejudice. The one repelled the encroachments of power by supplying his hearers with arguments against it; the other by rousing their passions and arming their resentment against those who would rob them of their birthright. Their vehemence and impetuosity arose also from very different feelings. In Chatham it was pride, passion, self-will, impatience of control, a determination to have his own way, to carry every thing before him; in Fox it was pure good nature, a sincere love of truth, an ardent attachment to what he conceived to be right; an anxious concern for the welfare and liberties of mankind. (7:316)[17]

Some of his critical observations were suprisingly acute:

> the difference between poetry and eloquence I take to be this: that the object of the one is to delight the imagination, that of the other to impel the will. The one ought to enrich and feed the mind itself with tenderness and beauty, the other furnishes

17. In "A Hazlitt Borrowing from Godwin" (*MLN* 58 [1943]: 69–70), S. C. Wilcox points out that one passage in the character of Fox was taken from a similar character by Godwin in the *Morning Chronicle* for November 22, 1806. Although Hazlitt did not copy the passage verbatim, and he acknowledged that it was borrowed, he failed to list his source as he had done when borrowing from Coleridge in his character of Pitt in *Free Thoughts on Public Affairs*.

it with motives of action. The one seeks to give immediate pleasure, to make the mind dwell with rapture on its own workings—it is to itself "both end and use": the other endeavours to call up such images as will produce the strongest effect on the mind, and makes use of the passions only as instruments to attain a particular purpose. The poet lulls and soothes the mind into a forgetfulness of itself, and "laps it in Elysium": the orator strives to awaken it to a sense of its real interests, and to make it feel the necessity of taking the most effectual means for securing them. The one dwells in an ideal world; the other is only conversant about realities. Hence poetry must be more ornamented, must be richer and fuller and more delicate, because it is at liberty to select whatever images are naturally most beautiful, and likely to give most pleasure; whereas the orator is confined to particular facts, which he may adorn as well as he can, and make the most of, but which he cannot strain beyond a certain point without running into extravagance and affectation, and losing his end. (7:299–300)

The volumes attracted little attention—and apparently sold poorly. John Murray brought out a second edition in 1808 with Hazlitt's name on the title page, but it was made up from the original sheets.[18] Of it a critic in the *Monthly Review* for June, 1809, wrote:

The criticisms, indeed, are of the boldest kind; and it would seem that their author is more anxious that his observations should excite sensation, than that they should produce conviction. His daring has in some instances struck out felicities, but, as is usually the case, has more frequently induced extravagancies. The essential requisites of a critic are not wanting in this writer; and he appears to offend more from a want of temper and of a strong or a properly directed moral sense, than from a deficiency of ability or judgment...: but his feelings seem to have undergone no discipline; caution he appears to disdain; it costs him little to judge peremptorily; and he does not affect to deny that he has no very lively anxiety that his decisions should be clear of injustice.

Hazlitt had indeed done what he wanted to do in writing: even a disapproving critic had to admit that he had style. He was improving with each new publication—and he was learning, this time from his study of the British orators. Inevitably, too, though his name was still unknown to the reading public, he was attracting the attention of the London booksellers.

While he was working on *The Eloquence of the British Senate*, he wrote for William Cobbett's *Weekly Political Register* a series of three letters signed "AO," which appeared in the issues of March 14 and May 16 and 23, criticizing the Reverend Thomas Malthus's *Essay on the Principle of Population as it Affects the Future Improvement of Society*. By August he had written

18. Another "Second Edition, Corrected and Improved" was issued by Cradock and Joy in 1812. Acutally it was in no way changed.

two more letters on the subject and made selections from Malthus's essay with critical comments, all of which he collected in a single volume brought out by Longman, Hurst, Rees, and Orme as *A Reply to the Essay on Population.*

Such piecemeal procedure did not make for unity of structure or tone, and the *Reply* is often diffuse, repetitious, and lacking in consistent method, as he himself admitted in his prefatory advertisement. Although he tried in his separate letters to attack specific aspects of Malthus's theory—his debt to Robert Wallace's *Various Prospects of Mankind, Nature, and Providence,* his assumption that population increases in a geometrical progression while the food supply increases arithmetically, his belief that an egalitarian society would result in scarcity for all—Hazlitt leapt ahead or doubled back on himself often, and he made use of whatever stylistic tool seemed feasible at the moment.

To those who complained that his style was "too flowery, and full of attempts at description," he replied in his advertisement: "If I have erred in this respect, it has been from design. I have indeed endeavoured to make my book as amusing as the costiveness of my genius would permit. If however these critics persist in their objection, I will undertake to produce a work as dry and formal as they please, if they will undertake to find readers" (1:179). Of course he did not mean to imply that he had decided to set up as a popular writer—only that he was, for the moment, trying to reach the common reader, those who might be expected to subscribe to Cobbett's *Register.* For once again he was alarmed at political events in England, and he wanted to awaken his countrymen to an imminent crisis and to a growing attitude which threatened to usurp their freedom.

The immediate crisis was Samuel Whitbread's bill to withdraw the dole from the poor and substitute education. Hazlitt did not approve of the poor laws as they stood, but he believed they provided the only possible protection for paupers until a better system could be developed. The attitude which he attacked was the reactionary belief that any attempt to better the state of the poor ran counter to the laws of nature. He traced that belief directly to Malthus's *Essay.*

Malthus had written the *Essay* originally in 1798 to combat Godwin's claim in *Enquiry Concerning Political Justice* that man could achieve utopia if left free to exercise his reason and his natural benevolence. Malthus had replied that such a thesis ignored the realities of nature: that a utopian society would quickly end in disaster, that apparent evils like war and disease and famine were nature's means of maintaining the population at a level that could be adequately served by the food supply, and that society must find ways of limiting population for the general welfare. He believed that men were motivated by self-love rather than benevolence, and he hoped to direct that self-love to the good of society by means of "prudential checks"—calling on men to delay marriage and limit their families to a number that they could support properly. But by the time the *Essay* reached its second edition in 1803 he had developed doubts about the efficacy of that scheme, and he urged abolition of the poor laws, which he thought were encouraging procreation among those least able to provide for themselves. Naturally rich men of both Tory and Whig parties, reacting to the excesses of the French Revolution and always eager to lower taxes, seized upon the *Essay* as justification for their selfish interests.

Hazlitt instinctively recoiled at such thinking, and he struck out at the book which he considered to be the root of it. In his advertisement he apologized for his personal attack on Malthus, but declared it unavoidable. As a believer in disinterestedness he had no patience with one who traced men's actions to self-love, and his treatment ranged from exasperation with this "conscience-keeper to the rich and great" (1:206) to irony at his "amorous complexion" (because he argued that men's sexual passions could not be controlled) (1:242). Meanwhile Hazlitt himself was blinded by his own intense emotions: he saw himself as the white knight of freedom assaulting the oppressor of men in thralldom. He accused Malthus of plagiarism, inaccuracy, inconsistency, and contradictions; he misinterpreted and misconstrued his words, often failing to distinguish between what Malthus had written and what his reactionary supporters inferred. And he fought back with theories quite as incapable of proof as Malthus's own, for neither attempted to document with hard facts his claims about how effectively men might exert "moral restraints" or whether vice and misery could be checked in an egalitarian society. The two were working from conflicting assumptions, and inevitably they arrived at conflicting conclusions. Like Burke's *Reflections* and Tom Paine's *Rights of Man*, the *Essay* and the *Reply* would, if bound up together, make one good book.[19]

However, Hazlitt's outcry was scarcely heard. Malthus, not he, had caught the temper of the times. Most of the critical journals ignored the *Reply*. And the *Monthly Review*, which noticed it in May, 1808, was scornful:

19. For a thorough analysis of the *Reply* in its historical context, see William P. Albrecht, *William Hazlitt and the Malthusian Controversy*, University of New Mexico Publications in Language and Literature, no. 4 (Albuquerque: University of New Mexico Press, 1950).

If an author will set modesty, breeding, and a sense of decency at defiance, be his talents and acquirements what they may, he is an objectionable public instructor: but if he be also found, as in the present instance, to possess qualifications as slender as his manner is disgusting and preposterous, we trust that we shall not be blamed if we dismiss him from our tribunal with slight notice: indeed, the share of it which he engages, he owes to our desire to exhibit his conduct as a warning to all others.

All in all, the *Reply* must have seemed to Hazlitt like one more failure to add to his list. Even his friend Godwin, the man whose theories he had been defending, took offense at a passing allusion—which Hazlitt had meant to be playful. He apologized promptly on August 6, but with more than a hint of annoyance. And he added a postscript which showed that his annoyance was not confined to Godwin: "No one has ever been more ready than I have to take part with my friends on all occasions. I have committed four or five riots in my zeal for the reputation of Coleridge & Wordsworth: & all the thanks I ever got for this my zeal in their favour was some of the last indignities that can be put upon any person. In my list of friends it has always been my good luck to come in like the tail of an etc. & to subsist only upon sufferance." [20]

Hazlitt had kept busy through most of the year 1807. He had finished two books and seen a volume of his father's sermons through the press. He had continued to paint and had at least started to work on a portrait of the publisher Joseph Johnson. [21] But he had gained little of the recognition which he craved, and he was resorting to the easy dodge that somehow his old friends had failed him—a dodge which his father had used in his time. Fortunately, however, he was presently engaged in a pursuit which promised to be more rewarding: he was paying court to Sarah Stoddart.

How or where they met is unknown. It might have been at any one of several houses, notably the Lambs'. However, Mary Lamb suffered an attack of madness in the summer of 1807 and was confined to an asylum in Hoxton. And her first surviving letter to Sarah after her release implied that the courtship was already well launched. She had been eagerly waiting, she declared, "to see how your comical love affair would turn out." Sarah had complained that Hazlitt had not written to her, and Mary replied:

You know, I make a pretence not to interfere; but like all old maids I feel a mighty solicitude about the event of love stories. I learn from the Lover that he has not been so remiss in his duty as you supposed. His Effusion, and your complaints of his inconstancy, crossed each other on the road. He tells me his was a very strange letter, and that probably it has affronted you. That it was a strange letter I can readily

20. Baker, p. 166.   21. See *The Hazlitts*, p. 423.

believe; but that you were affronted by a strange letter is not so easy for me to conceive, that not being your way of taking things. But however it be, let some answer come, either to him, or else to me, showing cause why you do not answer him. And pray, by all means, preserve the said letter, that I may one day have the pleasure of seeing how Mr. Hazlitt treats of love.

She concluded: "Farewell—Determine as wisely as you can in regard to Hazlitt; and, if your determination is to have him, Heaven send you many happy years together. If I am not mistaken, I have concluded letters on the Corydon Courtship [i.e., that of the young farmer Dowling] with this same wish. I hope it is not ominous of change; for if I were sure you would not be quite starved to death, nor beaten to a mummy, I should like to see Hazlitt and you come together, if (as Charles observes) it were only for the joke sake."[22]

By the time Mary wrote next, on December 21, Hazlitt and Sarah had come to an agreement. Members of their family said later that he proposed to her while she was putting on the teakettle—and it could well be, for Hazlitt was inordinately fond of tea. But though he may have acted on impulse, he was not blinded by passion. Sarah owned two houses, a malthouse, and a garden at Salisbury, not to mention some property in 5 percent annuities—and had prospects of more after her mother's death. Moreover, she was a sensible, intelligent woman who was likely to prove loyal to her husband. Earlier in the year he had remarked in his reply to Malthus: ". . . there are very few husbands who are not tolerably certain of being cuckolded by the first lord, or duke, who thinks it worth his while to attempt it. It is some consolation to us poor devils of authors, that we have no chance of getting a wife who is at all likely to meet with any such distinction" (1:276 n.). Like Goldsmith's Dr. Primrose, Hazlitt chose his wife for such qualities as would wear well. But having made the decision, he had no immediate cause for regret. For once, his efforts had been recognized—accepted.

All that was wanting now was the approval of Sarah's brother. Hazlitt had been cultivating his acquaintance—had even entertained him on December 8 at an unaccustomed dinner in his rooms with the Lambs, Godwin, and Joseph Hume.[23] Mary Lamb was concerned lest they withhold the news from him too long. "I think," she wrote to Sarah in her letter of the twenty-first,

you ought to tell your brother as soon as possible; for, at present, he is on very friendly visiting terms with Hazlitt, and, if he is not offended by a too long conceal-

22. *Lamb Letters*, 2:37–39. Hazlitt's "very strange letter" seems not to have survived.
23. Baker, p. 168 n.

ment, will do every thing in his power to serve you. If you chuse that I should tell him, I will; but I think it would come better from you. If you can persuade Hazlitt to mention it, that would be still better; for I know your brother would be unwilling to give credit to you, because you deceived yourself in regard to Corydon. Hazlitt, I know, is shy of speaking first; but I think it of such great importance to you to have your brother friendly in the business, that, if you can overcome his reluctance, it would be a great point gained. For you must begin the world with ready money— at least an hundred pound; for, if you once go into furnished lodgings, you will never be able to lay by money to buy furniture.

She reported that Hazlitt's brother John was "mightily pleased with the match; but he says you must have furniture, and be clear in the world at first setting out, or you will be always behindhand. He also said he would give you what furniture he could spare." She herself was determined to be optimistic: "I most heartily congratulate you on having so well got over your first difficulties," she told Sarah; "and now that it is quite settled, let us have no more fears. I now mean not only to hope and wish, but to persuade myself, that you will be very happy together."[24]

Mary's brother Charles was less sanguine; Hazlitt's decision to marry seemed to him virtually suicidal, and he toyed with that notion in a letter to Joseph Hume on December 29:

> I suppose you know what has happen'd to our poor friend Hazlitt. If not, take it as I read it in the Morning Post or Fashionable World of this morning:—
>
> "Last night Mr. H., a portrait painter in Southampton Buildings, Holborn, put an end to his existence by cutting his throat in a shocking manner. It is supposed that he must have committed his purpose with a pallet knife, as the edges of the cicatrice or wound were found besmeared with a yellow consistence, but the knife could not be found. The reasons of this rash act are not assigned; an unfortunate passion has been mentioned; but nothing certain is known. The deceased was subject to hypochondria, low spirits, but he had lately seemed better, having paid more than usual attention to his dress and person. Besides being a painter, he had written some pretty things in prose and verse."[25]

Hume showed the letter to Hazlitt, who, although he was ill and detested letter-writing, carried the joke along in a lengthy "humble petition and remonstrance" on January 10. He offered, first, a series of eight "proofs" that he was still alive, several of which offer glimpses of the indolent bachelor existence that he had been leading:

24. *Lamb Letters*, 2:39–40.
25. The exchange of letters of Lamb, Hazlitt, and Joseph Hume on this occasion can be found most easily in W. C. Hazlitt's *Lamb and Hazlitt* (New York, 1899), 64–102. Lamb's two letters are reprinted in *Lamb Letters*, 2:41–44.

And first, that he, the said W. Hazlitt, has regularly for the last month rang the bell at eleven at night, which was considered as a sign for the girl to warm his bed, & this being done, he has gone to bed, & slept soundly for the next twelve or fourteen hours.

Secondly, that every day about twelve or 1 o'clock he has got up, put on his clothes, drank his tea, & eat two plate-fulls of buttered toast, of which he had taken care to have the hard edges pared off as hurtful to the mouth & gums, & that he has then sat for some hours with his eyes stedfastly fixed upon the fire, like a person in a state of deep thought, but doing nothing.

Thirdly, that not a day has passed in which he has not eat & drank like other people. For instance, he has swallowed eight dozen of pills, nine boluses, & as many purgative draughts of a most unsavoury quality. What he has fed on with the most relish has been a mess of chicken-broth, & he has sent out once or twice for a paper of almonds & raisins. His general diet is soup-meagre with bread & milk for supper. That it is true that the petitioner has abstained both from gross feeding & from all kinds of intoxicating liquors; a circumstance, he conceives, so far from denoting a natural decay & loss of his faculties, that on the contrary it shews more wisdom than he was always possessed of.

Fourthly, that in regard to decency he has been known to walk out at least once a week to get himself shaved.

When he reached "Eighthly" he grew flippant:

be it known that the person, concerning whom such idle reports are prevalent, has actually within the given time written a number of love-letters, & that a man must be dead indeed, if he is not alive when engaged in that agreeable employment. And lest it should be suggested that these epistles resemble Mrs. Rowe's *Letters from the Dead to the Living*, being just such vapid, lifeless compositions, it may be proper to state, by way of counteracting any such calumny, that on the contrary they are full of nothing but ingenious conceits & *double entendres*, without a single *grave* remark or sickly sentiment from beginning to end. Farther that they had some life in them, he is assured by the quickness of the answers, which he received with that sort of pleasing titillation & gentle palpitation common to flesh and blood, reading them with alternate smiles & sighs, & once letting fall a tear at a description given by the lady of the ruinous state of a cottage or tenement which he hopes one day to call his own. . . .

That he has made several good resolutions to be put in practice as soon as he recovers, which he hopes shortly to do without undergoing the ancient ceremony of sacrificing a Cock to Aesculapius: as namely to live better than he has lately done, not to refuse an invitation to a haunch of venison, nor to decline drinking to a lady's health, to pay a greater attention to cleanliness, and to leave off wenching as injurious both to the health & morals.

He concluded by appointing Hume executor of his estate, which consists of several paintings and manuscripts of his own creation and "a small Claude

Lorraine mirror, which Mr. Lamb the other evening secretly purloined
after a pretended visit of condolence to his sick friend."

Hume promptly forwarded the letter to Lamb, who replied on January
12:

> The strange rumours which have been spread about since the death of our respected
> friend, as well as some things which have come under my observation, which I do
> not care to trust to the ordinary communication of a Post, but reserve them for the
> especial confidence of your most valued ear in private,—these things, without much
> help from a rainy day or time of the year which usually disposes men to sadness, have
> contributed to make me not a little serious and thoughtful of late. I have run over
> in my mind the various treatises which I have perused in the course of a studious,
> and, I hope, innocently employed life, on the nature of disembodied Spirits and the
> causes of their revisiting the earth. The fact I will take for granted; presuming that
> I am not addressing an Atheist. I find the most commonly assigned reason to be,
> *for the revealing of hidden Treasures which the Deceased had hoarded up in his or
> her Lifetime.* Now though I cannot sufficiently admire the providence of God who
> by this means has ofttimes restored great heaps of Gold and Silver to the circulation
> of the Living, thereby sparing the iterately plowed and now almost effete wombs of
> Peru & Mexico, which would need another Sarah's miracle to replenish, yet in the
> particular case of the Defunct I cannot but suspect some other cause, and not this,
> to have called him from his six foot bed of earth. For it is highly improbable that he
> should have accumulated any such vast treasures, for the revealing of which a miracle
> was needed, without some suspicion of the fact among his friends during his Life-
> time. I for my part alway looked upon our dear friend as a man rich rather in the
> gifts of his mind than in earthly treasures. He had few rents or comings in, that I was
> ever aware of, small (if any) landed property, and by all that I could witness he
> subsisted more upon the well-timed contributions of a few chosen friends who knew
> his worth, than upon any Estate which could properly be called his own. I myself
> have contributed my part. God knows, I speak not this in reproach. I have never
> taken, nor indeed did the deceased offer, any *written acknowledgments* of the various
> sums which he has had of me, by which I could make the fact manifest to the legal
> eye of an Executor or Administrator. He was not a Man to affect these niceties in his
> transactions with friends. He would often say, money was nothing between intimate
> acquaintances, that Golden Streams had no Ebb, that a Purse mouth never regorged,
> that God loved a chearful giver but the Devil hated a free taker, that a paid Loan
> makes angels groan, with many such like sayings: he had always free and generous
> notions about money. His nearest friends know this best.

Hume then rounded out the exchange with a short note to Hazlitt, enclosing
Lamb's letter, and a long letter to Lamb in reply to Hazlitt's "humble
petition." It was not up to the level of foolery maintained by the other two,
but a couple of his points are noteworthy:

3^{rdly} He talks of getting himself shaved. Now the ladies who were the most immediately acquainted with him, much to their uneasiness and probably (between you and I) at the expence of *their chins*, declare he never shaved at all. . . .

10^{thly} He was a man of spirit in his better days. He therefore would have been ashamed on his own account and much more so as an example for the well being of society, to cast out of human conduct the habit of wenching. Whereas our poor sneaking moralist (A Quaker, by G——d!) would debauch the lips of our friend by presuming he uttered his worse than sneer on the noble habit, by pretending that it was a deviation of moral rectitude.

Hume seems to have agreed with Lamb that Hazlitt's conduct and reputation hardly qualified him for a settled married life. Even Hazlitt himself had some doubts.

Yet at the same time he was proving that, though ailing, he could play the part of suitor very acceptably. He was self-conscious, obviously, when he sat down one Tuesday evening to write to Sarah, yet he managed to sound playfully affectionate. "My dear Love," he began,

Above a week has passed, and I have received no letter—not one of those letters "in which I live, or have no life at all." What is become of you? Are you married, hearing that I was dead (for so it has been reported)? Or are you gone into a nunnery? Or are you fallen in love with some of the amorous heroes of Boccaccio? Which of them is it? Is it with Chynon, who was transformed from a clown into a lover, and learned to spell by the force of beauty? Or with Lorenzo, the lover of Isabella, whom her three brethren hated (as your brother does me), who was a merchant's clerk? Or with Federigo Alberigi, an honest gentleman, who ran through his fortune, and won his mistress by cooking a fair falcon for her dinner, though it was the only means he had left of getting a dinner for himself? This last is the man; and I am the more persuaded of it, because I think I won your good liking myself by giving you an entertainment—of sausages, when I had no money to buy them with. Nay now, never deny it! Did not I ask your consent that very night after, and did you not give it? Well, I should be confoundedly jealous of those fine gallants, if I did not know that a living dog is better than a dead lion: though, now I think of it, Boccaccio does not in general make much of his lovers: it is his women who are so delicious. I almost wish I had lived in those times, and had been a little *more amiable*. Now if a woman had written the book, it would not have had this effect upon me: the men would have been heroes and angels, and the women nothing at all. Isn't there some truth in that? Talking of departed loves, I met my old flame [Sally Shepherd?] the other day in the street. I did dream of her *one* night since, and only one: every other night I have had the same dream I have had for these two months past. Now, if you are at all reasonable, this will satisfy you.

On the following Thursday morning, after receiving a book and a note from Sarah, he continued:

I liked your note as well or better than the extracts; it is just such a note as such a nice rogue as you ought to write after the *provocation* you had received. I would not give a pin for a girl "whose cheeks never tingle," nor for myself if I could not make them tingle sometimes. Now, though I am always writing to you about "lips and noses," and such sort of stuff, yet as I sit by my fireside (which I do generally eight or ten hours a day), I oftener think of you in a serious, sober light. For, indeed, I never love you so well as when I think of sitting down with you to dinner on a boiled scrag-end of mutton, and hot potatoes. You please my fancy more then than when I think of you in—no, you would never forgive me if I were to finish the sentence. Now I think of it, what do you mean to be dressed in when we are married? But it does not much matter! I wish you would let your hair grow; though perhaps nothing will be better than "the same air and look with which at first my heart was took."

And he concluded:

But now to business. I mean soon to call upon your brother *in form*, namely, as soon as I get quite well, which I hope to do in about another *fortnight;* and then I hope you will come up by the coach as fast as the horses can carry you, for I long mightily to be in your ladyship's presence—to vindicate my character. I think you had better sell the small house, I mean that at 4.10, and I will borrow 100 l. So that we shall set off merrily in spite of all the prudence of Edinburgh.

Good-bye, little dear![26]

Suddenly Hazlitt decided that he could not wait for Sarah to come up to town. On or about February 12 Mary Lamb wrote to Sarah that she had received from her a letter and drawing intended for Hazlitt and, since he was out of town, had forwarded them to Wem, where she supposed he had gone. "He left town on Saturday afternoon," she stated, "without telling us where he was going. He seemed very impatient at not hearing from you. He was very ill and I suppose is gone home to his father's to be nursed." She went on, then, to say that Dr. Stoddart strongly objected to their plan of having Sarah married from the Lambs' house. "His wife's father is coming to be with them till near the end of April," Mary reported, "after which time he shall have full room for you. And if you are to be married, he wishes that you should be married with all the proper decorums, *from his house*."[27]

26. *Memoirs*, 1:153–55. Howe (pp. 396–97) suggests that Hazlitt may have borrowed £100 from Richard ("Conversation") Sharpe, whom he met in the Lake District and whom he supposedly eulogized in "On the Want of Money" as one "who would lend his money freely and fearlessly in spite of circumstances (if you were likely to pay him, he grew peevish, and would pick a quarrel with you)" (17:185).

27. *Lamb Letters*, 2:44–45.

A few days later Lamb received a letter from Hazlitt's father. The letter and drawing addressed to William had arrived at Wem, William was not there, and his parents were worried. Where could he be? But by this time Lamb had learned his whereabouts: Hazlitt had written to his landlord asking him to send some shirts to him at Winterslow, "where the lady lives," as Lamb wrote to the Reverend Mr. Hazlitt, "whose Cottage, pictured upon a card, if you opened my letter you have doubtless seen, and though we have had no explanation of the mystery since, we shrewdly suspect that at the time of writing that Letter which has given you all this trouble, a certain son of yours (who is both Painter and Author) was at her elbow, and did assist in framing that very Cartoon which was sent to amuse and mislead us in town, as to the real place of destination."[28]

In due time Hazlitt returned from his clandestine trip, but plans for the marriage were still delayed. On February 26 Lamb wrote to his friend Thomas Manning: "A treaty of marriage is on foot between William Hazlitt and Miss Stoddart. Something about settlements only retards it. She has somewhere about £80 a year, to be £120 when her mother dies. He has no settlement except what he can claim from the Parish. *Pauper est Cinna, sed tamen amat.* The thing is therefore in abeyance."[29] Gradually, however, negotiations advanced. On March 18 Hazlitt entertained Dr. Stoddart at tea in his rooms with Godwin, the Holcrofts, Northcote, Lamb, Hume, George Dyer, and Crabb Robinson.[30] And at about the same time Mary Lamb wrote to Sarah asking what she, as bridesmaid, should wear at the wedding—"the gown you sprigged for me" or one made up from some silk of "a sort of dead-whiteish-bloom colour" which Manning had sent out from China. She regretted that she could not afford to give Sarah a wedding present, but she promised to "come with a willing mind, bringing nothing with me but many wishes, and not a few hopes, and a very little of fears of happy years to come."[31]

By mid-April Sarah was in London. So too was Wordsworth, who on April 19 wrote to Coleridge:

> I took the MSS [of " The White Doe of Rylstone"] to Lamb's to read it, or part of it, one evening. There unluckily I found Hazlitt and his Beloved; of course, though I had the Poem in my hand I declined, nay absolutely refused, to read it. But as they were very earnest in entreating me, I at last consented to read one Book, and when it was done I simply said that there was a passage which probably must have struck

28. Ibid., p. 46.   29. Ibid., p. 48.   30. Baker, p. 168 n.
31. *Lamb Letters*, 2:55-57.

Hazlitt as a *Painter* "Now doth a delicate shadow fall" etc. . . . We then had a short talk about that part and nothing more took place.[32]

Wordsworth had last seen Hazlitt at Grasmere the night when he had been fleeing from his humiliating escapade at Keswick. The two had never cared for each other; now Wordsworth felt uncomfortable in Hazlitt's presence. He later told Crabb Robinson that, "though he never refused to meet Hazlitt when by accident they came together, [he] did not choose that with his knowledge he should be invited." [33]

At last on Sunday, May 1, 1808, "William Hazlitt of the Parish of St. Andrews, Holborn, in the County of Middlesex, a Bachelor, and Sarah Stoddart of the Parish of Winterslow, in the County of Wilts, a Spinster," were married, under a special license dispensing with banns, at St. Andrews Church.[34] Charles Lamb remained skeptical about the match to the very last. "I was at Hazlitt's marriage," he wrote to Southey in 1815, "and had like to have been turned out several times during the ceremony. Any thing awful makes me laugh." [35]

After a breakfast at Dr. Stoddart's house the couple set off for Winterslow, where they had decided to settle. It was an ideal retreat for a man of Hazlitt's tastes and interests. The village lay on a wooded ridge a mile or two from the highway; below it stretched Salisbury Plain, where an enthusiastic walker could explore by the hour. Or he could visit Stonehenge, Wilton, Old Sarum, or Salisbury itself—all of them rich in historical associations. Living was cheap, and Sarah's cottage was comfortable, especially the little room hung with Claude Lorraine prints, on which he could "dwell forever" (10:315). "Here I came fifteen years ago, a willing exile," he wrote in "Is Genius Conscious of Its Powers"; "and as I trod the lengthened greensward by the low wood-side, repeated the old line, 'My mind to me a kingdom is!'" (12:121).

He was in and out of London frequently in the course of the next few months.[36] He had a couple of new literary projects in mind to keep the pot boiling: an English grammar for "Edwin Baldwin," as Godwin called himself in his new venture as publisher of children's books, and an abridged

32. *Letters of William and Dorothy Wordsworth: The Middle Years*, ed. E. de Selincourt, 2 vols. (Oxford: Clarendon Press, 1937), 1:196–97.

33. Robinson, 1:169–70.

34. *The Hazlitts*, p. 344.

35. *Lamb Letters*, 2:167.

36. Baker (p. 169) reports that Godwin's diary lists at least one meeting per month with him between May and November.

translation of Baron de Bourgoing's *Tableau de l'Espagne Moderne*.[37] But he was primarily interested now in proving himself as a painter, and at Winterslow he might have access not only to picturesque scenes but to several fine private collections of paintings. His sister Peggy, who visited him there, wrote later that

> painting was his great delight, and . . . it was his custom to go forth into the woods to sketch views from nature, taking with him his canvas, paints, etc., an hammer, and a nail, which he used to drive into a tree which served him as an easel to hang his picture on. A couple of eggs, boiled hard, and some bread and cheese for his dinner, but never any liquor of any kind. Usually coming home at four (except when we went to meet him in that beautiful wood), bringing with him some promising beginning of the beautiful views around, but fated, alas, never to be finished. Several of these I remember, one in particular, the view of Norman Court, the seat of [Charles Baring] Wall Esqr.[38]

It was an idyllic existence. And to add to his serenity, he learned, soon after his arrival at Winterslow, that Sarah was expecting a baby.

In October Hazlitt was back in London. On the twenty-ninth he called on Godwin,[39] probably to discuss his English grammar. But his stay in town was brief, and six weeks later, on December 10, Mary Lamb was writing to Sarah to complain that she had heard from the Hazlitts only through Dr. Stoddart. She urged that one of the two write back soon, since she and Charles were concerned about Sarah's health. "You cannot think how very much we miss you and H. of a Wednesday evening," she went on. "All the glory of the night, I may say, is at an end." But "the worst miss of all to me is, that, when we are in the dismals, there is now no hope of relief from any quarter whatsoever. Hazlitt was most brilliant, most ornamental, as a Wednesday-man; but he was a more useful one on common days, when he dropt in after a quarrel or a fit of the glooms."[40]

On January 15, 1809, at 4:15 P.M., Sarah bore a son, who was named William.[41] For Hazlitt, who had always been fond of children, having a son

37. Early in July Lamb wrote to George Dyer: "William Hazlitt, your friend and mine, is putting to press a collection of verses, chiefly amatory, some of them pretty enough. How these painters encroach on our province!" (*Lamb Letters*, 2:58). Cf. Lamb's reference to Hazlitt's "pretty things in prose and verse" in his letter of December 29, 1807, to Joseph Hume quoted above, p. 105. Like the Bourgoing translation, the volume of verse never appeared, and it may well have existed only in Lamb's imagination. He often enlivened his letters with spurious—and absurd—bits of news.

38. Moyne, pp. 109–10.   39. *Shelley and His Circle*, 1:442.

40. *Lamb Letters*, 2:59.

41. Sarah's own record of the births and deaths of her children and of her miscarriages is preserved in the British Museum (Add. MS 38898, fols. 3–4).

of his own must have capped the joy he had found at Winterslow. Yet it involved new responsibilities too, and he went to work promptly to meet them. He first thought of a series of articles on English philosophy, and he wrote a letter on the subject, signed "WH," which appeared in the February issue of the *Monthly Magazine*. It began with an attack on "the material or modern philosophy," deploring it as a "false system" which "has been gradually growing to its present height ever since the time of Lord Bacon, from a wrong interpretation of the word *experience*, confining it to a knowledge of things without us, whereas it in fact includes all knowledge, relating to objects either within or out of the mind, of which we have any direct and positive evidence." Bacon was justified in drawing men's attention to the importance of experience, long ignored by the schoolmen, but Hobbes, the "father of the modern philosophy," Locke, and French philosophers have erred in ignoring all but experience. He then launched into an argument to prove "that mind is something distinct from matter," but broke off suddenly, apologizing for the length of his letter and promising to continue it in a later issue of the magazine if readers seemed interested.[42]

He did not follow up on his promise; however, when another correspondent to the *Monthly Magazine* inquired, in the March issue, about the relative merits of Malthus's theories of population and those advanced in Thomas Jarrold's *Dissertations on Man*, Hazlitt replied, in the April issue, with a letter signed "Philo." In it he restated in a series of terse "queries" the main points of his *Reply* to Malthus, managing to express clearly and concisely the arguments which his "costive genius" had floundered over in the earlier work.[43] He had learned a good deal about the art of writing in the intervening two years.

Meanwhile he had decided that his proposed philosophical study warranted a book rather than a series of articles, and he arranged with R. Taylor and Company to print up a prospectus for a history of English philosophy to be published by subscription. He sent copies of the prospectus to several people of importance, among them (surprisingly enough) the Right Honourable William Windham, M.P., former secretary of war under Pitt, whom he

---

42. *Monthly Magazine* 27 (1809): 15–19. Hazlitt's authorship of the article was discovered by Geoffrey Carnall ("A Hazlitt Contribution," *TLS*, 19 June, 1953, p. 397), who points out that it contains passages which Hazlitt used later in his *Prospectus of a History of English Philosophy* and in his lecture on Hobbes in his *Lectures on English Philosophy*.

43. John Kinnaird, who first drew attention to the *Monthly Magazine* letter, discusses its significance in the development of Hazlitt's thinking in his article, "'Philo' and Prudence: A New Hazlitt Criticism of Malthus," *BNYPL* 69 (1965): 153–63.

addressed with a studied formality:

> Sir,—I take the liberty to offer to your notice the enclosed Prospectus. I have no
> other excuse to make for this intrusion than that I believe the design of the work is
> such as may meet with your approbation—& the natural wish of every one that
> what has employed many years of his life & many anxious thoughts may not be
> entirely lost. My principal view in it would be to chastise the presumption of modern
> philosophy. The advocates of this system, however, by an exclusive & constant claim
> to the privilege of reason, have so completely satisfied themselves, & so very nearly
> persuaded others to believe that they are the only rational persons in the world, that
> any attempt to disprove their doctrines is looked upon as flying in the face of reason
> itself & an attack upon first principles. An attempt like the present must therefore
> I believe fail of success, without some particular support; and my object in soliciting
> the names of a few persons distinguished for liberal knowledge, & elevated powers
> of mind as subscribers to the work, was to shew that an opposition to the fashionable
> paradoxes was not the same thing as formally declaring one's-self on the side of
> ignorance & error. I know no name, Sir, that would contribute to this end more
> than your own; the permission to make use of which would be thankfully & proudly
> acknowledged by, Sir, your obedient, very humble servant.[44]

But the prospectus attracted little interest—perhaps because Hazlitt had
made it clear that his history was to be more critical than factual—and the
volume was never published.

He was in London again for a while during the spring of 1809, seeing the
Lambs, who were staying temporarily in his old rooms in Southampton
Buildings. But his stay ended abruptly—and for a painful reason: as Mary
Lamb explained in a letter to Louisa Martin on March 28, "his child is
expected to die." Even in this extremity Charles could not take the Hazlitts
seriously, and in the nonsensical letter which he appended to Mary's he added:
"Hazlitt's child died of swallowing a bag of white paint, which the poor
little innocent thing mistook for sugar candy. It told its Mother just two
hours before it died, that it did not like soft sugar candy, and so it came out,
which was not before suspected. When it was opened several other things
were found in it, particularly a small hearth brush, two golden pippins and a
letter which I had written to Hazlitt from Bath." [45] For once Lamb's wit
is hard to share. Anything awful did indeed make him laugh.

Hazlitt was back in London in May and June, seeing Godwin frequently,
doubtless about his grammar.[46] The Lambs were planning to go down to
Winterslow in mid-July with Ned Phillips and Martin Burney. But Mary
was worried about the number of guests that Sarah would have, the length
of their visit ("they . . . talk of staying a whole month"), and the expense to

44. Howe, p. 107.   45. *Lamb Letters*, 2:66–67.   46. Baker, p. 169 n.

the Hazlitts. Young Burney was willing to give them five pounds, provided they could borrow blankets for him and thus save him the expense of putting up at an inn. They could count on another five from the Lambs, Mary wrote in a letter early in June, warning Sarah: "You are not to say this to Hazlitt, lest his delicacy should be alarmed; but I tell you what Martin and I have planned, that, if you happen to be empty pursed at this time, you may think it as well to make him up a bed in the best kitchen." [47]

The trip, however, was postponed because Mary suffered one of her attacks late in June. And it was as well that the Lambs did not carry out their plans because on July 5, after only six months of life, the Hazlitts' baby died.

Hazlitt was inconsolable. His sister, who reached Winterslow a day or two later, never forgot "the look of anguish . . . which at the first moment passed over his countenance." [48] And he himself wrote several years later:

> I have never seen death but once, and that was in an infant. It is years ago. The look was calm and placid, and the face was fair and firm. It was as if a waxen image had been laid out in the coffin, and strewed with innocent flowers. It was not like death, but more like an image of life! No breath moved the lips, no pulse stirred, no sight or sound would enter those eyes or ears more. While I looked at it, I saw no pain was there; it seemed to smile at the short pang of life which was over: but I could not bear the coffin-lid to be closed—it almost stifled me; and still as the nettles wave in a corner of the churchyard over his little grave, the welcome breeze helps to refresh me and ease the tightness at my breast! (8:326) [49]

"His grief, though deep, was silent," his sister wrote, "and he applied [himself] to his literary pursuits with the greatest diligence." [50] His English grammar was soon ready for publication, and Godwin and a committee of the friends of Thomas Holcroft commissioned him to prepare a biography of Holcroft from the journal and papers left behind after his death in March, 1809. Hazlitt wrote two undated notes to Godwin at about this time concerning publication of the grammar and specific details about Holcroft's life.

47. *Lamb Letters*, 2:72.
48. Moyne, p. 109.
49. Baker (p. 170 n.) assumes that this passage applies to the death of the Hazlitts' son John in 1816. But Hazlitt's phrase "years ago," written in 1820–21, suggests the earlier date. Moreover, his grief at the death of his first and only son must have been even more poignant than at that of his third, when his second son survived. In either case it is difficult to understand why Hazlitt would write that he had seen death only once. Evidently he refused to look at the body of one of the two dead children. If so, it would more likely have been the second, especially if he had found his first experience so shattering.
50. Moyne, p. 109.

Both were terse and restrained; there was even a hint of bitterness in his reply to Godwin's suggestion that he insert an attack on Lindley Murray, whose "standard" grammar they were hoping to supplant: "As to the attack upon Murray, I have hit at him several times, and whenever there is a question of a blunder, 'his name is not far off.' Perhaps it would look like jealousy to make a formal set at him. Besides I am already noted by the reviewers for want of liberality, and an undisciplined moral sense." [51]

A New and Improved Grammar of the English Tongue was published with *A New Guide to the English Tongue* by "Edward Baldwin" [Godwin] late in 1809, although the title page was dated 1810. Since it was intended as a textbook for use in elementary schools, it offered little scope for Hazlitt's talents. In his preface he complained that most English grammars were "little else than translations of the Latin Grammar into English" (2:5) which ignored the principles advanced twenty years earlier in Horne Tooke's *Diversions of Purley*. He himself, he admitted, could not subscribe to all Tooke's theories; but he was determined to make use of the best of them. And occasionally thereafter he adopted an unorthodox attitude—as when he wrote that "the grammatical distinctions of words do not relate to the nature of the things or ideas spoken of, but to our manner of speaking of them" (2:6), or that "the most common construction is always the least objectionable" (2:86–87). On the whole, though, the *Grammar* consisted merely of rules dogmatically stated and illustrated. Hazlitt did not try to enliven his instruction; he sought only to be exact and concise. Yet this sort of exercise may have helped to sharpen his style—and he could have profited from a close look at some of the niceties of syntax.

Godwin was well pleased with the job and almost immediately began work on an abridgment ("achieved . . . mainly by wholesale omissions")[52] which he issued under his usual pseudonym. He also sent a copy of Hazlitt's *Grammar* to the *Edinburgh Review* explaining that it was "written by one of my inward friends, Mr. William Hazlitt. He is a man of singular acuteness and sound understanding, and I think he has brought some new materials to elucidate a most ancient subject. . . . I need not say that it would be of the greatest advantage to me if the writers of the *Edinburgh Review* felt disposed to speak of the book according to what I hold to be its merits." [53]

51. C. Kegan Paul, *William Godwin: His Friends and Contemporaries*, 2 vols. (London, 1876), 2:175. For other evidence of Godwin's criticism and revision of Hazlitt's manuscript, see Baker, pp. 171–72 and n.

52. Geoffrey Keynes, "Hazlitt's Grammar Abridged," *The Library*, 4th ser. 13 (1932–33):97–98.

53. F. K. Brown, *Life of William Godwin* (London and Toronto: J. M. Dent and Sons, Ltd., 1926), pp. 235–36.

They were not so disposed, but the *Critical Review* for December was laudatory: "We entirely agree with the author of this useful work that there is something radically wrong in the common method of teaching English grammar by transferring the artificial roles of other languages to our own. . . . This appears to us, on the whole, a more rational, simple, and intelligible English grammar, than most of those in common use; and we think that it may with great benefit to the scholar, be introduced into our elementary schools." Unfortunately few teachers agreed, and the book failed to supersede Lindley Murray's;[54] in fact it is remembered primarily as the occasion for one of Lamb's more far-fetched puns: "Hazlitt has written a *grammar* for Godwin," he wrote to Thomas Manning on January 2, 1810; "Godwin sells it bound up with a treatise of his own on language, but *the grey mare is the better horse*. I don't allude to Mrs. Godwin, but to the word *grammar*, which comes near to *grey mare*, if you observe, in sound. That figure is called paranomasia in Greek. I am sometimes happy in it." [55]

In October, 1809, Lamb and his sister, now recovered from her illness, made their postponed visit to the Hazlitts at Winterslow. "The whole of the time they were here was very fine," Hazlitt wrote to his father on November 5, and Lamb later told Robert Lloyd that they had enjoyed "uniform fine weather, the only fine days which had been all the summer." [56] "We had many long, & some pleasant walks," Hazlitt continued, "to Stonehenge, Salisbury, Wilton, &c. & in the woods near our own house. We are I find just on the borders of Hampshire, & that part of the country which lies on the Hampshire side is as woody & pleasant as the Wilts side is bleak & desert. I suppose this was the origin of the two names, Hants, i.e., Haunts, & Wilts, i.e. Wilds. Miss Lamb continued in perfect health & spirits while she staid, & I hope the journey will be of service to her, as well as to him, for he neither smoked nor drank any thing but tea & small beer, while he was here."

Martin Burney had not been with them, but Ned Phillips, "a friend of Lamb's, & a very good-natured card-playing fellow, came down for the last ten days. He shot us a hare & pheasant, having been formerly an old sportsman, & an Oxonian of idle renown. He is one of those kind of people who are always very much pleased with every thing, & it is therefore pleasant

54. There is probably no basis for Thomas De Quincey's suggestion that the *Grammar* was suppressed "by some powerful publisher interested in keeping up the current reputation of Murray" (De Quincey, *Collected Writings*, 11:353).

55. *Lamb Letters*, 2:91.

56. Ibid., p. 88. Lamb also reported that, when told that eight people had dined at the top of the spire of Salisbury Cathedral, he had remarked, "They must be very sharp-set" (ibid., p. 90).

to be with him." [57] Others of the party gathered mushrooms "to throw into our hashed mutton at supper," and there were long discussions of Fielding and the many other writers whom they all admired (17:320).

It was an unforgettable holiday. After Mary Lamb had returned to London, she wrote early in November:

> The dear, quiet, lazy, delicious month we spent with you is remembered by me with such regret, that I feel quite discontent & Winterslow-sick. I assure you, I never passed such a pleasant time in the country in my life, both in the house & out of it, the card playing quarrels, and a few gaspings for breath after your swift footsteps up the high hills excepted, and those drawbacks are not unpleasant in the recollection. We have got some salt butter to make our toast seem like yours, and we have tried to eat meat suppers, but that would not do, for we left our appetites behind us; and the dry loaf, which offended you, now comes in at night unaccompanied; but, sorry I am to add, it is soon followed by the pipe and the gin bottle. We smoked the very first night of our arrival.

And later in the same letter: "I continue very well, & return you very sincere thanks for my good health, and improved looks which have almost made Mrs. Godwin die with envy; she longs to come to Winterslow as much as the spiteful elder sister did to go to the well for a gift to spit diamonds." In a postscript she added: "Charles told Mrs. Godwin, Hazlitt had found a well in his garden, which, water being scarce in your country, would bring him in two hundred a year; and she came in great haste the next morning to ask me if it were true." [58]

"Since they went," Hazlitt told his father in his letter of November 5, "I have set to pretty hard at Holcroft's Life, & have in the evenings (for I paint in the daytime) written 35 pages in the last week, in addition to near a hundred which I had before transcribed from his own narrative which comes down to his fifteenth year. This will be the best part of the work but I hope to make the rest out tolerably well from memorandums, anecdotes, his own writings, criticisms, &c. &c. I shall finish it, I hope, by Christmass, & certainly it will not be a hard job." [59] On December 4 Hazlitt wrote to his old friend Crabb Robinson, who, though then reading law at the Middle Temple, still had influential contacts as former foreign editor of the *Times*. He would be glad, he said, to write for Richard Cumberland's new *London Review*, adding: "I shall have done Holcroft's Life in a fortnight when I shall bring it up to town, & it will then be time enough to talk of the book or books to be reviewed. . . . I am pushing hard to get Holcroft done (all

57. *PMLA* 77 (1962):341.   58. *Lamb Letters*, 2:85–87.
59. *PMLA* 77 (1962):341.

but correcting & Heaven knows there will be enough of that wanted) by Tuesday, & I must therefore return to a most pathetic account of his being blown up by aqua fortis in 1800. I am tired to death of the work, having been at it unceasingly the last fortnight, & I hope you will therefore excuse brevity & stupidity." [60] On January 2, 1810, Lamb wrote to Thomas Manning that "Hazlitt has ... finished his life—I do not mean his own life, but he has finished a life of Holcroft, which is going to press." [61] And on the fifteenth Godwin recorded in his journal that Hazlitt had called on him and that the life of Holcroft was finished. [62] But it was not to be published for some time to come.

Now Hazlitt began casting about for a new project. His hopes of writing for the *London Review* had come to nothing when the magazine failed after four issues. [63] On February 26 he asked Crabb Robinson to inquire whether Tipper, publisher of the *Review*, would be interested in a translation of Chateaubriands's *Les Martyrs*. He wondered, too, if he might perhaps convert his proposed history of English philosophy into "a volume of Essays on the subjects mentioned in the prospectus." "One more push I must make," he wrote, "& then I hope to be afloat, at least for a good while to come. . . . I have in short many plots & projects in my head, but I am afraid none of them good ones." [64]

Instead of being "afloat," however, he was soon plunged in troubles. On March 6 his wife suffered a miscarriage, and a week or so later she wrote to Mary Lamb asking if she could come to town for a visit with the Lambs. Mary replied later in the month, saying that she was sorry "to hear of your mischance" and urging her to come up at once. She went on to report that there had been a considerable to-do about the life of Holcroft: "Mrs. Holcroft still goes about from Nicholson to Tuthil, and from Tuthil to Godwin, and from Godwin to Tuthil, and from Tuthil to Godwin, and from Godwin to Tuthil, and from Tuthil to Nicholson, to consult on the publication, or no publication, of the life of the good man, her husband. It

---

60. Howe, p. 112.   61. *Lamb Letters*, 2:89.

62. *Shelley and His Circle*, 2:548 n. Under the dates of January 23 and 26 Godwin wrote in his journal: "Ht. revise." Apparently he tried at first to make minor revisions in the manuscript before deciding to delay publication.

63. The last issue had, in fact, appeared before Hazlitt wrote to Robinson offering his services. In his letter he suggested reviewing Opie's *Lectures on Painting*, of which he later remarked that "delivery of them was what nobody but Opie would have undertaken, and that nobody but Mrs. Opie [the Quaker novelist Amelia Alderson] would have thought of their publication" (11:354).

64. Howe, p. 114.

is called the Life Everlasting." [65] The trouble was that Hazlitt had simpli-
fied his task by copying Holcroft's journal entire, rather than using it as a
source, and Godwin objected strenuously. In an undated letter to Mrs.
Holcroft he cited the scandalous—even actionable—remarks about his
friends, including his dead wife Mary Wollstonecraft, in the journal,
declaring emphatically that he would be "no part or party to such a
publication." [66]

Hazlitt, meanwhile, was at Winterslow. He had had a series of severe
blows: little William's death, Sarah's miscarriage, his failure to find a new
literary project, now this controversy over the Holcroft biography—which
doubtless held up payment for his work. He tried to console himself with
painting, but it too proved frustrating. One Sunday evening while Sarah was
still at the Lambs' he wrote to thank her for sending him some prints and to
explain why he had not gone up to London to see an exhibition of paintings
as she had suggested. "I just took out my little copy of Rembrandt to look
at," he told her, "& was so pleased with it, I had almost a mind to send it up,
& try whether it might not fetch two or three guineas. But I am not at
present much in the humour to incur any certain expence for an uncertain
profit." He went on then to discuss his problems with a painting of Jacob's
dream that he was attempting:

> With respect to my painting, I go on something like Satan [In *Paradise Lost*],
> through moist & dry, some [times] glazing & sometime scumbling, as it happens,
> now on the wrong side of the canvas & now on the right, but still persuading myself
> that I have at last found out the true secret of Titian's golden hue & the oleaginous
> touches of Claude Lorraine. I have got in a pretty good background, & a *conception*
> of the ladder which I learned from the upping stone on the down, only making the
> stone into gold, & a few other improvements. I have no doubt there was such another
> on the field of Luz, & that an upping stone is the genuine Jacob's Ladder. But
> where are the angels to come from? That's another question, which I am not yet
> able to solve.

He closed tenderly and a bit remorsefully: "You are a good girl, & I must
be a good boy. I have not been very good lately. I do not wish you to over-
stay your month, but rather to set off on the Friday. . . . It is supper time,
my dear, & I have been painting all day, & all day yesterday, & all the day
before, & am very, very tired, & so I hope you will let me leave off here, &
bid you good night."

He cheered up, however, at the thought that the Lambs were planning

65. *Lamb Letters*, 2:97–98.
66. Paul, *William Godwin*, 2:176–77.

another trip to Winterslow, and he added in a postscript: "Before you come away, get Lamb to fix the precise time of their coming down here." [67] And early in July the Lambs arrived in Winterslow, a bit the worse for their trip. "We purpose setting out for Oxford Tuesday fortnight," Charles wrote from Winterslow to Basil Montagu on July 12, "and coming thereby home. But no more night travelling. My head is sore (understand it of the inside) with that deduction of my natural rest which I suffered coming down. Neither Mary nor I can spare a morsel of our rest. It is incumbent on us to be misers of it. Travelling is not good for us—we travel so seldom." [68]

But the good life at Winterslow revived them, and their company cheered Hazlitt, who decided to travel to Oxford with them on their return trip. They set off in high spirits. Lamb had ordered a pair of breeches from a tailor at the village of Pitton, near Winterslow, and they had been made up in "lively Lincoln-green" rather than the "brown or snuff-coloured" material that he had specified. "I remember," Hazlitt wrote in 1819, "he rode in triumph in Johnny Tremain's cross-country caravan through Newberry, and entered Oxford, 'fearing no colours,' the abstract idea of the jest of the thing prevailing in his mind (as it always does) over the sense of personal dignity" (17:66–67). Hazlitt enjoyed pointing out the sights at Oxford; he "shewed them the seat of the Muses at a distance, . . . descanted on the learned air that breathes from the grassy quadrangles and stone walls of the halls and colleges—was at home in the Bodleian." Then when they went on to Woodstock to view the galleries at Blenheim he "quite superseded the powdered Ciceroni that attended us, and that pointed in vain with his wand to common-place beauties in matchless pictures" (8:188).

For the Lambs the trip "ended sadly," as Charles reported in a letter written shortly after their return to London. He himself was ill on the way back, and soon after their arrival Mary's "complaint came on, and she is now absent from home." He had learned to his distress that they had missed one of the features of Blenheim: the Titian Gallery, which "is never shown but to those who inquire for it," probably because the paintings there are "all naked pictures." "Well," he wrote mournfully, "I shall never see it. I have lost all wish for sights." [69] And on September 6, soon after the letter arrived, the Hazlitts too were saddened when Sarah suffered a second miscarriage.

At about the same time the August issue of the *Edinburgh Review* came out with a notice of Hazlitt's *Reply* to Malthus, now three years old, and of Robert Acklom Ingram's *Disquisitions on Population*. It was not truly a

67. *The Hazlitts,* pp. 432–44.   68. *Lamb Letters,* 2:101.   69. Ibid., p. 102.

review at all; the critic began: "We should scarcely have thought it worth while to take any notice of these disquisitions, which consist, in a great degree, of strange misapprehensions and misrepresentations of the doctrines they profess to discuss, if we had not observed, among many persons besides Mr. Ingram and his anonymous coadjutor, an ignorance of the principles of population, which seems to us nearly unaccountable, considering the careful and detailed manner in which the subject has been lately explained." Then he proceeded to point out what Malthus had actually said in his "excellent work" without attempting any criticism of the two books before him.

Hazlitt was infuriated. He could shrug off the carping comments of the *Monthly Review*, but not this slight from a highly respected liberal magazine like the *Edinburgh*. He replied to it in a hard-hitting letter to the *Political Register*. "Sir," he began,

> The title-page of a pamphlet which I published some time ago, and part of which appeared in the Political Register in answer to the Essay on Population, having been lately prefixed to an article in the Edinburgh Review as a pretence for making a formal eulogy on that work, I take the liberty to request your insertion of a few queries, which may perhaps bring the dispute between Mr. Malthus's admirers and his opponents, to some sort of issue. It will, however, first of all be proper to say something of the article in the Review. The writer of the article accuses the "anonymous" writer of the reply to the Essay, of misrepresenting and misunderstanding his author, and undertakes to give a statement of the real principles of Mr. Malthus's work. He at the same time informs us for whom this statement is intended, namely, for those who are not likely even to read the work itself, and who take their opinions on all subjects moral, political, and religious, from the periodical reports of the Edinburgh Review. For my own part, what I have to say will be addressed to those who have read Mr. Malthus's work, and who may be disposed to form some opinion of their own on the subject. (7:408–9)

And he again stated his case in a series of "queries," this time with a new and telling emphasis. Malthus and his Whig defenders, he charged, were basically opposed to any genuine social progress; they were convinced that "by the laws of God and nature, the rich have a right to starve the poor whenever they (the poor) cannot maintain themselves" (7:360–61). Hazlitt was learning the arts of forceful propaganda.

His letter appeared in the *Political Register* for November 24, and Lamb sent him a copy immediately, following it up with a letter on the twenty-eighth. [70] Yet it was cold comfort. He had gained little or nothing from his

70. *Lamb Letters*, 2:111–12. Lamb reported that Mary had been ill again—"that is, as ill as she can be to remain at home"—and he blamed a visit from Dorothy Wordsworth "and that damn'd infernal bitch Mrs. Godwin coming & staying so late." He had con-

writing—certainly no real recognition and, recently, not even a living income. His life of Holcroft was still pending, and he had not received a new assignment from one of the booksellers for more than a year. He could no longer afford to live on at Winterslow cultivating his talents as a painter.

Shortly after the beginning of the year 1811 he went up to London determined to set up as a painter of portraits. He settled again in rooms at 34 Southampton Buildings and, inevitably, saw a good deal of his old friends. Crabb Robinson was keeping a diary now, and he reported visiting him on February 18 and March 4, seeing him at the Lambs' on the sixth and thirtieth, entertaining him on the tenth, and attending a party at his rooms on the twenty-ninth.[71] Coleridge was in town too, making his headquarters at 32 Southampton Buildings, next door to Hazlitt. He was in poor health and distressed by the death of his old friend George Burnett; yet, as always, he monopolized the conversation wherever he went. Hazlitt found his company irksome; his reactionary opinions, infuriating. He told Robinson how Coleridge had lost him the patronage of Sir George Beaumont—spoke of him "with the feelings of an injured man," Robinson noted in his diary —and held him partly responsible for the Lambs' ill health.[72]

Yet he was faring surprisingly well in his new career; he had managed to attract several sitters: Robinson's brother Thomas, a Mr. Howel, the Quaker abolitionist Thomas Clarkson, and an unnamed "handsome young man." Then suddenly, as Crabb Robinson wrote in his diary on April 15, "poor Hazlitt left town in great agony." According to Godwin, he had finished and delivered his portrait of the young man, and it had been promptly returned with an angry letter from the young man's mother. He still had not finished his portrait of Thomas Robinson, and his portrait of Howel, though "a good caricature likeness" in Robinson's estimation, was "but a coarse painting." "He has not sent my brother's picture," Robinson wrote, "and I fear does not mean to let it go out of his hands; perhaps he has already destroyed it. And I fear he has not the money to refund. . . . I fear poor Hazlitt will never succeed. With very great talents and with uncommon powers of mind I fear he is doomed to pass a life of poverty and unavailing repinings against society and his evil destiny."[73]

---

cluded that they must have no more house guests, "& therefore I am sure you will take it in good part if I say that if Mrs. Hazlitt comes to town at any time, however glad we shall be to see her in the daytime, I cannot ask her to spend a night under our roof."

71. Robinson, 1:23–29.

72. Ibid., p. 24. Ironically, in a letter to John Rickman dated October 26, Coleridge blamed Hazlitt for Lamb's ill health (see below, p. 124).

73. Robinson, 1:30.

Eventually Thomas Robinson wrote to inquire about his portrait, and on July 10 Hazlitt replied from Winterslow: "I have the picture by me, & brought it down with a full intention to set about improving it immediately. I have however put it off from day to day & week to week first from an unfortunate habit that what I ought to do I seldom do, & secondly from a fear of doing away what likeness there is without mending the picture. I will however do what I can to it before I come to town in October, & will then leave it with your brother. Till then I do not forget that I am your debtor." He was glad, he added dispiritedly, "to hear that Mr. Clarkson's picture is thought like, & only wish it were what it should be." [74]

He had failed again. And this time his failure was the crueler because it came in the skill which he most cherished—and after months of seeking to perfect that skill. It came, too, at an especially critical moment, for Sarah was pregnant again, and on Thursday, September 26, at 3:40 A.M., she bore him a second son—another William.

On October 2 Mary Lamb wrote to congratulate Sarah on the birth of the baby, and Charles added a note, probably designed to cheer the harassed father: "Well, my blessing and heaven's be upon him, and make him like his father, with something a better temper and a smoother head of hair, and then all the men and women must love him." [75]

Later in the month Hazlitt turned up in London again. He was spending "5 evenings in the Seven" with Lamb, Coleridge complained in a letter to John Rickman dated October 26. "As long as Hazlitt remains in town," he continued, "I dare not expect any amendment in Lamb's Health, unless luckily H. should grow moody and take offence at being desired not to come till 8 o/clock." [76]

Actually, however, Hazlitt had a new scheme afoot to occupy his days: he was soliciting subscriptions to a series of lectures on English philosophy. There was a great demand for such lectures, especially by men and women of the middle class who were eager to enrich their limited education. Hazlitt still had the notes which he had prepared for his proposed history of English philosphy, and he could, without too much effort, work them up into a series of lectures. To be sure, he had probably never in his life attempted to speak in public. But he was desperate.

By October 29 he was back at Winterslow writing to Crabb Robinson to explain why he had not called on him during his recent trip to town: he was

74. Howe, p. 122. Although the original of Clarkson's portrait seems to have been lost, a reproduction of it appears in Thomas Taylor's *Life of Thomas Clarkson* (London, 1839).

75. *Lamb Letters*, 2:118.   76. *Coleridge Letters*, 3:340.

"held in durance vile" all the time he was in London "by one of the greatest miseries of human life, I mean a tight pair of boots." Then he got down to business: ". . . I am going (in spite of the muse that presides over eloquence, I do not know her name) to deliver lectures. . . . I have got 30 subscribers, & want ten or a dozen more if I can possibly get them. If therefore you could assist me by picking up one or two names, I can only say I shall be much obliged to you, & that the lectures will be as good as I can make them." He appended a synopsis of ten lectures, concluding: "The price to each subscriber is two guineas, & they will be delivered about January." [77]

On November 30 Hazlitt was in London again, and Robinson called and "chatted with him on his intended lectures." [78] On December 7 Robinson stopped off again at Hazlitt's lodgings "to pay him Subscription money for his Lectures" and found him "alone and gloomy." [79] A week later he wrote to his brother:

> W. Hazlitt is come to town. He means to spend the winter here, and on my asking him what he meant to do with your picture, he mumbled out that he should try to do something with it, or else he must—. The truth is that poor Hazlitt is so poor and so unhappy that I can't but feel more pity than displeasure. He announced you know lectures on the history of philosophy and wrote to me to procure him subscriptions. I informed him J. Buck and J. Collier would subscribe. He first sent me three tickets and then wrote to beg I would pay for them. J.B. and J.C. consented and I left the six guineas. When the lectures will be delivered I can not tell. He means to deliver them as he does to deliver your picture, and will probably do both sooner or later, but we must wait his time.[80]

But this time Hazlitt was determined. At Dr. Stoddart's suggestion he wrote to the committee in charge of the Russell Institution, a subscription library and reading room on Great Coram Street, Russell Square, asking them to sponsor the series. On December 19 the committee met and approved the suggestion, and on the twenty-sixth they announced that the series of ten lectures would begin on Tuesday, January 14, and continue weekly thereafter.[81]

Whatever the consequences, he could hardly withdraw now.

77. Howe, pp. 124–25. The troublesome boots may have been the handiwork of Thomas Hardy, the liberal bootmaker who was tried with Holcroft, Thelwall, and others in the state trials of 1794. In a letter dated from Winterslow on "Sun eve" Hazlitt apologized to Hardy because he did not "discharge my promise" before leaving London. He explained that he had failed to collect twenty pounds due him: ten for a picture and ten for revising a manuscript. He promised to pay his debt when he returned to town in October to deliver his lectures (Howe, p. 124 n.).

78. Ibid., p. 126.   79. Robinson, 1:54.   80. Howe, p. 126.
81. *Memoirs*, 1:192–94.

CHAPTER VI

New Directions
(1812–1815)

On Tuesday, January 14, 1812, Hazlitt faced his first audience in the rooms of the Russell Institution. His topic, as announced, was "The Writings of Hobbes, showing that he was the father of the modern system of philosophy." According to Crabb Robinson, the secretary of the institution, a Mr. Flack, told him just before the lecture that he must restrict himself to one hour. He had, unfortunately, material enough to last three hours—and he attempted to disgorge it all in an hour's time. The result was disastrous.

He began by reading passages from the prospectus which he had prepared for his history of English philosophy, declaring that he was interested not so much in tracing the history of English philosophy as in criticizing false philosophy and formulating more sensible principles. He was off to a bad start with those of his audience who had come for information rather than theory. And they must have grown increasingly restless as he developed his thesis—that modern philosophy stemmed from Hobbes, not Locke, and that Hobbes, though original, was dead wrong—by reading long excerpts from Hobbes's work with occasional critical comments of his own. To make matters worse, he "delivered himself in a low, monotonous voice," Robinson wrote in his diary,

> with his eyes fixed intently on his book, not once daring to look on his audience. He read, too, so rapidly that no one could possibly follow him; at the same time, the matter he read was of a kind to require reflection. No subject is in itself less adapted to a lecture than metaphysical philosophy; no manner less adapted to recommend abstruse matter than Hazlitt's. So that it is impossible Hazlitt's lectures should not

altogether fail of their subject, unless he should alter his style and delivery, which I fear is hardly in his power.

Robinson acknowledged that the content of the lectures had merit—but "he read ill a very sensible book; and, as he seems to have no conception of the difference between a lecture and a book, his lectures cannot possibly be popular, hardly tolerable."[1]

Hazlitt knew only too well that his lecture was a failure. The next day he received a letter of criticism from his brother-in-law, Dr. Stoddart, and by the time he reached the Lambs' that evening he was despondent. Inevitably the conversation veered around to the lectures, and suggestions were offered. Robinson "observed on the difference between a book and a lecture, and, perhaps more than I intended, betrayed my opinion. I spoke of the compassion I felt beholding Hazlitt so oppressed in delivering the lecture, and this he misunderstood." Hazlitt was so irritated that he declared he would abandon the series, at least at the Russell Institution. "He blamed himself for yielding to Dr. Stoddart in delivering them there, and considered the size of the room, the nature of the audience, etc., as the occasions of his not succeeding."[2] The following Monday evening he went to Basil Montagu's fine house at 25 Bedford Square to read his lecture to Lamb and some other friends who had not heard it at the Russell Institution. But half way through the reading he stopped suddenly and refused to finish it.

Yet the next evening, Tuesday, he appeared at the Russell Institution as scheduled and redeemed himself. "He delivered himself well, that is, loud," Crabb Robinson wrote, "and with a tone of confidence which, being forced, had sometimes the air of arrogance. This, however, did not offend (except perhaps a few), and he was interrupted by applauses several times." The content was better controlled too; "Mr. Burrell [a friend of Stoddart's] had abridged it, and well; except that he left two very tedious, because tautological, passages."[3]

1. Robinson, 1:57–58.   2. Ibid.
3. Ibid., p. 60. After Hazlitt's death his son published in *Literary Remains of the Late William Hazlitt* (London, 1836), the texts of five pieces which he took to be Hazlitt's lectures. P. P. Howe reprinted these five, plus an essay "On Abstract Rights" (also first printed in *Literary Remains*) in volume 2 of his *Complete Works*, pointing out that Hazlitt had probably hoped to publish them in the *London Magazine* in 1821. Although these may not be the lectures which Hazlitt delivered at the Russell Institution, they undoubtedly cover much the same ground. (They might well have been the essays mentioned in his letter to Crabb Robinson of February 26, 1810. See above, p. 119.) By comparing them with Crabb Robinson's comments on the original lectures, I have concluded that the first of the reprinted pieces corresponds to the first lecture as delivered and that the second

He failed, however, to finish what he wanted to say about Locke, and the next Tuesday evening, when the announced topic was "On Berkeley's Principles of Human Knowledge, and on Abstract Ideas," he continued his discussion of Locke, then, toward the end of the lecture, introduced a long excerpt from and discussion of Berkeley's arguments against the existence of innate ideas, remarking that he was doing so "as I do not know that I shall have a better opportunity" (2:172). But although he was having some difficulty handling his material, he handled himself admirably. Robinson considered that this lecture was "not less impressively delivered than the last." [4]

Thereafter the series moved along for five weeks without mishap. On February 4 Hazlitt was "still on Locke," and Robinson described his delivery as "now very respectable," although he "thought the lecture itself dry and unimpressive." He acknowledged, however, that he might himself be partly to blame, since his "quickness in perceiving the import and comprehending metaphysical reasoning was greatly lessened by the neglect of these pursuits." [5] On February 11 Hazlitt moved on to Disinterestedness, drawing largely on his *Principles of Human Action,* and there he remained for four weeks. He had announced one lecture on Self-Love, one on Hartley and Helvétius, one on Bishop Butler's theory of man, and two on Liberty and Necessity and Materialism; actually, however, the next four lectures treated Disinterestedness, Self-Love, Hartley, and Helvétius separately.

Robinson attended faithfully and continued to record his impressions. On February 11 the lecture "did not apparently please so much as others of less worth in reality. The attendance was thin." On the eighteenth he pronounced the performance "very dull, though it concluded eloquently." On the twenty-fifth, too, it was "very dull," but once again he thought himself partly at fault: "I am sorry to add that, either because I could not attend, or that my faculty of comprehending metaphysical reasoning is weakened by disuse, I was unable even to follow Hazlitt on his observations against the doctrine of associations." But on March 3 the lecture was "interesting and animated." [6] Meanwhile Robinson had recorded in his diary a telling entry: on February 27 he had dined at John Thelwall's with a

---

reprinted piece (considerably longer than any of the others) corresponds to the second, third, and possibly fourth lectures. The fourth piece reprinted almost certainly is the fifth lecture delivered, and the fifth and sixth reprinted seem to correspond to the seventh and ninth lectures. As is pointed out in the text below, Hazlitt did not follow the schedule of the lectures which he had announced, and he gave eleven lectures rather than ten.

4. Robinson., p. 62.   5. Ibid.   6. Ibid., pp. 63–65.

large party including "William Hazlitt, who said little and drank little, and therefore behaved inoffensively." [7]

Apparently Hazlitt's friends were used to his saying and drinking much and behaving offensively these days. The lectures had added new pressures to those which had been dogging him. On March 10, when the ninth lecture was scheduled, Robinson received a note announcing that the last two lectures had been postponed. "I fear his debts oppress him so that he cannot proceed," he wrote in his diary. "I wish I could afford him assistance, for I know of no state of suffering more dreadful than that of indigent genius. Nor is my pity less for Hazlitt, because my esteem for him is not great." [8] Robinson's patience was flagging.

Robinson missed part of the next lecture, on Free Will and Necessity, when Hazlitt finally gave it three weeks later, on March 31. There was another lapse of time before the tenth lecture, which he gave on April 14. Then—perhaps to compensate for his delays, perhaps to round out the promised topics—he gave a final, additional lecture on the twenty-eighth. Robinson noted in his diary that the April fourteenth lecture, on Horne Tooke's *Diversions of Purley*, revealed the "absurdity" of Tooke's philosophy "in a most convincing way." And he described the final lecture as "very well delivered and full of shrewd observation," singling out Hazlitt's concluding remarks "on the utility of metaphysics":

> He quoted and half assented to Hume's sceptical remark that perhaps they are not worth the study, but that there are persons who can find no better [way] of amusing themselves. Hazlitt then related an Indian legend of a Brahman who was so devoted to abstract meditation that he, in the pursuit of philosophy, quite forgot his moral duties and neglected ablution. For this he was degraded from the rank of humanity and transformed into a monkey. But even when a monkey he retained his original propensities, for he kept apart from other monkeys and had no other delight than in eating coconuts and studying metaphysics. "I, too," said Hazlitt, "should be very well contented to pass my life like this monkey, did I but know how to provide myself with a substitute for coconuts." [9]

For *metaphysics* read *psychology*. Hazlitt was still fascinated with human behavior, still convinced that man's mind was neither selfish nor inert. He rejected the notions of Hobbes and his empirical followers that sensations governed the operations of the mind. For him the mind could act

7. Ibid., p. 65.

8. Ibid., pp. 65–66. Hazlitt may, of course, have postponed his last lectures because he needed time for preparation. Thus far he had been dealing with the four English philosophers about whom he had already written most.

9. Ibid., pp. 69–70.

independently; it was "formative" as well as receptive, it could select from the sensations which played upon it, choose the good from the bad, and through the will, govern man's actions. It was not a machine but an independent force which raised man above the level of the other animals. And it was the object of his dearest study, that on which he would gladly have spent all his energies.

But always there was the problem of the substitute for coconuts for himself and his family. Once the lecture series was completed, he was again jobless. He made one more desperate attempt at painting. On May 28 Robinson and Mary Lamb called at his rooms and chatted with him, and on June 30 Robinson was there again while Hazlitt was "operating on Thomas"—that is, trying once more to finish his portrait of Thomas Robinson. On the following day he at last pronounced it done, and Crabb Robinson called to see it. Like others, he had misgivings: the painting seemed "now more tolerable than before, though still it has somewhat of the fierceness of the Saracen." [10] It proved to be Hazlitt's last attempt to make his living as a painter.

He continued to paint, from time to time, when he found a subject which caught his fancy. One day at a friend's house he asked if his hostess's daughter would pose for him. "I have always wished to paint Cupid and Psyche," he explained, "but I have never commenced, because I have never been able to see a Psyche—until to-day!" Then, his old self-doubt returning: "I don't know . . . that I shall ever succeed in painting a picture; but if not, I shall at least learn that I am unable to do so—and that is something." Again he tried—and failed. The friend who tells the story adds: "He was not quick and dexterous enough to catch ere they vanished all the transient and playful graces of childhood, nor could he revive them by that species of amusing dialogue, adapted to all ages, which is part of the accomplishment of a portrait-painter." In fact, on this occasion, the little girl soon tired and fell asleep. Yet "he bought colours and brushes, and a canvass [sic] or two every year, set to work with ardour, sketched, rubbed out, grew dissatisfied, gave up his labours as hopeless,—and resumed them again in the succeeding year!" [11] As late as 1826, in Paris, he was still trying—but copying Titian now rather than painting from life.

His failure as an artist was one of the greatest disappointments of his life.

10. Ibid., pp. 88, 104.

11. *New Monthly Magazine* 29 (1830), pt. 2, p. 472. The little girl who posed for Hazlitt was probably Anne Skepper, stepdaughter of Basil Montagu and later wife of Barry Cornwall [Bryan Waller Procter]. In 1812 she was thirteen years old.

His friend Benjamin Haydon insisted (no doubt unjustly) that it soured his judgments of all contemporary painters.[12] His sister believed that "what he had seen [at the Louvre], so far above all that he could hope to attain to, made him despise his own efforts. What he was most deficient in was the mechanical part. Shall I say that if he had had less talent and his perception of what was beautiful in art had been more dim, he would have been more successful."[13] He himself was less sure of the reason for his failure. He told Northcote that he thought he might have succeeded as a portrait-painter, but could never have painted "history" (that is, large canvases portraying groups in action); that he might have accomplished what Rembrandt or Titian did, but not what Raphael did (11:193). But William Bewick claimed that Hazlitt told him, "Had I possessed the executive part of the art sufficiently, and could I have drawn correctly, with facility, or to my satisfaction, the subject I feel I should have desired to realize would have been 'Jacob's Dream.' I have the arrangement, the composition, and, if I may be allowed to say so, the poetry of the picture in my mind."[14] Yet at bottom the several explanations agree: he could not realize his aspirations. As he wrote in "English Students at Rome," "I might have done as well as the others, I dare say, but from a desire to do too well. I did not consider that Nature is always the great thing, or that 'Pan is a god, Apollo is no more'" (17:139). The unfinished painting of Jacob's dream which he had begun at Winterslow in 1810 symbolized both his aspiration and his failure.

One day in late July of 1812 Hazlitt and Crabb Robinson met at Captain Burney's house. When someone brought up the subject of Philip Mallet, Hazlitt said, "He is a fellow who has a great reputation . . . because he did nothing. What can we think of a man, who being quite independent in his fortune, makes an abridgement of Locke and edits a book of Hobbes, and at the same time thinks he is doing nothing? I do not mean to say that it is necessary for a man to do anything. He may be a very excellent man without it."[15] Unfortunately for William Hazlitt's self-respect, he himself was doing nothing and had no appreciable reputation—and he had little reason to consider himself "a very excellent man."

The Society for the Diffusion of Knowledge upon the Punishment of Death commissioned him to write an essay "On the Punishment of Death" (19:324–29)—thanks, no doubt, to the president of the society, Lamb's affluent friend Basil Montagu, natural son of the earl of Sandwich. But the

12. See *Haydon Diary*, 2:433, 495–96, and *Autobiography and Journals of Benjamin Robert Haydon*, ed. Malcolm Elwin (New York: Coward McCann; London: Macdonald, 1950), pp. 187–88, 200 (hereafter cited as Elwin).

13. Moyne, pp. 108–9.   14. Landseer, 1:135.   15. Howe, pp. 132–33.

money he received for it was soon spent, and his debts continued to mount. On September 8 Crabb Robinson learned from Anthony Robinson that Hazlitt "some time ago borrowed of him £30, promising to repay it in a fortnight when he was to receive his money in the Society for Abolishing Capital Punishment. However, several fortnights have elapsed, and he had never heard from or seen H. since" (19: 368).

Crabb Robinson decided that someone must take action in Hazlitt's behalf. On September 21 he "called at Dr. Stoddart's with a view to speak to him about W. Hazlitt, but he was not at home."[16] A week later he tried again, found Stoddart at home, and "consult[ed] about Hazlitt and the getting him a situation under Walter" of the *Times*,[17] for whom Robinson had formerly served as foreign editor and Stoddart was now working. Two days later, on the thirtieth, he met Stoddart and Mary Lamb and again "chatted about Hazlitt." For a complication had risen: he had learned from Mrs. Thomas Clarkson that there might be an opening for Hazlitt on the *Morning Chronicle*. Hazlitt had himself approached James Perry of the *Chronicle* on the subject, and Lamb had written to John Dyer Collier of the *Chronicle* to recommend him, adding: "He is, indeed, at his wits' end for a livelihood; and, I should think, especially qualified for such an employment, from his singular facility in retaining all conversations at which he has been ever present."[18] The upshot of his friends' efforts was that Hazlitt suddenly had two prospects: Perry of the *Chronicle* had made him a "conditional promise," and Walter of the *Times* had "promised to do something" for him. It was a pleasant change; but Hazlitt's friends feared that he might offend one of his two benefactors. Crabb Robinson, however, consoled himself that "the prospect of his finding the means of subsistence is by this greatly improved."[19] And he celebrated his success by dispatching a letter to Hazlitt denying his request for a twenty-pound loan.

On October 10 Mrs. Clarkson wrote to Robinson that Hazlitt had been hired by the *Chronicle*. He was to receive four guineas per week, and, as Robinson wrote in his diary: "It is now in his power to live comfortably, if he be not altogether without the power of acting prudently."[20]

On Christmas Eve, when Robinson stopped in at the Lambs', he found Hazlitt "in high spirits"; his new job, he said, was "very easy, and the four guineas per week keep his head above water."[21] His duties were light: he attended the regular sessions of Parliament, took notes on the speeches delivered, and then reproduced the speeches in his own words. As Lamb had

---

16. Howe, p. 133.   17. Robinson, 1: 110.   18. *Lamb Letters*, 2: 124.
19. Robinson, 1: 110.   20. Ibid.   21. Ibid., p. 116.

remarked, he had a real gift for recalling conversations which eased his task. However, he was sometimes so carried away by the oratory that he forgot to take notes—and sometimes unconsciously improved on the speeches when he expressed them in his own words. Eventually he tired of the task,[22] but for the moment it made him "quite happy." He even promised to deliver the portrait of Thomas Robinson—and, Crabb Robinson wrote, "I believe I shall get it."[23]

For the first time in his thirty-five years of life Hazlitt now had a steady income. Accordingly he gave up his rooms in Southampton Buildings, took a substantial house at 19 York Street, Westminster, and moved Sarah and the baby up from Winterslow. On January 2, 1813, the Hazlitts entertained at a large party—the Lambs, the Burneys, and, among others, Crabb Robinson. "I found Hazlitt in a handsome room," Robinson wrote, "and his supper was comfortably set out,—enjoyments which have sprung out of an unmeaning chat with Mrs. Clarkson at Lamb's. On what frivolous accidents do the important events of our lives depend!"[24]

It was an unusual house. Milton—or, as people in the neighborhood had it, "*Milford*, a celebrated poet" (10:283)[25]—had lived there, and it now belonged to the philosopher Jeremy Bentham, whose garden it overlooked. The last occupant, James Mill, had moved out because he considered the house unhealthful; yet Hazlitt's friends, like Robinson, seem to have been agreeably surprised with it. The young painter William Bewick later wrote of it:

> The entrance was a sort of porch opening to a small anteroom, with very red brick floor and upright posts, that one rubbed one's shoulders against, and the staircase was narrow and dark. The room where Hazlitt received us was, as he informed us, in the same condition that it had been in Milton's time; the same dull-white painted wainscot, the same windows looking into a garden-like piece of ground, tricked out into grass-plots, shrubberies, and winding walks, with two noble trees crossing the windows. From these windows might occasionally be seen the celebrated law-giver Bentham, shuffling along in loose déshabille, his shirt-neck thrown open, the strings of his knee-breeches hanging about his shrunk legs, his loose habit of a coat seeming too large for his short puffy body.[26]

22. For Hazlitt's complaints about Parliamentary reporting, see 12:270–71.
23. Robinson, 1:116. As Baker has discovered (p. 183), Robinson later recorded that it "was never finished—and what was done was destroyed."
24. Robinson, 1:116.
25. Perhaps to clear up the confusion, Hazlitt placed on the facade a stone marked "To Milton / Prince of Poets" (11:323–24).
26. Landseer, 1:109–10.

Hazlitt soon made himself comfortable in his haphazard way. According to Bewick,

> The room we were in . . . was in keeping with the general negligence and pecu-
> liarity of Hazlitt's habits. There was little furniture, no appearance of books, no pic-
> tures or prints of any kind whatever!—a confusion and apparent want of comfort
> and domestic order reigned in the apartment. Over the mantel-shelf, upon the wains-
> cot, instead of picture or looking-glass, there was written, in good bold hand (Haz-
> litt's own writing) as high up as he could reach and covering the whole space, all
> manner of odd conceits (as they appeared to be), of abbreviations,—words,—names,
> —enigmatical exclamations,—strange and queer sentences, quotations,—snatches
> of rhyme,—bits of arithmetical calculations,—scraps of Latin,—French expressions,
> —words or signs by which the author might spin a chapter, or weave an elaborate
> essay. The chimneypiece seemed to be his tablet of mnemonics,—his sacred hiero-
> glyphics,—all jotted down without line, or form of any kind, some horizontal, some
> running up to the right, some down to the left, and some obliquely. They seemed
> thoughts and indications of things to be remembered, put down on the instant, and
> I concluded that this room might not be his study, but his living-room.[27]

Gradually Hazlitt made new friends in London. He had met the painter Benjamin Robert Haydon at Northcote's studio one day in 1812, praised his painting *Macbeth*, and become a regular caller at his studio, along with the artist David Wilkie and the poet extraordinary Leigh Hunt. In January, 1813, Haydon referred in his journal to "the daily contests with Hazlitt, . . . with Leigh Hunt and with Wilkie," who "all thought conclusively and differently on all subjects."[28] Hunt and his brother John went off to jail in February for describing the Prince Regent, in their newspaper, the *Examiner*, as "this Adonis in loveliness . . . a corpulent man of fifty"; but Hazlitt made a point of visiting both. John Hunt was quartered in a bare cell at Coldbath Fields. But his brother had the walls of his cell at Surrey Gaol papered with trellises of roses, the ceiling painted to represent sky and clouds, and the air sweetened with fresh flowers. "Even William Hazlitt, who there first did me the honour of a visit," he wrote in his autobiography, "would stand interchanging amenities at the threshold, which I had great difficulty in making him pass. I know not which kept his hat off with the greater pertinacity of deference, I to the diffident cutter-up of Tory dukes and kings, or he to the amazing prisoner and invalid who issued out of a bower of roses."[29]

27. *Ibid.*, pp. 118–19.
28. Elwin, p. 182.
29. *Autobiography of Leigh Hunt*, ed. J. E. Morpurgo, (New York: Chanticleer Press, 1948), p. 246.

The Hazlitts occasionally entertained at parties in the York Street house—not always as "comfortably set out" as the one Crabb Robinson attended on January 2. Sarah was born with few of the domestic talents, and she never cared to cultivate them: instead she relied on an ill-tempered maid named Becky who had a mind of her own.[30] Haydon never forgot one party at the Hazlitts'—planned to celebrate the christening of the new little William. Hazlitt doted on the boy, and "his eye glistened" when he invited Haydon to the affair. "Will ye come on Friday?" he urged.

On Friday Haydon arrived promptly at four o'clock, as directed.

> I walked up and found his wife ill by the fire in a bedgown—nothing ready for guests and everything wearing the appearance of neglect and indifference. I said: "Where is Hazlitt?" "Oh dear, William has gone to look for a parson." "A parson; why, has he not thought of that before?" "No, he didn't." "I'll go and look for him," said I, and out I went into the park through Queen's Square and met Hazlitt in a rage coming home. "Have ye got a parson?" "No, sir;" said he, "these fellows are all out." "What will you do?" "Nothing." So in we walked, Hazlitt growling at all the parsons and the church. When we came in we sat down—nobody was come—no table laid— no appearance of dinner.

Soon people began drifting in: "Charles Lamb and his poor sister—all sorts of odd clever people": "a young mathematician, who whenever he spoke, jerked up one side of his mouth, and closed an eye as if seized with a paralytic affection . . .; an old Lady of Genius with torn ruffles; his Wife in an influenza, thin, pale & spitty; and his chubby child, squalling, obstinate, & half-cleaned." "At last came in a maid who laid a cloth and put down knives and forks in a heap." Then came "a plate with a dozen large, waxen, cold, clayy, slaty potatoes. Down they were set, and down we sat also. . . . After waiting a little, all looking forlornly at the potatoes for fear they might be the chief dish, in issued a bit of overdone beef, burnt, toppling about on seven or eight corners, with a great bone sticking out like a battering ram; the great difficulty was to make it stand upright! but the greater to discover a *cuttable* place, for all was jagged, jutting, & irregular." "Neither Hazlitt nor Lamb seemed at all disturbed, but set to work helping each other; while the boy, half-clean and obstinate, kept squalling to put his fingers into the gravy."[31]

30. After she left the Hazlitt's service, Becky worked for the Lambs for fifteen years. Lamb described her as "ill-temperd" (*Lamb Letters*, 3:324), and Peter George Patmore recalled that she often gave the Lambs "'a bit of her mind' when they did anything that she considered 'odd' or out of the way" (*My Friends and Acquaintance*, 3 vols. [London, 1854], 1:41 [hereafter cited as Patmore]).

31. This account of the party has been compiled from two sources, *Haydon Diary*,

During the early months of 1813 Hazlitt was given an occasional assignment for the *Chronicle* in addition to his parliamentary reporting. On January 25, substituting for William Mudford, the dramatic critic, he wrote a long and generally glowing account of Coleridge's tragedy *Remorse*, comparing it favorably with Shakespeare.[32] Then on April 13 he somehow managed to place in the Tory *Courier* a brief but biting attack on Lord Wellesley, which was reprinted, in slightly abbreviated form, in the *Chronicle* the next day. "It is curious, though somewhat painful," it concluded,

> to see this lively little lord always in the full career of his subject, and never advancing a jot the nearer; seeming to utter volumes in every word, and yet saying nothing; retaining the same unabated vehemence of voice and action without any thing to excite it; still keeping alive the promise and the expectation of genius without once satisfying it—soaring into mediocrity with adventurous enthusiasm, harrowed up by some plain matter-of-fact, writing with agony under a truism, and launching a common-place with all the fury of a thunderbolt! (7:23)

A man who could express himself in such terms was not likely to be content long as a mere parliamentary reporter.

For the present, though, he confined himself largely to his rather tedious duties. When he met Crabb Robinson at the Lambs' on April 29, he seemed to be "made comfortable by a situation which, furnishing him with the necessaries of life, keeps his best faculties not employed, but awake." "I do not think," Robinson commented, "it is much to be feared that his faculties will, therefore, decline. He has a most powerful intellect, and needs only encouragement to manifest this to the world by a work which could not be overlooked."[33]

Before long Hazlitt acted to relieve the tedium of his job. In August he submitted some papers to Perry, explaining that he could supply others of the kind "such as—on classical education—on advantages & disadvantages of education in general—on love of posthumous fame—on taste and seeing—

1:303, and Elwin, pp. 188–89. Painter that he was, Haydon may well have added some imaginative coloring to the actual facts; however, of the two accounts, the one in the diary, written soon after the party, is the more detailed and colorful.

32. See 18:463–65. The review did not please Coleridge. Seizing upon Hazlitt's remark that one speech in the play was "too evidently copied from . . . Shakespeare," he wrote to John Rickman on the twenty-fifth: ". . . I hear that Hazlitt i[n the] M.C. has sneered at my presumption in [entering] the Lists with Shakespear's Hamlet in Teresa's Description of the two Brothers. . . . But mercy on us! is there no such thing as two men's having similar Thoughts on similar Occasions—?" (*Coleridge Letters*, 3:429).

33. Robinson, 1:128.

on love of nature—on patriotism—causes of methodism—on envy among
artists—characters of writers, painters, actors, &c." [34] On September 4 one
of these, "On the Love of Life," a two-paragraph essay, appeared in the
Chronicle under the heading "Commonplaces." Then on the eighteenth,
Hazlitt wrote a brief, ironic comment on the appointment of the former
radical Southey, rather than the ever loyal Walter Scott, as poet laureate
(7:24–25). And when a writer in the rival *Courier* criticized his remarks, he
replied in the *Chronicle* on the twentieth with more on the subject, again
emphasizing Southey's past record (19:115–17).

On the twenty-fifth the *Chronicle* contained two contributions by Hazlitt:
another "Commonplace," his short essay on the advantages of a classical
education (4:4–5), and a letter, signed "WH," debating a point made in an
article entitled "The English Stage," probably by William Mudford, in the
Chronicle for September 17. Hazlitt answered the question "Why are there
so few good modern comedies?" by arguing that "comedy naturally wears
itself out—destroys the very food on which it lives; and by constantly and
successfully exposing the follies and weaknesses of mankind to ridicule, in the
end leaves itself nothing worth laughing at" (4:10).[35] It was a challenging
idea; Hazlitt was inching his way into the realm of criticism.

On October 4 the *Chronicle* contained a reply, probably by Mudford, to
Hazlitt's letter and on the fifteenth (the day Sarah Hazlitt suffered her third
miscarriage) a withering criticism of that reply signed "H." The editors
had apparently decided to let the two settle their differences in public.

There was no question about the winner. Hazlitt wrote in his letter:

> the whole of our author's reasoning proceeds on a total misconception of the nature
> of the Drama itself. It confounds philosophy with poetry, laboured analysis with
> intuitive perception, general truth with individual observation. He makes the comic
> muse a dealer in riddles, and an expounder of hieroglyphics, and a taste for dramatic
> excellence, a species of second sight. He would have the Drama to be the most re-
> mote, and it is the most substantial and real of all things. It represents not only looks,
> but motion and speech. The painter gives only the former, looks without action or
> speech, and the mere writer only the latter, words without looks or action. Its business
> and its use is to express the thoughts and character in the most striking and instanta-
> neous manner, in the manner most like reality. It conveys them in all their truth and
> subtlety, but in all their force and with all possible effect. It brings them into action,
> obtrudes them on the sight, embodies them in habits, in gestures, in dress, in circum-
> stances, and in speech. It renders every thing overt and ostensible, and presents
> human nature not in its elementary principles or by general reflections, but exhibits

34. Baker, p. 193 n.
35. Concerning Coleridge's claim that the idea was originally his, see Howe, p. 141 n.

its essential quality in all their variety of combination, and furnishes subjects for perpetual reflection. (20:9–10)

In effect Mudford admitted defeat, for he resigned from the *Chronicle* and presently accepted a position as dramatic critic for the *Courier*, where, Hazlitt declared, he grumbled that "it is impossible for any one to understand a word I write" (8:294 n.). Meanwhile, on October 18, Hazlitt contributed to the *Chronicle* a brief but enthusiastic review of Catherine Stephens' performance in Thomas Arne's opera *Artaxerxes* and of John Liston's in *Love, Law, and Physic* (5:192–93). Then, on October 23, the *Chronicle* contained a curious review of a new production of *The Beggar's Opera* with Miss Stephens playing Polly. The author, an unabashed iconoclast, defied the critical tradition that John Gay's opera, though highly entertaining, was immoral and "low." "It not only delights, but instructs us," he insisted (5:193), and he defended his startling claim in forceful terms. William Hazlitt had made his appearance on the critical scene, and he was demanding a hearing in the self-confident tone which he could always muster—on paper.[36]

"I have reason to remember that article," he wrote later in "On Patronage and Puffing"; "it was almost the last I ever wrote with any pleasure to myself. I had been down on a visit to friends near Chertsey, and, on my return, had stopped at an inn at Kingston-upon-Thames, where I had got the Beggar's Opera, and had read it overnight. The next day I walked cheerfully to town. It was a fine sunny morning, in the end of autumn, and as I repeated the beautiful song, 'Life knows no return of spring,' I meditated my next day's criticism, trying to do all the justice I could to so inviting a subject. . . . I deposited my account of the play at the Morning Chronicle Office in the afternoon, and went to see Miss Stephens as Polly" (8:292),[37]

36. Hazlitt thought so well of this review that he reprinted the bulk of it almost verbatim three times: in the *Examiner* for June 8, 1815, in his Round Table essay "On the Beggar's Opera," and in the sixth of his *Lectures on the English Poets*. For a fuller discussion of the review and Hazlitt's later defense of the play, see R. M. Wardle "Hazlitt on *The Beggar's Opera*," South Atlantic Quarterly 70 (1971).

37. The friends near Chertsey were probably his parents, who settled at Addlestone, Surrey, after his father's retirement from his pastorate at Wem in 1813. According to W. C. Hazlitt (*The Hazlitts*, p. 210) the Reverend Mr. Hazlitt apparently received an annual grant from the Presbyterian Fund "occasionally supplemented by special allowances and doubtless by donations" from his Wem congregation. During his retirement he became a tireless writer of letters to the *Monthly Repository*. These letters, signed "WH," were on all sorts of topics: controversial points in theology, obituaries of friends, corrections of points in earlier articles, etc. At times he treated four or five subjects in a single letter; often he added such postscripts as the following: "Having still some room, I

having decided in advance that "her acting throughout was simple, unaffected, graceful, and full of tenderness" (5:194). She did not disappoint him; on October 30 he reviewed the play again, "repeating our praise of her, though, perhaps, by so doing, we shall only irritate the sullen fury of certain formidable critics" (5:195).[38] On November 16 he reviewed a new production of *Antony and Cleopatra*, complaining of the alterations made in Shakespeare's text, especially the attempt to superimpose on it "the forced mechanical style and architectural dialogue" of Dryden's *All for Love* (5:192). And on December 8 he wrote a perfunctory article on the new *Love in a Village* at Covent Garden, much of it devoted to praise of Miss Stephens (19:194).

Yet he did not confine himself to dramatic criticism. On October 28 he replied to a note in the *Edinburgh Review* on the character of Baron Grimm: literary men, he stated, seem "indifferent" only because "our feelings become more ideal; the impression of the moment is less violent, but the effect is more general and permanent" (4:135). On November 13 he wrote a laudatory review of Madame de Staël's *De l'Allemagne* (19:5–9). He continued to turn out political articles too, roused to action by Lord Liverpool's suggestion in Parliament that England seek an honorable peace with Napoleon. When "Vetus" [Edward Sterling] of the *Times* objected, demanding that the French forces be crushed, Hazlitt replied in a series of six impassioned articles between November 19 and January 5, deploring the

---

announce to you the opening of a very large Methodist Chapel at Bath. On the front of this building is inscribed, *Deo Sacrum*, in capitals. I wish to be informed what they mean by *Deo*. Do they mean the One Father of all, or do they mean Jesus Christ, contrary to his own declaration? Or do they mean Trinity, according to the idolatrous doctrine of the Church of Rome, and of some other churches?" (*Monthly Repository* 11 [1816]:649). For other letters by Hazlitt see 9 (1814):232–4, 330–31, 401–3; 10 (1815):29, 525–26; 11 (1816):69–70, 331, 200–201; 12 (1817):22–23, 223–24, 410, 681; 13 (1818):46, 616–17; 15 (1820):434. During the same period there were also letters in the *Repository* from another WH, who dated his correspondence first from Exeter and then from Dukinfield. They continued after the death of the Reverend Mr. Hazlitt in 1820.

38. In his essay "On Patronage and Puffing," Hazlitt wrote of his first review: "When I got back, after the play, Perry called out, with his cordial, grating voice, 'Well, how did she do?' and on my speaking in high terms, answered that 'he had been to dine with his friend the Duke, that some conversation had passed on the subject, he was afraid it was not the thing, it was not the true *sostenuto* style; but as I had written the article' (holding my peroration on the Beggar's Opera carelessly in his hand) 'it might pass!' I could perceive that the rogue licked his lips at it, and had already in imagination 'bought golden opinions of all sorts of people' by this very criticism, and I had the satisfaction the next day to meet Miss Stephens coming out of the Editor's room, who had been to thank him for his very flattering account of her" (8:293).

tactics of men who value "exclusive patriotism" above peace (7:33–34, 39–72). On December 1, certainly with Vetus in mind, he wrote a bitter "character" of "The Political Automaton" as a *"thing . . .* hired to soothe or inflame the public mind, as occasion requires; [which] succeeds in misleading the ignorant by a voluntary abuse of terms and an unlimited command over the figures of speech." "Its only principle," he charged, "is to make itself subservient to the will of its employer" (19:117). And five days later he jeered at a paragraph in the *Times* probably written by Vetus's employer, Hazlitt's brother-in-law Dr. Stoddart, urging that Wellington come to terms with those Frenchmen who might wish "to exchange the bloody tyranny of Bonaparte for the mild paternal sway of a Bourbon" (7:30).

Hazlitt must have awakened one morning late in 1813 and realized that he was a journalist. It was a cold awakening. Neither he nor his contemporaries thought highly of the profession, and he disdained the recognition it brought him. "I had not till then been in the habit of writing at all," he observed in 1829, "or had been a long time about it; but I perceived that with the necessity, the fluency came. Something I did, *took;* and I was called upon to do a number of things all at once. I was in the middle of the stream, and must sink or swim" (11:288).

Yet this new career was ideally adapted to his talents: his incisive mind, his quick impulsive temper, his fluency—which he already had, regardless of what he might say—all enabled him to turn out an article on literature or politics or morals or the theater—and presently on art—in rapid, masterful fashion. His confidence in first impressions helped too; for just as, at the Louvre, he had found his preliminary sketches superior to his finished paintings, so now he could send his first copy off to the printer with no qualms. Even his ingrained prejudices proved advantageous in journalism. Crabb Robinson, who saw him at the Lambs' on December 16, "disputed with him on politics" and, finding him "overbearing and rude," complained: "He mixes passion and ill-humour and personal feelings in his judgments on public events and characters more than any man I know, and this infinitely detracts from the value of his opinions, which, possessing as he does rare talents, would be otherwise very valuable. He always vindicates Buonaparte, not because he is insensible to his enormous crimes, but out of spite to the Tories of this country and the friends of the war of 1792. *Stulta in contraria currunt.*" [39] The Whig readers of the *Chronicle* did not resent his "spite to the Tories of this country"; when expressed in his forceful manner, it made for very lively reading. But Hazlitt himself and his foes—including

39. Robinson, 1:133.

some former friends—were in peril. It is dangerous to place a deadly weapon in the hands of an impulsive man. Hazlitt had such a weapon now, and he was a sure marksman.

During the early months of 1814 he contributed regularly to the *Chronicle*. In "On Patriotism—A Fragment," on January 5, he maintained that patriotism was not love of one's country (impossible in a nation of sixteen million people) but "little more than another name for the love of liberty, of independence, of peace, and social happiness" (4:68). In a review of Southey's *Carmen Triumphale, for the Commencement of the Year 1814*, on the eighth, he observed ironically that the new laureate "is the last man whom we should expect to see graceful in fetters" (7:25). Then on the eleventh, describing a play in which the clown Grimaldi sang a duet with a love-sick oyster, he declared that Southey's cheerful approval of the Bourbons was equally absurd (19:118). And in the issues for the twenty-first and twenty-seventh he denounced the Tory newspapers' insistence on crushing Napoleon and restoring the Bourbons and even defended Vetus when the *Times* silenced him for opposing restoration of the Bourbons (7:27–28, 34–39; 19:118–20).

Quite different were the "Fragments on Art: Why the Arts are not Progressive," which appeared in the *Chronicle* for January 11 and 15 with the challenging thesis: "What is mechanical, reducible to rule, or capable of demonstration, is progressive, and admits of gradual improvement: what is not mechanical or definite, but depends on genius, taste, and feeling, very soon becomes stationary or retrograde, and loses more than it gains by transfusion" (18:5–6). It was a variant of an argument often used in the old controversy of the Ancients versus the Moderns, and it attracted little attention stuck, as it were, into the corner of a morning newspaper. But it was a significant essay, for Hazlitt here declared his belief that great art springs not from careful craftsmanship but from an inner power. "There is a strength in the imagination," he declared, "that reposes entirely on nature, which nothing else can supply" (18:9).

He made another significant contribution in January: his notice of Edmund Kean's London debut on the twenty-sixth. "I went to see him the first night of his appearing in Shylock," he wrote in 1818. "I remember it well. The boxes were empty, and the pit not half full: 'some quantity of barren spectators and idle renters were thinly scattered to make a show.' The whole presented a dreary, hopeless aspect. I was in a considerable apprehension for the result. From the first scene in which Mr. Kean came on, my doubts were at an end. I had been told to give as favourable an account as I could; I gave a true one" (5:174–75). He assured his readers that "no actor has come out for many years at all equal to him," and he prophesied that Kean would be even more successful in other, more spirited parts (5:179–80). Then on February 2, after watching Kean play Shylock again: "It is not saying too much of him, though it is saying a great deal, that he has all that Mr. Kemble *wants* of perfection" (5:180). Hazlitt was, in fact, so taken with Kean's original interpretations and his dependence on passion rather than technique that he became his staunch supporter. Here was an actor who used his imagination! In the weeks ahead he lauded Kean's interpretations of Richard III, Hamlet, Othello, Iago, Macbeth, Romeo, and Luke (in an adaptation of Philip Massinger's *City Madam*), virtually ignoring all other actors except for purposes of comparison. It was rumored that Hazlitt had been paid £1500 by the management of Drury Lane to champion Kean, and he was credited with having saved the theater from financial ruin. "Perry was continually at me as other people were at him," Hazlitt wrote, "and was afraid it would not last. It was to no purpose. I said it *would last*" (8:293).⁴⁰ In fact he did a good deal to make it last.

Not all Hazlitt's contributions to the *Chronicle* were new and fresh: he quickly learned an old trick of the trade, the scissors-and-paste trick. And he used it to his own advantage in a long discussion, in four installments published between February 3 and April 8, of the "Account of German Philosophy and Literature" in Madame de Staël's *De l'Allemagne*. It consisted almost wholly of passages, often only slightly relevant, concerning the philosophy of Bacon, Hobbes, and Locke lifted from his lectures on English philosophy (20:12–36).

Meanwhile he branched out into art criticism: four articles (February 5 and 10 and May 7 and 10) reviewing paintings at the British Institution (18:10–16 and 21–24); one (May 3) on those at the Royal Academy (18:17–19); and a two-part critique (May 4 and 14) of his friend Haydon's painting *The Judgment of Solomon* (18:19–21).⁴¹ He continued his political

40. In a footnote Hazlitt added: "I cannot say how in this respect it might have fared if a Mr. M——, a fat gentleman, who might not have 'liked yon lean and hungry Roscius,' had continued in the theatrical department of Mr. Perry's paper at the time of this actor's first appearance; but I had been put upon this duty just before, and afterwards Mr. M——'s *spare* talents were not in much request. This, I believe, is the reason why he takes pains every now and then to inform the readers of the *Courier* that it is impossible for any one to understand a word that I write" (8:293 n.). "Mr. M——" was, of course, William Mudford.

41. Haydon later complained that Hazlitt "abused the picture in his spitish humour" when he first saw it exhibited; "but in coming round he met me, and holding out his two cold fingers with, 'By God, sir, it is a victory,' went away and wrote a capital crit-

articles, denouncing the *Courier* (February 26) and the *Times* (March 24) for their insistence on unconditional surrender of Napoleon and the capture of Paris (19:120–28).

But the abdication of Napoleon on April 6 left him speechless. Crabb Robinson wrote in his diary on the twenty-ninth: "Lamb says that Hazlitt is confounded by the conduct of Buonaparte; he is ashamed to show his face. He had but a little before the catastrophe told Lamb that *he* did not admire him on account of his infinite littleness." [42]

Before long James Perry realized that, with all his talent, Hazlitt was a dubious asset to the *Chronicle*. "I was generally sent out of the way," Hazlitt recalled in his essay "On Patronage and Puffing," "when any *debutant* had a friend at court, and was to be tenderly handled. For the rest, or those of robust constitutions, I had *carte blanche* given me. Poor Perry! what complaints he used to make, that by *running-a-muck* at lords and Scotchmen I should not leave him a place to dine out at!" (8:292). Hazlitt was prolix, too, as well as indiscreet. Mary Russell Mitford remembered "the doleful visage with which Mr. Perry used to . . . execrate 'the d——d fellow's d——d stuff' for filling up so much of the paper in the very height of the advertisement season. I shall never forget his long face. It was the only time of day that I ever saw it either long or sour." [43] On one occasion, reported by Robinson, Perry "called on Hazlitt one evening to answer on the spot an article or speech about the liberty of the Press. Hazlitt wrote one, he says not a good one. Perry looked it over. 'This is the most pimping thing I ever read. If you cannot do a thing of this kind off-hand you won't do for me.'" [44]

In May Perry decided that the *Chronicle* could dispense with Hazlitt. Robinson recorded Hazlitt's account of the incident:

> Perry said to him expressly that he wished Hazlitt to *look out for another* situation— the affronting language Hazlitt could not easily forget—as he was not fit for a reporter. Hazlitt said he thought he could do miscellaneous things. Perry said he would think of it. However, when Hazlitt afterwards went to the office for his salary

icism in the *Morning Chronicle.* / What a singular compound this man was of malice, candour, cowardice, genius, purity, vice, democracy and conceit" (Elwin, p. 200). But Haydon was out of sorts with Hazlitt when he made the charge, and it may have been exaggerated.

42. Robinson, 1:142. Evidently Hazlitt meant that Lamb was too small-minded to be able to appreciate Napoleon's greatness.

43. *Life of Mary Russell Mitford*, ed. Alfred Guy L'Estrange, 3 vols. (London, 1870), 2:47–48 (hereafter cited as L'Estrange).

44. Robinson, 1:154.

he was told Mr. Perry wished to speak to him. He went to Perry's room. Perry was not alone, and desired Hazlitt to wait. Hazlitt went to another room. Perry then seeing Hazlitt there, went out of the house. Hazlitt, in consequence, never called again. As there [was] no express refusal either to pay or to accept his services in another way than as a reporter, Perry has an excuse for saying he did not dismiss Hazlitt.[45]

According to Miss Mitford, Perry was piqued by "a very masterly but damaging critique [by Hazlitt] on Sir Thomas Lawrence, whom Mr. P., as one whom he visited and was being painted by, chose to have praised." [46] But undoubtedly the basic reason for Hazlitt's discharge, as he told Robinson, was the abdication of Napoleon, "by which . . . my articles were made in the event very unfortunate." [47]

Of course Hazlitt was resentful. "He complains bitterly of Perry's treatment of him," Robinson wrote, "and I believe his statement, for he is too proud and high-minded to lie. He says that during the last six months he wrote seventy columns for the *Chronicle*, that Perry himself confessed to him that Hazlitt's had done more for the paper than all the other writings, and in consequence of his approbation of what Hazlitt had done, advanced him a £100, of which £50 are due." "It is quite painful," he added, "to witness the painful exertions for a livelihood which Hazlitt is condemned to make. And how strongly it shows that a modicum of mechanical marketable talent outweighs an ample endowment of original thought, and the highest powers of intellect, when a man does not add to that endowment the other of making it turn to account. How many men are there connected with newspapers who live comfortably without a tithe of Hazlitt's powers as a writer!" [48]

Thanks to his friendship with the Hunts, Hazlitt had other resources, and he was soon writing for two weekly papers, the Hunts' *Examiner* and John Scott's *Champion*. Even before Napoleon's abdication he had placed in the *Champion* for April 3 an incendiary article "On the Late War" which Perry had rejected; in it he branded the war with France as an attempt

45. Ibid., pp. 153–54. Hazlitt always considered that he had been discharged. In 1823, when a foe referred to him as a "discarded servant" of the *Times*, Hazlitt replied that he had been discharged from the *Morning Chronicle*, but not from the *Times* (20:143).

46. L'Estrange, 2:48. The critique of Lawrence was undoubtedly Hazlitt's statement that Lawrence's portrait of Lord Castlereagh in the Royal Academy Exhibition of 1814 "is not a likeness. It has a smug, smart, upstart, haberdasher look" (18:18).

47. Robinson, 1:154. In a later essay "On the Qualifications Necessary to Success in Life" Hazlitt remarked that he had been discharged because his slouching manner and careless dress offended Perry (12:204–6). He did not, however, bear a grudge against Perry; in fact he spoke well of him on several occasions (e.g., 3:94; 16:223–24, and 18: introduction).

48. Robinson, 1:153–54.

to crush all liberalism (7:72–77). Then on May 22, five days after his last article appeared in the *Chronicle*, he published in the *Examiner* an essay "On Posthumous Fame," in which he first aired two theories which he was to recur to often in his future writing. He argued that Shakespeare's ability to enter into his characters was proof of a lack of egotism which made him careless of eventual fame—and that true genius springs from inspiration rather than effort exerted in a conscious quest for fame (4:21–24). He was, perhaps, showing Leigh Hunt that, given the opportunity, he could produce literary criticism that was as penetrating—and as readable—as any then appearing.

By June he was contributing regularly to both the *Champion* and the *Examiner*. For the *Champion* he acted as art critic; between June and October he wrote temperate criticisms of the paintings of Benjamin West (18:28–34), Richard Wilson (18:24–28), and Gainsborough (18:34–37), then followed up with three articles on the topic "The Fine Arts: Whether They Are Promoted by Academies and Public Institutions," in which he developed his theory, expressed in the *Chronicle* in January, that the arts are not "progressive" (18:37–51). But he showed much more enthusiasm for Hogarth's *Marriage à la Mode*, which he discussed in two articles in the *Examiner* in June; there was a life and a liveliness about Hogarth's paintings that delighted him: "He gives the extremes of character and expression, but he gives them with perfect truth and accuracy" (4:28). Not so the last opera of the season, which he reviewed in the *Examiner* for August 14; "without the aid of luxurious pomp," he asked, "what can there be to interest in this merely artificial vehicle of show, and dance, and song, which is purposely constructed so as to lull every effort of the understanding and feeling of the heart in the soft, soothing effeminacy of sensual enjoyment?" (5:196). On July 24 he reported his impressions of Kean's playing of Iago, which he found "not grave enough" (5:212). He continued his discussion in the issue of August 7, insisting that Iago represents not "absolute malignity, but a want of moral principle" (5:215). Then when Thomas Barnes, the regular dramatic critic for the *Examiner*, objected, he replied in a third article on September 11 (18:200–204). Somehow the *Examiner* seemed to bring out the best in him; his critical faculties were sharpening, he was learning what it was that he demanded of literature and art: that they offer a convincing picture of life heightened and animated by the artist's imagination.

He ventured into political commentary only once during these months— in "Prince Maurice's Parrot," a short, ironic treatment of some remarks about the slave trade made by Talleyrand at the Congress of Vienna. But he was so pleased with it that he published it in both the *Examiner* for July 3 and the *Champion* for September 18 (7:77–79).

Yet one of Hazlitt's critical efforts of this period was to bring him lasting distress: "The Character of Mr. Wordsworth's New Poem The Excursion," which appeared in the issues of the *Examiner* for August 21 and 28 and October 2. Even before it was written, it involved him in trouble. Because he had no copy of the poem, he persuaded Martin Burney to borrow Lamb's for him, knowing that Lamb had promised to review it for the *Quarterly*. Then he kept it so long that Lamb's review missed its deadline. On September 19 Lamb wrote to Wordsworth: "The unlucky reason of the detention of the Excursion was, Hazlitt and we having a misunderstanding. He blowed us up about 6 months ago, since when the union hath snapt." [49] Lamb was understandably annoyed; even he could not keep his patience with a man who accused him of "infinite littleness" in April and embarrassed him by failing to return a loan in September. But Lamb's resentment was mild compared with what lay ahead.

In many ways Hazlitt's review said a good deal in favor of Wordsworth and his poem. "In power of intellect," he began, "in lofty conception, in the depth of feeling, at once simple and sublime, which pervades every part of it and which gives to every object an almost preternatural and preterhuman interest, this work has seldom been surpassed" (19:9). [50] At the same time, however, he complained of Wordsworth's "intellectual egotism," his "ambiguous illustrations" of his principles, and his observations on Voltaire and the French Revolution. But the real damage was done in the third installment, on October 2, when, after observing that Wordsworth was a poet of sentiment rather than the imagination, Hazlitt launched into a tirade against the country people whom Wordsworth professed to admire.

"The conclusion of Hazlitt's Critique is come to us," Wordsworth's wife wrote to his sister Dorothy on October 29,

> —a curious piece, but it must benefit the sale of the book. You will be amused greatly at the abuse he levies at the Mountaineers—he says "all country People hate each other" and these more than others, and he gives the reason why and is confirmed in his opinions by the Poet who lets it out now and then—then he declaims against the Poverty of the country,—That *nothing good* is to be got—speaks of the want of every

49. *Lamb Letters*, 2:137.

50. Hazlitt later claimed (9:6) Wordsworth had been angry when he learned that Hazlitt had reviewed his poem favorably. Howe (p. 156) suggests that Hazlitt may have been annoyed when he read *The Excursion* because Wordsworth had modeled his Solitary after Joseph Fawcett. However, his evidence is dubious and dates from a later period.

thing that is intellectual and elegant, enumerates these wants, and amongst the items courtezans are found. A pretty comment upon these opinions would be to relate the study of the critics departure for [from?] this unaccommodating country.[51]

On November 11 Dorothy wrote to Mrs. Thomas Clarkson: ". . . amongst other evils he has the audacity to complain that there are no Courtesans to be found in the country."[52] She did not repeat the story of the critic's departure from the Lake District—but her brother was not so scrupulous. On December 28 Lamb replied to a recent letter from Wordsworth: "The ''scapes' of the great god Pan who appeared among your mountains some dozen years hence, and his narrow chance of being submerged by the swains, afforded me much pleasure. I can conceive the water nymphs pulling for him. He would have been another Hylas. W. Hylas."[53] But Wordsworth did not share his amusement.

During the last months of 1814 Hazlitt, unaware that trouble was brewing, continued his regular work for the *Champion* and the *Examiner*. For the *Champion* he wrote both dramatic and art criticism, still centering his attention in his dramatic critiques on the career of Edmund Kean. On October 9 he complained that Kean's playing of Richard III seemed to have suffered as a result of his stay in Ireland: "His pauses are twice as long as they were, and the rapidity with which he hurries over other parts of the dialogue is twice as great as it was. In both these points, his style of acting always bordered on the very verge of extravagance; and we suspect it has at present passed the line" (5:201). On November 13 he remarked that Kean's Macbeth was not sufficiently distinguished from his Richard III, pointing out that "the subtlety and nice discrimination" of Shakespeare's characters was one of the most remarkable facets of his genius (5:204). Meanwhile, on October 16 he had found a new favorite in Eliza O'Neill, then making her debut as Juliet. He reported at first that, "more than any late actress, [she] reminded us in certain passages, and in a faint degree, of Mrs. Siddons" (5:199); and by November 6, after she had played in *Venice Preserved* and Garrick's *Isabella*, he pronounced her "by far the most impressive tragic actress we have seen since Mrs. Siddons" (18:196). However, when Kean and Miss O'Neill played opposite each other in *Romeo and Juliet* just after the turn of the year, he was disappointed: Kean's "force of passion" and Miss O'Neill's "sensibility" were both affecting, but each fell short of

51. *Letters of Mary Wordsworth*, ed. Mary E. Burton (Oxford: Clarendon Press, 1958), p. 24.
52. *Letters of William and Dorothy Wordsworth: The Middle Years*, 2:607.
53. *Lamb Letters*, 2:146.

Mrs. Siddons, who, "in a wonderful manner, united both the extremes of acting here spoken of" (5:211).

In one article, his review of Miss O'Neill's debut, Hazlitt let fall some indiscreet personal remarks. Of William Augustus Conway, who played Romeo, he wrote: "There is, we suppose, no reason why this preposterous phenomenon should not be at once discarded from the stage, but for the suppressed titter of secret satisfaction which circulates through the dress-boxes whenever he appears. Why does he not marry?" (5:404).[54] But the bulk of Hazlitt's dramatic criticism for the *Champion* was devoted to per-cipient—though highly subjective—interpretations of Shakespeare's charac-ters. Yet his review of the Kean–O'Neill *Romeo and Juliet* on January 8, 1815, was the last that he wrote for that paper.

His most substantial contribution in art criticism to the *Champion* was the series of six articles on Sir Joshua Reynolds which ran from October 30 to January 8. In the first two, "Character of Sir Joshua Reynolds" (October 30 and November 6), he analyzed the artist's strengths and weaknesses as a painter with particular attention to his weaknesses, which, he believed, had been too often ignored. Sir Joshua was, he declared, "perhaps the most original imitator that ever appeared in the world" (18:53); he "did not possess either that high imagination or those strong feelings, without which no painter can become a poet in his art" (18:58).

In the four essays which followed Hazlitt considered Reynolds's *Discourses*, "the general merit of [which] is so well established that it would be needless to enlarge on it here" (18:62). Again he concentrated on Reynolds's shortcomings; he believed that the *Discourses* had too long been blindly venerated, when in truth, as he wrote in the first of the four essays (Novem-ber 27), "the rules . . . laid down, as general and comprehensive maxims, are in fact founded on a set of half principles, which are true only as far as they imply a negation of the opposite errors, but contain in themselves the germ of other errors just as fatal: which, if strictly and literally understood, cannot be defended, and which by being taken in an equivocal sense, of course leave the student as much to seek as ever" (18:62).

In "On Genius and Originality" (December 4) Hazlitt took issue with Reynolds's alleged belief "that genius and invention are principally shewn in borrowing the ideas, and imitating the excellences of others." On the contrary, he declared, "a work demonstrates genius exactly as it contains

54. When Hazlitt's criticism appeared in modified form in *A View of the English Stage* in 1818, Conway demanded—and received—a public apology from Hazlitt. See 5:404–5 and note the later use of the incident made in the *Blackwood's* article "Hazlitt Cross-Questioned," discussed below. See below p. 230 n.

what is to be found no where else, or in proportion to what we add to the ideas of others from our own stores, and not to what we receive from them" (18:64). Then after citing instance after instance to prove that great painters have shown most true genius when they have been most original, he concluded: "Sir Joshua, from his unwillingness to admit one extreme, has fallen into the other" (18:70); in stressing the need for industry he had overlooked the more valid claims of originality.

Similarly, in "On the Imitation of Nature" (December 25) Hazlitt maintained that Reynolds, in seeking to prove that *"the whole of art does not consist in copying nature,"* seemed "disposed to infer, that the whole of art consists in *not* imitating individual nature." To Hazlitt "the highest perfection of the art depends . . . on the union (as far as possible) of general truth and effect with individual distinctness and accuracy" (18:70). "The *gross* style," he declared, "consists in giving no details,—the *finical* in giving nothing else. . . . The union of both kinds of excellence, of strength with delicacy, as far as the limits of human capacity and the shortness of human life would permit, is that which has established the reputation of the greatest masters. Farther,—their most finished works are their best" (18:71). And again he cited the examples of great painters to prove his point, opposing to them the "slovenliness" of some contemporary painters and the "ineffectual microscopic finishing" of others. He applied his argument also to the area of expression: "Portrait-painting is the biography of the pencil, and he who gives most of the peculiarities and details, with most of the general character, —that is of *keeping*,—is the best biographer, and the best portrait-painter" (18:75).

The last essay in the series, "On the Ideal" (January 8, 1815), contested the principle that historical painting should be idealized rather than realistic. Hazlitt developed his point, curiously enough, by appealing to the practice of Hogarth, Fielding, and Shakespeare, all of whom blended the individual and the type in their characters. The same fusion prevailed, he added, in the Elgin marbles. And he concluded:

> If we are asked, then, what it is that constitutes historic expression or ideal beauty, we should answer, not (with Sir Joshua) abstract expression or middle forms, but consistency of expression in the one, and symmetry of form in the other.
>
> A face is historical, which is made up of consistent parts, let those parts be ever so peculiar or uncommon. Those details or peculiarities only are inadmissible in history, which do not arise out of any principle, or tend to any conclusion,—which are merely casual, insignificant, and unconnected,—which do not *tell*; that is, which either do not add to, or which contradict the general result,—which are not integrant parts of one whole, however strange or irregular that whole may be. (18:82)

Hazlitt's series may not strike a twentieth-century reader as revolutionary; he seems merely to be applying common sense to a set of half-truths perhaps deliberately exaggerated because Reynolds was addressing his remarks to students. Yet in 1814 a man needed courage to challenge the principles propounded by the most venerated of English painters—especially when that man had himself failed as a painter, was reduced to writing for the weekly newspapers, and had never before presumed to criticize more than an occasional painting or exhibition. His ideas were not as bold or original as he assumed, nor was he entirely fair when he treated Reynolds's theory and practice. Yet the series was important in Hazlitt's development, if not in that of criticism. He who had spent hours struggling to find "the true secret of Titian's golden hue & the oleaginous touches of Claude Lorraine" was convinced that the artist must exercise his own originality as well as study the masters, must try to combine the individual and the general, the real and the ideal. Although he had despaired of succeeding as a painter, his incisive mind went on questioning, analyzing, reaching for seasoned conclusions. In effect he believed that an artist could achieve greatness only if he tempered neoclassical dicta with Romantic individuality and close observation.[55]

Meanwhile, for the *Examiner*, Hazlitt was experimenting with a new kind of article. He titled them "Commonplaces," borrowing the heading from the series he had begun in the *Chronicle*, but they were essentially studies of human behavior, the subject which had long fascinated him. The first, "On Religious Hypocrisy" (October 9), dealt not so much with hypocrisy as with the self-deception and self-righteousness of devout people. "They see vice as an object always out of themselves," Hazlitt wrote, "with which they have no other concern than to denounce and stigmatise it. . . . They identify themselves with that perfect system of faith and morals, of which they are the professed teachers, and regard any imputation on their conduct as an indirect attack on the function to which they belong, or as compromising the authority under which they act" (4:129–30). The second (October 23) considered La Rochefoucauld's *Maxims*, charging that they, like Reynolds's *Discourses*, were based on half-truths, assuming, for example, that men are envious by nature when in truth "our admiration of others is stronger than our vanity" (20:41). The third (November 27), "On the Love of Nature," theorized that man's love of nature springs from associa-

55. For fuller discussions of Hazlitt's criticism of the *Discourses*, see Baker, pp. 272–82; C. H. Salter, "The First English Romantic Art Critics," *Cambridge Review* 78 (1956): 671–73; Eugene Clinton Elliott, "Reynolds and Hazlitt," *Journal of Aesthetics and Art Criticism* 21 (1962): 73–79; and Leonard M. Trawick, "Hazlitt, Reynolds, and the Ideal," *Studies in Romanticism* 4 (1964–65), 240–47.

tion of ideas "with the sports of our childhood, with air and exercise, with our feelings in solitude, when the mind takes the strongest hold of things, and clings with the fondest interest to whatever strikes its attention" (4:18), adding that, while our associations with persons are confined to the individual, our associations with objects extend to other objects of the same sort.[56]

On November 11 Crabb Robinson "read in court some of Hazlitt's articles in *Champion* and *Examiner*" and was moved to reflect: "How lamentable that so fine a writer should want a fit field for his exertions!"[57] Just six days later, when they met at the Lambs', Hazlitt had good news to report: he had "become an *Edinburgh* reviewer through the recommendation of Lady Mackintosh, who had sent to the *Champion* office to know the author of the articles on Institutions. Hazlitt sent those other writings to Jeffrey, and has been in a very flattering manner enrolled in the corps. This has put Hazlitt in good spirits; he now again has hopes that his talents will be appreciated, and become a subsistence to him."[58]

By mid-February Francis Jeffrey had accepted Hazlitt's first contribution, a review of Fanny Burney's new novel *The Wanderer*. Hazlitt was elated. "You need hardly be assured of the gratification I have felt in receiving your very obliging letter," he wrote to Jeffrey on February 15. As far as he was concerned, Jeffrey was free to revise the article as he saw fit "if you will be at the trouble of pruning its excrescencies." "The note about the Duke of Wellington I give up beforehand," he continued, "but I confess I should like to see his Majesty mounted *con amore*. But I know that I am somewhat 'splenetive & rash' & submit the whole to your decision." He seized eagerly on Jeffrey's suggestion that he review Sismondi's *De la Littérature du Midi de l'Europe:* "I will get Sismondi immediately. I should be glad to know whether you wish it for the next number of the review after the present one is out."[59] The next day he wrote again, suggesting further emendations which he "ought to have mentioned yesterday." He closed his letter cheerfully: "The coach is setting off, and I am going into the country for a few days to repose on the satisfaction which your letter has given me."[60]

56. Titled "On the Love of the Country" when reprinted in *The Round Table*.
57. Robinson, 1:153.
58. Ibid. As Stanley Jones has revealed ("Nine New Hazlitt Letters and Some Others," *Études Anglaises* 19 [1966]:264), an unpublished letter from Sir James Mackintosh to his wife dated November 16, 1814, suggests that "this recommendation is likely to have been more Hazlitt's idea than her own."
59. Baker, pp. 208–9. As Baker points out (p. 209 n.), Jeffrey discarded the note about the duke of Wellington, but respected Hazlitt's desire to retain the allusion to the king.
60. ALS [Autograph letter, signed], Yale University Library. Although I have

Hazlitt's review of *The Wanderer*, which appeared in the February issue of the *Edinburgh*, was a long, expansive, leisurely sort of essay surveying the history of the novel from Cervantes and LeSage through Richardson, Fielding, Smollett, and Sterne and praising them as "among the greatest ornaments and the best benefactors of our kind" (16:7). He could not say as much for contemporary novelists; with George III "constantly mounted on a great War-horse" people have paid too little attention to the novel. As for *The Wanderer*, Hazlitt dismissed its author as "a mere common observer of manners,—and also a very woman" (16:21). Obviously Hazlitt was gaining confidence in his trade. To appear in the *Edinburgh* was itself an achievement after his months of writing for the weekly papers; he was probably only half-joking when he wrote three years later: "To be an Edinburgh Reviewer is, I suspect, the highest rank in modern literary society" (12:365). Still it was remarkable that he, a novice, dared to defend the popular novel not only as a source of entertainment but as a serious literary form.

For the time being he continued as art critic for the *Champion*. On January 22 he reviewed Lucien Bonaparte's collection of paintings, then on sale, pronounced it "in general mere trash," and added some characteristic remarks on the lifelessness of "the French style of painting" (18:84–89). On February 5, 12, and 19 he commented, without much enthusiasm, on the paintings displayed at the British Institution, observing that if each new exhibition seems less good than the previous year's, it is because art is not progressive (18:89–96). And on March 5 he offered a general critique of David Wilkie's paintings, distinguishing between his serious realistic approach to his subject and Hogarth's lively satire (18:96–100). But this proved to be his last contribution to the *Champion* for many months.

This time he probably resigned from his post voluntarily—in part because he resented John Scott's growing disapproval of Napoleon but primarily because he had, for the first time in his life, a sense of security and even hope for the future. He could virtually bank now on regular work for the *Examiner* and frequent commissions from the *Edinburgh Review*. And Jeffrey had proved far more generous than the London editors: he had paid him twenty-five pounds for the review of *The Wanderer* and had shown genuine understanding in editing his text. On April 20 Hazlitt wrote him: "I have not yet seen the Review, but I am quite satisfied of the propriety of the

---

examined all the Hazlitt letters at Yale, I have given Baker as my source (as in the preceding note) for all those which he printed in their entirety in his book.

alterations (for I am very sensible of my want of Discretion in these matters) & I am very glad to have got off so well in my first adventure. I intend to do better before long." He promised that his next review, of Sismondi's book, would be ready "in about six weeks, if that will do" and that he would "attend to your suggestions in manufacturing it." He offered also to work up articles on Rousseau, on Johann Spurzheim the phrenologist ("I . . . think I could 'carve him like a dish fit for the Gods'"), and on Castlereagh and the Congress of Vienna. "I am not very well read in the modern novelists," he added: "for in truth I hate to read new books, & my general rule is never to read a book that I have not read before." However, he was evidently willing to review even novels, if necessary, for he remarked immediately: "Of this practice I begin however to repent." And he concluded: "I have only to thank you once more for the frankness & liberality of your very obliging letter." [61] Soon afterward, in an undated letter, he asked Jeffrey's "approbation for doing between this & Christmas two articles, one of Scott's edition of Swift, containing a view of the Literature of Queen Anne, & the other of Buhle's history of modern philosophy." In his enthusiasm he suggested that "my friend Mr. Hunt" would also be interested in reviewing for the *Edinburgh*.[62] And in a letter of May 1 he offered once again to write a critique of Spurzheim and suggested in a postscript: "Perhaps Schlegel would make a future article. . . . I am afraid you will begin to think me an *undertaker* more than a critic." [63]

He had also found, in the *Examiner*, another new and congenial outlet for his talents. In January Leigh Hunt had inaugurated in his paper a new series, "The Round Table," to consist of informal essays on miscellaneous topics by himself and others. Hazlitt dropped his "Commonplaces" immediately and began writing for this new series. "Round Table, No. 3" (January 15), his first contribution, was an expanded version of the essay "On the Love of Life" which he had originally written for the *Morning Chronicle* for September 4, 1813 (4:1–4). "Round Table, No. 7" (February 12), "On Classical Education," [64] was an expanded version of his "Commonplace" by the same title originally published in the *Chronicle* for September 25, 1813 (4:4–6). In the ninth and thirteenth papers of the series, published

61. ALS, Yale University Library.

62. Ibid. Baker (p. 209 n.) points out that Hazlitt seems to have submitted a review of Johann Gottlieb Bühle's book—and in 1822 asked Jeffrey to return it if he could locate it.

63. ALS, Yale University Library.

64. The Round Table essays in the *Examiner* appeared without titles. The titles now assigned to them were first listed in the index to the published volume.

in the *Examiners* for February 26 and April 9, he presented a lively essay in two parts restating his theory of the natural disinterestedness of the human mind—with an apology "for having thus plunged our readers all at once into the middle of metaphysics" (20:51). This time, however, he expressed his theory in highly readable form and added to it a glowing avowal of his delight in "metaphysics" which included a retelling of the story of the monkey and the coconuts which he had used to conclude his lecture series (20:51–52).

Gradually Hazlitt was venturing into the personal essay. And he practically admitted it in "Round Table, No. 10: On the Tatler," which appeared in the *Examiner* for March 5, the date of Hazlitt's last contribution to the *Champion*. It was a tribute to the most personal of all personal essayists then in print, a spirited article expressing the heretical notions that the *Tatler* was superior to the *Spectator*, Steele to Addison, originality to artificiality, and pathos to "moral dissertations and critical reasonings" (4:7–10). He had concluded, in effect, that popular appeal need not mar the literary merits of an essay or novel; it might even enhance them.

Yet his improved prospects had not sweetened his temper: he could be as abrasive as ever in company. On February 5, after dining with him at Thomas Alsager's house, Crabb Robinson remarked in his diary that "while he continued sober, [he] was excellent company." He was obviously in a quarrelsome mood though: he "abused Goethe for writing expressly on the principle of producing no effect"; he "became warm on politics and declaimed against the friends of liberty for their apostacy"; he refused to concede that there was as "great danger from the recent and unestablished tyranny of Buonaparte as from that of ancient governments"; he even "attacked" Robinson himself, "but was at the same time civil." [65] By the time they met again at Alsager's on April 15 Napoleon had returned from Elba, and Hazlitt was in a better frame of mind. Yet to Robinson he seemed "wrong as well as offensive in almost all he said. When pressed, he does not deny what is bad in the character of Buonaparte. And yet he triumphs and rejoices in the late events." [66] Later, when the conversation shifted to Wordsworth, "Hazlitt said in his ferocious way . . . that 'if Lamb in his criticism had found but one fault with Wordsworth he would never have forgiven him.'" [67]

Early in May, Wordsworth arrived in London for a visit. He and Hazlitt

---

65. Robinson, 1:161.   66. Ibid., p. 164.

67. Ibid., p. 166. Robinson records the remark in his entry for May 9, but notes that Hazlitt made the statement at Alsager's.

did not meet; since the *Examiner* review of *The Excursion* Wordsworth had
more reason than ever to avoid him. On Sunday, June 11, the poet called on
Leigh Hunt "to thank me," as Hunt put it, "for the zeal I had shown in
advocating the cause of his genius." [68] Hunt was embarrassed. Had Wordsworth seen that morning's *Examiner?* No, he had not.

When Wordsworth consulted the paper, he found no article about his
poetry. But tucked away in a section known as the "Theatrical Examiner"
was a quite gratuitous insult. For the past three months Hazlitt had been
writing occasional dramatic criticism[69] for the *Examiner*, and on the eleventh
he reviewed a production of Milton's *Comus*. Toward the end of his article
he declared,

> *We* have no less respect for the memory of Milton as a patriot than as a poet. Whether
> he was a *true* patriot, we shall not enquire: he was at least a *consistent* one. He did not
> retract his defence of the people of England; he did not say that his sonnets to Vane
> or Cromwell were meant ironically; he was not appointed Poet-Laureat to a Court
> which he had reviled and insulted; he accepted neither place nor pension; nor did
> he write paltry sonnets upon the "Royal fortitude" of the House of Stuart, by which,
> however, they really lost something.

And lest anyone might miss his intent he added in a footnote: "In the last
edition of the works of a modern Poet, there is a Sonnet to the King, com-
plimenting him on 'his royal fortitude.' The story of the Female Vagrant,
which very beautifully and affectingly describes the miseries brought on the
lower classes by war, in bearing which the said 'royal fortitude' is so nobly
exercised, is very properly struck out of the collection" (5:233).

Four days later Crabb Robinson called at Wordsworth's lodgings. They
discussed Hazlitt and the "malignant attack on Wordsworth by him in
Sunday's *Examiner*," and Wordsworth explained "his coolness towards
Hazlitt": "It appears that Hazlitt, when at Keswick, narrowly escaped
....." [70] And so the old story of Hazlitt's disgrace was repeated. Presently
Wordsworth told it again—apparently without any pledge of secrecy—to
Benjamin Haydon.[71] It was too good a story to keep to one's self, and it
must have passed from one person to another—and, sooner or later, back to
Hazlitt at a time when he was in no mood for raillery. For some time many

68. *Autobiography of Leigh Hunt*, pp. 253–54.
69. See 5:221–30.
70. Robinson, 1:169.
71. Wordsworth wrote to John Scott on June 11, 1816: "Haydon will tell you something about my quondam connection with Hazlitt, & how it was broken off" (*TLS*, 27
December 1941, p. 660).

of his oldest friends had resented his vehement allegiance to Napoleon. And just four weeks earlier Captain Burney had written that, because of Hazlitt's review of sister Fanny's *Wanderer*, he must insist on "the termination of our acquaintance." [72] On June 17 the two men were at a party at Lamb's house. "They did not speak," Crabb Robinson reported. "Hazlitt looked wild and uncomfortable." [73]

The following day dealt Hazlitt one of the harshest blows he had ever suffered. It was the day of Napoleon's downfall at Waterloo.

72. G. E. Manwaring, *My Friend the Admiral* (London: G. Routledge and Sons, Ltd., 1931), p. 250.
73. Robinson, 1:170.

CHAPTER VII

Good Hater
(1815–1816)

Hazlitt was stunned when he heard the news of Napoleon's downfall. "It is not to be believed," Haydon wrote in his autobiography, "how the destruction of Napoleon affected him; he seemed prostrated in mind and body: he walked about unwashed, unshaved, hardly sober by day, and always intoxicated by night, literally, without exaggeration, for weeks."[1] He had very little company in his misery; Crabb Robinson wrote: "Godwin, [Capell] Lofft, and Thelwall are the only three persons I know (except Hazlitt) who grieve at the late events."[2] Most Englishmen hailed Waterloo as a blessed deliverance, but to Hazlitt it spelt the death of the cause of human freedom in his time. He could talk of nothing else; he even argued at length with Haydon's model Salmon, who had fought against Napoleon in Spain and regretted that he had missed Waterloo—"but Sammons was proof, and always maintained the Duke [of Wellington] was the better man."[3]

During the last two weeks in June, Hazlitt wrote little or nothing. His brief critique of *The Beggar's Opera* in the *Examiner* for the eighteenth (4:65–66) and his lengthy review of Sismondi's *De la Littérature du Midi de l'Europe* in the June *Edinburgh* had probably both been written before Waterloo. The first was merely an expanded version of the review which he

1. Elwin, pp. 249–50. Despite Haydon's disclaimer, his statement may well be exaggerated. Yet Talfourd (2:170) described Hazlitt as "staggering under the blow of Waterloo" when he first met him in 1815.

2. *Diary, Reminiscences, and Correspondence of Henry Crabb Robinson*, ed. Thomas Sadler, 3 vols. (Boston and New York, 1898), 1:315–16 (hereafter cited as Sadler).

3. Elwin, p. 256.

had written for the *Chronicle* in October, 1813; the second fell short of his usual level. He quoted long excerpts from Sismondi's book, regretted that he too often relied on "French rules and German systems of criticism" (16:24), and warmed to his task only when he seized the occasion to compare the work of storytellers like Ariosto, Spenser, and Chaucer.

But he could not afford to stay idle long. And since Hunt was putting all his efforts into political articles, Hazlitt substituted for him as dramatic critic for the *Examiner*. He continued to follow Kean's career attentively, praising his "admirable comic talents" as Leon in Beaumont and Fletcher's *Rule a Wife*, though judging it inferior to Kemble's earlier interpretation of the part (5:233–34). And in the following months he found little to praise in the London theater. It was a poor season, apparently, and Hazlitt was in no mood to sit through plays of slight merit. His comments on them were usually perfunctory; even revivals of *The Tempest*, *As You Like It*, *Richard III*, *Tartuffe*, and his old favorite *School for Scandal* proved disappointing, and he was roused to enthusiasm only by the young Fanny Kelly (5:243–47) and by a revival of *The Beggar's Opera* (5:254–56). Kean as Bazajet in Rowe's *Tamerlane* was effective (18:205–7), but as Duke Aranza in John Tobin's *The Honey-Moon* he revealed "an infinite variety of talent, with a certain monotony of genius"; there was too much of Richard III in every part he played (5:263). Miss O'Neill pleased him less than she had earlier: she seemed to be trying, unwisely, to imitate Kean's energetic style (5:261–62). Or was it simply that Hazlitt was in a captious frame of mind?

During the summer he gradually resumed writing essays for the Round Table series, which Hunt had practically abandoned because of his concern with politics. Taking advantage of the elbow room offered by such a series, Hazlitt ranged from literary criticism to religion to his favorite topic of human behavior. In nos. 15 and 16 (August 6 and 20) he analyzed Milton's *Lycidas* and his versification, concluding that, despite Dr. Johnson's charges, he was an original and unaffected poet (4:31–41). In no. 26 (November 26) he praised Shakespeare's variety of characterization in *Midsummer Night's Dream* (4:61–64). No. 28 (December 24) consisted of a series of parallel passages of poetry, including one from Wordsworth with the comment: "We have been urged several times to take up the subject of Mr. Wordsworth's Poems, in order to do them justice. In doing this, we should satisfy neither his admirers nor his censurers. We have once already attempted the thankless office, and it did not succeed" (20:68). His comments on religion focused on nonconformist religion, which clearly tried his patience. "On the

Tendency of Sects," no. 19 (September 10), was summed up in the opening sentence: "There is a natural tendency in sects to narrow the mind" (4:47). "Of John Buncle," no. 20 (September 17), however, praised the vigor of Thomas Amory's "Unitarian romance" (4:51–57). But no. 22, "On the Causes of Methodism" (October 22), deplored the hypocrisy of this "most pitiful set" (4:57–61). Another pair of essays, nos. 17 and 18 (August 27 and September 3), stressed the importance of a person's "manner" in his relations with others—and, incidentally, chided Wordsworth for complaining about the indolence of a band of gypsies when he himself had recommended "a wise passiveness" (4:45 n.).[4] Yet no. 27, "On the Doctrine of Philosophical Necessity" (December 10), began with a quotation from "Tintern Abbey," followed by the words: "Perhaps the doctrine of what has been called philosophical necessity was never more finely expressed than in these lines of a poet, who, if he had written only half what he has done, would have deserved to be immortal" (20:60). Although Hazlitt was exercising his privilege of ranging widely in "The Round Table," Wordsworth seemed to be on his mind.

Most of his other work for the *Examiner* during these last months of 1815 was negligible: he reprinted two earlier essays from other periodicals[5] and wrote a brief article, "Chateaubriand—the Quack," damning the poet as a "political changeling" who had shifted his allegiance from Rousseau to Louis XVIII (19:128–29). But when a correspondent signing himself "Fair Play" objected to Hazlitt's interpretation, in this article, of Napoleon's execution of the duke d'Enghien, he replied in a series of four angry letters (September 24, October 8, November 19, and December 10) signed "Peter Pickthank" (19:129–50). His wrath at the enemies of Napoleon now boiled over, and he raged on for pages. He resented even his critic's use of the pseudonym "Fair Play":

> There is no such character nor no such thing. . . . Whoever supposes himself to be free from all bias or prejudice in questions of this kind is deficient in self-knowledge. . . . The cool, calculating, moderate patriotism which your Correspondent professes, will do very well to keep him on the safe side in opposition—from becoming obnoxious to persons of literal understandings and weak nerves, but it will not prevent him from being made a handle of by those who have the power and the will to go

4. Hazlitt would certainly have found Wordsworth's complaint annoying if he suspected that the poet had been addressing him in "The Tables Turned."

5. "On Modern Comedy," originally published in the *Chronicle* for September 25, 1813, was reprinted in the *Examiner* for August 20, 1815 (4:10–14); "Queries Relating to the Essay on Population," from the *Political Register* of November 24, 1810, appeared in the *Examiner* for October 29, 1815, as no. 23 of the Round Table series (7:357–61).

all lengths on the other side of the question, and who will be sure to convert his concessions of speculative and partial right into the means of practical and universal wrong. The cobwebs that entangle him will not stop them. The tide of corruption and oppression will not be stemmed by pretty speeches about purity and morality. The love of freedom is no match for the love of power, because the one is urged on by passion, while the other is in general the cold dictate of the understanding. (19:143–44)

Hazlitt published nothing at all in the *Edinburgh Review* during these months. Of all the topics he had suggested for articles, Jeffrey had singled out August Wilhelm von Schlegel's *Lectures on Dramatic Literature* and Hazlitt had gone directly to work on it, expecting to have it ready for the November issue of the magazine. But on November 20 he wrote that he had not finished his article because "circumstances absolutely prevented me." He hoped now to have it finished in two or three weeks.[6]

He must have been flattered and, to some extent, cheered when Macvey Napier of the *Edinburgh Review* staff invited him to write an article on fine arts for the proposed Supplement to the *Encyclopaedia Britannica*. Encouraged, Hazlitt approached Archibald Constable, publisher of the *Edinburgh*, to ask if he would consider bringing out a collection of his Round Table essays. When Constable reacted favorably, Hazlitt wrote to him on December 18, promising to "forward down to you half [of the] collection the latter end of the week" and enclosing a list of fifty essays to be included in the series and a contract empowering Constable and Messrs. Longman and Company, his London agents, to print a thousand copies of the book for fifty pounds.[7] Although he referred to himself in the letter as "a poor author," his prospects of making a decent living from his writing were improving.

Yet Hazlitt asked more of life than financial solvency, and the events of the year 1815—not only the defeat of Napoleon but the widespread poverty in England and the Castlereagh government's inhumane policies—enraged him. He chafed too at the kind of writing he was obliged to do; he still hoped to make his name as a philosopher rather than a writer of ephemeral trifles.

His unsettled state of mind did not make for serenity at the house on York Street. Life there grew increasingly disorderly. The maid Becky had left to work for the Lambs, and Sarah, pregnant for the sixth time in seven

6. Baker, p. 210.
7. See Jones, "Nine New Hazlitt Letters," pp. 263–77. As Jones points out, several of the essays listed in the letter had not yet been published.

years, had surrendered responsibility for the household to a Mrs. Tomlinson, a strong-minded woman who enjoyed displaying her authority upstairs and entertaining her soldier son-in-law below.[8] Hazlitt himself did not encourage order by his example, for he spent much of his time away from home, he adhered to his indolent habits, and he was drinking more than was good for him. All this must have built up resentment in Sarah, straining the tenuous bond that held them together. And it was not in Hazlitt's nature to be tolerant or understanding. In his essay "Education of Women" in the *Examiner* for February 12 he declared: "Women in general have no ideas, except personal ones. They are mere egotists. They have no passion for truth, nor any love of what is purely ideal. They hate to think, and they hate every one who seems to think of any thing but themselves. Everything is to them a perfect nonentity which does not touch their senses, their vanity, or their interest" (20:41). It does not sound like the remark of a zealous husband.

But beyond question Hazlitt doted on his son William, now four years old. One day when William Bewick was visiting the house, he heard a sound at the door, and presently little William came "creeping upon all fours." Hazlitt "jumped up from his seat, ran to him, and clasping his boy in his arms, hugged, and kissed, and caressed him, like some ardent loving mother with her first-born."[9] He must have found some relief from the anguish of the year 1815 when, on November 28, after two miscarriages, Sarah bore him a second son, named John.

Much of his time away from home was spent at the theater, now that he was reviewing plays regularly for the *Examiner*. But he found time, as always, for calls on his friends, though he must at times have been an unwelcome guest. Thomas Noon Talfourd described a typical evening at the Lambs', saying, "in *slouches* Hazlitt from the theatre, where his stubborn anger for Napoleon's defeat at Waterloo has been softened by Miss Stephens's angelic notes."[10] One night Lamb's brother John and Hazlitt fell to arguing over the subject of the coloring of Holbein's and Vandyke's paintings, and the elder Lamb became so annoyed that he knocked Hazlitt down. For once Hazlitt restrained his wrath: he got to his feet, shook hands with Lamb, and said, "I am a metaphysician, and do not mind a blow; nothing but an *idea* hurts *me*."[11]

8. *Memoirs*, 1:215–16.   9. Landseer, 1:118.

10. Talfourd, 2:122.

11. *Memoirs, Journals, and Correspondence of Thomas Moore*, ed. Lord John Russell, 8 vols. (London, 1853), 3:146. Cf. Robinson, 1:200, and *Haydon Diary*, 3:319–20.

He turned up regularly at Hunt's house, too, and at Haydon's studio. Both were hospitable men who gave merry parties, and Hazlitt must have joined in the merriment on occasion despite his testy mood. He could not have spent all his waking hours in a white rage; in fact, one day when Haydon stopped at York Street, he found him "arranging his hair before a glass, trying different effects, and asking my advice whether he should show his forehead more or less. In that large wainscotted room Milton had conceived, and perhaps written, many of his finest thoughts, and there sat one of his critics admiring his own features." [12]

He found frequent distraction in the game of fives, or rackets. From it he gained the exercise and relaxation that he had found in his long walks in the country, and he needed such relief just now. "It is," he wrote in 1819, "the finest exercise for the body, and the best relaxation for the mind. . . . He who takes to playing fives is twice young. He feels neither the past nor future 'in the instant'. . . . He has no other wish, no other thought, from the moment the game begins, but that of striking the ball, of placing it, of *making* it" (8:87). Having taken up the game, he determined to excel, of course, and threw all his energies into it. Friends marveled at his concentration; one of them described him as "a furious racket player," adding: "The whole of many, and the half of more days, were consumed in this amusement. The Fives Court . . . was the arena where he was then ambitious to figure; and rackets occupied almost his whole existence." [13] And later: "Hazlitt used to play at rackets for five or six hours at a time; sometimes quarreling with his adversary, but not bearing malice. He liked a stout antagonist. 'That fellow,' said he, speaking of one who showed himself disheartened, 'will never do any thing in the world; he never plays well, unless he is successful. If the chances go against him, he always misses the ball; he cries *Craven!*'" [14]

When Hazlitt asked William Bewick to come watch him play one day, Bewick was surprised,

as I had no idea of his skill in a game requiring so much physical exertion and activity. Besides, he would often lament his want of accomplishments of every kind. "Egad," he said, "he could do nothing like most men. There is Mrs. ——— plays exquisitely upon the flute; there is Mr. ——— sings his own songs, and accompanies himself upon the piano, will dash off a leader for a morning paper, or write an important note to the Secretary of State, whilst discoursing in a room full of company;

12. Elwin, p. 200.
13. *New Monthly Magazine* 29 (1830), pt. 2, pp. 473–74.
14. Ibid., p. 479.

and I could name many who thus possess genius and varied capacity, whilst I can literally do *nothing* nor ever could," &c. &c.

But he proved on the court that he did indeed excel at fives. Bewick looked on with interest, taking in every detail as Hazlitt struggled to win, then exulted in his victory, and finally showed his disregard for conventional appearances. Bewick's account, reflecting his artist's discerning eye, is the most vivid that survives of Hazlitt in action:

My friend, having stripped to his shirt, looked all alive, and being anxious to do his best, soon displayed himself not only an adept, but an original in his style of play. It was peculiar and characteristic of the man, and his sighs, groans, and lamentations left no doubt that he was becoming warm in the spirit of the game, and sad trouble he had to hitch up his trousers, it being his custom to be free of braces. He was the only one despoiled of his upper garments, so that I had no difficulty in following his rapid movements, and as his excitement warmed in the course of the game, so his exclamations became more vehement, and with his difficulties his ardour increased, until he lashed himself up to desperation, and looked more like a savage animal than anything human. The spectators below me appeared to be well aware of the ability and eccentricity of this hero of the game, as they peered forward to witness any extraordinary feat of play. When a difficult ball was driven to such a distance from him, and so skilfully dropped close to the wall, that it seemed an impossibility to come near it in time, or catch it with the racket if he did, he would run with desperate speed, make a last spring, and bending down his head to meet the concussion with the wall, crushing his hat flat over his eyes, dexterously tip the ball, sending it to its intended mark with unerring truth amid murmurs of applause. Then jerking himself upright again, his eye following the ball in its lightning speed, he would pursue it, however difficult the course. Thus he would repeat his feats of agility and success, excited all the while to a desperation and madness beyond belief. It is impossible to give an idea of his expressions. His ejaculations were interlarded with unintentional and unmeaning oaths that cannot be repeated, but may be imagined. In this way he would stamp and rave:—"Nothing but my incapacity,—sheer want of skill, of power, of physical ability,—of the Devil knows what! There again! Ever see such play? Egad, I'd better not take hold of the racket again if I do not do better. Ah! well, that is better, but still bad enough—sheer incapacity, egad!" And so he ran on all the time he played, so that the energies of mind and body were fretted and embittered. The frenzy of his irritability, although curious as characteristic, yet became, if not alarming, at least not pleasant to witness. And as he came occasionally to set his back against the post under me, and rub himself to and fro with the force of irascible impatience, repeating the exclamations to himself, I could not but wish that all might end well, and that the game might close in favour of my friend's party. Fortunately it was soon over, and, as I wished, William Hazlitt had won his game at tennis. I could perceive him in all the joyous triumph of boyish pleasure, stooping low, his racket in both hands, and, bounding from the ground, throw it high up to the roof, exclaiming to himself, "Hurrah! hurrah!" and as he waved his right arm over his head, catch with dexterity his falling racket, retiring with the satisfied beam of triumph in his face, to put on his coat and waistcoat.

Hazlitt came smiling with delight, and said, "Well, we had a hard run for it, but we beat after all." When we came to the street, he pointed to his cravat, and said to me with a somewhat mock servility,—"You see I am without my shirt; it was so wet with perspiration that I left it behind to get dried. You must not be seen walking with a person who has no shirt on his back, therefore we part here: you go that way, I this." [15]

During the first weeks of 1816 Hazlitt was kept busy turning out his regular articles for the *Examiner* and working up the fine arts entry for Napier. The latter took longer than he expected, and he appealed for an extension of his deadline. In the meantime he fretted because he had heard nothing from Constable about the Round Table essays which he had submitted or from Jeffrey about his Schlegel article. On February 19 he wrote to Constable:

> I sent off the first half of the Round Table some weeks ago, & I begin to fear some accident has happened to it or that you do not approve of the contents. Neither have I heard of the Review from Mr. Jeffrey, so that I am getting *blue-devilish* on that score also. You would oblige me by letting me know at your leisure whether anything has been done with the essays, & whether I shall send off the remainder. I had a letter from Mr. Napier this day giving me till the middle of March for the article on the Fine Arts, a respite which was very agreeable to me. I will send off the copy from here on the twelfth, if possible. [16]

The fine arts article was actually dispatched to Napier on March 20. It was a spirited, if rather dogmatic, essay on the subject, defending the real as opposed to the ideal as the ruling principle in art and unabashedly praising Hazlitt's favorite painters, Raphael, Titian, and Rembrandt (18:111–24). "It contains the best part of what I know about art," he wrote to Napier. But he was concerned about the occasional political allusions which he had allowed to creep into it. Did the gentlemen in Edinburgh consider him injudicious? "As to political innuendoes, and one or two other things relating to proposed articles, you can omit or retain them at your pleasure." [17] The following day, still having heard nothing from Constable about the Round Table essays, he wrote, again ingratiatingly:

15. Landseer, 1:136–40.

16. Jones, "Nine New Hazlitt Letters," p. 269.

17. *Athenaeum*, 8 August, 1919, p. 712. Hazlitt also wrote a spirited biographical sketch of the artist James Barry for the *Encyclopaedia* and translated five other similar entries from the *Biographie Universelle* (20:408–9).

I wrote to you about a fortnight ago respecting the Round Table, as I began to be apprehensive from my not having heard anything respecting it that some objection or difficulty had occurred. I should hope that is not the case, but I should be obliged if you could let me know shortly how the work stands. I should not trouble you about it but that just at present my affairs press, & I am anxious to know as nearly as possible what my resources are. I can send the remainder of the essays whenever you wish. I would make any alteration you might suggest as to particular passages that might require to be softened. But I cannot help thinking the work would answer at least sufficiently to pay expenses & trouble as I know they are talked of in London, & the Examiner has received several inquiries to know if it was not intended to collect them into a separate publication. I suppose the Edinburgh [containing his review of Schlegel] will soon be out to which I shall look with some anxiety.[18]

In reply Constable sent him a letter originally drafted on February 10 but, for some reason, not sent until March 27. Enclosed were proofs of the first four sheets (eight essays) of the Round Table volumes. "The printing will proceed regularly," Constable assured him, "and I should hope may be finished in April." He added that he hoped to get "a few subscribers" for "your work on the Philosophy of the Human Mind."[19] Hazlitt seems to have had a new project in his head—another attempt to distinguish himself as a metaphysician.

At about the same time he received a "very flattering" letter from Napier suggesting some emendations in the fine arts article. On April 2 he wrote back apologetically:

I dare say that your objections to several of the observations are well-founded. I confess I am apt to be paradoxical in stating an extreme opinion when I think the prevailing one not quite correct. I believe however this way of writing answers with most readers better than the logical. I tried for some years to express the truth & nothing but the truth, till I found it would not do. The opinions themselves I believe to be true, but like all abstract principles, they require deductions, which it is often best to leave the public to find out.

18. Jones, "Nine New Hazlitt Letters," p. 270. Hazlitt dated the letter March 19, but the postmark, March 23, and his reference to sending his fine arts article "yesterday" indicate that it was probably written on the twenty-first.

19. Ibid., p. 271. Jones assumes that Constable was referring to the history of English philosophy which Hazlitt had projected in 1809 and which had been the basis of his lectures at the English Institution in 1812. But his letter of April 20, 1817, to Jeffrey, quoted below, p. 191, seems to make a distinction between "my work on Metaphysics," to which he hopes to "return," and his articles on modern philosophy," which he expects to finish and send to Jeffrey "as soon as possible." I suggest that "the articles on modern philosophy" were the reworkings of his earlier material and that the "work on Metaphysics" referred to a new and original contribution to the field.

But there was another matter on his mind:

> I understood you to state in a former letter as the bookseller's arrangement that the money for any article would be paid when the article was printed. I suppose you will have nearly got through this so as to know the general size of it by this time. I have, Sir, a bill to take up to-morrow week 10 April, & if you could possibly transmit me fifteen pounds by that time, it would be a great assistance to me. The stagnation of money matters in this town is such that it is impossible to procure either by loan or anticipation, a single sixpence. I find this circumstance press particularly hard upon me at a time when I am clearing off the arrears into which my affairs had fallen owing to the aforesaid *logical way of writing*.[20]

The letter was dated from 34 Southampton Buildings, Hazlitt's address before he took the York Street house. He and Sarah may well have been temporarily separated.

April passed, and he heard no more from Constable about the progress of the Round Table volumes. On May 3, however, the delayed February issue of the *Edinburgh Review* appeared at last with his criticism of August Wilhelm von Schlegel's *Lectures on Dramatic Literature*. It was more a supplement than a critique: he used passages from Schlegel's book as a basis for his own perceptive comments on the difference between classical and romantic or the beauties of Greek art or the character of the French people or the merits of Shakespeare. On the last he dwelt especially, objecting that Schlegel ignored Shakespeare's faults, yet declaring that his remarks should be included in every edition of the plays to serve as antidote to the errors of earlier critics (16: 59, 95). Presently he had second thoughts on who might best do justice to Shakespeare.

The June issue of the Edinburgh contained a review of Leigh Hunt's poem *The Story of Rimini*. Hazlitt had written the article originally, but it had not met with Jeffrey's approval, and Jeffrey had revised it so extensively that he later considered it his own work (16:420). For once Hazlitt's critical judgment had been blinded by generosity.

He continued to grind out his weekly stint of articles for the Hunts. Although his work for Constable paid well and flattered his pride, he still relied on the *Examiner* for a steady income. He continued as dramatic critic all through the year 1816, managing generally to be more charitable than he had been in the previous year—except when he was obliged to review operas.[21] He followed Kean's progress closely, proclaiming on January 7 that "Othello is his best character, and the highest effort of genius on the

20. *Athenaeum*, 8 August, 1919, p. 712.
21. See 5:314–16 and 324–28.

stage," though wishing he would play the part less "fiercely" (5:271). As Sir Giles Overreach in Massinger's *New Way to Pay Old Debts* (January 14) he was "not at a single fault" (5:274), but the leading role in Massinger's melodramatic *Duke of Milan* (March 17) proved to be "one of his least impressive, and least successful [parts]" (5:290). Yet Hazlitt remained his staunch supporter, and when Kean failed to appear for a performance of this play on March 20 and the newspapers implied that he had been drunk, Hazlitt defended him vigorously, declaring that "the extravagance of actors . . . is not to be wondered at: they live from hand to mouth; they plunge from want to luxury; they have no means of making money *breed*, and all professions that do not live by turning money into money, or have not a certainty of accumulating it in the end by parsimony, spend it" (5:293).[22] On April 7 he retracted his criticism of Kean's interpretation of Shylock (5:294–96), and for the rest of the year he had little but praise for his playing of the lead in Charles Maturin's new tragedy *Bertram* (5:304–8), of Kitely in *Every Man in His Humour* (5:310–12), and of Mortimer in George Colman the Younger's *Iron Chest* (5:342–45).

When John Philip Kemble, in turn, played Sir Giles Overreach, Hazlitt reacted quite differently. Kemble, he thought, seemed almost apologetic— as if he were pleading, "*You have thrust me into this part, help me out of it, if you can; for you see I cannot help myself*" (5:303). Yet when Kemble announced his retirement that autumn, Hazlitt judged his portrayals of Macbeth, Cato, King John, and Coriolanus more kindly. "We wish we had never seen Mr. Kean," he wrote. "He has destroyed the Kemble religion; and it is the religion in which we were brought up" (5:345). When William Charles Macready made his debut as Orestes, in Ambrose Phillips's *Distressed Mother*, Hazlitt announced on September 22 that he was "by far the best tragic actor that has come out in our remembrance, with the exception of Mr. Kean" (5:334). But when Macready attempted Othello he seemed only "more than respectable in the part," definitely not in Kean's class (5:338–41).

Hazlitt reacted less favorably to his favorite actresses' performances this year. When Mrs. Siddons come out of retirement to play opposite Kemble in *Macbeth*, he felt obliged to say, reluctantly, on June 16 that her return was a mistake (5:312–14). Miss O'Neill continued to disappoint him in practically every part she attempted; as Lady Teazle she was "a complete

22. Kean seems actually to have suffered an accident. On March 30, 1816, he wrote to Hazlitt: "I have met with an awkward accident. Having been hurled out of a gig, and got a dislocated arm (not to speak of divers bruises and a severe shaking), I shall be unable to appear at your dinner party, or play for some nights in the Duke of Milan" (5:400).

failure" (5:291). The only actress whom he consistently approved was Fanny Kelly, whose charms drove a distracted suitor, George Barrett, to shoot at her during a performance at Covent Garden in June.[23] And he waxed suddenly (and surprisingly) effusive over three dancers, "the Miss Dennetts," whom he described as "three kindred Graces cast in the same mould: a little Trinity of innocent delights" (18:209–10). However, he wrote the most appealing lines of all the Theatrical Examiners for the year when he signalized the tenth anniversary of the failure of Lamb's farce *Mr. H.* Lamb, who could never stay angry with Hazlitt for very long at a time, was so pleased with the passage that he reprinted it when he published the play in 1818 (18:210–11).

Throughout the year Hazlitt continued to dominate "The Round Table," still leaping from subject to subject, though concentrating on analytical rather than personal essays. He reworked some of his favorite theories: in no. 31 (February 25) and no. 34 (March 5), the unrecognized debt of modern philosophers, especially Locke, to Thomas Hobbes (20:69–83); in no. 38 (May 12), Shakespeare's skill in distinguishing between similar characters like Richard II and Henry VI. In nos. 42 and 43 (July 21 and 28) he analyzed Milton's and Shakespeare's characterization of women and decided that Milton described Eve's charms specifically while Shakespeare let his heroines win readers' sympathy by their tenderness and unawareness of personal charms (4:105–11; 20:83–89). In no. 37 (April 21) he speculated, rather incoherently, "On Different Sorts of Fame" (4:93–97), and in no. 39 (May 19) on the "Character of John Bull," contrasting it with French character as he had sketched it in his *Edinburgh* review of Schlegel (4:97–100). The liveliest of his essays was the last of the series, no. 48, "On Actors and Acting" (January 5, 1817), in which he hailed players as both teachers and entertainers. "They are," he said, "the only honest hypocrites"; "they shew us all that we are, all that we wish to be, all that we dread to be"; the stage is "a bettered likeness of the world, with the dull part left out" (4:153). And his abiding love of the theater shone through his wistful desire that "all the celebrated actors, for the last hundred years could be made to appear again on the boards of Covent Garden and Drury-Lane, for the last time, in all their most brilliant parts" (4:157).

Some of the Round Table essays were exercises in basic aesthetic criticism, often with original twists. No. 29, "On Beauty" (February 4), in effect a continuation of his *Champion* criticisms of Reynolds's *Discourses*, stressed novelty, symmetry, and motion as components of beauty (4:68–72). No.

23. For Hazlitt's reviews of Miss Kelly, see 5:314–16 and 329–32.

39, "On Imitation" (February 18), offered new substance for a threadbare fabric: working from the discovery which he had explained to Coleridge at Linton back in 1798, he argued that "one chief reason . . . why imitation pleases is, because, by exciting curiosity, and inviting a comparison between the object and the representation, it opens a new field of inquiry, and leads the attention to a variety of details and distinctions not perceived before" (4:73). No. 40, "On *Gusto*" (May 26), not only offered the now famous definition of *gusto* as "power or passion defining any object" (4:77) but pointed out instances of it in art and literature and, in effect, exemplified it in the very style of the essay. The importance of power and passion emerged again in nos. 32 (March 3) and 33 (March 10), "On Pedantry," where Hazlitt heartily approved the pedant—or anyone else—who could lose himself in his own pursuits (4:80–88), and in no. 47 (November 24), "On Common-Place Critics," where he denounced critics "who have no opinions of their own, but who affect to have one upon every subject you can mention" (4:136). Significantly, when he cited examples of such critics' opinions, they proved to be devoid of imagination as well as originality.

Occasionally he wrote critical essays for the *Examiner* in addition to those in the Round Table series. Two on the Elgin marbles (June 16 and 30) maintained that Greek sculpture of the classical era disproved Reynolds's theories of the *ideal* in art because the statues were in effect "casts from nature" (18:100–103, 145–46, 438–39). Three "On the Catalogue Raisonné of the British Institution" (November 3, 10, and 17) berated the author of the catalogue for his chauvinistic criticism of the old masters; he revealed beyond a doubt that "the English are a shopkeeping nation" (4:150). Hazlitt was striking hard, flaunting his independence and originality, revealing himself as a truly *humane* critic. To be sure, many of his principles could be classified as "Romantic": his belief in originality, in the imagination, in power and passion, and the like. But there was an earthy realistic strain that ran through his critical opinions; he demanded first of all that art and literature imitate life.

During the summer of 1816 he wrote several essays in political criticism for the *Examiner*. Two of them, in the issues for August 4 and September 1, pointed out the fallacies in Robert Owen's socialistic *New View of Society* (7:97–103 and 19:159–61). Three others (August 11, 18, and 25) considered recent speeches in Parliament on "The Distresses of the Country" and urged immediate increases in taxation and reduction of public and private spending as means to relieve the suffering poor (7:103–13; 19:151–57). Another, "A Modern Tory Delineated" (October 6), listed, in a series of hard-hitting sentences, the sins of the party as Hazlitt saw them (19:173–76).

Throughout the year, however, he vented his bitterest criticism on his old foes, the apostates, as he deemed them, of the Lake school. On February 10, when Crabb Robinson saw him at Alsager's, he was "bitter, as he always is, against Wordsworth, who, he says, is satisfied with nothing short of indiscriminate eulogy, and who cannot forgive Hazlitt for having passed him off with a slight reserve of blame—so as to Southey, Hunt, etc. etc.; and if a man has ever disliked Wordsworth's poetry no subsequent love of it can ever atone for the offence." [24] Then on April 14, in no. 36 of the Round Table, "On the Character of Rousseau," he made the shocking statement that Wordsworth, Rousseau, and Benvenuto Cellini were "the three greatest egotists that we know of, that is, the three writers who felt their own being most powerfully and exclusively" (4:92–93).

On June 2 he shifted his attention to Coleridge in a brief review of "Christabel" and "Kubla Khan" which began: "The fault of Mr. Coleridge is, that he comes to no conclusion. He is a man of that great universality of genius, that his mind hangs suspended between poetry and prose, truth and falsehood, and an infinity of other things, and from an excess of capacity, he does little or nothing." Then he proceeded to damn "Christabel" as generally incomprehensible and "Kubla Khan" as nonsense (19:32–34). There were, to be sure, scraps of praise scattered through the review, but the overall effect was brutal. Leigh Hunt was moved to exclaim, "O, ye critics, the best of ye, what havoc does personal difference play with your judgments!" [25]

On June 9, as if in self-defense, Hazlitt wrote, as no. 41 of the Round Table series, a curious essay "On Good Nature," in which he declared:

> If the truth were known, the most disagreeable people are the most amiable. They are the only persons who feel an interest in what does not concern them. They have as much regard for others as they have for themselves. . . . They are general righters of wrongs, and redressers of grievances. They not only are annoyed by what they can help, by an act of inhumanity done in the next street, or in a neighbouring country by their own countrymen, they not only do not claim any share in the glory, and hate it the more, the more brilliant the success,—but a piece of injustice done three thousand years ago touches them to the quick. . . . They are vexed to see genius playing at Tom Fool, and honesty turned bawd. It gives them a cutting sensation to see Mr. Southey, poet laureate; Mr. Wordsworth, an exciseman; and Mr. Coleridge, nothing. (4:101–2 and 380)

24. Robinson, 1:179.
25. *Leigh Hunt's Literary Criticism*, ed. L. H. Houtchens and C. W. Houtchens (New York: Columbia University Press; London: Oxford University Press, 1956), p. 62.

On June 11 Wordsworth wrote to John Scott: "What you mention about the mode in which I am treated in the Ex[aminer] does not surprize me though it accords little with Mr. H.'s verbal professions the only time I ever saw him. . . . He is a man of low propensities, & of bad heart, I fear, but doubtless very clever—to his own injury, mostly, and to that of his readers, for he is a perverse Creature as any whom it has been my lot to know. His sensations are too corrupt to allow him to understand my Poetry —though his ingenuity might enable him so to write as if he knew something about it." [26]

During the following week, on June 19, Hazlitt's baby son John died. Again Hazlitt was prostrated: as long as he lived, he kept a lock of the child's hair in a bit of paper marked "my dear little John's hair, cut off the day he died." [27] This was one more weight added to the burden of bitterness that Hazlitt was bearing. Leigh Hunt, a kindly man, was perhaps hoping to lift some of that burden when he published in the July 14 *Examiner* a poetical epistle "To W.H., Esq." hailing him as

> Dear Hazlitt, whose tact intellectual is such
> That it seems to feel truth, as one's fingers do touch,

and describing an ideal day of walking and conversation in his company. [28]

By that time, however, Hazlitt had returned to battle. The *Examiner* for July 7 and 14 contained a long two-part review of Southey's *Carmen Nuptiale*, written in honor of the Princess Charlotte's marriage. Hazlitt damned Southey as poet and thinker, revived the old charge of apostasy, and dismissed the poem as "beneath criticism; it has all sorts of obvious commonplace defects, without any beauties either obvious or recondite. It is the Namby-Pamby of the Tabernacle; a Methodist sermon turned into doggrel verse. It is a gossiping confession of Mr. Southey's political faith—the 'Practice of Piety' or the 'Whole Duty of Man' mixed up with the discordant slang of the metaphysical poets of the nineteenth century" (7:87). And so on—and on.

On September 8 Hazlitt lashed out at Coleridge again, this time in a review of "A Lay Sermon on the Distresses of the Country." His article, he admitted, had been "written before the Discourse which it professes to criticise had appeared in print, or probably existed any where, but in

26. *TLS*, 27 December 1941, p. 660.

27. *Memoirs*, 1:224–25. N.B. that the passage quoted above, p. 115, may refer to John's death rather than the first William's.

28. *Poetical Works of Leigh Hunt*, ed. H. S. Milford (London: Oxford University Press, 1923), pp. 228–30.

repeated newspaper advertisements" (7:114 n.). But he knew well enough what to expect of this "Dog in the Manger of literature ... who will neither let any body else come to a conclusion, nor come to one himself" (7:115); and he proceeded with a bitter denunciation of Coleridge as man and as philosopher—his bitterest to date.

Coleridge did not have Wordsworth's vanity to protect him. He was morbidly sensitive to even the mildest criticism, smarting as he was from the raw wounds inflicted by awareness of his guilt and degeneration. On September 17 he wrote to Hugh J. Rose:

> There has appeared a most brutal attack, as unprovoked as it is even to extravagance false, on me both as a man and an author, in the Examiner—written by a man named William Hazlitt, whom I befriended for several years with the most improvident kindness when he was utterly friendless—and whom both Southey and myself at our own hazard saved from infamy and transportation in return for his having done his best by the most loathsome conduct (known to all the neighbourhood of Keswick & Grasmere but ourselves and the Wordsworths) to bring disgrace on our names and families. ... Every one particular which he has put down he *knows* to be false. But what can one do? I could not condescend to give publicity to Guilt and Baseness, the excess of which would perplex Belief while the Detail outraged Modesty. Better submit to the annoyance as the appropriate punishment of that weak good nature and that disposition to overvalue Talent, which put it in the power of such a Wretch to sign and seal all his other vices with ingratitude.[29]

Eight days later, on the verge of hysteria, he wrote again to Rose:

> Hazlitt possesses considerable Talent; but it is diseased by a morbid hatred of the Beautiful, and killed by the absence of Imagination, & alas! by a wicked Heart of embruted Appetites. Poor wretch! he is a melancholy instance of the awful Truth—that man cannot be on a Level with the Beasts—he must be above them or below them. Almost all the *sparkles & originalities* of his Essays, however, echoes from poor Charles Lamb—and in his last libel the image of the Angel without hands or feet was stolen from a Letter of my own to Charles Lamb, which had been quoted to him.[30]

Even Lamb was distressed. He wrote to Wordsworth on September 23: "Have you read the review of Coleridge's character, person, physiognomy &c. in the Examiner—his features even to his *nose*—O horrible license far

29. *Coleridge Letters,* 4:669–70.

30. Ibid., pp. 685–86. Hazlitt had written, "His genius has angel's wings; but neither hands nor feet" (7:117). In an undated note in one of his notebooks Coleridge wrote: "Mr. H. in his lust of Slander and in the rampancy of his malice first commits a rape upon my words, and then arraigns them as unchaste" (*Inquiring Spirit: A New Presentation of Coleridge,* ed. Kathleen Coburn [London: Routledge and Kegan Paul, 1951], p. 207).

beyond the old Comedy." [31] But Lamb was a good-natured man, and he refused to let Hazlitt's bitterness—even when it touched him personally—mar their friendship. "There was a cut at me a few months back by the same hand," he told Wordsworth, "but my agnomen or agni-nomen not being calculated to strike the popular ear, it dropt anonymous, but it was a pretty compendium of observation, which the author has collected in my disparagement from some hundreds of social evenings which we had spent together,—however in spite of all, there is something tough in my attachment to H—— which these violent strainings cannot quite dislocate or sever asunder. I get no conversation in London that is absolutely worth attending to but his." [32]

On September 29 Hazlitt began a review of George Ensor's *On the State of Europe* by comparing it favorably with Wordsworth's *Convention of Cintra*, which "had nothing remarkable in it but the profound egotism of the style, and some lofty abuse of Lord Wellington, who has, we suppose, since made his peace with the author, by making or breaking the Convention of Paris" (19:161–62). And later in the article he entered a new name on his list of proscripts: that of another renegade, his brother-in-law, Dr. Stoddart, now editor of the *Times*. Ferdinand of Spain was, he declared, "a tyrant both by profession and practice. He has but one idea in his head, like the editor of the *Times*, that a King can do no wrong, and he acts up to it, as the Doctor raves up to it, or as Mr. Coleridge cants up to it, or as Mr. Southey rhymes up to it, or as Mr. Wordsworth muses up to it" (19:164–65).

Hazlitt's victims were given a respite later in the autumn while he visited his parents, who had moved from Addlestone to Combe Down, near Bath. [33] On November 3 he was back in London "pouring out the result of a week's thinking" in a three-hour session at Haydon's studio. "He told me," Haydon wrote in his diary,

of three new characters for the Round Table he had been thinking of. One was of a man who had always something to say on every subject of a certain reach, such as,

31. *Lamb Letters*, 2:195.

32. Ibid., p. 196. The "cut" was doubtless a footnote reference, in Hazlitt's review of Southey's *Carmen Nuptiale*, to "a mad wag,—who ought to have lived at the Court of Horwendillus, with Yorick and Hamlet,—equally desperate in his mirth and his gravity, who would laugh at a funeral and weep at a wedding, who talks nonsense to prevent the head-ache, who would wag his finger at a skeleton, whose jests scald like tears, who makes a joke of a great man, and a hero of a cat's paw" (7:96 n.).

33. At Bath the Hazlitts met Catherine Emmet, niece of the Irish patriot Robert Emmet. She lived with the family until her death in 1824 and left Peggy Hazlitt the interest on five hundred pounds in her will.

"That Shakespeare was a great but *irregular genius,*" &c. He said some fine things, things which when he writes them will be remembered for ever. I gave him a bottle of wine, & he drank & talked, told me all the early part of his life, acknowledged his own weaknesses and follies. We then disputed about Art. I told him he always seemed angry on that subject because he had given it up, and that the Art would succeed in spite of his predictions. He would then remember his opposition with pain & mortification. If it failed he would have also the pain of having contributed to it. He denied that he was angry. "I daresay," said he, "it will succeed, but where is the use of anticipation of success?" "But where is the use," said I, "of morbid anticipation of failure?" "Very true," he answered. When a man of Genius is in a humour of pouring out, he should never be opposed. Every man of Genius should have Friends who respect & will give him his way at such times. I know myself at such times, I fly to such Friends, & pour forth, till exhausted. Hazlitt came to me, & when Art was settled, I let him go on. Hazlitt is a man who can do great good to the Art. He practised Painting long enough to know it; and he carries into Literature a stock which no literary man ever did before him.

All his sneers & attacks at times at my views I take as nothing. My object is to manage such an intellect for the great purposes of art; and if he was to write against me for six months, still would I be patient. He is a sincere good fellow at Bottom, with fierce passions & appetites. Appeal to him & he is always conquered & yields, & before long I'll venture to predict he shall assist the good cause, instead of sneering at it. He is disposed if his prejudices did not check him. His answer to the vile Catalogue Raisonné is the first symptom.[34]

It was a revealing interview. Hazlitt was frank, willing to accept correction, and eager for friendship and support. And Haydon, like Lamb, could see that, irascible as the man was, he needed and deserved support.

Of course any supporter of Hazlitt needed extraordinary patience. He could be genial enough in an afternoon's conversation with a friend—but vicious as ever when he turned his attention to an enemy, especially when that enemy was a former friend who had proved an apostate to the cause of liberty. On December 1 he launched in the *Examiner* the first of four diatribes, "Illustrations of the Times Newspaper," directed against the paper itself and especially its editor, his brother-in-law. "This paper is a nuisance which ought to be abated," he began, "and we shall here set about it accordingly" (19:177). Then he proceeded to flay the *Times* for approving the doctrine of the divine right of kings and "the little pert pragmatical plebeian

34. *Haydon Diary,* 2:64–65. The character "who had always something to say on every subject" appeared in the essay "On Common-Place Critics" in the *Examiner* for November 24. The criticisms of the *Catalogue Raisonné* appeared in the *Examiners* for November 3, 10, and 17. Haydon later remarked that Hazlitt "attacked the Catalogue Raisonné to oblige me" (*Diary,* 2:495).

Editor of the *Times*, one of the common race of men," for condoning the evils of "legitimacy." "And is it possible," he asked,

> that the Writer in the *Times* can be sincere in all this? Oh yes; as sincere as any man who is an apostate from principle, a sophist by profession, a courtier by accident, and a very head-strong man with very little understanding and no imagination, who believes whatever absurdity he pleases, and works himself up into a passion by calling names, can be. We think his opinions very mischievous, but impute no harm to the man. Some persons think him mad, and others wondrous wise; but he is a mere machine, playing the madman, and trying to be wise. (19:182)

Stoddart must have known, as Wordsworth and Coleridge did, who had written the attack. So must his sister Sarah. They apparently kept their thoughts to themselves. But Coleridge was still smarting from his wounds. On December 5 he wrote frantically to R. H. Brabant:

> The man who has so grossly calumniated me in the Examiner and the Ed. Review is a Wm Hazlitt, one who owes to me more than to his own parents—for at my own risk I saved perhaps his Life from the Gallows, most certainly his character from blasting Infamy—His reason I give in his own words—"Damn him! *I hate him:* FOR I am under obligation to him."—When he was reproached for writing against his own convictions, and reminded that he had repeatedly declared the Christabel the finest poem in the language of it's size—he replied—"I grumbled part to myself while I was writing—but nothing stings a man so much, as making people believe Lies of him."—You would scarcely think it possible, that a monster could exist who boasted of guilt and avowed his predilection for it.—All good that I had done him of *every* kind, and never ceased to do so, till he had done his best to bring down infamy on three families, in which he had been sheltered as a Brother, by vices too disgusting to be named—& since then the only *Wrong*, I have done him, has been to decline his acquaintance.[35]

The *Examiner* for December 15 contained the second of Hazlitt's "Illustrations of the Times Newspaper"; in it he inveighed against those of his contemporaries who "go from one extreme to another," who were "patriots in 1793, and royalists in 1816," citing the changes, over the years, in the writings of Wordsworth, Coleridge, Southey, and especially the editor

---

35. *Coleridge Letters*, 4:692–93. Coleridge was probably referring in his first sentence to the review of "Christabel" in the September *Edinburgh Review;* the December issue, containing Hazlitt's review of Coleridge's *Statesman's Manual* was not published until after the turn of the year (see below, p. 178 n.). Recent critics have generally agreed that Hazlitt had no share in the "Christabel" review: see Howe, pp. 398–400; Elisabeth Schneider, "The Unknown Reviewer of *Christabel:* Jeffrey, Hazlitt, Tom Moore," *PMLA* 70 (1955):417–32; Baker, 356 n.; and Schneider, "Tom Moore and the *Edinburgh* Review of 'Christabel,'" *PMLA* 77 (1962):71–76. But cf. Hoover H. Jordan, "Thomas Moore and the Review of Christabel," *Modern Philology* 54 (1956):95–105.

of the *Times*—"Dr. Slop," as he now called him (7:131–34). "All that is low in understanding, vulgar and sordid in principle in city politics," he declared, "is seen exuding from the formal jaws of *The Times* newspaper, as we see in the filth, and slime, and garbage, and offal of this great city pouring into the Thames from the sewers and conduit-pipes of the scavenger's company. It is a patent water-closet for the dirty uses of legitimacy: a leaden cistern for obsolete prejudices and upstart sophistry 'to knot and gender in.' Is this an exaggerated account? No" (19:356).[36]

Six days later Crabb Robinson walked out to Highgate to call on Coleridge, now under the care of his friend James Gillman. "He mentioned Hazlitt's attack with greater moderation than I expected," Robinson wrote in his diary. "He complains, and with reason, I think, of Lamb, who, he says, ought not to admit a man into his house who abuses the confidence of private intercourse so scandalously. He denies Hazlitt, however, originality, and ascribes to Lamb the best ideas in Hazlitt's article. He was not displeased to hear of his being knocked down by John Lamb lately." [37]

The next day the *Examiner* contained Hazlitt's third article on the *Times*, which concluded with remarks on a certain Jacobin poet "who founded a school of poetry on sheer humanity, on ideot boys and mad mothers, and on Simon Lee, the old huntsman," but who now

admires nothing that is admirable, feels no interest in any thing interesting, no grandeur in any thing grand, no beauty in any thing beautiful. He tolerates nothing but what he himself creates; he sympathizes only with what can enter into no competition with him, with "the bare earth and mountains bare, and grass in the green field." He sees nothing but himself and the universe. He hates all greatness, and all pretensions to it but his own. His egotism is in this respect a madness; for he scorns even the admiration of himself, thinking it a presumption in any one to suppose that he has taste or sense enough to understand him. He hates all science and art; he hates chemistry, he hates conchology; he hates Sir Isaac Newton; he hates logic, he hates metaphysics, which he says are unintelligible, and yet would be thought to understand them; he hates prose, he hates all poetry but his own; he hates Shakespeare, or what he calls "those interlocutions between Lucius and Caius," because he would have all the talk to himself, and considers the movements of passion in *Lear, Othello,* or *Macbeth,* as impertinent, compared with the Moods of his own Mind; he thinks every thing good is contained in the "Lyrical Ballads," or, if it is not contained there, it is good for nothing; he hates music, dancing, and painting; he hates Rubens, he hates Rembrandt, he hates Titian, he hates Vandyke; he hates the antique; he hates the Apollo Belvidere [*sic*]; he hates the Venus de Medicis. He hates all that others love and admire but himself. He is glad that Bonaparte is sent to St. Helena,

36. Hazlitt deleted this passage before he reprinted the essay in his *Political Essays.*
37. Robinson, 1:200.

and that the Louvre is dispersed for the same reason—to get rid of the idea of any thing greater, or thought greater than himself. The Bourbons, and their processions of the Holy Ghost, give no disturbance to his vanity; and he therefore gives them none. (7:144–45)

That evening, when Robinson met Hazlitt at Basil Montagu's house, he

could not abstain from adverting to a scandalous article in this morning's *Examiner* in which he attacks Wordsworth. Hazlitt, without confessing himself the author, spoke as if he were but did not vindicate himself boldly. He said: "You know I am not in the habit of defending what I do. I do not say that all I have done is right." In the same tone, and after I had said that I was indignant at certain articles I had read, and at the breach of private confidence in the detail of conversation, Hazlitt said: "It may be indelicate, but I am forced to write an article every week, and I have not time to make one with so much delicacy as I otherwise should." To this I replied by alluding to the anecdote of the French minister who answered the libeller who said he must live: "I do not see the necessity." Hazlitt then made a distinction. He said he would never take advantage of a slip in a man's conversation, and repeat what was not such a person's real opinion; but where what he had said was his notorious opinion not said to one person only, but generally, he thought such things might without justice be repeated. I said, "One aggravation is wanting in such a case, and your distinction amounts to this: I won't lie, I will only violate the confidence of friendship." Hazlitt then adverted to the tergiversation of these persons. He thought it, he said, useful to expose people who otherwise would gain credit by canting and hypocrisy. I admitted the attack on Southey's *Carmen Nuptiale* to be unexceptionable; but Hazlitt admitted that he believes Southey to be still a perfectly honest man. Wordsworth was not named. Coleridge he seemed very bitter against. Basil Montagu seemed inclined to take part with Hazlitt. He said, "It is difficult to draw the line in such cases. If I were in the House of Commons, and I heard a man applaud a measure of government publicly which he had privately reprobated to me the day before, should I be censurable in rising up and declaring this?"

I carefully abstained from shaking hands with Hazlitt. We were, of course, stiff towards each other, and I having praised a picture by Domenichino, engraved by Müller, of St. John, he said to Mrs. Montagu, in a marked way: "A very bad thing, ma'am." [38]

Hazlitt was clearly on the defensive now. Yet still he persisted.

By the twenty-ninth Coleridge's "Lay Sermon" had appeared, with the title *The Statesman's Manual*, and Hazlitt reviewed it mercilessly in the *Examiner*. He denied emphatically that the Bible, the statesman's manual, inculcated the divine right of kings; he mocked Coleridge's fawning appeals to the upper classes, his religious compromise, his apostasy; and he concluded that "greater nonsense the author could not write, even though he

38. Ibid., pp. 200–201.

were inspired expressly for the purpose" (7:128). Then in the December *Edinburgh Review* he reviewed it again,[39] in much the same spirit. "Our Lay-preacher," he stated, "in order to qualify himself for the office of a guide to the blind, has not, of course, once thought of looking about for matters of fact, but very wisely draws a metaphysical bandage over his eyes, sits quietly down where he was, takes his nap, and talks in his sleep—but we really cannot say very wisely" (16:100).

So ended the year 1816. If Hazlitt had been of a sanguine disposition, he might have taken inventory on December 31 and concluded that it had been a year of remarkable progress in the career for which he seemed destined. He had gained a key position on the staff of the *Examiner;* he had contributed articles to three of the four quarterly issues of the *Edinburgh Review;* and the editors had thought highly enough of his work to solicit contributions from him for the *Encyclopaedia Britannica* and to accept his Round Table essays for publication in lasting form.

Moreover, at about this same time he achieved another, more personal triumph: he stopped drinking. He had drunk to excess after the battle of Waterloo "until," as Haydon wrote, "at length wakening as it were from his stupor, he at once left off all stimulating liquors, and never touched them after." [40] And that victory, too, was reassuring.

However, Hazlitt was decidedly of a melancholic disposition, and he doubtless despaired when he looked over the debit side of his ledger of accomplishments. In the course of the year 1816 he had lost one of his two beloved sons, and his marriage was in jeopardy. His success as a journalist meant little to him, for he still longed to distinguish himself as a philosopher. As for his work for Constable and Company, it had all undergone revision, his review of *The Story of Rimini* emerging as hardly recognizable. And his Round Table volumes had still not been published. On July 24 he had written to Constable, then visiting in London, "may I hope to see some more *Round Tables* before I die?" [41] And although Constable had promptly sent

39. Hazlitt had not originally been assigned to review *The Statesman's Manual.* On January 3, 1817, he wrote Jeffrey that he had been unable to finish his articles on literature and philosophy because he had been ill, adding that he was sending a review of *The Statesman's Manual* instead (see Baker, p. 358 n.). The *Edinburgh* was, as often, running behind schedule.

40. Elwin, p. 250. Cf. Barry Cornwall, as quoted in Howe, p. 215. Haydon's mention of his drinking a bottle of wine on November 3, 1816 (quoted above, p. 174), is the last reference to his taking any kind of alcoholic liquor except for his own mention of drinking ale in Edinburgh in 1822 (see below, p. 318).

41. Jones, "Nine New Hazlitt Letters," p. 272.

him more proof and he had returned it as promptly, the volumes had still not been released.

The only book he had published during the course of the year was the three-volume *Memoirs of the Late Thomas Holcroft*, which Longman brought out in August after a six-year delay.[42] Godwin's proposed revision of the manuscript had probably amounted to little more than canceling a few passages which might have been considered offensive. And rather than shoring up Hazlitt's self-esteem, the book as published must have seemed downright embarrassing. It had been a hasty job; back in November, 1809, Hazlitt had told his father: "Above half the volume will . . . be mere strait forward transcription, & the rest will be merely picking out memorandums &c. from different places, & bringing them together, except such few reflections as I shall have to make, which will not be very long or deep." [43] At best it was loosely put together; he had made virtually no effort to impose either unity or interest on the mass of miscellaneous materials he presented. He reproduced Holcroft's diary for nine months, then disposed of the last eleven years of his life in one-fifth as many pages. His real ability came to the surface only in his "reflections"—on the reasons for ribaldry among actors (3:68) or on the glories of the French Revolution and the liberal cause (3:155–56).[44] Yet, ironically, reviewers were surprisingly complimentary. The *Eclectic Review* for February, 1817, stated flatly that Holcroft's account of his early life was "the only interesting part of this book." But the *European Magazine*, reviewing the book in its July, 1816, issue, cited "the unassuming simplicity of [the editor's] arrangement—the copious extracts from the diary—and the judicious selections from the correspondence." And the *Gentleman's Magazine* for April assured its readers that Hazlitt's additions to Holcroft's diary were managed "so ably, that the interest is not in the least diminished. The liberal impartiality with which this Editor has accomplished his task, cannot fail meeting with the most decided approbation of all parties." But surely Hazlitt himself knew better.

All in all, it had been a year of both profit and loss. And there was one

---

42. Baker, p. 180. Kenneth Neill Cameron (*Shelley and His Circle*, 2:548 n.) speculates that Godwin's calls on Hazlitt on May 29 and June 8 and Hazlitt's on Godwin on June 10 and July 5 (all recorded in Godwin's journal) may have been devoted to discussions of the text of the *Memoirs*.

43. Ernest J. Moyne, "An Unpublished Letter of William Hazlitt," *PMLA* 77 (1962): 341–42.

44. For fuller critical discussions of the book, see the editor's preface to Elbridge Colby's edition (London: Constable and Co., Ltd., 1925) and Virgil R. Stallbaumer, "Hazlitt's *Life of Thomas Holcroft*," *American Benedictine Review* 5 (1954): 27–44.

item on the debit side of the ledger that he doubtless ignored. He had fallen into the dangerous habit of wasting his talents in outpourings of pure venom—of which no sampling can give an adequate notion—venom which had embittered some of his oldest friends, shocked others, and made the few still loyal apologize for their very loyalty: Charles Lamb lamely argued that he could not forego Hazlitt's conversation and Mary Lamb explained to Crabb Robinson: "You are rich in friends. We cannot afford to cast off our friends because they are not all we wish." [45]

Hazlitt could, and did, assure himself that he had written nothing that did not need to be proclaimed to the world—and that he had been wounded by the apostasy of men like Wordsworth, and especially, Coleridge, his first idol, far more than they could ever be wounded by his words. He could, and did, insist that he placed principle above mere friendship. Still his venom was inexcusable. And it was also dangerous. For some time his victims had been striking back at him privately. Sooner or later he was bound to hit someone who would strike back publicly.

45. Sadler, 1:352.

Man of Letters
(1817)

Hazlitt's fury did not burn itself out at the close of the year 1816. He marked the beginning of the new year by publishing in the *Examiner* for January 12 a fourth installment of his "Illustrations of the Times Newspaper," this one bearing the provocative subtitle "On the Connexion between Toad-Eaters and Tyrants." It purported to be "an explanation of some of the causes which impede the natural progress of liberty and human happiness" (7:145), and it laid the blame clearly on the "modern apostates," beginning with Burke, who had betrayed the principles of liberalism and toadied to tyrants:

> We shall not go over the painful list of instances; neither can we forget them. But they all or almost all contrived to sneak over one by one to the side on which "empty praise or solid pudding" was to be got; they could not live without the smiles of the great (not they), nor provide for an increasing establishment without a loss of character; instead of going into some profitable business and exchanging their lyres for ledgers, their pens for the plough (the honest road to riches), they chose rather to prostitute their pens to the mock-heroic defence of the most bare-faced of all mummeries, the pretended alliance of kings and people! We told them how it would be, if they succeeded; it has turned out just as we said; and a pretty figure do these companions of Ulysses (*Compagnons du Lys*), these gaping converts to despotism, these well-fed victims of the charms of the Bourbons, now make, nestling under their laurels in the stye of Corruption, and sunk in torpid repose (from which they do not like to be disturbed by calling on their former names or professions), in lazy sinecures and good warm berths! Such is the history and mystery of literary patriotism and prostitution for the last twenty years. (7:147)

In the same issue of the *Examiner* a letter signed "Semper Ego Auditor" contrasted Coleridge's *Statesman's Manual*, as reviewed in the December 29 issue, and the thrilling appeal for separation of church and state which the writer, obviously Hazlitt, had heard him deliver in January, 1798. He was, he maintained, perplexed:

> I ask Mr. Coleridge, why, having preached such a sermon as I have described, he has published such a sermon as you have described? What right, Sir, has he or any man to make a fool of me or any man? I am naturally, Sir, a man of plain, dull, dry, understanding, without flights or fancies, and can just contrive to plod on, if left to myself: what right, then, has Mr. C., who is just going to ascend in a balloon, to offer me a seat in the parachute, only to throw me from the height of his career upon the ground, and dash me to pieces? (7:129)[1]

On January 29 Crabb Robinson called on Charles Lamb. "The conversation was on Hazlitt's attack on Coleridge and Wordsworth." Lamb admitted "he had quarrelled with Hazlitt about it," yet he still tried to defend his friend; Hazlitt had, he insisted, recognized Coleridge's genius and had even wept when he felt obliged to criticize *The Excursion* unfavorably. Robinson was not convinced; "I do not believe the fact that Hazlitt cried," he wrote in his diary, "and I hardly think Lamb serious in his vindication of Hazlitt."[2] Neither man, apparently, could understand that Hazlitt's love of liberty was stronger than his allegiance to any friend or benefactor.

In truth Hazlitt's preoccupation was so strong these days that it colored even the dramatic reviews which he wrote for the *Examiner*. On the fifth of the month he interrupted his critique of a production of Rowe's *Jane Shore* at Drury Lane to comment that a tragedy "which is founded on the dreadful calamity of hunger, is hardly proper to be represented in these starving times" (18:211). On the twenty-sixth he departed from his praise of Kean's success in Thomas Southerne's *Oroonoko* to comment ironically: "The political allusions throughout, that is, the appeals to common justice and humanity, against the most intolerable cruelty and wrong, are so strong and palpable, that we wonder the piece is not prohibited" (18:217). And on February 2, contrasting the merits of Drury Lane and Covent Garden theaters, he remarked that he favored the former because he was a lover of old books and old plays and old faces. But, he added, "there is one face which we never liked, and never shall like, which is the face of Tyranny, and the older it gets, the uglier it gets in our eyes" (18:219).

The February 2 issue of the *Examiner* also contained the first installment of a review, concluded the following week, of *Interesting Facts relating to the Fall and Death of Joachim Murat, King of Naples*, by Francis Macirone,

1. This letter was the germ of Hazlitt's later "My First Acquaintance with Poets."
2. Robinson, 1:202.

the Englishman who had been aide-de-camp to Murat. It began with a
tirade against the "old rotten demirep" Legitimacy: "What a tissue of
patches and of paint! What a quantity of wrinkles and of proud flesh!...
What treacheries and lies upon her tongue! What meanness and malice in
her heart! What an old hypocritical hag it is! What a vile canting, mumbling,
mischievous witch!" (7:153). Then Hazlitt's anger focused on Castlereagh,
the foreign secretary, and Wellington, whom he accused of perfidy toward
Murat, substantiating his charges with generous summaries of and excerpts
from Macirone's book.

Yet Hazlitt could and did relax at times with the friends whom he had
not yet alienated. He seems to have seen most, these days, of Hunt, who
shared his opinions, and Haydon, who very definitely did not. He especially
enjoyed Haydon's regular Sunday dinners. "He would say to his little boy,
after breakfast, as a way of introducing his intentions, 'Well, sir; shall we
go and eat Haydon's mutton?'" [3] And off he would stalk to the stimulating
gatherings where the company "discussed their favourite subjects, debated
over classics, fought Napoleon's campaigns with the fierceness of partisans
—Hazlitt always supporting Napoleon, Haydon always against him, and
in favor of the Duke—very often, it seems, breaking up their evenings in
a violent heat, to forget their differences, or meet and renew them on the
next occasion." [4]

Hazlitt spent two Sundays during the month of February, 1817, at
Hunt's house in the Vale of Health in Hampstead, where the young poet
Percy Shelley and his new wife, the daughter of Godwin and Mary
Wollstonecraft, were visiting. On the ninth Charles Cowden Clarke and
Walter Coulson were there for dinner and an informal concert; then the
company launched into a discussion of the merits of monarchy and republicanism, with Hunt and Coulson defending monarchy and Hazlitt
and Shelley defending republicanism. It lasted until three o'clock the following morning,[5] yet it did not make for any strong fellow feeling between
the two republicans. Shelley's heart was in the right place, surely, but his
feet were too far off the ground to please William Hazlitt.

The following Sunday, February 16, Hazlitt was at the Hunts' again,
this time with his wife. The Shelleys were still there, and Godwin
and Basil Montagu joined them for dinner. Others came in for music

3. *The Hazlitts*, p. 168.   4. Stoddard, pp. 62–63.

5. *Mary Shelley's Journal*, ed. F. L. Jones (Norman: University of Oklahoma Press,
1947), p. 77. Cf. Charles Cowden Clarke and Mary Cowden Clarke, *Recollections of
Writers* (London, 1878), p. 26.

afterwards, and Hunt entertained the group by reading some poems—one of them a quite remarkable sonnet "On First Looking into Chapman's Homer"—written by a twenty-year-old protégé of his named John Keats.[6] Hazlitt had met the young man through Haydon during the preceding autumn and was to see a good deal of him in the months ahead. He was an eager little fellow, bursting with enthusiasm and imagination and yet essentially down to earth—more Hazlitt's sort of man than the visionary Shelley. Keats had some hopes of a career in poetry and was looking for guidance. Cowden Clarke and Hunt had both been helpful, but he had begun to question their essential taste; he had read what seemed like sounder critical principles in some of Hazlitt's *Examiner* articles.

The following Thursday, February 20, Mary Shelley recorded in her journal that she was reading *The Round Table*, which Constable and Longman had finally published in two volumes six days earlier. It contained fifty-two essays, twelve of them by Leigh Hunt, the remainder by Hazlitt, whose name appeared alone on the title page. Although all forty of his essays had appeared before—and he doubtless considered them as ephemeral trifles, considerably below the level of his "philosophical" writings[7]—Hazlitt must have found some satisfaction in having them collected at long last. The world could now see his broad range of knowledge and interests; truly nothing human—or humane—was alien to him. He complained in his advertisement of a "want of variety" in subject matter because Hunt had had little time for essay writing after Napoleon's return from Elba; however, Hazlitt's essays revealed his understanding of literature, art, the theater, education, religion, aesthetics, and ethics. They varied from "On Classical Education" to "Character of John Bull," from "On Milton's Versification" to "On Religious Hypocrisy." Twenty-three of them had appeared in the Round Table series in the *Examiner;* the other seventeen were reprinted from the *Morning Chronicle* and the *Examiner*—or, the one political essay of the lot, his old favorite "Character of the Late Mr. Pitt," from *Free Thoughts on Public Affairs.*

Regardless of subject matter, the style was consistently arresting. Hazlitt remarked in his essay on the *Tatler* that he preferred Steele's essays to Addison's because "they are more like the remarks which occur in sensible conversation, and less like a lecture" (4:8). In the personal essay, he said,

6. *Mary Shelley's Journal*, p. 77.

7. Stanley Jones ("Nine New Hazlitt Letters," p. 266–68) discusses the differences between the list of essays in Hazlitt's letter of December 15, 1815, to Constable and those included in the published volumes, pointing out that he discarded essays on philosophical topics.

"the reader is admitted behind the curtain, and sits down with the writer in his gown and slippers" (4:7); elsewhere he observed that "the perfection of letters is when the highest ambition of the writer is to please his readers" (4:83). And so it was here. He avoided contemporary politics, excising from the essays as originally published sentences which might prove offensive.[8] The reader is carried along from subject to subject, often challenged by the novelty of the ideas expressed, invariably delighted by the author's manner of expressing them. For Hazlitt's style is never that of banal conversation; it is the conversational style of an alert, intelligent man, sensitive to the meaning and the overtones of the words he uses, who can enrich his remarks with a wealth of pertinent materials drawn from his reading or his experience. Above all it is the style of a man who aspires to please his reader—and, in the terms of his essay "On *Gusto*," to "leave a sting in the mind." It is hard to believe that this man could ever have written the obnoxious "Illustrations of the Times Newspaper."

Of course not all readers were captivated by the charms of *The Round Table*. The liberal *Monthly Magazine* reviewed it generously in its April issue, citing "the well-known fineness of tact of the two contributors, and the exquisite originality of mind, and breathing freedom displayed in their critical observations, especially upon the poets; and above all, upon Shakespeare" and prophesying that "this small work will find a welcome place in the libraries of the polished and cultivated portions of British society." But the more orthodox journals professed to be shocked. The April *Eclectic Review* singled out the "blasphemous ribaldry" of Hazlitt's essay "On the Causes of Methodism" and observed ruefully: "One might almost admire the honesty, the sort of moral courage which is manifested in this open hostility against religion, contrasted with the insidious decency of air with which the attack is sometimes conducted, did it not seem to indicate that want of shame which, forbidding all hope of repentance, seals up the character in utter worthlessness." And the *Literary Gazette* seized upon the book as the pretext for three letters, signed "A New Examiner," in its issues for May 3 and 17 and June 7, deploring the brand of morality displayed in the book—and originally in a newspaper intended for Sunday breakfast tables. The reviewer singled out Hazlitt's remarks about country

8. Howe records Hazlitt's revisions in his notes to volume 4 of the *Complete Works*. Note, however, that Hazlitt deleted from his "Observations on Mr. Wordsworth's Poem The Excursion" several favorable passages in the original *Examiner* review. For a discussion of the significance of these changes, see B. Bernard Cohen, "William Hazlitt: Bonapartist Critic of *The Excursion*," *MLQ* 10 (1949): 158–67.

people in his review of Wordsworth's *Excursion* and about English character in his essay "On the Character of John Bull." "These Sunday-morning preceptors," he raged, "make their fellow subjects doubt and fear and hate each other. They scatter suspicions, exasperations, firebrands, and discords through the two islands. We repeat it, that we know of no parallel to this cold-blooded malignity; this unappeasable, unprovoked, and wanton craving for the indiscriminate slaughter of public and private character; this horrid fiend-like eagerness to traduce defenceless women, and foment local hatreds and national divisions among their countrymen."

Hazlitt could afford to laugh off these hysterical charges; readers of the *Eclectic* and the *Literary Gazette* would be unlikely to buy his book under any circumstances. The limited sale of the book (which was never reprinted in his lifetime) probably annoyed him more; yet he already had a new and more ambitious project in mind. And though he may never have known it, the book had made a lasting mark: it had stimulated the imagination of one reader, his young admirer John Keats. Keats had already read some of the essays when they first appeared in the *Examiner;* had, in fact, meditated on Hazlitt's suggestion, in the essay "On Milton's Versification," that Johnson and Pope would have converted Milton's vaulting Pegasus into a rocking-horse (4:40) and had turned it to verse in his poem "Sleep and Poetry" as

> They sway'd about upon a rocking horse,
> And thought it Pegasus.

He admired Hazlitt's vigorous approach to life and to literature; in a letter to his friend John Hamilton Reynolds on March 9 he exclaimed, "It is the finest thing by God—as Hazlitt wo^d say." [9] In the same month he took up the phrase "the mighty dead," which he probably found in Hazlitt's essay "On Classical Education" (4:5), and used it in a letter to Haydon—and later in his poem *Endymion*. And on May 11, in another letter to Haydon, he wrote: "I am very near Agreeing with Hazlit that Shakspeare is enough for us" and went on to praise a recent article by Hazlitt in the *Examiner*. [10]

On September 21 Keats was at Oxford visiting his friend Benjamin Bailey. "How is Hazlitt?" he wrote to Reynolds. "We were reading his Table last night—I know he thinks himself not estimated by ten People in the world—I wishe he knew he is." [11] Beyond question Hazlitt had

9. *Letters of John Keats, 1814–1821,* ed. Hyder E. Rollins, 2 vols. (Cambridge, Mass.: Harvard University Press, 1958), 1:123 (hereafter cited as *Keats Letters*).

10. Ibid., 1:124 and n., 143.

11. Ibid., p. 166. For other evidence of Keats's knowledge of *The Round Table,* see Harold E. Briggs, "Two Notes on Hazlitt and Keats," *PMLA* 49 (1944):596–98.

found a disciple. This young man who had instinctively "*hoisted* himself up, and looked burly and dominant" when he first encountered the phrase "sea-shouldering whales" in Spenser[12] would naturally respond to an essay like Hazlitt's "On *Gusto*"; he would never be content, as he said later, to be "a versifying pet lamb"—he wanted his poetry to leave a sting in the mind. One who was thirsting for new ideas about poetry, about beauty, about philosophy, could find them in abundance in such essays as "On Beauty," "On Imitation," "On the Elgin Marbles," or "Why the Arts Are Not Progressive." Indeed ideas leapt up at Keats from strange sources: hints in Hazlitt's critique of *The Excursion* and in the essays "On Living to One's Self" and "On Posthumous Fame" prompted him to ponder the question of the poet's approach to his material: Wordsworth's "egotistical sublime" was not enough—one must strive for the "negative capability," as Keats later called it, of Shakespeare. For the moment these were only seeds of ideas to be fertilized as he read more of Hazlitt's criticism and cultivated as he mulled them over in his mind and in his letters to his friends. He even got hold of a copy of Hazlitt's *Principles of Human Action* in his eagerness to glean all that the man had to offer.[13] Hazlitt had thought long and fruitfully on the subject of the imagination and the poet's relation to society, and Keats's poetry and letters were the richer for his exposure to Hazlitt's conclusions.[14]

During the months of February and March, 1817, Hazlitt's contributions to the *Examiner* fell off sharply. He continued to write the weekly Theatrical Examiners, paying special attention to the debut of Junius Brutus Booth, who was being featured at Covent Garden as a rival to the great Kean. On February 16 Hazlitt declared Booth's playing of Richard III too much like Kean's and urged him to "come forward in his own person" (5:354). A week later, when the managers of Drury Lane had lured Booth away and cast him as Iago opposite Kean's Othello, Hazlitt was better pleased, although he still complained that Booth was imitating Kean. For

12. Cowden Clarke, *Recollections of Writers*, p. 126.

13. J. M. Bullitt argues (*PQ* 24 [1945]:355–56) that Hazlitt's denial of self-love in *Principles of Human Action* is "one of the fundamental elements in Keats's conception of poetry and the imagination."

14. Of the many studies of the relationships of Hazlitt and Keats, the most inclusive and useful are Clarence D. Thorpe's "Keats and Hazlitt," *PMLA* 62 (1947):487–502; Herschel M. Sikes's "The Poetic Theory and Practice of Keats: the Record of a Debt to Hazlitt," *PQ* 38 (1959):401–12; Kenneth Muir's "Keats and Hazlitt" in *John Keats: A Reassessment* (Liverpool: Liverpool University Press, 1959); and Claude Lee Finney's *The Evolution of Keats's Poetry*, 2 vols. (Cambridge, Mass.: Harvard University Press, 1963), passim.

him Kean had no rivals; his playing of Othello was "beyond all praise" (5:357). But on the whole Hazlitt expressed scant enthusiasm for any of the productions which he was obliged to review. On March 2, after Booth had returned to Covent Garden as Richard III, he deplored the conduct of the managers, who had first underpaid Booth and then outbidden Drury Lane for his services; then once again he accused Booth of copying Kean (5:357–58). On the ninth he reported that "Mr. Booth continues to give his imitations of Mr. Kean" at Covent Garden and that peace had been restored, partly because of a public apology from Booth, partly because of "the administration of club-law. . . . We have here an example of the *imperium in imperio*" (18:221). This was Hazlitt's last contribution to the *Examiner* for three weeks, his last Theatrical Examiner for five.

There was good reason for the falling off: Hazlitt was again a sick man. On March 4 he wrote to Francis Jeffrey: "I have been so ill as to be unable to do almost any thing."[15] And on the thirteenth, apologizing to Macvey Napier for his failure to complete six biographical articles for the *Encyclopaedia Britannica*: "I conceive that nobody has been to blame in this business but myself. In fact, I have been very ill all the winter, & have had more to do than I could have got through properly, if I had been well."[16] Yet he was seeking new assignments: in his letter to Jeffrey he offered to write for the *Edinburgh Review* an article on the principles of modern philosophy, another on recent novels and romances, featuring Godwin's forthcoming *Mandeville* and "a flying article" on Southey's *Wat Tyler;* in his letter to Napier he wrote: "I . . . shall be happy at any time to do what I can for the *Supplement*. But I would have you to understand at first that I am a very unscientific person, & am therefore always liable to blunder on such matters. All that I know anything about (except things of amusement) is metaphysics, & I know more of my own metaphysics than any body else's. I should think that the article Buonaparte might be made something of a little different from the Biography."

Neither Jeffrey nor Napier, apparently, approved his suggestions. But the *Examiner* was less discriminating, and presently he launched another series of blasts at Southey and Coleridge. The issue for March 9 contained an article ironically contrasting a *Quarterly Review* essay on parliamentary reform, presumably by Southey, and the laureate's *Wat Tyler*, written when he was still an "Ultra-jacobin" and recently published against Southey's wishes; it consisted largely of a series of eight *morceaux* from the poem for

15. *London Mercury* 12 (1925):411.
16. *Athenaeum*, 8 August 1819, pp. 712–13.

comparison with the "Ultra-royalist" thinking of the *Quarterly* article (7:168–76). Three weeks later, on the thirtieth, Hazlitt replied to an article by Coleridge in the *Courier* defending Southey from the charge of apostasy. He summed up Coleridge's defense with mordant irony:

> *That Mr. Southey was a mere boy when he wrote* Wat Tyler, *and entertained Jacobin opinions: that being a child, he felt as a child, and thought slavery, superstition, war, famine, bloodshed, taxes, bribery and corruption, rotten boroughs, places, and pensions, shocking things; but that now he is become a man, he has put away childish things, and thinks there is nothing so delightful as slavery, superstition, war, famine, bloodshed, taxes, bribery and corruption, rotten boroughs, places, and pensions, and particularly, his own.* (7:181)

He followed this up with an ingenious letter in the April 6 *Examiner*, dated from Bristol and signed "Vindex." The writer deplored the defense of Southey written by "this hack writer of the *Courier*," then proceeded to identify him from internal evidence as the author of *Conciones ad Populum*, two lectures delivered by Coleridge in Bristol in 1795. The *coup de grâce* came when he recalled that Coleridge "*may* remember *publicly*, before several strangers, and in the midst of a public library, turning into the most merciless ridicule 'The dear Friend' whom he now calls Southey the philologist—Southey the historian—Southey the poet of the *Thalaba*, and *Madoc*, and the *Roderic!* Mr. Coleridge recited an Ode of his dear Friend, in the hearing of these persons, with a tone and manner of the most contemptuous burlesque, and accused him of having stolen from Wordsworth images which he knew not how to use" (19:198).

"A Sketch of the History of the Good Old Times," which began in the same issue and continued through the issues of April 13 and 20, contained a summary of a published history of France, "the title of which we dare not give," showing that the woes of that country did not date from the French Revolution. There were incidental barbs aimed at Wordsworth, Coleridge, Southey, and Dr. Stoddart, culminating in the final sentence: "And there we close the book. But whoever after this sketch shall have the face to talk of 'the good old times,' of mild paternal sway, and the blessings of Legitimacy, that is, of power restrained only by its own interests, follies, vices, and passions, and therefore necessarily sacrificing to them the rights, liberties, and happiness of nations, we shall pronounce to be either a consummate hypocrite or 'a fool indeed'" (19:196).

By this time Hazlitt's style was unmistakable; friends and foes alike knew whom to blame for these vitriolic attacks. Wordsworth wrote in a letter to

Haydon on April 7: "The miscreant Hazlitt continues, I have heard, his abuse of Southey, Coleridge, and myself, in the Examiner.—I hope that you do not associate with the Fellow, he is not a proper person to be admitted into respectable society, being the most perverse and malevolent Creature that ill luck has ever thrown in my way. Avoid him—hic niger est—And this, I understand is the general opinion wherever he is known, in London." [17] Haydon had no defense to offer, only the explanation that Hazlitt's conduct stemmed from injured pride. "With respect to Hazlitt," he replied on April 15, "I think his motives are easily enough discernible. Had you condescended to visit him when he praised your 'Excursion,' just before you came to town, his vanity would have been soothed and his virulence softened. He was conscious of what an emergency you had helped him from: he was conscious of his conduct while in your neighborhood, and then, your taking no notice of his praise added to his acrid feelings. I see him scarcely ever, and then not at my own house." [18] He was, he claimed, bracing himself for a sudden attack. "My turn will come with Hazlitt," he assured Wordsworth,

> for he has the malignant morbidity of early failure in the same pursuit. I have had several side stabs about "great" pictures, etc., and the absurdity of Art ever existing in England; but he shall see, if he cuts me (up) openly, it shall not be with impunity. In the "Edinburgh Encyclopaedia," speaking of English Art, he mentioned every living painter now eminent, but me! By leaving me out, the blockhead, he made people remark it; and so he has, in fact, done me good. One night, when I saw him half-tipsy, and so more genial than usual, I said to him, "Why do you sneer so at the prospects of English Art? you know this is the country where it will next succeed." "I dare say it will," he replied, "but what is *the use of predicting success?*" He served me a dreadful trick with Wilkie. He asked of me a letter of introduction to see Wilkie's pictures. I gave it, and the very next Sunday out came an infamous attack on Wilkie's genius! You may depend, my dear sir, that men of eminence are considered food for such propensities and nothing better. [19]

Meanwhile Hazlitt continued the weekly Theatrical Examiners which he had resumed on April 13. His health had evidently improved—but not his temper. Reviewing a production of Colley Cibber's *Double Gallant* at Drury Lane on the thirteenth, he presumed to quarrel with Alexander Pope because of the "great piece of injustice" done Cibber in the *Dunciad*, and he went on to laud the *double-entendres* in Cibber's play, pronouncing

17. *Letters of William and Dorothy Wordsworth: The Middle Years*, 2:781–82.
18. *Life, Letters, and Table Talk of Benjamin Robert Haydon*, ed. R. H. Stoddard (New York, 1876), p. 196 (hereafter cited as Stoddard).
19. Ibid., pp. 197–98.

them "luscious" in comparison with the "cautious purity of the modern drama" (5:359–60). On the twentieth he fumed at the sheeplike audiences who flocked to the opera on Saturday, the "fashionable" day, and who professed to find "sublimity" in Mozart's *Don Giovanni* (5:363). On the twenty-seventh, in a review of William Dimond's *Conquest of Taranto* at Covent Garden, he scoffed at the popularity of such "*purely romantic*" plays, in which the author "contracts with the managers to get up a striking and impressive exhibition in conjunction with the scene-painter, the scene-shifter, the musical composer, the orchestra, the chorusses on the stage, and the *lungs* of the actors" (5:366).

The truth of the matter was that Hazlitt had tired of his job. He had been working on a new project which, he hoped, might release him from the constant pressures of journalism. On April 20 he wrote to Francis Jeffrey:

> I take the liberty of troubling you with a copy of a work I have just finished relating to Shakespear. I thought perhaps if you approved of it you might take a brief notice of it in the Edinburgh Review. I should not make this abrupt proposition, but from the necessity of circumstances. My friends may praise what I write, but I do not find that the public read it, & without that, I cannot live. If I could dispose of the copyright of the Round Table & of this last work, I could find means to finish my work on Metaphysics, instead of writing for three newspapers at a time to the ruin of my health & without any progress in my finances. A single word from you would settle the question, & make what I write a marketable commodity. The booksellers have kept me in a hole for the last ten years: do, Dear Sir, extend a friendly hand to help me out of it. I would not ask such a favour for myself, if I thought the mere notice of either of the trifles above alluded to would be any discredit to the high character of your Journal. I have had to write a new Preface to the Characters (a very bad one, as it usually happens in such cases) which has prevented me from sending the articles on modern philosophy. But I will finish & send it off as soon as possible,—I hope in time for the next number, if it is admissible in other respects.[20]

Yet the next few days brought a strange twist in Hazlitt's plans. The issue of the *Times* for April 30 contained a review of the new *Macbeth* at Drury Lane. Mrs. Hill, a newcomer from Dublin, was accorded some "negative praise" for her playing of the part of Lady Macbeth. But she was no Mrs. Siddons! And the author launched into a rhapsody: to have seen Mrs. Siddons as Lady Macbeth "but once, was never to forget her afterwards. It was no more possible to forget her than if we had seen some more than mortal vision. . . . Her voice was power: her form was grandeur" (18:227).

Obviously the reviewer was Hazlitt—he who, a bare three months ago, had poured his venom on the *Times* and its editor, his brother-in-law. But

20. Baker, p. 214.

Stoddart had been discharged from the paper and had taken over editorship of *The Day*, which he named *The Day and New Times*. Thomas Barnes, his successor, had recommended to the manager, John Walter, that Hazlitt be appointed dramatic critic, and Walter had consulted Crabb Robinson. Robinson read him "On the Causes of Methodism" from *The Round Table* and urged him to appoint Hazlitt "at the same time that I did not encourage him to form a personal intimacy with him."[21] And Hazlitt had accepted, probably because the *Times* paid well.

In the weeks that followed he reviewed plays regularly for both the *Times* and the *Examiner*. To do so without repeating himself presented a challenge, and he responded to it cleverly. Having reviewed *Macbeth* for the *Times* on April 30, he wrote only a brief comment on it for the *Examiner* of May 4, appending it to a longer notice of *John Gilpin*, the farce presented on the same program. Since he had little to say about the farce, he filled out his article by recalling his enjoyment of some prints of John Gilpin's ride "hung round a little parlour where we used to visit when we were children" (18:222). Similarly, in the *Times* for May 15, he wrote a full-length review of Kean's playing of Eustace in George Colman Jr.'s *Surrender of Calais*, while in the *Examiner* of the eighteenth he appended a brief review of Colman's play to a longer one of the opera *Don Giovanni*. In the *Times* he declared that the part of Eustace was no challenge to Kean's talents as actor (18:228); in the *Examiner*, that Kean had a perfect right, "like other actors, sometimes [to] have a part to walk through" (18:225).

There came a time, however, when Hazlitt's subterfuge collapsed. Late in May, Kean presented a benefit performance of John Brown's *Barbarossa* and sang in *Paul and Virginia*, the musical afterpiece, at Drury Lane; in the following week Mrs. Siddons returned to Covent Garden for a production of *Macbeth*. Neither of these events could be slighted, and Hazlitt reviewed both plays for both papers (5:372–73; 18:230, 232–33). Alert readers might have noticed distinct similarities between the two articles. He must have decided then that he could not review for the two papers at once. The Hunts may even have issued an ultimatum, for the article on Mrs. Siddons was his last contribution to the *Examiner* for a year.

His contributions to the paper had been falling off. In May he had done only one article besides his dramatic critiques, a three-part review of Southey's *Letter to William Smith, Esq., M.P.* in the issues for May 4, 11, and 18. Smith had charged his fellow members in the House of Commons to compare

21. *History of "The Times"*, 5 vols. (London: Office of the Times, 1935–47), 1:164–65.

Southey's *Wat Tyler* with the recent *Quarterly Review* article on parliamentary reform—possibly as a result of Hazlitt's *Examiner* article on the subject on March 9. Southey had apologized in an open letter for the radical sentiments of his play, attributing them to his youth and inexperience. Of course Hazlitt would accept no such explanation; he repeated his old charges of apostasy, adding a running commentary on selected passages from Southey's *Letter*. For example:

His engagement to his first love, the Republic, was only upon liking; his marriage to Legitimacy is *for better, for worse*, and nothing but death shall part them. Our simple Laureate was sharp upon his hoyden Jacobin mistress, who brought him no dowry, neither place nor pension, who "found him poor and kept him so," by her prudish notions of virtue. He divorced her, in short, for nothing but the spirit and success with which she resisted the fraud and force to which the old bawd Legitimacy was forever resorting to overpower her resolution and fidelity. He said she was a virago, a cunning gipsey, always in broils about her honour and the inviolability of her person, and always getting the better in them, furiously scratching the face or cruelly tearing off the hair of the said pimping old lady, who would never let her alone, night or day. But since her foot slipped one day on the ice, and the detestable old hag tripped up her heels, and gave her up to the kind keeping of the Allied Sovereigns, Mr. Southey has devoted himself to her more fortunate and wealthy rival: he is become uxorious in his second matrimonial connexion; and though his false Duessa has turned out a very witch, a foul, ugly witch, drunk with insolence, mad with power, a griping, rapacious wretch, bloody, luxurious, wanton, malicious, not sparing steel, or poison, or gold, to gain her ends—bringing famine, pestilence, and death in her train—infecting the air with her thoughts, killing the beholders with her looks, claiming mankind as her property, and using them as her slaves—driving every thing before her, and playing the devil wherever she comes, Mr. Southey sticks to her in spite of every thing, and for very shame lays his head in her lap, paddles with the palms of her hands, inhales her hateful breath, leers in her eyes and whispers in her ears, calls her little fondling names, Religion, Morality, and Social Order, takes for his motto

> "Be to her faults a little blind,
> Be to her virtues very kind"—

sticks close to his filthy bargain, and will not give her up, because she keeps him, and he is down in her will. Faugh! . . . The above passage is, we fear, written in the style of Aretin, which Mr. Southey condemns in the *Quarterly*. It is at least a very sincere style: Mr. Southey will never write so, till he can keep in the same mind for three and twenty years together. Why should not one make a sentence of a page long, out of the feelings of one's whole life? The early Protestant divines wrote such prodigious long sentences from the sincerity of their religious and political opinions. Mr. Coleridge ought not to imitate them. (7:193–94)

John Keats read these lines with delight. "By the by what a tremendous Southean Article [Hazlitt's] last was," he wrote to Haydon on May 11. And to Hunt on the tenth: "I must mention Hazlitt's Southey—O that he had left out the grey hairs!—Or that they had been in any other Paper not concluding with such a Thunderclap—that sentence about making a Page of the feelings of a whole life appears to me like a Whale's back in the Sea of Prose." [22]

Coleridge, the victim of several by-blows in Hazlitt's article, was understandably less admiring. Writing to the Reverend Francis Wrangham on June 5 he declared:

> both my Health & my circumstances have been such, that my powers of Volition, constitutionally weak, have sunk utterly under the weight of embarrassments, disappointments, and infamous Calumny. For instance, the author of the Articles in the Edinburgh Review, and the Examiner (W. Hazlitt) after efforts of friendship on my part which a Brother could not have demanded, my House, Purse, Influence —& all this, tho' his manners were dreadfully repulsive to me, because I was persuaded that he was a young man of great Talent and utterly friendless—his very Father & Mother having despaired of him—after having baffled all these efforts at the very moment, when he had been put in the way of honorable maintenance by the most unmanly vices, that almost threatened to communicate a portion of their own Infamy to my family, and Southey's, and Wordsworth's, in all of which he had been familiarized, and in mine & Southey's domesticated—after having been snatched from an infamous Punishment by Southey and myself.

And he dredged up the old Keswick story, with a few new and more lurid details:

> (there were not less than 200 men on horse in search of him)—after having given him all the money, I had in the world, and the very Shoes off my feet to enable him to escape over the mountains—and since that time never, either of us, injured him in the least degree—unless the quiet withdrawing from any further connection with him (& this without any ostentation, or any mark of Shyness when we accidentally met him)—not merely or chiefly on account of his Keswick Conduct, but from the continued depravity of his Life—but why need I say more? [23]

Coleridge had, obviously, been driven close to distraction.

During the months of June and July, Hazlitt continued his regular dramatic criticism in the *Times*. But the reviews were in general disappointing —partially because the plays were undistinguished, perhaps also because

---

22. *Keats Letters*, 1:144, 137–38. The reference to Southey's "few contemptible grey hairs" appears at the beginning of the article (7:187).

23. *Coleridge Letters*, 4:735.

Hazlitt was still in a testy mood, but primarily because he had less room to expand his thoughts than ever before. He was used to literary elbowroom—for space to dilate on his memories of Mrs. Siddons, or the prints of John Gilpin's ride, or whatever else happened to catch his fancy. The *Times* reviews, however, never so wander. They sound as if he had been limited to 250–300 words for each production. They have a perfunctory air about them which is far removed from the leisurely manner of his usual writing. He seems to be doing his job conscientiously rather than enthusiastically. And when, in 1818, he selected the reviews which were to be reprinted in his *View of the English Stage,* he chose only two of the forty-four which he had written for the *Times.*

Little is known of his personal life during the spring and early summer of 1817. He was seeing less of the Lambs and Crabb Robinson and, probably, of Leigh Hunt and Haydon as well. He was at Hunt's house on June 30[24] and on May 6 had a single sitting for a "head" by Haydon, who wrote in his diary that he "never had so pleasant [a] sitter." Haydon seized the opportunity to test his pet theory about Hazlitt:

> I told him I thought him sound on every thing but Art; that he appeared to me to think there would never be another Raphael. He said, "Am I not right, *bating* the present time?" "Certainly," I said. "Then," said he, "I have nothing to do with the present time; my business is with what has been done." "Very true," said I, "and if you have nothing to do with the present time, why attack it? Let it alone, at any rate." Thus his real thoughts were evident. The success of Painting is to Hazlitt a sore affair after his own failure.[25]

One evening at Basil Montagu's house Hazlitt was introduced to Sir Anthony Carlisle, professor of anatomy at the Royal Academy. When Carlisle spoke scornfully of "the uselessness of poetry," Hazlitt was appalled —yet curious to know him better. He asked William Bewick to take him to one of Carlisle's lectures, which were famous for their demonstrations: six or eight naked Life-guardsmen performing a sword exercise to exhibit muscular action, or some Indian or Chinese jugglers to reveal how supple the human body can become through training. The evening Hazlitt was present Carlisle handed around a human heart and a human brain, each on a dinner plate. According to Bewick, Hazlitt "shrank back in sensitive horror, closed his eyes, turned away his pale, shuddering countenance, and

24. See Hunt's letter to C. C. Clarke dated July 1, 1817, and reprinted in *Four Generations,* 1:174.

25. *Haydon Diary,* 2:110. The "head" was doubtless for inclusion in Haydon's painting *Christ's Entry into Jerusalem* (see below, p. 258).

appeared to those near him to be in a swooning state." He soon rallied, however, and "whispered in nervous accents, 'Of what use can all this be to artists? Surely the bones and muscles might be sufficient.'" And when he saw Carlisle lecturing "in full court dress, with bag wig, curled and powdered, his cocked hat, and lace ruffles to his wrists," he burst out laughing. "'I should not have known my unpoetic acquaintance in that disguise,'" he declared; "'he seems like an owl peeping and winking in an ivy-bush upon some ancient turret, and I cannot conceive of such an arrant puppy finding anything good or of *use*, or beauty in poetry. I now know *the man*.'" [26]

He still saw Godwin from time to time and, through him, made two new acquaintances: Dr. John Wolcot (better known as "Peter Pindar," the satirical poet) and John Philpot Curran. He spent an evening at Godwin's house while Shelley was visiting there from May 22 to 26, and on the twenty-eighth Godwin and he had supper at Wolcot's rooms in Somers Town. [27] Hazlitt was fascinated by Wolcot, who held forth over a decanter of rum like a fine old monk—"old and blind, but still merry and wise" (6:168). "He was the life and soul of the company where he was," Hazlitt recalled in 1829, "—told a story admirably, gave his opinion freely, spoke equally well, and with thorough knowledge of poetry, painting, or music, could 'haloo an anthem' with stentorian lungs in imitation of the whole chorus of children at St. Paul's, or bring the black population of the West Indies before you like a swarm of flies in a sugar-basin, by his manner of describing their antics and odd noises" (20:226). Once when Hazlitt was present the old fellow argued the merits of Dryden's "Alexander's Feast" with Curran, another spry veteran with "a flash of the eye, a musical intonation of voice, such as we have never known excelled" (20:231).

Hazlitt relished the company of men like these two; they had gusto. Godwin had a good deal less of it; his conversation was "flat as a pancake," Hazlitt said; "he has not a word to throw at a dog" (12:198). Still he respected Godwin as an old friend, a staunch liberal, and an acute thinker. The respect was mutual: when the publisher Archibald Constable offered to include a portrait of Godwin in his forthcoming novel *Mandeville*, Godwin "mentioned the question to one or two friends" and reported to Constable in a letter of June 12: "Mr. Hazlitt said at once, 'Such an impertinence suits wonderfully well with Lady Morgan, and is indeed a copy of the lady's mind, but it would completely let you down from the

26. Landseer, 1:141–42.
27. See N. I. White, *Shelley*, 2 vols. (Cambridge, Mass.: Harvard University Press, 1940), 1:520; *Mary Shelley's Journals*, p. 80; and *Letters of Mary W. Shelley*, ed. F. L. Jones, 2 vols. (Norman: University of Oklahoma Press, 1944), 1:29.

rank to which you justly have a claim.'"[28] That settled the matter for Godwin. And when the novel was published, he suggested that Hazlitt review it for the *Edinburgh Review*.[29]

Hazlitt's relations with his wife were less cordial. Sarah Hazlitt could be good company; she had a certain wry humor about her and a vigorous, if mannish, style. But she was never a gracious hostess or even a tolerable housewife: one of her very few recorded attempts at entertaining was the dreadful fiasco intended to celebrate the baptism of her son. If she was irritable on occasion, she had ample cause, for Hazlitt was no model of a husband: he spent evening after evening away from home (at least two a week at the theater while he was reviewing for the *Times*); he rarely took her to the dinners or suppers which he attended; he had treated her only brother outrageously and at least offended her closest friends, the Lambs. Moreover, he was often ill-tempered (and, until recently, drunk), he was seldom out of debt, and he doubtless never even pretended to be faithful to her.[30] She must often have reflected that, after all her efforts to find a husband, she had made a wretched bargain.

Meanwhile Hazlitt continued to hope for better days, once his new study of Shakespeare was published. It had probably been shaping in his mind ever since February, 1816, when he reviewed Schlegel's *Lectures on Dramatic Literature* for the *Edinburgh*. There was a need, certainly, for a study of Shakespeare which took into account the changes in critical attitudes since Johnson wrote his preface to the plays, and William Hazlitt seemed the logical man for the job. In the course of his career as a dramatic critic he had seen and reviewed dozens of performances of Shakespeare's plays; he had studied the interpretations of numerous actors and actresses and had concluded that Mrs. Siddons and Kean came closest to catching the true spirit of Shakespeare. For *The Round Table* he had written an essay on the characters of *Midsummer Night's Dream*, another on the character of Shakespeare's women, a third "On Shakespeare's Exact Discrimination of Nearly Similar Characters."[31] He could turn out a book such as he had in mind with relatively little effort.

Although Hazlitt sent a copy of the book to Francis Jeffrey on April 20, it was not officially published until July. Hazlitt had evidently concocted

---

28. Thomas Constable, *Archibald Constable and His Literary Correspondents*, 3 vols. (Edinburgh, 1873), 2:91–92.

29. See below, p. 208.

30. See Sarah's statements in her journal, quoted below, pp. 249, 319, 323.

31. The latter two, published in the *Examiner* for July 28, 1816, and May 12, 1816, were not included in the collected edition of the essays.

an ingenious scheme to spare himself frustrating transactions with the booksellers: his friend C. H. Reynell had printed the book, and Hazlitt was hoping to find a publisher who would buy up the printed edition and offer it to the public. Hence his letter to Jeffrey, which he followed up with a note to Archibald Constable on May 29:

> I some time ago sent Mr. Jeffrey a volume which I have written for a friend, who wishes to dispose of the edition of 1000 copies for 200 guineas. Perhaps you might be willing to purchase it. I do not know what Mr. Jeffrey's opinion of it is, but I enclose you an extract from the Times newspaper which may have some weight with it. I am afraid to ask after the Round Table: but I hope it will find its way.[32]

Appended was this notice from the *Times* of the twenty-eighth:

> *Shakespear:* The lovers of the drama, and more particularly of the great master of it, may derive, we apprehend, considerable pleasure from a work written by Mr. W. Hazlitt entitled *Characters of Shakespear's Plays.* The observations have much of the ingenuity and depth of the famous German commentator Schlegel, without his efforts at system.

Constable failed to accept the offer, but Jeffrey wrote to Hazlitt, apparently promising to notice the new book in the *Edinburgh* and offering a suggestion or two. "With respect to the Shakespear," Hazlitt replied on June 13, "I shall be satisfied if you find any thing to praise in it. I know it has plenty of faults." As usual, he accepted Jeffrey's criticism humbly: "With respect to what you say of my writing, I have no other objection to make than that it is too favourable. I confess to all the faults. I am sorry to say in reference to your very friendly suggestion that I am afraid I am unfit for almost any other profession than that of an author." Yet he was more cheerful than usual: a promised remittance from Jeffrey would, he stated, "very nearly clear me of my old arrears, & at present my immediate receipts are greater than my outgoings." [33]

The Characters of Shakespear's Plays was presently accepted for publication by Charles Ollier and Rowland Hunter, who had succeeded his late uncle Joseph Johnson at the famous shop in St. Paul's Churchyard. It was officially released to the public on July 9, with a flyleaf bearing the affectionate dedication: "To Charles Lamb, Esq., this volume is inscribed, as a mark of old friendship and lasting esteem."

Hazlitt certainly enjoyed writing the book. By the time he had finished it, he was steeped in Shakespeare. His review of Southey's *Letter to William*

32. Jones, "Nine New Hazlitt Letters," p. 274.
33. ALS, Yale University Library.

Smith in May contained no less than nineteen quotations from Shakespeare; the five brief articles which he wrote for the *Morning Chronicle* in June and July[34]—his only periodical contributions for these months apart from the dramatic reviews in the *Times*—contained nine. These were in no sense literary or personal essays such as might naturally call up echoes from an author's past reading; they were political articles, fiery propaganda, in Hazlitt's now familiar vein, all of them deploring the tyranny exercised by the Castlereagh government at home and abroad—with occasional barbs aimed in passing at defenders of that government like Coleridge, Southey, and Dr. Stoddart.[35]

In the preface to the book Hazlitt quoted Pope's celebrated remarks about Shakespeare's originality and characterization, then added: "The object of the volume here offered to the public is to illustrate these remarks in a more particular manner by a reference to each play." Schlegel, he acknowledged, had given "the best account of the plays of Shakespear that has hitherto appeared," but Schlegel's work had two shortcomings: "an appearance of mysticism in his style" and lack of "illustrations from particular passages of the plays" (4:170–71). These faults Hazlitt promised to avoid in his book. His opinions, he warned, were far removed from those expressed in Johnson's famous preface, but he did not apologize: Johnson was "neither a poet nor a judge of poetry"; "he was a man of strong common sense and practical wisdom, rather than of genius or feeling"; he "found the general species of *didactic* form in Shakespear's characters" but ignored their "individual traits, or the *dramatic* distinctions which Shakespear has engrafted on this general nature" (4:174–76). Moreover, Hazlitt believed, Johnson's fondness for balanced sentences led him to seek out a fault to counterpoise each merit which he mentioned.

"Poor Shakespear!" Hazlitt exclaimed toward the end of his preface, and the exclamation was sincere. He was an unabashed Bardolater, convinced that his idol had been shamefully abused. Shakespeare's plays, he acknowledged, were great popular favorites, but the professional critics failed to yield him the honor that was his due. Accordingly, Hazlitt set himself up as

34. "On the Spy-System" (June 30 and July 15), "The Treatment of State Prisoners" (July 5), "On the Treatment of State Prisoners" (July 17), "The Opposition and 'The Courier'" (July 19), and "England in 1798" (August 2) (see 7:208–19; 19:199–202). By this time James Perry had resigned from editorship of the *Chronicle*.

35. The last of the five pieces was hardly an article at all: merely a statement of Southey's in the *Quarterly* implying disbelief in the *Monthly Review*'s claim that England had caused the death of 5,800,000 Europeans—followed by a long passage from Coleridge's pacifistic poem "Fears in Solitude" written in 1798.

Shakespeare's defender, one interested in revealing his extraordinary powers rather than analyzing the plays thoroughly and balancing merits against defects. (Johnson had done enough of that!) And for Hazlitt Shakespeare's greatest power was his skill in detecting the subtleties of human character—which, indeed, was a favorite pastime of Hazlitt himself.

The result approached what has since been termed impressionistic criticism—and often disdained because of its abuse in the hands of lady or lady-like Victorians who lacked Hazlitt's judgment and discriminating taste. He enjoyed seeing or, even more, reading Shakespeare's plays, and he wanted to increase others' enjoyment. Furthermore, he wanted his readers to enjoy the process of reading *about* Shakespeare's plays, and he strove to put them at their ease. He had said in *The Round Table* that he preferred "Steele's occasional selection of beautiful poetical passages, without any affectation of analyzing their beauties, to Addison's fine-spun theories" and Steele's "sensible conversation" to Addison's lecturing (4:8–9). Accordingly, he sought to single out "beauties" or subtleties rather than to analyze them, and he maintained always an informal tone. At times his "conversation" with the reader slipped into rhapsody, when his enthusiasm carried him away, but he never sounded remote or condescending. One of his favorite quotations was Bacon's phrase "coming home to men's bosoms and business," and throughout his book he tried to bring Shakespeare close to readers and to stay close to them himself. In effect he used the techniques of the personal essay to enliven literary criticism; he even lifted bodily from the Round Table series in the *Examiner* his essay on *Midsummer Night's Dream* and reprinted it (with a paragraph from another of his essays) in this new book.

But the lasting value of the essays sprang not from Hazlitt's manner but from his perceptive criticism. He was, of course, no scholar; he had only a superficial knowledge of Shakespeare's reading or the work of his predecessors or the intellectual temper of his time; he discussed Shakespeare's villains without mention of Machiavelli, his heroines without mention of Lyly or Greene, his heroes without mention of Holinshed. He attempted little in the way of comparison with other dramatists earlier or later; he looked only at Shakespeare, who, for him, was sufficient in himself. But he looked hard, his perception was sharp; he had familiarized himself thoroughly with the plays on the stage and in print, and he was a keen intuitive psychologist who could appreciate Shakespeare's insight into "the mixed motives of human character." For him Shakespeare's "subtlety exceeds that of all other dramatic writers" (4:245); he was "scarcely more remarkable for the force and marked contrasts of his characters than for the truth and subtlety with which he has distinguished those which approached nearest to each other" (4:293). He "has been accused of inconsistency . . . only because he has kept up the distinction which there is in nature, between the understandings and the moral habits of men, between the absurdity of their ideas and the absurdity of their motives" (4:237). In short, "the true spirit of humanity, the thorough knowledge of the stuff we are made of, the practical wisdom with the seeming fooleries . . . have no parallel any where else. In one point of view, they are laughable in the extreme; in another they are equally affecting, if it is affecting to show *what a little thing is human life*, what a poor forked creature man is!" (4:283).

Hazlitt was quick to admit that, unlike Johnson, he did not like the comedies "half so well" as the tragedies (4:314). Tragedy, he believed, ennobles our emotions, exercises our sympathies, in a way which comedy cannot. "It has been said," he wrote in his essay on *Othello*,

> that tragedy purifies the affections by terror and pity. That is, it substitutes imaginary sympathy for mere selfishness. It gives us a high and permanent interest, beyond ourselves, in humanity as such. It raises the great, the remote, and the possible to an equality with the real, the little and the near. It makes man a partaker with his kind. It subdues and softens the stubbornness of his will. It teaches him that there are and have been others like himself, by showing him as in a glass what they have felt, thought, and done. It opens the chambers of the human heart. (4:200)

Lear he pronounced "the best of all Shakespear's plays, for it is the one in which he was the most in earnest. . . . The passion which he has taken as his subject is that which strikes its root deepest into the human heart" (4:257). Further, Shakespeare sought to tell us not what he thought but what others thought; he "appears to have been all the characters, and in all the situations he describes" (4:284). He showed not a trace of "egotism"— at least in the plays. The poems and sonnets, where he sought to express his own feelings, had far less value and interest for Hazlitt and received only slight notice. For him Shakespeare's greatness sprang from his matchless sympathetic imagination.

There was very little system about the book. Hazlitt considered the plays as his fancy directed; generally speaking, he discussed the tragedies first, then the histories and the comedies, and finally the poems and sonnets. But he did not always adhere to this plan, and when he did, he seems to have been prompted by personal preferences rather than by any desire for order. Unfortunately, the total effect of the book is distinctly anticlimactic; the gusto which brightens the first essays flickers and dies long before the end of the book. Furthermore, the essays themselves are similarly wanting in order or climax. Hazlitt followed no consistent pattern of development; usually he concentrated on characterization, but he might (or might not) provide also a summary of the plot, describe a fine scene in detail, quote a purple passage, rhapsodize on Mrs. Siddons's unforgettable Lady Macbeth, or work in a discussion of the nature of tragedy, a critique of Wordsworth's "Intimations of Immortality," or even (as in the essay on *Coriolanus*) a tirade against tyranny and war. The essay on *Richard III*, for example, contains, first, remarks on Kean's interpretation of Richard, then criticism of Cibber's revision of the play, then a couple of fine passages and a brief discussion of the leading character. And the essay on *Troilus and Cressida* fades out with "we must conclude this criticism; and we will do it with a quotation or two" (4:226).

But although the haphazard organization may be annoying, the vivid style compensates. Hazlitt outdid himself to make his enthusiasm infectious. He discussed the characters as if they were real people well known to the reader and himself. He wrote to convince the reading public that Shakespeare could both entertain and enlighten them. To twentieth-century readers he may seem overfond of generalizations, careless, inaccurate, sometimes rhetorical, frequently superficial; but they must acknowledge that he makes them listen as few critics before or since his time have done. And usually their attention is amply rewarded, often with original insights that have never been superseded.

One of his best known passages is a case in point—the lines on the character of Hamlet:

> Hamlet is a name; his speeches and sayings but the idle coinage of the poet's brain. What then, are they not real? They are as real as our own thoughts. Their reality is in the reader's mind. It is *we* who are Hamlet. This play has a prophetic truth, which is above that of history. Whoever has become thoughtful and melancholy through his own mishaps or those of others; whoever has borne about with him the clouded brow of reflection, and thought himself "too much i' th' sun"; whoever has seen the golden lamp of day dimmed by envious mists rising in his own breast, and could find in the world before him only a dull blank with nothing left remarkable in it; whoever has known "the pangs of despised love, the insolence of office, or the spurns which patient merit of the unworthy takes"; he who has felt his mind sink within him, and sadness cling to his heart like a malady, who has had his hopes blighted and his youth staggered by the apparitions of strange things; who cannot be well at ease, while he sees evil hovering near him like a spectre; whose powers of action have been eaten up by thought, he to whom the universe seems infinite, and himself nothing; whose bitterness of soul makes him careless of consequences, and who goes to a play as his best resource to shove off, to a second remove, the evils of life by a mock representation of them—this is the true Hamlet. (4:232–33)

And the true Hazlitt? For surely to a receptive reader exposed hitherto only to objective criticism, the passage conveyed new insights: through exercise of his sympathetic imagination Hazlitt seemed truly to have identified with the character, to be in a position to understand and appreciate it in all its complexity.

And receptive readers responded eagerly. Leigh Hunt greeted the new book enthusiastically in a prepublication notice in the *Examiner* for June 20: the Theatrical Examiner for that issue consisted of an excerpt from Hazlitt's chapter on *The Merchant of Venice* with Hunt's admiring comment and a statement that "it is the least of all its praises to say that it must inevitably supersede the dogmatical and half-informed criticisms of Johnson." [36] Constable's *Edinburgh Magazine* for November was similarly complimentary, declaring that "Mr. Hazlitt's Characters of Shakespeare . . . appear to us the most animated, intelligent, and prepossessed criticism on the 'great heir of fame'" and describing Hazlitt as "the best writer of a short essay since Goldsmith." [37] But Hazlitt must have been more concerned to learn the reaction of the *Edinburgh Review*, for he believed that this new book merited serious consideration. On August 12 he wrote to Jeffrey asking whether he thought it likely he could "*insinuate* The Shakespear Characters in the next no." and assuring him that "your notice would at once lift me from the character of a disappointed author to that of a successful one." [38] And when the delayed August issue of the *Edinburgh* appeared, he had the satisfaction of reading these judicious words by Jeffrey:

> This is not a book of black-letter learning, or historical elucidation;—neither is it a metaphysical dissertation, full of wise perplexities and elaborate reconcilements. It is, in truth, rather an encomium on Shakespeare, than a commentary or critique on him—and is written, more to show extraordinary love, than extraordinary knowledge of his productions. Nevertheless, it is a very pleasing book—and, we do not hesitate to say, a book of very considerable originality and genius. The author is not merely an admirer of our great dramatist, but an idolater of him; and openly professes his idolatry. We have ourselves too great a leaning to the same sentiment, to blame him very much for his enthusiasm: and though we think, of course, that our own admiration is, on the whole, more discriminating and judicious, there are not

36. Hunt later reprinted the article in his *London Journal;* and in the *Examiner*s for October 26, November 2, and November 23 he reviewed the book more fully (see *Leigh Hunt's Dramatic Criticism*, ed. L. H. Houtchens and C. W. Houtchens [New York: Columbia University Press, 1949], pp. 167–79).

37. In "Hazlitt Reviews Hazlitt?" (*Modern Language Review* 64 [1969], 20–26) John O. Hayden argues that Hazlitt might have written the review himself.

38. ALS, Yale University Library.

many points on which, especially after reading his eloquent exposition of them, we should be much inclined to disagree with him.

The book, as we have already intimated, is written less to tell the reader what Mr. H. *knows* about Shakespeare or his writings, than to explain to them what he *feels* about them—and *why* he feels so—and thinks that all who profess to love poetry should feel so likewise. What we chiefly look for in such a work, accordingly, is a fine sense of the beauties of the author, and an eloquent exposition of them; and all this, and more, we think, may be found in the volume before us.

Even better than the reviews was the favorable response of the public. Hazlitt reported happily in his letter to Jeffrey that the book was selling well; in fact, the first edition sold out in six weeks, and the publishers Taylor and Hessey bought up the copyright and prepared to issue a second edition. Nothing quite like it had ever before been available in the bookshops. To be sure, earlier critics like Maurice Morgann had discussed Shakespeare's characters in similar fashion, and Coleridge in his lectures and Lamb in his critical essays had anticipated some of the points made; but no one had ever attempted a comprehensive study of all of Shakespeare, play by play, that readers could read and reread with pleasure as a guide to their understanding and appreciation. Young John Keats read the book with enthusiasm, underlining passages that captured his imagination and scribbling comments in the margins—especially in the essay on *King Lear*.[39] He found new fuel to kindle the ideas already sparked by *The Round Table:* Hazlitt's comments on Shakespeare's objectivity, for example, or his contrast between Chaucer's "consecutive" mind and Shakespeare's "intuition." And across the Atlantic, in Boston, Massachussetts, the book found another eager reader, an unscrupulous publisher who brought out a pirated edition in the following year.

With the book well launched, Hazlitt could hope soon to be out of debt,[40] and he seems to have gone down to the Fox and Hounds Inn at Burford Bridge on the river Mole in the valley of Mickleham and there to have spent his time reading, tramping the fields, perhaps trying his hand again at sketching. In *The Spirit of the Age* he recalled finding the Reverend Thomas Chalmers's *Sermons on Astronomy* "in the orchard at Burford-bridge near Boxhill, and passing a whole and very delightful morning reading it, without

39. See Amy Lowell, *John Keats*, 2 vols. (Boston and New York: Houghton Mifflin Co., 1925), 2:587–90.

40. In his August 12 letter to Jeffrey he had acknowledged receipt of "your remittance of £50" and added: "Perhaps if you like my Biographical article [i.e., his review of Coleridge's *Biographia Literaria*] *very much*, I might apply in *forma pauperis* for one of 30£ in advance for the one which I meditate on modern novels" (ALS, Yale University Library).

quitting the shade of an apple-tree" (11:45 n.). He might also have walked over to Fredley Farm nearby to visit "Conversation" Sharpe, his old benefactor. The inn proved such a restful retreat that he evidently recommended it to John Keats, who went there in the following November to finish work on his new poem, *Endymion*.[41]

On August 13 the *Champion* (no longer under John Scott's editorship) contained a signed article by Hazlitt "On the Effects of War and Taxes" urging the newly appointed Finance Committee of the House of Commons to distinguish between productive and unproductive labor when they tried to balance the national budget—and to observe how much of the tax income was spent on unproductive warfare and on luxury for the privileged few (7:219–25).[42] Then when the August issue of the *Edinburgh Review* appeared, it contained Hazlitt's lengthy critique of Coleridge's *Biographia Literaria*.

Although he was less virulent in this than in many of his recent attacks, he spared Coleridge nothing. He regarded the volume as pure apology, and he lashed out not only at Coleridge's defense of Southey, Wordsworth, and Burke, but even at his estimates of the philosophical contributions of Hobbes and the "monstrous absurdity" Kant. The article rose to a telling envoi:

> Mr. C., with great talents, has, by ambition to be every thing, become nothing. His metaphysics have been a dead weight on the wings of his imagination—while his imagination has run away with his reason and common sense. He might, we seriously think, have been a very considerable poet—instead of which he has chosen to be a bad philosopher and a worse politician. There is something, we suspect, in these studies that does not easily amalgamate. We would not, with Plato, absolutely banish poets from the commonwealth; but we really think they should meddle as little with its practical administration as may be. They live in an ideal world of their own; and it would be, perhaps, as well if they were confined to it. Their flights and fancies are delightful to themselves and to every body else; but they make strange work with matter of fact; and, if they were allowed to act in public affairs, would soon turn the world upside down....
>
> This is the true history of our reformed Antijacobin poets; the life of one [of] whom is here recorded. The cant of Morality, like the cant of Methodism, comes in most naturally to close the scene: and as the regenerated sinner keeps alive his old raptures and new-acquired horrors, by anticipating endless ecstasies or endless tortures in another world; so, our disappointed demagogue keeps up that "pleasurable poetic

41. See Walter Jackson Bate, *John Keats* (Cambridge, Mass.: Harvard University Press, 1963), p. 229.

42. The article was reprinted without Hazlitt's signature in the October issue of the *Edinburgh Magazine*, the monthly which Archibald Constable had inaugurated as a successor to the old *Scots Magazine*.

fervour" which has been the cordial and the bane of his existence, by indulging his maudlin egotism and his mawkish spleen in fulsome eulogies of his own virtues, and nauseous abuse of his contemporaries—in making excuses for doing nothing himself, and assigning bad motives for what others have done.—Till he can do something better, we would rather hear no more of him. (16:137–38) 43

In September and October Hazlitt was back in London writing two or three reviews of plays each week for the *Times*. Usually he confined himself to detailed discussions, usually favorable, of the actors' performances, but occasionally he took time to describe the new decor at Covent Garden (18:243) or criticize the experiment at the English Opera House of presenting two performances in a single evening (18:251). The reviews brightened up when Kean returned to London after a tour; Hazlitt declared that Kean outdid himself in *Macbeth*, falling short only of Mrs. Siddons's achievement (18:260–61). And Kean's Othello was still "we suppose, the finest piece of acting in the world" (18:262–63).

During the same two months he wrote occasional articles for other papers. The *Morning Chronicle* for September 2 contained his "Examination of Mr. Malthus's Doctrines," rejecting both the supposed geometric ratio of population growth and the arithmetic ratio of growth of subsistence as untenable theories used "as a lucky diversion against all Utopian projects of perfectibility, and against every practical advance in human improvement" (7:336). And for a few weeks he resumed regular work for the *Champion*. For the September 28 issue he wrote "On the Regal Character," angrily contrasting the self-centered nature of kings in general and the character of the true "patriot King, who without any other faculty usually possessed by Sovereigns, has one which they seldom possess—the power in imagination of changing places with his people" (7:287). Then in the issues for October 12, 19, and 26 came a long article "What is the People?" an impassioned defense of the theory *vox populi vox Dei*—"the rule of all good Government: for in that voice, truly collected and freely expressed . . . we have all the

43. Hazlitt reprinted a passage of the review concerning Burke (minus the final paragraph) in the *Champion* for October 5, 1817. The article in the *Edinburgh Review* contained a long footnote, signed with Francis Jeffrey's initials, replying to "averments of a personal and injurious nature" in the *Biographia Literaria* (see 16:426–27). Later Jeffrey listed the entire article as his, but it bears every indication of being Hazlitt's work. It was probably this article about which he later wrote: "I happened to be saying something about Burke, and was expressing an opinion of his talents in no measured terms, when this gentleman interrupted me by saying, he thought, for his part, that Burke had been greatly over-rated, and then added, in a careless way, 'Pray did you read a character of him in the last number of the ———?' 'I wrote it!'—I could not resist the antithesis, but was afterwards ashamed of my momentary petulance" (8:286).

sincerity and all the wisdom of the community" (7:268). Along with it went an equally impassioned attack on "the old doctrine of Divine Right, new-vamped up under the style and title of Legitimacy" (7:260). Hazlitt allowed himself passing slaps at Southey and Stoddart, but on the whole he exercised a becoming restraint: for once he chose to uphold cherished ideals rather than to degrade fellow mortals.

Ironically, just as Hazlitt was showing signs of moderation, the opposition decided to square accounts with him. In August the belated April issue of the *Quarterly Review* appeared with a critique of *The Round Table*, probably by James Russell, a colleague of Robert Southey.[44] Instead of screaming in horror at the liberal principles displayed in the essays, the critic chose the much more damaging device of ridicule. "Whatever may have been the preponderating feelings with which we closed these volumes," he began,

> we will not refuse our acknowledgments to Mr. Hazlitt for a few mirthful sensations which he has enabled us to mingle with the rest, by the hint that his Essays were meant to be "in the manner of the Spectator and Tatler." The passage in which this is conveyed happened to be nearly the last to which we turned; and we were about to rise from "the Round Table" heavily oppressed with a recollection of vulgar descriptions, silly paradoxes, flat truisms, misty sophistry, broken English, ill humour and rancorous abuse, when we were first informed of the modest pretensions of our host. Our thoughts then reverted with an eager impulse to the urbanity of Addison, his unassuming tone, and clear simplicity; to the ease and softness of his style, to the cheerful benevolence of his heart. The playful gaiety too, and the tender feelings of his coadjutor, poor Steele, came forcibly to our memory. The effect of the ludicrous contrast thus presented to us, it would be somewhat difficult to describe. We think that it was akin to what we have felt from the admirable nonchalance with which Liston, in the complex character of a weaver and an ass, seems to throw away all doubt of his being the most accomplished lover in the universe, and receives, as if they were merely his due, the caresses of the fairy Queen.[45]

What followed was in much the same scornful tone. Hazlitt was dismissed as "a sour Jacobin" whose writing is "mere trash."

Crabb Robinson came upon the article when he picked up a copy of the April *Quarterly* at the Surrey Institution on October 24. Much as he disapproved of Hazlitt's attacks, he was shocked at this "very bitter and scornful

44. Here and elsewhere information about publication dates of the *Quarterly Review* and authorship of its articles is drawn from Hill Shine and Helen Chadwick Shine, *The Quarterly Review under Gifford* (Chapel Hill: University of North Carolina Press, 1949).

45. The allusion in the final lines is to Liston, the popular comedian, playing the part of Bottom in *Midsummer Night's Dream*.

review." "I hope Southey was not the author of it," he wrote in his diary. "If not, I suspect some friend of the Laureate's wrote with laboured malice to avenge his friend. The severity of the criticism has defeated its object in great measure, I have no doubt. The *Quarterly* exceeds the *Edinburgh* in acrimony and vulgarity." [46]

But this was only the beginning. In the October issue of *Blackwood's Magazine*, the rising Tory journal published in Edinburgh, the new editors, John Wilson and John Gibson Lockhart, presented the first installment of "The Cockney School of Poetry." Their target was Leigh Hunt and his *Story of Rimini*, but the article concluded with an ominous hint: "Mr. Jeffrey does ill, when he delegates his important functions into such hands as those of Mr. Hazlitt. It was chiefly in consequence of that gentleman's allowing Leigh Hunt to pass unpunished through a scene of slaughter, which his execution might so highly have graced, that we came to the resolution of laying before our readers a series of essays on *the Cockney School*—of which here terminates the first." [47]

The October 26 issue of the *Examiner* contained the first installment of Hunt's enthusiastic review of *The Characters of Shakespear's Plays*, but it offered little consolation: Hazlitt was beginning to question Hunt's judgment and perhaps to object to the common coupling of their names. "Hazlitt spent Sunday evening with me, talking of [Hunt's] self delusion and conceit," Haydon wrote in his diary on October 13. "I told him some one said, 'let him be in a delusion & a sleep.' 'Yes,' said Barnes, 'but he *kicks* in his sleep.' 'I don't know as to his *kicking*,' said Hazlitt, 'but I know he talks & writes in his sleep.' The same Friend complained that the Quarterly Review said he preceded Bristol Hunt as Voltaire did Marat & Danton. 'I don't know whether he *precedes* Bristol Hunt, but I am sure he comes *after* Voltaire,' said Hazlitt." [48]

At the same time some of Hazlitt's friends were beginning to have second thoughts about his own judgment. When Godwin suggested that Hazlitt review his *Mandeville* for the *Edinburgh Review*, Jeffrey replied on October 30 that Hazlitt "seems to be a person whose judgement is somewhat at the mercy of partialities and prejudices . . . ." [49] As for Crabb Robinson, although he admitted that Hazlitt was "greatly improved in his manners

46. Robinson, 1:210.

47. The authors were alluding to the review of *Rimini* in the June, 1816, *Edinburgh Review* which was probably more Jeffrey's work than Hazlitt's (see discussion above, p. 166).

48. *Haydon Diary*, 2:134. "Bristol" Hunt was the radical politician Henry Hunt.

49. Howe, p. 218.

. . . almost gentlemanly compared to what he was" when they met at Basil Montagu's on November 2, he was relieved when Hazlitt "studiously avoided" him and refused to speak. "It is what I wished," he wrote in his diary.[50] Even Keats, though still a loyal admirer, had learned that Hazlitt was not infallible. In May he had objected to his reference to Southey's "grey hairs"; now on September 28 he remarked in a letter to Haydon that the artist Cripps had "the fault that you pointed out to me in Hazlitt—on the constringing and diffusing of substance." [51] And on October 29, in a letter to Benjamin Bailey, he puzzled over Hazlitt's remark that Wordsworth, the advocate of "a wise passiveness," should not complain of the indolence of a band of gypsies. "I think he is right," Keats declared, "and yet I think Hazlitt is right and yet I think Wordsworth is rightest. Wordsworth had not been idle had he not been without his task—nor had they Gipseys—they in the visible world had been as picturesque an object as he in the invisible." [52]

During November and December Hazlitt wrote little. He reviewed no plays for the *Times* between October 27 and November 29. Then he resumed his regular articles, contrasting on December 2 the extravagant style of Miss O'Neill in *Venice Preserved* with Kean's more restrained acting; he added, characteristically, that Mrs. Siddons had been equally adept at both (18:265–67). On the sixteenth he hailed Kean's return to the stage in *Richard III* after an illness of six weeks (18:269). And on the nineteenth he wrote a very brief review of Kean's performance in the comedy *Riches; or, the Wife and Brother* (18:270–71)—which proved to be his last for the *Times*. Later, in his preface to *A View of the English Stage*, he explained that he had been "forced to quit . . . by want of health and leisure" (5:174).[53]

He had complained of illness more than once during the year; doubtless he was already suffering from the chronic digestive complaint which was to plague him as long as he lived. But he had not been robbed of his leisure by heavy pressures from the periodicals: in recent months, since he had stopped writing for the *Examiner*, he had been writing occasionally for the *Morning Chronicle*, the *Champion*, and the *Edinburgh Magazine*. And he had produced fewer articles than in the past. His only periodical contribution for December, apart from his *Times* reviews, was a critique of Benjamin West's painting *Death on a White Horse* in the *Edinburgh Magazine*,

50. Robinson, 1:211.   51. *Keats Letters*, 1:167.   52. Ibid., pp. 173–74.

53. Cf. Hazlitt's emphatic statement, quoted above p. 144 n., that, although he was discharged from the *Morning Chronicle*, he left the *Times* voluntarily.

praising the artist's skill but lamenting his lack of gusto and deploring the extravagant praise of the painting provided in the descriptive catalogue (18:135–40).

The real reason for his resignation from the *Times* was, undoubtedly, that he had had his fill of writing for the newspapers and magazines. He had drifted into it against his will, and, for a time, it had served its purpose. But he was ready now for work which would be less demanding and more rewarding. He had, in fact, a new project in mind: a series of lectures on English poetry. His series on English philosophy had been reasonably successful, and the sale of *The Characters of Shakespear's Plays* proved that readers were looking for guidance from a critic who spoke their language.

It was worth a try, surely. It would involve less pressure than regular journalism, less of a tax on his health. It would free him from the endless squabbles of the newspapers; it would let him steep himself, instead, in the masterpieces of literature which he loved. And always, if he could contrive to have the lectures published, he could collect double pay for his efforts.

CHAPTER IX

Moment of Triumph
(1818)

In due time Hazlitt proposed to the committee in charge of the Surrey Institution that he present for them a series of six lectures on the English poets. Members of the committee, one of whom was Lamb's friend Thomas Alsager, acted on the proposal, and Hazlitt stopped in at the committee room one day to hear the verdict from the secretary of the institution, Peter George Patmore.

When Patmore entered the room, he saw "a pale anatomy of a man, sitting uneasily, half on half off a chair, with his legs tucked awkwardly underneath the rail, his hands folded listlessly on his knees, his head drooping on one side, and one of his elbows leaning (not resting) on the edge of the table by which he sat, as if in fear of its having no right to be there. His hat had taken an odd position on the floor beside him, as if that, too, felt itself as much out of its element as the owner."[1] The stranger half rose from his chair, but said nothing. After he learned that the committee had approved his proposal, he confessed to Patmore that he had written none of the lectures. Yet he asked him if he could secure "whole or part" payment in advance.

While the two men were completing arrangements for the lectures, Patmore called one day at Hazlitt's house on York Street. "On knocking at the door," he wrote,

> it was, after a long interval, opened by a sufficiently "neat-handed" domestic. The outer door led immediately from the street (down a step) into an empty apartment,

1. Patmore, 2:250. Patmore erroneously assumed throughout his report that he was writing about Hazlitt's later lectures on the comic poets.

indicating an uninhabited house and I supposed I had mistaken the number; but, on asking for the object of my search, I was shown to a door which opened (a step from the ground) on to a ladder-like staircase, bare like the rest, which led to a dark bare landing-place, and thence to a large square wainscotted apartment. The great curtainless windows of this room looked upon some dingy trees: the whole of the wall, over and about the chimney-piece, was entirely covered, up to the ceiling, by names written in pencil, of all sizes and characters, and in all directions.[2]

The room was furnished only with a table (strewn with breakfast dishes, although it was two o'clock in the afternoon), a sofa, and three chairs. Sarah was stretched out on the sofa; Hazlitt sat at the table and held forth "for a couple of hours, without intermission" on Wordsworth, Coleridge, and whatever else happened to come to his mind. When Patmore suggested that he review the lectures for *Blackwood's Magazine*, Hazlitt was wary. But he finally agreed to lend him the manuscripts as they were completed.

During the month of January, before the lecture series began, Hazlitt contributed two papers to the *Yellow Dwarf*, a new weekly published by Leigh Hunt's brother John. "The Press—Coleridge, Southey, Wordsworth, and Bentham," which appeared in the initial number on January 3, presented a statement made in "the French House of Commons" that "liberty of the Press is less necessary in a Representative Government than in any other" (19:202), reviewed the records of the four Englishmen named in the title of the article, and concluded that Bentham was the only honest man of the four. In the same issue came the first installment of "On Court-Influence," which was continued in the January 10 *Yellow Dwarf*. Hazlitt began with the thesis that "the temptation to men in public life to swerve from the path of duty, less frequently arises from a sordid regard to their private interests, than from an undue deference to popular applause" (7:230), citing the cases of Burke and Southey to illustrate his point. He then pointed out how court influence had corrupted Castlereagh, Southey, Coleridge, and—a new candidate—William Gifford, editor in chief of the *Quarterly Review*. "It is hard for any one to be an honest politician who is not born and bred a Dissenter," he declared at last. "Nothing else can sufficiently inure and steel a man against the prevailing prejudices of the world, but that habit of mind which arises from non-conformity to its decisions in matters of religion" (7:239-40). And "in discharge of an old debt" he sketched the character of a Dissenting minister, obviously his father:

> Their sympathy was not with the oppressors, but the oppressed. They cherished in their thoughts—and wished to transmit to their posterity—those rights and privileges for asserting which their ancestors had bled on scaffolds, or had pined in dungeons, or

2. Ibid., p. 261.

in foreign climes. Their creed too was "Glory to God, peace on earth, good will to man." This creed, since profaned and rendered vile, they kept fast through good report and evil report. This belief they had, that looks at something out of itself, fixed as the stars, deep as the firmamaent, that makes of its own heart an altar to truth, a place of worship for what is right, at which it does reverence with praise and prayer like a holy thing, apart and content: that feels that the greatest being in the universe is always near it, and that all things work together for the good of his creatures, under his guiding hand. This covenant they kept, as the stars keep their courses: this principle they stuck by, for want of knowing better, as it sticks by them to the last. It grew with their growth, it does not wither in their decay. It lives when the almond-tree flourishes, and is not bowed down with the tottering knees. It glimmers with the last feeble eyesight, smiles in the faded cheek like infancy, and lights a path before them to the grave!—This is better than the life of a whirligig Court poet. (7:242)

In a letter to J. J. Morgan dated January 7 Coleridge apologized for not speaking to him at a recent party at the Lambs' "because that unhappy man Hazlitt . . . is always there," and he complained bitterly of the unfairness of Hazlitt's *Yellow Dwarf* article.[3] Ten days later, writing to John Payne Collier, he referred to "the rancorous hatred of Hazlitt, provoked (as far as my consciousness extends) wholly and solely by acts of friendship towards him."[4] But Hazlitt acted solely by his own lights: he could be both loyal and loving toward one who was faithful to the cause he revered. His father, who had moved to Crediton in Devonshire, was eighty-three years old now —so frail as barely to have escaped being dragged into the water by a swan one day. He had grown playful in his old age—and rather childish too, delighting in the snuff and barley-sugar candy which he carried about together in a leather-lined waistcoat pocket. Yet Hazlitt respected him for his steadfastness, over the years, to the cause of human freedom, even as he deplored Coleridge's alleged defection from that cause. He judged a man not for his acts of personal kindness but for his principles.

On Tuesday, January 13, Hazlitt delivered his first lecture "On Poetry in General" at the Surrey Institution. According to later reports, he was carefully dressed but nervous, lost his voice once or twice during the lecture, yet managed to get through the trying evening reasonably well despite a rather thin and sometimes restless audience.[5] William Bewick, to whom Hazlitt had given a ticket to the series, left a much more vivid account of the performance:

The friends who knew the sensitive and wayward character of Hazlitt were prepared for a disappointment from his failure in self-possession and confidence. They therefore placed themselves in readiness,—but what did take place?

3. *Coleridge Letters*, 4:798.   4. Ibid., p. 813.   5. *Memoirs*, 1:236.

The time arriving, and the audience expressing unequivocal signs of impatience, our lecturer, pallid as death, and hesitating, like some unhappy being about to meet his doom, approached the table, lecture in hand, and tried to clear his choking voice, but all his efforts failed to overcome his nervousness. The auditory, perceiving his timidity, clapped and applauded, crying, "Bravo, Hazlitt!" This seemed to encourage him, and he began in faint and tremulous accents; but as the noise subsided, and he became conscious of the sound of his own voice, lifting his too-observant eyes to the "sea of heads" before him, all watching and gazing at him, his small modicum of voice and confidence oozed out, and fidgeting confusedly at his waistcoat pockets, he came to a full stop, closed his manuscript, and bolted off in quick retreat. In the room he passed into, however, he found friends ready to prevent his disappearance. They came round him, encouraged and persuaded him; he heard too the hubbub of applause, the shouting of his name, with many expressions of encouragement, and he slowly returned to the lecture-table, amidst vociferous clamours of "Bravo, Hazlitt!" &c. He commenced once more his difficult task, and warming to his subject while he was stimulated by the frequent acknowledgments of his striking thoughts or brilliant language, before he had finished his first lecture he became quite at home with the indulgent friends before him.[6]

But the content of the lectures made up for any faults of delivery. It was the most fully developed statement of his poetic creed that he ever attempted. "The best general notion which I can give of poetry," he began, "is that it is the natural impresssion of any object or event, by its vividness exciting an involuntary movement of imagination and passion, and producing, by sympathy, a certain modulation of the voice, or sounds, expressing it" (5:1). In the course of his lecture he would, he announced, "speak first of the subject-matter of it, next of the forms of expression to which it gives birth, and afterwards of its connection with the harmony of sound" (5:1). Then followed a dazzling, yet provocative, series of generalizations: "Poetry is the language of the imagination and the passions"—"Poetry is the universal language which the heart holds with nature and itself"— "Poetry . . . is an imitation of nature, but the imagination and the passions are a part of man's nature"—"Poetry is the high-wrought enthusiasm of fancy and feeling" (5:1–4)—and so on. Hazlitt developed and discussed his points in detail—and obviously enjoyed the process—stressing always that poetry is the product of the imagination and the passions, rather than rhyme and meter. "It is not a branch of authorship," he declared: "it is 'the stuff of which our life is made.' The rest is 'mere oblivion,' a dead letter: for all that is worth remembering in life, is the poetry of it. Fear is poetry,

6. Landseer, 1:144.

hope is poetry, love is poetry, hatred is poetry, contempt, jealousy, remorse, admiration, wonder, pity, despair, or madness, are all poetry" (5:2).

However, he was not advocating a mere spontaneous overflow of subjective feelings; he thought always in terms of the *sympathetic* imagination. "Impassioned poetry," he maintained, "is an emanation of the moral and intellectual part of our nature, as well as of the sensitive—of the desire to know, the will to act, and the power to feel; and ought to appeal to these different parts of our constitution, in order to be perfect." Indeed "the tragedy of Shakespeare, which is true poetry, stirs our inmost affections; abstracts evil from itself by combining it with all the forms of the imagination, and with the deepest workings of the heart, and rouses the whole man within us" (5:6).

All this was strong fare for most of his audience. T. N. Talfourd, who was present, remarked later on "their imperfect sympathy"; the group, he declared,

> consisted chiefly of Dissenters, who agreed with him in his hatred of Lord Castlereagh, and his love of religious freedom, but who "loved no plays;" of Quakers, who approved him as the earnest opponent of slavery and capital punishment, but who "heard no music;" of citizens, devoted to the main chance, who had a hankering after "the improvements of the mind;" but to whom his favourite doctrine of its natural disinterestedness was a riddle; of a few enemies who came to sneer; and a few friends, who were eager to learn, and to admire.[7]

By the time Hazlitt had finished arguing that the language of poetry must not be reduced "to the standard of common sense and reason" (5:8), that "the progress of knowledge and refinement has a tendency . . . to clip the wings of poetry" (5:9), that "painting gives the event, poetry the progress of the events: but it is during the progress . . . that the pinch of the interest lies" (5:10), that poetry begins "as often as articulation passes naturally into intonation" (5:12), and the like, most of his audience must have been puzzled and dazed. Then came the astonishing claim that *Pilgrim's Progress*, *Robinson Crusoe*, and Boccaccio's tales "come as near to poetry as possible without absolutely being so" (5:13). Not until he reached his concluding remarks on Homer, the Bible, Dante, and Ossian did he offer what they had come to hear, and these were so rapid and sparkling that they were left baffled.

But those few friends who were "eager to learn, and to admire" were elated. Hazlitt had spoken for the new generation of poets, had opened new paths for them to explore, had, in fact, proved himself a major critic.

7. Talfourd, 2:174.

Patmore insisted on the honor of escorting him home. When he offered his arm, Hazlitt pulled away; when Patmore persisted, Hazlitt held it only *"gingerly* with the tips of his fingers" "as if it had been a bar of hot iron" and punctuated every third sentence with a "Sir." [8] He was not sure he could trust this fellow who was reviewing the lectures for the Tory *Blackwood's.*

The following Sunday John Keats dined with Hazlitt and Haydon. Word had gone out about the brilliance of that first lecture, and Keats was determined to be present at the second. He had become more and more convinced that Hazlitt's judgments about poetry and the fine arts were worth listening to. On December 22, 1817, describing West's painting *Death on a White Horse* in a letter to his two brothers, he had complained, quite in the manner of Hazlitt, that the painting offered "nothing to be intense upon." In another letter to his brothers on January 13—and in a third to Haydon on the tenth—he declared that "if there were three things superior in the modern world, they were 'the Excursion,' 'Haydon's Pictures' & Hazlitts depth of Taste." [9] Moreover, in his copy of *The Characters of Shakespear's Plays* he wrote on the title page: ". . . he hath a kind of taste."

Unfortunately he was confused about the time of the second lecture, "On Chaucer and Spenser," and he arrived at the Surrey Institution an hour late, just as the audience was leaving. Hazlitt, Bewick, John Hunt and his son Henry, "all the Landseers"—"Aye & more" . . . "pounced upon" him, and he determined to be prompt on the following Tuesday. [10] Although they had apparently been well pleased with the lecture, it had fallen short, inevitably, of the first. Hazlitt had spent most of the hour pointing out the "beauties" of Chaucer and Spenser and reading long excerpts from *Canterbury Tales* and *The Faerie Queene.* The less knowledgeable members of the audience probably found it far more to their taste than the first lecture.

Keats was almost certainly present for the third lecture "On Shakspeare and Milton," given on the twentieth, but he did not record his impressions of it. Crabb Robinson was there and admitted in his diary that Hazlitt "delighted me much by the talent he displayed." Although he began with a reading of his Round Table essay "Why the Arts Are Not Progressive" and included much of another, "On Milton's Versification," he soon gave

---

8. Patmore, 2:275–76. Cf. pp. 276–77, where Patmore describes Hazlitt's embarrassment when they were approached by "petitioners" (i.e., streetwalkers).

9. *Keats Letters,* 1:204–5. Cf. p. 203.

10. Ibid., p. 214.

vent to all his enthusiasm for the talents of the two poets whom he so heartily admired. The lecture flashed with brilliant comparisons of the two poets and of their work and that of Spenser and Chaucer; there were fewer excerpts from the poems discussed (probably because he assumed that his audience would be relatively familiar with Shakespeare and Milton), more revealing insights memorably phrased. He concluded with a penetrating critique of *Paradise Lost* which offered, in miniature, the kind of tribute to Milton that *The Characters of Shakespear's Plays* had accorded to Shakespeare. Keats might well rejoice in Hazlitt's depth of taste. And there was a special challenge for a rising young poet in his passing allusion to "a modern school of poetry" which relies on "a mere effusion of natural sensibility" or, worse, "the morbid feelings and devouring egotism of the writers' own minds" (5:53). The audience interrupted with applause at this point, but Crabb Robinson doubted "whether he was generally understood." To him this was just one more outburst of Hazlitt's bitterness of spirit.[11]

Hazlitt seems to have delivered no lecture on the following Tuesday, January 27. He was approaching less familiar periods of literature, and he probably needed time for preparation. On February 3 his subject was Dryden and Pope, and he did a creditable job of acknowledging the merits of these masters of "the artificial style of poetry," as he called them. Hazlitt never subscribed to the theory that Pope was not a poet; he recognized his talents, but placed them definitely below those of the "natural" poets who had preceded him. Since he felt less enthusiasm for his subject, he was not at his best in this lecture; it was shorter than the earlier ones and ended with a cursory review of Dryden's longer poems and the works of nine minor poets of the seventeenth century. He disposed of John Donne in three lines: "Of Donne I know nothing but some beautiful verses to his wife, dissuading her from accompanying him on his travels abroad, and some quaint riddles in verse, which the Sphinx could not unravel" (5:83).

The next two lectures, "On Thomson and Cowper" (February 10) and "On Swift, Young, Gray, Collins, etc." (February 17), seem to have been hurriedly thrown together. In the first Hazlitt discussed and compared the two poets named in the title of the lecture, examined the work of Robert Bloomfield and George Crabbe, then took up the subject of pastoral poetry in general and concluded by reading his Round Table essay "On the Love of the Country."[12] At the outset of the second he announced that he would "endeavour to give a cursory account of the most eminent of our poets"

11. Robinson, 1:218.
12. Howe (5:392) records Hazlitt's use in this lecture of other materials already in print.

from the early eighteenth century to the present, but after presenting brief critiques of the works of ten eighteenth-century poets and comparing the wit of Swift, Voltaire, and Rabelais, he merely listed twenty-five others whom he lacked time to discuss, then finished off with remarks on Thomas Chatterton, whom he dismissed as a precocious youth but not a genius.

But although these lectures were loosely organized and superficial (Hazlitt was trying to sum up the history of English literature to date in six one-hour lectures!), they often opened up new vistas to his loyal young admirers. On February 11 William Bewick wrote to his brother: "Hazlitt is giving lectures on poetry; they are said to be the finest lectures ever delivered. He is the Shakespeare prose writer of our glorious country; he outdoes all in truth, style, and originality—you must read his Shakespeare's characters." 13 "By his request," Bewick recalled later, "I often called upon him and accompanied him to the Surrey Institution. He was generally sitting alone in front of the looking-glass, putting the last touches to the lecture of the evening. After which he would chat away in great good-humour, making pertinent remarks upon the requirements of popular lecturing, observing that 'He at all events must endeavour to express his own thoughts upon what he undertook to do, and not to be led away by the mistake of pleasing the million, or speaking for the present hour.'" 14

Keats too was now attending the lectures faithfully. Of the February 11 lecture he remarked, in a letter to his brothers written on or about the fourteenth, that Hazlitt "praised Cowper & Thompson but he gave Crabbe an unmerciful licking." And three days after the February 18 lecture he wrote again to his brothers: "I hear Hazlitt's Lectures regularly—his last was on Gray Collins, Young &c and he gave a very f[ine] piece of discriminating criticism on Swift, Vo[ltaire] And Rabelais—I was very disappointed at his treatment of Chatterton—I generally meet with many I know there." 15

Crabb Robinson took a more jaundiced view of the lectures; to him Hazlitt seemed "bitter, sprightly, and full of political and personal allusions." "In treating of Prior," Robinson wrote in his diary, he "quoted his

13. Landseer, 1:41–42.
14. Ibid., 1:144–45.
15. *Keats Letters*, 1:227 and 237. H. W. Garrod (*Keats*, Oxford: Clarendon Press, 1926, p. 64 n.) suggested that Keats might have been moved to write "The Pot of Basil; or, Isabella" after hearing Hazlitt's remark in his lecture "On Dryden and Pope" that translations of some of Boccaccio's or Chaucer's tales "as that of Isabella, the Falcon, of Constance, The Prioress's Tale, and others, if executed with taste and spirit, could not fail to succeed in the present day" (5:82).

unseemly verses against Blackmore to a congregation of saints. He drew an ingenious but not very intelligible parallel between Swift, Rabelais, and Voltaire, and even eulogized the modern infidel, so indiscreet and reckless is the man."[16]

Hazlitt must have heard that some members of his audience had objected to his treatment of Chatterton because he began his next lecture "On Burns and the Old Ballads" (February 24) with an apology to those whom he might have offended. However, he did not retract; he was convinced that Chatterton's poetry revealed precocity rather than true genius, and he derided the extravagant praise that contemporary critics had showered on him. He turned then to Burns, and at last the lectures sprang to life again. Here was the sort of person Hazlitt could respond to, "sympathize" with: he was a creature of warmth and feeling who left a sting in the mind of his reader. Wordsworth had attempted a defense of him which disclosed, Hazlitt believed, Wordsworth's utter inability to understand a man like Burns. But Hazlitt left no doubt that he could understand Burns and could appreciate his poetry—especially "Tam O'Shanter," which he quoted entire. In his zest he lingered so long over Burns that the old ballads received very scant notice.

Crabb Robinson was present for only a part of this lecture; he "hurried away to attend Mrs. Smith to Coleridge's lecture," for Coleridge by this time was giving his second series of lectures on Shakespeare at the Crown and Anchor Tavern. Just as he was leaving the Surrey Institution, however, Robinson heard Hazlitt's strictures on Wordsworth, and he was so enraged that "I lost my temper and hissed; but I was on the outside of the room. I was led to burst out into declamations against Hazlitt which I afterwards regretted, though I offered nothing but the truth. Hazlitt abused Wordsworth in a vulgar style, imputing to him the mere desire of representing himself as a superior man." Later, after the lecture had been published, Robinson read it and reflected that "it is amusing to observe how the animal vigour of the Scotch peasant is eulogized as if this were glory as well as felicity, while the purity and delicacy of the Philosopher of the Lakes is sneered at as a sort of impotence."[17] If he had read these words, Hazlitt would have retorted that he did indeed prefer vigor to delicacy in both life and literature.

At the last lecture "On the Living Poets" (March 3) Hazlitt dilated on the nature of fame: the true genius, he declared again, concentrates on

16. Robinson, 1:219. The author of the lines on Blackmore was John Gay rather than Prior.

17. Ibid., pp. 220 and 223.

doing his job well, oblivious of fame. Not so the modern poet, who is pre-occupied always with himself and his immediate success. Crabb Robinson tartly summed up the substance of what followed when he read the published lecture later in the year:

> he flippantly and cavalierly, but with eloquence occasionally, breaks the staff over the heads of the living poets. He bepraises Coleridge with outrageous eulogy, at the same time that he reproaches him bitterly. Praises Wordsworth warmly but in a sentence or two, while he dwells with malignity on his real and imputed faults, and treats Southey absolutely with contempt. Rogers he passes over as if he were a lady whom he was not at liberty to abuse. Does not name Crabbe, and rather avoids meeting public opinion on the merits of Lord Byron. Indeed, it is easy to give evasive judgment by dwelling on accidents only. Moore he seems desirous of favouring, and he is kind to Walter Scott.[18]

Actually Hazlitt came surprisingly close to anticipating the verdicts of posterity on all these men.

By this time his interest was flagging, and he was encountering some resistance from his audience. When he disposed of Hannah More's poetry by remarking casually that she had written a great deal which he had not read, one of his listeners cried, "More pity for you!"[19] He was not the man to feign an interest which he did not feel, and he concluded the series by confessing candidly: "I have thus gone through the task I intended, and have come at last to the level ground. I have felt my subject gradually sinking from under me as I advanced, and have been afraid of ending in nothing. The interest has unavoidably decreased at almost every successive step of the progress, like a play that has its catastrophe in the first or second act. This, however, I could not help. I have done as well as I could" (5:168).

Despite his apology, however, the lectures had not been a failure. Words-worth, Coleridge, Southey, and their supporters, like Crabb Robinson, were obviously not going to be pleased. Coleridge, more than the others, continued to seethe; and in a letter of February 5 to James Perry he repeated his charge that Hazlitt had explained his attitude toward Coleridge by remarking: "Because I HATE him."[20] But the Wordsworths were evidently unruffled; at least Charles Lamb felt he could adopt a tone of gentle irony when he wrote to Mrs. Wordsworth on February 18: "W.H. goes on lecturing against W.W. and making copious use of quotations from said W.W. to give a zest to said lectures. . . . I have not heard either [Coleridge] or H."[21]

18. Ibid., p. 222. Hazlitt had discussed Crabbe's poetry in his February 10 lecture.
19 Talfourd, 2:175.   20. *Coleridge Letters*, 4:831.
21. *Lamb Letters*, 2:227.

The editors of the *Examiner* were enthusiastic, claiming that Hazlitt had drawn ever larger audiences and that the final lecture, when the hall was crowded to the ceiling, had been followed by a rousing "Bravo!"[22] James Perry, now retired from the editorship of the *Morning Chronicle*, decided that he had underestimated Hazlitt in the past and, according to Mary Russell Mitford, invited him to dine with some friends who were eager to hear what this new lion had to say. "The lion came—smiled and bowed," Miss Mitford wrote, "—handed Miss Bentley to the diningroom —asked Miss Perry to take wine—said once 'Yes' and twice 'No'—and never uttered another word the whole evening."[23]

Keats was delighted with the series—even the harsh treatment of contemporary poets. He was surer than ever now that Hazlitt was the man he should look to for guidance. "Hazlitt has damned the bigotted and bluestockined how durst the Man?!" he wrote to Haydon on March 21. "He is your only good damner and if ever I am damned (damn me if) I should'nt like him to damn me. . . ."[24] And on April 27 he wrote to John Hamilton Reynolds: "I have written to George for some Books—shall learn Greek, and very likely Italian—and in other ways prepare myself to ask Hazlitt in about a years time the best metaphysical road I can take."[25]

Thanks to Patmore's reviews in the February and March *Blackwood's*, the lectures were reaching a wider audience. And Hazlitt was well pleased with the way Patmore was handling the assignment. When he read the manuscript of the first installment, he wrote to Patmore: "I am well satisfied with the article, and obliged to you for it. I am afraid the censure is truer than the praise. It will be of great service if they insert it entire, which, however, I hope."[26] He was cheered too by the publishers Taylor and Hessey's offer of one hundred pounds for rights to bring out the lectures in book form. Soon he was busy preparing them for the press; on March 6 he returned two corrected proofs to the publishers and promised to submit more copy that same evening.[27] And presently he was invited to repeat the series

22. Baker, p. 253.   23. L'Estrange, 2:48.   24. *Keats Letters*, 1:252.

25. Ibid., p. 274. Concerning Keats's later use of ideas which may have been suggested by Hazlitt's lectures, see Sikes, "The Poetic Theory and Practice of Keats," pp. 401–4; Finney, *The Evolution of Keats's Poetry*, 1:342, and Douglas Bush, *John Keats* (New York and London: Macmillan Co., 1966), pp. 70, 146–47. In "Some Problems concerning Keats and Hazlitt" (*Keats-Shelley Memorial Bulletin* 8 [1957]: 33–37), Rotraud Muller points out that Keats marked with two crosses the *Lectures on the English Poets* in a list of new books included in his copy of Leigh Hunt's *Literary Pocket Book*.

26. Patmore, 2:278 n.

27. *The Keats Circle: Letters and Papers 1816–1878*, ed. Hyder E. Rollins, 2 vols. (Cambridge, Mass.: Harvard University Press, 1948), 1:13 (hereafter cited as *Keats Circle*).

at the Crown and Anchor Tavern in the Strand, where Coleridge had been lecturing on Shakespeare.[28] Hazlitt's new profession was proving rewarding indeed!

Inevitably his work for the periodicals had fallen off sharply while he was giving the lectures. For the *Yellow Dwarf* he had written a three-installment article "On the Clerical Character," which appeared in the issues for January 24 and 31 and February 7. It was, in effect, a sequel to the remarks about the Dissenting clergy which had concluded his January 10 article "On Court Influence." Now, however, he focused his attention on the faults of the clergy, especially the Established clergy. Their dress sets them off from other men, he charged, and tends to make them priggish; in their desire to convey an impression of sanctity, they are likely to become hypocritical. In effect, Established religion encourages dishonesty in its clergy— and Hazlitt seized the occasion to attack the alliance of church and state, adding for good measure a few incidental slaps at Southey and Wordsworth (7:242–59).

On February 14 it was Coleridge's turn again. The *Courier* for February 9 had included a favorable review of his first lecture on Shakespeare, in which he had compared Caliban with the Jacobins. Hazlitt's article, "Mr. Coleridge's Lectures," derided Coleridge for mixing politics and criticism and, inevitably, reminded him of the days when he had heartily approved of Jacobins (19:206–10). Another article, "On the Question Whether Pope was a Poet," in the February *Edinburgh Magazine* (20:89–92), was lifted almost bodily from Hazlitt's fourth lecture. And in March, April, and May the *Yellow Dwarf* contained three articles, all of which were merely reprints of essays written for and published in other periodicals during the preceding year.[29]

For the *Yellow Dwarf* of April 4 Hazlitt also wrote "Pulpit Oratory, No. 4: the Rev. Herbert Marsh, Bishop of Landaff [*sic*]," a scornful attack on Marsh and especially the sermon on "the renewal of our knowledge of one another in a future state" which he had preached "two or three Sundays ago . . . at the Chapel Royal . . . before the Prince Regent." John Hamilton Reynolds had written the three earlier essays of the series, but he was ill in

28. On March 25 Haydon wrote to Keats: "Haslitt is going to lecture at Crown & anchor I am sorry for it, tho' he will get money, it is letting his talents down a little" (*Keats Letters*, 1:259).

29. The reprinted articles were "What is the People?" from the *Champion* of October 12, 19, and 26, 1817; "An Examination of Mr. Malthus's Doctrines" from the *Morning Chronicle* of September 2, 1817; and "On the Regal Character" from the *Champion* of September 28, 1817.

April, and Hazlitt evidently filled in for him.[30] But it was not until later in the month that he returned to regular writing for the magazines. On the twenty-fifth he reviewed Thomas Moore's new poem *The Fudge Family in Paris*, hailing the author as a poet and a patriot, "neither a coxcomb nor a catspaw,—a whiffling turncoat, nor a thorough-paced tool, a mouthing sycophant, 'a full solempne man,' like Mr. Wordsworth,—a whining monk, like Mr. Southey,—a maudlin Methodistical lay-preacher, like Mr. Coleridge" (7:287–88), and so on. He even managed to include a gratuitous attack on the editor of the *New Times*.[31]

The *Yellow Dwarf* for May 2 contained Hazlitt's review of canto 4 of Byron's *Childe Harold's Pilgrimage*—"an indigestion of the mind," he termed it. He made a great point of his disappointment in the poem: "All our prejudices are in favour of the Noble Poet," he insisted, "and against his maligners." But he could not condone the "mass of discordant things, incoherent, not gross"; the cynicism, more objectionable than Wordsworth's egotism; the picture of this "spoiled child of the Muses—and of Fortune" (19:35–41). At the same time he quoted liberally from the poem with obvious relish. Byron was, after all, like Burns and Shakespeare, Hazlitt's kind of man.

He wrote one more article for the May 23 number of the *Yellow Dwarf*, which expired with that issue. It was an essay "On the Opera," in which he vented his distaste for that "most artificial of all things." He branded its profuseness ("one may be stifled to death with roses," he lamented), its catering to the shallowest of audiences. Yet he conceded that it was peculiarly appropriate to the dismal times in which he was living: "It may serve to assist the *euthanasia* of the British character, of British liberty, and British morals, by hardening the heart, while it softens the senses, and dissolving every manly and generous feeling in an atmosphere of voluptuous effeminacy" (20:96).

He had been hoping, meanwhile, to resume work for the *Edinburgh Review*—had sent Jeffrey an unsolicited article and, incidentally, asked his advice about repeating his lecture series in Edinburgh. On May 3 Jeffrey

30. The article was discovered and reprinted by William H. Marshall in "An Addition to the Hazlitt Canon: Arguments from External and Internal Evidence," in *Papers of the Bibliographical Society of America* 55 (1961):347–70.

31. Hazlitt had been more critical of Moore when he discussed his work in the last of his Lectures on the English poets in February (5:151–52). Moore responded to the favorable review of *The Fudge Family* by sending him a presentation copy of the book. Their friendship soon cooled, however, and in his essay "On the Jealousy and the Spleen of Party" Hazlitt struck out vehemently against Moore (see discussion below, pp. 419–20, and compare my forthcoming article, "Moore's Present to Hazlitt").

replied, aplogizing for his failure to publish "your little paper on Dr. Reid's book" and advising him not to attempt the lecture series. What followed is revealing: Jeffrey was sorry, he said, to hear that Hazlitt had been unwell; he was aware that Hazlitt needed money desperately; he assured him that "we cannot let a man of genius suffer in this way," and he enclosed an advance of one hundred pounds, "a great part of which I shall owe you in a few weeks," adding that another hundred pounds was "heartily at your service" if needed.[32] Despite the success of the lectures and *The Characters of Shakespear's Plays*, Hazlitt had still not extricated himself from the worries which had dogged him for months.

On May 12 he wrote to thank Jeffrey for the remittance. "I hope it will set me on my legs again," he remarked, "as I shall pass the summer in the country, doing little, & thinking less." However, he was planning "among other nothings" to submit "two pretty long reviews, which may I fear tire your patience." He had "some thoughts of making an article on Drake's book, taking the amusing anecdotes, & adding a little speculation on the age of Elizabeth, Protestantism, the Bible, translations from the classics, &c." But he was still struggling with "the metaphysics" and promised to "send [it] first—that there may be time to alter the subject if necessary."[33]

Presently Taylor and Hessey published Hazlitt's *Lectures on the English Poets*—on the same day that they brought out a second edition of *The Characters of Shakespear's Plays*. John Taylor was excited about the publication of the *Lectures:* he assured his brother, in a letter of June 4, that it was "a Work of extraordinary Ability."[34] Unfortunately, however, editors of the major magazines failed to share his enthusiasm, and the book went practically unnoticed until the beginning of the following year, when the July, 1818, number of the *Quarterly Review* appeared.

Meanwhile the publisher Robert Stodart brought out still another volume bearing Hazlitt's name—this one a mere job of bookmaking, a collection of his dramatic reviews issued with the title *A View of the English Stage*. He announced in the preface to the volume that a detailed account of contemporary acting "might not be wholly without its use" because plays and players

32. Constable, *Archibald Constable and His Literary Correspondents*, 2:217-19. "Dr. Reid's book" was Thomas Reid's *Inquiry into the Human Mind*.

33. ALS, Yale University Library. The review of Nathan Drake's *Shakespeare and His Times* (1817) never appeared in the *Edinburgh*. Hazlitt's "speculation," probably derived in part from C. W. Dilke's introduction to *A Continuation of Dodsley's Old English Plays*, may well have formed the nucleus of the first lecture of *Lectures on the Dramatic Literature of the Age of Elizabeth* (see below, p. 252 and n.).

34. Edmund Blunden, *Keats's Publisher: A Memoir of John Taylor (1781–1864)* (London: Jonathan Cape, 1936), p. 54 (hereafter cited as Blunden).

are "the epitome of human life and manners" and the actor's art is so ephemeral; yet the book was pretty clearly designed primarily to help him work his way out of debt. The reviews were drawn from all four periodicals that he had served as dramatic critic: the *Morning Chronicle*, the *Champion*, the *Examiner*, and the *Times*. He advised "any one who has an ambition to write, and to write *his best*, in the periodical press, to get if possible 'a situation' in the *Times* newspaper, the Editor of which is a man of business, and not of letters" (5:173–74). Yet he reprinted in the collection only two of the forty-two reviews which he had written for the *Times*.

He seems to have followed no consistent principles in his choice of the essays which he reprinted. Although he remarked in the preface that he considered the criticisms of Kean in the *Morning Chronicle* to be his best, he did not reprint all of them. Nor did he select all those which were enlivened by his chatty comments on matters of more general interest. Sometimes he omitted the brief notes about performances elsewhere which he appended to his reviews of the new plays at Drury Lane or Covent Garden; usually he discarded his cursory reviews of farces or afterpieces; occasionally he excised a sentence or two of a controversial cast.[35] But he followed no discernible pattern of selection—and he may well have reprinted those reviews which happened to be most easily accessible.

Even in its own time the book had little more than historical interest. A reader might enjoy Hazlitt's accounts of the most successful performances of his favorites: Kean and Miss O'Neill in tragedy, Liston and Miss Kelly in comedy, and, of course, Mrs. Siddons in anything. He could, now and then, share Hazlitt's delight in a bit of subtle acting or a well-turned phrase. But the bright spots were dimmed by the detailed accounts of commonplace performances which stretched between them. Crabb Robinson pronounced it "a very inferior book," though he admitted that it amused him.[36]

A View of the English Stage went virtually unnoticed by the reviewers.[37]

35. Hazlitt's revisions of the original texts are recorded in Howe's notes to volume 5 of the *Complete Works*.

36. Robinson, 1:226. Mary Russell Mitford found reading the book "rather like dining on sweetmeats and supping on pickles. So poignant is he, and so rich, everything seems insipid after him" (L'Estrange, 2:47).

37. Eventually it fell into the clutches of the pietistic *British Review*, which presented a long retrospective critique of it, *The Round Table*, *The Characters of Shakespear's Plays*, and *Lectures on the English Poets* in their May, 1819, issue. The reviewer charged that Hazlitt seemed to be trying to "destroy the very foundations of morality and decorum" and begged him to reform his ways before "the decline of life." Anyone who could respect actors, enjoy *The Beggar's Opera*, condone Shakespeare's lack of morality, admire Boccaccio, Voltaire, and Rousseau, and approve of Bonaparte seemed to him to be "a

But the January issue of the *Quarterly Review*, running behind schedule as usual, came out in June with a devastating critique, probably by James Russell, of *The Characters of Shakespear's Plays*. The author damned Hazlitt's cavalier treatment of Johnson's preface to Shakespeare, his style, his politics, and his critical principles at length, concluding:

> We should not have condescended to notice the senseless and wicked sophistry of this writer, or to point out to the contempt of the reader his "didactic forms" and "logical diagrams," had we not considered him as one of the representatives of a class of men by whom literature is more than at any former period disgraced, who are labouring to effect their mischievous purposes *non vi sed saepe cadendo;* and therefore conceived that it might not be unprofitable to show how very small a portion of talent and literature was necessary for carrying on the trade of sedition. The few specimens which we have selected of his ethics and his criticism are more than sufficient to prove that Mr. Hazlitt's knowledge of Shakespeare and the English language is exactly on a par with the purity of his morals and the depth of his understanding.

Hazlitt later declared, doubtless with some exaggeration, that Taylor and Hessey "never sold another copy" of *The Characters of Shakespear's Plays* after the review in the *Quarterly* appeared (8:99).

He struck back in the *Examiner* for June 14 with an article entitled "The Editor of the Quarterly Review," denouncing William Gifford, whom he held personally responsible for the attack, as a "cat's paw," "a Government critic" delegated "to keep a strict eye over all writers who differ in opinion with His Majesty's Ministers, and to measure their talents and attainments by the standard of their servility and meanness" (19:210–11). Leigh Hunt wrote delightedly to Shelley on August 4: "Hazlitt has written a masterly character of Gifford, much more coolly done than these things of his in general; and *this* single circumstance shows what sort of feelings the poor creature generates."[38]

Hazlitt himself was in no mood for rejoicing; he was hounded by ill health, debts, the savage attack in the *Quarterly*—and, no doubt, the failure of his marriage. In the course of the next month he probably wrote three articles—one of them, a slight piece entitled "Mr. Wordsworth and the Westmoreland [*sic*] Election," published in the *Examiner* for July 15, chiding the poet for a grammatical error (he who had criticized one of his political foes for a fault in grammar—yet posed as an admirer of rustic

---

scoffing infidel." But he urged Hazlitt to "take in good part our observations on the tendency of his writings, in the assurance that not one word of what we have felt it our duty to offer has been set down in malice, but has been written more in sorrow than in anger."

38. *Correspondence of Leigh Hunt*, ed. Thornton Hunt, 2 vols. (London, 1862), 1:124.

speech!) (19:213–14). In the second, "On the Ignorance of the Learned," which appeared in the July *Edinburgh Magazine*, he seemed to be airing his resentment of the intellectual life in general: he poured scorn on learned bookworms who are ignorant of real life, on a system of education which is "but a foil to common sense; a substitute for true knowledge" (8:70), which relies on rote learning and enables the drudge to outshine his abler fellows. "You will hear more good things on the outside of a stage-coach from London to Oxford," he declared, "than if you were to pass a twelve-month with the Under-graduates or Heads of Colleges of that famous University" (8:75). In much the same vein was his third essay "On Respectable People" in the August *Edinburgh Magazine*. People are generally called respectable, he argued, when nothing specific can be said in their favor: "Respectability means a man's situation and success in life, not his character or conduct" (12:363). As for the "respectable" writer, he is "a literary pimp." But there was a touch of irony in the final sentence of the article: "To be an Edinburgh Reviewer is, I suspect, the highest rank in modern literary society" (12:365). To be sure, he had attained that rank. But Jeffrey had still not printed his latest contribution, the review of Thomas Reid's book, and he may have had some fears that Jeffrey's hundred-pound advance had been intended as a dismissal.[39]

He needed a respite from the pressures that were bearing down upon him, and his mind naturally turned to Winterslow. On July 28 he wrote to Archibald Constable asking if he could have "on account the sum of fifty pounds" because he was "going in the country for the rest of the summer" and wanted to "leave all accounts clear behind me." He promised, in return, to send "articles to that amount for the Magazine within the next two months . . . which the Editors would then have ready by them for the next year."[40]

He traveled down to Winterslow alone, probably on foot; in an essay

39. Hazlitt certainly feared later that he had been "expelled" from the *Edinburgh Review*. When the charge was made in *Blackwood's*, he asked Jeffrey if it were true (see below, p. 231). And in a letter to Archibald Constable probably written in September, he asked if Constable knew the contents of the next issue, said he had submitted a long article for it, but concluded that he had been dropped from the staff (*TLS*, 21 March, 1936, p. 244).

40. Baker, p. 255. Hazlitt may have been acknowledging a loan from Constable when he wrote him an undated letter enclosing "a note of hand for 40£" (see *London Mercury* 7 [1922–23]: 496). Howe, who reprinted the note, assumed that Hazlitt's reference to seeing Reynolds and arranging "about the lectures" applied to the publication of the *Lectures on the English Poets*. However, since John Hamilton Reynolds seems to have reviewed the *Lectures on the English Comic Writers* for the *Edinburgh Magazine* from Hazlitt's manuscripts, the letter probably refers to that series and should be dated later than Howe supposed.

written in 1823 he recalled the "luxury" of reading Congreve's *Love for Love* "after a sultry day's walk in summer between Farnham and Alton" (12:126). And at Winterslow he stayed not at his wife's cottage in the village but at The Hut, an inn a mile or two away on the high road between London and Salisbury. There he could find the quiet which he needed to prepare for the new series of lectures which he had agreed to deliver during the winter ahead. He could immerse himself in the old English writers whom he so loved but had never studied systematically. Such reading was indeed a luxury for one whose knowledge of literature was so scattered. And he found relief, surely, in being by himself, free to walk across Salisbury Plain, to revisit Stonehenge or Wilton, enjoy the excitement of an occasional cockfight, gossip with the simple people who gathered at the inn—people who cared nothing about his reputation as a writer but loved to tell of the escaped lioness who had attacked the London coach there three years before. At Winterslow he could escape from all the pressures which, along with his blasted hopes for a better world, had made life a burden.

In addition to reading and preparing his lectures, he could, when he was in the proper mood, dash off an article or two for the *Edinburgh Magazine*. When Macvey Napier invited him to write an article on the drama for the *Britannica* Supplement, he replied on August 26 that he was "obliged, from want of health and a number of other engagements, which I am little able to perform, to decline the flattering offer." One of these other engagements was "writing *nonsense*" for Constable "as fast as I can." [41]

Soon afterwards he was back in London, probably not with his family at the York Street house, but in lodgings on King Street, Somers Town. [42] And just before or after his return he suffered an even more damaging personal attack—from a new source, *Blackwood's Magazine*. It probably came not as a complete surprise: the unscrupulous Tories on the *Blackwood's* staff had allowed Leigh Hunt and his friends no quarter; their "Cockney School" articles by "Z" [John Gibson Lockhart] had become notorious. Yet they had published Patmore's favorable reviews of Hazlitt's lectures and had included in their June issue an article "Jeffrey and Hazlitt," which, though not always complimentary, at least acknowledged the two to be the foremost critics of the age. But there were ominous clouds on the horizon. In the section "To Correspondents" included in the February issue the editors had commented: "We have no objection to insert Z.'s Remarks on

41. *Selection from the Correspondence of the Late Macvey Napier, Esq.*, ed. Macvey Napier, Jr. (London, 1879), p. 21.
42. *The Hazlitts*, p. 365.

Mr. Hazlitt's Lectures, after our present Correspondent's Notices are completed. If Mr. Hazlitt uttered personalities against the Poets of the Lake School, he reviled those who taught him all he knows about poetry." Then in the March issue the rhyming "Notices" alluded in passing to "pimpled Hazlitt's coxcomb lectures." And at the end of Patmore's review of the lectures in April the editors inserted a cautionary note:

> When we undertook to give the foregoing abstract of Mr. Hazlitt's Lectures, it was not our intention to have accompanied it by a single observation in the shape of judgment, as to their merits or defects; but we find, that our own opinions have been strangely supposed to be identified with those we have done nothing more than detail. We choose, therefore, to say a few words on the impression we have received from these, and from Mr. Hazlitt's previous writings on similar subjects. . . .
>
> As we have not scrupled to declare, that we think Mr. Hazlitt is sometimes the very best living critic, we shall venture one step farther, and add, that we think he is sometimes the very worst. One would suppose he had a personal quarrel with all living writers, good, bad, or indifferent. In fact, he seems to know little about them, and to care less. With him, to be alive is not only a fault in itself, but it includes all other possible faults. He seems to consider life a disease, and death as your only doctor. He reverses the proverb, and thinks a dead ass is better than a living lion. In his eyes, death, like charity, "covereth a multitude of sins." In short, if you want his praise, you must die for it; and when such praise is deserved, and given really *con amore*, it is almost worth dying for.
>
> By the bye, what can our Editor's facetious friend mean by "pimpled Hazlitt?" if he knows that gentleman's person, he cannot intend the epithet to apply to *that*; and how "pimpled" may be interpreted with reference to *mind*, we are not able to divine.

In the May issue a "Letter from Z. to Leigh Hunt" referred to Hazlitt's pimpled nose, and the third Cockney school article in July mocked "Bill Hazlitt" as "that foundered artist"

> whose tact intellectual is such,
> That it seems to feel truth as one's fingers do touch.

Moreover, there was a clear threat in the final sentences of the article: "It was indeed a fatal day for Mr. Jeffrey, when he degraded both himself and his original coadjutors, by taking into pay such an unprincipled blunderer as Hazlitt. He is not a coadjutor, he is an accomplice. The day is perhaps not far distant, when the Charlatan shall be stripped to the naked skin, and made to swallow his own vile prescriptions." [43]

43. The verse was quoted from Leigh Hunt's poem "To W.H." (see above, p. 171).

The threatened exposure came in the August issue of *Blackwood's*, which contained also the infamous Cockney school review of Keats's *Endymion*. The article, entitled "Hazlitt Cross-Questioned" and signed "An Old Friend with a New Face," consisted of eight direct questions. They began:

> Query I. Mr. William Hazlitt, ex-painter, theatrical critic, review, essay, and lecture manufacturer, London, Did you, or did you not, in the course of your late Lectures on Poetry, &c. infamously vituperate and sneer at the character of Mr. Wordsworth —I mean his personal character; his genius even you dare not deny?
>
> II. Is it, or is it not, true that you owe all your ideas about poetry or criticism to gross misconceptions of the meaning of his conversation; and that you once owed your personal safety, perhaps existence, to the humane and firm interference of that virtuous man, who rescued you from the hands of an indignant peasantry whose ideas of purity you, a cockney visitor, had dared to outrage?

The next five questions were focused on Hazlitt's published work, in effect accusing him of ignorance, dishonesty, and obscenity; the last read merely: "Do you know the Latin for a goose?"[44]

Obviously the editors of *Blackwood's* were athirst for blood. In the same issue, a review of Lamb's recently published works included the observation the Lamb "does not condescend to say one syllable" about "'pimpled Hazlitt,' notwithstanding his 'coxcomb lectures' on Poetry and Shakespeare." And, still in the August issue, the author of an article on Shakespeare's sonnets remarked of *The Characters of Shakespear's Plays:* "To [Hazlitt] truth and falsehood are indifferent. He cannot write one syllable on any subject, unless he has an opinion before him, and then he very magnanimously and intellectually contradicts that opinion. He stands with his back turned on the whole writing world, and need not therefore be surprised to get an occasional kick or two."

Hazlitt was stung by these remarks, so much bitterer and more personal than anything even the *Quarterly* had dealt him. J. A. Hessey sent his partner, John Taylor, a copy of the August *Blackwood's* and wrote him in a letter of September 5: ". . . Hazlitt has been here and he is very much moved—He thinks & so do I that he had better remain quiet and let them take their Course."[45] Within the next few days Hazlitt sent Archibald Constable a copy of the article, declaring that he did not "feel tempted to

44. Hazlitt was asked, among other questions, if he had not "wantonly and grossly and indecently insulted Mr. Conway the actor, and published a Retracting Lie in order to escape a caning" (see above, p. 148 n.).

45. *Keats Circle*, 1:37.

this kind of personal warfare," but promising to "see about it" if Constable so advised. In passing he remarked that he expected to receive two hundred, rather than one hundred, pounds for publication rights for his forthcoming lectures.[46]

But he spoke too soon. By September 16 he had conferred with Hessey and had learned that the publishers dared not risk so large an outlay for a book by a man recently under scandalous attack. Hessey complained to Taylor that Hazlitt was irked because they had not agreed to the original terms. He added that Hazlitt "says he is in better Health and Spirits than he has been for some years," that he was planning to go to the seaside to finish his lectures, and that (despite Jeffrey's advice) he hoped to repeat his lectures in Edinburgh.[47] He was in an aggressive mood.

On September 19 he wrote again to Constable. "In making my bargain the other day," he explained, "the various fabrications in [*Blackwood's*] article were objected to me as lessening the value of my literary e[state]." He had decided to take the matter to court and, by way of formality, he enclosed a note to William Blackwood threatening to sue him immediately if he did not supply the name of the author of the slanderous article.[48]

He had already taken steps to start proceedings. He had written to Francis Jeffrey asking him to act as his counsel in the suit, and Jeffrey replied on the twentieth that he would be glad to do so but could not recommend a solicitor for him because "I have no personal acquaintance with you." He had looked over the *Blackwood's* article and suspected that it was actionable; he warned, however, that Hazlitt must be able to disprove the statements in the article. Yet his tone was distinctly friendly: he assured Hazlitt that *Blackwood's* claim that he been "expelled" from the *Edinburgh Review* was "*quite false*," though he could not provide "a formal warrant for saying so" because the *Edinburgh* never revealed authorship of its articles. And as if to prove his good faith he added that he would try to work Hazlitt's review of Reid's book into the next issue and asked him to send along "anything brilliant or striking" that he might have on other subjects. He suggested especially an article on the fine arts, since he had heard that Hazlitt was "profound" on that subject.[49]

The next day Keats wrote to C. W. Dilke: "I suppose you will have heard that Hazlitt has on foot a prosecution against Blackwood—I dined with him a few days sinc[e] at Hessey's—there was not a word said about [it],

46. *TLS*, 21 March, 1936, p. 244.   47. Blunden, p. 65.
48. Jones, "Nine New Hazlitt Letters," pp. 276–77.
49. Constable, *Archibald Constable and His Literary Correspondents*, 2:220–21.

though I understand he is excessively vexed." [50] And the *Times* for the twenty-first contained a notice of the suit, describing *Blackwood's* as "a book filled with private slander." Hazlitt was gaining strong support.

News of the suit spread fast. Mrs. Sarah Coleridge wrote from Keswick to Thomas Poole before the end of the month:

> I understand Mr Wm Hazlitt is about to commence a prosecution against the Editor of [*Blackwood's*] for a libel. . . . I was annoyed at hearing of the intended prosecution, because Southey and Wordsworth may be troubled to give their evidence to the truth of the assertions in the article which would be very disagreeable, & as Master Hazlitt will cut a very ridiculous figure, I wonder he chuses to make a stir in it. I think I told you the ridiculous story of Hazlitt's behaviour to a Peasant Girl when he was here 12 or 14 years ago: some person has taken up this tale, mentioning the kindness of Mr Wordsworth and others to him on this occasion, & commenting on his ingratitude: W. spoke of it here last week & seemed vexed that his name was connected with the thing in any way; but so it is. [51]

Meanwhile William Blackwood had sent Hazlitt a curt note on the twenty-first refusing to divulge authorship of the article, and on the twenty-fifth Hazlitt wrote to James Balfour of Edinburgh authorizing him to bring suit against the publisher.[52]

At first Blackwood was scornful. When John Murray, a shareholder in the magazine, wrote in alarm that "the clamour against its personality [is] almost universal," Blackwood assured him that he supposed "this fellow merely means to make a little bluster, and try if he can pick up a little money"; and he promised a "most powerful" attack on Hazlitt as the lead article in the October issue of the magazine. He sent Murray a long letter composed by John Wilson and John Gibson Lockhart, the authors of "Hazlitt Cross-Questioned," assuring Murray that he had nothing to fear from Hazlitt. But by October 6, when he received a summons to appear before the Court of Sessions to defend himself against Hazlitt's suit for two thousand pounds' damages, Blackwood himself took fright. To add to his concern, an anonymous pamphlet, *Hypocrisy Unveiled, and Calumny Detected*, came out in the middle of the month, damning *Blackwood's* for its sins past and present, with special attention to its treatment of Hazlitt. "The libeller of MR. HAZLITT," wrote the author of the pamphlet,

> avows himself to be an *old friend* with a *new face*,—a face which certainly, whatever features it may have at one time displayed, exhibits only those of a demon. . . . The

50. *Keats Letters*, 1:368.
51. *Minnow Among Tritons*, ed. Stephen Potter (London: Nonesuch Press, 1934), p. 64.
52. Jones, "Nine New Hazlitt Letters," p. 277.

attack on Mr. Hazlitt comes with a worse grace from these persons, inasmuch as they praised him warmly in the outset, holding him up as the first poetical critic of the day, and afterwards devoting an article to a parallel between him and Mr. Jeffrey; but the secret of all is, that Mr. Hazlitt furnished several very able articles to the *Scots* or *Edinburgh Magazine;*—articles which display more original thinking than all that have yet appeared in Blackwood's work. . . . Hazlitt is an abomination in their sight because he is rising into consequence.[53]

At this point Wilson and Lockhart lost their heads and, by sending challenges to the publisher of the pamphlet, revealed that they were the authors of the offensive article. Murray was frantic. He assured Blackwood that "three fourths of the talent of the Bar are in hostility to you, and . . . any jury will be prejudiced against you." Then followed elaborate negotiations, carried on between Sharon Turner, acting for Murray, and P. G. Patmore, acting for Hazlitt. At length they came to terms, and Hazlitt agreed to drop the suit upon payment of one hundred pounds' damages and costs.[54] The *Scotsman* for January 30, 1819, announced that the case had been settled out of court.[55]

Inevitably the last months of the year 1818 had been an unpleasant period for Hazlitt. In spite of himself he had become a public figure: the forces of reaction seized upon his name as symbolic of all they regarded as most hateful. In October and November a writer for the *New Monthly Magazine* joined the general outcry with the first two installments of "The Cockney School of Prose," a nasty attack labeling Hazlitt as a "cankered Cockney," a "pimpled coxcomb," "the dirty dandy of literature," and so forth.[56] On October 22 Keats met Hazlitt on his way to a game of rackets—probably to work off some of his frustration.[57]

Yet there were compensations: his foes would never have been so vicious if they had not regarded him as a serious threat. As the author of *Hypocrisy Unveiled* had put it, he was "an abomination in their sight because he is rising into prominence." Accordingly, when he decided to prepare a written reply to *Blackwood's* in the midst of all the furor, he was able to express

53. *Hypocrisy Unveiled and Calumny Detected* (London, 1818), quoted in Howe, pp. 269–70.

54. The complete texts of Blackwood's and Murray's letters appear in Margaret Oliphant, *Annals of a Publishing House: William Blackwood and His Sons*, 3 vols. (New York, 1897), 1:162–70, and Samuel Smiles, *A Publisher and His Friends*, 2 vols. (London, 1891), 1:482–93.

55. See *TLS*, 22 August, 1935, p. 525.

56. *New Monthly Magazine* 10 (1818):198–202, 299–304.

57. *Keats Letters*, 1:402.

himself calmly, reasonably, and above all, with dignity. "Sir," he began,

> Before I answer your questions, give me leave to tell you my opinion of the person who asks them. I think then that you are a person of little understanding, with great impudence, a total want of principle, an utter disregard to truth or even to the character of common veracity, and a very strong ambition to be picked up and paid as a cat's paw. If I were in the habit of using the words, Liar, Fool, Coxcomb, Hypocrite, Scoundrel, Blackguard, &c., I should apply them to you, but this would be degrading them still lower unnecessarily, for it is quite as easy to prove you the *things* as to call you the *names*. (9:3)

He depreciated his success as a popular writer, which his attacker had scorned; he pointed, proudly, instead, to his *Principles of Human Action*, a book which Coleridge had once praised. "When," he wrote,

> this gentleman, of whom I have at various times spoken the truth, the whole truth, and nothing but the truth, formerly knew me, when I passed for an idiot, he used to say of me (and by so doing he excited a Surprise and incredulity which only his eloquence and persuasive tones could overcome) that "I had the most metaphysical head he ever met with," and when by his advice, and in order as he said that I might laugh at the tittle-tattle about my private follies, I put my metaphysics on paper, answering for myself, he turned his back upon me. ... This same person used at the same time to cocker me up with such expressions as these, that "if ever I got language for my ideas, the world would hear of it, for that I had guts in my brains." And now that I have got language for *my* ideas, he says they are *his* ideas, that my brains are in his and Mr. Wordsworth's head (I deprecate this last utterly) and he gets such a fellow as Z . . . to say that I am a charlatan. (9:3-4)

Then he turned to the specific questions directed at him in the *Blackwood's* article:

> 1. You ask me "if I do not infamously vituperate and sneer at the character of Mr. Wordsworth, *videlicet* his personal character; his genius even I dare not deny." Why not: because I dare not deny my own convictions: certainly I am bound by public opinion to acknowledge [it] in very unsparing terms, and I have in fact gone on the forlorn hope in praising him. As to his personal character, I have said nothing about it: I have spoken of his intellectual egotism (and truly and warrantably) as the bane of his talents and of his public principles. It is because you cannot answer what I have said on the Lake School of Poetry, that you ask me eight impertinent questions. . . .
>
> 3. You ask me whether I do not owe my personal safety, perhaps existence, to the interference of that virtuous man in my behalf, &c. I beg to be excused answering this question except as it relates to my supposed ingratitude, and on that subject my answer is as follows. (9:5-6)

And he told how pleased Wordsworth had reportedly been with the *Examiner* critique of *The Excursion* until he learned that Hazlitt had written it. The story was hardly relevant, but Hazlitt was wise to avoid reviving the details of the Keswick scandal. He answered the remaining questions clearly and decisively, and rested his case. But the reply was not published. He may have hoped to place it in a rival publication like the *Edinburgh Magazine*. But either he failed to place it or he decided, in the long run, to "remain quiet," as he had originally intended, rather than to draw further attention to the nasty interlude. He seems to have sent his reply to Jeffrey, adding marginal notes to aid Jeffrey in preparing his case against Blackwood.

During the autumn months he had three articles published in the *Edinburgh Magazine*—probably some of the "nonsense" that he had been writing at Winterslow during the summer. The September issue contained two: one "On Nicknames" and another "On Fashion." The first, a discussion of what would today be termed "name-calling," was undoubtedly prompted by *Blackwood's* writers' irresponsible use of "nicknames" to brand their foes. "No matter how undeserved the imputation," Hazlitt wrote, "it will stick; for, though it is sport to the bye-standers to see you bespattered, they will not stop to see you wipe out the stains" (17:48). The second article deplored the absurdity of constantly changing fashion and the vulgarity of those who take it seriously (17:51–56). Then in the October issue he offered the first installment of "Thoughts on Taste," a more penetrating essay in which he made the distinction: "Genius is the power of producing excellence; taste is the power of perceiving the excellence thus produced in its several sorts and degrees, with all their force, refinement, distinctions, and connections. In other words, taste (as it relates to the productions of art) is strictly the power of being properly affected by works of genius" (17:57). William Hazlitt, obviously, was a man of taste.

At about this same time he began writing the brief critical introductions which he provided for the plays included in William Oxberry's anthology, *New English Drama*.[58] Most of the plays were already familiar to him; he had read them, seen them, even reviewed many of them at one time or other, and occasionally he borrowed from his reviews. He was gaining a name for himself among the booksellers as a man of taste with a ready supply of literary lore which he could quickly turn to account. Even in mere hackwork like this he wrote with gusto, calling his readers' attention

---

58. P. P. Howe reprints Hazlitt's eighteen introductions, written between 1818 and 1825, in volume 9 (pp. 63–94) of *Collected Works* and records Hazlitt's borrowing from his earlier works in the notes to the volume.

to the merits of each play and, always, sharing with them his delight in the characterization.

Most of his efforts during the last months of the year were directed to his new series of lectures on the English comic poets. On Tuesday, November 3, he gave the first lecture "On Wit and Humour," again at the Surrey Institution. "Man is the only animal that laughs and weeps," he stated at the outset, "for he is the only animal that is struck with the difference between what things are, and what they ought to be" (6:5). There were other remarks in a similar vein, perceptive, sometimes with wistful overtones; for example: "To explain the nature of laughter and tears, is to account for the condition of human life; for it is in a manner compounded of these two! It is a tragedy or a comedy—sad or merry as it happens" (6:5). But most of the lecture was given over to definition and analysis of wit and humor: "Humour," he stated, "is the describing the ludicrous as it is in itself; wit is the exposing it, by comparing or contrasting it with something else" (6:15). He obviously relished this sort of exercise: he could draw on his innate understanding of human nature, his reading and experience, and his skill in trenchant expression. He rounded out his remarks with capsule critiques of Aristophanes, Lucian, Molière, and Rabelais, candidly admitting that he said very little about the first two because he knew very little about them.

Faithful William Bewick attended the new series regularly and reported later with satisfaction that Hazlitt had recovered from his stage fright. Now when he called for Hazlitt before the lectures, "he would sip his cup of strong tea, and laugh and joke at the difficulty he had to surmount at his first series of lectures." [59] Another friend declared that Hazlitt "read his lectures in an abrupt yet somewhat monotonous voice, but they were very effective. If he failed in communicating by his manner, the lighter graces of his authors, he established their graver beauties, and impressed on his auditors a due sense of their power." [60]

The subject of the second lecture on November 10 was "On Shakspeare and Ben Jonson," and inevitably the section on Shakespeare outshone that on Jonson, whose plays, Hazlitt admitted, he had never enjoyed. Yet once again he stated his preference for Shakespeare's work in tragedy: his comedy is "too good-natured and magnanimous . . .; it does not take the highest pleasure in making human nature look as mean, as ridiculous, and contemptible as possible" (6:35). Crabb Robinson was present, probably

59. Landseer, 1:145.
60. *New Monthly Magazine* 29 (1830), pt. 2, p. 473.

against his better judgment, and pronounced the lecture "a dull performance. He raised a tumult by abusing Gifford, which a few hissed at and many applauded; but the best thing he did was reading a glorious passage from Ben Jonson's *Alchemist.*"[61]

The third lecture, on the seventeenth, "On Cowley, Butler, Suckling, Etheredge, &c.," began with Dr. Johnson's definition of metaphysical poetry and proceeded with brief discussions of the poets named in the title, cursory glances at half a dozen others, and a final overview of minor seventeenth-century dramatists. Hazlitt had never before shown any real interest in or knowledge of this period; the writers who flourished then showed too little concern with the subtleties of human character to please him. Moreover, because he tried to touch on many writers rather than to concentrate on a few of the most rewarding, the lecture was superficial and incoherent. Crabb Robinson decided: "He is sinking as a lecturer very fast."[62]

Hazlitt took a two-week recess before the next lecture, ostensibly because of the death of Queen Charlotte, though he may have welcomed the chance to put in some additional preparation, realizing that he was not performing at his peak.[63] Fortunately he could feel sincere enthusiasm for his next subject, the Restoration comedy, which he discussed on December 8. He was dealing again with drama, with life; in fact he considered the comedies of Wycherley, Congreve, Vanbrugh, and Farquhar the finest of the genre in English, and he enlivened his lecture with animated accounts of the plays and generous excerpts. He could only deplore the reforming zeal of Jeremy Collier which led to the sentimental comedy of the next century. Crabb Robinson suspected him of deliberately "touching the sore spots of the saints" in the audience, "being always on the brink of obscenity and palpably recommending works of the most licentious character. . . . This lecture was, after all, but dull," he wrote, "and his audience grew thin."[64]

The lecture on December 15 "On the Periodical Essayists" had as its

---

61. Robinson, 1:225. The lecture as published contained no reference to Gifford. Robinson may have been referring to the passage in the opening paragraphs where Hazlitt again cited Samuel Johnson's insensitivity to poetry. Gifford had castigated a similar passage in his review of *The Characters of Shakespear's Plays.* However, Catherine Macdonald Maclean (*Born under Saturn* [London: Collins, 1943], pp. 396–98) points out, from the *Examiner* report of the lecture, that Hazlitt introduced an attack on Canning by referring to him as dedicatee of Gifford's edition of Ben Jonson.

62. Ibid.

63. Eleven days before the beginning of the series Hazlitt had prepared little more than half the lectures. On October 23 J. A. Hessey reported to John Taylor that "he has got, he says, the first 4 Lectures written & much of the others" (*Keats Circle*, 1:53).

64. Robinson, 1:225.

epigraph (at least in the printed version) a dictum which Hazlitt could approve wholeheartedly: "The proper study of mankind is man." Since the periodical essay was another of his favorites, he was again buoyed up as he discussed Addison and Steele (as usual, favoring Steele), Johnson (lauding his character, as revealed by Boswell, rather than his essays), and Goldsmith (declaring him "more observing, more original, more natural and picturesque" than Johnson). Crabb Robinson considered it "all for the greatest part a repetition of The *Round Table*," [65] and in truth much of his discussion of Addison and Steele was lifted from his Round Table essay on the *Tatler*.

Hazlitt also drew liberally on his earlier writings in the next two lectures, "On the English Novelists" (December 22) and "On the Works of Hogarth —On the Grand and Familiar Style of Painting" (December 29).[66] In both, the subject was again human nature, realistically yet imaginatively drawn, and Hazlitt maintained a high pitch of enthusiasm throughout. He did not apologize for treating the novel as a serious literary form or for airing personal preferences. He rated Fielding's "superior insight into the springs of human character" (6:116) above Richardson's "artificial reality" (6:117), Ann Radcliffe's imaginative romances above Fanny Burney's detailed pictures of contemporary life. In the Hogarth lecture he praised the lifelike expressions of the figures in Hogarth's paintings, contrasting them with those of Wilkie, the "serious, prosaic, literal narrator of facts" (6:139). Yet he granted that Hogarth was not a painter to be compared with Rubens and he concluded with a nostalgic recollection of his days with the old masters in the Louvre.

The final lecture "On the Comic Writers of the Last Century" (January 5) was again anticlimactic. Hazlitt could generate little enthusiasm for the comic writers of the eighteenth century. Again he drew on materials already in print: his Round Table essay "On Modern Comedy" (attributing the decline of comedy to the tendency of literature and education to make people more alike), a critique of the actor Liston from a *Times* review, and a defense of Colley Cibber from the *Examiner*. The audience may have complained about his borrowings because he concluded his published lecture by admitting them—insisting, however, that they constituted "a very small proportion to the whole" (6:168). Except for his zestful remarks about Sheridan as dramatist and orator, this final lecture was commonplace; once

65. Ibid., p. 226.

66. In the notes to volume 6 of the *Complete Works*, Howe records Hazlitt's borrowing from his *Edinburgh Review* article "On Standard Novels and Romances" and his Round Table essay "On Hogarth's Marriage a la Mode."

again he filled out a meager sketch with odds and ends of information, rather ill digested, about minor playwrights and actors.

None the less the introductory lecture and those on Restoration drama, the novel, and Hogarth were ably handled, and few in the audience would have agreed with Crabb Robinson's sour comments on the series. Bewick left a quite different impression: "Hazlitt became a favourite at the Surrey Institution," he wrote,

> and stood up in his place at the lecture-table with all confidence, in the consciousness of having friends and admirers about him. In his flights of sarcasm, or bursts of censure upon the favourite authors of some of his hearers—Lord Byron, for instance —he would occasionally meet with disapprobation; and, as he calmly looked towards the place whence the hissing came, turning back the leaf of his copy, and deliberately repeating the sentiments with greater energy and a voice more determined than before, he exclaimed with slow emphasis, "If my Lord Byron will do these things, he must take the consequences; the acts of Napoleon Bonaparte are subjects of *history*, not for the disparagement of the Muse." Then tossing over the leaf with an air of independence and iron firmness, as if he was not to be influenced by opinions differing from his own on these subjects, he exhibited a striking contrast to the timidity and nervousness of his first appearance at the Surrey Institution.[67]

Although Keats did not attend these lectures, he arranged to borrow Hazlitt's manuscript copies of them.[68] They probably made no very lasting impression on him; after all, they had much less to offer him than did the lectures on the English poets. Yet he was sufficiently taken with Hazlitt's remarks about Godwin in the sixth lecture to copy them at some length in a letter to his brother and sister-in-law in America as "a specimen of [Hazlitt's] usual abrupt manner, and fiery laconiscism."[69]

The summary review of the series, probably by John Hamilton Reynolds, in the *Edinburgh Magazine* was, of course, highly commendatory, as were the reports in the *Examiner* and the *Morning Chronicle*. The *Monthly Review*, which considered these lectures along with *The Characters of Shakespear's Plays* and *Lectures on the English Poets* in their May, 1820, issue, hailed Hazlitt as "perhaps the most sparkling prose-writer of the present day" and prophesied: "All these volumes will be read with luxury on account of their brilliant execution, and with instruction on account of the many delicate remarks which are interspersed among the declamation." But most reviewers ignored the lectures, though they were duly published

67. Landseer, 1:147–48.
68. *Keats Letters*, 2:24 n. Cf. Leonidas M. Jones, "New Letters, Articles and Poems by John Hamilton Reynolds," *Keats-Shelley Journal* 6 (1957):102.
69. Ibid., p. 24.

by Taylor and Hessey in the following year. They probably did not pay
Hazlitt the two hundred pounds which he had asked for publication rights,
and nothing came of his scheme to deliver them in Edinburgh. However, he
was again asked to repeat the series at the Crown and Anchor Tavern,
where Coleridge was still lecturing on Shakespeare.[70] He allowed himself
only a week's respite, then gave his first lecture at the Crown and Anchor
on January 10, 1819.

All in all, Hazlitt's fortunes had improved in the course of the year 1818.
He rounded it out with a long review of Horace Walpole's recently published letters to George Montagu, a cheerful essay which appeared in the
December issue of the *Edinburgh Review*. Although his earlier review of
Reid's *Inquiry into the Human Mind* never appeared in the *Edinburgh* and
the article on the fine arts, suggested by Jeffrey, seems never to have been
written, he was back now in Jeffrey's fold. And his review of Walpole's
letters glowed with pleasure; for although he recognized Walpole's shortcomings as a political thinker, his vanity, and his insensitivity, he praised
him as "the very prince of Gossips." He quoted the letters at length, declaring that personal letters were "the honestest records of great minds"
(16:141). He complained only about the cost of the book; it was a pity,
he wrote, that so few readers could afford to enjoy, as he had, "this lively
volume" (16:152).

In the terms of his lecture "On Wit and Humour" Hazlitt could look
back on his life during the past twelve months as more comedy than tragedy,
more merry than sad. He was still plagued by a loveless marriage and by
open hostility from Tory critics. Yet he had made some gains: his health
had improved during his summer at Winterslow, and the *Blackwood's*
rascals were in retreat. Moreover, he seemed to be in a fair way to solving
his perennial money problems; for though Hessey complained in his October

70. Two newspaper articles of this period quoted by Kathleen Coburn in her edition
of Coleridge's *Philosophical Lectures* ([London: Routledge and Kegan Paul, 1949], pp.
34–35) seem to imply that Hazlitt and Coleridge were regarded as rival authorities on
Shakespeare. In the *Champion* for January 10, 1819, John Thelwall wrote that Coleridge's
interpretation of Hamlet "accords with, *if he has not availed himself of*, the opinions of
Hazlitt and of another Lecturer [Thelwall himself] whose disquisitions on the character
of Hamlet during the last season, excited very popular attention." And an anonymous
writer in the *Courier* wrote after Coleridge's lecture on *Lear* on January 28, that he had
"none of the glib nonsense of Mr. Hazlitt; no tinkling sentences of pretty phraseology,
where big words ramble along without meaning, till the reader stares and wonders what it
can be that is so utterly unintelligible. Mr. Hazlitt evidently never read a play of Shakespeare through, and the style in which he criticizes him, always reminds us of Bradbury,
the clown, dancing upon stilts, where a great clutter, ungainly labour, and violent
distortion, are substituted for agility, ease, and elegance."

23 letter to Taylor that Hazlitt had called on him two days in succession "of course . . . for more money," [71] he had found at last a decent livelihood. Lecturing had proved more profitable than he had anticipated; as he told Francis Jeffrey in his letter of May 12, he "got in all (Lectures & copyright included) 200 guineas for them, which is very well for ten weeks work." [72] It had other advantages too: it did not demand his constant presence in London, it involved a good deal of solitary reading and thinking such as he enjoyed, and it might, with luck, eventually free him from the abrasive warfare of contemporary journalism.

71. *Keats Circle*, 1:53.

72. ALS, Yale University Library. Hazlitt was referring to the *Lectures on the English Poets.*

CHAPTER X

Withdrawal
(1819–1820)

During the months of January and February, 1819, while he was repeating his lectures at the Crown and Anchor Tavern, Hazlitt contributed only two brief articles to periodicals: a letter in the January *Edinburgh Magazine* citing parallel passages in Shakespeare's *Henry VIII* and George Cavendish's *Negociations of Cardinal Wolsey* (20:410) and a sprightly article in the February 7 *Examiner*, "Death of John Cavanagh," affectionately hailing the famous fives player as a true professional.[1] Although he might continue to turn out an occasional article for the magazines or to write reviews for Francis Jeffrey, he regarded lecturing as his major occupation; he was, in fact, negotiating with the Surrey Institution for a new series—this one on the dramatic literature of the Age of Elizabeth.[2]

However, he had a piece of unfinished business in hand, for in January the belated July, 1818, issue of the *Quarterly* came out with a blistering review of his *Lectures on the English Poets*, probably by William Gifford and Eaton S. Barrett. Incensed by Hazlitt's article "The Editor of the Quarterly Review" in the June 14 *Examiner*, they damned the style, the obscure critical principles (especially the heterodox definitions of poetry), the vague critiques of individual poets, the cavalier treatment of Pope, and the general "ignorance" displayed in the *Lectures*. "Upon the whole," they concluded, "the greater part of Mr. Hazlitt's book is either completely unintelligible, or exhibits only faint and dubious glimpses of meaning; and the little portion

1. The article was incorporated into Hazlitt's later Table Talk essay "The Indian Jugglers" (8:77–89).
2. See his letter of February 4, 1819, reprinted in *Complete Works*, 6:385–86.

The Reverend William Hazlitt. Miniature by John Hazlitt.

Hazlitt as a child. Miniature by John Hazlitt. (See p. 25.)

The Parsonage at Wem, Shropshire.

Hazlitt's house at No. 19, York Street,
Westminster.

Hazlitt as a young man. Painting by John Hazlitt. (See p. 64.)

Charles Lamb in the costume of a Venetian senator. Painting by John Hazlitt. (See p. 82.)

Christ's Entry into Jerusalem. Painting by Benjamin Haydon. (See p. 258.)

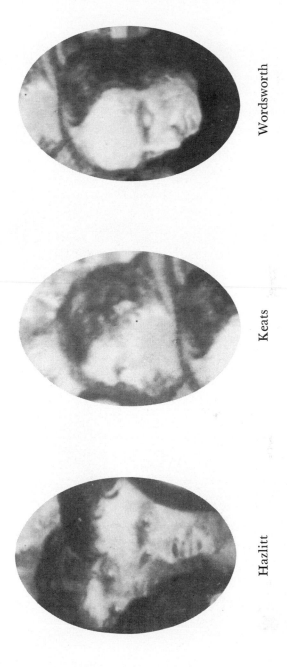

Wordsworth

Keats

Hazlitt

Hazlitt in 1824. Drawing by William Bewick. (See p. 383.)

of it that may be understood is not of so much value as to excite regret on account of the vacancy of thought which pervades the rest. . . . Connected thought may be retained, but no effort of recollection has any power over an incoherent jumble of gaudy words."

There was nothing in the article that was actionable, but much that could not go unanswered. Hazlitt wrote to Whitmore and Fenn, proprietors of a circulating library, asking them to lend him the issues of the *Quarterly* containing the reviews of *The Round Table, The Characters of Shakespear's Plays,* and the *Lectures on the English Poets*.[3] Then he applied himself to the task of a single quashing reply, *A Letter to William Gifford.* He opened with a restatement of his "character" of Gifford in the *Examiner,* adding a few details and shifting from third to second person; then: "Such, Sir, is the picture of which you have sat for the outline:—all that remains is to fill up the little mean, crooked, dirty details. The task is to me no very pleasant one; for I can feel very little ambition to follow you through your ordinary routine of pettifogging objections and barefaced assertions, the only difficulty of making which is to throw aside all regard to truth and decency, and the only difficulty in answering them is to overcome one's contempt for the writer. But you are a nuisance, and should be abated" (9:17). He replied then, point by point, to Gifford's criticisms of his three books, sometimes with the hard-driving earnestness of the earlier article in the *Examiner,* sometimes with an air of outraged innocence, but always cogently, always stressing Gifford's sophistry and casuistry and insisting on his own love of truth and liberty. Finally, as in his reply to *Blackwood's,* he cited his original "metaphysical discovery" as the achievement by which he rightly should be judged. "For this cause it is," he wrote,

that I have gone on little discomposed by other things, by good or adverse fortune, by good or ill report, more hurt by public disappointments than my own, and not thrown into the hot or cold fits of a tertian ague, as the Edinburgh or Quarterly Review damps or raises the opinion of the town in my favour. I have some love of fame, of the fame of a Pascal, a Leibnitz, or a Berkeley (none at all of popularity) and would rather that a single inquirer after truth should pronounce my name, after I am dead, with the same feelings that I have thought of theirs, than be puffed in all the newspapers, and praised in all the reviews, while I am living. I myself have been a thinker; and I cannot but believe that there are and will be others, like me. If the few and scattered sparks of truth, which I have been at so much pains to collect,

3. See 9:251. Actually Hazlitt asked for the issues "for August 1817, & that for June last year, & the present one." By the first and second he undoubtedly referred to the issues for April, 1817, and January, 1818, which appeared late.

should still be kept alive in the minds of such persons, and not entirely die with me, I shall be satisfied. (9:58–59)

The *Letter to Gifford* was published by John Miller and sold for three shillings. Inevitably its appeal was limited: it attracted few buyers[4] and no critical notice. Yet it gladdened victims of Gifford's acid pen. Writing to Mary Shelley on March 9 Leigh Hunt described it as "a most bitter *gnothi seauton* letter." [5] And John Keats was so taken with it that he copied out an extended excerpt in a long journal-letter to his brother and sister-in-law on March 13. "The manner in which this is managed," he commented: "the force and innate power with which it yeasts and works up itself—the feeling for the costume of society; is in a style of genius—He hath a demon as he himself says of Lord Byron." [6] In the same letter he offered a capsule rating of contemporary literary figures: "he [i.e., Keats himself] . . . doth not admire Sheild's play, Leigh Hunt, Tom Moore, Bob Southey & M[r] Rogers; & does admire W[m] Hazlitt: more over . . . he liketh half of Wordsworth, & none of Crabbe." [7]

Before he settled down to prepare his next lecture series, Hazlitt decided to collect his political essays for publication, probably because he intended to write no more of the sort. Godwin tried to persuade Taylor & Hessey to publish the volume, but they declined.[8] However, Hazlitt had found a new friend in the publisher William Hone. On February 3 Hone wrote to John Childs: "I dined at John Hunt's on Sunday with Mr. Hazlitt, for whose work on the prospectus I have just concluded a bargain." [9] Earlier, on January 25, Hone had contracted to publish the *Political Essays, with Sketches of Public Characters.*[10] He was not the sort of man who would quail at controversial materials. In December, 1818, he had been prosecuted for his unorthodox publications, but had defended himself so brilliantly that sympathizers had raised a subscription of three thousand pounds for him. His keen mind and his liberal opinions naturally recommended him to Hazlitt. P. G. Patmore wrote later that Hone was "the person among all Hazlitt's

4. In 1820 Robert Stodart bought up the unsold sheets and offered them to the public as a "second edition."

5. *Correspondence of Leigh Hunt*, 1:128.

6. *Keats Letters*, 2:76. 7. Ibid., p. 69.

8. *Shelley and His Circle*, 1:222 and n.

9. Frederick William Hackwood, *William Hone* (London: T. F. Unwin, 1912), p. 212 The prospectus which Hazlitt agreed to write was for a history of parody which was never completed or published.

10. The contract is preserved among the Hazlitt papers in the Lockwood Memorial Library of the State University of New York at Buffalo.

intimates in whose society he seemed to take the most unmingled pleasure." [11]

Hazlitt prefaced his collection with an outspoken essay which accurately defined his political stance. "I am no politician," he declared,

> and still less can I be said to be a party-man: but I have a hatred of tyranny, and a contempt for its tools; and this feeling I have expressed as often and as strongly as I could. I cannot sit quietly down under the claims of barefaced power, and I have tried to expose the little arts of sophistry by which they are defended. I have no mind to have my person made a property of, nor my understanding made a dupe of. I deny that liberty and slavery are convertible terms, that right and wrong, truth and falsehood, plenty and famine, the comforts or wretchedness of a people, are matters of perfect indifference. That is all I know of the matter; but on these points I am likely to remain incorrigible, in spite of any arguments that I have seen used to the contrary. (7:7)

And later:

> The question with me is, whether I and all mankind are born slaves or free. That is the one thing necessary to know and to make good: the rest is *flocci, nauci, nihili, pili.* Secure this point, and all is safe: lose this, and all is lost. There are people who cannot understand a principle; nor perceive how a cause can be connected with an individual, even in spite of himself, nor how the salvation of mankind can be bound up with the success of one man. It is in vain that I address to them what follows. (7:9–10)

With equal force he explained his unswerving loyalty to Napoleon:

> If Buonaparte was a conqueror, he conquered the grand conspiracy of kings against the abstract right of the human race to be free; and I, as a man, could not be indifferent which side to take. If he was ambitious, his greatness was not founded on the unconditional, avowed surrender of the rights of human nature. But with him, the state of man rose too. If he was arbitrary and a tyrant, first, France as a country was in a state of military blockade, on garrison-duty, and not to be defended by mere paper bullets of the brain; secondly, but chief, he was not, nor he could not become, a tyrant by right divine. Tyranny in him was not sacred: it was not eternal: it was not instinctively bound in a league of amity with other tyrannies; it was not sanctioned by all the laws of religion and morality. (7:12)

And his attitude toward English politics was implicit in his "characters" of the Reformer, the Whig, and the Tory. The Reformer he described as "a speculative (and somewhat fantastical) character" (7:15); the Tory, as one who "considers not what is possible, but what is real," who "gives might the preference over right" (7:17); the Whig, as "a Trimmer . . . a cloak for corruption, and a mar-plot to freedom" (7:21). Hazlitt was indeed not

11. Patmore, 3:74, 80–82.

a party man; his politics were distinctly his own, based on his love of freedom and, underlying it, his love of humanity.

The essays which he gathered in the volume seldom achieved the ringing nobility of the preface. They seem to have been chosen at random—perhaps, again, from those which happened to be most easily accessible. They included articles from the Tory *Courier*, the *Morning Chronicle*, the *Champion*, the *Examiner*, and the *Yellow Dwarf*; there were two "characters" of Burke, one from Hazlitt's *Edinburgh Review* article on Coleridge's *Biographia Literaria*, another from *The Eloquence of the British Senate*; there were characters of Chatham and Fox, also from the latter volume, and the rather shopworn one of William Pitt from *Free Thoughts on Public Affairs*, none of them arranged according to any consistent pattern of subject or chronology. Hazlitt mischievously reprinted also an essay by Coleridge on Pitt and Bonaparte written for the *Morning Post* of March 19, 1800— an essay which Hazlitt heartily approved but which was now anathema to Coleridge.

Hazlitt may well have had some notion that he was choosing the best of his essays, but it is not apparent; he seems not to have singled out those of a more general or lasting interest or to have given preference to either longer or shorter essays; he reprinted the first installment of a review of Robert Owen's *New View of Society*, but not the second; he included "On the Courier and Times Newspapers" from the *Morning Chronicle* of January 21, 1814, but without its last four paragraphs; and he made frequent revisions in many of the essays, but not, apparently, to make them more acceptable to the general reader.[12] Apart from the striking preface, the book consisted largely of topical essays which had outlived their immediate interest. Hazlitt himself could take pride in it as evidence of his steadfast defense of human liberty during his years as a journalist. But most of his contemporaries were repelled by his bitter personal attacks. Crabb Robinson dismissed the essays as "malignant party squibs," observing in his diary that the later pieces were "more ferocious and malignant, more laboured and stuffed with ornament than his earlier writings."[13] And it proved a poor investment for Hone. He kept the book on his list for three years, then sold the remaining sheets to two other publishers, who in 1822 brought out a "second edition," unchanged except for its title page.

Reviewers generally overlooked the book. But there was one notable

---

12. Howe records Hazlitt's revisions in the notes to volume 7 of *Complete Works;* he reprints the political essays which Hazlitt excluded from this collection in volume 19.

13. Robinson, 1:236–37.

exception, for a critic for the *Quarterly*, probably William Gifford himself, seized upon it as a means of settling accounts with Hazlitt, and in the July issue he flayed "the Hazlitt" as one of the "insects of the moral world," citing the number of distinguished men "traduced" in the book, finding "something . . . symptomatic of mania, and rather tragical" in "these wanderings of the author," and concluding:

> Many will think that we have, on this and other occasions, wasted more time on him than he deserved. We are ourselves of that opinion: but when the Hazlitt first appeared within our province, it struck us that it was of a new species; its activity, disagreeable hum, and glittering blackness—but, above all, the value of the objects, which it seemed to be its nature to defile, excited our attention. We did not know, moreover, but that it might then be only in its *larva* or grub state; and there was no saying to what extent, if it should change to the perfect *image*, it might increase its numbers. We confess, however, that we wanted skill in entomology. It is plain that it had reached its perfection when we first noticed it; that its powers of mischief hardly extend beyond the making of some dirt and some noise: that it does not belong to our climate, nor can multiply here; but that its presence is owing to the late extraordinary seasons, which have brought us so many new plagues. Its minutes were nearly over, and it would have perished as the heats declined. Yet, perhaps, it may not be entirely without advantage that we have fastened it down upon a sheet of paper amongst our other specimens.

In the following month the *Anti-Jacobin Review* assailed the book with righteous indignation. "This is said to be the age of *book-making*," the reviewer began; "and certainly one of the most impudent of all *book-makers* is Mr. William Hazlitt. Not content with sending his hearers to sleep at the *Surrey*, while listening to his ill-disguised plagiarisms, and puny and illiberal criticism; and afterwards picking their pockets . . . by publishing his lectures . . . he has here thrown together a collection of things he calls 'essays,' and 'Sketches of Character'. . . ." Then he damned Hazlitt as spokesman for all the evil forces that would undermine English government and religion, submitting that "such conduct is a contempt of law, and a defiance of authority, which calls for the most severe reprehension and condign punishment." Even the liberal *Monthly Review*, which delayed its notice until November, 1820, did not attempt to defend the essays. The critic commented at length on the irony that Hazlitt could pour such vitriol on individual men while championing the welfare of mankind. "We participate with him in all his hatred of tyranny and contempt for its tools," he wrote, "whatever station in life they occupy, and with whatever rank or title they are decorated and disgraced: but we have no relish for diffuse, personal, and declamatory invective, and of this we have too much in the volume before us." *Political Essays* served only to make the public more aware of Hazlitt's past indiscretions. It was perhaps as well that the volume sold poorly: twenty years later the "second edition" was still being advertised.[14]

Inevitably Hazlitt chafed at such treatment and felt increasingly alienated from society. And now that he was separated from his family and no longer writing regularly for the periodicals, he had time to kill. He often sought company at the homes of friends like the Hunts, Haydon, or the Lambs.[15] His moods ran to extremes: sometimes he was as mute as he had been at James Perry's dinner party in 1818;[16] on occasion, however, he could dominate the conversation. Bewick recalled his appearing at Haydon's with

> some of his lucubrations, which he would, at a fitting opportunity, and with modest awkwardness, draw from his coat-pocket. Then explaining the subject of his paper, he would read it with feeling and freshness, as though it engrossed all his mind. Glancing occasionally to observe what effect his language had upon his hearers, he would sometimes rise from his seat, and in the interest of the subject pour forth in impassioned tones, excited expression, and animated action, the violence of his emotion. It was in this way he read his Letter to Gifford,—The Description of a Prize Fight,—On the Death of Kavannah, &c. &c. If the paper so read seemed to have the desired effect, he would send it to the press.[17]

Sarah Hazlitt visited some of the same houses, but probably not at the same times. Crabb Robinson reported seeing her at the Lambs' on May 11 and Hazlitt there on June 17.[18]

Their separation became, in effect, final sometime during the year 1819, when Hazlitt gave up the York Street house altogether. Bentham, his landlord, probably forced him out because he was behind in his rent: two years later, in a letter to Leigh Hunt, Hazlitt recalled that Bentham had "philosophically put an execution in my house."[19]

The separation itself, however, was hardly painful; by this time neither Hazlitt nor Sarah could have had any strong desire to preserve the flimsy attachment between them. Hazlitt was thinking of himself, surely, when he wrote in 1821: "How few out of the infinite number of those that marry . . . wed with those they would prefer to all the world; nay, how far the

14. Geoffrey Keynes, *Bibliography of William Hazlitt* (London: Nonesuch Press, 1931) p. 38 (hereafter cited as Keynes).

15. *Correspondence of Leigh Hunt*, 1:108, and Blunden, p. 141.

16. See *Keats Letters*, 2:14.   17. Landseer, 1:122–23.

18. Robinson, 1:230 and 232.   19. *Four Generations*, 1:134.

greater proportion are joined together by mere motives of convenience, accident, recommendation of friends, or indeed not unfrequently by the very fear of the event, by repugnance and a sort of fatal fascination: yet the tie is for life, not to be shaken off but with disgrace or death: a man no longer lives to himself, but is a body (as well as mind) chained to another, in spite of himself" (8:96). They had reached an impasse, for, as Haydon put it, "the poor woman, irritated by neglect, irritated him in return."[20]

Nonetheless a separation is a break, a laceration that leaves a wound. And Hazlitt felt keenly the separation from his son, now eight years old. The boy was hopelessly spoiled. In a letter to George and Georgiana Keats on February 14, John Keats referred to him as "that little Nero."[21] He had never had any consistent discipline. His formal education had been sporadic: Mary Lamb had taught him and little Mary Novello (later Mary Cowden Clarke) for a while,[22] and he had been enrolled in at least three schools before he was eleven years old. At home his parents' haphazard existence had failed to provide any stabilizing force. But it was Hazlitt's misguided affection which did most to spoil his son. He used to give the boy money when he went out in the morning, specifying that it must be spent before the day was over—this, so that young William would learn "generous notions." Inevitably "a rather promiscuous circle of acquaintances from the neighbourhood" soon swarmed around the house.[23] But that was not the worst. Sarah complained later that Hazlitt took the boy to "the Fives Court and such places," even "when he went picking up the girls on the town"—to which, she claimed, Hazlitt rejoined that "he did not know that it was any good to bring up children in ignorance of the world."[24] With such a background he was bound to be unruly. Yet Hazlitt cherished him as his only surviving child, his posterity.

Late in June or early in July Hazlitt left London for Winterslow to work on his next series of lectures. He had already offered the publication rights to Archibald Constable, but Constable had turned them down in a letter of June 25.[25] Barry Cornwall wrote in later years that Hazlitt "knew little

20. *Haydon Diary*, 2:373.
21. *Keats Letters*, 2:59. W. C. Hazlitt (*Four Generations*, 1:106) seriously suggested that Keats probably called the boy Nero because of his black curly hair.
22. *Mary and Charles Lamb*, ed. W. C. Hazlitt (London, 1874), pp. 124–25.
23. *The Hazlitts*, p. 323.
24. *Journals*, p. 196. In 1826 Northcote told Haydon that Hazlitt "brought London strumpets into his Lodgings when his boy of 10 years old was reading" and "the boy was so shocked, he either kicked or abused them away" (*Haydon Diary*, 3:132).
25. See Stanley Jones, "Hazlitt in Edinburgh: An Evening with Mr. Ritchie of *The Scotsman*," *Études Anglaises* 17 (1964): 16 n.

or nothing" about the Elizabethan dramatists "with the exception of Shakespeare" and that he asked Lamb and Cornwall to recommend the books that he should read. Cornwall supplied him with a dozen volumes, and he settled down at the Hut to master his subject.[26]

This time, however, the company at the inn irked him. He was annoyed when the landlord asked if he had any object in reading all those books, or when he heard "a fellow disputing in the kitchen, whether a person ought to live . . . by pen and ink" (17:68). He channeled his annoyance into an essay "Character of the Country People," which appeared in the *Examiner* for July 18. "They are *ferae naturae*," he declared, "and not to be tamed by art" (17:67). And he bemoaned their rudeness, their intolerance, their ignorance, credulity, immorality, and whatnot.

But the countryside itself had not lost its charm for him, nor had his books. As he read over the Elizabethan playwrights, he wrote, "I almost revived my old passion for reading, and my old delight in books" (12:226). It was a pleasant, relaxed summer. "There are neither picture-galleries nor theatres-royal on Salisbury-plain where I write this," he presently assured his lecture audience;

> but here, even here, with a few old authors, I can manage to get through the summer or the winter months, without ever knowing what it is to feel *ennui*. They sit with me at breakfast; they walk out with me before dinner. After a long walk through unfrequented tracks, after starting the hare from the fern, or hearing the wing of the raven rustling over my head, or being greeted by the woodman's "stern good-night," as he strikes into his narrow homeward path, I can "take mine ease at mine inn," beside the blazing hearth, and shake hands with Signor Orlando Friscobaldo [a character in Dekker's *Honest Whore*], as the oldest acquaintance I have. Ben Jonson, learned Chapman, Master Webster, and Master Heywood, are there; and seated round, discourse the silent hours away. Shakespear is there himself, not in Cibber's manager's coat. . . . I should have no objection to pass my life in this manner out of the world, not thinking of it, or it of me; neither abused by my enemies, nor defended by my friends; careless of the future, but sometimes dreaming of the past, which might as well be forgotten. (6:247)[27]

26. *Cornwall Recollections*, pp. 73–74. Cf. Hazlitt's remark in his essay "On Coffee-House Politicians": "We had a pleasant party one evening at B—— C——'s. A young literary bookseller who was present went away delighted with the repast, and spoke in raptures of a servant in green livery and a patent-lamp. I thought myself that the charm of the evening consisted in some talk about Beaumont and Fletcher and the old poets, in which every one took part or interest, and in a consciousness that we could not pay our host a better compliment than in thus alluding to studies in which he excelled, and in praising authors whom he had imitated with feeling and sweetness" (8:203).

27. W. C. Hazlitt (*Memoirs*, 2:14–16) fancied that Hazlitt fell in love with a Miss

He was still at Winterslow on September 15, when John Hunt wrote to him from Taunton asking him to settle a bill of fifty pounds from Messrs. Rees and Eaton. Evidently Hunt had endorsed the bill for Hazlitt, Rees and Eaton were threatening to sue Hunt, and he wanted Hazlitt to act at once. Hazlitt wrote to Leigh Hunt, presumably asking him to forward the bill to him, and Hunt replied that Barry Cornwall had sent it to Southampton Buildings, not knowing that Hazlitt was still at Winterslow.[28] Then on September 25 Hazlitt wrote to Francis Jeffrey:

> I blush when I sit down to write this letter. But you some time ago said if I wanted it & would send to you for *another* 100£ you would let me have it. It would at this present moment interpose between me & almost ruin. I do not know that since that time I have done any thing to deserve your less favourable opinion. I shall receive 150£ for my next Lectures (on the age of Elizabeth) at Christmas, but I shall be prevented from completing them in time to deliver [them] (next month) to the utter discomfiture of all my hopes, if I am not enabled to parry an immediate blow (a bill for 66£) with which I am threatened down here, which I see no means of meeting but through your often experienced liberality. . . . Permit me to add, I have a good 50£ note of hand which has six months to run & which I would transmit you immediately, & my own note of hand for 50£ at 3 months, which I could be certain of honouring, when I receive my money from the Surry Institution. The 100£ which I am in your debt I hope still to write out in Edinburgh Reviews![29]

Evidently the crisis passed, but it demanded some fast juggling on Hazlitt's part. The note made out to him which he offered to send Jeffrey was from Haydon,[30] who wrote in his autobiography that in 1819 Hazlitt offered to sell him for forty pounds the copies of the masterpieces in the Louvre which he had painted in 1802. Haydon generously assured him that they were worth fifty pounds (although he noted that they were "not artistic, but as if done by a literary man with great feeling for the beauties of High Art") and gave him a note for that amount.[31]

Windham of Norman Court, near Salisbury, during his stay at Winterslow. But as Howe (p. 332 n.) points out, no Windham ever occupied Norman Court. Howe suggests that the passage which W. C. Hazlitt assumed to be addressed to "Miss Windham" probably referred to Sally Walker.

28. The two letters are printed in *Memoirs*, 1:253–55.

29. Baker, pp. 261–62.

30. On May 2, 1820, Hazlitt wrote Jeffrey: "I don't know whether I ought or ought not to remind you (lest you should have forgotten) that Mr. Haydon's bill becomes due about this time, & that it was—what shall I say?—a good one. He told me the other day, it had not been presented" (ALS, Yale University Library).

31. Elwin, p. 339. Haydon reported the sequel of the sale thus: "I paid half this sum on the maturity of the bill, but not being able to do my duty to all, after six years' devotion

Ironically, on September 22, while Hazlitt was trying to worm his way out of his financial straits, John Keats was writing to his friend Charles Armitage Brown: "I shall apply to Hazlitt, who knows the market as well as any one, for something to bring me a few pounds as soon as possible." [32] Of course Keats was right; Hazlitt knew the literary market as well as anyone. Yet, hard pressed as he was, he was practically ignoring it. The only contribution that he sent out from Winterslow, apart from the essay "On the Character of the Country People," was another "Historical Illustrations of Shakespeare" published in the September *Edinburgh Magazine*, citing parallels between *Julius Caesar* and Plutarch and between *The Tempest* and Magellan's *Voyage to the South Seas* (20:410). Debts or no debts, he was spending his time at Winterslow in congenial pursuits: enjoying the countryside, reading, and preparing his lectures.

On Friday, November 5, he was back in London, giving the first lecture on the dramatic poets of the Age of Elizabeth at the Surrey Institution.[33] This time he did not need to define and analyze terms as he had done in his two preceding series; he was dealing with a period rather than with types of literature, and he opened with a spirited tribute to the titans of the Elizabethan era, saluting them as "truly English" (6:175). The neglected dramatists of the period were, he declared, "a constellation of bright luminaries" (6:181) inferior to Shakespeare, certainly, but equaled in dramatic poetry and tragedy by only one English dramatist since their time: Thomas Otway. He then identified the causes of this remarkable literary flowering: the questioning spirit of the Reformation, the translations of the Bible and classical literature, the discovery of the New World, and the like—rising to a

---

to one work, a writ was issued for the £25 left; and so utterly ignorant was I of the nature of the thing, I did not know what the copy meant. I went down and paid the debt and costs, but felt as if from that hour the curse had lighted on me, and so it proved." In the margin of the note which Hazlitt sent him appealing for help (reproduced in Baker, p. 243) Haydon wrote: "I gave him fifty to relieve his wants—all *my* misfortunes—he told Mary he should get them again *cheap*—He (at least a Friend of his for him) bought for 5 or 6 pounds & now chuckles at having got *them again*—This is the meanest thing Haslitt ever did." As Baker points out (p. 244 n.) Haydon referred to Hazlitt's perfidy on three other occasions. The friend who bought the paintings from Haydon was presumably P. G. Patmore, who reported (Patmore, 3:105–10) that he bought two copies of Titian when Haydon's property was sold and that he in turn sold them to Hazlitt for ten pounds.

32. *Keats Letters*, 2:177. Cf. Keats's letter of the same date to Richard Woodhouse: "I shall enquire of Hazlitt how the figures of the market stand" (ibid., 174).

33. As William Garrett has shown ("Hazlitt's Debt to C. W. Dilke," *Keats-Shelley Memorial Bulletin*, no. 15 [1964], pp. 37–42) this lecture was apparently based on Dilke's introduction to *A Continuation of Dodsley's Old English Plays* (1815).

stirring climax in his praise of "the natural genius of the country" (6:191) which "gave a unity and common direction to all these causes" (6:191).

It was a brilliant job; yet no one present recorded its effect on the audience. Keats, who already had a keen interest in the Elizabethans, wrote to Joseph Severn on November 10: "I have been so very lax, unemployed, unmeridian'd, and objectless these two months that I even grudge indul[g]ing (and that is no great indulgence considering the Lecture is not over till 9 and the lecture room seven miles from wentworth Place) myself by going to Hazlitt's Lecture." [34] Later in the letter he added: "If you should be at the Lecture tomorrow evening I shall see you." [35] But on the night of the twelfth, when Hazlitt was delivering his second lecture, Keats was at home writing to his brother George and his wife: "Hazlitt has begun another course of Lectures on the Writers of Elizabeth's reign—I hear he quoted me in his last Lecture." [36] And he seems not to have indulged himself in the pleasure of attending any of the later lectures. Crabb Robinson was at the second lecture, however, and pronounced it "very inferior to his former works." [37]

Robinson had a point; there was a distinct falling off in the second and third lectures. Hazlitt announced at the outset that he would take up the less known dramatists before proceeding to such major figures as Beaumont and Fletcher and Jonson. Consequently, the second and third lectures were "On . . . Lyly, Marlow, Heywood, Middleton, and Rowley" and "On Marston, Chapman, Deckar, and Webster." He assumed that his audience would be unfamiliar with these authors, and he contented himself with a general introduction to each (stressing, of course, truth of character and richness of imagination) and very generous excerpts. The fourth lecture, "On Beaumont and Fletcher, Ben Jonson, Ford, and Massinger," went better, but the fifth, "On Single Plays, Poems, etc.," and the sixth, "On Miscellaneous Poems," were loose collections of odds and ends with no unifying principle and little of Hazlitt's usual enthusiasm. He was probably addressing himself as well as his audience when he said defensively in his sixth lecture:

> I conceive that what I have undertaken to do in this and former cases, is merely to read over a set of authors with the audience, as I would do with a friend, to point out

34. *Keats Letters*, 2:227.
35. Ibid., p. 228. Keats meant "the day after tomorrow" rather than "tomorrow."
36. Ibid., p. 230. Hazlitt *mis*quoted Keats's poem "Sleep and Poetry" in his November 5 lecture.
37. Robinson, 1:237.

a favourite passage, to explain an objection; or if a remark or theory occurs, to state it in illustration of the subject, but neither to tire him nor puzzle myself with pedantic rules and pragmatical *formulas* of criticism that can do no good to any body. . . . I do not think that is the way to learn "the gentle craft" of poesy or to teach it to others: —to imbibe or to communicate its spirit; which if it does not disentangle itself and soar above the obscure and trivial researches of antiquarianism is no longer itself, "a Phoenix gazed at by all." At least, so it appeared to me (it is for others to judge whether I was right or wrong). In a word, I have endeavoured to feel what was good, and to "give a reason for the faith that was in me" when necessary, and when in my power. This is what I have done, and what I must continue to do. (6:301–2)

The seventh lecture, on Bacon, Sir Thomas Browne, and Jeremy Taylor, was devoted largely to comparison of the prose styles of the three authors and, accordingly, was more coherent than its predecessors. But the last of the series was incoherent and—worse—irrelevant. In it Hazlitt commented on some "latter-day poetic dramatists" (Sheil, Tobin, Lamb, and Cornwall), identified four types of tragedy (the antique or classical, the Gothic or romantic, "the French or common-place rhetorical," and "the German or paradoxical" [6:347]), read a long passage from his *Edinburgh Review* article on Schlegel's *Lectures on Dramatic Literature* to describe the first three, traced the development of English tragedy after the Restoration, and rounded out the whole with a critique of modern German drama, recognizing its flaws but admitting its power over him ever since he first saw Schiller's *The Robbers* as a boy. The envoy to the audience began with an apology:

I have done: and if I have done no better, the fault has been in me, not in the subject. My liking to this grew with my knowledge of it: but so did my anxiety to do it justice. I somehow felt it as a point of honour not to make my hearers think less highly of some of these old writers than I myself did of them. If I have praised an author, it was because I liked him: if I have quoted a passage, it was because it pleased me in the reading: if I have spoken contemptuously of any one, it has been reluctantly. It is no easy task that a writer, even in so humble a class as myself, takes upon him; he is scouted and ridiculed if he fails; and if he succeeds, the enmity and cavils and malice with which he is assailed, are just in proportion to his success. (6:363–64)

It closed with a bitter acknowledgment of defeat:

An author wastes his time in painful study and obscure researches, to gain a little breath of popularity, meets with nothing but vexation and disappointment in ninety-nine instances out of a hundred; or when he thinks to grasp the luckless prize, finds it not worth the trouble—the perfume of a minute, fleeting as a shadow, hollow as a

sound; "as often got without merit as lost without deserving." He thinks that the
attainment of acknowledged excellence will secure him the expression of those feelings in others, which the image and hope of it had excited in his own breast, but instead of that, he meets with nothing (or scarcely nothing) but squint-eyed suspicion,
idiot wonder, and grinning scorn.—It seems hardly worth while to have taken all
the pains he has been at for this!

In youth we borrow patience from our future years: the spring of hope gives us
courage to act and suffer. A cloud is upon our onward path, and we fancy that all
is sunshine beyond it. . . . Life is a continued struggle to be what we are not, and to
do what we cannot. But as we approach the goal, we draw in the reins; the impulse
is less, as we have not so far to go; as we see objects nearer, we become less sanguine
in the pursuit: it is not the despair of not attaining, so much as knowing there is
nothing worth obtaining, and the fear of having nothing left even to wish for, that
damps our ardour, and relaxes our efforts; and if the mechanical habit did not increase
the facility, would, I believe, take away all inclination or power to do any thing.
We stagger on the few remaining paces to the end of our journey; make perhaps one
final effort; and are glad when our task is done. (6:364)

The speaker sounds like a tired, unhappy man. All the anxieties of the
past months seem to be weighing him down. He had pinned his hopes on
lecturing—and had found that it was not, after all, going to solve his problems, personal or financial. Lecturing about writers whom one had read for
years was one thing; patching together a series about an unfamiliar period in
the course of a summer was quite another. Instead of the enthusiastic response of admirers like Bewick or Patmore or Keats or Cornwall, he now
sensed only "squint-eyed suspicion, idiot wonder, or grinning scorn." He
was disheartened, surely; he had reached the end of his career as a lecturer,
and an ignominious end it was. The only account of the series that was to
survive, apart from Crabb Robinson's acid comment on the second lecture,
was the report of an anonymous member of the audience who recalled that
Hazlitt kept hitching up his trousers, which slipped down regularly for want
of braces, and that he recited the refrain of the old song "Back and side, go
bare" with a curious emphasis: "Of jolly good ale and *OLD*." 38

Hazlitt did not repeat these lectures at the Crown and Anchor Tavern.
Nor did Taylor and Hessey publish them; they had already more of Hazlitt's lectures on their shelves than they could dispose of: John Taylor wrote
to Michael Drury of Philadelphia on January 26, 1820, asking if he could
sell a thousand copies of the second edition of *Lectures on the English Poets* "for
more than waste paper, exclusive of the Freight." 39 Hazlitt had offered the
new lectures to Archibald Constable and been told that Constable's schedule

38. *Memoirs*, 1:256–57.   39. *Keats Circle*, 1:101.

was already too full.[40] The firm of Stoddart and Steuart brought them out presently, but they evidently sold poorly, and the remaining sheets were bound up as a "second edition" by the publisher John Warren in 1821.

Yet, curiously enough, the published *Lectures on the Dramatic Literature of the Age of Elizabeth* was reviewed more widely than Hazlitt's two earlier volumes of lectures. John Scott, editor of the new *London Magazine*, wrote a long review for his second issue in February, 1820, praising Hazlitt's originality, defending him against hostile critics, and hailing him for his "comprehension of innate character, absolutely unequalled by any of his contemporaries," for "a finer and more philosophical taste than any other critic on poetry and art whose name we can cite," and for his "intense feeling of the pathetic, the pure, the sublime, in quality, action, and form." In the following month another magazine of the same name but more conservative opinions lauded Hazlitt's originality and his style, but urged him to "avoid the cockneys and all manner of politics" because "he beats them hollow." And the reviewer for the *Monthly Magazine* cited his "powers of mind, which united to an enthusiasm for their subject, render him as conspicuously eminent for a critic, as the authors he treats of were for genius and wit." "We may safely appeal to the judgment of the literary public," he concluded, "whether the articles contained in the Quarterly Review upon similar subjects, are at all comparable to the enlightened spirit of truth, and critical discrimination which abound in the single volume before us." The September *Monthly Review*, however, was inclined to be censorious: "He presents himself as before," their critic wrote; "he persists in the swimming walk and spangled shoes, and pushes elegance of step almost to affectation; he advances in the same luxurious dress, in which the flowers of fancy, the jewels of allusion, the tinsel of conceit, and the ribbands of sentiment, mingle in gay embroidery, with too much ostentation to be either entirely unheeded or entirely approved." And later: "Much as we admire the superior talents of Mr. Hazlitt, we think that they are not inexhaustible, and that already something of repetition is discernible in his successive works." The *Edinburgh Review* also had its reservations. A writer in the November issue declared:

> He has no lack of the deepest feelings, the profoundest sentiments of humanity, or the loftiest aspirations after ideal good. But there are no great leading principles of taste to give singleness to his aims, nor any central points in his mind, around which his feelings may revolve, and his imaginations cluster. There is no sufficient distinction between his intellectual and his imaginative faculties. He confounds the truths

40. See above, p. 249.

of imagination with those of fact—the processes of argument with those of feeling—
the immunities of intellect with those of virtue. Hence the seeming inconsistency of
many of his doctrines. Hence the want of all continuity in his style. Hence his failure
in producing one single, harmonious, and lasting impression on the hearts of his
hearers.

They were harsh words, but they were not vindictive; all things considered,
the published *Lectures on the Dramatic Literature of the Age of Elizabeth*
fared surprisingly well.

But Hazlitt had no way of anticipating these heartening reviews, and
long before they appeared he had taken the obvious course—back to writing
for the periodicals. He naturally turned first to the *London Magazine*,
which Scott was developing as a rival to *Blackwood's*. For the first issue he
submitted two articles: a chatty review of recent events in the London
theater and an essay of some sort which Scott felt obliged to reject. "I am
sorry to say," he wrote on January 20, 1820, to Cradock and Baldwin,
publishers of the new magazine, "that I cannot honestly tell you that Mr.
Hazlitt's manuscript is likely to suit us in the mag. It falls into all those errors
which I know are his besetting ones, but which I hope to keep him clear of
when he is directed to particular topics, such as the drama, etc. His talent
is undoubted, and his wish to serve us, I believe, at present very sincere."
Evidently Hazlitt had suggested that his essay might be the first of a series
which Cradock and Baldwin would eventually publish in book form; but
Scott, though well disposed toward Hazlitt, was hesitant. "Since I last saw
you," he continued,

> the friend at whose house I met Hazlitt on Sunday has called upon me to make a sort
> of semi-authorised communication from the gentleman. The fact is, as you sur-
> mized, that Mr. H. is in want of a certain sum of money, and he says that, this sum
> in his power, he would be very free in every respect, and would devote the whole
> power of his mind to the preparation of the dramatic [articles], or anything else we
> might suggest. If so, he would be a very valuable contributor. . . . I will engage for
> the gentleman, from what I know of his character, that he would be most ready to
> listen to suggestions, and to strain every nerve for us in return for a service. He is
> naturally grateful, and although an original, is an honest one. I have not spoken to
> him for several years until last Sunday, but I see that in a very short time I shall be
> able to influence him to proper subjects and to the proper manner of handling them
> —I mean *proper* in regard to the Magazine, as, generally speaking, I should have
> little claim to be his judge or guide. Would it therefore suit you to say to him that,
> with regard to the Essays, of which one has been sent, you beg leave to think a little
> farther over the matter, and claim the privilege of suggesting what may occur to
> you; but that on the general score of dramatic articles, and such other contributions

as might hereafter be arranged between himself and you on mutual agreement, you
have no objection to treat as for the volume *immediately?* [41]

Thus Hazlitt found himself back almost where he had started—reporting
on developments in the theater in an essay, "The Drama," which became
a regular feature of the new magazine.

It was an agreeable assignment for a man of his temperament because it
offered him plenty of scope. He was not confined to a factual report of the
latest performance at one of the theaters; he could, in effect, write a personal
essay on the drama in general, discussing whatever facet of the subject
chanced to arrest his fancy. In "The Drama, No. 1" in the January issue
he was in a retrospective mood: the drama in recent years had changed, he
declared, but not, as some would have it, degenerated; "we have got striking
melo-drames for dull tragedies; and short farces are better than long ones of
five acts" (18:271). He considered the changes in acting from one generation to another, then the nature of audiences, "among the most sociable,
gossiping, good-natured, and humane members of society" (18:272). He
permitted himself some nostalgic recollections of actors of the past (notably,
of course, Mrs. Siddons, who had now fully retired) and, finally, a comparison of the merits of some of his favorites: Mrs. Siddons, Kean, Miss O'Neill,
and others. "The Drama, No. 2," in February, began with a farewell
tribute to Miss O'Neill, who had just married and retired from the stage,
and ended with rather unenthusiastic comments on five current plays,
among them a production of *Coriolanus* in which Kean, in the leading role,
disappointed him by attempting too "patrician" a part for his style of acting
(18:280–91).

Late in February Hazlitt went down to Somerset to visit John Hunt,
probably in response to the invitation which Hunt had extended in the
previous September.[42] He may have stopped off at Crediton to see his
parents and his sister Peggy. But he was back in London on March 25 for
the first exhibition of Haydon's mammoth painting *Christ's Entry into
Jerusalem,* for which Wordsworth, Keats, and Hazlitt himself had all
posed—Hazlitt "as an investigator" who apparently had some doubts about
the new Messiah. Haydon reported in his journal that the exhibition was a
striking success: "The Room was full. Keats and Hazlitt were up in a
corner, really rejoicing." [43]

During the spring of 1820 Hazlitt continued his drama articles for the

41. *Four Generations,* 1:135–38.
42. *Memoirs,* 1:253–54.
43. Elwin, p. 332. Hazlitt did not wholly approve of the new painting. In his review of

London Magazine. In March he told how much he enjoyed attending the smaller theaters in London, then conjured up recollections of the strolling players he had seen as a boy in Wem. He next criticized the performances at the minor theaters (Covent Garden and Drury Lane having been closed for most of the month because of the death of the king and the duke of Kent); then, probably to counteract his harsh remarks about Kean's *Coriolanus* in February, he concluded by reprinting the praise of Kean's *Othello* which he had written for the *Examiner* back in October, 1817 (18:291–302).

When he wrote the April installment of "The Drama," he was far from the London theaters on his Somerset trip—"sitting in an arm-chair by a sea-coal fire," first at Ilminster, "a pretty town in the Vale of Taunton," later at "the Lamb at Hindon, a dreary spot" (18:368). Ignoring his remarks in the January installment, he developed the proposition that "there has hardly been a good tragedy or a good comedy written within the last fifty years" (18:303). The reason, he explained, was that the French Revolution had focused men's attention on politics: "we are more in love with a theory than a mistress" (18:306). Next he chattered on about the failure as dramatists of several distinguished men of letters—Godwin, Wordsworth, Coleridge—before switching to accounts of two dramatic adaptations of Scott's novels and a brief critique of two new comedies. In passing he sounded a warning when he remarked of George Soane's *The Hebrew:* "Mr. Kean's acting in it, in several places, was such as to terrify us when we find from the play-bills that he is soon to act Lear" (18:315).

Writing "The Drama" was agreeable enough, no doubt, but not very profitable. In four months Hazlitt had published only these four essays; he needed to find a more substantial project. In a letter to John Scott that spring, he asked if the publishers of the *London Magazine* would be interested in a series of eight articles on modern philosophy at five guineas each —presumably the eight lectures on modern philosophy which he had delivered back in 1812 and offered to Jeffrey in 1816. In the same letter he

---

Farington's *Life of Sir Joshua Reynolds* in the August *Edinburgh Review* he wrote: "Mr. Haydon is a young artist of great promise, and much ardour and energy; and has lately painted a picture which has carried away universal admiration. Without wishing to detract from that tribute of deserved applause, we may be allowed to suggest (and with no unfriendly voice) that he has there, in our judgment, laid in the groundwork, and raised the scaffolding, of a noble picture; but no more. There is spirit, conception, force, and effect: but all this is done by the first going over of the canvas. It is the foundation, not the superstructure of a first-rate work of art. It is a rude outline, a striking and masterly sketch" (16:209).

announced that his address during the coming weeks would be The Hut at Winterslow.[44] He was still in London on April 20, when Crabb Robinson saw him again at the Lambs',[45] but soon he was back in the country, musing and writing:

> Taste is a luxury for the privileged few: but it would be hard upon those who have not the same standard of refinement in their own minds that we suppose ourselves to have, if this should prevent them from having recourse, as usual, to their old frolics, coarse jokes, and horse-play, and getting through the wear and tear of the world, with such homely sayings and shrewd helps as they may. Happy is it, that the mass of mankind eat and drink, and sleep, and perform their several tasks, and do as they like without us—caring nothing for our scribblings, our carpings, and our quibbles; and moving on the same, in spite of our fine-spun distinctions, fantastic theories, and lines of demarcation, which are like the chalk-figures drawn on ball-room floors to be danced out before morning! In the field opposite the window where I write this, there is a country-girl picking stones: in the one next it, there are several poor women weeding the blue and red flowers from the corn: farther on, are two boys, tending a flock of sheep. What do they know or care about what I am writing about them, or ever will—or what would they be the better for it, if they did? (12:27)

At Winterslow Hazlitt seems to have written "The Drama, No. 5" for the May *London Magazine*. It was another leisurely, gossipy piece more or less based on plays he had seen in London during the spring. He chided Robert Elliston, manager of Drury Lane, for suspending the free list during Kean's coming appearance in *King Lear* and for postponing the production "lest . . . the immortal Shakespeare should meet with opponents" (18:316).[46] He criticized Charles Mathews's performance in *The Country Cousins*, recalled that Mathews had resented his criticism in the *Times* in 1817, then dilated on the folly of resenting constructive criticism.[47] He praised Junius Brutus Booth's playing in *Lear*, though he lamented the managers' mingling of Nahum Tate's love scenes with Shakespeare's original text. All this boded ill for Kean's long-promised *Lear*.

44. *The Hazlitts*, pp. 451–52.
45. Robinson, 1:239.
46. The "opponent" was Junius Brutus Booth, who was currently playing Lear at Covent Garden. Hazlitt reported a rumor that Drury Lane was about to claim exclusive rights to the production of Shakespeare's plays.
47. In the course of this passage Hazlitt quoted a sentence of his own, "He might exhibit it every night for a month, and we should go to see it every night!" which P. G. Patmore had used, without acknowledgment, in a review for *Blackwood's*. In a footnote he remarked: "We should put a stop to the practices of 'such petty larceny rogues'—but that it is not worth while." Patmore recognized the allusion and broke with Hazlitt. Later, however, the two met at a dinner at John Scott's, Hazlitt acted "as if nothing had happened between them," and the two became friends again (Patmore, 2:279, 283–85).

Gradually now he began to resume work for other periodicals. For the May *Edinburgh Review* he wrote a long critique of Joseph Spence's *Anecdotes of Pope*, declaring that Spence was no Boswell, that he presented only "shreds and patches, and not cut out of the entire piece" (16:156). And he speculated on how brilliantly Boswell could have presented the titans of the early eighteenth century.

On May 2 he wrote from Winterslow to Francis Jeffrey to suggest more articles that he might write. He mentioned a review of Joseph Farington's *Memoirs of the Life of Sir Joshua Reynolds*, observing: "The text is in bungling openstitch & presents plenty of loop-holes for *apercus* on the subjects of patronage, public taste, portrait painting, & the grand style of art as pursued in this country by Barry, West, Fuseli, Haydon, etc. But I had better do the thing, & then you will judge." He hesitated to attempt an article on the Elizabethan era, as Jeffrey had asked, because he had "nearly exhausted my little stock of knowledge" on the subject, though he added that, "if anything occurs, I will bear in mind your suggestion." But he had other possibilities in mind: "I have been reading the Sketch-Book of Geoffrey Crayon, Gent. [Washington Irving], & think something might be made of it in the way of an extract or two, & of a prefatory sketch of the character of American Literature as here exemplified. Southey's Life of Wesley I am half afraid to ask for." [48]

In June he wrote two articles for the *Examiner*. On the fourth he replied, in "Illustrations of a Hack Writer," to a statement in the *Courier* that "flatterers of the people" are every bit as sycophantic as alleged flatterers of kings. And he sketched a "character" of a successful hackwriter, pretty clearly based on the career of William Mudford, his old rival of the *Morning Chronicle*, who was now editor of the *Courier* (19:214–15). Then on the twenty-fifth, when Leigh Hunt was ailing, he wrote the "Theatrical Examiner," first comparing Macready's interpretation of Macbeth with Kean's and Kemble's—and pronouncing Kemble's the finest—then praising Miss Stephens's singing at a benefit performance. The latter moved him to reminisce:

Those were the happy days when first Miss Stephens began to sing! . . . They were the sweetest notes we ever heard, and almost the last we ever heard with pleasure! For since then, other events not to be named lightly here, but "thoughts of which can never from the heart"—"with other notes than to the Orphean lyre," have stopped our ears to the voice of the charmer. But since the voice of Liberty has risen once more in Spain, its grave and its birth place, and like a babbling hound has

48. ALS, Yale University Library.

wakened the echos in Galicia, in the Asturias, in Castile and Leon, and Estremadura, why, we feel as if we "had three ears again" and the heart to use them, and as if we could once more write with the same feelings (the tightness removed from the breast, and the pains smoothed from the brow) as we did when we gave the account of Miss Stephens's first appearance in the Beggar's Opera. Life might then indeed "know the return of spring,"—and end, as it began, with faith in human kind! (18:342–43)

Momentarily Hazlitt's spirits seem to be reviving. The revolution in Spain, King Ferdinand's acceptance of a liberalized constitution—these buoyed him up, even though his own affairs showed little sign of improvement.

In "The Drama, No. 6" in the June *London Magazine* he reported at last on Kean's performance in *King Lear*, which had finally been presented. "We need not say," he wrote, "how much our expectations had been previously excited to see Mr. Kean in this character, and we are sorry to be obliged to add, that they were very considerably disappointed" (18:331). In the first place, the text used was Tate's adaptation of the play; in the second, although Kean had assured London audiences that this was his finest part, it proved, Hazlitt believed, to be beyond his abilities. "There are pieces of ancient granite that turn the edge of any modern chisel," he wrote: "so perhaps the genius of no living actor can be expected to cope with Lear. Mr. Kean chipped off a bit of the character here and there: but he did not pierce the solid substance, nor move the entire mass.—Indeed, he did not go the right way about it. He was too violent at first, and too tame afterwards. He sunk from unmixed rage to mere dotage" (18:332–33). Then he analyzed Kean's performance point by point, occasionally remarking on the playing of the other actors and admitting only grudgingly that "the tragedy was, in general, got up better than we expected" (18:338).[49]

In the same issue of the *London Magazine*[50] Hazlitt succeeded in placing another sort of contribution, an essay "On the Qualifications Necessary to Success in Life." It was headed "Table-Talk, No. 1," and it launched the series which he had been hoping since January to write for the *London Magazine.* It was, in a sense, a new sort of venture for him—similar in

49. As originally published in the *London Magazine*, the essay closed with a notice of *The Lady and the Devil*, an afterpiece at Drury Lane, and a very favorable critique of James Sheridan Knowles's *Virginius* at Covent Garden. Neither was the work of Hazlitt, whose account of *Virginius* appeared in "Drama, no. 7" in the following month (See below, pp. 264–65).

50. E. L. Brooks (*NQ* 199 [1954]:355–56) has suggested that Hazlitt may have written also the pre-publication notice of Shelley's *Prometheus Unbound* which appeared in the June, 1820, issue of the *London Magazine*—in fact, that he may have contributed regularly to the monthly "Literary and Scientific Intelligence."

many respects to the personal essays which he had written for the Round Table series, yet considerably longer, more analytical, essentially a study of human behavior. This was, of course, his favorite topic, and when he set himself to pondering any aspect of it, his ideas rushed forth in such profusion that he set them down as they struck him, with little concern for logical progression. In an essay like this he could draw on his long years of reflection on life and human nature and on his reaction to his immediate experiences. In doing so he revealed much about his inmost thoughts at a time when he was under great emotional pressure, yet wrote few letters. In this first essay of the Table Talk series, while exploring the qualifications for success in life, he brooded a good deal on his own apparent failure.

His conclusions were hardly surprising: "Fortune does not always smile on merit:—'the race is not to the swift, nor the battle to the strong': and even where the candidate for wealth or honours succeeds, it is as often, perhaps, from the qualifications which he wants as from those which he possesses; or the eminence which he is lucky enough to attain, is owing to some faculty or acquirement, which neither he nor any body else suspected" (12:195). And presently: "The way to secure success is to be more anxious about obtaining than about deserving it" (12:196). Or "even in the pursuit of arts and science, a dull plodding fellow will often do better than one of a more mercurial and fiery cast—the mere unconsciousness of his own deficiencies, or of any thing beyond what he himself can do, reconciles him to his mechanical progress, and enables him to perform all that lies in his power with labour and patience" (12:197). Hazlitt acknowledged that a deserving man might succeed, but cautioned: "The way to fame, through merit alone, is the narrowest, the steepest, the longest, the hardest of all others—(that it is the most certain and lasting, is even a doubt)" (12:196). He then considered the specific qualifications for success, illustrating each point by instances drawn from literature and life, usually contemporary life, with the person involved often identified by name. When he came at last to consider the man who has not succeeded, he needed no identification:

> A writer, whom I know very well, cannot gain an admission to Drury-lane Theatre, because he does not lounge into the lobbies, or sup at the Shakespear—nay, the same person having written upwards of sixty columns of original matter on politics, criticism, belles-lettres, and *virtù* in a respectable Morning Paper, in a single half-year, was, at the end of that period, on applying for a renewal of his engagement, told by the Editor "he might give in a specimen of what he could do!" One would think sixty columns of the Morning Chronicle were a sufficient specimen of what a man could do. But while this person was thinking of his next answer to Vetus, or his account of Mr. Kean's performance of Hamlet, he had neglected "to point the toe," to hold

up his head higher than usual (having acquired a habit of poring over books when young), and to get a new velvet collar to an old-fashioned great coat. (12:204–5)

Equally unmistakable was the subject of the following lines:

He who can truly say, *Nihil humanum a me alienum puto,* has a world of cares on his hands, which nobody knows any thing of but himself. This is not one of the least miseries of a studious life. The common herd do not by any means give him full credit for his gratuitous sympathy with their concerns; but are struck with his lack-lustre eye and wasted appearance. They cannot translate the expression of his countenance out of the vulgate; they mistake the knitting of his brows for the frown of displeasure, the paleness of study for the languor of sickness, the furrows of thought for the regular approaches of old age. They read his looks, not his books; have no clue to penetrate the last recesses of the mind, and attribute the height of abstraction to more than an ordinary share of stupidity. "Mr. ——— never seems to take the slightest interest in any thing," is a remark I have often heard made in a whisper. (12:206)

Hazlitt remarked bitterly on the effect which rank may have on a man's rise to literary success:

An author now-a-days, to succeed, must be something more than an author,—a nobleman, or rich plebeian: the simple literary character is not enough. "Such a poor forked animal," as a mere poet or philosopher turned loose upon public opinion, has no chance against the flock of bats and owls that instantly assail him. It is name, it is wealth, it is title and influence that mollifies the tender-hearted Cerberus of criticism—first, by placing the honorary candidate for fame out of the reach of Grub-street malice; secondly, by holding out the prospect of a dinner or a vacant office to successful sycophancy. This is the reason why a certain Magazine praises Percy Bysshe Shelley and vilifies "Johnny Keats:" they know very well that they cannot ruin the one in fortune as in fame, but they may ruin the other in both, deprive him of a livelihood together with his good name, send him *to Coventry,* and into the Rules of a prison; and this is a double incitement to the exercise of their laudable and legitimate vocation. (12:208)

Yet, given an occasion, he could brighten up and enjoy himself fully. On May 4 Barry Cornwall had written to Leigh Hunt: "A new Tragedy on a subject of Roman History is accepted and forthcoming at Covent Garden. As the Author is an old acquaintance of Hazlitt's (to whom I am going to write in a day or two about the matter) you will I know be glad to mention the thing, to say nothing of its being a piece of news for the paper."[51] Eventually Hazlitt heard the news: the play was a tragedy called *Virginius;* the author was young James Sheridan Knowles, whom Hazlitt had prob-

51. Richard W. Armour, *Barry Cornwall* (Boston: Meador Publishing Co., 1935), p. 54.

ably not seen since the two of them had practiced ropedancing some twenty years before. He hurried up to London and, although the play had already been reviewed once in the *London Magazine*, he reviewed it again in his "Drama, No. 7" for the July issue. He led into the essay casually, observing that, despite his love of the theater, he loved it best "at a distance." "We like to be a hundred miles off from the Acted Drama in London," he wrote, "and to get a friend (who may be depended on) to give an account of it for us; which we read, at our leisure, under the shade of a clump of lime-trees" (18:344). However, "we heard from good authority that there was a new tragedy worth seeing, and also that it was written by an old friend of ours. *That* there was no resisting. So 'we came, saw, and were satisfied.' Virginius is a good play:—we repeat it. It is a real tragedy; a sound historical painting" (18:345). Then he defended the play against hostile critics, lauded Macready's playing of the leading role as "his best and most faultless performance," and lamented that the play as presented at Covent Garden had been purged of some of the liberal sentiments which appeared in the printed text. He went on to discuss Kean's recent benefit at Drury Lane, finding flaws in his playing both in *Venice Preserved* and in the farcical afterpiece. Somehow Hazlitt had lost his old enthusiasm for Kean.

While he was in London Knowles entertained him, Macready, and a few others at a dinner of salmon and boiled leg of mutton at a coffeehouse in Covent Garden. "Hazlitt was a man whose conversation could not fail to arrest attention," Macready wrote later in his *Reminiscences*. "He found in me a ready listener, and in the interest of our discussion became irritated by the boisterous boyish sallies of Knowles's irrepressible spirits, rebuking him for his unseasonable interruptions, and, as one having authority, desiring him not 'to play the fool.' The poet was in truth a very child of nature, and Hazlitt, who knew him well, treated him as such."[52] In his review of *Virginius* Hazlitt had hailed Knowles as "the same boy-poet, after a lapse of years, as when we first knew him; unconscious of the wreath he has woven round his brow, laughing and talking of his play just as if it had been written by any body else, and as simple-hearted, downright, and honest as the unblemished work he has produced" (18:348). There were limits, obviously, to Hazlitt's patience with boyish simplicity; still he must have found some comfort in the success of this young man who, Macready said, "considered himself greatly indebted" to Hazlitt's "early advice and tutorship." And at about the same time he received from John

52. *Macready's Reminiscences*, ed. Sir Frederick Pollock, 2 vols. (London, 1875), 1:213.

Keats a copy of his newly published poem *Lamia* inscribed "To Wm Hazlitt Esqre with the Author's sincere respects." [53] A happy few valued his efforts!

The *London Magazine* for July contained a second Table Talk essay "On the Difference between Writing and Speaking." It was a long essay, but much less searching than the first of the series; Hazlitt argued that "the writer and speaker have to do things essentially different. Besides habit, and greater or less facility, there is also a certain reach of capacity, a certain depth or shallowness, grossness or refinement of intellect, which marks out the distinction between those whose chief ambition is to shine by producing an immediate effect, or who are thrown back, by a natural bias, on the severer researches of thought and study" (12:263). Yet he clearly revealed his acute powers of mind when he analyzed the conversation, oratory, and writing of public figures ranging from Burke and Chatham to Jack Davies, "the unrivalled racket player" (12:273). He concluded the essay with "a definition of the character of an author," dwelling on his need for solitude: "The intervention of other people's notions, the being the immediate object of their censure or their praise, puts him out. What will tell, what will produce an effect, he cares little about; and therefore he produces the greatest. The *personal* is to him an impertinence; so he conceals himself and writes. Solitude 'becomes his glittering bride, and airy thoughts his children.' Such a one is a true author; and not a member of any Debating Club, or Dilettanti Society whatever" (12:279). Again he was looking inward.

The August issue of the *Edinburgh Review* contained Hazlitt's review of Farington's *Memoirs of the Life of Sir Joshua Reynolds.*[54] He gave the book short shrift; it was, he declared at the outset, "a superfluous publication" (16:181) because Farington really had only one point to make, and his supplementary observations on original genius, the dearth of English art, the decline of Italian art, and the achievement of the Royal Academy were all misguided. Hazlitt soon lost sight of Farington altogether, preferring to comment on art in general and on contemporary English painting in particular. As so often, his subject ran away with him—and he did not hesitate to admit it. "We had quite forgotten," he wrote in his final paragraph, "the chief object of Mr. Farington's book, Sir Joshua's dispute with the Academy about Mr. Bonomi's election [as Professor of Perspective]; and it is too late to return to it now" (16:211).

53. Lowell, *John Keats*, 2:425.

54. In a letter dated August 11, 1820, Hazlitt told Haydon that Jeffrey had accepted his review of Farington "with some corrections" (Baker, p. 404 n.).

His essay "The Drama, No. 8," in the August *London Magazine,* consisted largely of general comments on the theaters, large and small, and actors, past and present, although it worked at last into specific criticisms of two minor comedies at the Haymarket Theater and of Madame Vestris's playing of Macheath in *The Beggar's Opera.* Early in the essay Hazlitt wrote: "We like a play-house in proportion to the number of happy human faces it contains (and a play-house seldom contains many wretched ones)" (18:352). Yet he seems to have been attending the theaters less and less, perhaps even relying, as he had declared in "The Drama, No. 7," on news of the theater sent to him in the country by an accommodating friend. In the same essay he had maintained that the only installment of the series "that has given us entire satisfaction" (18:343) was written when the theaters were closed for several weeks and he was free "to take a peep into the raree-show of our own fancies" (18:343).

Hazlitt was spending little time in the city these days, escaping more and more to Winterslow. He had convinced himself that solitude was essential to a literary man, that, to serve his fellow creatures best, he must withdraw from society. But surely such protests were in large part defensive; surely his desire to escape from human contact stemmed primarily from his fear of being rejected—hurt—by others. If he was in a fair way toward becoming a recluse, it was not truly, as he liked to think, by choice.

Late in July he received word from his sister Peggy that his father had died on July 16.[55] The news could hardly have caused him deep grief; the old man was eighty-four years old now and had grown increasingly feeble. "I did not see my father after he was dead," Hazlitt wrote later, "but I saw death shake him by the hand and stare him in the face" (8:373). And he had the consolation of knowing that, though he had disappointed his father long ago, he had, in a sense, carried on his father's work: he had become a preacher of sorts, a missionary of the gospel of human freedom. Yet he had never gained the self-assurance which had sustained the old man.

Peggy asked in her letter whether Hazlitt intended to prepare an obituary of their father for the *Monthly Repository.* He never did,[56] but he may well have written the brief notice which appeared in the *Examiner* for August 1

55. Not knowing where her brother was living, Peggy sent him word of their father's death through their niece Mary in London. It was only when Sarah Hazlitt arrived at Crediton on July 27 that Peggy learned where Hazlitt was staying (*The Hazlitts,* p. 449).

56. The issue of the *Monthly Repository* for November, 1820, contained an obituary notice of the Reverend Mr. Hazlitt signed by the Reverend G. P. Hinton, Minister of the Unitarian Chapel at Crediton. It included the lines describing a Dissenting clergyman from Hazlitt's essay "On Court Influence," quoted above, pp. 212–13.

hailing the Reverend Mr. Hazlitt as "a man who through his whole life was a friend to truth and liberty." [57] Later in the year, deliberating on "The Pleasures of Painting," he recalled affectionately the time when he and his father had been drawn together by their interest in his portrait of the old man.[58] Yet even his respect and affection for his father were blighted by his sense of his own inadequacy. According to Haydon, he once exclaimed: "Say nothing about my father; he was a good man. His son is a devil, and let him remain so." [59]

If Hazlitt went down to Crediton when he heard of his father's death, he stayed there only briefly. By August 13 he was in London again moving into a back room on the second floor at 9 Southampton Buildings, Chancery Lane, which he had rented for fourteen shillings per week. His landlord was a tailor named Micaiah Walker, whose eldest daughter had married Robert Roscoe, son of one of Hazlitt's former patrons at Liverpool. On the sixteenth a younger daughter, Sally, came to Hazlitt's room "to wait on him." She was not a pretty girl; in a lucid moment Hazlitt allegedly told his wife that "her eyes were the worst and had the worst expression he had ever seen, of hypocrisy and design, and had a poor slimy watery look, yet she was well made and had handsome arms."[60] Barry Cornwall described her face as "round and small" and her eyes as "motionless, glassy, and without any speculation (apparently) in them," adding that "her steady, unmoving gaze upon the person whom she was addressing was exceedingly unpleasant." Yet he was fascinated by her "movements in walking . . . for I never observed her to make a step. She went onwards in a sort of wavy, sinuous manner, like the movement of a snake. . . . She was silent," he added, "or uttered monosyllables only, and was very demure. . . . The Germans would have extracted a romance from her, endowing her perhaps with some diabolic attribute." [61] Sarah Hazlitt was, understandably, less enchanted with the girl; she dismissed her as "thin and bony as the scrag end of a neck of mutton." [62] Hazlitt, however, was immediately "struck with her appearance and elegant manners, and told her so," whereupon "she turned round and stared him full in the face." [63]

57. *Four Generations*, 1:124.

58. See above, p. 65.   59. Stoddard, p. 292.   60. *Journals*, pp. 246–47.

61. *Cornwall Recollections*, pp. 82–83. Cf. Hazlitt's remark in his essay "Travelling Abroad" in the *New Monthly Magazine* for June, 1828: "If I want to know what real grace is, I ask myself, How the Venus de Medicis would move from her pedestal? Not like a French woman, but like———" (17:339). Note also Hazlitt's statement in *Liber Amoris:* "Your ordinary walk is as if you were performing some religious ceremony" (9:108).

62. *Journals*, p. 247.   63. Ibid., p. 246.

Hazlitt was forty-two years old, a scholar and a philosopher, as he liked to style himself. Sally, probably in her late teens, was an accomplished flirt. She made, he later claimed, "a dead set at him," and he was helpless. He who had been so often spurned, rejected, who had longed for solitude and defended himself against oppressors real and fancied, had no defenses to offer against a coquette. He surrendered at once.

"I do not think that what is called *Love at first sight* is so great an absurdity as it is sometimes imagined to be," the hapless man wrote a few months later.

> We generally make up our minds beforehand to the sort of person we should like, grave or gay, black, brown, or fair; with golden tresses or with raven locks;—and when we meet with a complete example of the qualities we admire, the bargain is soon struck. We have never seen any thing to come up to our newly discovered goddess before, but she is what we have been all our lives looking for. The idol we fall down and worship is an image familiar to our minds. It has been present to our waking thoughts, it has haunted us in our dreams, like some fairy vision.

Then, addressing himself to the "goddess": "Oh! thou, who, the first time I ever beheld thee, didst draw my soul into the circle of thy heavenly looks, and wave enchantment round me, do not think thy conquest less complete because it was instantaneous; for in that gentle form (as if another Imogen had entered) I saw all that I had ever loved of female grace, modesty, and sweetness!" (8:310–11).

The scholar-philosopher was smitten!

CHAPTER XI

A Very Child in Love
(1820–1821)

Hazlitt suddenly found himself thrust into a perilous situation: an impulsive man who had long felt himself spurned, he was confronted with a flirtatious girl who welcomed attention, especially from gentlemen above her station. He was, as he later assured her, "a very child in love" (9:114); she was "the only woman that ever made me think she loved me, and that feeling was so new to me, and so delicious, that it 'will never from my heart'" (9:109). Within a week, he wrote, "you sat upon my knee, twined your arms about me, caressed me with every mark of tenderness consistent with modesty" (9:107). And she continued to do so—but no more—almost every day "by the hour together," he claimed, for a year and a half (9:146). Hazlitt was intoxicated, blind to the fact that Sally was only dallying with him. He convinced himself that she was "half inclined to be a prude"; he admired her "as a 'pensive nun, devout and pure'" (9:102); he believed her "the precise little puritanical person she set up for" (9:127–28). His critical and analytical powers failed him entirely; he was indeed a very child in love.

Yet he was probably happier than he had been for years; he could feed himself now on hopes. He respected Sally's chastity, assuring himself that eventually she would be his. For more than six months he was happily unaware of any obstacle (except his own marriage, which he hoped to dissolve) to fulfillment of their love.[1]

1. The only hint that he may have had momentary doubts of Sally's constancy early in their courtship occurs in the passage from *Troilus and Cressida* beginning "Oh if I thought it could be in a woman" which he inserted in *Liber Amoris* under the heading "A Proposal of Love [Given to her in our early acquaintance]" (9:115). And here he seems to be expressing doubts of women in general, not of Sally.

The September issue of the *London Magazine* contained two articles, both probably written before the fateful meeting on August 16. One, the ninth installment of "The Drama," contained some sharp criticism of Elliston, manager of the Drury Lane Theater, for his cavalier attitude toward the managers of the summer theaters (18:360–66). Then followed reviews of four new plays, among them a production of *Othello* in which Kean had attempted a new interpretation of the leading role. It did not please Hazlitt; so far as he was concerned, "There is but one perfect way of playing Othello, and that was the way in which he used to play it" (18:362).

The other article in the September *London* was "Table-Talk, No. 3: On the Conversation of Authors," an essay in much the same vein as its predecessors in the series. "An author is bound to write—well or ill, wisely or foolishly: it is his trade," Hazlitt declared at the outset,

> But I do not see that he is bound to talk, any more than he is bound to dance, or ride, or fence better than other people. Reading, study, silence, thought, are a bad introduction to loquacity. It would be sooner learnt of chambermaids and tapsters. He understands the art and mystery of his own profession, which is book-making: what right has any one to expect or require him to do more—to make a bow grace-fully on entering or leaving a room, to make love charmingly, or to make a fortune at all? . . . Introduce him to a tea-party of milliner's girls, and they are ready to split their sides with laughing at him: over his bottle he is dry: in the drawing-room, rude or awkward: he is too refined for the vulgar, too clownish for the fashionable: —"he is one that cannot make a good leg, one that cannot eat a mess of broth cleanly, one that cannot ride a horse without spur-galling, one that cannot salute a woman, and look on her directly:"—in courts, in camps, in town and country, he is a cypher or a butt: he is good for nothing but a laughing-stock or a scare-crow. You can scarcely get a word out of him for love or money. (12:24–25)

For the moment he seemed to be thinking of his own shortcomings, though with none of his usual resentment. But he soon moved on to a more general view of the subject, remarking that "the conversation of authors is not so good as might be imagined: but, such as it is (and with rare exceptions) it is better than any other" (12:30). And he treated his readers to another nostalgic account of the old Thursday evening parties at the Lambs', followed by vivid sketches of the conversational powers of able talkers of his acquaintance: Leigh Hunt, James Northcote, Horne Tooke, John Philpot Curran, "Peter Pindar," and the like. The essay was sharpened by frequent barbs aimed at Coleridge, the master of interminable, unfathomable con-versation, but softened at last by a warm tribute to "the mere book-worm" George Dyer, who "lives all his life in a dream of learning, and has never once had his sleep broken by a real sense of things" (12:43).

It is a splendid exercise in the art of the essay, one which defies any quick summary. Hazlitt's characteristic trenchant observations on human nature are here, brightened by acute vignettes of notable men he has known, unmarred by the bitterness of earlier, more subjective essays. Lamb wrote Hazlitt that his sister Mary had read it just before one of her seizures and found "unmix'd delight" in it. "The Article is a treasure to us for ever," he added. Even Hazlitt's estranged brother-in-law was pleased with it. "Stoddart sent over the magaz^e to know if it were yours," Lamb wrote, "and says it is better than Hogarth's 'Mod. Midn. Conversation,' with several other most kind mentions of it." [2]

Hazlitt tore himself away from Southampton Buildings for part of September and October and went down to Winterslow again, where he doubtless kept busy writing Table Talk essays—some for the *London*, others for a volume of essays which the publisher John Warren had commissioned. He did not write "The Drama, No. 10," which appeared in the October *London Magazine;* it was probably the work of John Hamilton Reynolds. Hazlitt's only contribution to the October issue was "Table-Talk, No. 4: On the Present State of Parliamentary Eloquence," which he described in his opening paragraph as "a marginal note or explanatory addition" (17:5) to his essay "On the Difference between Writing and Speaking."

It was not one of his striking successes, and he seems to have known it. "It is a subject of which I wish to make clear work as I go," he observed, "for it is one to which, if I can once get rid of it, I am not likely to recur" (17:5). He proceeded then to analyze the abilities of a dozen members of Parliament and to comment briefly on the inferior powers of half a dozen members of the House of Lords, always, of course, favoring those who enlivened their speeches with imagination or passion. He praised the writer who is a "good hater," who puts his heart into his task, rather than the reasonable, impartial reporter of facts. "Fling yourself into the gap at once," he urged, "—either into the arms, or at the heads of Ministers!" (17:7). He came out strongly in favor of the fiery Irish in Parliament rather than the icy Scots. Indeed he criticized the icy Scot Henry Brougham so sharply that John Scott felt obliged to insert a footnote assuring readers of the *London* that "we must not be understood as at all participating in these sentiments" (17:385).

2. *Lamb Letters*, 2:283. Stoddart's praise showed uncommon generosity on his part: not only did he have old grievances against Hazlitt, but he might well have recognized himself in the essay as the "very ingenious man" who excels at "common chit-chat" but is completely irrational when he attempts to argue (12:33–34).

In November Hazlitt published no article in the *London* or any other magazine; he was, presumably, spending his time writing essays for the projected volume of Table Talk. In December he was back in London with his fifth Table Talk essay, "On the Pleasures of Painting," another piece in his reflective analytical vein enriched by his recollections of the past. He must have thought highly of it because it was the only one of the *London Magazine* series which he included in the published volume of Table Talk, where, divided into two parts, it appeared as the first and second essays.

He made some interesting points about the difference between writing and painting. Although he declared that he had "long since given up all thoughts of the art as a profession" (8:17), he recalled nostalgically the solace he had found in painting. "From the moment that you take up the pencil, and look Nature in the face," he maintained, "you are at peace with your own heart" (8:5). Writing, by contrast, yields far less satisfaction. "I have not much pleasure in writing these Essays," he confessed,

> or in reading them afterwards; though I own I now and then meet with a phrase that I like, or a thought that strikes me as a true one. But after I begin them, I am only anxious to get to the end of them, which I am not sure I shall do, for I seldom see my way a page or even a sentence beforehand; and when I have as by a miracle escaped, I trouble myself little more about them. I sometimes have to write them twice over: then it is necessary to read the *proof*, to prevent mistakes by the printer; so that by the time they appear in a tangible shape, and one can con them over with a conscious, sidelong glance to the public approbation, they have lost their gloss and relish, and become "more tedious than a twice-told tale." (7:6)

Yet for all his protestations he seemed to find a good deal of pleasure in the very process of describing the thrill of painting his first portrait—of the old woman in the bonnet—or the happy hours which went into his painting of his father, now "gone to rest, full of years, of hope, and charity!" (8:13).

The same serenity pervaded the second half of the essay, when he treated the painter's enjoyment of the works of other artists. When he visits a collection of paintings in one of the great country houses, "he goes away richer than he came, richer than the possessor" (8:14). When he himself was first initiated into "the mysteries of the art" at the Orleans Gallery in London, or, even more, when he first viewed the breath-taking gathering of old masters at the Louvre, he, as a "true adept," knew a delight far beyond what a "mere man of taste and natural sensibility" could ever realize. On and on he went, summoning up fond memories and savoring the words which recreated them. He concluded at last with a long quotation from

Jonathan Richardson's "Discourse on the Science of a Connoisseur," citing "some striking examples of the felicity and infelicity of artists" and a touching envoy to "Poor Dan. Stringer," whose skills as a painter were dissipated when he "fell a martyr (like Burns) to the society of country-gentlemen, and then of those whom they would consider as more his equals" (8:21).

Hazlitt seemed suddenly to have achieved a detached, yet humane, posture as he regarded the world about him. He spoke as a philosopher in retirement rather than a bitter recluse. His temper may have been sweetened by the novel sensation of loving and (as he thought) being loved, but beyond question his interest in writing had revived when he happened upon this new type of essay. He had always judged art and literature largely for their truth to life; his political essays had been shaped by his longing to improve the lot of man. Now he was dealing with life itself—and utilizing all his skills. His sharp eye could pierce the surface of human life and action; his keen mind could detect subtle meanings in his discoveries; his wealth of experience as painter, philosopher, political commentator, reporter, and critic—his knowledge of literature and the theater—all provided material to enliven his points. And his extraordinary flair for expressing himself—almost entirely spontaneous if we can believe his own statement in "On the Pleasure of Painting"—enriched the whole with grace and charm. For the first time in his career he could engage in the "metaphysical" speculation which he prized, while still giving rein to the "colorings of the imagination" which came so easily to him. William Hazlitt had found his true vocation.

The December *London Magazine* contained another article by him, "The Drama, No. 11." This was a halfhearted job which began with an ironic apology for his failure to complete the usual installment for the November issue: the friend who was to join him for a mutton chop and an evening at the theater (with Charles Kemble playing in Kotzebue's *The Stranger*) had failed to appear, he claimed, and he had missed the play. Incidentally, he glanced back over the earlier installments of the series and offered a mocking comment on each.[3] Clearly his interest in the series was waning; in fact he remarked: "If theatrical criticisms were only written when there is something worth writing about, it would be hard upon us who live by them. . . . No; the duller the stage grows, the gayer and more edifying must we become in ourselves: the less we have to say about that, the more room we have to talk about other things" (18:369). Then he ruefully listed the meager fare available at the London theaters and filled out the article

3. True to form, Hazlitt did not bother to check the dates of the installments which he was discussing. Howe points out his inaccuracies in *Complete Works*, 18:474.

with a review of Macready's performance in Edward Young's *Revenge*. To add a touch of spice to his essay, he wrote the review in a parody of Coleridge's convoluted style.

Thus ended Hazlitt's first year as dramatic critic for the *London Magazine* —and his last, for he never wrote another article in the series.[4] It had, for a while, served him well: it had provided him with a regular income when he sorely needed it, and he had taken advantage of the freedom it afforded him to discuss general principles as well as specific plays or authors. But in the Table Talk essays he had found an outlet much more to his liking.

Thomas Noon Talfourd took over the drama articles in Hazlitt's place. When Crabb Robinson heard of the change, he noted in his diary on December 27: "It will be, I fear, a falling off, for Hazlitt, though a mannerist in style, is a thinker at least." He went on: "Hazlitt's *Table Talk* in the *London* is full of acute observation. If spleen did not throw an offensive hue over all he writes, and were not his style spoiled by an ambition of ornament, he would be a very first-rate writer. As it is, I read all he writes with zest."[5] Like Dr. Stoddart, Robinson was charmed by the Table Talk essays, even though he disapproved of their author.

Hazlitt seems to have seen little of his old friends during the last months of the year 1820. Lamb wrote him one Saturday that autumn asking him not to call next day because Mary was ailing.[6] He was at Basil Montagu's house with Barry Cornwall, Crabb Robinson, and Mrs. Horace Twiss on December 10.[7] He later declared that he spent several hours a day while in London sitting in the Walkers' second floor back with Sally on his knee. But there were also congenial haunts nearby: during the day he could relax at the Southampton Coffee House, where "no one . . . has the slightest notion of any thing that has happened, that has been said, thought, or done out of his own recollection" (8:193); he could sit far into the night "silent and as a spectator" or join in the animated discussion of politics or literature at the Southampton Arms tavern (8:201). He must also have spent a good deal of time, in London or at Winterslow, meditating and writing essays for his coming volume of Table Talk.

At the same time he continued to turn out similar essays for immediate publication in the *London Magazine*. Readers aware of the identity of the

4. He did, however, offer to write another one for Taylor and Hessey after they assumed managership of the magazine (Blunden, p. 148). But no such article appeared in the *London*.

5. Robinson, 1:260.

6. *Lamb Letters*, 2:283.

7. Robinson, 1:258.

Table Talker must have been taken aback when they read the sixth essay of the series, "On the Look of a Gentleman," in the January, 1821, issue; he who had so often belittled the social graces acknowledged respectfully that "an habitual self-possession determines the appearance of a gentleman" (12:209). And he developed his thesis by citing examples of gentlemanly conduct as he had observed it, especially during his days as parliamentary reporter. At times his attitude was almost wistful: "I confess . . . that I admire this look of a gentleman, more when it rises from the level of common life, and bears the stamp of intellect, than when it is formed out of the mould of adventitious circumstances" (12:212). These were strange words for the scholar-philosopher. He was perhaps learning, in his new role of suitor, that a measure of gentlemanly self-possession might have distinct advantages.

On January 18 and 19 he dated from Winterslow Hut another essay, "On Living to One's Self," intended for his projected volume of Table Talk. "I never was in a better place or humour than I am at present for writing on this subject," he began. "I have a partridge getting ready for my supper, my fire is blazing on the hearth, the air is mild for the season of the year, I have had but a slight fit of indigestion to-day (the only thing that makes me abhor myself)" (8:90). He explained presently that by living to one's self he meant "living in the world, as in it, not of it: . . . it is to be a silent spectator of the mighty scene of things, not an object of attention or curiosity in it; to take a thoughtful, anxious interest in what is passing in the world, but not to feel the slightest inclination to make or meddle with it" (8:91). There are melancholy undertones in the essay as he reviews his own active life or reflects on the world around him. But he insists that he has done now with feverish ambition, that he longs only to "regain the obscurity and quiet that I love, 'far from the madding strife,' in some sequestered corner of my own, or in some far-distant land" (8:100). His chronic resentment has yielded to resignation and acceptance, attitudes ideally adapted to the stance of a philosophical essayist.

Never before in his mature years had he come so close to contentment. He even entered at times into the camaraderie of the able staff of the *London*, carrying on a friendly rivalry especially with Lamb, whose "Essays of Elia" were competing with his own for attention in the magazine. "That 'young master' will anticipate all my discoveries, if I don't mind," he wrote to Scott early in the year.[8] For the first time in his life Hazlitt was enjoying recognition both as a writer and as a suitor: he was being paid at the rate of

8. *Four Generations*, 1:140.

a guinea per page for his essays,[9] and Sally Walker was at least not discouraging his advances.

Soon after the beginning of the year 1821 he suffered a heavy blow. Sally told him the story—which has the ring of pure fiction—of her loyalty to a former love, one who had been "far distant" for "two long years," separated from her because "pride of birth . . . would not permit him to think of a union" (9:104–5). Suddenly, instead of answering his constantly recurring question with "You should judge by my actions" or "Do I seem indifferent?" (9:108), she said always, "No—never" (9:99). But he soon regained his equilibrium, assuring himself that the girl was disclosing her innate nobility. Once he had gained her affections, she would prove as faithful to him.

He continued to turn out his monthly essays for the *London*. The February issue contained "Table-Talk, No. 7: On Reading Old Books," in which he mused along in leisurely fashion. He declared his preference for old books rather than new ones ("I have more confidence in the dead than the living") (12:220); he admitted that "contemporary writers may be generally divided into two classes: one's friends or one's foes" (12:220); he shared with the reader his satisfaction in rereading old favorites like *Tom Jones* or *The Tatler*, Rousseau, Richardson, or Burke—and relived his first encounters with them. But suddenly he announced: "Books have in a great measure lost their power over me; nor can I revive the same interest in them as formerly. I perceive when a thing is good, rather than feel it" (12:225). Yet he admitted that "the reading of Mr. Keats's Eve of St. Agnes lately made me regret that I was not young again. The beautiful and tender images there conjured up 'come like shadows—and so depart.' The 'tiger-moth's wings,' which he has spread over his rich poetic blazonry, just flit across my fancy; the gorgeous twilight window which he has painted over again in his verse, to me 'blushes' almost in vain 'with blood of queens and kings'" (12:225).

But this was only a momentary mood; Hazlitt's new character of philosophical spectator had not stifled his innate gusto. He may, in fact, have been trying obliquely to make amends to Keats for an ill-natured allusion to him in "The Drama, No. 11" two months earlier. There he had quoted the phrase "mouth with slumbery pout" from *Endymion*, labeled it "a vile phrase, worse than Hamlet's 'beautified' applied to Ophelia," and added: "Indeed it has been remarked that Mr. Keats resembles Shakspeare in the novelty and eccentricity of his combinations of style. If so, it is the only

9. See below, p. 292 n.

thing in which he is like Shakspeare" (18:368). He went on then to defend Keats against the merciless attacks of the Cockney-baiters in *Blackwood's*. Even so, the scornful comparison of Keats and Shakspeare remained, and Hazlitt must have regretted it when he learned that Keats had gone to Rome in failing health.

By the time the Table Talk volume had appeared, Keats had died on February 25 in Rome, and Hazlitt inserted in his essay "On Living to One's Self" a plaintive allusion to "Poor Keats," the "'bud bit by an envious worm'" who "withdrew to sigh his last breath in foreign climes" (8:99). His later references to Keats were in much the same vein.[10] He never reviewed one of Keats's publications, but he included several of his poems in the anthology *Select British Poets* (1824), observing that Keats "gave the greatest promise of genius of any poet of his day" (9:244). Hazlitt probably never knew, though, how much Keats had looked to him for guidance in developing his talents and mastering his faults. Keats had read his books and attended his lectures, had listened closely to his conversation when they met, and had given him presentation copies of *Endymion* and *Lamia*. But his true acknowledgment of Hazlitt's influence lay buried in personal letters to family and friends which Hazlitt was never to read.

Hazlitt was much more immediately concerned with another tragic event, the death of John Scott, editor of the *London Magazine*, on February 27, after a duel with Jonathan Henry Christie fought at Chalk Hill Farm in Hampstead on the sixteenth. Hazlitt seems to have played no direct part in the dispute between Scott and John Gibson Lockhart which led up to the duel, though he had urged Scott not to compromise.[11] Yet he surely felt personally involved in its results: the death of a liberal colleague and the escape with impunity of the loathed "Z" of the Cockney school attacks. It was a sordid story; it had begun months earlier with attacks back and forth between the two magazines; it grew suddenly serious when Lockhart demanded a public apology or "satisfaction" and Scott in turn demanded that Lockhart "distinctly declare the nature of his connection" with

10. See, for example, 8:211, 254; 12:123; 16:237, 269.

11. *Four Generations*, 1:140. In *Fifty Years' Recollections* (3 vols. [London, 1858], 2:225), Cyrus Redding claimed that Thomas Campbell "declared to me that Hazlitt had been a means of irritating John Scott to such a degree, that he was one cause of his going out in the duel in which he fell." Redding acknowledged, however, that Horace Smith "thought and said, that I must be under a mistake. . . . The remark of Smith [in his *Graybeard's Gossip about his Literary Acquaintances*] was, 'Campbell was too prone to believe whatever he might hear in disparagement of Hazlitt, and in this instance I have reason to think he was misinformed'" (see also Redding's *Past Celebrities*, 2 vols. [London, 1863], 1:85).

Blackwood's. It reached its tragic climax after endless confusion and recrimination, when Scott challenged Christie, Lockhart's agent in the proceedings, to the fatal duel.

Inevitably Scott's death precipitated a crisis in the offices of the *London.* Hazlitt abandoned his pose of detached philosopher and rallied to the cause at once, volunteering to do what he could to fill the gap. On March 5 Robert Baldwin, publisher of the magazine, wrote in reply:

> My dear Sir,—I must not any longer neglect to avail myself of your kind offer to assist in filling up the chasm made by the death of our lamented friend in the Magazine; and I know not any subject which would be thought more interesting than a continuation of the Living Authors [a series which Scott had been writing], nor any pen so fitted for the subject as yours. Pray select any one you may think most fit, and render us your powerful assistance towards making our next number equal to its predecessors.
>
> In a day or two I shall probably request an interview with you on the subject of an editor.[12]

In the event, no new editor was appointed; Baldwin himself apparently filled the post until Taylor and Hessey took over publication of the magazine in the following May. Meanwhile Hazlitt seems to have solicited articles for the next few issues: he arranged for Leigh Hunt and Thomas Jefferson Hogg to submit pieces,[13] asked Barry Cornwall to write an essay on Shakespeare's *Pericles,*[14] and perhaps helped persuade Thomas Griffiths Wainewright to resume regular contributions to the magazine.[15] And, most helpful of all, he himself turned out an unprecedented four articles for the May issue. He took such an active part in the affairs of the magazine that some people believed he had succeeded Scott as editor. John Landseer wrote to him one Tuesday evening: "I wish you would be at the trouble of informing me, by post, if my letters can *not* appear in your next magazine— that is to say—as soon as you get another from Mr. Baldwin."[16]

12. *The Hazlitts,* p. 465.   13. *Four Generations,* 1:135.   14. Blunden, p. 146.

15. Wainewright, who wrote under the pseudonyms "Janus Weathercock" and "Egomet Bonmot," had been a regular contributor to earlier issues of the *London Magazine,* but had contributed nothing for seven months until his article on the British Exposition was published in the April, 1821, issue. He talked of resuming regular contributions, but by August he was bidding farewell to the other contributors, including Hazlitt. The two had quarrelled in the pages of the *London* in 1820, but probably all in good fun. Wainewright, a fop whose hands were "bespangled with regal rings," later achieved lasting fame as a poisoner and ended his days in Van Diemen's Land. His extraordinary history is recorded in Jonathan Curling's *Janus Weathercock* (London: T. Nelson and Sons, Ltd., 1938).

16. *Memoirs,* 2:10.

In the meantime the March and April issues of the *London* had appeared with two more Table Talk essays, probably written before the crisis occurred. "No. 8: On Personal Character" was another study of human behavior which opened with the flat statement: "No one ever changes his character from the time he is two years old; nay, I might say, from the time he is two hours old" (12:230). Any confidence that Hazlitt might have had in Locke or in human perfectibility, any hopes of remaking himself in a more winsome image, seem to be blasted as he argues that "there is an involuntary, unaccountable family-character, as well as family face" (12:232), that women differ essentially in character from men, that races and nationalities have distinctive traits of character, that "the slothful [never] becomes active, the coward brave, the headstrong prudent, the fickle steady, the mean generous, the coarse delicate, the ill-tempered amiable, or the knave honest" (12:236). Moreover, "a self-tormentor is never satisfied, come what will. He always apprehends the worst, and is indefatigable in conjuring up the apparition of danger. He is uneasy at his own good fortune, as it takes from him his favourite topic of repining and complaint. Let him succeed to his heart's content in all that is reasonable or important, yet if there is any one thing (and *that* he is sure to find out) in which he does not get on, this embitters all the rest. I know an instance. Perhaps it is myself" (12:238). Thanks to his weeks of reflection on human character Hazlitt was advancing from self-defense to self-knowledge.

"Table-Talk, No. 9," in the April issue of the *London,* was "On People of Sense"—that is, hardheaded, unimaginative people. Of course Hazlitt had little to say in their favor: ". . . all the grave impostures that have been acted in the world," he believed, "have been the contrivance of those who set up for oracles to their neighbours" (12:242). They make "a point of scouting the arts of painting, music, and poetry, as frivolous, effeminate, and worthless, as appealing to sentiment and fancy alone, and involving no useful theory or principle" (12:245). He cited his former landlord, Jeremy Bentham, as a classic example of the man of sense, deploring especially Bentham's "technical and conventional jargon, unintelligible to others and conveying no idea to himself in common with the rest of mankind" (12:249–50). More surprisingly, he singled out Shelley's recently published *Prometheus Unbound* for criticism—not because Shelley was "a man of sense," but because he failed to create the "sympathy with nature" that is requisite to poetry:

> Shakespear was, in this sense, not only one of the greatest poets, but one of the greatest moralists that we have. Those who read him are the happier, better, and

wiser for it. No one (that I know of) is the happier, better, or wiser, for reading Mr. Shelley's Prometheus Unbound. One thing is that nobody reads it. And the reason for one or both is the same, that he is not a poet, but a sophist, a theorist, a controversial writer in verse. He gives us, for representations of things, rhapsodies of words. He does not lend the colours of imagination and the ornaments of style to the objects of nature, but paints gaudy, flimsy, allegorical pictures on gauze, on the cobwebs of his own brain, "Gorgons and Hydras, and Chimeras dire." He assumes certain doubtful speculative notions, and proceeds to prove their truth by describing them in detail as matters of fact. This mixture of fanatic zeal with poetical licentiousness is not quite the thing. (12:245–46)

Nor was this his last word on the subject; he had more to say about Shelley's poetry in the volume *Table-Talk; or, Original Essays* which was published by John Warren of Old Bond Street in this same month of April.

This was a collection of sixteen essays, only two of which (the two parts of "On the Pleasure of Painting") had previously appeared in the Table Talk series of the *London Magazine*. Hazlitt included in the volume his essay "On the Ignorance of the Learned," which had appeared originally in the *Edinburgh Magazine* for July, 1818, and he incorporated his "Death of John Cavanagh" from the *Examiner* of February 7, 1819, into his essay "The Indian Jugglers." The other twelve pieces in the collection were entirely new.

The essays differ considerably in subject matter: one, "Character of Cobbett," can be classified as literary criticism; two, the two parts of "On Certain Inconsistencies in Sir Joshua Reynolds's Discourses" (a restatement of the principles expressed in the *Champion* between November, 1814, and January, 1815), as art criticism; but the great majority of the essays are miscellaneous in content (ranging from Indian jugglers to will making), rambling and personal in manner, on the order of the Table Talk essays in the *London Magazine*. When Hazlitt published a second volume of Table Talk in 1822, he subtitled it "Original Essays on Men and Manners." They are just that. The term *personal essay* does not adequately describe them; although the tone is relaxed and the style conversational, they are far more thoughtful and searching than most personal essays. Hazlitt was aware of the discrepancy between content and style and defended it when he brought out the Paris edition of *Table-Talk* in 1825:

The title may perhaps serve to explain what there is of peculiarity in the style or mode of treating the subjects. I had remarked that when I had written or thought upon a particular topic, and afterwards had occasion to speak of it with a friend, the conversation generally took a much wider range, and branched off into a number of indirect and collateral questions, which were not strictly connected with the original view of the subject, but which often threw a curious and striking light upon it, or upon human life in general. It therefore occurred to me as possible to combine the advantages of these two styles, the *literary* and *conversational;* or after stating and enforcing some leading idea, to follow it up by such observations and reflections as would probably suggest themselves in discussing the same question in company with others. This seemed to me to promise a greater variety and richness, and perhaps a greater sincerity, than could be attained by a more precise and scholastic method. The same consideration had an influence on the familiarity and conversational idiom of the style which I have used. (8:333)

Again he was engaging in the "metaphysical" discussion which he enjoyed, couching it in the familiar manner which held the interest of the common reader.

He allowed himself ample scope, now meditating "On Living to One's Self" or "On People with One Idea," presently speculating "On the Past and Future" or "On Genius and Common Sense." If there is a linking theme, it is his interest in the human faculties which are innate rather than acquired, instinctive rather than rational in origin. He delighted in investigating the essential nature and the capacities of genius or common sense (by which he meant natural intelligence, not practical sense); he enjoyed defining and analyzing such qualities as cleverness or the imagination, of making subtle distinctions between talent and genius, common sense and "vulgar opinion," or coarseness and vulgarity. Again and again he warned his reader of the limitations of pure reason or the inefficacy of fixed rules.

Yet his primary concern was not to admonish but merely to investigate the fascinating complexities and paradoxes of human nature. In "On Paradox and Common-place" he remarked: "I have been sometimes accused of a fondness for paradoxes, but I cannot in my own mind plead guilty to the charge" (8:146). Here, however, he was using the word to mean perverseness or singularity. Certainly he enjoyed revealing the contradictions in human behavior; in fact this is probably what he meant when he spoke of making "a very bad antithesis" with impunity (8:80–81).[17] He amused himself often with such antitheses: the ignorance of the learned, the limitations of men of practical achievements, the importance of the will rather than the understanding in accomplishing great actions, the enigmatic character of William Cobbett—"a very honest man with a total want of principle" (8:55)—or of George Canning, "the most equivocal character among

17. Elsewhere, in his article "The Periodical Press," in the May, 1823, *Edinburgh Review,* Hazlitt referred to "the extreme paradoxes of the author of Table-Talk" (16:231).

modern politicians [who] was the cleverest boy at Eton" (8:72). He even admitted to a strange quirk in his own nature: a romantic interest in the trappings of wealth and success (8:112) which belied his ardent liberalism.

Throughout the book Hazlitt expanded his points from the store of anecdotal material which he had gathered over the years—from his reading, from hearsay, and from personal experience. And although the essays were not truly subjective, they occasionally hinted at the state of his mind during these early months of his courtship of Sally Walker. On the whole he seemed unruffled; only occasionally did he reveal a shadow of distress or anger.[18] Yet the essay "On Living to One's Self" contained a startling passage:

> Even in the common affairs of life, in love, friendship, and marriage, how little security have we when we trust our happiness in the hands of others! Most of the friends I have seen have turned out the bitterest enemies, or cold, uncomfortable acquaintance. . . . He who looks at beauty to admire, to adore it, who reads of its wondrous power in novels, in poems, or in plays, is not unwise: but let no man fall in love, for from that moment he is "the baby of a girl." (8:95–96)

And there was almost certainly autobiographical significance in the note which he appended to the essay "On Thought and Action":

> A thorough fitness for any end implies the means. Where there is a will, there is a way. A real passion, an entire devotion to any object, always succeeds. The strong sympathy with what we wish and imagine, realises it, dissipates all obstacles, and removes all scruples. The disappointed lover may complain as much as he pleases. He was himself to blame. He was a half witted, *wishy-washy* fellow. His love might be as great as he makes it out: but it was not his ruling-passion. His fear, his pride, his vanity was greater. Let any one's whole soul be steeped in this passion, let him think and care for nothing else, let nothing divert, cool, or intimidate him, let the *ideal* feeling become an actual one and take possession of his whole faculties, looks, and manner, let the same voluptuous hopes and wishes govern his actions in the presence of his mistress that haunt his fancy in her absence, and I will answer for his success. But I will not answer for the success of a "dish of skimmed milk" in such a case. I could always get to see a fine collection of pictures myself. The fact is, I was set upon it. Neither the surliness of porters, nor the impertinence of footmen could keep me back. I had a portrait of Titian in my eye, and nothing could put me out in my determination. If that had not (as it were) been looking on me all the time I was battling my way, I should have been irritated or disconcerted, and gone away. But

18. See, for example, his apostrophe to Tudorleigh Woods in "On the Past and Future" (8:24–25) and his outburst against the public in "On Living to One's Self" (8:100). Neither seems more than a temporary (and, with Hazlitt, conventional) mood; in fact the first should probably be read as an expression of his longing for Sally's company at Winterslow (see 8:337 and cf. Howe, p. 332 n.).

my liking to the end conquered my scruples or aversion to the means. I never understood the Scotch character but on these occasions I would not take "No" for an answer. If I had wanted a place under government, or a writership to India, I could have got it from the same importunity, and on the same terms. (8:112 n.)[19]

In short, Hazlitt's attitude toward his infatuation was itself paradoxical: he saw himself now as a helpless victim, now as the staunch warrior determined to fight for victory.

The essays were generally free from personal attacks. Hazlitt avoided political comment, although he scored Canning for his "common-place" preference for "centuries of experience" over "visionary schemes of ideal perfectibility" (8:153). As for his old foes of the Lakes, he spared Coleridge altogether and lauded Wordsworth as "the greatest, that is, the most original poet of the present day," although he modified his praise with the words "only because he is the greatest egotist" (8:44) and followed up with specific evidence of that egotism.[20]

However, he was less sparing of his friends and allies. When he remarked of his colleague "Janus Weathercock," "I must therefore make an example of him *in terrorem* to all such hypercritics" (8:160), he was only continuing the playful quarrel that the two had carried on in the *London Magazine*.[21] But his treatment of Leigh Hunt was less genial; at least Hunt thought he detected reflections of his own character just after an incidental reference to "LH" in the essay "On People with One Idea." Hazlitt was discussing "vivacious mannerists in their conversation, and excessive egotists," and he remarked:

Though they run over a thousand subjects in mere gaiety of heart, their delight still flows from one idea, namely, themselves. Open the book in what page you will, there is a frontispiece of themselves staring you in the face. . . . If they talk to you of the town, its diversions, "its palaces, its ladies, and its pomp," they are the delight, the grace, the ornament of it. If they are describing the charms of the country, they give no account of any individual spot or object, or source of pleasure but the circumstance of their being there. . . . If they tell a love-tale of enamoured princesses, it is plain they fancy themselves the hero of the piece. If they discuss poetry, their encomiums still turn on something genial and unsophisticated, meaning their own style: if they enter into politics, it is understood that a hint from them to the poten-

19. It may not be assuming too much to read Hazlitt's name into the blank space in a sentence in the same essay: "The Dutch went mad for tulips, and ⸺ ⸺ for love" (8:104).

20. For other references to Wordsworth, though not by name, see 8:65 and 68. For one in the *Edinburgh Magazine* version of "On the Ignorance of the Learned" deleted from the text of the published *Table-Talk*, see 8:343.

21. See, for example, 18:344–45.

tates of Europe is sufficient. In short, as a lover (talk of what you will) brings in his mistress at every turn, so these persons contrive to divert your attention to the same darling object—they are, in fact, in love with themselves; and, like lovers, should be left to keep their own company. (8:69)[22]

Hunt was further annoyed at a quite gratuitous attack on Shelley in the essay "On Paradox and Common-place":

> The author of the Prometheus Unbound ... has a fire in his eye, a fever in his blood, a maggot in his brain, a hectic flutter in his speech, which mark out the philosophic fanatic. He is sanguine-complexioned, and shrill-voiced. ... He is clogged by no dull system of realities, no earth-bound feelings, no rooted prejudices, by nothing that belongs to the mighty trunk and hard husk of nature and habit, but is drawn up by irresistible levity to the regions of mere speculation and fancy, to the sphere of air and fire, where his delighted spirit floats in "seas of pearl and clouds of amber." ... Bubbles are to him the only realities:—touch them, and they vanish. Curiosity is the only proper category of his mind, and though a man in knowledge, he is a child in feeling. ... Mr. Shelley has been accused of vanity—I think he is chargeable with extreme levity; but this levity is so great, that I do not believe he is sensible of its consequences. He strives to overturn all established creeds and systems: but this is in him an effect of constitution. He runs before the most extravagant opinions, but this is because he is held back by none of the mechanical checks of sympathy and habit. He tampers with all sorts of obnoxious subjects, but it is less because he is gratified with the rankness of the taint, than captivated with the intellectual phosphoric light they emit. ... With his zeal, his talent, and his fancy, he would do more good and less harm, if he were to give up his wilder theories, and if he took less pleasure in feeling his heart flutter in unison with the panic-struck apprehensions of his readers. (8:148–49)

The passage contained some shrewd criticism and some home truths which Hazlitt had long entertained. But to Shelley's admirers it inevitably seemed unnecessarily severe treatment for one who was an ally, if not a close friend.

22. Hazlitt may well have had Hunt in mind also when he described, in "The Indian Jugglers," "an individual who if he had been born to an estate of five thousand a year, would have been the most accomplished gentleman of the age," but who is "too versatile for a professional man, not dull enough for a political drudge, too gay to be happy, too thoughtless to be rich," who "wants the enthusiasm of the poet, the severity of the prose-writer, and the application of the man of business" (8:83–84). Moreover, in the essay "On the Conversation of Authors" in the *London Magazine* for the preceding September, Hazlitt had drawn attention to Hunt's egocentricity as well as his more genial characteristics (12:38–39). Hunt might have pointed out that in the meantime he had paid Hazlitt a studied compliment in the *Indicator* for February 28: "We cannot refer to what Mr. Hazlitt said of [Lyly's *Campaspe*]; his books, as we are always having reason to find, when we most want them, being of that description of property which may be called borrowable."

Table-Talk was surprisingly well received. The reviewer in the May *London Magazine* was naturally highly complimentary. "This work," he declared,

> contains some of the most valuable of those treasures which its author has produced from his vast stores of feeling and of thought. Admirable as his critical powers are, he is, perhaps, most felicitous when he discusses things rather than books—when he analyzes social manners, or fathoms the depths of the heart,—or gives passionate sketches of the history of his own past being. We are acquainted with no other living writer, who can depict the intricacies of human character with so firm and masterly a hand—who can detect with so fine an intuition the essences of opinion and prejudice —or follow with so unerring a skill the subtlest windings of the deepest affections.

And he pronounced the book "the most substantial of any that he has written." More surprisingly, the august *Gentleman's Magazine* praised his "natural and unaffected style" in its November issue, and added:

> The good-humoured remarks interspersed throughout appear to be gleaned chiefly from actual observation of men and manners, and considerable intercourse with society. The peculiar characteristics of different individuals are admirably pourtrayed. The Essay "on People with one Idea" is an excellent pourtraiture of the eccentricities of human nature. The "Character of Cobbett" is humourously drawn. In short, many original ideas are introduced, which may afford ample compensation for the time devoted to the perusal of this Volume.

Lamb too reviewed the book, hailing Hazlitt as "one of the ablest prose-writers of the age," but regretting his treatment of his friends in print. But for some reason the review was never published.[23]

Naturally the *Quarterly Review* did not join the chorus of praise. John Matthews wrote airily in the October issue: "Mr. Hazlitt . . . having already undergone the wholesome discipline of our castigation, without any apparent benefit, a repetition of it would be useless, as far as regards himself: for the sake of our younger class of readers, however, it may not be entirely fruitless to take some brief notice of these crude, though laboured lucubrations." He then branded the essayist a "SLANG-WHANGER . . . *'One who makes use of political or other gabble, vulgarly called slang, that serves to amuse the rabble.'*" And he triumphantly quoted Hazlitt's own words in "The Indian

23. George L. Barnett ("An Unpublished Review by Charles Lamb," *MLQ* 17 [1956]: 352–56) suggests that the review may have been written as a substitute for the one which Hunt had withdrawn from the *Examiner* and that it in turn was withheld because Hunt feared lest the remarks about Hazlitt's treatment of his friends might reawaken his wrath. The manuscript of the review, a portion of which is printed in *Lamb Letters*, II, 300–1, is preserved in the Berg Collection of the New York Public Library.

Jugglers": "What abortions are these Essays! What errors, what ill-pieced transitions, what crooked reasons, what lame conclusions! How little is made out, and that little how ill! Yet they are the best I can do."

Leigh Hunt was outraged when he read the book. On Friday, April 20, he wrote to Hazlitt:

> I think, Mr. Hazlitt, you might have found a better time, and place too, for assaulting me and my friends in this bitter manner. A criticism on "Table Talk" was to appear in next Sunday's *Examiner*, but I have thought it best, upon the whole, not to let it appear, for I must have added a quarrelsome note to it; and the sight of acquaintances and brother-reformers cutting and carbonadoing one another in public is, I conceive, no advancement to the cause of liberal opinion, however you may think they injure it in other respects. In God's name, why could you not tell Mr. Shelley in a pleasant manner of what you dislike in him? If it is not mere spleen, you make a gross mistake in thinking that he is not open to advice, or so wilfully in love with himself and his opinions. His spirit is worthy of his great talents. Besides, do you think that nobody has thought or suffered, or come to conclusions through thought or suffering but yourself? You are fond of talking against vanity: but do you think that people will see no vanity in that very fondness—in your being so intolerant with everybody's ideas of improvement but your own, and in resenting so fiercely the possession of a trifling quality or so which you do not happen to number among your own? I have been flattered by your praises: I have been (I do not care what you make of the acknowledgment) instructed, and I thought bettered, by your objections; but it is one thing to be dealt candidly with or rallied, and another to have the whole alleged nature of one's self and a dear friend torn out and thrown in one's face, as if we had not a common humanity with yourself.

In a postscript he added:

> Since writing this letter, which I brought to town with me to send you, I have heard that you have expressed regret at the attack upon myself. If so, I can only say that I am additionally sorry at being obliged to send it; but I should have written to you, had you attacked my friends only in that manner.[24]

Hazlitt was shaken. He had merely written the truth as he saw it. He spent Saturday, the twenty-first, playing fives, probably to relieve his tension. Then in the evening he replied to Hunt in a pathetically self-revealing letter. "My dear Hunt," he began,

> I have no quarrel with you, nor can I have. You are one of those people that I like, do what they will; there are others that I do not like, do what they may. I have always spoken well of you to friend or foe, viz. I have said you were one of the

24. *Memoirs*, 1:305–7. Hunt's first draft of the letter has been reprinted by George L. Barnett in "Leigh Hunt Revises a Letter," *Huntington Library Quarterly* 20 (1956–57), 284–91.

pleasantest and cleverest persons I ever knew; but that you teazed any one you had
to deal with out of their lives. I am fond of a theory, as you know: but I will give
up even that to a friend, if he shews that he has any regard to my personal feelings.
You provoke me to think hard things of you, and then you wonder that I hitch them
into an Essay, as if that made any difference. I pique myself on doing what I can for
others; but I cannot say that I have found any suitable returns for this, and hence
perhaps my outrageousness of stomach! For instance, I praised you in the *Edinburgh
Review*, and when in a case of life and death I tried to lecture, you refused to go
near the place, and gave this as a reason, saying it would seem a collusion, if you said
any thing in my favour after what I had said of you. 2. I got Reynolds to write in
the *Edinburgh Review*, at a time when I had a great reluctance to ask any favour of
Jeffrey, and from that time I never set eyes on him for a year and a half after. 3. I
wrote a book in defence of Godwin some years ago, one half of which he has since
stolen without acknowledgment, without even mentioning my name, and yet he
comes to me to review the very work and I write to Jeffrey to ask his consent, thinking myself, which you do not, the most magnanimous person in the world in the
defence of a cause. 4. I have taken all opportunities of praising Lamb, and I never
got a good word from him in return, big or little, till the other day. He seemed struck
all of a heap, if I ever hinted at the possibility of his giving me a lift at any time. 5.
It was but the other day that two friends did all they could to intercept an article
about me from appearing in the said *E.R.*, saying "it would be too late," "that the
Editor had been sounded at a distance, and was averse," with twenty other excuses,
and at last I was obliged to send it myself, graciously, and by main force, as it were,
when it appeared just in time to save me from drowning. Coulson had been backwards and forwards between my house and Bentham's for between three or four years,
and when the latter philosophically put an execution in my house, the plea was he
had never heard of my name; and when I theorized on this the other day as bad
policy, and *felo de se* on the part of the Radicals, your nephew and that set said:
"Oh, it was an understood thing—the execution, you know!" My God, it is enough
to drive one mad. I have not a soul to stand by me, and yet I am to give up my only
resource and revenge, a theory—I won't do it, that's flat. Montagu is, I fancy, cut
at my putting him among people with one idea, and yet, when the Blackwoods
(together with your) shirking out of that business put me nearly underground, he
took every opportunity to discourage me, and one evening, when I talked of going
there, I was given to understand that there was "a party expected." Yet after this I
am not to look at him a little *in abstracto*. This is what has soured me, and made me
sick of friendship and acquaintanceship. When did I speak ill of your brother John?
He never played me any tricks. I was in a cursed ill humour with you for two or
three things when I wrote the article you find fault with (I grant not without reason).
If I complained to you, you would only have laughed; you would have played me
the very same tricks the very next time; you would not have cared one farthing about
annoying me; and yet you complain that I draw a logical conclusion from all this,
and publish it to the world without your name. As to Shelley, I do not hold myself
accountable to him. You say I want *imagination*. If you mean invention or fancy,

I say so too ; but if you mean a disposition to sympathize with the claims or merits of others, I deny it. I have been too much disposed to waive my own pretensions in deference to those of others. I am tired with playing at rackets all day, and you will be tired with this epistle. It has little to do with you ; for I see no use in raising up a parcel of small, old grievances. But I think the general ground of defence is good.

W.H.

In a postscript he suggested that Hunt write a character of him for the next issue of the *London Magazine*. And he concluded earnestly: "I want to know why everybody has such a dislike to me." [25]

It was a revealing letter: Hazlitt lamented that he had not a soul to stand by him, that he was sick of friendship and acquaintanceship; he talked, significantly, of death, of drowning, of being placed under ground; he wanted to know why everyone disliked him. He could not understand why others resented his criticism, yet a mere scratch disclosed the festering sense of rejection beneath his own skin.

Hunt did not choose to anatomize Hazlitt's character for the edification of readers of the *London Magazine;* instead, he replied on the following Monday:

Dear Hazlitt,—If you do not want to quarrel with me, I certainly do not want to quarrel with you. I have always said, to my own mind and to those few to whom I am in the habit of speaking on such things, that Hazlitt might play me more tricks than any man ; and I conceive you have played me some. If I have teased you, as you say, I have never revenged myself by trampling upon you in public ; and I do not understand you when you say there is no difference between having an ill opinion of one in private and trying to make everybody else partake it. But I am not aware how I can have teased you to the extent you seem to intimate. How can anybody say that I talked about the collusion you speak of? It is impossible. I both spoke of your lectures in the *Examiner,* and came to hear them ; not indeed so often as I could wish, but Mrs. Hunt knows how I used to fret myself every evening at not being able to go. . . . I have often said, I have a sort of irrepressible love for Hazlitt, on account of his sympathy for mankind, his unmercenary disinterestedness, and his suffering ; and I should have a still greater and more personal affection for him if he would let one ; but I declare to God I never seem to know whether he is pleased or displeased, cordial or uncordial—indeed his manners are never cordial—and he has a way with him, when first introduced to you, and ever afterwards, as if he said, "I have no faith in anything, especially your advances: don't you flatter yourself you have any road to my credulity: we have nothing in common between us." Then you escape into a corner, and your conversation is apt to be sarcastic and incredulous about all the world as your manner. Now, egregious fop as you have made me out in your book, with my jealousy of anything bigger than a leaf, and other marvels—who is to be fop enough to suppose that any efforts of his can make you more comfortable? Or how can you so repel one, and then expect, not that we should make no efforts (for those we owe you on other accounts), but that it could possibly enter our heads you took our omission so much to heart? The tears came into the eyes of this heartless coxcomb when he read the passages in your letter where you speak of not having a soul to stand by you.

He commented then on Hazlitt's complaints against his other friends, concluding in his kindly way:

But I will leave these and other matters to talk over when I see you, when I will open myself more to you than I have done, seeing that it may not be indifferent to you for me to do so. At any rate, as I mean this in kindness, oblige me in one matter, and one only, and take some early opportunity of doing justice to the talents and *generous qualities* of Shelley, whatever you may think of his mistakes in using them. The attack on me is a trifle compared with it, nor should I allude to it again but to say, and to say most honestly, that you might make five more if you would only relieve the more respectable part of my chagrin and impatience in that matter. You must imagine what I feel at bottom with regard to yourself, when I tell you that there is but one other person from whom I could have at all borne this attack on Shelley; but in one respect that only makes it the less bearable.[26]

Doubtless Hunt was only one of many who had failed to perceive that Hazlitt's brusqueness was only skin-deep.

In the following month, May, 1821, the *London Magazine* contained the four articles which Hazlitt had written to help fill the gap made by John Scott's death. One, "On Antiquity," the tenth Table Talk essay, was a series of loosely related speculations on the passage of time (12:252–62). The other three were critical articles, each of which he used to state one of his favorite principles. In "Mr. Crabbe," the fifth essay of the "Living Authors" series which Scott had been writing, Hazlitt described Crabbe as "a most potent copyist of actual nature, though not otherwise a great poet"

26. *Memoirs*, 1:308–12. Hunt presently reported the incident to Byron in Italy, commenting: "I was sorry for it on every account, because I really believe Hazlitt to be a disinterested and suffering man, who feels public calamities as other men do private ones; and this is perpetually redeeming him in my eyes. I told him so, as well as some other things, but you shall see our correspondence by and by" (ibid., p. 313). Cf. Hunt's letters to Shelley on the subject (*Correspondence of Leigh Hunt*, 1:166) and Shelley's own comment in a letter of January 25, 1822: "As to Reviews, don't give Gifford or his associate Hazlitt a stripe the more for my sake. The man must be enviably happy whom Reviews can make miserable. I have neither curiosity interest, pain nor pleasure in [or] for any thing, good or evil they can say of me" (*Letters of Percy Bysshe Shelley*, ed. Frederick L. Jones, 2 vols. [Oxford: Clarendon Press, 1964], 2:382–83).

(19:60). "Poetry," he wrote, "should be the handmaid of the imagination, and the foster-nurse of pleasure and beauty: Mr. Crabbe's Muse is a determined enemy to the imagination, and a spy on nature" (19:59). Even less enthusiastic was the review of Byron's new tragedy, *Marino Faliero, Doge of Venice*. "We know not much about the plot," Hazlitt complained,

> about the characters, about the motives of the persons introduced, but we know a good deal about their sentiments and opinions on matters in general, and hear some very fine descriptions from their mouths; which would, however, have become the mouth of any other individual in the play equally well, and the mouth of the noble poet better than that of any of his characters. We have, indeed, a previous theory, that Lord Byron's genius is not dramatic, and the present performance is not one that makes it absolutely necessary for us to give up that theory. (19:44)

In the third article, a critique of Haydon's latest painting, *Christ's Agony in the Garden* (an engraving of which was included in the magazine), Hazlitt found fault with both the size and the execution of the piece. Yet he advised Haydon to follow his natural bent. "A man may avoid great faults or absurdities by the suggestion of friends," he cautioned the painter: "he can only attain positive excellence, or overcome great difficulties, by the unbiassed force of his own mind" (18:144).[27]

After the May issue of the *London*, however, Taylor and Hessey took over the management of the magazine, and Hazlitt's contributions fell off sharply. Only four articles by him appeared before the close of the year, three of them Table Talk essays. The new publishers opened offices on Waterloo Place and themselves acted as editors, with Thomas Hood serving as their assistant.[28] They entertained their contributors at monthly dinners and literary discussions—general discussions rather than editorial planning sessions. But

27. Haydon inserted a copy of the article in his diary under the date of January 15, 1812 (see *Haydon Diary*, 2:356).

28. Taylor and Hessey may have offered Hazlitt the editorship of the magazine when they took it over. On May 9 Robert Baldwin wrote to him: "The arrangement with Messrs. Taylor and Hessey is completed, and Mr. Taylor will take an early opportunity of calling on you, unless you should think proper to look in upon them in a day or two. I sincerely hope that such an arrangement will be made as shall be quite satisfactory to yourself; I am sure it is to their interest that it should be so" (*Memoirs*, 2:8). Then on the twenty-ninth Hessey wrote to Hazlitt: "Mr. Taylor was all this morning on the point of setting out to call upon you, as he wanted much to have some conversation with you, but a constant succession of callers-in prevented him. Will you do us the favour to take your breakfast with us in the morning, between nine and ten, when we shall have a chance of being uninterrupted for an hour or two" (ibid., p. 9). However, the publishers may have met with Hazlitt only to discuss terms for his regular contributions to the *London*. As late as August 1 some people believed him to be the editor of the magazine. On that day Washington Irving wrote to John Howard Payne: "I called on Hazlitt a day or two after my arrival. He is not the Editor of the Magazine, but writes for it at the

Hazlitt seems seldom to have attended the affairs. Ever since the publication of his *Lectures on the English Poets* his relations with Taylor and Hessey had been strained.[29]

Hazlitt seems, in fact, to have seen little of any of his literary friends during the year 1821. Crabb Robinson reported seeing him at the Lambs' on four occasions (February 21, May 16, July 20, and December 19) and remarked that they were now speaking to each other again, though far from cordially.[30] Surviving letters reveal that on May 29 James Hessey invited him to have breakfast with Taylor and him and that on July 16 Thomas Pittman invited him to visit the fives court at Canterbury.[31] But there is no proof that he accepted either invitation. And it is more than likely that he was spending more and more of his time at 9 Southampton Buildings.

The euphoria of the early months of the year was wearing thin. He was making no progress in his courtship of Sally: though she continued to sit on his knee and fondle him, she refused to give any sort of encouraging answer to his proposals. Barry Cornwall remarked that, when he appeared at the *London Magazine* dinners, "he was a rather silent guest, rising into emphatic talk only when some political discussion (very rare) stimulated him." [32] And he was writing very little; in addition to the four articles published in the *London Magazine*, he published only two others during the last seven months of the year. And one of those exposed him to another painful experience.

---

rate of 16 guineas a sheet. (I.E. a guinea a page) The Mag: is at present owned by Taylor & Hessey. He told me he would speak to them on the subject, and thought it probable they would be induced to take writings from you, on experiment, at the same rate. Though of course they would not want above half a sheet, say 8 pages, from one author per month, as they like to have a variety of styles and authors. He told me he would either call on me or write to me after he had seen Taylor & Hessey. I have heard nothing from him as yet." On August 23 Irving wrote to Payne: "Hazlitt has gone out of town without letting me hear from him on the subject of the Magazine; though he had frequently promised to do so" ("Correspondence of Washington Irving and John Howard Payne (1821–1828)," ed. Thatcher T. Payne Luquer, in *Scribner's Magazine* 48 [1910]:466–67).

29. Hood could not recall seeing Hazlitt at any of the dinners; Barry Cornwall thought he attended only once or twice; John Clare recalled one dinner when Coleridge dominaated the conversation "to the exclusion of every one else, notably of William Hazlitt, who sat close to him." And Hazlitt and De Quincey are said to have met at one of the dinners after De Quincey began writing for the *London Magazine* in September, 1821 (see *Thomas Hood and Charles Lamb*, ed. Walter Jerrold [London: E. Benn, Ltd., 1930], p. 122; *Cornwall Recollections*, p. 110; Frederick Martin, *Life of John Clare* [London and Cambridge, 1865], p. 181; and Howe, p. 298). One might well question whether Coleridge and Hazlitt would have remained long in each other's company.

30. Robinson, 1:261, 264, 265, 278.

31. See above, p. 291, and *Memoirs*, 2:3–5.

32. *Cornwall Recollections*, p. 110.

His one contribution to the *London* in June was "Pope, Lord Byron, and Mr. Bowles," a lengthy review of the third edition of Byron's *Letter . . . on the Rev. W. L. Bowles's Strictures on the Life and Writings of Pope* on the merits of Pope's poetry.[33] In it he called down a plague on the houses of both Byron and Bowles; he damned Byron for his arrogance, Bowles for his servility; Byron for overstressing the morality of Pope's writing, Bowles for discussing the poet's personal morality. But the core of the article concerned the relative importance of nature and art in poetry. "A man can make any thing," he wrote,

> but he cannot make a sentiment! It is a thing of inveterate prejudice, of old association, of common feelings, and so is poetry, as far as it is serious. A "pack of cards," a silver bodkin, a paste buckle, "may be imbued" with as much mock poetry as you please, by lending false associations to it; but real poetry, or poetry of the highest order, can only be produced by unravelling the real web of associations, which have been wound round any subject by nature, and the unavoidable conditions of humanity. (19:75)

He illustrated his point nicely by means of the little candle that sheds its beams so far in act 5 of *The Merchant of Venice:*

> It is not the splendour of the candle itself, but the contrast to the gloom without,—the comfort, the relief it holds out from afar to the benighted traveller,—the conflict between nature and the first and cheapest resources of art, that constitutes the romantic and imaginary, that is, the poetical interest, in that familiar but striking image. There is more art in the lamp or chandelier; but for that very reason, there is less poetry. (19:76)

Finally, to clinch the point for Byron, he spelled it out in a series of four axioms, each accompanied by appropriate illustrations.

The argument adds up to a cogent defense of the poetic theory which Hazlitt espoused—and which, he believed, Byron practiced even while he renounced it. Leigh Hunt was delighted with the article; in the *Examiner* for July 15 he declared that it had "completely settled" the Bowles–Byron controversy.[34] But Byron was in no mood to accept suggestions from William Hazlitt. On January 26 of this year he had compared K. W. F. Schlegel in his diary with Hazlitt, "who *talks pimples*—a red and white corruption

---

33. The article was composed in part of excerpts from two earlier papers, "The Opera" in the *Yellow Dwarf* of May, 1818, and "On the Question Whether Pope Was a Poet" in the *Edinburgh Magazine* of February, 1818 (19:342).

34. *Leigh Hunt's Literary Criticism,* p. 152.

rising up (in little imitation of mountains upon maps), but containing nothing, and discharging nothing, except their own humours." [35]

Hazlitt's only published essay in July was "Capital Punishments," his first contribution to the *Edinburgh Review* in nearly a year. It was a long study of the *Report of the Select Committee on Criminal Laws* of the House of Commons, with liberal quotations from the report itself and from legal authorities to prove that contemporary laws were so stringent that they were seldom enforced—and crime too often went unpunished. Hazlitt may have written it at the request of his friend Basil Montagu, an ardent proponent of penal reform who had testified before the committee.[36] But it was no hack job; Hazlitt meant every word when he urged the public not to reject the proposals of the committee as mere theory, and he supplemented the review with a forceful appeal that England adopt a "standard of *natural justice*, judged of by the sentiments of the community, and of every man in it" (19:225).

In August he resumed his Table Talk essays in the *London Magazine* with No. 11 of the series, "On a Landscape of Nicolas Poussin." He was effusive in his praise of Poussin's work, especially the painting of Orion then on exhibition at the British Institution; he hailed Poussin as "the most poetical" of all painters, comparing him to Milton because both succeeded in improving upon nature. He seized the opportunity to restate a cherished theory:

> To give us nature, such as we see it, is well and deserving of praise; to give us nature, such as we have never seen, but have often wished to see it, is better, and deserving of higher praise. He who can show the world in its first naked glory, with the hues of fancy spread over it, or in its high and palmy state, with the gravity of history stamped on the proud moments of vanished empire,—who by his "so potent art," can recal time past, transport us to distant places, and join the regions of imagination (a new conquest) to those of reality,—who teaches us not only what nature is, but what she has been, and is capable of being,—he who does this, and does it with simplicity,

35. *Letters and Journals of Lord Byron*, ed. Rowland E. Prothero, 6 vols. (London: John Murray; New York: Charles Scribner's Sons, 1922), 5:191. At about the same time he sent John Murray for publication a long note replying to Hazlitt's claim in *Lectures on the English Poets* that he had altered his original opinion of Napoleon. It did not appear, however, until after Byron's death (see *Poetical Works of Lord Byron*, ed. E. H. Coleridge, 7 vols. [London: John Murray; New York: Charles Scribner's Sons, 1905], 6:12 n., and *Byron's Don Juan, Variorum Edition*, ed. Willis W. Pratt, 4 vols. [Austin: University of Texas Press, 1957], 4:17–18).

36. See above, p. 131, re Hazlitt's earlier paper on the same subject for Montagu's Society for the Diffusion of Knowledge upon the Punishment of Death.

with truth, and grandeur, is lord of nature and her powers; and his mind is universal, and his art the master-art! (8:169)

This seems like high praise to apply to the work of Nicolas Poussin. Yet Hazlitt thought so well of the essay that he singled it out as the one "Table-Talk" from the *London Magazine* to be included in the second volume of essays which he presently published. Moreover, he placed it first in the volume—and rightly, because it was a noble essay—perhaps nobler than the painting which it celebrated.

In September and October Hazlitt published no articles in any of the periodicals. He had been at Winterslow in July and August, feeling "indifferent," living sparely,[37] and perhaps writing essays for his forthcoming second volume of Table Talk. It was probably there, too, that he wrote an article, intended for the *London Magazine*, which precipitated still another personal crisis.

The subject of the paper was the infamous Guy Fawkes (or Faux, as Hazlitt spelled the name), the one character in history not only scorned but actively derided once a year by loyal Englishmen. Hazlitt, the champion of lost causes, chose, however, to defend him: Fawkes was a "good hater," a man after Hazlitt's heart; he was a fanatic, to be sure, but not a coward.

As early as Friday, July 22, Taylor and Hessey had seen the manuscript and had notified him that they could not print it as it stood. He wrote them that day from Winterslow: "Could you return me the Guy Faux; & I will either alter it or try another experiment on some less obnoxious subject?"[38] The matter was still pending in early October after Hazlitt had returned to London. By this time he was furious. Hessey called at his lodgings one morning, found him at breakfast, and tried to mollify him. On October 5 he wrote to his partner:

> On my asking him if we were to expect a No. of the Living Authors he observed that he felt no Interest in them or their works and that he considered such Papers as mere fat work which cost him no effort and brought him no fame. He then spoke of the Table Talks as being the papers on which he valued himself and which he wished to continue but said that he felt so annoyed and cramped in his mind by the fear of alteration or objection or perhaps rejection altogether that he could not write freely as he was accustomed to do.—He spoke of Guy Faux and its rejection, and very

37. Hazlitt complained of his "indifferent" health in his July 22 letter to Taylor and Hessey (ALS, Yale University Library). W. C. Hazlitt claimed to have seen his August board bill, in which rice and tea were often listed. He was paying eighteenpence for breakfast and supper and from eighteenpence to three shillings for dinner (*The Hazlitts*, p. 147).
38. ALS, Yale University Library.

much pressed its admission saying at length that he must candidly confess that if Guy Faux were not inserted he should never write a line with pleasure for the Magazine. I told him we had decided objections to certain parts, but for those parts (as is always the case) he feels the greatest Affection and he proposed again the qualifying of them by a Note. He said he wished much to see the Magazine write down all its rivals by superiority of talent, and expressed a desire to assist in the good work by all the means in his Power. All he wished was to have his Liberty in the Table Talks and in everything else he was ready to do whatever we wished. But Guy Faux seemed to be the sine quâ non. I told him I did not think we could with any regard to our own safety insert the Article, but I brought it away with me to look it over again and see what alterations might make it passable, for I did not wish to cut with him and in fact I scarcely knew what were the passages actually objected to.—It does however appear to me that we could not insert it as it is, and therefore I must either tell him so and say that when you return you and he can decide as to any alterations if you think that when altered it may be admitted—or else I will say we cannot receive it at all, and leave him and Mr. Baldwin to settle the matter themselves.[39]

If there were any further negotiations, they broke down. But Hazlitt was determined to see the article in print, and he submitted it to Leigh Hunt for publication in the *Examiner*. Hunt, who was less cautious than the editors of the *London*, accepted it, and it appeared in three installments in the issues of the *Examiner* for November 11, 18, and 25. By this time Hazlitt had developed a real sense of identification with Fawkes, who had been willing to sacrifice everything for a principle which he revered. "I like the spirit of martyrdom, I confess," he wrote: "I envy an age that had virtue enough in it to produce the mischievous fanaticism of a Guy Faux. . . . To have an object always in view dearer to one than one's self, to cling to a principle in contempt of danger, of interest, of the opinion of the world,—this is the true *ideal*, the high and heroic state of man" (20:99). Considerably later in the article, after he had analyzed both fanaticism and courage at length, he concluded: "Mental courage is the only courage I pretend to. I dare venture an opinion where few else would, particularly if I think it right. I have retracted few of my positions. Whether this arises from obstinacy or strength, or indifference to the opinions of others, I know not. In little else I have the spirit of martyrdom: but I would give up any thing sooner than an abstract proposition" (20:122).

Whether he wrote those words before or after Taylor and Hessey rejected his article, he must have applied them to that incident. It rankled in his mind and, as he had prophesied, robbed him of the pleasure he had found in

39. Blunden, pp. 137–38.

writing Table Talk essays for the *London*. In the two essays which appeared in the magazine in November and December he was in a defensive, even contentious, mood. They sound as if he had written them expressly to enlighten Taylor and Hessey on a couple of salient points.[40]

The first of the essays, "Table-Talk, No. 12: On Consistency of Opinion," acclaimed the man who sticks resolutely to the principles which he has adopted in early youth. He himself, he was convinced, had not altered any of his principles since he was sixteen years old. Although Coleridge had told him that "this pertinacity was owing to a want of sympathy with others," he disagreed flatly; he believed, rather, that the man of fixed ideas was one who had "carefully examined [his belief] in all its bearings" (17:23) before adopting it. And by way of contrast he rehearsed once again the inconsistencies of Wordsworth, Coleridge, and Southey.[41]

The second of the two essays, "No. 13: On the Spirit of Partisanship," in the December issue of the *London*, was, in effect, a sequel to the November essay. Hazlitt here declared himself an admirer of intensity as well as consistency of opinion. "I have in my time known few thorough partisans," he began;

> at least on my own side of the question. I conceive, however, that the honestest and strongest-minded men have been so. In general, interest, fear, vanity, the love of contradiction, even a scrupulous regard to truth and justice, come to divert them from

40. Hazlitt may have decided later that the two essays were marred by ill temper, for he excluded them not only from his second volume of *Table-Talk* but also from the later *Plain Speaker* which contained several of the Table Talk essays from the *London Magazine* not included in the earlier volumes. The two essays were first reprinted by his son after his death—"On Consistency of Opinion" (with some passages omitted) in *Winterslow* (1850) and "On the Spirit of Partisanship" in *Sketches and Essays* (1839).

41. One of the anecdotes which Hazlitt told concerned a gentleman who had been reprimanded by "a romantic acquaintance" for burning two candles "while many a poor cottager had not even a rush-light to see to do their evening's work by" (17:26). Later, however, when he had a lord as guest at dinner, he insisted on having six candles at the table. Although Wordsworth was not named, he was the "romantic acquaintance"; the gentleman was Charles Lloyd, from whom Hazlitt had heard the story. Wordsworth wisely refrained from making any public comment on the story, but his wife wrote in an undated letter to Thomas Monkhouse: "What a wretch that Hazlitt is, but if C. Lloyd could be accounted sane, I should say he was the worse of the two" (*Letters of Mary Wordsworth*, p. 83). And on February 20, 1822, after Lloyd had sent him a memorial of his deceased mother, Wordsworth replied in a note deploring his manners, though not denying the truth of the story. Lloyd replied that Wordsworth had said much worse of him on occasion, adding, in extenuation of his own action, that he had been unaware of Hazlitt's hostility toward Wordsworth when he repeated the story in his presence (P. M. Zall, "Hazlitt's 'Romantic Acquaintance': Wordsworth and Charles Lloyd" *MLN* 71 [1956]:11–14).

the popular cause. It is a character that requires very opposite and almost incompatible qualities—reason and prejudice, a passionate attachment founded on an abstract idea. He who can take up a speculative question, and pursue it with the same zeal and unshaken constancy that he does his immediate interests or private animosities, he who is as faithful to his principles as he is to himself, is the true partisan. (17:34)

He inveighed then against those who are too good-natured or prudent or temperate to be "good haters." He wrote not in his usual Table Talk strain, enlivening his points with anecdotes; the bitterness of his old political essays revived, and he seemed more to scold his readers than to entertain them. The fun had suddenly been drained out of the essays.

His contentious mood undoubtedly was not due solely to his quarrel with Taylor and Hessey; he was distressed also by an unexpected turn in his courtship of Sally. Sometime during October a young man named Tomkins had moved into quarters at 9 Southampton Buildings. The very night that he arrived, Sally's attitude toward Hazlitt changed. She insisted that he must not court her on the stairs lest Tomkins "take [her] for a light character." Soon she was running "blushing & breathless to meet him." [42] She had found a new prey. And Hazlitt, of course, was in torture.

In November he took refuge again at Winterslow, determined to write. Jeffrey had asked him to review a new volume by Lady Morgan, and he was hard at it. "Would you send me word," he wrote Jeffrey on November 26, "when will be the latest time for forwarding the article if I can succeed in it?" He had sent Jeffrey "some proof sheets of the new volume of Table-talk," hoping for "a notice in the next number" of the *Edinburgh.* And he explained that he understood Henry Colburn would publish the book, since John Warren, who had brought out the first volume, had recently failed.[43]

On December 1 Hazlitt wrote to Thomas Talfourd, who was acting as his intermediary with Colburn. Once again he was weighed down by debts —and full of schemes for extricating himself from his predicament. He was, he declared, "driven almost into a corner. What with uneasiness of mind & this failure of Warren's, I hardly know what to do. Could you ask Colburn (with whom I have already communicated) whether he will give me £200 for 20 Essays, advancing One Hundred, that is, the amount for the first Ten essays, which I will engage to complete & deliver in Two months from the present time, & which he may make use of either for the magazine or in a Volume with what title he pleases—only in the former case I wish to

42. ALS, Lockwood Memorial Library, State University of New York at Buffalo.
43. Baker, p. 409 n. The volume he was reviewing was probably Lady Morgan's *Italy* (1821).

reserve right of copy." He added later in a postscript: "A thought has just struck me, that if Colburn chose to buy Warren's volume, he might use the Essays for the magazine [i.e., the *New Monthly Magazine*, of which Colburn was publisher] in the first instance (they are all *virgins* but one) & publish the book afterwards, & in the meantime I will write a new series; that is, I will sell him 40 Essays or *Table-Talk* for £400, to do what he pleases with, he advancing me £100 down, & I giving him up half the copy *instanter*. The subjects are not at all blown upon."

He told Talfourd that he was "busy about Lady Morgan, & will do it *con amore* if I can but get out of this present hobble." He had a debt of fifty pounds coming due as soon as he returned to town, "which the Review of Lady M. alone would do, but I am too uncomfortable, I fear, to get through it properly, circumstanced as I am." And finally he came out with it: "The truth is, I seem to have been hurt in my mind lately, [and contin]ual effort to no purpose is too [much for] any patience, & mine is nearly exhausted. My dear Talfourd, if you have a girl that loves you, & that you have a regard for, lose no time in marrying, & think yourself happy, whatever else may happen." Incidentally he asked his friend to "propose to [Colburn] (if you please) the *Picturesque Tour in Italy* [with] an account of the Vatican at the same price [£200], with one Hundred for my expences." [44] If all else failed, he might decide to escape entirely from London and all his troubles. He might even hope to entice Sally into going with him.

44. *The Hazlitts*, pp. 475–76.

CHAPTER XII

REJECTED!
(1822)

Sometime about the turn of the year 1822 Hazlitt's prospects took a turn for the better. After considerable urging his wife consented to sue for divorce, and he abandoned all thoughts of his "picturesque tour" of Italy. It was more important for him to gain his freedom as soon as possible so that he could offer Sally an honorable marriage. Nothing came of his proposed review of Lady Morgan's book, but his most pressing financial problems were resolved, once he was assured that Colburn would make the Table Talk series a regular feature of his *New Monthly Magazine* and would publish the volume which Hazlitt had been preparing for John Warren.

The January issue of the *New Monthly* contained the first of the series, "On Going a Journey," one of the most joyous essays Hazlitt ever wrote. He did not try to analyze—or penetrate to any truths more profound than the relative merits of walking alone or with others, in town or in country, at home or abroad. "No one likes puns, alliterations, antitheses, argument, and analysis better than I do," he wrote; "but I sometimes had rather be without them" (8:182). And he gave himself over almost entirely to an infectious expression of the delight he had found in cross-country walks: "I laugh, I run, I leap, I sing for joy"—spicing his points with genial recollections of Coleridge, Wordsworth, and Lamb, of the inns where he had put up during his tramps, the meals he had eaten, and the books he had read. There is not a trace of the turmoil which had soured his recent essays.

He did not break completely with Taylor and Hessey when he began writing for the *New Monthly*. For the January issue of the *London Magazine* he reviewed *The Pirate*, the new novel "by the author of *Waverley*."

Although he found fault with Scott's plotting, his attempts at moralizing, his characterization, his style, and even his grammar, he warmly praised his overall achievement as a novelist. "This is not the best," he wrote, "nor is it the worst (the worst is good enough for us) of the Scotch Novels" (19:85).

For the February issue of the *London* he wrote the first installment of an essay "On the Elgin Marbles," an expanded version of the article which he had published in the *Examiner* for June 30, 1816.[1] Once again he opposed Reynolds's theory of idealization in art, this time presenting detailed studies of the Elgin marbles to prove that the Greek sculptors of the classical age relied on nature, rather than "ideal forms," for their models (18:145–50).[2]

Of more lasting interest, however, were the two articles which he wrote for the February *New Monthly*. One of these was "The Fight," his unforgettable account of his first prize fight—the bloody match between Bill Neate and Tom Hickman, the arrogant Gas-man, fought at Hungerford, Berkshire, on December 11, 1821. Hazlitt relished every minute of his new experience, and he recounted with gusto the coach trip down and back, the sprightly conversation, the night at the inn—but, most of all, the fight itself. "This is the high and heroic state of man!" he exclaimed as he described the two fighters bouncing back into the fray after each half-minute rest between rounds. And he responded fully to the awful climax when the underdog Neate delivered the knockout blow and Hickman's "face was like a human skull, a death's head, spouting blood. The eyes were filled with blood, the nose streamed with blood, the mouth gaped blood" (17:83).

Hazlitt seems to lose himself completely in the excitement of the occasion. In the essay as published there was only one hint that his mind was still weighed down: "I will not libel any life," he wrote, "by comparing it to mine, which is (at the date of these presents) bitter as coloquintida and the dregs of aconitum!" (17:76). But the original manuscript of the essay contained at least three passages, later deleted, which show his true feelings. For example:

1. On January 23 Hessey sent Hazlitt a check for twenty pounds, acknowledged receipt of "the paper on the Marbles" (which he thought would "pretty nearly balance" their account), and wished him "a pleasing journey" (Howe, p. 308). Incidentally, Hazlitt was husbanding his words, if not his funds, these days: although he omitted from the new article a passage from Pliny's *Natural History* which had appeared in the introduction to the original article in the *Examiner*, it did not go to waste; he used it as the conclusion of the essay "On Great and Little Things" in the February *New Monthly*.

2. In "Two Critics of the Elgin Marbles" (*Journal of Aesthetics and Art Criticism* 14 [1955–56]:462–74), Frederic Will points out that Hazlitt's stress on naturalness was a significant departure from conventional criticism of the time, which was based on observation of "idealized" Hellenistic sculpture.

And now, reader, let me tell thee a secret: thou hast perhaps hitherto thought me gay, vain, insolent, half-mad—no tongue can tell the heaviness of heart I felt at that moment. No foot-steps ever fell more slow, more reluctantly than mine, for every step, that carried me nearer to Brentford, bore me farther from her with whom my soul & every thought lingered. Dark was the night without me, dark & silent: but a greater dark [page missing] should I return to her, after what had happened? Where go to live & die far from her? Oh! thou dumb heart, lonely, sad, shut up in the prison house of this rude form, that hast never found a fellow but for an hour & in very mockery of thy misery, speak, find bleeding words to express thy thoughts, break thy dungeon-gloom, pronouncing the name of thy Clarissa [*Infelice* substituted below the line] or die & wither of pure scorn!...[3]

In another of the deleted passages Hazlitt reveals that his companion "Jack Pigott" (Peter George Patmore), "a sentimentalist" who was carrying a volume of *La Nouvelle Heloise*, proved to be "a man cut out by nature, circumstances, & education for a confidant:—so 'in dreadful secrecy impart I did' some part of the depth of my despair & the height of her perfections, & we are become inseparable from the interest he takes in the subject."[4] Patmore was presently to prove very useful.

When Cyrus Redding, assistant editor of the *New Monthly*, read the manuscript of the essay, he was scandalized—not because of the sentimental digressions but because Hazlitt had presumed to write about a prize fight. "It was a thoroughly blackguard subject," Redding wrote in later years. "It was disgracing our literature in the eyes of other nations—why not a paper on American gouging, Stamford bull-baiting, or similar elegancies. It was a picture of existing manners, it was true, the more the pity, and that it could not sooner be a record of our barbarities." However, the essay was finally accepted. "Colburn had spoken of it to several persons, and Hazlitt's friends were expecting it. I believe, too, that omitting it would have been thought to sanction the belief in the poet's dislike to the writer."[5] Hazlitt

3. Stewart C. Wilcox, *Hazlitt in the Workshop: the Manuscript of "The Fight"* (Baltimore: Johns Hopkins Press, 1943), pp. 17–18. Wilcox reprints the surviving pages of the manuscript of the essay, now preserved in the Pierpont Morgan Library, italicizing the three digressions concerning Sally Walker which were omitted from the published essay. By comparing the number of words in the essay as published with the number probably included in the lost pages of the manuscript, he estimates that Hazlitt must have deleted other passages amounting to approximately five hundred words. In his notes (pp. 56–57) Wilcox points out Hazlitt's later use in *Liber Amoris* of the lines quoted above.

4. Ibid., p. 48.

5. Redding, *Fifty Years' Recollections*, 2:277–78. (For other accounts by Redding of this incident, see Wilcox, *Hazlitt in the Workshop*, pp. 5–7.) By "the poet's dislike to the writer" Redding means the resentment of Thomas Campbell, editor of the *New Monthly*, because Hazlitt had charged, in *Lectures on the English Poets*, that Campbell had borrowed

may have heard other objections from readers of the magazine after his article appeared; at all events he never wrote another essay of the kind, and he never reprinted "The Fight." [6]

His other contribution to the February *New Monthly*, "Table-Talk, No. 2: On Great and Little Things," also brought repercussions.[7] Hazlitt was here writing in his analytical—and paradoxical—vein; he made much of the fact that small annoyances are often more troublesome than larger ones, then moved on to other aspects of his subject, eventually coming to "the misery of unequal matches":

> The woman cannot easily forget, or think that others forget, her origin; and with perhaps superior sense and beauty, keeps painfully in the background. It is worse when she braves this conscious feeling, and displays all the insolence of the upstart and affected fine-lady. But shouldst thou ever, my Infelice, grace my home with thy loved presence, as thou hast cheered my hopes with thy smile, thou wilt conquer all hearts with thy prevailing gentleness, and I will shew the world what Shakespear's women were!—Some gallants set their hearts on princesses; others descend in imagination to women of quality; others are mad after opera-singers. For my part, I am shy even of actresses, and should not think of leaving my card with Madame V——. I am for none of these *bonnes fortunes;* but for a list of humble beauties, servant-maids and shepherd-girls with their red elbows, hard hands, black stockings and mob-caps, I could furnish out a gallery equal to Cowley's, and paint them half as well. (8:235–36)

He even sketched in an emotional biography, still in the first person:

> I always was inclined to raise and magnify the power of Love. I thought that his sweet power should only be exerted to join together the loveliest forms and fondest hearts; that none but those in whom his Godhead shone outwardly, and was inly felt, should ever partake of his triumphs; and I stood and gazed at a distance, as unworthy to mingle in so bright a throng, and did not (even for a moment) wish to tarnish the glory of so fair a vision by being myself admitted into it. I say this was

---

the line "Like angel's visits, few and far between" in "The Pleasures of Hope" from Robert Blair.

6. It was first reprinted by his son in *Literary Remains* (1836) and it apparently continued for some time to be regarded as in dubious taste. When Alexander Ireland included it in his *William Hazlitt, Essayist and Critic: Selections from His Writings* in 1889, he remarked in his prefatory memoir: "I have been advised not to reprint this paper, but Hazlitt must be shown in every phase; an ardent admirer pronounces it his *chef d'oeuvre.*"

7. Hazlitt later told his wife that he had not intended to have the essay printed in the *New Monthly* (see below, p. 344). As Howe suggests (8:363) Hazlitt's words "Mr. Davison might both print and publish this volume" (8:236) seem to bear out the claim, since Thomas Davison was the printer of the first volume of *Table-Talk* but not of the *New Monthly*.

my notion once, but God knows it was one of the errors of my youth. For coming nearer to look, I saw the maimed, the blind, and the halt enter in, the crooked and the dwarf, the ugly, the old and impotent, the man of pleasure and the man of the world, the dapper and the pert, the vain and shallow boaster, the fool and the pedant, the ignorant and brutal, and all that is farthest removed from earth's fairest-born, and the pride of human life. Seeing all these enter the courts of Love, and thinking that I also might venture in under favour of the crowd, but finding myself rejected, I fancied (I might be wrong) that it was not so much because I was below, as above the common standard. I did feel, but I was ashamed to feel, mortified at my repulse, when I saw the meanest of mankind, the very scum and refuse, all creeping things and every obscene creature, enter in before me. I seemed a species by myself. I took a pride even in my disgrace: and concluded I had elsewhere my inheritance! The only thing I ever piqued myself upon was the writing the *Essay on the Principles of Human Action*—a work that no woman ever read, or would comprehend the meaning of. . . . And thus I waste my life in one long sigh; nor ever (till too late) beheld a gentle face turned gently upon mine! . . . But no! not too late, if that face, pure, modest, downcast, tender, with angel sweetness, not only gladdens the prospect of the future, but sheds its radiance on the past, smiling in tears. (8:237)

Hazlitt, or one of the editors, added a footnote: "I beg the reader to consider this passage merely as a specimen of the mock-heroic style, and as having nothing to do with any real facts or feelings" (8:238 n.). Yet knowledgeable readers of the *New Monthly* must have felt reasonably sure that they were listening to an avowal of love—and not for Sarah Hazlitt!

While his essay "The Fight" was still in proofs, he had written to Colburn that he was leaving for Scotland during the following week and would set to work then on the new volume of *Table-Talk*.[8] And by the time the two articles appeared in the February *New Monthly*, Hazlitt was in Scotland fulfilling the forty-day residence required of applicants for a divorce. Sarah was to follow him shortly. He had probably insisted on a Scottish divorce because the law there permitted remarriage after divorce, as English law did not. For middle-class people like themselves even to consider divorce was defying convention, but Sarah had never quailed at unconventional behavior. Besides, she was fond of travel. Mary Shelley claimed that Mary Lamb "in vain endeavoured to make her look on her journey to Scot[la]nd in any other light than a jaunt."[9] And she bore her husband no ill will; according to James Kenney, when the two met one day shortly before Hazlitt left London, he greeted her, "Ah you there—and how do you do?" To which she replied, "Oh very well Wm & how are you?" Then when he

8. *Four Generations*, 1:193–94.
9. *Letters of Mary W. Shelley*, 1:257.

told her that he was "just looking about" for his dinner, she said, "Well mine is just ready a nice boiled leg of pork—if you like Wm to have a slice." And off the two went to dine.[10]

Yet Hazlitt had set out one Sunday before mid-January in considerable distress. He had stopped first at Stamford (presumably to view the earl of Exeter's collection of paintings at Burleigh House) and, being detained longer than he expected, had tried to relieve his distress by writing a series of dialogues recording memorable scenes in his courtship. The first four showed Hazlitt eagerly wooing Sally, accepting her favors gratefully, and anticipating the day when he would be free to propose marriage. When, after six months, she told him of her former love, he was jolted but not disheartened. "No person who is in love," he wrote in 1829 in his *Characteristics*, "can ever be entirely persuaded that the passion is not reciprocal" (20: 239).

But when the new lodger, Tomkins, arrived at the house and Sally began flirting with him, Hazlitt was frantic. In the sixth dialogue of the *Liber Amoris*, "The Quarrel," he recreated the painful scene, burned into his memory, when he confronted her with his suspicions: "Oh! my God! after what I have thought of you and felt towards you, as little less than an angel, to have but a doubt cross my mind for an instant that you were what I dare not name—a common lodging-house decoy, a kissing convenience, that your lips were as common as the stairs—" (9: 106). Why, he asked, had her little sister Betsey cried, "He thought I did not see him!" when she saw them kissing? Was their courtship a common joke in the household? "There is a difference," he assured her, "between love and making me a laughing-stock" (9: 106). And what of the conversation he had overheard down in the kitchen the night before?

He did not repeat the conversation in his dialogue as published, but later, in a letter to P. G. Patmore, he recorded it:

> *Betsey.* "Oh! if those trowsers were to come down, what a sight there would be!" (*A general loud laugh.*)
> *Mother.* "Yes! he's a proper one. Mr. Follett is nothing to him."
> *Cajah (aged 17).* "Then, I suppose he must be seven inches."
> *Mother W.* "He's quite a monster. He nearly tumbled over Mr. Hazlitt one night."
> *Sarah.* (At that once, that still & ever dear name, ah! why do I grow pale, why do I weep & forgive?) said something inaudible, but in correction.
> *Cajah.* (*Laughing*) "Sarah says. . . ."
> *Sarah.* "I say, Mr. Follett wears straps."[11]

10. Ibid.
11. The person under discussion was evidently the lodger Griffiths (see below, p.

In the original manuscript of the dialogues he recorded also an offensive remark of Mrs. Walker's: he had asked her not to pull up Sally's skirts, as he was told she did, and she had retorted: "Oh, there's nothing in that, for Sarah often pulls up mine." [12] Such talk and actions hardly became one whom he had regarded as an angel.

He recalled then her insistence, the first night Tomkins arrived, that Hazlitt must not court her on the stairs lest the new lodger "take [her] for a light character." "Was that all?" he asked. "Were you only afraid of being *taken* for a light character?" (9:109). And again, in a letter to Patmore, he commented bitterly: "I was very well as a stop-gap, but I was to be nothing more. The instant Tomkins came, she flung herself at his head in the most barefaced way, & used to run blushing & breathless to meet him."

Sally refused to be moved: Hazlitt had no monopoly on her affections. "You say your regard is merely friendship," he told her,

> and that you are sorry I have ever felt anything more for you. Yet the first time I ever asked you, you let me kiss you; the first time I ever saw you, as you went out of the room, you turned full round at the door with that inimitable grace with which you do everything, and fixed your eyes full upon me, as much as to say, "Is he caught?"—that very week you sat upon my knee, twined your arms round me, caressed me with every mark of tenderness consistent with modesty; and I have not got much farther since. Now if you did all this with me, a perfect stranger to you, and without any particular liking to me, must I not conclude you do so as a matter of course with everyone?—Or, if you do not do so with others, it was because you took a liking to me for some reason or other. (9:107)

337). Cajah was Sally's brother, named after his father, Micaiah.

When no other source is given, all quotations from Hazlitt's letters to Patmore in this chapter are copied from the originals now preserved in the Lockwood Memorial Library of the State University of New York at Buffalo. These letters, which differ markedly from the versions which Hazlitt printed in *Liber Amoris*, were included in the "privately printed" edition of *Liber Amoris* brought out by Richard Le Gallienne and W. Carew Hazlitt in 1894; however, the editors sometimes copied inaccurately and occasionally censored the texts. When quoting letters to Patmore for which the originals are not among the eleven letters in the Lockwood Library, I have followed the versions in P. P. Howe's edition of *Liber Amoris* in volume 9 of the *Complete Works* and have identified my source, as usual, in parentheses. I have drawn liberally on the eleven original letters, partly because earlier biographers have made little use of them, but primarily because they reveal Hazlitt with his defenses down, disclosing without restraint his intense, mercurial nature, his longing for acceptance, and his fear of rejection.

12. *Liber Amoris*, ed. Richard Le Gallienne (Privately printed, 1894), p. 224. Although Sally Walker seems to have been called Sarah, I have referred to her always as Sally to avoid confusion with Sarah Hazlitt.

She replied only: "It was gratitude, Sir, for different obligations"—to which Hazlitt added in the original manuscript an angry footnote not included in the published dialogue: "Upwards of £30 worth—a trifle. Among others, is my hair in a golden heart, which I see set down in the Jeweller's bill, *A gold chased heart. A chased* heart indeed, but not given for a *chaste* heart." [13]

Yet the odds were on Sally's side: her emotions were in no way involved, while Hazlitt's were helplessly entangled. The following day, as he recorded it in his final dialogue, "The Reconciliation," he was contrite. "The words I uttered," he told her—with no little truth—"hurt me more than they did you. . . . —Ah, Sarah! I am unworthy of your love: I hardly dare ask for your pity; but oh! save me—save me from your scorn: I cannot bear it— it withers me like lightning" (9:109). Did she feel, perhaps, some fundamental antipathy toward him, "an original dislike, which no efforts of mine can overcome"? (9:110). No, she told him; she was merely being faithful to her lost lover.

He pressed his case: he would be quite content to be married to her if she would only give him "the love, or regard, or whatever you call it, you have shown me before marriage, if that has only been sincere" (9:111). He later told Patmore that he even suggested that she live with him "as a friend"—to which she replied, "I don't know: and yet it would be no use if I did, you would always be hankering after what could never be" (9:118). But he persisted: "I asked her if she would do so at once—the very next day? And what do you guess was her answer—'Do you think it would be prudent?' As I didn't proceed to extremities on the spot, she began to look grave, and declare off. . . . Would she live with me in her own house—to be with me all day as dear friends, if nothing more, to sit and read and talk with me? . . . She would make no promises, but I should find her the same" (9:118).

Again his suspicions were aroused. "Is it not that you prefer flirting with 'gay young men' to becoming a mere dull domestic wife?" At that she bridled. "You have no right to throw out such insinuations: for though I am but a tradesman's daughter, I have as nice a sense of honour as anyone can have" (9:111).

He repented immediately of his boldness. "Talk of a tradesman's daughter! you would ennoble any family, thou glorious girl, by true nobility of mind." And when she told him that her former lover resembled the little statue of Napoleon on his mantelpiece, he insisted that she accept it as a keepsake.

13. Ibid., p. 192 n.

Now that she had received another "obligation" from him, she "immediately came and sat down, and put her arm around my neck, and kissed me. . . . Is it not plain we are the best friends in the world," he asked her, "since we are always so glad to make it up?" And he concluded the dialogue with the words: "Is it possible that the wretch who writes this could ever have been so blest? Heavenly delicious creature! Can I live without her? —Oh! no—never—never. . . . Let me but see her again! She cannot hate the man who loves her as I do" (9:112).

From Stamford he went on to Renton, on the Eye Water, thirty miles southeast of Edinburgh. He stopped at the "lone inn . . . on a rising ground (a mark for all the winds, which blow here incessantly)" with "a woody hill opposite" and "a winding valley below" (9:116). There he settled down to spend the first month of his required residence. The divorce proceedings were bound to put him even deeper in debt, and he was determined to write enough new essays to fill out his second volume of *Table-Talk*.

From Renton he wrote to Sally sometime in February assuring her that he had been working hard. "I regularly do ten pages a day, which mounts up to thirty guineas' worth a week, so that you see I should grow rich at this rate, if I could keep on so; *and I could keep on so*, if I had you with me to encourage me with your sweet smiles, and share my lot." [14] He was willing, it would seem, to buy her affections if all else failed. Or to beg them, for he added presently: "You once made me believe I was not hated by her I loved; and for that sensation, so delicious was it, though but a mockery and a dream, I owe you more than I can ever pay. I thought to have dried up my tears for ever, the day I left you; but as I write this, they stream again." [15] He had received only one letter from her, a noncommittal note dated January 17, shortly after his departure, signed "yours Respectfully, S. Walker," and concerned only with such matters as the disposal of his mail. He was in despair, yet he feared that he might offend her by his appeals for sympathy. "Forgive what I have written above," he pleaded; "I did not intend it; but you were once my little all, and I cannot bear the thought of having lost you for ever, I fear through my own fault." And he asked if she and her mother would go as his guests to see Miss Stephens in *Love in a Village* and Kean in *Othello*. [16]

Her reply was chilling—a "cold, prudish answer," he described it to Patmore, "beginning *Sir*, and ending *From your's truly*, with *Best respects from herself and relations*"—refusing, too, his offer of the theater tickets (9:116). He wrote to her again in March, complaining that her letters

14. Ibid., p. 85.   15. Ibid., pp. 85–86.   16. Ibid., p. 86.

"are so short; and then scarce one kind word in them *in the way of friend-ship*. You are such a girl for business." Yet he would not scold, he told her; "Not for the world would I send thee an unkind word so far away. I may be rash and hasty when I am with thee, but deliberately can I never say or do aught to cast the slightest blame upon thee. You are my idol—the dear image in my heart as 'that little image' on the mantlepiece (*or somebody like it*) is in thine." He reported that his writing was coming along well: "*It will take another month to finish*, but all the labour and anxiety is over." And he recalled tenderly the night he took her and her mother to see Mac-ready play in *Romeo and Juliet*:

> Can I ever forget it for a moment—your sweet modest looks, your infinite propriety of behaviour, all your sweet ways—your hesitating about taking my arm as we came out till your mother did—your laughing about losing your cloak—your stepping into the coach without my being able to make an inch of discovery—and oh! my sitting down beside you, you whom I loved so well, so long, and your assuring me I had not lessened your pleasure at the play by being with you, and giving me that dear hand to press in mine—I seemed to be in Heaven,—that slight, exquisitely turned form contained my all of heaven upon earth—I sat beside the adorable creature by her own permission—and as I followed [folded?] you, yes, you my best Sarah, to my heart, there was, as you say, "a tie between us," you did seem to be mine for a few short moments, in all truth and honour and sacredness. Oh! could we but be always so—do not mock me for I am indeed a very child in love.[17]

Yet he was not really as docile as he pretended. At about the same time, writing to Patmore in a more rational mood, he gave a quite different picture of the events which he had described so plaintively in the last two dialogues of *Liber Amoris*:

> We had a famous parting-scene, a complete quarrel and then a reconciliation, in which she did beguile me of my tears, but the deuce a one did she shed. What do you think? She cajoled me out of my little Buonaparte as cleverly as possible, in manner and form following. She was shy the Saturday and Sunday (the day of my departure) so I got in dudgeon, and began to rip up grievances. . . . If you had seen how she flounced, and looked, and went to the door, saying "She was obliged to me for letting her know the opinion I had always entertained of her"—then I said,

17. The text given here is that of the original letter, first published in *John Bull* on June 22, 1823, and reprinted by Stanley Jones in *Review of English Studies*, n.s. 17 (1966): 163–70. The version in *Liber Amoris* is much shorter and advances the claim that Hazlitt has written "a volume in less than a month" (9:113). Jones suspects that Theodore Hook, the unscrupulous editor of *John Bull*, might have secured the letter through John Wilson Croker of the *Quarterly Review*, whom Hazlitt had attacked, especially in his essay "On the Aristocracy of Letters" in the second volume of *Table-Talk*.

"Sarah!"—and she came back and took my hand, and fixed her eyes on the mantle-piece—(she must have been invoking her idol then—if I thought so, I could devour her, the darling—but I doubt her). (9:116–17)

Soon afterwards he wrote again to Patmore, this time enclosing a copy of "little YES and NO's" second letter. He was annoyed at her curtness—and suspicious as well, because the letter had been posted under a frank which he could not identify. "See if you can decypher it by a Red-book," he asked Patmore. Yet he took heart when he reflected that she wrote her letter the very day after hearing from him. He was grasping for straws—for straws in the wind. "I suspect her grievously of being an arrant jilt, to say no more," he admitted, "—yet I love her dearly" (9:118).

During his five weeks at Renton Inn he had written a good deal for a man torn, as he was, by warring emotions. In a letter to Patmore in March he listed nine essays already finished and two in progress—all evidently intended for the projected second volume of *Table-Talk*, although only five of them were actually included in it. At Renton, too, he probably wrote an account of the collection of paintings which he had seen at Burleigh House, a review of Byron's *Sardanapalus* for the *Edinburgh Review*,[18] and "Table-Talk, No. 3: On Milton's Sonnets." In the last, which appeared in the March *New Monthly*, he proved clearly that his analytical powers had not atrophied under emotional pressures. He deftly contrasted the "sincerity, the spirit of political patriotism" of Milton's poems with Shakespeare's "overcharged and monotonous" sonnets and those of Wordsworth, who "has not [Milton's] high and various imagination, nor his deep and fixed principle" (8:175–76). And he warmly defended Milton against hostile criticism, pointedly praising him as a man of unflagging loyalty to his beliefs. "Our first of poets," he declared, "was one of our first of men" (8:176).

On Sunday, March 3, he wrote to Colburn from Renton: "By the time you receive this, the New Volume will be done, & ready, if you desire it, to go to press with, or to send up in lumps of 50 pages at a time for the Magazine. It contains, I hope, better things than any I have done. I thank God for my escape, & have now done with essay-writing forever. . . . I have worked at it, I assure you, without ceasing & like a tyger. I am on the whole

18. In his March 30 letter to Patmore, Hazlitt wrote, "My Sardanapalus is to be in." The belated February issue of the *Edinburgh* contained a review of the poem which Jeffrey later included in his own *Contributions to the Edinburgh Review*. As Howe suggests (16:421), the review was doubtless Hazlitt's originally, but was so extensively revised by Jeffrey that he considered it his own work.

better in health, & hope to take a trip into the Highlands before I return."
And he asked Colburn to send him "30£ by return of post, or I shall be obliged to write to Jeffrey for money to get away from here, which I wish to
do immediately after my task is done" (9:261).

Two of the essays written at Renton, but not immediately published,
revealed, by contrast, Hazlitt's mercurial nature, even in this period of
emotional distress. One, "On Dr. Spurzheim's Theory," later printed in
The Plain Speaker, was a cogent examination of the science of craniology
(or phrenology) expressing nothing but scorn for the "unmeaning, *quackish*
sort of common-place" (12:143) advanced by this "Baron Munchausen of
marvelous metaphysics" (12:138).[19] The second, "Advice to a School-boy,"
later published in the Paris edition of *Table-Talk* as "On the Conduct of
Life," was a poignant letter addressed to "My dear little Fellow."

"I had a letter from my little boy the other day," Hazlitt had written to
Sally from Renton Inn, "and I have been writing him a long essay in my
book on his conduct in life, shewing him how to avoid his father's errors,
and particularly pointing out to him the dangers of love, you may well
laugh at this."[20] For Hazlitt, however, it was no laughing matter. He loved
the boy and was painfully aware of his own shortcomings as a parent.
Although both Hazlitt and Sarah were devoted to their son, he had suffered
from their quarrels both before and after the separation; at the same time,
he had learned to play one against the other for his own advantage. In an
undated note to his mother he wrote: "I shall come up in a day or two.
Father has been very unkind to me. And I shall try if you will be not so.
I am just going out, I don't know where, to bide out a good while."[21]

Before Hazlitt had left London, he had entered the boy in a school kept
by a Mr. Dawson on Hunter Street. Young William had gone unwillingly
and, as "Advice to a School-boy" shows, had complained about his school-
fellows, their dress, and their treatment of him. For the first time in his life
he was confronting the outside world alone, and he was revealing, as his
father admitted, that he was "a spoiled child" (17:87). The picture of the
boy that emerges from the essay is pathetic; the picture of his father, no less

19. In a related essay, "On Dreams," also written at Renton and published in *The
Plain Speaker*, Hazlitt attacked Franz Gall and Johann Kaspar Spurzheim's claim that a
somnambulist's ability to see proves that some organs may be active while others are dor-
mant. The essay contained some interesting remarks about Hazlitt's own experiences as a
somnambulist (12:19) and some striking anticipations of Freudian theory (12:23).

20. *Review of English Studies*, n.s. 17 (1966):165.

21. The note, apparently never before published, is preserved in the Lockwood Memorial Library at the State University of New York at Buffalo.

so: "As my health is so indifferent," he wrote, "and I may not be with you long, I wish to leave you some advice (the best I can) for your conduct in life, both that it may be of use to you, and as something to remember me by. I may at least be able to caution you against my own errors, if nothing else" (17:86).

He knew only too well what his errors were: he trusted his son would not "look with too jaundiced an eye at others" and overrate his "own peculiar pretensions" (17:88). He should learn to dance, that he may develop a "graceful carriage" (17:90); he must cultivate "openness, freedom, self-possession" (17:90); he must avoid overapplication to books—for "Whatever may be the value of learning, health and good spirits are of more" (17:91). One surly William Hazlitt in the world was enough.

When he looked into the future, Hazlitt still thought in terms of his own failures: "I should wish you to be a good painter, if such a thing could be hoped," he wrote (17:99). As for love and marriage:

> If you ever marry, I would wish you to marry the woman you like. Do not be guided by the recommendation of friends. Nothing will atone for or overcome an original distaste. It will only increase from intimacy; and if you are to live separate, it is better not to come together. There is no use in dragging a chain through life, unless it binds one to the object we love. Chuse a mistress from among your equals. You will be able to understand her character better, and she will be more likely to understand yours. Those in an inferior station to yourself will doubt your good intentions, and misapprehend your plainest expressions. All that you swear is to them a riddle or downright nonsense. . . . Do not fancy every woman you see the heroine of a romance, a Sophia Western, a Clarissa, or a Julia; and yourself the potential hero of it, Tom Jones, Lovelace, or St. Preux. Avoid this error as you would shrink back from a precipice. All your fine sentiments and romantic notions will (of themselves) make no more impression on one of these delicate creatures, than on a piece of marble. Their soft bosoms are steel to your amorous refinements, if you have no other pretensions. It is not what you think of them that determines their choice, but what they think of you. . . . Do you, my dear boy, stop short in this career, if you find yourself setting out in it, and make up your mind to this, that if a woman does not like you of her own accord, that is, from involuntary impressions, nothing you can say or do or suffer for her sake will make her, but will set her the more against you. (17:98–99) [22]

Hazlitt's mind was as sharp as ever. Sally had bewitched only his heart.

22. For the cynical analysis of female character which Hazlitt wrote, but omitted from the essay as published, see 17:395–97. For example: "Love in women . . . is a merely selfish feeling. It has nothing to do (I am sorry to say) with friendship, or esteem, or even pity."

By March 30 he had moved to Edinburgh—as tortured as ever. He had been "in a sort of Hell," he wrote to Patmore, and he could see "no prospect of getting out of it. I would put an end to my torments at once," he added, "but I am as great a coward as I am a fool." He had still received no reply to his last letter to Sally. "I wrote to her in the tenderest, most respectful manner," he declared,

poured my soul at her feet, & this is the way she serves me! Can you account for it except on the admission of my worst suspicion, that she has. . . . Oh! my God! can I bear to think of her so, or that I am scorned & made a sport of by the creature to whom I had given my very heart? I feel like one of the damned. To be hated, loathed as I have been all my life, & to feel the utter impossibility of its ever being otherwise while I live—take what pains I may! If you *do* know any thing, good or bad, tell me, I intreat you. I can bear any thing but this horrid [suspense. If I knew] she was a mere abandoned creature I should try to forget her: but till I do know this, nothing can tear me from her, I have sucked in poison from her lips too long—alas! mine do not poison again. I sit & cry my eyes out, my weakness grows upon me & I have no hopes left unless I could lose my senses quite. I think I should like this—to forget, ah! to forget—there would be some thing in that—to be an ideot for some few years & then to wake up a poor wretched old man, to recollect my misery as past, & die!

To add to his frustration, he was making no progress toward the divorce. His wife had not arrived in Scotland, and he feared he might be obliged to return to London without having gained his freedom. He was determined, however, not to stay at the Walkers' house. Yet he asked plaintively, "Can I breathe away from her?"

Undoubtedly he was, to some extent, indulging in histrionics. He was a highly emotional man who had long felt that the world had paid him too little attention, and in the sentimentalist Patmore he had found a receptive audience. At Renton he had been able to rouse himself from his morbid state long enough to write several first-rate essays. And at Edinburgh he at least maintained appearances. In a postscript he told Patmore that he had met "the great little man" Francis Jeffrey and confided to him that he was "dull & out of spirits." He added, however, that Jeffrey "says he cannot perceive it."

On or about April 7 he wrote to Patmore from the lodgings which he had taken with a Mrs. Dow at 10 George Street, in Edinburgh. He still had not heard from Sally, but a letter from Patmore had made him feel "somewhat easier," knowing of his friend's "interest in my vexations." He had received word, too, that his wife would arrive in Edinburgh during the following week. "How it will end, I can't say," he wrote;

and don't care except with reference to the other affair. I should like to have it in my power to make [Sally] the offer direct & unequivocal, to see how she'd take it. It would be worth something at any rate to see her superfine airs upon it; & if she should take it into her head to turn round her sweet neck, drop her eyelids, & say, "Yes, I will be yours"—treason domestic, foreign levy, nothing could touch me further. By Heaven, I doat on her. The truth is, I never had any pleasure, like love, with any one but her. Then how can I bear to part with her?"

And again the old longing overpowered him: "Do you know I like to think of her best in her morning gown, in her dirt & her mob cap; it is so she has oftenest sat on my knee with her arms round my neck—Damn her, I could devour her, it is *herself* that I love. I went with a girl that was what they call [illegible] I fancied she was 15 & though it's what I hate, I adored her the more for it. When I but touch her hand, I enjoy perfect happiness and contentment of soul." But suddenly his doubts returned:

Yet I think I am in the wrong box. What security can I have that she does not flirt or worse with every one that comes in her way when I recollect how she took my first advances? How can I think she has any regard for me when she knows the tortures she puts me to by her silence? And what can I think of a girl who grants a man she has no particle of regard for the freedoms she has done to me? My idea is that in refusing to marry she has made up her mind to a sporting-life (keeping safe as well as she can) between disappointment & wantonness & a love of intrigue. I think she would sooner come & live with me than marry me. So that I have her in my arms & *for life*, I care not how; I never could tire of her sweetness, I feel as if I could grow to her, body & soul!

Then: "A thought has struck me." And he told Patmore that he owed Sally's father ten pounds. If Colburn would advance him that amount, Patmore could deliver it to the Walkers' house and suggest that Sally write "mentioning the receipt of the same & stating that no great harm had been done by the delay." This, he declared, would be a favor *"greater than an angel's visit."*

He continued: "You might add (supposing her to seem gracious) that you believe I have been hurt, thinking I had offended her." But then he had second thoughts: "Yet I doubt about all this; only I am afraid of being kept some time longer in the dark—yet that is better than the Hell of detecting her in an impudent intrigue with some other fellow. I don't see how I should stand it. I must say Farewel, for the thought drives me mad."

Before he posted the letter, he returned to it, overwriting across the page: "It won't do at all. The way would be (if you got the stuff) to call & ask for Mr. W. & treat it as a mere matter of business & if they ask how I am, say 'not very well.' And if she comes poking out, to say I desired my love to her, or some thing of that grave easy sort. But ask her for nothing, for whatever you do, she'll refuse, except kisses! But use your own discretion about it." Later he squeezed still another frantic postscript into the top of the first page: "Don't go at all. I believe her to be a common lodging-house drab, & that any attempt to move only hardens her. All she wants is to be tickled & go all lengths but the last—to be thrown on the floor & felt & all & still resist & keep up the game. To think that I should feel as I have done for such a monster."

Yet despite his addled state of mind, he kept writing essays. He concentrated on criticism, probably because he could discipline his powers better when he was examining a specific work of literature or art than when his thoughts were ranging widely over the complexities of human behavior. At Edinburgh he finished the second installment of his essay "On the Elgin Marbles" for the *London Magazine* (18:150–66). On April 10 Hessey wrote to Taylor: "Hazlitt desired his wife to call and say he should send a paper by the latter end of next week."[23] And that same day Hazlitt sent off the essay and promised to review the collection of water colors of Greece by Dr. Hugh Williams on exhibition in the Calton Convening Rooms in Edinburgh. This, he wrote, "will make up the sheet & I hope nearly balance our account." He added that he was planning to visit Robert Owen's colony New Lanark and would prepare a description of it for the *London* "tandem." "Will you have it for next month?" he asked. "If so, & you could send me £10 upon it by return of post, it would be an especial favour."[24] On the sixteenth he wrote again thanking the publishers for their letter and its contents and saying that he expected to be in London to "do the *Leonardo* unless W[ainewright] likes."[25]

In the meantime, thanks no doubt to William Ritchie of the weekly *Scotsman*, he had been asked to review for that paper the Fourth Annual Exhibition of Living Artists then in progress at the Waterloo Rooms in Edinburgh. The article, which appeared in the April 20 issue and was signed "By a Stranger," was hardly calculated to win friends among the Scots. "Scotland," he announced in his opening paragraph,

23. Blunden, p. 139.

24. *London Mercury* 7 (1922–23): 497. The Williams article (discussed below, pp. 331–32) appeared in the May *London Magazine*, but the description of New Lanark never appeared (and probably never was written) although Hazlitt visited the town on April 28 (*Journals*, p. 194).

25. *The Hazlitts*, p. 471.

seems to have been hitherto the country of the Useful rather than of the Fine Arts. We are more prone to study realities than appearances: we are not a luxurious people, and have paid little attention to the most evanescent of all luxuries, the luxury of the eye. A stranger is struck, in visiting Edinburgh, to see no looking-glasses in the best-furnished rooms. Is this the effect of ancient bigotry, which banished them as symbols of vanity and of the pride of human life? Or is it a systematic economy, which allows of nothing superfluous? Or is it indifference to the mere shows and glittering shadows of things? On any of these suppositions, the bare walls of our houses augur ill for the progress and cultivation of art. (18:167)

Scotland, he believed, was not yet sufficiently civilized to foster the arts:

Probably the crust of prejudice, and antipathy to painting as a frivolous or meretricious art, has lain too long upon the national understanding for it to thaw at once in the ray of royal and doubtful patronage. The cold, dry, barren, unmanured soil cannot be expected to shoot forth into luxuriance with the first breath of a northern spring. The mind must be gradually prepared; the seed must be sown; prejudices must be removed; the habits of a people must undergo a change,—must become comparatively soft and effeminate. Whether this is "a consummation devoutly to be wished," is a question beyond our fathom: but the change must take place, before the Fine Arts, those *deliciae humanae generis*, can be had in perfection. (18:167–68)

The collection has "a *pauper* appearance," he complained. "It seems to have just emancipated itself from the forge, the workshop, and the factory. It looks meagre, dry, hard, mechanical, ill-fed. Instead of being seated on a throne, it is placed upon a cutty-stool;—for a robe whose woof is Iris-dipped, it shivers in a cold, scanty penance-sheet. Kirk Assemblies have over-laid it: public opinion has pinched and nipped it into nothing; and by force of being despised, it has become mean and despicable" (18:168).

These were strong words to address to a people who prided themselves on their sophistication—whose city had been often called the most beautiful in the world. But Hazlitt was in no mood to enjoy his environment. Later he was to praise the "situation and buildings" of Edinburgh, but to insist that it "would have even a more imposing and delightful effect if Arthur's Seat were crowned with thick woods, if the Pentland-hills could be converted into green pastures, if the Scotch people were French, and Leith-walk planted with vineyards" (10:98). In *Liber Amoris* he addressed the city as "Stony-hearted Edinburgh," calling it a "City of palaces, or of tombs—a quarry, rather than the habitation of men," complaining that "the dust of [its] streets mingles with my tears and blinds me" (9:126). As usual he felt excluded, rejected; he fancied that the Scots disapproved of him on principle. In the essay "On the Scotch Character," which appeared in *The Liberal* for the following January, he wrote: "If a word is said against your moral character, they shun you like a plague-spot. They are not only afraid of a charge being proved against you, but they dare not disprove it, lest by clearing you of it they should be supposed a party to what had no existence or foundation. They thus imbibe a bad opinion of you from hearsay, and conceal the good they know of you both from themselves and the world. If your political orthodoxy is called in question, they take the alarm as much as if they were apprehensive of being involved in a charge of high treason" (17:104).

Though Hazlitt had written for both the *Edinburgh Review* and the *Edinburgh Magazine*, he saw little of the literary people of the city. The exception was William Ritchie, who had reviewed some of his works for the *Scotsman*, and who now aided him in arrangements for the divorce. On April 17 Ritchie entertained him at supper in his house at 22 Nicolson Street with two other members of the *Scotsman* staff, J. R. M'Culloch and Thomas Hodgskin, and the lawyer-phrenologist George Combe. But the party was evidently not a success; Combe later reported that Hazlitt "drank no wine or strong liquor, but an enormous quantity of tea," and the conversation seems to have dragged. Hazlitt, who was "still sitting" when Combe left at 1:30 A.M., would have been irked if he had known that Combe was silently making a phrenological analysis of him which he relayed in a letter to his friend the Reverend David Welsh.[26] If Hazlitt's new friends were at first disposed to see more of him, they probably changed their minds when they read his review of the Exhibition of Living Artists in the *Scotsman* four days later.

Hazlitt apparently called on Jeffrey only the once. He told Patmore in his letter of March 30 that Jeffrey was "very gracious to me—et sa femme aussi!" But he was not very gracious in return. He objected to the "large sprawling Danae" over the mantel in Jeffrey's office, "where he received Scotch parsons and their wives on law business." Though Jeffrey might have placed it there in order to "triumph over Presbyterian prudery and prejudice," it was, to Hazlitt's way of thinking, ugly, and nothing could redeem it. "You can only have put it there because it is naked, and that alone shows a felonious intent," he told Jeffrey—and later repeated for the benefit of readers of *Conversations with Northcote*. "Had there been either beauty or expression, it would have *conducted off* the objectionable part"

26. Stanley Jones, "Hazlitt in Edinburgh: An Evening with Mr. Ritchie of *The Scotsman*," *Études Anglaises* 17 (1964):9–20; 113–27.

(11:295–96).[27] Nothing in Edinburgh seemed to suit him quite. Later, after Jeffrey had stopped in at his lodgings with a loan of a hundred pounds, Hazlitt apparently did not bother to return his call.[28]

However, on Sunday, April 21, his spirits revived when his wife finally arrived in Edinburgh. She had landed at Leith on the packet *Superb*, and she went directly to the Black Bull on Catherine Street to stay temporarily. Hazlitt may have met her there. At least he was at the inn earlier in the day drinking ale when he wrote to Patmore announcing that "Mrs. H—— is actually on her way here." The good news had come to him quite by chance: ". . . coming up Leith Walk I met an old friend [Adam Bell], come down here to settle, who said, 'I saw your wife at the wharf. She had just paid her passage by the Superb.'"

In the journal which Sarah kept during her stay in Edinburgh she said nothing of meeting her husband that first day. She noted, however, that she "dined at three on mutton chops," then "walked up to Edinburgh Castle, and on the Calton Hill," returned in time for tea, "had ham for supper," and "went to bed at half past twelve."[29] Sarah was indeed regarding her trip as a "jaunt."

Her husband, of course, was elated. Sarah's arrival, he wrote to Patmore, "has brought me to life," and he was planning his strategy. His friend Adam Bell, he decided, was "the very man to negotiate the business between us." Even Patmore's last letter scolding him for his treatment of Sally and defending her conduct failed to dishearten him. Although her failure to write worried him, he now had hopes that all would be well. "Should the business succeed," he wrote to Patmore, "& I should be free, do you think S.W. will be Mrs. ————? If she *will*, she *shall*; & to call her so to you, or to hear her called so by others, will be music to my ears, such as they never heard. Do you think if she knew how I love her, my depressions & my altitudes, my wanderings & my pertinacity, it would not melt her? She knows it all, & if she is not a bitch, she loves me or regards me with a feeling next to love."

Negotiations for the divorce began at once. On Monday, April 22, Adam Bell called at the Black Bull and took Sarah to meet a barrister, George Cranstoun, who was to take charge of the suit. She was worried because

27. Hazlitt probably had Jeffrey's "Danae" in mind when he complained, later in the year, of people "who think that to have an indecent daub hanging up in one corner of the room, is proof of a liberality of *gusto*, and a considerable progress in *virtù. Tout au contraire*" (10:14).

28. See Hazlitt's apology, quoted below, p. 349.

29. *Journals*, p. 185.

she had heard that if she took the oath of calumny, swearing that there had been no collusion about the suit, she might be liable to prosecution and even transportation. After all, she admitted, Hazlitt had told her "that he should never live with me again, and as my situation must have long been uncomfortable, he thought for both our sakes it would be better to obtain a divorce and put an end to it." Cranstoun assured her that the courts would not regard such an agreement as collusion since "repeated adulteries had been committed for years before." She consented, then, to proceed with the divorce, and she promptly engaged a solicitor named John Gray and moved into lodgings at a Mr. Bracewell's house, 6 South Union Place, for which, she conscientiously reported in her journal, she paid "fourteen shillings a week, and two shillings firing." [30]

The next day Gray told her that she must "ascertain the name and place of abode of the woman Mr. Hazlitt visits whether she was the mistress of the house, or a lodger." He added that the suit would probably last two months and cost fifty pounds. She dutifully took steps to get the needed information and some other papers necessary in the suit and to send her husband "the paper signed by Mr. Hazlitt, securing the reversion of my money to the child . . . to get it properly stamped." Then on Wednesday, the twenty-fourth, she picked up at a law stationer's shop a copy of the oath of calumny which differed markedly from the one which she had been shown earlier, and she decided that she could not in conscience subscribe to it. She promptly sent a note to Hazlitt notifying him that she must drop the suit. [31]

He rallied his forces at once. That afternoon William Ritchie called on Sarah "to beg me as a friend to both, (I had never seen or heard of him before) to proceed in the divorce" and thus "relieve all parties from an unpleasant situation." He assured her that "with my appearance, it was highly probable that I might marry again, and meet with a person more congenial to me, than Mr. Hazlitt had unfortunately proved," adding that her husband was "in such a state of nervous irritability that he could not work or apply to any thing, and that he thought he would not live very long if he was not easier in his mind."

Sarah was not much moved by the appeal. "I told him," she wrote in her journal, "I did not myself think he would survive me; but the life he had led would fully account for it: and that I certainly had scruples about taking the Oath, though I was of opinion that both reason and justice were on my side. Yet I was not quite so sure about the law." [32]

30. Ibid., p. 186.   31. Ibid., pp. 186–87.   32. Ibid., p. 188.

That same evening Adam Bell called to tell her that a person later identified as Hazlitt had been followed to the house of a Mrs. Knight. And the next day, Friday, the twenty-sixth, John Gray stopped in to report that Mrs. Knight had admitted that "a little dark gentleman" had called on one Mary Walker, a lodger at her house, and that the same gentleman, who said that he wrote for the *Edinburgh Review* and was married, but separated from his wife, had brought other women to the house and "been shut up with them." 33 Gray also gave her a copy of the charges which he had drawn up against Hazlitt, and Sarah transcribed them, word for word, into her journal. She then apparently decided to yield to Hazlitt and his agents, for the following day she gave Bell a copy of a contract specifying that Hazlitt must pay all expenses of the divorce, must provide for their son's education and living expenses (allowing her "free access to him at all times, and occasional visits from him"), and will give her a note of hand for fifty pounds payable in six months. With that, she walked down to Holyrood House and made a thorough tour of the place—all but the gallery of portraits of Scottish monarchs. Staunch liberal that she was, she balked at paying an extra shilling to look at pictures of kings.

On Sunday, the twenty-eighth, having taken stock of her resources, she sent word to Hazlitt that she had "only between five and six pounds of my quarter's money left, and therefore if he did not send me some immediately, and fulfil his agreement for the rest, I should be obliged to return [to London] on Tuesday, while I had enough to take me back." Hazlitt replied through

33. Ibid., p. 189. Hazlitt seems to have circulated quite different accounts of how evidence for the divorce was handled. Seymour Kirkup told John Forster that, when Hazlitt visited Landor in Italy, he told Landor and Kirkup that he and Sarah "took the steamboat to Leith, provided themselves each with good law advice, and continued on the most friendly terms in Edinburgh till everything was ready: when Hazlitt described himself calling in from the streets a not very respectable female confederate, and, for form's sake, putting her in his bed, and lying down beside her. 'Well, sir,' said Hazlitt . . ., 'down I lay, and the folding-doors opened, and in walked Mrs. H., accompanied by two gentlemen. She turned to them and said, Gentlemen, do you know who that person is in bed along with that woman? Yes, Madam, they politely replied, 'tis Mr. William Hazlitt. On which, sir, she made a courtsey, and they went out of the room, and left me and my companion *in statu quo*'" (John Forster, *Walter Savage Landor*, 2 vols. [London, 1869], 2:208). Benjamin Haydon had another version: "He advises his wife to let him go down & commit adultery, & then for her to come down & proceed against him. Down he goes, sleeps in a brothel, with a strumpet *one eyed from disease*! (his own acct.), his wife brings her action, & he [is] divorced! . . . The bawd & the strumpet come into court. The Judge says, 'did you ever see this Gentleman?' 'Yes, Sir,' said the girl, looking at him with one eye! 'How long?' 'Three hours at a time, may it please your Lordship.' 'Then you have known this gentleman carnally?' 'Yes, Sir, & please your Lordship'" (*Haydon Diary*, 2:373–74).

Adam Bell that "he would give the draft for fifty pounds at three months instead of six, when the proceedings had commenced"—"meaning I suppose," Sarah noted parenthetically, "when the Oath was taken, for they had already commenced." 34

After trying in vain to get any further word from her husband through Adam Bell, she decided on the following Tuesday evening to take drastic action: she set off, veiled, at dusk, to Hazlitt's lodgings.

It was a disagreeable session. As Sarah recorded it in her journal, it began with a discussion of finances:

> He told me he expected thirty pounds from Colbourn on Thursday, and then he would let me have five pounds for present expences, that he had but one pound in his pocket, but if I wanted it, I should have that. That he was going to give two Lectures at Glasgow next week, for which he was to have £100 and he had eighty pounds beside to receive for the Table Talk in a fortnight out of which sums, he pledged himself to fulfil his engagements relative to my expences: and also to make me a handsome present when all was over (£20) as I seemed to love money. Or it would enable me to travel back by land, as I said I should prefer seeing something of the country to going back in the steam boat, which he proposed. Said he would give the note of hand for fifty pounds to Mr. Ritchie for me, payable to whoever I pleased; if he could conveniently at the time, it should be for three months, instead of six, but he was not certain of that.

When he asked her if she had taken the oath of calumny, she saw her chance to strike a bargain:

> I told him I only waited a summons from Mr. Gray, if I could depend on the money, but I could not live in a strange place without: and I had no friends, or means of earning money here, as he had; though, as I had still four pounds, I could wait a few days. I asked him how the child's expences; or my draught were to be paid, if he went abroad. and he answered, that if he succeeded in the divorce, he should be easy in his mind, and able to work, and then he should probably be back in three months; but otherwise, he might leave England for ever. He said that as soon as I had got him to sign a paper giving away a hundred and fifty pounds a year from himself; I talked of going back, and leaving every thing; as if I meant to bamboozle him. I told him to recollect, that it was no advantage for myself that I sought; nor should I get a halfpenny by it: it was only to secure something to *his* child, as well as mine. He said he could do very well for the child himself; and that he was allowed to be a very indulgent kind father; some people thought too much so. I said, I did not dispute his fondness for him; but I must observe, that though he got a great deal of money; he never saved, or had any by him; or was likely to make much provision for the child.

34. *Journals*, p. 194.

Inevitably, then, they descended to recriminations:

> Neither could I think it was proper, or for his welfare, that he should take him to
> the Fives Court, and such places: and carry him out with him when he went picking
> up the girls on the town: it was likely to corrupt and vitiate him, and bring him up to
> like such ruinous practices. He said perhaps the last was wrong; but that he did not
> know that it was any good to bring up children in ignorance of the world. I observed
> that he was a very affectionate, kind-hearted and good child, both to him and me:
> and he replied that he had taught him all that; but that I was frequently, telling him
> that his father did not behave well to his mother. I told him the child made his own
> observations; and was pretty competent to judge of that matter: but that I had always
> told him he was a very kind father to him, though he did not behave well to me. He
> said I had always despised him, and his abilities. I asked if the women with whom he
> associated, were any better judges of them. and told him, that in spite of his assertion,
> that he did not wish them to know or understand that he had abilities; nobody was
> more sore on that point: but, I added, that all recrimination was now useless, as
> probably all intercourse between us had for ever ended.

At that point Hazlitt softened; he assured Sarah that he meant to be "very good friends" with her if she "carried through the business"—though he added that, if she failed to do so, he would never see her again. When they finally parted, he warned her that she had better not call on him again, and Sarah assured him that she would not do so "without a necessity." [35]

The dreary proceedings dragged along. On Thursday, May 2, Sarah rented cheaper lodgings on the third floor of the house where she had been staying. That same day Adam Bell notified her that Hazlitt would sign the financial agreement and send her five pounds the next day. But the emotional strain was beginning to tell on Sarah. She suffered "a violent bowel complaint" all that day and was "still very poorly" on Friday when she moved into her new quarters. To add to her misery, she learned from John Gray that she must mark time for three more weeks before she could take the oath. And he regaled her with a lurid description of Mrs. Knight's house, where her husband had been a regular visitor:

> He told me that he was never more astonished, than on going to No 21 James Street;
> for that the people he found there, was a set of the lowest, abandoned blackguards
> he had ever met with: who told him they would not say a word till he treated them
> with Mulled Port: but that when they were half intoxicated he got out of them suf-
> ficient for his purpose. That the appearance of the house, people, and every thing
> about it, was more infamous than any thing that he had before any idea existed in
> Edinburgh at the present day. I said, I was not at all surprised at it; as those were the

35. Ibid., pp. 195–96.

kind of people he associated with in London: he had a taste that way. To which he replied, it was a very depraved one. I said that many people had been surprised that he preferred such society to mine; but so it was: and would render my procuring other proofs of Adultery in London, somewhat difficult.[36]

Sarah waited out the next week in Edinburgh. Sunday, Monday, and Tuesday she was too ill to leave the house, but Wednesday, the eighth, she walked to Roslin Castle and back—a distance of seventeen miles, "a great part of it very hilly." Most of the rest of the week she was kept indoors by cold, stormy weather, but on Sunday she walked to Holyrood before dinner and to Stockbridge and back afterwards. Then on Monday, May 13, to pass the time before she could take the oath, she set out on a week's trip to Glasgow through the Trossachs—by boat from Newhaven to Stirling, but the rest of the way on foot—a distance of 170 miles in one week, "having set out on Monday at twelve o'clock, and returned at 1. The next Monday," as she wrote in her journal.[37]

Meanwhile Hazlitt too had been to Glasgow. Through the efforts of his friend Sheridan Knowles he had been invited to deliver two lectures at the Andersonian Institution there. He gave the first, on Shakespeare and Milton, on Monday evening, May 6; the second, on Thomson and Burns, on Monday, the thirteenth, the day Sarah set out from Edinburgh. Both lectures had, of course, been published some time before, but as George Combe reported to a friend he had "actually got his published lectures in MS. and means to read them, trusting to the public's ignorance of literature for escaping detection."[38]

The lectures were generally well received. The Glasgow *Herald* remarked that the first lecture "made a powerful impression upon an audience composed of some of the most distinguished characters and most respectable inhabitants of our city"; the *Chronicle* declared that the "sterling bullion of his matter" in the second lecture "might have entitled him to a manner more impassioned." However, the Tory *Sentinel* was not so well disposed; its reviewer branded Hazlitt as a Cockney, complained of his "bad voice" and "intolerable pauses," observed that the second lecture was "very thinly attended," deplored the "tawdriness" of his treatment of Thomson and the harshness of his remarks when he dealt with Wordsworth's criticism of Burns's morals. He concluded: ". . . we are sure we are speaking the sentiments of many when we say that 5 s. are too much for an old lecture read at

36. Ibid., p. 197.
37. Ibid., p. 209.
38. Letter to the Reverend David Welsh, May 10, 1822, in Charles Gibbon's *Life of George Combe*, 2 vols. I (London, 1878), 151–52.

the Surrey Institution."[39] Hazlitt's secret was out. Still, he was well paid for his reading: although he did not receive the hundred pounds which he had expected, he was, Sarah claimed, paid fifty-six pounds—as much as he normally earned for writing fifty-six pages of original material for the magazines.

While he was in Glasgow, Hazlitt went to the Tron Church to hear the celebrated "metaphysical divine" Dr. Chalmers preach (20:115). Then, the day after his second lecture, he and Knowles started out on a trip to the Highlands. They underwent a change of heart, however, when they found that they could not climb Ben Lomond because of the snow. And since he had no pressing reason for returning to Edinburgh, Hazlitt boarded the *City of Edinburgh* the next day, May 15, to sail to London.

Once there, he went directly to the Walkers' house. What happened then he recorded in the letters to "JSK" (Knowles) which form the third section of *Liber Amoris*. Sally was reticent at first, but eventually she relented. She had been upset because Hazlitt's son had shown some hostility toward her, but Hazlitt brought them together, and the boy apologized. When he saw that she had put the little statue of Napoleon back on his mantelpiece, he insisted that she keep it for herself. Later he talked earnestly with her, and she was demure as could be. Yet when it came time for her to go downstairs, she refused to kiss him goodnight.

Somehow that was too much. All the frustration of his weeks in Edinburgh suddenly burst in a paroxysm of rage: he tore from his neck the locket containing a strand of her hair, he "dashed the little Buonaparte on the ground, and stamped upon it," he "shrieked curses on her name, and on her false love" (9:145). Sally's parents and the other lodgers rushed to his door. "She's in there! He has got her in there!" Mrs. Walker wailed. He threw open the door and rushed from the house shouting, "She has murdered me!—She has destroyed me for ever! She has doomed my soul to perdition!"

But once outside the house "the desolation and the darkness became greater, more intolerable"; "the eddying violence of [his] passion" drove him back (9:146). He met Sally's father, to whom he told the whole story of his frustrating courtship. Walker apparently had had no inkling of what was going on, and he seemed genuinely distressed. He told Hazlitt, however, that he would not object to Sally's marrying him (9:148).

The next day Hazlitt felt "almost as sailors must do after a violent storm

39. See *Memoirs*, 2:41–42; and Stanley Jones, "Hazlitt as Lecturer: Three Unnoticed Contemporary Accounts," *Études Anglaises* 15 (1962):15–24.

over-night, that has subsided toward daybreak" (9:148). That evening, deciding that he should go down to Winterslow for a while, he gathered the fragments of his locket and the statue, wrapped them in a piece of paper on which he wrote *"Pieces of a broken heart, to be kept in remembrance of the unhappy. Farewell"* (9:148), and sent them to her. And the following day, as he prepared to leave the house, he wrote her a note asking if she would accept copies of *The Vicar of Wakefield, The Man of Feeling,* and *Nature and Art*[40] in exchange for three volumes of his own writings which he had given her.

That afternoon he found on his table a package containing several books which he had given her during their courtship. He asked her sister Betsey to return them to her, explaining that "it is only those of my own writing that I think unworthy of her."

At this Betsey "raised herself on the other side of the table where she stood, as if inspired by the genius of the place, and said, 'AND THOSE ARE THE ONES THAT SHE PRIZES THE MOST!'" (9:149).

Immediately the poor man's hopes soared again; he was "childish, wanton, drunk with pleasure." In his elation he gave Betsey a pound note as a reward. He dropped his plans for the trip to Winterslow and stayed on at the Walkers', although he saw nothing of Sally for several days.

Then one evening he called her up to his room. When she appeared, he insisted that she sit in his arm-chair while he "knelt to her adoring" (9:150). But she would give him no encouragement. "I always told you I had no affection for you," she said, and she complained of his "exposing [her] to the whole house" during his recent outburst (9:150–51). She had, she admitted, been "guilty of improprieties," but he had repeated them "not only in the house, but out of it; so that it has come to my ears from various quarters, as if I was a light character" (9:151). Yet after a while she relented enough to let him hold her hands.

He tried now to learn who had replaced him in her affections. Was it Tomkins? No, he had stayed at the house for only a short time. "Well, then, was it Mr. ———?" After some hesitation, and then faintly, she replied, "No," and added that "she could make no more confidences." But she insisted that she had "no tie" at present, that she did not "intend ever to marry at all" (9:152).

Would she be friends with him then?—She could not promise. On her own terms?—She would make no terms. And suddenly she left him.

40. In an undated letter of this period Hazlitt wrote to Taylor and Hessey, asking them to send him copies of these three novels "prettily bound" (*Four Generations,* 1:194).

Once again Hazlitt was thrown into a frenzy, which he duly reported to Knowles:

> The cockatrice, I said, mocks me: so she has always done. The thought was a dagger to me. My head reeled, my heart recoiled within me. I was stung with scorpions; my flesh crawled; I was choked with rage; her scorn scorched me like flames; . . . I saw the tables, the chairs, the places where she stood or sat, empty, deserted, dead. I could not stay where I was; I had no one to go to but to the parent-mischief, the preternatural hag, that had "drugged this posset" of her daughter's charms and falsehood for me, and I went down and (such was my weakness and helplessness) sat with her for an hour, and talked with her of her daughter, and the sweet days we had passed together, and said I thought her a good girl, and believed that if there was no rival, she still had a regard for me at the bottom of her heart; and how I liked her all the better for her coy, maiden airs: and I received the assurance over and over that there was no one else; and that Sarah (they all knew) never staid five minutes with any other lodger, while with me she would stay by the hour together, in spite of all her father could say to her (what were her motives, was best known to herself!); and while we were talking of her, she came bounding into the room, smiling with smothered delight at the consummation of my folly and her own art; and I asked her mother whether she thought she looked as if she hated me, and I took her wrinkled, withered, cadaverous, clammy hand at parting, and kissed it. Faugh!
> (9:153–54)

So ended another chapter of the lugubrious story. Yet, with all his raging, Hazlitt behaved much as usual during his stay in London. Patmore, who saw him frequently, later wrote that he dined at least once at Haydon's house and once at the house of another friend, where he entertained the guests with gossipy anecdotes that he had picked up here and there. The two men called on John Hunt, again shut up at Coldbath Fields Prison, found him strolling about the sparse garden, then went to his cell, where he had hung Hazlitt's portrait of the old woman in the bonnet. Hazlitt was touched to find it there, and again he regaled his friends with anecdotes—this time of Jeffrey and Scott particularly, drawing on his Edinburgh experiences.[41]

But when he wrote to Patmore on May 30 aboard the steamer that was carrying him back to Scotland,[42] he insisted that he was truly beside himself with grief. "What have I suffered since I parted with you!" he began.

> A raging fire is in my heart and in my brain, that never quits me. . . . I can neither escape from her, nor from myself. . . . —I believe you thought me quite gay, vain,

---

41. Patmore, 3:20–27, 102–4.

42. In *Liber Amoris* the letter is dated only "Written in May." However, Hazlitt says in a postscript that he is mailing the letter from Scarborough, and he began his next letter, postmarked May 31: "I wrote yesterday from Scarborough."

insolent, half mad, the night I left the house—no tongue can tell the heaviness of heart I felt at that moment. No foot steps ever fell more slow, more sad than mine; for every step bore me farther from her, with whom my soul and every thought lingered. I had parted with her in anger, and each had spoken words of high disdain, not soon to be forgiven. Should I ever behold her again? Where go to live and die far from her?... I stopped, faultered, and was going to turn back once more to make a longer truce with wretchedness and patch up a hollow league with love, when the recollection of her words—"I always told you I had no affection for you"—steeled my resolution, and I determined to proceed. You see by this she always hated me, and only played with my credulity till she could find some one to supply the place of her unalterable attachment to *the little image*.

"I am a little, a very little better to-day," he continued. "Would it were quietly over; and that this misshapen form (made to be mocked) were hid out of the sight of cold, sullen eyes! The people about me even take notice of my dumb despair, and pity me. What is to be done? I cannot forget *her*; and I can find no other like what *she seemed*." But he was still not ready to acknowledge defeat. "I should wish you to call, if you can make an excuse, and see whether or no she is quite marble—whether I may go back again at my return, and whether she will see me and talk to me sometimes as an old friend. Suppose you were to call on M—— [i.e., Roscoe, Sally's brother-in-law] from me, and ask him what his impression is that I ought to do. But do as you think best. Pardon, pardon" (9:121–22).

Yet when he wrote to Patmore the next day, he was raging again, tormented now by suspicion that he had a new rival. "I wrote yesterday by Scarborough," he began,

to say that the iron had entered my soul—forever. I have since thought more profoundly about it than even before, & am convinced beyond a doubt that she is a regular lodging-house decoy, who leads a sporting life with every one who comes in succession, & goes different lengths according as she is urged or inclined. This is why she will not marry, because she hankers after this sort of thing. She has an itch for being slabbered & felt, & this she is determined to gratify upon system, & has a pride in making fools of the different men she indulges herself with & at the same time can stop short from the habit of running the gauntlet with so many. The impudent whore to taunt me that "she had always told me she had no affection for me" as a salvo for her new lewdness—& how did she tell me this, sitting in my lap, twining herself round me, letting me enjoy her through her petticoats, looking as if she would faint with tenderness & modesty, admitting all sorts of indecent liberties & declaring "however she might agree to her own ruin, she would never consent to bring disgrace upon her family," as if this last circumstance only prevented her, & all this without any affection—is it not to write whore, hardened, impudent, heartless whore after her name? Her look is exactly this. It is that of suppressed lewdness

& conscious & refined hypocrisy, instead of innocence or timidity or real feeling. She never looks at you, nor has a single involuntary emotion For any one to suffer what she has done from me, without feeling it, is unnatural & monstrous. A common whore would take a liking to a man who had shewn the same love of her & to whom she had granted the same incessant intimate favours. But her heart is seared, as her eyes gloat, with habitual hypocrisy & *lech* for the mere act of physical contact with the other sex. "Do you let any one else do so," I said to her when I was kissing her. "No, not now," was her answer—that is, because there was nobody in the house to do it with her. While the coast was clear, I had it all my own way: but the instant Tomkins came, she made a dead set at him, ran breathless upstairs before him, blushed when his foot was heard, watched for him in the passage, & he going away, either tired of her or without taking the hint, she has taken up in my absence with this quack-doctor, a tall, stiff-backed able bodied half blackguard that she can make use of & get rid of when she pleases. The bitch wants a *stallion*, & hates a lover, that is, any one who talks of affection, & is prevented by fondness or regard for her from going or attempting to go all lengths. I at present think she liked me to a certain extent as a friend, but still I was not good enough for her. She wanted to be courted not as a bride, but as a common wench. "Why, could we not go on as we were, & never mind about the word, *forever*?" She would not agree to "a tie," because she would leave herself open to any new pretender that answered her purpose better, & *bitch* me without ceremony or mercy, & then say—"she had always told me she had no regard for me"—as a rea[son for] transferring her obscenities (for such they were without [doubt] from) me to her next favourite. Her addicting herself to Tomkins was endurable, because he was a gentlemanly sort of man, but her putting up with this prick of a fellow, merely for bone & measurement & gross manners, sets me low indeed. The monster of lust & duplicity! I that have spared her so often because I hoped better things of her & to make her my future wife, & to be refused in order that she may be the trull of an itinerant apothecary, a fellow that she made a jest of & despised, till she had nobody else in the way to pamper her body & supply her morning's meal of studied wantonness. "That way, madness lies." I do not feel as if I can ever get the better of it: I have sucked in the poison of her seeming modesty & tenderness too long. I thought she was dreaming of her only love, & worshipped her equivocal face, when she wanted only a codpiece & I ought to have pulled up her petticoats & felt her. But I could not insult the adored of my heart, to find out her real character; & you see what has become of me. I was wrong at first in fancy[ing] a wench at a lodging house to be a Vestal, merely for her demure looks. The only chance I had was the first day: after that, my hands were tied & I became the fool of Love. Do you know the only thing that soothes or melts me is the idea of taking my little boy whom I can no longer support & wandering through the country as beggars, not through the wide world, for I cannot leave the country where she is. Oh God! oh God! The slimy, varnished, marble fiend to bring me to this when three kind words would have saved me.

But even as he leveled the charges, he longed to refute them, or at worst to have them proved beyond doubt: "Yet if I only knew she was a whore, *flagrante delicto*, it would wean me from her, & burst my chain. Could you ascertain this fact for me, by any means or through any person (E. for example) who might try her as a lodger? I should not like her to be seduced by elaborate means, but if she gave up as a matter of course, I should then be no longer the wretch I am or the God I might have been, but what I was before, poor plain W.H."

Hazlitt's imagination was diseased, his mind close to distraction. To compound his agony, he found, when he arrived back in Edinburgh, that the divorce suit was at a standstill. During his absence Sarah had returned from Glasgow, prepared to take the oath of calumny on May 24. She had learned from John Gray, however, that Hazlitt had appointed a solicitor named Prentice to defend him and that the oath-taking had been postponed for three more weeks in order to allow time for Prentice to prepare his case. "So here I am," she wrote sadly in her journal, "lonely, in a strange place, my quarter's money and the four pounds all gone, and obliged to borrow; instead of having the £37–10–0 repaid me to lay by, and money in my pocket for present expences, as Mr. Hazlitt repeatedly promised: and can neither see or hear from my boy, who is my dearest comfort!" Adam Bell heightened her misery by telling her that her husband was "at variance at present" with Sally, "as she had told him she preferred another man." Bell told her, too, that "he had seen some passages of her letters, and they were such low, vulgar, milliners or servant wenches sentimentality, that he wondered Mr. Hazlitt could endure such stuff." He advised her to settle in Edinburgh with her son and "take about eight young ladies at a high price, to instruct which would be both profitable and respectable."[43] But Sarah would have none of the scheme, and on Friday, May 31, having received five pounds each from Bell and William Ritchie, she set off on another walking trip to the Highlands.[44]

Hazlitt stayed on in Edinburgh. Though he yearned to be near Sally, he was still torn by doubts. He wrote to Patmore:

> try to ascertain for me whether I had better return there or not, as soon as this affair is over. I cannot give her up without an absolute certainty..Only however sound the matter by saying for instance that you are desired to get me a lodging, & that you believe I should prefer being there to any where else. You may say that the affair of the divorce is over and that I am gone on a tour of the Highlands. Ascertain if that wretched rival is there still. I am almost satisfied she is a wretched creature

43. *Journals*, pp. 209–10.
44. On this tour she covered 112 miles. Understandably, she complained on July 13 that she had worn out all her shoes but a pair of light ones (*Journals*, p. 243).

herself, but my only hope of happiness rests on the alternative. Ours was the sweetest friendship—oh! might the delusion be renewed that I might die in it! If there is any insolence—TRY HER through some one (any one) E. for example, who will satisfy my soul I have lost only a lovely frail one that I was not like to gain by true love. Oh! that I was once back to London. I am going to see Knowles to get him to go with me to the Highlands, & talk about *her*. I shall be back Thursday week, to appear in court *pro formâ* the next day, & then for Heaven or for Hell.

He concluded: "Send me a line about my little boy."

When he wrote again on June 9 he was calmer. Francis Jeffrey ("to whom I did a tale unfold") had brought him a hundred pounds "to give me time to recover." [45] And a letter from Patmore had cheered him, since Patmore was convinced that Sally was a good girl "if there is goodness in human nature." At the same time he had promised to find someone to test her virtue, and Hazlitt hoped that his doubts would soon be resolved.

Yet a hint in Patmore's letter that Hazlitt would really like to break off the connection put him on the defensive:

You say I want to get rid of her. I hope you are more right in your conjectures about her than in this about me—Oh no! believe it, I love her as I do my own soul, my heart is wedded to her, be she what she may, & I would not hesitate a moment between her and an angel from Heaven. I grant all you say about my self tormenting madness; but has it been without cause? Has she not refused me again & again with scorn & abhorrence, after going all lengths with a man for whom she disclaims all affection, and what security can I have for her continence with others, who will not be restrained by feelings of delicacy towards her, & whom she must have preferred to me for their very grossness? "She can make no more confidences!"—These words ring forever in my ears, & will be my death-watch.

Once more he had been rejected. Soon he was wallowing in self-pity. "Who is there so low as me?" he asked.

Who is there besides, after the homage I have paid her & the caresses she has lavished on me, so vile, so filthy, so abhorrent to love, to whom such an indignity could have happened? When I think of this, (& I think of it forever, except when I read your letters), the air I breathe stifles me. I am pent up in burning, impotent desires which can find no vent or object. I am hated, repulsed, bemocked by all I love. I cannot stay in any place, & find no rest or intermission from the thought of her contempt & ingratitude. I can do nothing. What is the use of all I have done? . . . My state is that I feel I shall never lie again at night nor rise up of a morning in peace, nor ever behold my little boy's face with pleasure while I live,—unless I am restored to her favour. Instead of that delicious feeling I had when she was heavenly-kind to me, & my heart

45. According to Sarah, Hazlitt told her that he "squeezed £100 out of Jeffrey, like so many drops of blood" (*Journals*, p. 236).

softened & melted in its own tenderness & her sweetness, I am now inclosed in a
dungeon of despair. The sky is marble like my thoughts, nature is dead without me as
hope is within me, no object can give me one gleam of satisfaction now or the prospect
of it in time to come. . . . I wake with her by my side, not as my sweet bedfellow but
as the corpse of my love, without a heart in her, cold, insensible or struggling from
me; & the worm gnaws me & the sting of unrequited love & the canker of a hopeless,
endless sorrow. I have lost the taste of my food by feverish anxiety, and my tea which
used to refresh me when I got up has no moisture in it. Oh! cold, solitary, sepulchral
breakfasts, compared to those which I made when she had been standing an hour by
my side, my Eve, my guardian-angel, my wife, my sister, my sweet friend, my all,
& had blest a wretch with her cherub kisses! Ah! what I suffer only shews what I
have felt before.

He added in a postscript: "I would give a thousand worlds to believe her
any thing but what I suppose. I love her, Heaven knows." Then: "You say
I am to try her after she agrees to have me, No; but I hate her for this, that
she refuses me. The oath is to be taken (God willing) to-morrow. Oh! let
me be free that I may *not* make her an offer. The hideous little hypocritical
anomaly! . . . I'm mad! So much for sentiment."

He had abandoned his plan to tour the Highlands with Knowles; instead
he was going back to Renton "to see if I can work a little in the three weeks
before it will be over, if all goes well." He added: "Tell Colburn to send the
Table talk to [Jeffrey], 92 George Street, Edinburgh, unless he is mad, &
wants to ruin me & the book."

For the second volume of *Table-Talk*, much of it the product of his
earlier stay at Renton, had just been published, and he was still hoping to have
it reviewed in the *Edinburgh*. In recent weeks he had written only the
article "Williams's Views in Greece" for the May *London Magazine*.
"Pictures at Burleigh House," which had appeared in the April *New
Monthly* as "Table Talk, No. 4," had been finished at Renton.

Neither was a major effort. "Pictures at Burleigh House," the first of
his accounts of the picture galleries of England, began with a melancholy
contrast between his feelings during his recent visit to the gallery and those
of his two earlier visits more than twenty years ago, when he "could not
write a line— . . . could not draw a stroke . . . was no better than a changeling" (10:63). But he could then enjoy the beauties of the place as he could
no longer do. And he proceeded to describe the paintings at Burleigh House,
leaving the reader to guess what had robbed him of his happiness.

The review of Hugh Williams's water colors on exhibition at the Calton
Convening Rooms in Edinburgh was quite different. Hazlitt approved of
the paintings, but was more interested in mocking the puzzled Scots who

came to see them. "Mr. Williams," he wrote, ". . . has stretched out under the far-famed Calton Hill, and in the eye of Arthur's Seat, fairy visions of the fair land of Greece, that Edinburgh belles and beaux repair to see with cautious wonder and well-regulated delight. . . . There played the NINE on immortal lyres, and here sit the critical but admiring Scottish fair, with the catalogue in their hands, reading the quotations from Lord Byron's verses with liquid eyes and lovely vermillion lips—would that they spoke English, or any thing but Scotch!" But his mockery soon turned to scorn: "Poor is this irony! Vain the attempt to reconcile Scottish figures with Attic scenery!" (10:171). Such remarks perhaps served to relieve his testy mood, but they were bound, sooner or later, to bring reprisals.

Even the seventeen essays contained in the new volume of *Table-Talk* did not measure up to the standard of the first series.[46] Instead of observing life complacently, savoring its paradoxes, he now looked inward; his mind was absorbed with its own concerns, and he recurred constantly—often defensively—to himself. He even spared his usual butts; except for passing thrusts at Byron, Gifford, and John Wilson Croker of the *Quarterly Review* in "On the Aristocracy of Letters," the essays were almost free from personal attacks.

Not all the essays were morbidly introspective; some were random gossip —but gossip based on his own recollections of conversations heard (and he remarked that he liked to listen unless the topic was congenial) at the Southampton Coffee House (in "On Coffee-house Politicians") or of evenings at the theater (in "Whether Actors Ought to Sit in Boxes"). There were essays on literary subjects too—"On the Aristocracy of Letters" and "On Patronage and Puffing," for example—but they also tended to center around Hazlitt's own experience as a writer, often told with some bitterness. Even the memorable essay "On Familiar Style," fine as it was, amounted, in effect, to a defense of his own style, as did the passage on literary style in "On Effeminacy of Character." Never before had he depended so much on his own memory, so little on his reading or the experience of others.

46. Only four of the essays had been published previously: "On a Landscape of Nicholas Poussin" in the *London Magazine* and "On Milton's Sonnets," "On Great and Little Things," and "On Going a Journey" in the *New Monthly*. Of the remaining thirteen, "Whether Actors Ought to Sit in Boxes," "On the Disadvantages of Intellectual Superiority," "On Patronage and Puffing," "On the Knowledge of Character," and "On the Fear of Death" were listed among those written at Renton in a letter to Patmore in March (*Memoirs*, 2:68); and "On the Picturesque and the Ideal" is dated August 2–28, 1821, by A. C. Goodyear (8:372). The others were probably written at Winterslow during the summer and autumn of 1821.

The most obviously introspective essays were those which purported to be analytical. There were exceptions: "On Criticism" was a mine of solid information on what criticism should and should not be; "Of Corporate Bodies" trenchantly anatomized the stultifying effects of group thinking. But in "Why Distant Objects Please" he drew repeatedly on nostalgic memories of his lost youth: visits to the Montpelier tea gardens, watering the kitchen garden at Wem, the taste of barberries in winter in New England. In "On the Fear of Death" he recalled his little son's death and anticipated his own:

> If I had lived *indeed*, I should not care to die. But I do not like a contract of pleasure broken off unfulfilled, a marriage with joy unconsummated, a promise of happiness rescinded. My public and private hopes have been left a ruin, or remain only to mock me. I would wish them to be re-edified. I should like to see some prospect of good to mankind, such as my life began with. I should like to leave some sterling work behind me. I should like to have some friendly hand to consign me to the grave. On these conditions I am ready, if not willing, to depart. I could then write on my tomb—GRATEFUL AND CONTENTED. (8:325–26) [47]

In "On Intellectual Superiority" he seems to be talking about himself most of the time—and in a plaintive strain, as when he refers to a landlord and his daughter who are quick to condemn a writer lodging with them when his writing is attacked (8:284), or to "men of letters, artists, and others" who "are no match for chamber maids, or wenches at lodging-houses" (8:287–88), or to his surprising desire "to pass for a good-humoured fellow" (8:283), or to his even more surprising admission that he "like[s] to be pointed out in the street, or to hear people ask . . . *which is Mr. H——?*" (8:286). And in "On the Knowledge of Character" he focuses his attention even more on his immediate problems when he speaks of a landlady who increases a lodger's bill after he has given her daughter a present (8:309); or of "the greatest hypocrite" he ever knew, "a little, demure, pretty, modest-looking girl, with eyes timidly cast upon the ground, and an air

47. In the original manuscript of the essay Hazlitt added: "I want an eye to cheer me, a hand to guide me, a breast to lean on; all which I shall never have, but shall stagger into my grave without them, old before my time, unloved and unlovely, unless—. I would have some creature love me before I die. Oh! for the parting hand to ease the fall" (*Memoirs*, 2:11). Hazlitt may have omitted the passage from *Table-Talk* because he had decided to use it (in altered form) in *Liber Amoris* (See 9:114). He also omitted a passage describing his father's death (8:373) and a final paragraph suggesting that "we die every moment of our lives" (8:374). In "A Manuscript Addition to Hazlitt's Essay 'On the Fear of Death'" (*MLN* 55 [1940]: 45–47), Stewart C. Wilcox cites a letter from Colburn to Hazlitt indicating that this last passage was omitted because of a delay in the proof.

soft as enchantment" (8:305); or, in a contrasting mood, of the validity of love at first sight.[48] He certainly had himself in mind when he wrote in the same essay:

> I know a person to whom it has been objected as a disqualification for friendship, that he never shakes you cordially by the hand. I own this is a damper to sanguine and florid temperaments, who abound in these practical demonstrations and "compliments extern." The same person, who testifies the least pleasure at meeting you, is the last to quit his seat in your company, grapples with a subject in conversation right earnestly, and is, I take it, backward to give up a cause or a friend. Cold and distant in appearance, he piques himself on being the king of *good haters*, and a no less zealous partisan. The most phlegmatic constitutions often contain the most inflammable spirits—as fire is struck from the hardest flints. (8:306)

These are personal essays indeed—painfully personal. Hazlitt himself complains, still in "On the Knowledge of Character":

> What is it to me that I can write these TABLE-TALKS? It is true I can, by a reluctant effort, rake up a parcel of half-forgotten observations, but they do not float on the surface of my mind, nor stir it with any sense of pleasure, nor even of pride. Others have more property in them than I have: *they* may reap the benefit, I have only had the pain. Otherwise, they are to me as if they had never existed: nor should I know that I had ever thought at all, but that I am reminded of it by the strangeness of my appearance, and my unfitness for every thing else. (8:305)[49]

Inevitably the pain comes across to the reader and mars his enjoyment of the essays. Instead of sharing in a zestful session of table talk, he is subjected, too often, to the sentimental reverie of one who is begging for sympathy.

48. The passage is quoted above, p. 269. Howe (8:371) regards the contrast between this passage and the remarks about "the greatest hypocrite" as evidence of "Hazlitt's practice of 'writing in' passages in proof." Yet Hazlitt's letters to Patmore reveal that he could leap from protestations of love for Sally to bitter accusation—and back again— within a single letter. Howe also remarks a significant difference in the original wording of the "love at first sight" passage. In the first and second editions of *Table-Talk* it read: "An argument immediately draws off my attention from the prettiest woman in the room. I accordingly succeed better in argument—than in love!" (8:372). In later versions of the essay these two sentences are expressed in the third person; that is, the essay was more subjective, when originally published, than it now appears.

49. There are significant differences between this passage and the similar one in "On the Pleasure of Painting" quoted above, p. 273. In the earlier passage Hazlitt complained that he found "not much pleasure in writing these Essays," but admitted that he met "now and then . . . with a phrase that I like, or a thought that strikes me as a true one"; in the later, that he experienced no "sense of pleasure" or "even of pride." In the earlier passage also he professed to be bored by the tediousness of the process and declared that the essays lost "their gloss and relish" as a result; in the later one, he was "reluctant" even to begin the essays and found nothing but "pain" in the process.

Reviewers were not inclined to offer such sympathy. Most of them paid no attention to the new volume. Francis Jeffrey failed to heed Hazlitt's appeal for a notice in the *Edinburgh*, and the *Quarterly* ignored the book. But *Blackwood's*, after its long armed truce,[50] struck again. In their March issue they had seemed ready to bury the hatchet. The author of "London Chit-Chat, 11" had remarked: "The review of [Scott's] the Pirate, in Taylor and Hessey's Magazine, was written by Hazlitt, and is considered here to be a delightful piece of criticism. It is much to be wished that he and the other critics *militant*, would more often abate their mutual asperity, and look after the excellences, as well as the defects of authors opposed to them, in literary and political party." And in the first of the celebrated "Noctes Ambrosianae" the editor had gone so far as to say, "Oh, Hazlitt's a real fellow in his small way. He has more sense in his little finger, than many who laugh at him have in their heads, but he is bothering too long at that *table-talk*." In the course of the next five months, however, most of their good will evaporated, and they devoted ten pages of their August issue to a slashing review of *Table-Talk*. "The whole surface of these volumes," the critic charged, "is one gaping sore of wounded and festering vanity; and, in short . . . our table-talker is rather AN ULCER than A MAN." And later: "his prevailing topics are THREE;—first, the stupidity of the world, in not acknowledging his merits; second, the absurdity of those prejudices, which lead mankind in general to approve of the literary productions of men born gentlemen, and educated like gentlemen . . . ; thirdly, the shocking anti-cockneyism of Blackwood's Magazine and the Quarterly Review." Then, as if to prove his own lack of prejudice, he concluded: "By the way, Hazlitt shewed great want of trap by not coming to sup with us at Ambrose's during his late northern progress. We could not have supposed him to be so decidedly a spoon. Before we had always given him credit for playing a good knife and fork."

Eventually Hazlitt's allies came to the defense of *Table-Talk*. Yet even they hinted that the essays were often self-conscious. The author of the review in the *Monthly Review* for May, 1823, denied that the style of the essays was truly conversational. "It is," he argued, "rather a series of soliloquies, admirably declaimed, but declaimed for admiration;—a set of florid

50. For the past three years *Blackwood's* had scarcely mentioned Hazlitt's name. In no. 5 and 6 of the "Cockney School" series (April and October, 1819) and in "Ancient National Melodies, No. 1" (December, 1821), they had aimed only by-blows at him in the course of attacks on Leigh Hunt. In this last article, however, they had referred to Hazlitt's "Stable-Talk," although they were themselves handling the sale of the volume in Edinburgh.

speeches, which, without affecting the formality of a lecture, are still made to be overheard. . . . [The] essays are meditations, rhapsodies, harangues, any thing but chit-chat, any thing but 'Table-Talk.' Still a bottle with a false label may contain good wine; and a misdirected letter may contain pleasing information." And in the following month the *London Magazine*, which had already reviewed the first volume of *Table-Talk*, was of two minds about the second. "Each essay," the reviewer declared,

> is the pure gathering of the writer's thoughts upon the subject of which it treats; and if it be not always strictly just in its deductions, and complete in its conclusions, it is sure to strike out some bold and original thinking, and to give some vigorous truths in stern and earnest language. The style of the book is singularly nervous and direct, and seems to aim at mastering its subject by dint of mere hard hitting. There is no such thing as manoeuvring for a blow. The language strikes out, and if the intention is not fulfilled, the blow is repeated until the subject falls. Those readers who like the graces of a dancing dazzling style will be disappointed in Mr. Hazlitt's pages; for his sentences have no "limbs and outward flourishes;" they are determined bodies only! His periods do not chime round like a peal of well-ordered bells; but they go right on, until they run against a full stop.

But Hazlitt had too much on his mind to care how his essays were received. During his second stay at Renton he was so distraught by his anguish that he could write nothing. "Othello's occupation, alas! is gone," he wrote Patmore on June 18. He was "musing over my only subject . . . seeking for rest & finding none." He had "hit upon a truth that if true explains all & satisfies me, I hope forever. This is it. You will by this time probably know something from having called & seen how the land lies that will make you a judge how far I am stepped into madness in my conjectures. If you think me right, all engines set at work at once that punish ungrateful woman." "By this time," he continued, "you probably know enough to know whether this following solution [situation?] is *in rerum natura* at No. 9 S.B." Then he copied down, as he remembered it, the conversation which he had heard in the Walkers' kitchen the night before he first left for Edinburgh.[51] "I ask you candidly," he wrote, "whether on hearing this I ought not to have walked quietly out of the house & never have thought of it again. She also said to me the other evening when I told her (I don't know what), that she had heard enough of that sort of conversation. No wonder, when she had heard for years this kind of kitchen-stuff." He returned then to the subject of his supposed new rival:

51. See above, p. 305.

Who do you think this hero, this Hercules, this plenipotentiary was? Why, I recollect the person who once tumbled over me half-drunk was this very Griffiths who keeps possession of his ten-shilling Garrett, in spite of an offer of marriage from *me* & a hundred guineas a year for his apartment. Can there be a doubt, when the mother dilates in this way on codpieces & the son replies in measured terms, that the girl runs mad for size. Miss is small, & exaggerates dimensions by contrast. Misjudging fair! Yet it is she whom I spared a hundred times from witnessing this consummation devoutly wished by the whole kitchen in chorus, after she has been rubbing against me, hard at it for an hour together; [and I] thinking to myself, "The girl is a good girl," &c. & means no harm—it is only [her fond]ness for me, not her lech after a man.

One moment he raged: "I think she would make the most delicious whore alive, but, by God, I do not stomach her as a wife in my present humour— you will say circumstances." The next, he relented: "Oh no! the very thought that she may have in spite of all appearances a true & tender regard for me, *namely*, that she would have me & therefore does not *hate* me, makes my heart glow with its old tenderness & melt in heavenly sweetness toward the little cherub."

Once again he issued orders to Patmore: "Don't go to Roscoe, nor let me have any more formal refusals, till I am quite free at any rate & then, if she gives herself airs, she must be *tried*. But I think you might go & take away the MSS. & if you see her, say 'You think it is a pity we should part otherwise than friends, for that you know I had the truest regard for her, & that I should never think of any other lodging, but that I feared she had a dislike to seeing me there' in consequence of my past misconduct." Then: "I have hit it. *Say that I shall want it very little the next year, as I shall be abroad for some months, but that I wish to keep it on to have a place to come to when I am in London & not to seem to have parted in anger, when I feel nothing but friendship & esteem.* If you get a civil answer to this, take it for me, & send me word." Finally he resorted once more to testing her virtue: "Otherwise, get E. or any body to see what flesh she is made of, & send her to hell if possible. She may then, you know, take compassion on me, as Killigrew's cousin said. I have half a mind to come up in the Steam-Boat, to watch the operation. Learn first whether the great man of Penman-Mawr [i.e., Griffiths] is still there. You may do this by asking after my hamper of books which were in the back parlour. . . . Hint that I am free and that I have had a severe illness." A postscript reads: "Alas, alas for me! Keep these letters. Above all, use your own discretion. Treat me as a child. Q. a Child Harold." [52]

52. Concerning "Killigrew's cousin" in *Memoirs of Count Grammont* see 8:200. The

In due time he returned to Edinburgh, where he learned that Sarah had taken the oath of calumny on Friday, June 14. Her patience was practically exhausted. The oath-taking itself had been an ordeal, Adam Bell had been making a nuisance of himself,[53] she had been violently ill, and her appeals for money had been ignored. Now young William's holidays were about to begin, and there was no one in London to receive him. "I fretted that he should be left there," she wrote in her journal, "and thought he would be very uneasy if they had not sent him to Winterslow, and feel quite unhappy and forsaken." [54]

She determined to see Hazlitt at any cost, and on Monday, June 17, she went to the Bells' house when they said he would be there. When he failed to appear, she called at his lodgings twice, then finally met him by chance on the street. He gave her ten pounds and promised to send more soon. She "asked about the child, and he said he was going to write that night to Mr. John Hunt about him; so that the poor little fellow is really fretting, and thinking himself neglected." [55] She offered to call at Hazlitt's lodgings that evening to discuss their financial arrangements, but he insisted that they must not be seen together. Yet at least she was ten pounds richer, and the next morning she sensibly took a canal boat to Glasgow, where she crossed over to Ireland for ten days.

Hazlitt too was concerned about his son. On or about June 20 he wrote to Patmore: "Will you call at Mr. Dawson's school, Hunter Street, & tell the little boy I'll write to him or see him on Saturday morning? Poor little fellow!" But he was more concerned about himself. "The deed is done," he told Patmore,

> & I am virtually a free man. Mrs. H. took the oath on Friday (they say *manfully*) & nothing remains but to wait a week or two longer for the sentence of divorce. What had I better do in these circumstances? I daren't write to her [Sally], I dare not write to her father, or else I would. She has shot me through with poisoned arrows, & I think another "winged wound" would finish me. It is a pleasant sort of balm she has left in my heart. One thing I agree with you in, it will remain there forever, but yet not very long. It festers & consumes me. If it were not for my little boy, whose face I see struck blank at the news, & looking through the world for pity & meeting with contempt, I should soon settle the question by my death. That is the only thought

contrast between Hazlitt's original letters and the published versions is nowhere more striking than when one compares the passage above with the rhapsodic lines which he substituted for it in letter 10 of *Liber Amoris* (9:129–31).

53. Bell had first indulged in drunken accusations and insults, then apologies and amorous advances (*Journals*, pp. 222–23).

54. *Journals*, p. 227.   55. Ibid., p. 228.

that brings my wandering reason to an anchor, that excites the least interest, or gives
me fortitude to bear up against what I am doomed to feel for the ungrateful. Otherwise, I am dead to all but the agony of what I have lost. She was my life—it is gone
from me, & I am grown spectral.

Then, after a good deal more in a similar strain, he shifted suddenly to: "Do
you know I think G. (the fellow in the back parlour) is the very man her
mother was commending to her daughter's lecherous thoughts (if she has
any) that night in the seven inch conversation: for I recollect he tumbled
over me one night half drunk, which was one of the circumstances related
as a proof of his huge prowess. Do you think this might not sink into the
nun's mind in my absence . . . ?" But soon he was lyrical: "The gates of
paradise once were open to me, & I blushed to enter but with the golden
keys of love! I would die, but her lover, my love of her, ought not to die.
When I am dead, who will love her as I have done? If she should be in
misfortune, who will comfort her? When she is old, who will look in her
face, & bless her?" And finally: "Would there be any harm in speaking to
Roscoe *confidentially* to know if he thinks it would be worth while to make
her an offer the instant I am free—or suppose you try the 100£ a year
whenever the apartment [is vacant.]"

A few days later, on June 25, he was rehearsing the whole affair from
beginning to end: "I was very well as a stop-gap, but I was to be nothing
more. . . . I thought her warmth was reserved for the *little image*, till I saw
her always running upstairs with [Tomkins]. . . . It was then my mad
proceedings commenced." He revived the old accusations: she is "a common
lodging-house decoy"; he might, he believes, "have had her in the *sporting-
line*"; she is a "cruel, heartless destroyer."

But at the thought of seeing her again, he resumed his scheming:

> If Roscoe's answer is positive & final, it is plain she hates me, because I neglected
> certain opportunities, & has got some one to supply my inattentions. In that case, I
> intreat you to get some one to work to ascertain for me, without loss of time, whether
> she is a common sporter, or not. Nothing else but the knowledge of her being common
> can reconcile me to myself, after what has passed.—It has occurred to me that as
> Roscoe was thought by the family to be like the bust of Buonaparte, it might be a
> brother of his: & that in these circumstances the affair has been renewed. If that were
> the case, I should be happy even to lose her for her heart's love: but to any one else
> (except by way of learning what she is) I will not part with her, to that I have made
> up my mind.—You don't know what I suffer or you would not be so severe upon
> me. My death will I hope satisfy every one before long.

Yet he confessed that he had written her "a very quiet, rational letter, begging pardon & professing reform for the future & all that." It read:

> *Evil to them that evil think*, is an old saying; and I have found it a true one. I have
> ruined myself by my unjust suspicions of you. Your sweet friendship was the balm
> of my life; and I have lost it, I fear for ever, by one fault and folly after another.
> What would I give to be restored to the place in your esteem, which, you assured me,
> I held only a few months ago! Yet I was not contented, but did all I could to torment
> myself and harass you by endless doubts and jealousy. Can you not forget and for-
> give the past, and judge of me by my conduct in future? Can you not take all my
> follies in the lump, and say like a good, generous girl, "Well, I'll think no more of
> them?" In a word, may I come back, and try to behave better? A line to say so would
> be an additional favour to so many already received by
>
> Your obliged friend,
And sincere well-wisher.
>
> (9:132–33)

But Sally ignored the appeal, and Hazlitt wrote in a postscript to his letter
to Patmore: "I have no answer from her. I *wish* you to call on Roscoe in
confidence to say that I intend to make her an offer of marriage, & that I
will write to her father to that purpose the instant I am free (next Friday
week) & to ask him whether he thinks it would be to any purpose, & what he
would advise me to do." At the last minute he squeezed in two other after-
thoughts: "Write for God's sake to let me know the worst" and "There has
been another delay (pro forma) of ten days."

On Sunday, the twenty-ninth, he received a note from his wife stating
that she had returned from Ireland with only four shillings, sixpence, in
her pocket. She enclosed a letter from their son, sent to her because the boy
did not know how to reach his father. That afternoon Hazlitt called at
Sarah's lodgings with ten pounds, but made it clear that he did not feel
obliged to underwrite her trips about the countryside. Again the meeting
ended in a squabble, with Sarah defending her expenditures, complaining of
his treatment, and assuring him that she was putting up with considerable
inconvenience for his sake, Hazlitt vindicating himself as best he could.[56]

He was on the defensive again when he wrote to Patmore on July 3.
Patmore had intimated in a letter that Sally was repelled by Hazlitt's
"outrageous conduct," and in reply Hazlitt regaled him once again with an
account of "the ambiguity of her situation with respect to me, kissing,
fondling a married man as if he were her husband," "the different *exposés* from
the conversations in the kitchen," and all the other familiar details. His
conduct had not been "outrageous," he protested, but "too gentle": "I did
not . . . follow up my advantage by any action which should say, 'I think

56. Ibid., p. 236.

you a whore,' or will lay aside the feeling of love & adoration I cherish for you to see whether you are not a Miss Wills." He spoke again of her "lust," her *"sporting-life."* "She was not by any means so horrified," he charged, "when in our first intimacy I asked to go to bed to her, & she only answered in her pretty, mincing way, 'It would be of no use if you did, for Betsey sleeps with me!' That I should have spared the traitress when I had her melting in my arms, after expressions like this & when I must know that if I did not, she would get somebody else that would, astonishes me when I look back to it."

The thought of his new rival set his imagination groveling:

> I see the young witch seated in another's lap, twining her serpent arms round him, her eyes glancing, & her cheeks on fire—Damn the unnatural hag. Oh! oh! why does not the hideous thought choke me? It is so, & she can make no more confidences. The gentleman who lodges in the old room is a fat, red faced, pot-bellied powdered gentleman of sixty—a pleasant successor! For what am I reserved? The bitch likes the nasty, the wilful, the antipathetic. That was why she pitched upon me, because I was out of the ordinary calculation of love. I'll say no more about that, however. You will say if I have only lost a Miss Wills, a girl that will be a bawd to elderly gentlemen, & that with her own person, enjoying the incongruity of the combination, what have I lost? If I had known it from the first, nothing—but as it is, I have lost her, myself, Heaven, & am doomed to Hell.

Again he raised the question of trying her virtue: "Where is E.? Why tarry the wheels of his chariot? Where, how, shall I be released from these horrors?" And in a postscript inserted at the head of the letter: "Get some one to try her, or I am destroyed for ever. To go & see E. there after [word or words illegible] her for the asking, would lift my soul from Hell. It would be sweet & full revenge. *You* may try her, if you like—a pot-belly & a slender waist match by contrast. Do they not? I shall soon be in town, & see. Pity me. . . ."

In another postscript to the same letter he dallied with the notion that his new rival might be her first love. "How would I lift up my hands in thankfulness to be so discarded, how would I fall down & worship him & her!" he exclaimed. But a moment later he started off in a new direction:

> The mother also said that while I was away, Sarah thought it best not to encourage a passion that perhaps might never be fulfilled. But she did not give over encouraging till the end of the five weeks. Q.E.D. If it is the same old fellow that was there before, I shall go mad. Besides, she kept repeating that she 'despised looks,' & objected to Tomkins as a new lodger, so that it takes time to insinuate the feeling of obscenity into her veins. Life is hideous to me, & death horrible. What shall I do? Oh! that I knew she was a strumpet, & that she knew I did.

Yet he seemed calm enough on Saturday, July 6, when he met his wife by chance at Dalkeith, where both had gone to see the duke of Buccleuch's house and paintings—she on foot and he in a gig with a friend named Henderson. They talked reasonably about their son and discussed plans for their return to London—preferably not on the same boat, he advised. He told her, she wrote in her journal, that he

> meant to go to Winterslow and try if he could write, for he had been so distracted the last five months that he could do nothing, and perhaps he would let me know another time what he had suffered. that he might also go to his mother's for a short time, and that he meant to take the child from school at the half quarter and take him with him, and that after the holidays at Christmas he should return to Mr. Dawson's again. Said he had not been to town. and that we had better have no communication at present, but that when it was over he would let me have the money as he could get it.[57]

Soon afterward he received from Patmore a letter dated July 4 giving the results of his second interview with Roscoe. "Now my dear H——," he cautioned, "let me entreat and adjure you to take what I have to tell you, *for what it is worth*—neither for less, nor more" (9:134). And he reported that neither Roscoe nor the Walkers would stand in the way of Sally's marriage to Hazlitt, but they felt she should make her own decision —and she seemed "at present indisposed to the marriage." However, he added, the family were "by no means *certain* that SHE may not, at some future period, consent to it; or they would, for her sake as well as their own, let you know as much flatly, and put an end to the affair at once" (9:135). Roscoe himself believed that it should be broken off immediately; however, he sympathized with both Hazlitt and Sally and had agreed to ask her if she would consent to see him again. All might still be well, Patmore believed, if only Hazlitt could maintain a "wise and prudent conduct," for at present Sally herself and all her family were frightened of Hazlitt and "as to what might be your treatment of her if she was your's" (9:136). Most heartening of all, however, was Roscoe's assurance that Sally was "a *good girl*, and *likely to make any man an excellent wife*.... And once, in speaking of *his* not being a fit person to set his face against 'marrying for love,' he added 'I did so myself, and out of that house; and I have had reason to rejoice at it ever since'" (9:136–37).

"I can only say that you have saved my life," Hazlitt wrote back on July 8. "If I make enemies with her now, I deserve to be hanged, drawn, &

57. Ibid., p. 239.

quartered. She is an angel from heaven, & you can not say I ever said to the contrary! . . . Do you know I mean to be the very *ideal* of a lodger when I get back, & if ever I am married, & if I don't make her the best bedfellow in the world, call me *cut*. . . . She is a saint, an angel, a love . . . ," he went on. "If she deceives me again, she kills me. . . . Bless her, may God bless her for not utterly disowning & destroying me!" And presently: "I have been thinking of her little face these two last days looking like a marble statue, as cold, as fixed & graceful as ever statue did, & I could not believe the lies I told of her. No, I think I'll never believe again that she will not be mine, for I think she was made on purpose for me." Then came a shocking revelation: "I had half begun a new amour, but it's all off, God bless you!" [58]

He was eagerly anticipating his return to London now. "How ought I to behave when I go back?" he asked Patmore. "I think not romantic, but mild & somewhat melancholy. Eh? Advise a fool, who had nearly lost a Goddess by his folly." He leapt to conclusions: "The thing is, I could not think it possible she could ever like *me*. Her taste is singular, but not the worse for that. . . . She'll have enough of my conversation & of something else before she has done with me, I suspect. . . . I hope your next letter won't reverse all, & then I shall be happy till I see her—one of the blest when I do see her, if she looks like my own beautiful love."

Three days later, on Thursday, July 11, he met his wife on Catherine Street. She was still worrying about money, especially her solicitor's bill, and wondering when the divorce case would be settled. Hazlitt mollified her for the moment, but the next day she received a bill for twenty pounds from John Gray, which she took immediately to Adam Bell's house. However, "he and Mr. Hazlitt went out at the back-door as I came in at the front." She then sent him a letter through the mail, and the next day he called at her lodgings to tell her that Gray's fee was included in the amount already paid to Prentice.

He was in an unruly mood. When Sarah suggested that Prentice send her the twenty pounds due to Gray, Hazlitt replied that "there was no occasion; Mr. Gray would not care a damn who paid him the money." He complained that Sarah "was always starting off, and turning round short at something or other. Said he had also notice to appear at 11 o'clock on Wednesday. and that the more he had tried to hurry them the more they had delayed. and

---

58. In her journal (p. 246) Sarah reported that Mrs. Dow, Hazlitt's landlady in Edinburgh, wanted him to marry her daughter—"and the impediment to that was that she had bad teeth and a foul mouth."

he wanted very much to be off." She told him that she had decided not to return to London by steamboat and asked his opinions of the paintings at Dalkeith. He pronounced them "very poor" except for two which were "tolerable"—one of them "a female figure, floating on the water in an historical picture, which he thought a copy of some good picture." [59]

When he wrote again to Patmore on Tuesday, July 16, he was suffering misgivings. "To-morrow is the decisive day that makes me or mars me," he began. "You must know I am strangely in the dumps at this present writing. My reception with her is doubtful, and my fate is then certain . . . on my forehead alone is written—REJECTED!" But gradually he regained some of his optimism, and soon he was writing: "Still I hope for the best. If she will but *have* me, I'll make her *love* me" (9: 137–38).

The next morning the divorce case was settled at last. That afternoon, after two attempts, Sarah found Hazlitt at dinner in his lodgings and stayed to drink tea with him. Both aired their grievances against Adam Bell and his wife, who had been bearing tales back and forth between them. When Sarah repeated Bell's remarks about Sally's letters, Hazlitt exclaimed, "What a lying son of a Bitch!" He subjected her to a detailed account of his courtship of Sally: her fondling, her devotion to the absent lover—all the long tale of her puzzling behavior, the family quarrels, her mother's willing-ness to permit "girls of the town" to visit him. He added that "he was deter-mined to ascertain what the real state of things was, and was going to the house to watch her narrowly. and perhaps he might kill her and himself too when he got there." When Sarah ventured to remark that he had done "a most injudicious thing" in publishing the passage about Infelice in the *New Monthly*, he replied that it had gone in by mistake.[60] He asked about her plans for the immediate future and told her "he wished he could marry some woman with a good fortune, that he might not be under the necessity of writing another line . . . and that now his name was known in the literary world he thought there was a chance for it; though he could not pretend to any thing of the kind before." Finally he announced that he could give her no money and suggested that she send to her brother in London for a loan of five pounds which he would repay later.[61]

His friend Henderson, who was with him at the time, urged him to join him in a tour of the Highlands. But Hazlitt decided against it and embarked

59. *Journals*, p. 242. Hazlitt was probably referring to the painting *Hope Finding Fortune in the Sea* which pleased him because the female figure reminded him of Sally (see *Liber Amoris*, p. 236, and *Journals*, p. 247).

60. See above, p. 303.   61. *Journals*, pp. 246–49.

by steamer for London at 8:00 A.M. the following day, Thursday, July 18. When Adam Bell complained to Sarah that he had rushed off without bothering to thank him for his good offices, she told him grimly that "it was what I never knew him to do to any body." [62]

In London he returned to his room at the Walkers' house. At first Sally seemed to be avoiding him, although she was affable enough when they happened to meet. One day when he asked her to sew some frills on a shirt for him, she replied, "With the greatest pleasure" (9:154). When he suggested that she have the damaged statue of Napoleon repaired, she consented. And of course he took heart.

He recorded the painful sequel in the letters to JSK (Sheridan Knowles) which form the third section of *Liber Amoris*. He told how one evening, when he sent for her and she failed to appear, he left the house "in great vexation at my disappointment" (9:155). But when he learned later from her mother that she had been dressing to go out to have the statue repaired, he was overcome with remorse—and offered to rent "nearly the whole of the lodgings at a hundred guineas a year" so that Sally would have more time to herself (9:156).

The following Monday she brought him the mended statue, and he "shook hands with her again in token of reconciliation." Then "she went waving out of the room, but at the door turned round and looked full at me, as she did the first time she beguiled me of my heart" (9:156). He was tempted to suggest that they set out for Scotland that very week, with her mother as chaperone, so that they could be married at once. But "something," he wrote, "withheld me" (9:156).

That evening when he sent for her again, her sister Betsey told him that she had gone to Somers Town to visit their grandmother. He was suspicious, and went directly to Somers Town, where he saw her coming towards him down King Street—with Tomkins. "Will you believe it," he wrote, "after all that had passed between us for two years, after what had passed in the last half-year, after what had passed that very morning, she went by me without even changing countenance, without expressing the slightest emotion, without betraying either shame or pity or remorse or any other feeling that any other human being but herself must have shown in the same situation" (9:157). Then: "I turned and looked—they also turned and looked —and as if by mutual consent, we both retrod our steps and passed again, in the same way. I went home. I was stifled. I could not stay in the house, walked into the street and met them coming towards home" (9:157).

62. Ibid., p. 261.

Back in his rooms, he called for her, and "she came smiling." When he questioned her, she showed no embarrassment about what had happened. They "parted friends" and he "felt deep grief, but no enmity against her." "I thought," he wrote, "[Tomkins] had pressed his suit after I went, and had prevailed. There was no harm in that—a little fickleness or so, a little over-pretension to unalterable attachment—but that was all. She liked him better than me—it was my hard hap, but I must bear it" (9:158).

He went out then "to roam the desert streets" and, by chance, met Tomkins. He hailed him, asked for a few minutes' conversation, and they talked for four hours. Thus

> it came out that for three months previous to my quitting London for Scotland, she had been playing the same game with him as with me—that he breakfasted first, and enjoyed an hour of her society, and then I took my turn, so that we never jostled; and this explained why, when he came back sometimes and passed my door, as she was sitting in my lap, she coloured violently, thinking if her lover looked in, what a *denouement* there would be. He could not help again and again expressing his astonishment at finding that our intimacy had continued unimpaired up to so late a period after he came, and when they were on the most intimate footing. She used to deny positively to him that there was anything between us, just as she used to assure me with impenetrable effrontery that "Mr. [Tomkins] was nothing to her, but merely a lodger." (9:158)

"I did not sleep a wink all that night," he told Knowles;

> nor did I know till the next day the full meaning of what had happened to me. With the morning's light, conviction glared in upon me that I had not only lost her for ever—but every feeling I had ever had towards her—respect, tenderness, pity—all but my fatal passion, was gone. . . . She is dead to me; but what she once was to me, can never die! The agony, the conflict of hope and fear, of adoration and jealousy is over; or it would, ere long, have ended with my life. I am no more lifted now to Heaven, and then plunged into the abyss; but I seem to have been thrown from the top of a precipice, and to lie grovelling, stunned, and stupefied. I am melancholy, lonesome, and weaker than a child. The worst is, I have no prospect of any alteration for the better: she has cut off all possibility of a reconcilement at any future period. Were she even to return to her former pretended fondness and endearments, I could have no pleasure, no confidence in them. I can scarce make out the contradiction to myself. I strive to think she always was what I now know she is; but I have great difficulty in it, and can hardly believe but she still *is* what she so long *seemed*. Poor thing! (9:160)

Again he reviewed and analyzed the whole series of events. As a student of human behavior, he found a curious fascination in it: "A more complete experiment on character was never made," he decided. "Her hypocritical high-flown pretensions, indeed, make her the worse; but still the ascendancy of her will, her determined perseverance in what she undertakes to do, has something admirable in it, approaching to the heroic. She is certainly an extraordinary girl!" As a lover he sought purgation in reliving the melancholy tale. He concluded his final letter to Knowles and the *Liber Amoris* itself with the plaintive envoy: "Alas! thou poor hapless weed, when I entirely lose sight of thee, and for ever, no flower will ever bloom on earth to glad my heart again" (9:160–62).

The tragic farce was played out now, concluding in bathetic anticlimax. A more self-assured man might have taken refuge in scorn; Hazlitt could only feel that he had been once more rejected. Yet he could not ring down the curtain. He had told his story over and over—to Patmore, to Sarah, to Knowles, doubtless to many others. Now he told it to anyone who would listen. On August 9 Haydon wrote in his diary: "Hazlitt called last night in a state of absolute insanity about the girl who has jilted him." [63] According to Barry Cornwall,

> Upon one occasion I know he told the story of his attachment to five different persons in the same day, and at each time entered into minute details of his love story. "I am a cursed fool," said he to me, "I just saw J—— going into Wills' Coffee-house yesterday morning; he spoke to me. I followed him into the house; and whilst he lunched, I told him the whole story. Then" (said he) "I wandered into the Regent's Park, where I met one of M——'s sons. I walked with him some time, and on his using some civil expression, by God! sir, I told him the whole story." (Here he mentioned another instance, which I forget.) "Well, sir" (he went on), "I then went and called on Haydon; but he was out. There was only his man, Salmon, there; but, by God! I could not help myself. It all came out; the whole cursed story! Afterwards I went to look at some lodgings at Pimlico. The landlady at one place, after some explanations as to rent, etc., said to me very kindly, 'I am afraid you are not well, sir?'—'No, Ma'am,' said I, 'I am not well;' and on inquiring further, the devil take me if I did not let out the whole story, from beginning to end!" [64]

Yet he could not indulge himself in this luxury forever. Although he had remarked again and again that he had not long to live—even hinted at suicide—he was apparently not going to die of a broken heart. And beneath all the hysteria he had a fund of common sense which told him that he must

63. *Haydon Diary*, 3:375–76. Haydon added, "Poor Hazlitt, his candour is great, & his unaffected frankness is interesting."

64. *Cornwall Recollections*, pp. 81–82.

meet certain responsibilities: he must provide for his son's education, make the quarterly payments on Sarah's allowance, discharge the debts incurred during the divorce proceedings—as well as provide a decent living for himself. He had talked of escaping to Europe, of finding a wealthy wife to support him. But these were only delusions; he had no choice: he must master his emotions and settle down to the arduous business of writing.

CHAPTER XIII

Catharsis
(1822–1824)

On August 23, 1822, Hazlitt bestirred himself to resume writing. He wrote that day to Francis Jeffrey asking if he could review "Napoleon in Exile" and Allan Cunningham's dramatic poem *Sir Marmaduke Maxwell* for the *Edinburgh*. "I have since I returned," he told Jeffrey, "found out the person I told you of to be a regular lodging-house decoy. I hope the state of distraction I was in about that affair will plead my excuse for any oddnesses I might be guilty of while in Edinburgh. I am better a good deal, but feel much like a man who has been thrown from the top of a house." [1]

At about the same time he set to work on an essay "On the Prose Style of Poets" which was not published until 1826, when it appeared as the leading essay in *The Plain Speaker*. Again he wisely chose a subject which was critical in nature rather than one which might involve his emotions, and he seemed quite in command of his powers as he argued that a poet, when he attempts to write in prose "is looking for beauty, when he should be seeking for truth" (12:9). Though his style may abound in "pleasing excrescences," it lacks the rhythm and cadence of good prose; "there is," Hazlitt believes, "a natural measure of prose in the feeling of the subject and the power of expression in the voice, as there is an artificial one of verse in the number and co-ordination of the syllables; and I conceive that the trammels of the last do not (where they have been long worn) greatly assist the freedom or the exactness of the first" (12:8). In short, "the prose-writer

1. ALS, Yale University Library. By "Napoleon in Exile" Hazlitt meant Barry O'Meara's *Historical Memoirs of Napoleon*, a translation of Gaspard Gougaud's *Mémoires pour servir à l'Histoire de France en 1815*, written from Napoleon's dictation.

is master of his materials: the poet is the slave of his style" (12:9). And he illustrated his thesis by analyzing the prose of Burke, the poet Robert Montgomery, Coleridge, and Southey. Leigh Hunt he cited as "among the best and least corrupted of our poetical prose-writers" (12:16).

He had not yet recovered from the results of his emotional crisis. But he had in hand a project which he hoped would bring some release. On September 8 Haydon wrote to Mary Russell Mitford:

> Hazlitt at present gives me great pain by the folly with which he is conducting himself. . . . The girl really excited in him a pure, devoted, and intense love. His imagination clothed her with that virtue which her affected modesty induced him to believe in. . . . He has written down all the conversations without color, literal as they happened; he has preserved all the love-letters, many of which are equal to anything of the sort, and really affecting; and I believe, in order to ease his soul of this burden, means with certain arrangements, to publish it as a tale of character. He will sink into idiotcy if he does not get rid of it.

Haydon was torn between sympathy for the man and scorn for his absurd conduct. "Poor Hazlitt!" he told Miss Mitford:

> He who makes so free with the follies of his friends, is of all mortals the most open to ridicule. To hear him repeat in a solemn tone and with an agitated mouth the things of love he said to her (to convince you that he made love in the true gallant way), to feel the beauty of the sentiment, and then look up and see his old, hard, weather-beaten, saturnine, metaphysical face—the very antidote of the sentiment—twitching all sorts of ways, is really enough to provoke a saint to laughter. He has a notion that women never have liked him. Since this affair he has dressed in the fashion, and keeps insinuating his improved appearance. *He springs up to show you his pantaloons!* What a being it is! His conversation is now a mixture of disappointed revenge, passionate remembrances, fiending hopes, and melting lamentations. I feel convinced that his metaphysical habits of thinking have rendered him insensible to moral duty &c. . . .[2]

Haydon continued to put up with Hazlitt's vagaries; on September 26 he wrote in his diary: "Hazlitt dined with us and was full of his Sally Walker."[3] But not all Hazlitt's friends were so tolerant, and he must have suffered the pangs of rejection once again. Back in April Crabb Robinson had recorded that Mary Lamb was disgusted by Hazlitt's behavior; he suspected, however, that she lacked the strength to break off her friendship with him.[4] But on November 3 he wrote in his diary with some satisfaction: "I was not sorry to find from Mrs. [Basil] Montagu that she views Hazlitt as I do, and I infer from what she said that he no longer visits the house. I

2. Stoddard, pp. 210–11.   3. *Haydon Diary*, 2:382.   4. Robinson, 1:282.

hope to hear this confirmed. She intimates that Lamb has broken with him."[5] Others, especially among Hazlitt's married friends, must have been similarly repelled—if not by the sordid details of the divorce, by his maudlin laments on his loss.

Still he kept busy. On October 2 he wrote again to Jeffrey asking if he might review the Marquis de Montholon's *Mémoires* for the *Edinburgh*. "I have been thinking, at your suggestion," he continued, "of doing an article on the Newspaper & Periodical Press, taking in the Times, Chronicle, Magazines, Reviews, etc. . . . I am better than I was," he assured Jeffrey, "& able to work. . . . I have come away *alive*, which in all the circumstances is a great deal." He apologized for his failure to call before he left Edinburgh, explaining that "the truth is, *I hated the sight of myself* & fancied every body else did the same. Otherwise I do assure you it would have been the greatest relief my mind was then capable of." He announced, too, that he was living now at No. 4 Chapel Street West, Curzon Street.[6] Jeffrey replied that he would be glad to consider an article on the periodical press.

A week later Hazlitt was apparently at Winterslow. He had received some encouragement from Taylor and Hessey and was busy working up articles for the *London Magazine*. "Hazlitt wrote to me to send him down Cunningham's Poems," Hessey wrote his partner on October 9, "he is doing Angerstein, he says, and a capital Paper he will make I have no doubt."[7] He had a new scheme in mind: a series of articles on the great English collections of paintings in the manner of the essay on the earl of Exeter's gallery at Burleigh that he had written for the April *New Monthly Magazine*. He was already at work on a criticism of John Julius Angerstein's collection —later the nucleus of the National Gallery. And during his stay at Winterslow he visited the celebrated Fonthill Abbey, which had only recently been opened to the public by its new owner, John Farquhar.

On November 4 he was back in London, where he dropped in on Hessey at eight o'clock in the evening and stayed until one. His head was full of plans. "He came," Hessey wrote to Taylor the next day, "to mention a project of his, a Series of Maxims and Reflections that he has begun to write and which he would put into the Magazine if we like, three or four pages at a Time—they may be afterwards made into a Volume—a little Volume like the *Opium Eater* or *Rochefoucault*. He thinks he can make up about

5. Ibid., p. 286. Thomas Carlyle wrote in his *Reminiscences* (ed. J. A. Froude, 2 vols. [London, 1881], 1:232) that Hazlitt "was not now of the 'admitted' (such the hint) [at the Montagus' house in 1824]; at any rate kept strictly away."

6. Baker, p. 418.   7. Blunden, p. 140.

three Magazine Sheets of really good ones and he is desirous of doing his best as a sort of sample Book of what he can do." That same day he viewed the collection of paintings at Dulwich College, then left town again. "He goes to Oxford to-day," Hessey wrote Taylor, "and by Thursday or Friday will give us the account of Blenheim." [8]

Hazlitt's energies were reviving—and coming under control. And he had found a new outlet for his talents in *The Liberal, Verse and Prose from the South,* the magazine which Byron, Shelley, and Leigh Hunt had established in Italy before Shelley's tragic drowning in July. The first issue, published by John Hunt on October 15, had been almost universally damned, largely because it contained Byron's irreverent "Vision of Judgment." But Hazlitt was not the man to be frightened off by damnation. As early as October 19, in the first of three reviews of *The Liberal,* volume 1, in the *Literary Gazette,* William Jerdan had announced that Byron wanted Hazlitt to join Hunt and him at Pisa "to throw a little spirit into future Numbers, and prevent their being so inhumanly disgraced by Lordly spleen and sycophantic, even if congenial, prostitution." [9] Byron and Hazlitt had traded some rather harsh remarks in recent months, yet Byron evidently was willing to ignore them. On October 26 Leigh Hunt wrote to his brother John: "Is Hazlitt preparing anything yet? . . . Lord Byron admires Hazlitt's writings." [10]

Hazlitt's first two articles to be published after the end of his affair with Sally appeared in the November *London Magazine.* One was a critique of *Sir Marmaduke Maxwell,* the dramatic poem by Allan Cunningham which he had earlier offered to review for Jeffrey; the other, a description of Fonthill Abbey and the collection which William Beckford had assembled

8. Ibid., pp. 141–42.

9. William H. Marshall, *Byron, Shelley, Hunt, and "The Liberal"* (Philadelphia: University of Pennsylvania Press, 1960), p. 102.

10. *His Very Self and Voice,* ed. E. J. Lovell (New York: Macmillan Co., 1954), p. 327. Byron's approval, if it truly existed, was short-lived. Dr. Henry Muir reported, after a meeting with him on October 10, 1823: "Speaking of Hazlitt, Lord B. expressed himself in the most bitter terms, and would not allow that he could write good English" (ibid., p. 451). And Hunt himself later acknowledged: "Lord Byron in truth was afraid of Mr. Hazlitt; he admitted him like a courtier, for fear he should be treated by him as an enemy; but when he beheld such articles as the 'Spirit of Monarchy,' where the 'taint' of polite corruption was to be exposed, and the First Acquaintance with Poets, where Mr. Wordsworth was to be exalted above depreciation, 'In spite of pride, in erring reason's spite—' (for such was Mr. Hazlitt's innocent quotation) his Lordship could only wish him out again, and take pains to show his polite friends that he had nothing in common with so inconsiderate a plebeian" (*Lord Byron and Some of His Contemporaries* [London, 1828], pp. 63–64).

there. In the first he intimated that Cunningham's powers were more lyrical than dramatic and questioned his use of Scots dialect and of "spiritual machinery" (ghosts, that is), then suddenly broke off with: "But enough, and indeed too much of captious criticism" and devoted the bulk of the review to passages illustrating "the beauty and felicity of execution to be found in this attractive performance."[11] The article on Fonthill Abbey was much less favorable: Hazlitt relentlessly damned the taste displayed throughout the collection. "Mr. Beckford," he asserted, "has undoubtedly shown himself an industrious *bijoutier*, a prodigious virtuoso, an accomplished patron of unproductive labour, an enthusiastic collector of expensive trifles —the only proof of taste (to our thinking) he has shown in this collection is *his getting rid of it*" (18:174). Instead of criticizing the collection seriously, he offered a vivid description of Titian's *St. Peter Martyr*—which Beckford had reputedly offered to buy from Napoleon for 200,000 guineas—then gave a sampling of the catalogue of oddities at Fonthill, added some anecdotes about his friend Richard Cosway, and concluded with a brief paragraph describing "with charity" the few objects that appealed to him at all.[12]

In December the *London* contained Hazlitt's description of the Angerstein collection, which he pronounced "the finest gallery, perhaps, in the world" (10:7). He began ecstatically with an apostrophe to "Art, lovely Art!" Then: "We know of no greater treat than to be admitted freely to a Collection of this sort, where the mind reposes with full confidence in its feelings of admiration, and finds that idea and love of conceivable beauty, which it has cherished perhaps for a whole life, reflected from every object around it. It is a cure (for the time at least) for low-thoughted cares and uneasy passions. . . . Here is the mind's true home" (10:7). He had found a subject which solaced his heart and sparked his enthusiasm, and he regained much of his old verve as he savored the beauty of the paintings,

11. The article was identified and reprinted for the first time by Herschel M. Sikes in "Hazlitt, the *London Magazine*, and the 'Anonymous Reviewer,'" *BNYPL* 65 (1961): 159–74.

12. In "William Beckford, Man of Taste" (*History Today* 10 [1960]: 686–94), Boyd Alexander argues that Hazlitt's criticism was unfair because he overlooked many of Beckford's best purchases and failed to consider adequately the beauty of the architecture and landscaping. Some of Hazlitt's harshness may have been due to his resentment at the lavish expenditures at Fonthill. In 1826 he complained that "thirty pampered domestics sat down in the servants' hall at Fonthill Abbey, to dine on Westphalia hams boiled in Maderia wine, and other luxuries of the same stamp, while old age staggered under its load of labour, or sickness fainted for want of a glass of wine or a morsel of bread in the neighbourhood" (19:280).

especially Ludovico Carracci's *Susannah and the Elders*, which he had first seen in the Orleans Gallery. There was a touch of his old tartness as well in his comment, after learning that one of Angerstein's paintings had been taken to the Royal Academy for students to copy: "Well—*better late than never*" (10:12).

Meanwhile he had finished and submitted to Jeffrey his article "On the Periodical Press," "a few weeks" had passed, and he had heard no word in reply. On December 23 he wrote to Jeffrey: "Might I request the favour of a line from you to say whether it came safe to hand, & whether you think of using it? I should be very sorry indeed if you do not think it good enough for the Review, but in that case you would perhaps let me have it again." He was clearly apprehensive, for he continued, "If you think I am at all in a vein of writing, shall [I] attempt a sort of critical parallel for the next No. between Lord Byron's Heaven & Earth, & T. Moore's Loves of the Angels?" 13 In good time he received the reassuring news that his "Periodical Press" article would appear in a coming issue of the *Edinburgh* and that Jeffrey would be willing to consider the "critical parallel" of Byron and Moore.

In the January, 1823, issue of the *London* Hazlitt reviewed the paintings at Dulwich College. Again he began with a lyrical outburst—this one with personal overtones prompted by the sight of schoolboys in their state of blissful ignorance. "See him there, the urchin, seated in the sun, with a book in his hand, and the wall at his back," he wrote.

> He has a thicker wall before him—the wall that parts him from the future. He sees not the archers taking aim at his peace; he knows not the hands that are to mangle his bosom. He stirs not, he still pores upon his book, and, as he reads, a slight hectic flush passes over his cheek, for he sees the letters that compose the word FAME glitter on the page, and his eyes swim, and he thinks that he will one day write a book, and, have his name repeated by thousands of readers, and assume a certain signature, and write Essays and Criticisms in a LONDON MAGAZINE, as a consummation of felicity scarcely to be believed. Come hither, thou poor little fellow, and let us change places with thee if thou wilt; here, take the pen and finish this article, and sign what name you please to it; so that we may but change our dress for yours, and sit shivering in the sun, and con over our little task, and feed poor, and lie hard, and be contented and happy, and think what a fine thing it is to be an author, and dream of immortality, and sleep o' nights! (10:18)

But the nostalgic mood soon passed, giving way to a lively running commentary on the paintings in the collection.

13. ALS, Yale University Library.

In this same month the second number of *The Liberal* appeared with two bold essays by Hazlitt. The first, "On the Spirit of Monarchy," marked his return to political commentary; in it he argued that, just as men in barbarous ages set up idols resembling themselves, so men of later eras "have got living idols, instead of dead ones" (19:259). "Tyranny, in a word," he declared, "is a farce got up for the entertainment of poor human nature; and it might pass very well, if it did not so often turn into a tragedy" (19:256). He went on, then, to claim that merit has no place in the appointment of a king or in his choice of his aides or their conduct: "The stream of corruption begins at the fountain-head of court influence. . . . The right and the wrong are of little consequence, compared to the *in* and the *out*. The distinction between Whig and Tory is merely nominal: neither have their country one bit at heart" (19:261).

Hazlitt hit hard throughout the essay. Immediately after this statement about Whigs and Tories he interjected: "P[s]haw! we had forgot—Our British monarchy is a mixed, and the only perfect form of government; and therefore what is here said cannot properly apply to it" (19:261). But he presently described satirically a coronation at which Castlereagh and Prince Leopold were present. "What does it all amount to?" he asked. "A shew— a theatrical spectacle!" (19:264). And he concluded with a passage from Jeremy Taylor warning kings against abusing their powers.

His other article, "On the Scotch Character, A Fragment," was less ambitious but more venomous. His resentment against Scots overflowed in a splenetic assault on their alleged clannishness, their parochialism, their prejudice. "Nothing goes down but Scotch Magazines and Reviews, Scotch airs, Scotch bravery, Scotch hospitality, Scotch novels, and Scotch logic," he charged (17:100). "An Englishman is satisfied with the character of his country, and proceeds to set up for himself; an Irishman despairs of that of his, and leaves it to shift for itself; a Scotchman pretends to respectability as such, and owes it to his country to make you hate the very name by his ceaseless importunity and intolerance in its behalf" (17:102). He struck at *Blackwood's* ("a troop of Yahoos" [17:106]) and managed incidental slurs at Sir Walter Scott, even at the *Edinburgh Review* (17:103). He branded the average Scot as "a bigot to the shadow of power and authority, a slave to prejudice and custom, and a coward in every thing else" (17:104). And he closed with an ultimatum that "a Scotchman is a machine, and should be constructed on sound moral, and philosophical principles, or should be put a stop to altogether" (17:106). Even the audacious editors of *The Liberal* were apprehensive, and they inserted at the end of the article: "N.B. A Defence of the Scotch, shortly" (17:398).

Hazlitt was in a bellicose mood: he was plagued not only by his disappointment in love but also by mounting debts. On February 12 he wrote from 5 Coleman Buildings to Thomas Noon Talfourd that he had been arrested and hoped Talfourd would call on him to "see if your influence could procure me any terms of accommodation."[14] At about the same time he wrote to Taylor and Hessey: "I have been able to do nothing, & have the thing [his arrest? his distress about Sally?] hanging over me." He asked them to advance him thirty pounds "for copy-right on ten articles of the Galleries." He was evidently still confined, because he asked in a postscript if they would "send over to Hone's for a copy of my Political Essays, which I want to refer to."[15] He had decided to expand his *Examiner* letter on Coleridge's "Lay Sermon," reprinted in *Political Essays,* into a longer piece recalling his first encounters with Coleridge and Wordsworth. It was soon finished; on February 25 John Hunt wrote to his brother Leigh in Italy that he had received the manuscript of "My First Acquaintance with Poets" and "a set of 'Maxims'" from Hazlitt and had paid him twenty-eight pounds for his two essays in the January *Liberal,* which added up to twenty-eight pages.[16]

Hazlitt had weathered another financial crisis, but he could not afford to relax his efforts. He continued to solicit assignments from Jeffrey. Mary Russell Mitford wrote hopefully to William Macready that Hazlitt, who approved of her new novel *Julian,* had "applied to Mr. Jeffrey for his sanction" to review it for the *Edinburgh.*[17] If Hazlitt actually made the request, nothing came of it. And when his review of Moore's "Loves of the Angels" and Byron's "Heaven and Earth" appeared in the February issue of the *Edinburgh,* Jeffrey had, once again, revised and expanded it almost beyond recognition.[18]

In the February number of the *London Magazine* Hazlitt reported on the marquis of Stafford's collection of paintings at Cleveland House, introducing his essay with a complaint which had distinct misanthropic undertones: "There are only three pleasures in the world, pure and lasting, and all derived from inanimate things—books, pictures, and the face of nature. What is the world but a heap of ruined friendships, but the grave of love?" (10:27). But he was cheered by the fine paintings he described—"probably the most magnificent Collection this country can boast" (10:36), he pronounced it,

14. *The Hazlitts,* p. 472.

15. *London Mercury* 7 (1922–23): 498.

16. Marshall, *Byron, Shelley, Hunt,* pp. 148, 174.

17. Vera Watson, *Mary Russell Mitford* (London: Evans Bros., ca. 1949), p. 155 n.

18. Howe reprints the sections which he judges to be Hazlitt's work—largely a comparison of Moore as a poet of fancy and Byron as a poet of passion (16:411–15).

apparently forgetting that he had applied a more inclusive superlative to the Angerstein Gallery. He described in considerable detail and with lavish praise the Raphaels and Titians at Cleveland House, lingering especially over those which he had formerly seen in the Orleans Gallery. Yet while commenting on the universal appeal of Rubens's paintings, he remarked quite gratuitously: "The Scotch understand nothing but what is Scotch. What has the dry, husky, economic eye of Scotland to do with the florid hues and luxuriant extravagance of Rubens? Nothing. They like Wilkie's *pauper* style better. Out upon it that there should be such a people! No, if there is a single Scotchman that understands Rubens, we will agree to eat him, and that would be no savoury morsel!" (10:29, 312).

Rancor again colored the review, also in the February *London Magazine*, of *Peveril of the Peak*, the new novel "by the author of *Waverley*." Hazlitt accorded high praise to the novel, which he was convinced was the work of Sir Walter Scott. But he was equally convinced that Sir Walter was the silent partner in *Blackwood's Magazine*, and he seized the opportunity to say so: ". . . the reputed author is accused of being a thorough-paced partisan in his own person,—intolerant, mercenary, mean; a professed toad-eater, a sturdy hack, a pitiful retailer or suborner of infamous slanders, a literary Jack Ketch, who would greedily sacrifice any one of another way of thinking as a victim to prejudice and power, and yet would do it by other hands, rather than appear in it himself" (19:95). These were shocking words to apply to a man venerated as Scott was, yet somehow they slipped through the press and appeared in the first copies of the magazine to be distributed. They were noticed then, and the passage was suppressed in later issues. There were to be repercussions later.

Beyond question Hazlitt was in an angry frame of mind; the wound he had suffered was still festering. All the inflated rhetoric of his letters, all the agonized rehearsals of his distress, all his venomous outpourings had failed to purge him. And now, seven months after the end of the affair with Sally, he determined to make a final test of her virtue. He was still not sure whether she was truly the "lodging-house decoy" that he had so often branded her. And he must know—positively.

He found an agent to perform the test—one whom he referred to as "Mr. F.," presumably not the same person as the "E." whom he had earlier urged Patmore to assign to the task.[19] And he who had apparently never

19. Bonner (*Journals*, p. 269 n.) suggests that "F" might have been Patmore himself. However, it seems unlikely that Hazlitt would have tested Sally by means of one who had called at her house earlier and whom she would recognize as Hazlitt's friend.

before kept a diary now recorded step by step the details of Sally's trial as F reported them.[20]

F engaged a room at the Walkers' house on March 4 and moved into it on the fifth. That same day he met Sally in the back parlor as she was about to leave the house—"to meet Tompkins," Hazlitt suspected. On her return she threw her bonnet and shawl over F's coat as it lay on a chair. "This is her first move," Hazlitt commented in his journal, "thus putting these little matters together & mingling persons by proxy." When she left the room, she gave F "one of her set looks at the door."

The next morning, Hazlitt wrote, "she comes up to light his fire, & he wanting his pantaloons brushed, she comes to take them out of his hands, as he gives them to her naked at the door. She is not dressed to wait at breakfast, but is very gracious & smiling, & repulses a kiss very gently. She afterwards expressly forgives this freedom, & is backwards and forwards all day. On his asking for a newspaper or a book, she brings him up the *Round Table*, with my name & sincere regards written in the title-page."

The next day Sally "regularly answers the bell, yet does not bring up the things that are wanted, smirks & backs out of the room in her marked manner." When F queried her brother Cajah about Hazlitt, he was told that "Mr. H. always drank water & they didn't like it [at] the Southampton Arms." He added that Hazlitt was "rather an odd man, a little flighty," he believed, and added smilingly that he had been in love. "F. did not ask with whom," Hazlitt wrote in his journal, "but said the manner & tone convinced him more than anything that the whole was a regularly understood thing, & that there was nothing singular in gentlemen's being *in love* in that house."

On the evening of March 8, F asked Sally "to stay tea which she declined, but he followed her to the door, & kissed her several times on the stair case, at which she laughed. While this passed he had hold of one hand, & the other was at liberty, but she did not once attempt to raise it so as to make even a show of resistance." Hazlitt commented bitterly: "This is what she calls 'being determined to keep every lodger at a proper distance.'"

The following day F saw Sally "in close conference with T[omkins] across the way from the Walkers' house." In anguish, Hazlitt wondered "what divine music he poured into her ear, to which my words were harsh discord."

That evening F insisted that Sally remain in his room while he drank his

20 The following report of the "trial" is based on Hazlitt's own account in *Journals*, pp. 269–77, and all quoted passages are copied from it.

tea, and he asked her opinions on various writers—Hazlitt among them. She replied only briefly, probably because she had read little, and F concluded that "she is quite incapable of understanding any real remark, & shut up her lips . . . for fear of being found out for what she is, a little mawkish simpleton." Yet it seemed to Hazlitt's warped imagination that "she cackled on with her new gallant; T. being in the street with her every night & I in hell for this grinning, chattering ideot."

The next morning, March 10, Sally answered F's first call in her "bedgown," but returned ten minutes later "dressed all in her best [ruff]." When he pictured the scene, Hazlitt burst out: "Decoy! Damned, treble damned ideot! . . . When shall I drive her out of my thoughts?—Yet I like to hear about her—that she had her bed-gown or her ruff on, that she stood or sat, or made some insipid remark, is to me to be in Heaven—to know that she is a whore or an idiot is better than nothing. Were I in Hell, my only consolation would be to learn of her. In Heaven to see her would be my only reward."

And so it went, with F reporting regularly on his progress and Hazlitt analyzing and recording—and agonizing over each detail. On the twelfth Sally sat down in F's room and "he laid his hand upon her thigh, to which she made not the slightest objection. [He] then put his arm round her neck, & began to play with her necklace & paddle in her neck, all which she took smilingly"—"being determined," Hazlitt added with poignant irony, "to keep every lodger at a proper distance, having been guilty of improprieties enough with me." When F reported to him that day, Hazlitt asked him

> if he wanted to take a girl into keeping would he allow her half a guinea a week to be his whore? & he said, No, for one might get girls that would have some conversation in them for that, & she had not. He thought at first she would not talk, but now he was convinced she could not. He asked what was to be done if she consented to come to bed to him. I said Why you had better proceed. He did not seem to like the idea of getting her with child, & I said I supposed he didn't like to have a child by a monster, which he said was really his feeling. In this child-getting business we are however reckoning without our host, for she has evidently some evasion for that. It remains to be seen what her theory & practice on this subject are.

On the thirteenth F saw little of Sally until she answered his bell in the evening. "She would not come in," he told Hazlitt: "she could hear where she was." "Her old word," Hazlitt commented angrily. But

> F. got up & sat near her. He began to say he was sorry he staid out at night & was afraid she thought him wild. She said she was not his keeper. He then said he could

bear to live by himself [if] he could [have] something to kiss & fondle & muss. They should make good company. She asked if [he thought it would be] proper. Oh! he said, hang propriety. . . . Would it be seemly? Oh, he said, as to seemly there was nobody to see them but themselves. While this delicate negotiation was going on, she kept sobbing and crying all the time & at last said she must go now. But she could come and sit with him when they were gone to bed. She made no promise & so it stands. F. swears he'll put it home to her today; but I doubt she has already denied him.

The next day "F. got her between his legs so that she came right into contact with him. She made no resistance nor complaint. She retired a step or two & he followed & then she retreated a little further. . . . He said 'M[iss] I will kill you with kissing, if I catch you.' 'But you must catch me first,' she said, & bounded down stairs & stood looking up & laughing in the first landing place."

Hazlitt was beside himself now. "By God," he wrote, "there isnt such another scheming punishing [?] devil in the world." He feared that F had fallen in love with Sally "& thinks she likes him & I shant be able to get him to move." On Saturday, the fifteenth, as Sally was drawing the curtains for the night, F "kissed her & saying he was determined to give her a good tickling for her tricks in running away from him the day before, put his hand between her legs on that evening. She only said, 'Let me go Sir.', & retiring to the door, asked if he would have the fire lighted." "She was altered in her manner," Hazlitt noted, "& probably begins to make something." "In lighting F. upstairs," he added, "she waits for him to go first, & on his insisting on her leading the way, they had a regular scamper for it, he all the way tickling her legs behind. Yet she expressed no resentment nor shame. This is she who murdered me that she might keep every lodger at a proper distance." Then: "I met Tomkins in the street who looks bad. I fancy we are all in for it."

On the sixteenth F invited Sally to have tea with him, but she "answered 'she never drank tea with gentlemen', and was high." Then that evening he met her walking along Lincolns Inn Fields and followed her as she went down Queen Street toward the New Inn—where, evidently, Tomkins was living. When F offered to escort her, she "stood stock still, immoveable, inflexible—like herself & on his saying he could not then press her & offering his hand, she gave it him, & then went on to her lover." F returned to the house, where he told her brother, "I just met your sister," and Cajah replied, "Why she is gone to her grandmother's."

"Let her be to hell with her tongue—. She is as true as heaven wished her heart & lips be," Hazlitt concluded his journal incoherently. He knew beyond a doubt what he had long suspected. Yet he still had not ridded himself of his malady. "I also am her lover," he wrote, "& will die for her only, since she can be true to any one."

Yet, distraught as he was, he managed to keep writing. Although he was concentrating on the three major projects which he had undertaken, he found time to turn out two magazine articles in March and April.[21] The first, in the March *London Magazine*, was "The Pictures at Windsor Castle," another essay in his galleries series, written with little enthusiasm: he found Windsor "chill and comfortless . . . filled with too many rubbishly pictures of kings and queens" (10:37). In April his only published work was "My First Acquaintance with Poets" in the third number of *The Liberal*. Although it attracted little notice at the time and was never reprinted during Hazlitt's lifetime, this essay contrasted sharply with his other writings of the past year: it shone with his former admiration for the great men he described. Yet every now and then his anguish clouded the page: "So have I loitered my life away, reading books, looking at pictures, going to plays, hearing, thinking, writing on what pleased me best. I have wanted only one thing to make me happy; but wanting that, have wanted everything!" (17:116).

Soon he had a new source of distress when the *Blackwood's* men renewed their attacks on him. His *Liberal* essay "On the Scotch Character," with its allusion to the "flagrant impudence and dauntless dulness" of "Mr. Blackwood's shop," was not to be borne in silence. In their January, 1823, issue they warned of their intentions in a footnote to their review of Byron's "Heaven and Earth": "No. 2 [of *The Liberal*, in which Byron's poem appeared] is like a lion with a fine shagged king-like head, a lean body, hungered lips, and a tawdry tail—Byron—Hazlitt—Hunt. We shew now the lion's head. Carcase, hips, and tail by and bye." In the March issue they settled down in earnest; in three separate articles they alluded to Hazlitt's association with *The Liberal*. The most damaging of the three[22] was "On the Scotch Character—By a Flunky," a series of excerpts from Hazlitt's essay with an angry comment on each. When, for example, Hazlitt complained that Scots are suspicious of a stranger's principles, the author of the

21. The March *New Monthly Magazine* contained "Table-Talk, No. 6: Dreaming," which he had written during his stay at Renton in February, 1822 (see discussion of "On Dreams" above, p. 311 n.). He had resumed the series in December, 1822, with "Table-Talk, No. 5: On the Conversation of Authors," a reprint of an essay of the same title which had appeared originally as no. 3 of the *London Magazine* series in September, 1820.

22. The other two were "The Candid, No. 2" and "Noctes Ambrosianae, No. 7."

article countered: "No wonder you are irritated: for, like Caesar's wife, you should have been above suspicion. Did they object to your principles or your ———? . . . Alas! Poor Yorick! The truth will out: and Rousseau himself has not been more candid in his Confessions. . . . What good did the people of Scotland ever know of this Cockney that they should conceal it? And what kind of good must that be, that can be so effectually concealed from the world."

Hazlitt was infuriated. On April 17 he wrote to Thomas Cadell, *Blackwood's* London agent, threatening to sue "for damages sustained from repeated slanderous and false imputations in that work on me."[23] Cadell was alarmed and wrote the next day to William Blackwood asking how to "avert the impending storm."[24] Blackwood managed to calm Cadell's fears with the help of one of his contributors, the reckless William Maginn, LL.D., of Cork. On May 13 Maginn wrote to Blackwood that he was about to set out for London and would gladly undertake "to palaver [Cadell] out of sticking to Hazlitt."[25] And by that date Hazlitt had already provided the Blackwoodians with a means of striking back hard—and with impunity.

Liber Amoris; or, the New Pygmalion was published by John Hunt during the first week of May.[26] It appeared anonymously with an advertisement stating that the book had been transcribed from a manuscript left behind by "a native of North Britain, who left his country early in life" and who had died "in the Netherlands—it is supposed, of disappointment preying on a sickly frame and morbid state of mind" (9:97). Hazlitt could hardly have believed, however, that his subterfuge would succeed— he had told his story too many times to too many people, and he had too many enemies who would be delighted to expose his humiliation. Yet he himself saw nothing shameful in his account of his hapless love for Sally Walker; it had lasting value on two counts: to the reading public as a study of human passion and to himself as a therapeutic device. "Damn him," he said once when discussing one of Leigh Hunt's pet theories, "it's always coming out like a rash. Why doesn't he write a book about it and get rid of it?"[27] With luck he might be able to rid himself of the specter of Sally Walker once and for all.

---

23. *Four Generations*, 1:142.   24. Ibid., p. 143.

25. Oliphant, *Annals of a Publishing House*, 1:390–92.

26. For some reason, perhaps because Hunt was under indictment for printing "The Vision of Judgment" in the first number of *The Liberal*, C. H. Reynell, the printer (whose daughter later married Hazlitt's son), paid Hazlitt the hundred pounds due him for the copyright.

27. *Cornwall Recollections*, p. 86.

The process may have been painful, but it demanded little effort. He had most of his materials already at hand: he had written down the dialogues a year earlier, and he had asked Patmore to keep the letters which he had composed in the heat of his passion. All that remained was to refine and polish those letters, to fill in the sketch with a few fragments like the apostrophe to "stony-hearted Edinburgh," and perhaps to write up the three letters addressed to JSK which rounded out the action. He seems to have deliberately avoided any coherent narrative: neither the dialogues nor the letters to Patmore are presented according to chronological order. As a result the book gives not only an impressionistic effect but also a feeling of spontaneity which lends immediacy.[28]

Most readers of the book were scandalized. To Crabb Robinson it was "disgusting"—"nauseous and revolting"—"low and gross and tedious and very offensive"; he believed that "it ought to exclude the author from all decent society."[29] The reviewer in the *Literary Gazette* for May 31 slyly remarked that the book had "been cruelly ascribed by some malignant enemy to Mr. Hazlitt" and expressed surprise that "a writer so prone to resent attack has not leaped forth to disclaim the foul reproach, through all the channels of Cocaigne-periodical literature." He added piously that "to criticise such a production would be indeed a prostration of intellect, and entitle the critic to no small portion of the contempt which immeasurably attaches to the Liber Amoris. But it is our duty to warn the public against imposture, as well as to point out the pleasing paths of letters, and to this we must sacrifice a brief space of our publication." The *New European Magazine* for June was aghast: ". . . a more disgraceful specimen of rhapsodical nonsense has never before been submitted to our critical scrutiny," the reviewer wailed, adding "that a man should publish to all the world, that he was such a downright fool, is almost beyond the comprehension of common sense to imagine." The book was, he assured his readers,

the actual history of a man who sets himself up as a critic, a moralist, a judge of human nature, and—*horresco referens,*—a reformer of the morals and the politics of the people! But what will the majority of his countrymen now think of this virtuous Essayist? Will they not regard him with all the horror and detestation which he deserves? Will they not, when they hear even his name mentioned, shudder at the

28. There may have been other reasons for the neglect of chronology: it might have been sheer carelessness on the part of one who was no lover of orderly development and whose mind at the time was more than usually disordered, or it might have been cultivated as a means of confusing readers and thus concealing his authorship the better. He might even have been anticipating some of the experiments in chronology made by later novelists.

29. Robinson, 1:296.

sound, and pray to Heaven that their children may die ignorant of his existence? If the writer's object be notoriety, doubtless, his end will be attained; but the fame he will acquire is from a poisoned and pestiferous source, which, like the noxious exhalations of a sepulchre, taints all coulours it touches with it's own.

The editors of *Blackwood's* seized upon the book with delight. All their harshness toward the Cockneys was now vindicated, they declared in their June issue; "we have long wished that some of this precious brotherhood would embody in a plain English narrative, concerning plain English transactions, the ideas of their school concerning morality, and the plain household relations of society. We now have our wish; and it is certainly not the less desirably accomplished, because this work is not a novel, but a history; not a creation of mere Cockney imagination, but a *veritable* transcript of the feelings and doings of an individual living LIBERAL." They assured the "Good public" that, "since we first took pen in hand, nothing so disgusting as this has ever fallen in our way." They called down upon the author's head "and upon the heads of those accomplished reformers in ethics, religion, and politics, who are now enjoying his *chef-d'œuvre*, the scorn and loathing of every thing that bears the name of MAN. Woman!— But it would be an insult to go farther." And they were able to vent their righteous spleen without running the risk of a libel suit; taking advantage of the author's anonymity, they referred to him only as "H———."

A few of Hazlitt's sympathetic friends were more tolerant. De Quincey insisted that he thought the better of Hazlitt after reading the book because it revealed that he was "capable of stronger and more agitating passions than I believed to be within the range of his nature." [30] Miss Mitford told a friend that Hazlitt revealed himself to be "in love for the first time in his life, to desperation and folly; but it is fine passion and therefore affecting." [31]

But the book found few defenders, and sales were poor. In time the price was reduced from seventeen and six to seventeen shillings; yet still there was no demand for a second edition. Throughout the nineteenth century critics relegated *Liber Amoris* to the category of literary mistakes—or embarrassments. It did not even enjoy a *succès de scandale*.

In more recent years the book has found occasional apologists. Paul Elmer More hailed it as "one of the very few expressions of genuine passion in the English Language." [32] P. P. Howe pleaded that it be judged as a piece of

30. *Collected Writings*, 3:79.

31. *Letters of Mary Russell Mitford*, 2d ser., ed. Henry Chorley, 2 vols. (London, 1872), 1:126.

32. *Shelburne Essays*, 2d ser. (Boston and New York: Houghton Mifflin Co., 1930), p. 84.

imaginative fiction, ignoring the moral issues involved.[33] Leonard Woolf argued that Hazlitt's "bad taste consisted in the fact that his mistress was called Sarah Walker instead of Lesbia or Cynthia." [34] And in his preface to a new edition of the book in 1948 Charles Morgan championed Hazlitt's candor and inveighed against Victorians who had been startled by the raw human passions exposed. But most readers today would agree that both its literary value and its merit as a study of human passion are weakened by the sentimental rhetoric with which Hazlitt overlaid the original letters. The latter provide a far more powerful study of human passion—and its triumph over human intelligence.

Shortly after the publication of *Liber Amoris* the firm of Simpkin and Marshall brought out anonymously Hazlitt's *Characteristics: In the Manner of Rochefoucault's Maxims*, the collection which he had offered earlier to Taylor and Hessey. This was a project well adapted to Hazlitt's talents: he could set down the host of ideas that flashed into his mind as he contemplated the world around him, yet he was spared the labor of developing them into coherent essays. He had always found such labor irksome; in fact, in Characteristic no. 180 he wrote: "I like very well to speak my mind on any subject (or to hear another do so) and to go into the question according to the degree of interest it naturally inspires, but not to have to get up a thesis on every topic" (9:194). And he was in no mood at present to get up theses —to write Table Talk essays.

The 434 maxims in the little book cover a great variety of subjects: friendship, love, envy, the theater, painting, the nature of women, the character of Frenchmen or Scots as opposed to that of Englishmen—and so on. Hazlitt followed no system; he did not arrange the maxims under topic headings, yet successive items may concern the same or related subjects—to which he may or may not recur later in the series. They sound often like the sort of entry which an author might jot down in a notebook, to be more fully developed later. Hazlitt acknowledged in the title and the preface that he had modeled his work on Rochefoucauld's, but his maxims were, on the whole, longer than Rochefoucauld's and less terse. Hazlitt was never a man of few words—at least written words—and although he remarked in his preface that a maxim should be epigrammatic, "with a certain pointedness and involution of expression" and should be "so developed as of itself to suggest a whole train of reflections to the reader" (9:165), his characteristics disappoint because they fall short as

33. *Fortnightly Review* 105 (1916): 300–310.
34. *Essays* (New York: Harcourt, Brace and Co., 1927), p. 25.

epigrams, yet lack the succession of original insights which readers prize in his essays.

Hazlitt differed from Rochefoucauld in another respect: he refused to echo the master's cynicism. He still clung to his belief in the disinterestedness of man. "The error in the reasonings of Mandeville, Rochefoucault, and others," he wrote in no. 105 "is this: they first find out that there is something mixed in the motives of all our actions, and they then proceed to argue, that they must all arise from one motive, *viz.* self-love. They make the exception the rule. It would be easy to reverse the argument, and prove that our most selfish actions are disinterested" (9:184). And he seemed determined to maintain his confidence in human disinterestedness despite all that his recent experience might suggest to the contrary. Sometimes he seemed to be working against considerable odds, as when he remarked in no. 417: "Vice is man's nature: virtue is a habit—or a mask" (9:226).

Throughout the collection, especially in the opening pages, he seems preoccupied, in one way or other, with human relationships: magnanimity, envy, women's attitudes toward men, the scholar's feeling of isolation, prejudices, man's feelings of superiority or inferiority toward others, and the like. He is clearly concerned about his relationships with others, eager to retain his faith in man. At best he is, as Stewart C. Wilcox phrased it, "disillusioned without being cynical." [35]

One of the sources for his disillusionment recurs periodically. In Characteristic no. 278, citing "persons among my acquaintance who have been ruined with their eyes open by some whim or fancy," he refers to a man who "divorced his wife to marry a wench at a lodging-house, who refused him, and whose cruelty and charms are the torment of his own life and that of his friends" (9:207). In no. 126: "The affected modesty of most women is a decoy for the generous, the delicate, and unsuspecting; while the artful, the bold, and unfeeling either see or break through its slender disguises" (9:188). But in no. 313 he shows some signs of regaining his equilibrium when he admits: "It is impossible to love entirely without being loved again. Otherwise the fable of Pygmalion would have no meaning. Let any one be ever so much enamoured of a woman who does not requite his passion, and let him consider what he feels when he finds her scorn or indifference turning to mutual regard, the thrill, the glow of rapture, the melting of two hearts into one, the creation of another self in her—and he will own that he was before only half in love!" (9:212).

The volume attracted little attention. The *Monthly Review* for February, 1824, accorded it a brief notice, remarking that "the pointed epigrammatic

35. "Hazlitt's Aphorisms," *MLQ* 9 (1948): 418–23.

and authoritative tone, which a collection of aphorisms should possess, is well suited to Mr. Hazlitt's paradoxical and caustic genius; and accordingly his 'Characteristics' contain many sound truths, mixed up with not a few bold misrepresentations of human nature." But other reviewers found the *Liber Amoris* more challenging, and the book suffered the fate of many of Hazlitt's works: as late as 1837 the first edition was not sold out, and the remaining sheets were bound up as a second edition and issued with a new preface by R. H. Horne.

The May *Edinburgh Review* contained Hazlitt's third major product for this month, the article "On the Periodical Press" which he had sent to Jeffrey late in 1822. He began by defending contemporary criticism, declaring that it filled an important need in evaluating the great works of the past for an age which could not hope to equal them. Then came individual estimates of the leading newspapers and magazines, several of which Hazlitt had known from the inside—or about which he had gathered revealing anecdotal information. From them he went on to a hard-hitting attack on the abusive and insinuating tactics of the "Ministerial press," as he chose to label such ultraconservative periodicals as the *Quarterly Review* and the *John Bull*, different as they were in most respects. Yet he offered only an incidental slur at his archenemy: "Of the *Magazines*, which are a sort of *cater-cousins* to ourselves, we would wish to speak with tenderness and respect. There is the Gentleman's Magazine, at one extremity of the series, and Mr. Blackwood's at the other" (16:230). But it was enough to stir up again the wrath of his old foes.

By late June Hazlitt seemed to be settling back into a normal routine of writing and visiting: on the twenty-second he heard the Reverend Edward Irving preach at the Caledonian Chapel in Hatton Garden (20:121); three days later he called on Haydon, who was eager to hear what Northcote had said about him;[36] and on the thirtieth he spent a convivial evening with Taylor and Hessey. The next day Hessey wrote to his partner: "We had a very delightful Evening. . . . Hazlitt walked with me as far as to this side of Temple Bar & was very pleasant." [37]

For the *London Magazine* he continued to write only his accounts of the English galleries, which were falling into a rather uninspired pattern. "I cannot but think *the London* drags heavily," Lamb had written to his Quaker friend Bernard Barton on May 3. "I miss Janus [Wainewright]. And O how it misses Hazlitt." [38] "The Pictures at Hampton Court," in the June issue, largely echoed the account of the Windsor Castle gallery in March: it opened with a brief passage describing the beauty of the site, deliberately

36. *Haydon Diary*, 2:418.   37. *Keats Circle*, 2:444.   38. *Lamb Letters*, 2:385.

ignored the royal portraits in the collection, and then singled out a few items —notably the Raphael cartoons—for consideration (10:42–49). "Lord Grosvenor's Collection of Pictures" in July was in much the same mode: an introductory passage celebrating the stately homes of England, then the usual descriptions, this time concentrating on the Rembrandts and Rubenses assembled at Grosvenor House (10:49–55).

His better efforts now were going to *The Liberal*, the fourth number of which, in July, contained two articles which exercised his powers of analysis and development as they had been seldom engaged for the past year. One, "Pulpit Oratory—Dr. Chalmers and Mr. Irving," compared the preaching —both content and delivery—of the two eminent Scottish clergymen. Predictably Hazlitt preferred Irving who, despite his florid style, had "something humane in his appeals, striking in his apostrophes, graceful in his action, soothing in the tones of his voice" (20:118) while Chalmers merely "succeeds by the force of sophistry and casuistry" (20:116). But although he treated both respectfully, he once again aired his pet prejudice: "The Scotch at present seem to bear the bell, and to have 'got the start of the majestic world.' They boast of the greatest novelists, the greatest preachers, the greatest philanthropists, and the greatest blackguards in the world. Sir Walter Scott stands at the head of these for Scotch humour, Dr. Chalmers for Scotch logic, Mr. Owen for Scotch Utopianism, and Mr. Blackwood for Scotch impudence" (20:113). He was practically begging for reprisals.

His other article in the July *Liberal*, "Arguing in a Circle," began strategically by celebrating "the progress that has been made in public opinion and political liberty" in England (19:268), then proposed that Englishmen should therefore defend the cause of liberty in all struggles between monarchs and their subjects on the Continent. He blamed Burke, "that brilliant sophist" (19:271), and Pitt, master of "deep-mouthed *commonplaces*" (19:271) for prejudicing the English people against the cause of liberty. And he launched then into a fine attack on apostasy, especially the apostasy of Robert Southey, quite in the old manner. For the moment he seemed to be regaining his analytical and rhetorical powers; publishing *Liber Amoris* and seeing Sally's character exposed seemed to have purged him of the preoccupation with his personal woes which had tainted so many of his recent articles.

Unfortunately *The Liberal*, which had been printing most of his best work, failed to prosper, and the fourth issue proved to be its last. In its place the Hunts brought out a new weekly, the *Literary Examiner*, which contained, in its August 2 issue, a brief article by Hazlitt, "Judging of

Pictures," emphatically denying "the exclusive right and power of painters to judge of pictures" (18: 182).[39] "I am far from saying," he declared, "that *any* one is capable of duly judging pictures of the higher class. It requires a mind capable of estimating the noble, or touching, or terrible, or sublime subjects which they present—but there is no sort of necessity that we should be able to put them upon the canvas ourselves" (18: 183).

More substantial was his contribution to the August *New Monthly:* "Table-Talk, No. 7: On Londoners and Country People," his first new essay in the series since his return from Edinburgh. It was quite in the old vein of Table Talk essays: an ironic, yet good-humored piece characterizing "the true Cockney" as one who knows and cares about nothing beyond the confines of his beloved London. Hazlitt summoned up delightful recollections of Londoners whom he had known; in fact he became so absorbed with them that he allowed the "country people" only one disapproving paragraph toward the end of the essay, then referred the reader to his remarks about country people in his *Round Table* review of Wordsworth's *Excursion* (12:66–77).

But before any of these July or August articles appeared, Hazlitt had fled to Winterslow. The angry reaction to *Liber Amoris* had set in. Cruellest of all was the attack of Theodore Hook's *John Bull,* which on June 9 accused "this impotent sensualist" of having inserted a favorable notice of his own book in the *Times;* then two weeks later they printed the full text of one of his letters to Sally.[40] On July 19 he wrote to Thomas Hood apologizing for his failure to go to Petworth, probably by appointment to see Lord Egremont's collection of paintings. He explained that something had happened which "hurt my mind." "I had only the heart to come down here," he went on, "and see my little boy, who is gone from hence." Then after promising to "do *Blenheim*"—that is, review the duke of Marlborough's collection—"for next month," he added: "I used to think she read and perhaps approved these articles. But whatever I can do, implying an idea of taste or elegance, only makes me more odious to myself, and tantalises me with feelings which I can never hope to excite in others—wretch that I am, and am to be, till I am nothing!"[41] At about the same time he wrote his essay "Whether Genius Is Conscious of Its Powers,"[42] maintaining that

39. The article opened with remarks on the envious nature of painters which might well have grown out of Haydon's conversation about Northcote on June 25 (see above, p. 367).

40. See above, pp. 308–309 and n.   41. *The Hazlitts,* pp. 473–74.

42. Howe (12:398) dates the essay "autumn 1823" without presenting his evidence for so doing. But Hazlitt's account of the lily and daisies outside his window as he writes

genius is spontaneous, not cultivated, that the man of genius works not to compete with others or to win fame but because of an "involuntary, silent impulse" (12:119). But his thoughts were elsewhere, and he broke off suddenly with "I am not in the humour to pursue this argument any farther at present, but to write a digression" (12:121).

The subject of the digression was himself. He told of his first visit to Winterslow fifteen years earlier, his frequent returns since then, the beneficial effects of the place on his powers of expression; presently he was recalling the "cry of abuse" that he had been "followed with . . . *for not being a government-tool*," the failure of his essays and lectures and of *The Characters of Shakespear's Plays*, the downfall of Napoleon, the Tory critic Jerdan's praise of his work—until he learned the identity of its author. He spoke of Keats and Leigh Hunt, who likewise had "fallen a sacrifice to the obloquy attached to the suspicion of doubting, or being acquainted with any one who is known to doubt, the divinity of kings" (12:123). He concluded his digression: "Really, it is wonderful how little the worse I am for fifteen years' wear and tear, how I come upon my legs again on the ground of truth and nature, and 'look abroad into universality,' forgetting that there is any such person as myself in the world!" (12:123).

But obviously he had not forgotten himself or his troubles. "I have let this passage stand (however critical)," he added, "because it may serve as a practical illustration to show what authors really think of themselves when put upon the defensive—(I confess, the subject has nothing to do with the title at the head of the Essay!)—and as a warning to those who may reckon upon their fair portion of popularity as the reward of the exercise of an independent spirit and such talents as they possess" (12:123–24). And although he virtually admitted that he had spoken out "in a fit of spleen and impatience," he returned to his original subject only to the extent of explaining what had kept him writing in spite of neglect and opposition: "The stimulus of writing is like the stimulus of intoxication, with which we can hardly sympathize in our sober moments, when we are no longer under the inspiration of the demon, or when the virtue is gone out of us" (12:125). He closed on a more cheerful note, recalling the pleasures he once found in reading—and adding that "as my life began, so I could wish that it may end" (12:126).

Yet in its total effect the essay echoed the mood of Hazlitt's letter to

---

suggests a period earlier in the year. The essay was first published in *The Plain Speaker* in 1826, but its first sentence appeared as "Common Place, No. 20" in the *Literary Examiner* for September 13, 1824 (20:124).

Hood: the inventory of his achievements to date is a record of failure; he finds no satisfaction in his writing, only the faintest glimmer of happiness in the future.

On August 18 Mary Shelley imparted a curious bit of gossip in a letter to Leigh Hunt:

> I asked [James Kenney] about Hazlitt—This love-sick youth, jilted by Infelice has taken to falling in love. He told Kenny that whereas formerly he thought women silly, unamusing toys, & people with whose society he delighted to dispense—he was now only happy where they were & given up to the admiration of their interesting foibles and amiable weaknesses. He is the humble servant of all marriageable young ladies. . . . K. met H. in the Ham^std fields—Well sir—he said—I was just going to Mr. ——— there's a young lady there—I don't know—But said K. there was another a young lady of colour you were about to marry—has she jilted you like Infelice? —"No, sir, but you see sir, she had relations—kind of people who ask after character, & as mine [is] [?small], sir, why it was broken off."[43]

In September Haydon wrote Miss Mitford a bit of news which would seem to cancel out Mrs. Shelley's: Hazlitt, he said, had come up to town "for a night or two, and passed nearly the whole of each watching Sally's door!" However, Haydon's next sentence was a surprise: "He had another flame, who is at Hampton; down he went to tempt her for Gretna; but her brother, an officer in the Navy, happened to be with her; and 'officers,' said Hazlitt, 'you know, are awkward fellows to deal with!' Oh, the gallant, gay Lothario!"[44] Hazlitt's emotions were in a turmoil; he was apparently determined to find acceptance somewhere, somehow.

Haydon remarked in passing that Hazlitt had been to Fonthill Abbey, where Phillips, the auctioneer overseeing the sale of the property, had "fixed him to write up, for fifty guineas, what he wrote down from his conscience last year." And Peter George Patmore, who was preparing a series of essays on English galleries for the *New Monthly Magazine*, wrote several years later that he and Hazlitt had spent eight or ten days at Fonthill and visited Sir Richard Colt Hoare's collection of paintings at Stourhead. He recalled Hazlitt's "almost childish delight" when he met with a familiar painting and the satisfaction he took from introducing his friend to his

---

43. *Letters of Mary W. Shelley*, 1:255–57.

44. Stoddard, p. 213. This "flame" may well have been Isabella Bridgwater, whom Hazlitt married in the following spring. As Stanley Jones ("Isabella Bridgwater: A Charade by Hazlitt?" *Review of English Literature* 8 [1967]: 91–95) has noted, the essay "On the Old Age of Artists," published in the *New Monthly Magazine* for September, 1823, quoted Pope's tribute to Lady Bridgwater and cited Boccaccio's heroine Isabella within a few lines.

favorites. One day they walked the twelve miles to Salisbury "in a broiling sunshine," and Patmore commented on "the extraordinary physical as well as moral effect produced on Hazlitt by the sight and feel of 'the country'": "he was like a being of another species; his step firm, vigorous, and rapid; his look eager and onward, as if devouring the way before it—and his whole air buoyant and triumphant." [45] He told too of the curious friendship which Hazlitt struck up with Tom, the footboy who brought up his breakfast at Fonthill. Flattered, Tom told his hero what he knew of the lore of the place and its late eccentric owner, Beckford—and managed "to procure him an inordinate quantity of cream for his breakfast and tea." [46]

Nature, art, and friendship doubtless helped to console him for the general vilification he was suffering, for the vicious reviews of *Liber Amoris* gave way to scornful comments on his "Periodical Press" article. The *Times* scored his "malignity" and referred to him as a "discarded servant" of the paper, to which he replied in a brief note in the *Examiner* for September 8 (20:142–43). By that time the unscrupulous William Maginn, in "Letters of Timothy Tickler, No. 8," in the August *Blackwood's*, had written a scathing critique of the last number of the *Edinburgh Review*, with special attention to Hazlitt's article. He charged that Jeffrey must have excised the attack on *Blackwood's* which Hazlitt would certainly have included in his article, and he offered a mock lament that Jeffrey

> has suffered William Hazlitt, author of the *Liber Amoris*, an old newspaper-monger —a gentleman of the press, that has lived all his days by scribbling dramatic criticisms, and leading paragraphs, and so forth, for the different London newspapers and magazines;—he has suffered this low, vulgar, impudent gentleman of the press—the writer of that filthy book, which, but for its dulness, and the obscurity of its author, must long ere now have been burnt by "the hands of the common hangman;"—he has suffered this despicable member of the Cockney School to write an Essay in the Edinburgh Review on "the Periodical Press of Britain." Francis Jeffrey has been obliged to swallow this bitter pill.

Fortunately Hazlitt had a couple of innocuous projects to occupy him during these difficult days. He was working on "a new collection of Elegant Extracts, in which the Living Poets are included," as Mary Shelley described it in a letter to Leigh Hunt on the ninth. [47] And the September *New Monthly* contained a new Table Talk essay, "No. 8: On the Old Age of Artists," a series of vivid, affectionate sketches of elderly artists—Nollekens, who had just died, Northcote, Fuseli, West, and Cosway—who had been

45. Patmore, 3:65–66.   46. Ibid., p. 72.
47. *Letters of Mary W. Shelley*, 1:260. Mrs. Shelley had heard the news from Lamb, who, she said, had "corrected" the edition for Hazlitt.

lucky enough to live their last days as prosperous members of the Royal Academy (12:88–97).[48]

He needed, however, to find new outlets for his writing. *The Liberal* was extinct now, and the *London* was failing. Lamb wrote again to Bernard Barton in September on the subject: "I linger among its creaking rafters, like the last rat. It will topple down, if they don't get some Buttresses."[49] Moreover, Hazlitt himself had already remarked in passing that the Table Talk series in the *New Monthly* was "nearly done" (12:122). On October 10 he contributed to the *Morning Chronicle* a review of *Vathek*, the novel which Beckford had written almost forty years earlier. Hazlitt reviewed it now, probably, because he had recently been to Fonthill, had read or reread the novel, and wanted to turn his efforts to account. He praised especially the "misanthropic view of human nature" which Beckford had managed to convey with such "gaiety and good humour" (19:98). He himself could have used a similar detachment.

The major result of his trip to Fonthill appeared in the October *London Magazine* as "Pictures at Wilton, Stourhead, etc.," a perfunctory treatment of four separate collections, two of which he could describe only from memory because they had been closed to the public. When he discussed the collection at Fonthill, he hardly confirmed Haydon's prophecy that he would now "write up" what he had previously "written down." He allowed that Beckford's "genius, as a writer, 'hath a devil' [but] his taste in pictures is the quintessence and rectified spirit of *still-life*" (10:59). At Stourhead he was delighted more by the idyllic village outside the mansion than the paintings inside. And he concluded with an appeal to his readers to visit Petworth, the seat of Lord Egremont, where they would find "the coolest grottos and the finest Van Dykes in the world" (10:61). He did not attempt to describe these in detail—and for good reason: as his letter of July 19 to Thomas Hood reveals, he had failed to go to Petworth himself.[50]

In much the same hasty mood was the article "Pictures at Oxford and Blenheim" in the November issue of the *London*. Hazlitt was able to work up some enthusiasm for the venerable atmosphere at Oxford, but little for the paintings there. And although he described lyrically the Rubenses and Vandykes at Blenheim—not to mention the supposed Titians, kept under lock and key because of the nude figures in them—he concluded the article and the series itself with a rather flat envoy:

48. The account of Cosway was copied almost verbatim from the essay on Fonthill Abbey which Hazlitt had published in the *London Magazine* for the previous November.
49. *Lamb Letters*, 2:394–95.   50. See above, p. 369.

We now take leave of *British Galleries of Art*. There are one or two others that we had intended to visit; but they are at a great distance from us and from each other; and we are not quite sure that they would repay our inquiries. Besides, to say the truth, we have already pretty well exhausted our stock of criticism, both general and particular. The same names were continually occurring, and we began sometimes to be apprehensive that the same observations might be repeated over again. One thing we can say, that the going through our regular task has not lessened our respect for the great names here alluded to; and, if we shall have inspired, in the progress of it, any additional degree of curiosity respecting art, or any greater love of it in our readers, we shall think our labour and our anxiety to do justice to the subject most amply rewarded. (10:319)

The article proved to be Hazlitt's last regular contribution to the *London Magazine*.

In November the *New Monthly* contained "Table-Talk No. 9: On Sitting for One's Picture," a perceptive study of the delicate relationship which prevails between painter and sitter by one who had been both. Again Hazlitt developed his points by means of anecdotes—ranging from his own recollections of painting his father's portrait to accounts of some of Reynolds's experiences with illustrious sitters (12:107–16).

During the last four months of the year 1823 the Hunts printed in their *Literary Examiner* a series of eighty-six "Common Places" by Hazlitt in nine sporadic installments.[51] These were much in the manner of the earlier *Characteristics*, except that they tended to become longer in the later installments, sometimes qualifying more as brief essays than as maxims. Again Hazlitt ranged widely in subject manner; again, too, the maxims occasionally had personal overtones. But when he touched, as he did in the installment for November 15, on disappointment in love, he seemed to be attaining a salutary ironic detachment:

LXIV. Is it a misfortune or a happiness that we so often like the faults of one we love better than the virtues of any other woman; that we like her refusals, better than all other favours; that we like her love of others, better than any one else's love of us?

LXV. If a man were refused by a woman a thousand times, and he really loved her, he would still think that at the bottom of her heart she preferred him to every one else. Nor is this wonderful, when we consider that all passion is a species of madness; and that the feeling in the mind towards the beloved object is the most amiable and

51. These may well have been the set of maxims which John Hunt referred to in his letter of February 25 (quoted above, p. 356) and which did not appear in *The Liberal*. The dates of the installments and the numbers of the maxims included in each are listed by Howe in his notes to the series (20:413).

delightful thing in the world. Our love to her is heavenly, and so (the heart whispers us) must hers be to us—though it were buried at the bottom of the sea; nay, from the tomb our self-love would revive it! We can never persuade ourselves that a mistress cares nothing about us, till we no longer care about her. No! It is certain that there is nothing truly deserving of love but love, and

> "In spite of pride, in erring reason's spite,"

we still believe in the justice of the blind God!

LXVI. It would be easy to forget a misplaced attachment, but that we do not like to acknowledge ourselves in the wrong. (20:133–34)

During the weeks when the "Common Places" were appearing, Hazlitt became involved in two minor literary controversies. One developed when he read in the October *London Magazine* an article by Thomas De Quincey advancing two arguments which Hazlitt had anticipated in his reply to Malthus. On October 20 James Hessey wrote to John Taylor: "Hazlitt has done me a great Service by sending a Letter which will fill up the Lions Head [a regular feature of the *London*] capitally—he writes to the Editor to claim the credit of having ten or more years ago made the very same replies to Malthus as De Quincey has in his *Notes* last month. He speaks very respectfully of De Q. but says, as he has been a good deal abused for differing from Malthus, he may as well claim the credit of priority in publishing his Opinions—they exactly coincide with the Opium Eater's." [52] Actually, however, there may have been a touch of irony in Hazlitt's letter enclosing the two passages from his *Reply*: "I am glad to find our ingenious and studious friend the *Opium-Eater* agrees with me on this point . . . almost in so many words." [53]

The other dispute, which touched Hazlitt only incidentally, stemmed from an article by Southey in the January *Quarterly Review* questioning Lamb's orthodoxy. Lamb denied the charge in his "Letter of Elia to Robert Southey" in the October *London Magazine*, then went on to defend his friendship with men like Leigh Hunt and Hazlitt. Of Hazlitt he wrote:

> What hath soured him, and made him to suspect his friends of infidelity towards him, when there was no such matter, I know not. I stood well with him for fifteen years (the proudest of my life), and have ever spoke my full mind of him to some, to whom his panegyric must naturally be least tasteful. . . . I wish he would not quarrel with the world at the rate he does; but the reconciliation must be effected by himself,

52. *Keats Circle*, 2:450.
53. *The Hazlitts*, p. 475. De Quincey replied in a letter printed in the December issue of the *London;* he acknowledged Hazlitt's claim, but denied any suggestion of plagiarism (*Collected Writings*, 9:23–31).

and I despair of living to see that day. But, protesting against much that he has written, and some things which he chooses to do; judging him by his conversation, which I enjoyed so long, and relished so deeply; or by his books, in those places where no clouding passion intervenes—I should belie my own conscience, if I said less, than that I think W.H. to be, in his natural and healthy state, one of the wisest and finest spirits breathing. So far from being ashamed of that intimacy, which was betwixt us, it is my boast that I was able for so many years to have preserved it entire; and I think I shall go to my grave without finding, or expecting to find, such another companion.[54]

For Hazlitt, of course, the words were heartening. He had complained to Hunt in April, 1821, that Lamb "seemed struck all of a heap, if I ever hinted at the possibility of his giving me a lift at any time." [55] Now he had provided a lift when it was sorely needed, and he followed it up in his essay "Guy Faux" in the next issue of the *London*. There he quoted Hazlitt's *Examiner* article on Fawkes, alluding playfully to the author as a "very ingenious and subtle writer, whom there is a good reason for suspecting to be an Ex-Jesuit, not unknown at Douay." [56]

Hazlitt was willing and eager to be reconciled with his old friend. In his essay "On the Pleasure of Hating," written at this time, he analyzed the basic hostilities in human nature, inevitably coming around to himself: "I have quarrelled with almost all my old friends, (they might say this is owing to my bad temper, but) they have also quarrelled with one another. What is become of 'that set of whist-players,' celebrated by ELIA in his notable *Epistle to Robert Southey, Esq.* (and now I think of it—that I myself have celebrated in this very volume) 'that for so many years called Admiral Burney friend?'" (12:130–31). And later: "I think I must be friends with Lamb again, since he has written that magnanimous Letter to Southey, and told him a piece of his mind!" (12:132). However, Lamb's gesture of friendship had not dissipated all Hazlitt's bitterness toward his fellows; he was still a good hater, and he ended his essay on a misanthropic note:

Seeing all this as I do, and unravelling the web of human life into its various threads of meanness, spite, cowardice, want of feeling, and want of understanding, of indifference towards others and ignorance of ourselves, seeing custom prevail over all excellence, itself giving way to infamy—mistaken as I have been in my public and private hopes, calculating others from myself, and calculating wrong; always disappointed where I placed most reliance; the dupe of friendship, and the fool of love;

54. *Works of Charles and Mary Lamb*, ed. E. V. Lucas 5 vols. (New York: Macmillan Co., 1913), 1:274.

55. See above, p. 288.

56. *Works of Charles and Mary Lamb*, 1:278.

have I not reason to hate and to despise myself? Indeed I do; and chiefly for not having hated and despised the world enough. (12:136)

The essay was not printed until Hazlitt's *Plain Speaker* was published in 1826. But word of Hazlitt's gratitude reached Lamb—perhaps through Sarah Hazlitt, since Lamb wrote in a postscript to a letter to her early in November: "I am pleased that H. liked my letter to the Laureate." [57] And soon the two men were friends again. Crabb Robinson reported seeing (but ignoring) Hazlitt at Lamb's cottage in Islington on January 25.[58]

In the meantime Hazlitt showed increasing signs of regaining his former powers of concentration. The December *New Monthly* contained "Table-Talk, No. 10: On Application to Study," an analysis of various aspects of the subject in the manner of the best of the early Table Talk essays. Again he dealt with the operations of genius—the subject from which he had been so quickly distracted to his own concerns when he last approached it in "Whether Genius Is Conscious of Its Powers." Contrary to popular opinion, he declared, geniuses are both prolific (witness the numbers of paintings by Raphael and Rubens surviving in collections) and painstaking (witness Shakespeare's success in finding always the exact word to serve his purpose). He insisted that "the more we do, the more we *can* do" (12:60). He declared: "I do not conceive rapidity of execution necessarily implies slovenliness or crudeness. On the contrary, I believe it is often productive both of sharpness and freedom" (12:62). And of his own writing: ". . . if what I write at present is worth nothing, at least it costs me nothing. But it cost me a great deal twenty years ago. I have added little to my stock since then, and taken little from it. I 'unfold the book and volume of the brain,' and transcribe the characters I see there as mechanically as any one might copy the letters of a sampler. I do not say they came there mechanically— I transfer them to the paper mechanically. After eight or ten years' hard study, an author (at least) may go to sleep" (12:61–62). He had no patience with those who "spend whole years in mere corrections for the press, as it were—in polishing a line or adjusting a comma" (12:64) or with those who are always preparing for great achievements but never accomplishing them. The essay was, in effect, a defense of his own methods of composition— perhaps, too, a sign of growing self-respect.

The next issue of the *New Monthly*, that for January, 1824, carried another Table Talk essay, "No. 11: On the Spirit of Obligations." This was an analysis of human benevolence with a surprisingly misanthropic

57. *Lamb Letters*, 2:406.   58. Robinson, 1:301.

tone: Hazlitt questioned the motives of friends and philanthropists; he declared that "true friendship is self-love at second-hand" (12:84) and that "entire friendship is scarcely to be found, except in love" (12:85). And he finally admitted:

> I used to think better of the world than I do. I thought its great fault, its original sin, was barbarous ignorance and want, which would be cured by the diffusion of civilization and letters. But I find (or fancy I do) that as selfishness is the vice of unlettered periods and nations, envy is the bane of more refined and intellectual ones. . . . The worst is, you are no better off, if you fail than if you succeed. You are despised if you do not excel others, and hated if you do. . . . Instead of being raised, all is prostituted, degraded, vile. Every thing is reduced to this feverish, importunate, harassing state. I'm heartily sick of it, and I'm sure I have reason if any one has. (12:87)

Yet in spite of these hints of misanthropy Hazlitt seems to have begun the year 1824 in a more mellow frame of mind than he had enjoyed for some time. He was no longer haunted by memories of Sally Walker, and, after a series of glancing blows during the autumn,[59] the *Blackwood's* men had lifted their siege. Their motives were not humane; on January 22 William Maginn wrote to William Blackwood: "You are blamed for attacking obscure Londoners—most particularly Hazlitt. He is really too insignificant an animal. Make it a rule that his name be *never* mentioned by any of your friends: I for one will keep it." [60] Hazlitt, however, probably assumed that his threat to sue Thomas Cadell had brought about the respite. And he had some reason for optimism about his future; for he was planning a new series of essays to take the place of the "Table-Talks" in the *New Monthly*, he had been commissioned by Jeffrey to write two major reviews for the *Edinburgh*, and he had probably met the woman who was to give him, for a time at least, a measure of contentment.

The new series of essays, "The Spirits of the Age," began with a study of Jeremy Bentham in the January *New Monthly;* it ended with the publication of eighteen such papers in *The Spirit of the Age* in 1825. Hazlitt sought to characterize for his contemporaries—and, as it worked out, for posterity—the men of his era who seemed to him most representative, whether good or bad. He was admirably equipped to do the job: he had known many of these men personally, or at least seen them in action; he

---

59. See "Letters of Timothy Tickler, Nos. 9 and 10" and "The General Question" (September), "Noctes Ambrosianae, No. 12" (October), and "Letters of Timothy Tickler, No. 11" (November).

60. *MLN* 57 (1942): 460.

had an innate respect for greatness; and, as always, his powers of analysis and expression enabled him to make searching observations in a striking manner. Moreover, and equally important: writing these sketches proved to be a salutary exercise. Although he assured Walter Savage Landor, "you can hardly suppose the depression of body and mind under which I wrote some of these articles," [61] they served to pull his attention away from his personal woes—to direct his analytical skills toward other men rather than himself.

In the essay on Bentham he described his subject as he had known him— seen him, from the windows of the York Street house, as the old philosopher paced about his garden—then summarized the principles of Bentham's utilitarianism and probed to the source of its basic flaw: his ignorance of human nature. "If the mind of man," Hazlitt stated, "were competent to comprehend the whole of truth and good, and act upon it at once, and independently of all other considerations, Mr. Bentham's plan would be a feasible one, and *the truth, the whole truth, and nothing but the truth*, would be the best possible ground to place morality upon. But it is not so" (11:9). And he proceeded to examine the weaknesses of Bentham's arguments, finishing off with complaints about his *"topical"* reasoning (11:14) and his "barbarous" style (11:15)—adding, quite anticlimactically, a final paragraph about his personal habits. The essay was no masterpiece of orderly presentation, yet the need to center his attention on one figure gave it a unity which Hazlitt's discursive mind often failed to achieve. Even Crabb Robinson was compelled to accord it qualified praise; on February 14, after reading the article in the *New Monthly*, he noted in his journal: "The shrewdness and acuteness of Hazlitt render it absolutely a matter of grief that his moral obliquities should deprive his writings of the charm they would otherwise have." [62]

Hazlitt settled down now to write similar estimates of other contemporaries for the *New Monthly*. The subject of "Spirits of the Age, No. 2," in the February issue, was the Reverend Edward Irving, whom he had compared with Dr. Chalmers in the fourth number of *The Liberal*. Again he stressed (and vividly described) the sheer physical attractiveness of the man, the force of his personality, declaring: "He has, with an unlimited and daring licence, mixed the sacred and the profane together, the carnal and the spiritual man, the petulance of the bar with the dogmatism of the pulpit, the theatrical and the theological, the modern and the obsolete;—what wonder that this splendid piece of patchwork, splendid by contradiction and contrast, has

61. *Four Generations*, 1:184.   62. Robinson, 1:301.

delighted some and confounded others?" (11:39). Hazlitt was among the delighted, obviously; he could not resist such gusto, even while he deplored the "trashy and hackneyed" (11:45) volume of *Orations* which Irving had published. And he compared him again with Dr. Chalmers, concluding that "the one [Chalmers] is most indebted to his mind, the other to his body" (11:47). "Very maliciously but very ably done," Crabb Robinson wrote of the essay on February 20.[63]

In the March number of the *New Monthly* Hazlitt anatomized Horne Tooke in the third paper of the series, characterizing him as "the finest gentleman (to say the least) of his own party" (11:47), but branding him as a trimmer too self-centered to succeed as a politician or to contribute significantly as a member of Parliament. His real contribution, Hazlitt believed, was *The Diversions of Purley*, his philosophical investigation of the principles of grammar. And Hazlitt, whose own *English Grammar* had drawn on Tooke's principles, proceeded with an exposition of *The Diversions of Purley* and criticism of Lindley Murray's text, which had managed to dominate its field, though long outdated. In the course of the first three essays in his "Spirits of the Age" series he had moved from political theory to theology to grammar—with an ease that few of his contemporaries could have matched.

Sir Walter Scott was the subject of the April essay. And now Hazlitt's prejudices colored his judgment. He had no firsthand knowledge of Scott: he had seen him only briefly in Edinburgh while Scott was acting as clerk of Sessions.[64] But he did not hesitate to speak his mind: he dismissed Scott's poetry as lacking in "*character*";[65] he stated that the Scotch novels were wanting in invention, though unparalleled as "a new edition of human nature" (11:64); and he attacked Scott as a supporter of legitimacy, warning him that his glamorous pictures of "the good old times" would never accomplish their purpose of winning converts to his cause.[66]

By the time the essay appeared in the *New Monthly* Hazlitt was settled at the inn at Melrose, in Scott's own neighborhood—with his bride. How

63. Ibid., pp. 301–2.

64. See 11:276–77, 369, and cf. Landseer, 1:172.

65. The editors felt obliged to add a cautionary note at this point: "The writer of this paper, and not the Editor, must be considered as here presuming to be the critical arbiter of Sir Walter's poetry. A journal such as this cannot be supported without the aid of writers of a certain degree of talent, and it is not possible to modify all their opinions so as to suit everybody's taste" (11:333–34).

66. Hazlitt's stunning last sentence, quoting Pope's lines on "Atticus" and piling accusation upon accusation against Scott, did not appear in the *New Monthly* but was added to the essay as published in *The Spirit of the Age* (see 11:335).

the courtship developed, no one knows; the second Mrs. Hazlitt remains a shadowy figure who came into and left her husband's life with very little impact. Her given name was Isabella; her maiden name is unknown; she was supposedly twenty-eight years old when she married Hazlitt. According to the most reliable information available, she had been born in Scotland but had gone to the island of Grenada, in the British West Indies, in her late teens and there married Henry B. Bridgwater, an army officer who rose to the rank of lieutenant colonel before he died in 1819, leaving his widow an annuity of three hundred pounds or thereabouts. She returned then to Scotland and, reputedly, met Hazlitt by chance in the course of a stagecoach ride. They were married, presumably in Edinburgh—or at least in Scotland—not only because of her connections there but also because Hazlitt's divorce was not recognized in England.

Mary Shelley told Leigh Hunt that the new Mrs. Hazlitt was said to be "a nice kind of woman"; Haydon rated her "a very superior woman" and prophesied that she would make Hazlitt "a decent being in regard to washing his face and hands (et cetera)." [67] She must have been an intelligent woman if, as Charles Armitage Brown told Crabb Robinson,[68] she was drawn to Hazlitt because of his writing—and a tolerant one, at least if she had read his attacks on her countrymen. She must have had courage, as well, to defy convention and marry a divorced man whose moral indiscretions were no secret.

Hazlitt himself seldom mentioned the lady. He wrote few personal letters during the last years of his life, and his essays contained far less of a personal nature. However, two remarks that he made some time before this marriage may have some bearing on his motives. One was an incidental observation in a footnote to his "Guy Faux" article in November, 1821: "A man who has been jilted of his first choice marries out of spite the first woman he meets" (20:105 n.). The other was made to his first wife just after the divorce: that he "wished he could marry some woman with a good fortune, that he might not be under the necessity of writing another line." [69]

Characteristically Hazlitt did not plan his wedding journey in advance. He told William Bewick that when he and his bride climbed into the post chaise after the ceremony, the driver asked him what direction to take, and it suddenly dawned on Hazlitt that he had not given the matter a moment's thought. "Looking out before me," he told Bewick, "I observed two pointed

67. *Letters of Mary Shelley*, 1:303; Stoddard, p. 225. 68. Robinson, 1:387.

69. *Journals*, p. 249. It is worth noting that Hazlitt did not say that he wished to stop writing, but that he be relieved of the necessity for writing.

hills, and asked where are those hills? 'Melrose, Sir.' 'Then drive there;' and to Melrose we came." [70]

Hazlitt kept busy during their stay at Melrose. On April 16, when he wrote to Taylor and Hessey, he promised to read immediately some books that they had sent him and announced that he was returning the proof of *Sketches of the Principal Picture-Galleries in England*, which they were about to publish as a separate volume. [71] On April 25 he sent Jeffrey a review of Landor's *Imaginary Conversations* for the belated March issue of the *Edinburgh* and promised to have a review of Lady Morgan's *Life and Times of Salvator Rosa* finished by the end of the week (16:435). He was reading for pleasure too: he borrowed the Duc de Sully's *Mémoire* from "a small but well-stocked circulating library," but found it so "slippery with blood" that he turned for relief to Ann Radcliffe's *Sicilian Romance*, which proved to be equally distressing (17:321).

Two young friends, Sheridan Knowles and William Bewick, visited him during his stay at Melrose. [72] In later years Bewick wrote a detailed—perhaps suspiciously detailed—report of his visit, revealing how sensitive Hazlitt was, these days, to both beauty and pain. When he took Bewick to meet Knowles, who was out fishing, he cautioned him to be silent so that they might observe Knowles's grace and dexterity with the fishing rod. "Could a sculptor have struck him out in marble, standing on the rock, in one of his fine positions," Hazlitt told Bewick, "the statue would have made his fame, as the Gladiator did for the Greek sculptor." [73] One day, he declared, he had watched him for an hour from behind a bush.

Bewick described too how Hazlitt shrank from looking at the dead fish in Knowles's basket, but how he cried out, when the fish was held up to the sunlight, "How silvery! what rainbow hues and tints glisten and flit across its shining surface!" and quoted apposite lines from Waller, Lovelace, and another poet whose verse he had read when he was a boy. [74] Another day Hazlitt called Bewick's attention to "the beautiful variation of colour and tint on the stones and moss of an old wall opposite the window of the inn." But suddenly, when he saw an injured man being carried into the house, he rushed across the room, covered his eyes, and, according to Bewick, begged: "Don't let me hear anything of it; the man is dead, I dare say, but I cannot look at anything of the kind, death or the appearance of it, and pray do not

70. Landseer, 1:171.   71. *London Mercury* 10 (1942): 73.

72. Bewick's account of his visit at Melrose implies that Hazlitt met Knowles at Melrose by accident, but invited Bewick to visit him.

73. Landseer, 1:158.   74. Ibid., p. 160.

speak of it."[75] The same sensitivity underlay his reaction to a scene which they happened on one evening: "a low mound upon which stood a small stone building in ruins, and by its side an animal quietly grazing . . . in deep shade against a star-lit sky." "There is a picture," said Hazlitt, and proceeded, Bewick claimed, to dwell on "the sentiment that pervades it, the wonderful breadth and harmony and depth of effect that 'hangs upon the beating of the heart'"—none of which a painter could hope to reproduce.[76] Yet this same sensitivity could make him turn on the villagers as they stood gaping at this eccentric stranger in their midst and denounce them as "staring hawbucks" and "gaping Scotch ninnies."[77]

While Bewick was at Melrose he made the chalk drawing which was said to have caught the best likeness of all the portraits of Hazlitt that survive.[78] Hazlitt enjoyed the process; he prided himself on being, as he had written in the previous November, "an excellent sitter" (12:109). And Bewick was a keen observer of character; he later wrote of Hazlitt's "pale and contemplative face, . . . his head inclined on one side, and his searching expressive eyes bent in silent meditation" and of his "long black hair clustering in massy locks about a forehead and features the very image of intellectual refinement, of deep or critical investigation";[79] and all these he managed to convey in his sketch. Hazlitt himself was pleased with it and had Bewick set it up over the mantelpiece while they ate dinner. "He frequently laid down his knife and fork," Bewick says, "to contemplate the likeness, gazing earnestly and long, asking if really his own hair was anything like that of the drawing." When Mrs. Hazlitt assured him, "Oh! it is exactly your own hair, my dear," Hazlitt remarked, "Well, surely that puts me in mind of some of Raphael's heads in the cartoons. Ah! it is, however, something to live for, to have such a head as *that*." Knowles was so taken with the sketch that he wrote a sonnet on it, beginning, "Thus Hazlitt looked! There's life in every line. . . ."[80]

Naturally Hazlitt did not call on Sir Walter Scott while he was in his neighborhood. But Bewick walked over to Abbotsford "to see the place, its scenery, and its mysterious belongings" and was so interested in a portrait

---

75. Ibid., pp. 164–65.   76. Ibid., pp. 167–68.   77. Ibid., p. 163.

78. The original is preserved today in the Maidstone Museum. Copies by Bewick himself are in the National Portrait Gallery and in the possession of John Carter of London.

79. Landseer, 1:159. Patmore's description of Hazlitt (2:303–5) reinforces Bewick's by its similarity. However, he also singled out the "peculiar character about the nostrils, like that observable in those of a fiery and unruly horse" and the mouth, which "could scarcely be described, except as to its astonishingly varied power of expression." Both are remarkable in Bewick's drawing.

80. Ibid., pp. 166–67.

of Mary Queen of Scots that he later asked permission to make a drawing of it. Scott wrote granting permission, and Bewick returned to Abbotsford, made his drawing, and stayed overnight. Before he left the next day, Scott asked him how Hazlitt happened to be staying at Melrose. When Bewick told him about the recent marriage, "Sir Walter observed, with great apparent sincerity, that 'Mr. Hazlitt was one of our most eloquent authors, and a man, as far as he could be allowed to judge, of great natural and original genius; that it was a pity such great powers were not concentrated upon some important work, valuable to his country, to literature, and lasting to his fame.'" [81]

Bewick hurried back to Melrose, eager to repeat Scott's words. But during his absence Hazlitt had set out for London at short notice, leaving a note, and, as a farewell gift, the two volumes of Lady Morgan's *Salvator Rosa* which he had been reviewing.

In London the Hazlitts probably stayed at the lodgings at 10 Down Street, Piccadilly, which Hazlitt had taken earlier in the year, doubtless with his marriage in mind. It was a more genteel neighborhood than any he had previously inhabited. Sarah Hazlitt called on them and was "much taken with her successor," as Mary Shelley wrote in a letter to Leigh Hunt on July 29. [82]

Soon after their return the March *Edinburgh Review* came out with Hazlitt's extensive critique of the first two volumes of Landor's *Imaginary Conversations*. He had not been completely satisfied with the article when he submitted it to Jeffrey on April 25, [83] and it may well have undergone some "alterations and additions," as Patmore claims Hazlitt himself reported. [84] It opened with an emphatic statement quite in Hazlitt's manner: "This work is as remarkable an instance as we have lately met with of the strength and weakness of the human intellect. It displays considerable originality, learning, acuteness, terseness of style, and force of invective—but it is spoiled and rendered abortive throughout by an utter want of temper, of self-knowledge, and decorum" (16:240). Then followed a host of examples of Landor's "luxuriant crop of caprice, dogmatism, extravagance, intolerance, quaintness, and most ridiculous arrogance" (16:240). Yet Hazlitt recognized that Landor was "excellent, whenever excellence is compatible with singularity" (16:244).

81. Ibid., p. 197.

82. *Letters of Mary W. Shelley*, 1:303. "This is fact," Mrs. Shelley added, as if she could hardly credit her own words.

83. See Keynes, p. 83. Howe (16:435) speculates that Jeffrey made changes in only one of the passages about which Hazlitt expressed doubts.

84. Patmore, 3:160.

The discussions of the separate Conversations demanded a considerable knowledge of history, literature, and philosophy, at which Hazlitt would hardly have flinched—although Jeffrey might have found it necessary to correct some of the details—and it was probably Hazlitt who drew the line at discussing the "very new and learned principles" expressed by Prince Maurocordato and General Colocotroni in their Conversation because "we have no skill in wood craft nor in flat-bottomed boats" (16:260). Jeffrey might have seen fit also to tone down Hazlitt's praise of Napoleon or his criticism of Southey. But the penetrating analysis of human motives which took up a good share of the review was almost certainly Hazlitt's own.

In July Hazlitt published two more of his "Spirits of the Age" essays. One, "Lord Eldon," appeared in the regular series in the *New Monthly*; the other, "Character of Mr. Canning," in the *Examiner* for July 11, perhaps because the editors of the *New Monthly* found it too strong for their tastes. Both had the same faults as the earlier essay on Scott: Hazlitt had had no direct contact with either of the men he was treating, and his violent anti-Tory prejudice blinded him to their merits. He dealt in broad generalizations—often pure rhetoric—rather than the specific details which had given life to the first essays in the series. And he allowed his subjects no quarter: Eldon is "a thoroughbred Tory," an "*out-and-outer*" (11:145); he may seem good-natured, but"mere good nature . . . is often no better than indolent selfishness" (11:142); his "impartiality and conscientious exactness . . . in the stated routine of legal practice" may be "proverbial" (11:144)— yet "on all the great questions that have divided party opinion or agitated the public mind" he "has been found uniformly and without a single exception on the side of prerogative and power and against every proposal for the advancement of freedom" (11:146). Canning fared even worse: "He has no steady principles, no strong passions, nothing original, masculine, or striking in thought or expression. There is a feeble, diffuse, showy, Asiatic redundancy in all his speeches—something vapid, something second-hand in the whole cast of his mind" (11:151). Moreover, "the word *Legitimacy* . . . is the key with which you 'pluck out the heart of his mystery'" (11:156). The only relief from this shower of abuse came when Hazlitt condescendingly singled out for praise the parodies which Canning had written for the *Anti-Jacobin* twenty-five years earlier.

The July issue of the *Edinburgh Review* contained two articles by Hazlitt, the one on Lady Morgan's *Life and Times of Salvator Rosa* which he had been writing at Melrose and another on Shelley's *Posthumous Poems*, in which he did not scruple to express his honest opinions as frankly as he would have done if Shelley had been alive. "Mr. Shelley, with all his faults, was a man of genius," he acknowledged (16:266), and he wished "to speak of the errors of a man of genius with tenderness" (16:267). But he could not wholly admire the work of a poet who, as he put it, "had no respect for any poetry that did not strain the intellect as well as fire the imagination—and was not sublimed into a high spirit of metaphysical philosophy" (16:265). Nor could he praise the "filmy, enigmatical, discontinuous, unsubstantial" verse that Shelley wrote (16:274). "Almost all is effort," he maintained, "almost all is extravagant, almost all is quaint, incomprehensible, and abortive, from aiming to be more than it is" (16:265). Yet he paused to pay homage to Byron and Keats as well as Shelley—the three promising poets whose lives had so recently been cut off. Mary Shelley, understandably, was not pleased with the review, although she acknowledged to Marianne Hunt on October 10 that she did not know whether it was meant to be favorable or unfavorable.[85] Hazlitt could have told her that it was meant, above all, to be honest.

Lady Morgan's *Salvator Rosa* offered much less of a challenge to Hazlitt's critical faculties. He admitted at the outset of the review that he was "not among the devoted admirers of Lady Morgan" (16:284), although he deplored the treatment accorded her by Tory critics. He could not condone her reliance on imagination and speculation rather than fact, or her pretentious style, and he developed his essay largely by means of summary and excerpts which revealed the "showers of roses and clouds of perfume" (16:295) which obscured her biographical information. "Her prose-Muse is furnished with wings," he observed; "and the breeze of Fancy carries her off her feet from plain ground of matter-of-fact, whether she will or no" (16:299). He stated: "The art of writing may be said to consist in thinking of nothing but one's subject; the art of book-making, on the contrary, can only subsist on the principle of laying hands on every thing that can supply the place of it" (16:300). Lady Morgan's liberal principles might be laudable, but they were not enough to compensate, in Hazlitt's estimation, for her lamentable practices as an author.

At about this same time Hazlitt wrote an essay "On Egotism" which he later included in his *Plain Speaker*. "Of all modes of acquiring distinction and, as it were, 'getting the start of the majestic world,'" he stated, "the most absurd as well as disgusting is that of setting aside the claims of others in the lump, and holding out our own particular excellence or pursuit as the only one worth attending to" (12:158). And he proceeded, in the manner of

85. *Letters of Mary W. Shelley*, 1:307.

his Table Talk essays, to examine many facets of his subject—distinguishing between "sanguine" and "morbid" egotists, the latter of whom "not only want to be at the head of whatever they undertake, but if they succeed in that, they immediately want to be at the head of something else, no matter how gross or trivial" (12:167). In the course of his argument he drew, with his usual economy, on the lives of Salvator Rosa and Lord Eldon to help develop his points; and, almost inevitably, he referred to another case in point: "A prose-writer would be a fine tennis-player, and is thrown into despair because he is not one, without considering that it requires a whole life devoted to the game to excel at it; and that, even if he could dispense with his apprenticeship, he would still be just as much bound to excel in rope-dancing, or horsemanship, or playing at cup and ball like the Indian jugglers, all which is impossible" (12:168). And finally: "To conclude with a piece of egotism: I never begin one of these *Essays* with a consciousness of having written a line before; and endeavour to do my best, because I seem hitherto to have done nothing!" (12:168).

The general impression conveyed by this essay, as well as the other pieces written at this time, is that Hazlitt is in a better frame of mind than usual. And well he might be; he had had three long reviews published in the last two issues of the *Edinburgh*, he had begun a new series which eventually could be worked up into a new book, and he had two volumes about to be published. Once again he had escaped from the demands of daily or weekly journalism. And he had found a gentle helpmeet whose income, combined with his own, provided more financial security than he had ever before known.

The first of his new volumes, *Select British Poets*, was published by W. C. Hall during the summer of 1824. Hazlitt seems to have worked on it for several years, off and on,[86] and Lamb to have corrected his manuscript. In the preface he announced that the anthology was intended to improve on the Reverend Vicesimus Knox's *Elegant Extracts in Verse*, "at least a third" of which "was devoted to articles either entirely worthless, or recommended only by considerations foreign to the reader of poetry" (9:233). Hazlitt presumably chose the poems included and wrote the "Critical List of Authors," consisting of terse estimates of each of the poets represented. Some of them were remarkably cogent and deft; of Dryden, for example, he wrote that he

> stands nearly at the head of the second class of English poets, *viz.* the *artificial*, or those who describe the mixed modes of artificial life, and convey general precepts

86. See Keynes, pp. 74–75.

and abstract ideas. He had invention in the plan of his Satires, very little fancy, not much wit, no humour, immense strength of character, elegance, masterly ease, indignant contempt approaching to the sublime, not a particle of tenderness, but eloquent declamation, the perfection of uncorrupted English style, and of sounding, vehement, varied versification. The *Alexander's Feast*, his *Fables* and *Satires*, are his standard and lasting works. (9:238)

Unfortunately the volume ran into trouble almost as soon as it was released because it contained selections from contemporary poets reprinted without permission. It was withdrawn almost immediately, but reprinted by Thomas Davison and published by Thomas Tegg without the contemporary selections in the following year.[87]

Hazlitt's other new volume, published by Taylor and Hessey, was his *Sketches of the Principal Picture-Galleries in England*, which included the description of the earl of Exeter's collection at Burleigh originally written for the *New Monthly* and the essay "On Hogarth's Marriage a-la-Mode" from *The Round Table* as well as the essays which had appeared in the *London Magazine*.[88] None of the essays had undergone substantial revision. Hazlitt had changed their order and had deleted his gratuitous remarks about Scotchmen's inability to appreciate Rubens. But most of the changes were minor corrections such as an editor might have made, and no one, author or editor, seems to have noticed that Angerstein's collection was still hailed as "the finest gallery, perhaps, in the world" (10:7) and Lord Stafford's as "probably the most magnificent Collection this country can boast" (10:36). And although he rearranged the order of the essays, Hazlitt was apparently not seeking to strengthen the unity or cumulative effect of the volume; it trails off at the conclusion, even as the individual essays do.

The book did not attract wide attention. A reviewer for the *Gentleman's Magazine* wrote: "On opening this volume we anticipated much information. But how great was our surprise on its perusal, to find that instead of containing some rich stores of information, it abounded with reflections, the generality of which have not the least reference to the subject." He added that the essays were "adapted to pass away an idle hour in the closet; but as guides they will never be of much utility." And most readers would agree:

87. As Keynes points out (p. 75) Tegg seems to have taken over publication of the book before the 1824 edition was released, although Hall's name appeared on the title page.

88. The first announcement of the volume stated that it would contain Hazlitt's essay on the Elgin marbles from the *London Magazine* of February and May, 1822, but "Marriage a la Mode," a critical essay on Hogarth's series of that name, was unaccountably substituted (10:307).

Hazlitt's irrelevant introductory passages to each essay are often forced, and his brief descriptions of the paintings have little value as criticism. They were almost wholly subjective, reporting "the feelings which [the paintings] naturally excite in the mind of a lover of art" (10:3) rather than analyzing them. In an age when fine paintings were confined almost entirely to private collections available to the public only by appointment, there was an audience for such books; Patmore's similar series, "British Galleries of Art," in the *New Monthly* also was published as a separate volume. However, that audience was evidently limited, for Hazlitt's book was never reprinted during his lifetime, and it ranks as only a minor contribution to art criticism.

As soon as he had prepared his two volumes for publication Hazlitt was in a position to take the trip to Italy that he had long planned. Before he went to Edinburgh for his divorce, he had offered to write a "Picturesque Tour in Italy" for Colburn. Now he broached the scheme to Hessey and Taylor, asking for a fifty-pound advance, but Taylor refused.[89] He modified his original plan then; instead of confining himself to criticism of Italian art, he decided to compose a series of letters treating all phases of a journey on the Continent. And now or later he succeeded in persuading the editors of the *Morning Chronicle* to print the letters serially.

Soon he was involved in preparations for his trip. He probably wrote up several more "Spirits of the Age" essays, which Colburn agreed to bring out in a volume. He arranged for young William, now enrolled at a school kept by a Unitarian pastor William Evans at Park Wood, near Tavistock, to spend the long summer vacation and the Christmas holidays with his grandmother and Aunt Peggy at Alphington. On July 21, her seventy-eighth birthday, the elder Mrs. Hazlitt wrote to her grandson to assure him that she was looking forward to his visits. She had been pleased, she told him, to learn from him that "your Father and Mrs. Hazlitt were comfortable together." And she urged: "Tell Father to write to me by you, and now and then besides, and before he goes abroad." Then, doubtless recollecting her own foreign travel, so many years ago, that had cost her two of her six children: "I don't like his going: so many die there; such stagnant waters surrounding the towns, and all over the country."[90]

But nothing could deter Hazlitt. And toward the end of August he and his new wife set off by coach to Brighton, where they were to take the steam packet to Dieppe.

89. See Taylor's letter to the Reverend J. C. Hare dated April 19, 1825, and printed in Blunden, p. 163.

90. *Memoirs*, 2:107 n.

There were obvious advantages in getting away from London for a while. He badly needed a rest. Mary Shelley wrote to Marianne Hunt on October 10: ". . . when I saw him I could not be angry [at his review of Shelley's *Posthumous Poems*]—I never was so shocked in my life—gaunt and thin, his hair scattered, his cheek bones projecting—but for his voice and smile I sh[oul]d not have known him—his smile brought tears into my eyes, it was like a sun beam illuminating the most melancholy of ruins—lightning that assured you in a dark night of the identity of a friend's ruined and deserted abode." [91] Surely it would do him good to get a fresh start far from the scenes where he had suffered so much frustration and abuse. Even as he left, his friend Haydon was fuming at his remarks "on Academies and men of Genius" in his *Edinburgh* review of *Salvator Rosa*.[92] And the *Blackwood's* men were starting to resume their attacks: their July issue contained an article "Cockney Contributions for the First of April," which included a clever parody, "Table Talk, A New Series, No. 1: On Nursery Rhymes in General." Then in the August issue the ingenious Maginn, who had happened on the attack on Sir Walter Scott deleted from later copies of Hazlitt's review of *Peveril of the Peak* in the February, 1823, *London Magazine*, had written a damning article, "Profligacy of the Periodical Press," blaming John Taylor for the offensive attack. "The article was by Hazlitt," Maginn wrote to William Blackwood, ". . . but it is better to say Taylor for it will vex much more and perhaps bring an explanation." [93] And having hit on this convenient means of attacking Hazlitt without mentioning his name, he proceeded to reply to Hazlitt's review of Shelley's *Posthumous Poems* in "Letters of Mr. Mullion, No. 1" in the September *Blackwood's*. This time he pretended that Barry Cornwall had written the review under attack, and he flayed both him and Shelley mercilessly. He reached the nadir of poor taste when he encountered Hazlitt's remark that Shelley had drowned with a volume of Keats's poetry in his pocket: "But what a rash man man Shelley was, to put to sea in a frail boat with Jack's poetry on board! Why, man, it would sink a trireme. . . . Seventeen ton of pig-iron would not be more fatal ballast. Down went the boat with a 'swirl!' I lay a wager that it righted soon after ejecting Jack."

Fortunately for Hazlitt, he probably never read the words. By the time the article appeared, he had escaped from London and all its painful memories—for the time being.

91. *Letters of Mary W. Shelley*, 1:307.
92. *Haydon Diary*, 2:493–96.
93. *MLN* 57 (1942): 461.

CHAPTER XIV

Citizen of the World
(1824–1825)

Hazlitt set forth on his travels with an open mind and a quizzical eye. "The rule for travelling abroad," he told readers of his letters, "is to take our common sense with us, and leave our prejudices behind. . . . Let us think what we please of what we really find, but prejudge nothing" (10:89). He was determined to be a philosophical traveler, to reflect and learn as well as observe.

The coach ride to Brighton was marred by a tiresome monologue delivered "in a nasal tone by a disciple of [the Quakeress] Mrs. Fry and amanuensis of philanthropy in general," but he found relief in "some very charming scenery; Reigate is a prettier English country-town than is to be found anywhere—out of England!" (10:90–91). And as they arrived in Brighton, they heard a Frenchman strumming on his guitar and singing. "The genius of the South," Hazlitt decided, "had come out to meet us" (10:91).

The season at Brighton was at its peak, and the inns were filled. But a young Cockney accosted them and, out of sheer good will, volunteered to take them to the White-Horse Hotel, where he was stopping and where he knew they could find lodgings. "Amiable land of *Cockayne*," Hazlitt wrote, "happy in itself, and in making others happy! Blest exuberance of self-satisfaction, that overflows upon others! Delightful impertinence, that is forward to oblige them!" (10:90). He was obviously in a holiday mood, happy to be able to think the best of his fellows.

The town itself delighted him: "the bare cliffs," the "glazed windows to reflect the glaring sun," the "black pitchy bricks shining like scales of fishes," all "the finery and motion" of a resort town in full swing (10:90). He did not care for the celebrated pavilion; it looked to him like "a collection of stone pumpkins and pepper-boxes" (10:90). But he was stirred by the prospect of the sea, "that vast Leviathan, rolled round the earth, smiling in its sleep, waked into fury, fathomless, boundless, a huge world of water-drops" (10:90).

On the first of September the Hazlitts embarked on the steam packet to cross over to Dieppe. Their fellow passengers proved to be "pleasant and unobtrusive"—yet interesting to a student of nature, and Hazlitt singled out no fewer than eight of them for description and comment. His forbearance was severely tested, however, when the packet was delayed overnight outside the harbor at Dieppe and then, when they landed, by two couples who pushed ahead of them in the line at the passport office. "Persons in a certain class of life," he declared, "are so full of their own business and importance, that they imagine every one else must be aware of it—I hope this is the last specimen I shall for some time meet with of city-manners" (10:91). He had evidently not left all his prejudices at home.

At Dieppe the travelers put up at Pratt's Hotel in a delightful room over-looking the river—"and we should have thought ourselves luckily off, but that the bed, which occupied a niche in the sitting-room, had that kind of odour which could not be mistaken for otto of roses" (10:92). The town itself presented "a very agreeable and romantic appearance"; Hazlitt was charmed by the canals and drawbridges, the lime trees on the quay, the fine houses with high-walled courtyards, even the "huge, mis-shapen, but venerable-looking Gothic Church" (10:92). The inhabitants interested him even more: their clothing, their good-natured faces, their gesticulations. "You see the figure of a girl sitting in the sun," he wrote, "so still that her dress seems like streaks of red and black chalk against the wall; a soldier reading; a group of old women (with skins as tough, yellow, and wrinkled as those of a tortoise) chatting in a corner and laughing till their sides are ready to split; or a string of children tugging a fishing-boat out of the harbour as evening goes down, and making the air ring with their songs and shouts of merriment" (10:93). The French, he found, were charming when they were content to be natural; their life was much more comfortable than that in England. "This town is a picture to look at," he declared; "it is a pity that it is not a nosegay" (10:92). But he objected when the barber added citron juice to his shaving lather; it was "a false refinement . . . to which I was averse" (10:95).

From Dieppe the Hazlitts went by diligence to Rouen—a distance of thirty-six miles for eight francs each, plus two for the postilion, as Hazlitt carefully pointed out, adding that "travelling is much cheaper in France than in England" (10:95). The diligence cut "a very awkward figure, compared with our stagecoaches," yet it was "roomy and airy, and remarkably easy in its motion" (10:95); it reflected the Frenchman's interest in "the essential only" as opposed to English concern for "show and finish." And he continued to play his favorite game of observation and analysis as they rode, with harness bells jingling, at a rate of six miles per hour along the broad roads past peasants in wagons that looked like hencoops across "richly cultivated" plains divided by rows of trees instead of hedges. He wondered why the apple trees were allowed to overhang the roads; was it because of "the honesty of the inhabitants, or the plenty of the country"? (10:95). He noticed that the ploughs were driven by one man, as in Scotland. And he remarked on the number of women working in the fields—the older ones with "strangely distorted visages, and those horrid Albert-Durer chins and noses, that have been coming together for half a century" (10:95).

At Rouen they stopped at the Hotel Vatel, where the rooms were bare and dirty, but the food tasty. He was delighted with the view of the city from the surrounding hills; it alone was worth the trip to France. "The town is spread out at your feet (an immense, stately mass of dark grey stone)," he reported, "the double towers of the old Gothic Cathedral, and of the beautiful Church of St. Antoine rise above it in all their majestic proportions, overlooking the rich sunny valleys which stretch away in the distance" (10:98). He was disturbed, though, by the cripples who howled and begged their way along the hill known as Mont des Malades. "Would any people but the French," he asked his readers, "think of giving it so inauspicious a title?" (10:98). And thus he continued, observing, inquiring, reflecting, analyzing, interpreting. Even the green parrot at the hotel prompted speculations: "It is wonderful how fond the French are of holding conversation with animals of all descriptions, parrots, dogs, monkeys. Is it that they choose to have all the talk to themselves, to make propositions, and fancy the answers; that they like this discourse by signs, by *jabbering*, and gesticulation, or that the manifestation of the principle of life without thought delights them above all things? The sociableness of the French seems to expand itself beyond the level of humanity, and to be unconscious of any descent" (10:97). They were, beyond question, a puzzling lot.

The day Hazlitt was scheduled to leave Rouen he was "too late, or rather too ill" to take the diligence at six o'clock in the morning.[1] He set out later

1. From this point, until his departure from Paris for Italy, Hazlitt abandons the "we"

on foot "under a scorching sun and over a dusty road" in no mood to enjoy "the vast, marshy-looking plains of Normandy, with the Seine glittering through them like a snake, and a chain of abrupt chalky hills, like a wall or barrier bounding them" (10:100–101). At Louviers he boarded a diligence for Évreux, expecting to transfer there to one going on to Paris. He had as traveling companion an Englishman who had been on the packet from Brighton with him, but they "pretended not to recognize each other, and yet our saying nothing proved every instant that we were not French" (10:102). At Évreux he learned that the next diligence to Paris would not leave until the following evening. Back he went then the next morning to Louviers, where he set out once more, this time wedged into a coach with a screaming little boy, three talkative Frenchmen, and a dog. "It was impossible," he complained, "to suffer more from heat, from pressure, or from the periodical 'exhalation of rich-distilled perfumes'" (10:105).

As they drew near Paris, however, he forgot all his discomfort. "The approach to the capital on the side of St. Germain's," he wrote, "is one continued succession of imposing beauty and artificial splendour, of groves, of avenues, of bridges, of palaces, and of towns like palaces, all the way to Paris, where the sight of the Thuilleries completes the triumph of external magnificence, and oppresses the soul with recollections not to be borne or to be expressed!" (10:105).

Soon he was settled at the Hôtel des Étrangers, Rue Vivienne, where he received a call from—of all people—Sarah Hazlitt, who had been in Paris since early July. "He is most splendidly situated as to rooms," she wrote their son on September 25, "and gets his food cooked in the English way, which is a very great object to him; but, as may be supposed, it is terribly expensive." [2]

"The first thing I did when I got to Paris," Hazlitt wrote to his *Morning Chronicle* readers—doubtless with some exaggeration—"was to go to the Louvre" (10:106). He approached the galleries with some hesitation because he feared that most of his favorite paintings would be missing— returned to the places from which Napoleon had seized them. He knew, too, that he would inevitably be reminded of the downfall of his hero, and he

---

of the earlier and later narrative and speaks only of what "I" did. His wife was perhaps visiting elsewhere in France.

2. *Journals,* p. 260. Sarah, who had stopped by to ask for money and had received only "2 Napoleons of what he owed," had some reason to resent Hazlitt's lavish living arrangements.

allowed himself a passage of melancholy rhetoric on that score. His regrets
were sharpened when he encountered the liveried servants who had replaced the rude guards who had once irked him with their cry of "Citoy-
ens!" But he had long yearned to revisit the Louvre, and nothing could
stop him.

He was surprised to discover that only a few paintings had disappeared
from the Grande Galerie. Those remaining seemed, moreover, to have
mellowed in the twenty years since his last visit. Soon he was moving through
the galleries eagerly, seeing again the Claudes and Poussins, the Dutch and
then the Italian paintings, describing his favorites lovingly, and concluding
that this collection was "equal . . . to Mr. Angerstein's, the Marquess of
Stafford's, the Dulwich Gallery, and Blenheim put together" (10:113).
He was less enthusiastic when he described the sculpture: most of the fine
old pieces had been removed, and the modern statues in the "French
Saloon" seemed to him to show "labour and study" but to lack "taste and
genius" (10:168). French sculptors would do well, he believed, to cross
over to London and observe in the Elgin marbles the true spirit of classical
sculpture. Incidentally he admitted that his personal taste had always run
to painting rather than sculpture—partly, perhaps, because of his practical
experience as a painter, but also because "painting is more like nature"
(10:163).

Hazlitt visited the collection of French "historical paintings" at the
Luxembourg Gallery, too, but was not much impressed with what he found
there. "The fault . . . that I should find with this Collection of Pictures,"
he wrote, "is, that it is equally defective in the imitation of nature, which
belongs to painting in general; or in giving the soul of nature—expression,
which belongs more particularly to history-painting" (10:130). These
were fundamental principles in his aesthetic creed, and painters who ignored them might please him momentarily, but could never call up the
emotional response which he felt in the presence of truly great art.

He was encouraged, however, when he visited an exhibition of contemporary paintings, to learn that the new generation of French artists were
making their figures more animated. For his report to readers of the *Morning
Chronicle* on October 8 he composed a dialogue discussion between an
Englishman (one deeply imbued with Hazlitt's own artistic principles) and
a Frenchman who had been taught to revere the conventions of earlier
French art. The Englishman tries again and again to rouse his friend's
admiration for the spirit which enlivens these new paintings, but the Frenchman is guarded in his praise; to him the paintings are not "finished." The

Englishman argues that "they are finished as nature is finished" (10:127), but in vain.

Of course Hazlitt seized the opportunity to attend the theaters in Paris—the Théâtre Français, the Théâtre des Variétés, the Opera, the Salle Luvois. Talma and Mademoiselle Georges, "the great props of French tragedy" (10:154), whom he had seen before, were unfortunately not playing. But he saw Mademoiselle Mars as Célimène in Le Misanthrope at the Théâtre Français and pronounced her "an accomplished comic actress" (10:147). The entire company seemed to him to play flawlessly; they created an allusion so complete that "you forgot you were sitting at a play at all, and fancied yourself transported to the court or age of Louis XIV!" (10:150). Three years later he wrote of that perfect performance: "Nothing that we know of is a specific for conjuring up this shadow of the past, and making you (if you are in the mood) feel like a great booby school-boy, with a large bouquet at your breast, or an antiquated fop with a bag-wig and sword—but sitting at the Théâtre Français with Mademoiselle Mars and the whole corps dramatique drawn up on the stage" (18:380).

The other theaters he attended disappointed him. At the opera he remarked on the small attendance; the French are not fond of music, he decided, "it interrupts their talking" (10:169). And he found the opera itself dull, the ballet graceless; in fact the only person on the stage who held his attention was the "jerking, twisting, fidgeting, wriggling, starting, stamping" prompter (10:171). At the Salle Luvois, where the Italian opera played, he liked the performance better, but was annoyed by the inattention of the people of quality. French aristocrats, he noticed, "behave well at their own theaters, but it would be a breach of etiquette to do so anywhere else" (10:175).

He never stopped observing and comparing. He was an unabashed sight-seer who wanted to take in everything available, and he could recreate vividly all that he saw. He told his readers the bad as well as the good; Paris, he declared, is "a beast of a city to be in—to those who cannot get out of it" (10:155). "Fancy yourself in London," he suggested,

with the footpath taken away, so that you are forced to walk along the middle of the streets with a dirty gutter running through them, fighting your way through coaches, waggons, and hand-carts trundled along by large mastiff-dogs, with the houses twice as high, greasy holes for shop-windows, and piles of wood, greenstalls, and wheelbarrows placed at the doors, and the contents of wash-hand basins pouring out of a dozen stories—fancy all this and worse, and, with a change of scene, you are in Paris. The continual panic in which the passenger is kept, the alarm and the escape from it, the anger and the laughter at it, must have an effect on the Parisian character, and make it the whiffling, skittish, snappish, volatile, inconsequential, unmeaning thing it is. (10:155)

Yet, with all its faults, he admitted, "Paris, where you can get a sight of it, is really fine" (10:156). And he thoroughly enjoyed strolling the length and breadth of the city: across the river to the Champ de Mars, to the Jardin des Plantes at the opposite end of the city, to Montmartre, where the air "is truly vivifying and the view inspiring" (10:161). He especially liked the newly developed section near the Place Vendôme, where "there is a double side-path to walk on, the shops are more roomy and richer, and you can stop to look at them in safety" (10:157). But his favorite walk was to the Tuileries; it and Titian's "Man in Black" (*Young Man with Glove?*) were, he decided, the two things in Paris that he liked best (10:159–60). The gardens at the Tuileries seemed like "a powdered beau" or "nature to advantage drest"; those at the Luxembourg were "more extensive, and command a finer view," but looked "dilapidated and desultory" (10:159). The views from the bridges over the Seine especially delighted him: "The mass of public buildings and houses, as seen from the Pont Neuf," he wrote, "rises around you on either hand, whether you look up or down the river, in huge, aspiring, tortuous ridges, and produces a solidity of impression and a fantastic confusion not easy to reconcile. The clearness of the air, the glittering sunshine, and the cool shadows add to the enchantment of the scene. In a bright day, it dazzles the eye like a steel mirror" (10:156). He admired the architecture of the Chambre des Députés, the Tuileries and Luxembourg palaces, the Hôtel des Invalides, the Palais de Justice. And he made constant comparisons—of Paris and London, of the new Paris and the one he had known twenty years before. When he happened upon a Café Byron on one of the boulevards, he commented wryly that no one would be likely to open a Café Wordsworth in Paris.

He was most interested, of course, in the people—in all the details of their life which might help him to interpret their national character. The ubiquitous bookstalls surprised him. "They contain neatly-bound, cheap, and portable editions of all their standard authors, which of itself refutes the charge of a want of the knowledge or taste for books" (10:118). So did the number of people who were actually reading:

> You see an apple-girl in Paris, sitting at a stall with her feet over a stove in the coldest weather, or defended from the sun by an umbrella, reading Racine or Voltaire. . . . You see a handsome, smart *grisette* at the back of every little shop or counter in Paris, if she is not at work, reading perhaps one of Marmontel's Tales, with all the

absorption and delicate interest of a heroine of romance. . . . The French read with
avidity whenever they can snatch the opportunity. They read standing in the open
air, into which they are driven by the want of air at home. They read in garrets and
in cellars. (10:118–19)

At the French theaters "the attention was more like that of a learned society
to a lecture on some scientific subject, than of a promiscuous crowd collected
together merely for amusement, and to pass away an idle hour" (10:114).
Moreover, they showed a surprising knowledge of the plays themselves and
of the actors. After watching a performance of one of Racine's tragedies he
wrote: "The play was not much; but there seemed to be an abstract interest
felt in the stage as such, in the sound of the verse, in the measured step of the
actors, in the recurrence of the same pauses, and of the same ideas; in the
correctness of the costume, in the very notion of the endeavour after excellence, and in the creation of an artificial and imaginary medium of thought"
(10:115). All this hardly squared with conventional notions of French
levity. Yet he noted, at the same time, the ornamental clocks bearing the
legend "Le Tems fait passer l'Amour" (17:240).

He was fascinated by the people's faces—"grave and serious when they
are by themselves, as they are gay and animated in society" (10:119). He
was attracted, too, by the French women's way of walking, "that light,
jerking, fidgetting trip on which they pride themselves" and which he
attributed to "the awkward construction of their streets" or to "the round,
flat, slippery stones, over which you are obliged to make your way on tiptoe"
(10:156). He observed that "English women, even of the highest rank, look
like *dowdies*" (20:346) by comparison with the well-groomed Parisiennes.

When he walked outside the city, he was struck by the absence of sub-
urbs. "Not a hundred yards from the barrier of Neuilly" he encountered a
flock of sheep tended by "a dog and a boy, grinning with white healthy teeth,
like one of Murillo's beggar-boys" (10:158). The Bois de Boulogne offered
"a delicious retreat," with its endless "green-sward paths and shady alleys
. . . terminating in a point of inconceivable brightness" (10:158). He went
out along the river past Passy and to the Père Lachaise Cemetery, where he
mused over the graves of Abélard and Héloïse, of Molière, of the "double
traitor" Marshal Ney, of "Chancellors and *charbottiers*" (10:147). And he
marveled at the profusion of flowers about the place: the French had indeed
"made the grave a garden" (10:145).

He had little to say about his own social life in Paris. He wrote later of
seeing Stendhal, who had sent him a letter praising his *Characters of Shakespear's Plays*, and a Dr. Edwards, who had been one of his schoolmates at

Hackney thirty years before (10:246). He also referred, later, to a conversation about Shakespeare with a Frenchwoman (12:338), and his grandson reported that he had attended a reception given by the Duchesse de Noailles "in her bed-room";[3] but otherwise he seems to have been content to study life in Paris rather than to take an active part in it.[4]

Poor health may have prevented him from spending much time in company. Sarah Hazlitt told her son, in a letter of September 25, that his father had been too ill to write to him.[5] And when he was well, he needed, as always, to turn out enough literary work to meet his expenses. During the first part of his stay he recorded his impressions of France in thirteen articles which appeared sporadically in the *Morning Chronicle* between September 14 and November 17.

They were sprightly essays, crammed with vivid impressions of everything from the Cathedral of Nôtre Dame to the shapely legs of Frenchwomen. Hazlitt proved himself an incomparable guide: his artist's eye for detail and his writer's ear for language equipped him admirably for his task. So did his analytical mind, which was constantly at work—comparing Paris and London, French art and English art, French theaters and English theaters, even French cemeteries and English cemeteries—but most of all, French character and English character. This last was not as simple a matter as he had once supposed; the more he saw of the French, the more puzzling he found them. In many ways they reminded him of monkeys; "I confess," he wrote, "this . . . simile sticks a good deal in my throat; and at times it requires a stretch of philosophy to keep it from rising to my lips" (10:143). Yet Frenchmen could be bafflingly serious on occasion, and he was hard put to it to pin them down. "I change my opinion of the French character fifty times a day," he confessed, "because at every step, I wish to form a theory, which at the next step, is contradicted" (10:144). In one of his essays, "National Antipathies," he declared that prejudice sprang from feelings of inferiority, and he urged readers not to judge other peoples on the basis of flimsy evidence.

The essays suggest that Hazlitt was in an unusually expansive frame of mind; they are never darkened by self-pity or misanthropy. He allowed

---

3. *Lamb and Hazlitt*, ed. W. C. Hazlitt, pp. 55–56.

4. He may have deliberately avoided writing of his social life because he believed he should confine himself, in his articles for the *Morning Chronicle*, to matters of more general interest. He refers to his contacts with Stendhal and Edwards and the lady admirer of Shakespeare only later in his writing and incidentally as he is discussing more general matters.

5. *Journals*, p. 261.

himself an occasional thrust aimed toward Scott (10:158, 325) or Wordsworth (10:152 n.) or his long-suffering former brother-in-law (10:142 n.), but in general he seemed to be enjoying the change of atmosphere in Paris as well as the change of scene. The essays in the *Chronicle* were apparently well received, for on November 4 Henry Leigh Hunt, son and successor to John Hunt, wrote asking how much Hazlitt wanted for rights to publish the series in book form.[6]

Hazlitt wrote five other essays during his stay in Paris, three of them drawing on his recent experiences to confirm some of his cherished theories. One of these, "On a Portrait of an English Lady, by Van Dyke," was a rambling series of thoughts inspired by his visits to the Louvre. It began with a study of the lady in Vandyke's portrait, remarking that her face was distinctly English—and "natural" rather than French. Comparison with other portraits soon gave way to general remarks on the paintings in the collection. But they led to no specific conclusions. Probably the most salient point made was the statement "he then is the greatest painter who can put the greatest quantity of expression into his works, for this is the nicest and most subtle object of imitation" (12:290). The essay ended in a long paragraph distinguishing between his own taste and that of "princely collectors" like William Beckford—most of which had appeared as "Common Place No. 54" in the October, 1823, *Literary Examiner*.

Another essay written in Paris, "Sir Walter Scott, Racine, and Shakespear," opened with remarks on the relative merits of opera and tragedy, then went on to "the more immediate object" of the essay: the merits of the three writers named in the title. "Sir Walter's *forte*," Hazlitt concluded, "is in the richness and variety of his materials, and Shakespear's in the working them up" (12:344). He touched upon Racine only in the final paragraph, where he charged him with lack of original genius and imagination. "The genius of Shakespear is dramatic," he declared, "that of Scott narrative or descriptive, that of Racine is didactic" (12:346). And forgetting that he had warned against "national antipathies," he concluded the essay: "The French object to Shakespear for his breach of the Unities, and hold up Racine as a model of classical propriety, who makes a Greek hero address a Grecian heroine as *Madame*. Yet this is not barbarous—Why? Because it is French, and because nothing that is French can be barbarous in the eyes of this frivolous and pedantic nation, who would prefer a peruke of the age of Louis XIV to a simple Greek head-dress!" (12:346).

6. *Memoirs*, 2:124. In her letter to her son dated September 25 (*Journals*, p. 260), Sarah Hazlitt remarked that Hazlitt had failed to come to terms with Taylor and Hessey and would sell the rights to the book to the highest bidder.

Neither of these two essays appeared in any of the English magazines; they were published for the first time in *The Plain Speaker* in 1826. The other three essays written in Paris Hazlitt sent back to the *New Monthly Magazine*, where they appeared in the issues for January and February, 1825.

"Madame Pasta and Mademoiselle Mars," in the January issue, began, as might be expected, with a comparison of the two actresses' styles of acting, with Madame Pasta given preference because of her greater naturalness. Hazlitt then turned aside to a comparison of French and English character —and from that, to another of French and English art. Yet he found his way eventually back to the subject of acting and then clinched his point: "Natural objects convey given or intelligible ideas which art embodies and represents, or it represents nothing, is a mere chimera or bubble; and, farther, natural objects or events cause certain feelings, in expressing which art manifests its power, and genius its prerogative" (12: 334). Likewise: "Natural acting is ... fine, because it implies and calls forth the most varied and strongest feelings that the supposed characters and circumstances can possibly give birth to: it reaches the height of the subject" (12: 335). In short, truly great art and truly great acting must "anchor in nature" (12: 334).

Hazlitt's other article in the January *New Monthly*, "On Old English Writers," was inspired by his interest in the volumes of French standard authors which he found in Parisian bookstalls—and by an attempt to rouse interest in Shakespeare in France. He was not convinced that literature can be successfully imported into one country from another, but he heartily favored a revival of interest in the older English authors at home; their work has "a heartiness and determined resolution" about it (12: 315) that contrasts sharply with the flaccid products of contemporary writers. "Away then with this idle cant," he urged, "as if every thing were barbarous and without interest, that is not the growth of our own times and of our own taste; with this everlasting evaporation of mere sentiment, this affected glitter of style, this equivocal generation of thought out of ignorance and vanity, this total forgetfulness of the subject, and display of the writer, as if every possible train of speculation must originate in the pronoun *I*, and the world had nothing to do but to look on and admire" (12: 318). He offered then a rapid survey of English literature as it has descended "from the tone of the pulpit to that of the court or drawing-room, from the drawing-room into the parlour, and from thence, if some critics say true, into the kitchen and ale-house." And he added ominously: "It may do even worse than that!" (12: 323).

The last of the five essays, "On Novelty and Familiarity," which appeared in the February *New Monthly*,[7] was an exercise in analysis in his wide-ranging Table Talk manner. He stated the kernel of his idea early in the essay:

> Whatever art or science we devote ourselves to, we grow more perfect in with time and practice. The range of our perceptions is at once enlarged and refined. But—there lies the question that must "give us pause"—is the pleasure increased in proportion to our habitual and critical discernment, or does not our familiarity with nature, with science, and with art, breed an indifference for those objects we are most conversant with and most masters of? I am afraid the answer, if an honest one, must be on the unfavourable side; and that from the moment that we can be said to understand any subject thoroughly, or can execute any art skilfully, our pleasure in it will be found to be on the decline. . . . Thus in youth and childhood every step is fairy-ground, because every step is an advance in knowledge and pleasure, opens new prospects, and excites new hopes, as in after-years, though we may enlarge our circle a little, and measure our way more accurately, yet in ninety-nine cases out of a hundred we only retrace our steps, and repeat the same dull round of weariness and disappointment. (12:295–96)

He rambled on then, applying his theory to various aspects of life, usually with melancholy results. "The best part of our lives," he maintained, "we pass in counting what is to come; or in fancying what may have happened in real or fictitious story to others" (12:303). But he offered his readers some consolation at the end of the essay:

> Upon the whole, there are many things to prop up and reinforce our fondness for existence, after the intoxication of our first acquaintance with it is over; health, a walk and the appetite it creates, a book, the doing a good-natured or friendly action, are satisfactions that hold out to the last; and with these, and any others to aid us that fall harmlessly in our way, we may make a shift for a few seasons, after having exhausted the short-lived transports of an eager and enthusiastic imagination, and without being under the necessity of hanging or drowning ourselves as soon as we come to years of discretion. (12:310–11)

His weeks in Paris seem to have induced a rather mellow mood. These five essays, as well as the *Morning Chronicle* articles, suggest that Hazlitt had left his most pressing worries in London and was truly enjoying himself—walking, reading, attending the theater, visiting the galleries, and, of course, reflecting on all about him.

---

7. Actually the essay contains no internal evidence to indicate that it was written while Hazlitt was in Paris; in fact, the long autobiographical passage (12:303–5) might suggest earlier composition.

He took advantage of his stay in France to arrange with the publisher Galignani for a Paris edition of his *Table-Talk*. It did not involve any major effort on his part, since most of the essays included were selected from the two volumes already published in London. Galignani agreed also to bring out a Paris edition of *The Spirit of the Age; or, Contemporary Portraits*, which Colburn issued early in 1825.[8] The volume contained eighteen essays, five of which had already appeared in the "Spirits of the Age" series in the *New Monthly*. The thirteen new essays concerned, generally, men about whom Hazlitt had already written, yet he made, for him, surprisingly little use of his earlier articles.[9] In the past he had treated these men on special occasions: when reviewing one of their books or commenting on a specific action or, incidentally, when he found them useful to illustrate a general point. Here he could consider their total achievement to date, balancing the good and the bad, and attempt an assessment of the whole. In some of the essays, such as those on Wordsworth and Sir James Mackintosh, he took the opportunity to modify some of his earlier strictures.

It is notoriously difficult to gain proper perspective on what lies directly beneath one's nose, and Hazlitt did not always succeed. He had to strain hard to find any good in a Tory, especially a Tory convert, and his estimates of many of his subjects were clouded by prejudice. Yet he was a shrewd observer of human nature and a fearless man. Few of his contemporaries could have probed so expertly or would have dared to speak out so frankly. And none could have done the job with such style.

Inevitably in these brief, comprehensive essays, he dealt in broad generalizations based on intuitive analysis, often with little or no supporting evidence. He had written the essays rapidly, and he obviously spent little time in research or checking his facts. He made some egregious blunders—referring, for example, to Keats as "scarce twenty years old" when he died, and consistently spelling Washington Irving's name *Irvine*. Yet in the best of the essays he compensated, as usual, for such shortcomings by his revealing analysis of character and his engaging presentation.

He made few changes in the five essays which he reprinted from the *New Monthly*,[10] none of which indicate that he sought to reshape them to fit any

---

8. As Baker has pointed out (p. 433 n.), the book was in print before November 22, 1824. On that date Godwin returned a copy to Colburn with thanks.

9. The exception is the essay on George Crabbe, which was a revised and shortened version of the article on Crabbe which Hazlitt had written for the "Living Authors" series in the *London Magazine* in May, 1821 (see discussion above, pp. 290–91).

10. His two major changes were adding a paragraph about William Wilberforce to the essay on Lord Eldon and supplying the famous nonstop sentence at the end of his essay

general interpretation of the age such as was implied in the title of the book. They remain "Spirits of the Age" rather than facets of the spirit of the age. In some of the new essays, however, he was quite clearly working toward a definition of that spirit. He opened his essay on Godwin with the statement "the Spirit of the Age was never more fully shown than in its treatment of this writer—its love of paradox and change, its dastard submission to prejudice and to the fashion of the day" (11:16). The essay on Coleridge began: "The present is an age of talkers and not of doers; and the reason is, that the world is growing old. We are so far advanced in the Arts and Sciences, that we live in retrospect, and doat on past achievements. The accumulation of knowledge has been so great, that we are lost in wonder at the height it has reached, instead of attempting to climb or add to it; while the variety of objects distracts and dazzles the looker-on" (11:28–29).[11] And the essay on Wordsworth led off with "Mr. Wordsworth's genius is a pure emanation of the Spirit of the Age," then cited his use of "the simplest elements of nature and of the human mind" as the elements of his "new system of poetry" (11:86). There are other passing references to the spirit of the age, but none of them attempt to define it or even serve to provide a recurring pattern.[12] Hazlitt seems to be, as so often, more interested in finishing the job he has undertaken than in developing a thesis. The later essays in the volume are, as a rule, shorter and more hurried; he often treats two men in an essay, sometimes according one of them only a single paragraph. Moreover, his essay on Crabbe is a reworking of an earlier article, and that on Malthus ignores the man's character and merely presents another "reply" to his theory, including a generous excerpt from Godwin's essay *Of Population*. These later essays tend to lose force and interest—to decline in quality, generally. The volume closes

on Sir Walter Scott—applying to him Pope's biting judgment on "Atticus" in his "Epistle to Dr. Arbuthnot."

11. The last two paragraphs of the Coleridge essay, beginning, "It was a misfortune to any man of talent to be born in the latter end of the last century," did not appear in the first edition of *The Spirit of the Age*, but were added to the Paris and the second English editions.

12. Two of these occur in papers originally published in the *New Monthly:* Sir Walter Scott, Hazlitt stated, "would fain put down the *Spirit of the Age*" (11:66); the Reverend Edward Irving "has opposed the spirit of the age" (11:44). Five others occur in the later essays: Byron is described as one who "panders to the spirit of the age" (11:76) and Lamb as one who "has succeeded not by conforming to the *Spirit of the Age*, but by opposition to it" (11:178); the talent and tone of the *Edinburgh Review* are said to be "characteristic of the Spirit of the Age" (11:127); Jeffrey is "in advance of the age, and yet perfectly fitted both from knowledge and habits of mind to put a curb upon its rash and headlong spirit" (11:130); and "the spirit of the monarchy" is said to be "at variance with the spirit of the age" (11:37).

with an anticlimactic tribute to Sheridan Knowles added as a postscript to the final essay. Hazlitt may well have hurried through his task because he was eager to set out on his European jaunt. And although he rearranged the order of the essays for the Paris edition of the book and made other minor changes,[13] he gained nothing in the way of organization—and he virtually restored the original order in the second London edition of the book.

The individual essays are similarly wanting in organization: Hazlitt seems to be writing down his impressions of each man as they occur to him. The sort of revealing personal details which enliven many of the essays may appear at the conclusion as a sort of afterthought—or they may be missing altogether. Nor is there any attempt at climactic arrangement in the separate essays. In short, the faults of *The Spirit of the Age* are Hazlitt's chronic faults.

They are amply balanced, as usual, by his virtues: notably his perceptive analysis and his zestful style. Later readers are likely to prize most highly those essays which offer glimpses of famous men in everyday dress: Bentham, bustling about his garden; Wordsworth, reading his poems with beaming eye; Lamb, blurting out "the finest wit and sense in the world" (11:182). Unfortunately Hazlitt did not always provide such glimpses, even of men whom he knew well. He would probably have defended his practice by maintaining that he provided personal details only when they helped the reader to understand a character. Similarly, perhaps, he made use of comparison—of Byron and Scott, Coleridge and Godwin, the *Edinburgh* and *Quarterly* reviews—when they served his purpose. Some of these are brilliant exercises in analysis.

He is at his best, naturally, when he attempts a balanced estimate of a man whom he knows and respects. Although he may discern his subjects' limitations, he can sincerely honor their accomplishments. Often he traces their successes or their failures to sources in the character of the men or their time. The essay on Wordsworth is a case in point: Hazlitt singles out Wordsworth's originality for the highest praise, he explains his egotism as a reaction to public neglect, and he virtually retracts the charge of narrow-mindedness which he leveled at Wordsworth in his unfortunate "Illustrations of the Times Newspaper" in 1816 and repeated in his lecture "On the Living Poets."

13. For example, he added "Character of Cobbett" from *Table-Talk* (having omitted it from the Paris edition of *Table-Talk*) and "Character of Canning" from the *Examiner* for July 11, 1824.

Only a few of the essays have proved to have lasting interest. The best of them present incisive profiles of the distinguished men of a great era. However, the subjects of some, like the Reverend Edward Irving, have left no mark on history; others, like Thomas Campbell, seem hardly to deserve the praise which Hazlitt accords them. But more are stained with Hazlitt's prejudices—political prejudice in the treatment of Lord Eldon and Sir Walter Scott, personal prejudice in that of Lord Byron[14] and Thomas Moore. The most offensive, however, is the outpouring of pure invective in the essay on William Gifford, where Hazlitt's grudge is both personal and political. In it he dredges up his own old grievances against Gifford and airs them once again.

Incoherent, hasty, prejudiced—*The Spirit of the Age* is all these. However, the separate "portraits" of these philosophers, men of letters, and statesmen —good and bad, orthodox and radical, famous and obscure—all combine to form a vivid panorama of the age, one of the great eras of intellectual ferment in England, yet, to Hazlitt's distress, one which had fallen short of its promise. Although his name did not appear on the title page, the book was recognized immediately as his work: his mind and his manner were reflected in every paragraph.

It proved to be his most successful effort, passing through a second edition

14. Hazlitt broke off his essay on Byron suddenly with the announcement that he had just received word of Byron's death (April 19, 1824), adding that he would not alter what he had written because Byron himself would prefer to have it stand (11:77–78). Patrick L. Story ("Byron's Death and Hazlitt's *Spirit of the Age*," *English Language Notes* 7 [1969] 42–46) maintains that this final paragraph must have been added some weeks after Hazlitt had written the rest of the essay. But I cannot agree that all the essays in the volume were necessarily completed by April, 1824, as Story claims. In 1827 Hazlitt remarked in his essay "On Knowledge of the World" that he had told Jeffrey he had "composed a work in which [he] had 'in some sort handled' about a score of leading characters" (17:300). However, his use of "composed" need not mean that he had finished writing the essays. For that matter, there is no proof that the two men met in April, 1824, as Howe assumed (p. 337) and Story emphatically states. Hazlitt fails to mention such a meeting in his note of April 25 to Jeffrey, and he might well have told Jeffrey about his new work in a later letter which has not survived. Story's claim that Hazlitt's essay on Byron was written before that on Wordsworth is also suspect. He cites as proof Hazlitt's statement that he had already called Byron "the spoiled child of fortune." But in truth Hazlitt had used the phrase in two essays, an 1818 review of *Childe Harold's Pilgrimage* (19:35–43) and an 1821 article, "Pope, Lord Byron, and Mr. Bowles" (19:62–84), long before he had started work on *The Spirit of the Age*.

I must acknowledge, however, that I share Story's conviction that the conclusion of the portrait of Byron may have been "a separate and considered addition." Hazlitt could even, despite his disclaimer at the beginning of the essay, have written the entire piece after Byron's death and supplied the final sentences to protect himself against the charge that his frank appraisal of the dead poet was in questionable taste.

in London and one in Paris before the end of the year. Reviewers recognized immediately that it was a significant book, and it was noticed more promptly and more widely than any of Hazlitt's earlier publications. Most of the critics agreed that, though his interpretations might be questionable, he had done a brilliant job. The *Eclectic Review* for February declared that he could "hit off a likeness with a few artist-like touches, which may, indeed, be called a caricature, but still, the exaggeration is so dexterously managed as never to injure the likeness." The *New Monthly* for March hailed the book as "another volume from the reckless, extravagant, and hasty, but acute, brilliant, spirit-stirring, and always entertaining pen of the author of 'Table Talk'; for *his* it must be—or the devil's." The *Gentleman's Magazine* for the same month pronounced the author "a man of no ordinary powers, and were it not for a dash of the coxcomb in his criticisms, he would stand higher in the estimation of the world than he does. . . . His style is peculiar to himself, it is deeply impregnated with the spirit of the masters of our language, and strengthened by a rich infusion of golden ore dug from the pure mine of classic antiquity."

The *Monthly Review* treated the book in its leading article in the May issue. Yet the critic had reservations: Hazlitt had "considerable power," he acknowledged, "but it requires much discipline and regulation. It is his standing fault that he takes his pen with a strong determination, a malice prepense, to be impressive; and becomes, for that sole reason, obscure." The June 11 *Literary Gazette*, naturally, was even more dubious. "Where the author is intelligible," its reviewer wrote, "there is some spirited writing; but as for the truth of the portraits, it is quite evident that the limner had no sufficient opportunities for studying them from the originals; and that his pencil has been guided by personal feelings rather than by a regard to fidelity and likeness." One of the least favorable notices appeared in the *London Magazine*—not as a regular review but as a long "Letter from an Absent Contributor" who complained that half the book was Cherokee to him. "Mr. Hazlitt," he acknowledged, "is undoubtedly a very clever man; but, either from too great faith in his own genius, or from too comfortable a reliance on the obtuseness of the public, he publishes a vast quantity of verbiage which overlays and smothers his better sense."

The *Quarterly Review* ignored the new book—but not *Blackwood's*. In their May issue a reviewer railed:

Now that the Pillory is (perhaps wisely) taken down, what adequate and appropriate punishment is there that we can inflict on this rabid caitiff? The old Germans used to enclose certain criminals in wicker creels, and sink them in mud and slime. "Is there a man in all Scotland," or in merry England, that would not give his vote for the temporary immersion of this unnatural liar in the jakes? Who, if that punishment were carried into effect by the hands of a mudlark, would not laugh at the incurable culprit as he wriggled himself, in laborious extrication, from the penal ordure, and dropping at every faultering step filth from his body almost as loathesome as that which he had discharged from his soul, rushed for refuge into some obscene receptacle of the infamous and excommunicated, in the pestilent regions of Cockaigne?[15]

By the time the reviews began appearing, Hazlitt was too far away to be affected by either the praise or the blame. He had lingered in Paris far longer than he intended. In her letter of September 25, 1824, Sarah Hazlitt told young William that his father was planning to spend three weeks in Paris.[16] But October, November, and December passed, and he was still there at the turn of the year.

Finally, in mid-January of 1825, he and his wife left by diligence for Lyons en route to Italy. He later gave readers of the *Morning Chronicle* a lively account of the eccentric *conducteurs*, fellow passengers, innkeepers, waiters, and general onlookers whom he encountered along the way—and of the endless inconveniences and frustrations of travel in the year 1825. "Certainly," he commented wryly, "mine was not a Sentimental Journey" (10:178).

The trip to Lyons was trying, but the passage over the Alps via Mont Cenis in January was harassing. Although he had reserved two places inside the coach, he learned at the last minute that after they left Chambéry they would be assigned to one inside seat and one "in the *coupé*, which turned out to be a cabriolet, a place in front with a leathern apron and curtains, which in winter time, and in travelling over snowy mountains and through icy valleys, was not a situation 'devoutly to be wished'" (10:183). However, after suffering "a very purgatory of heat, closeness, confinement, and bad smells" (10:184) inside the carriage, they decided that the coupé would be preferable.

At first Hazlitt was thrilled with his new situation.

We had come a thousand miles to see the Alps for one thing, and we *did* see them in perfection, which we could not have done inside. The ascent for some way was striking and full of novelty; but on turning a corner of the road we entered upon a narrow defile or rocky ledge, overlooking a steep valley under our feet, with a headlong turbid stream dashing down it, and spreading itself out into a more tranquil river

15. Francis Jeffrey's review of *The Spirit of the Age*, in the April *Edinburgh Review*, is discussed below, pp. 421–22.

16. *Journals*, p. 261.

below. . . . and as the road wound along to the other extremity of this noble pass, between the beetling rocks and dark sloping pine-forests, frowning defiance at each other, you caught the azure sky, the snowy ridges of the mountains, and the peaked tops of the Grand Chartreuse, waving to the right in solitary state and air-clad brightness.—It was a scene dazzling, enchanting, and that stamped the long-cherished dreams of the imagination upon the senses. (10:188–89)

But eventually the novelty wore thin:

The wind cut like a scythe through the valleys, and a cold, icy feeling struck from the sides of the snowy precipices that surrounded us, so that we seemed enclosed in a huge well of mountains. . . . We travelled through a scene of desolation, were chilled in sunless valleys or dazzled by sunny mountain-tops, passed frozen streams or gloomy cavities, that might be transformed into the scene of some Gothic wizard's spell, or reminded one of some German novel. Let no one imagine that the crossing the Alps is the work of a moment, or done by a single heroic effort—that they are a huge but detached chain of hills, or like the dotted line we find in the map. They are a sea or an entire kingdom of mountains. (10:190–91)

There were moments of comic relief—as when a customs official discovered that one of Hazlitt's trunks was filled with books, and ordered that it remain "corded and *leaded*" as long as it was passing through the territory governed by the king of Sardinia. But most of the time the trip was a harrowing experience.

At length they reached Italy and Turin, where Hazlitt rejoiced in the "clean, spacious streets" (10:195), the view of the Alps, "the broad and rapid Po" (10:196), the "soft and balmy" air, the delicious dinner at the Pension Suisse—and the chance to change his clothing after the long journey. Only the number of beggars who "expose their diseased, distorted limbs" (10:197) and the confused, noisy opera which he attended marred his pleasure.

Next came an eight-day trip to Florence, including short stops at Parma and Bologna. Hazlitt enjoyed traveling along level ground, for a change, through "one continuous garden" (10:199), though he admitted that eventually the very lushness grew monotonous. It was carnival time, and he sketched vivid pictures of the costumes and the general gaiety for the benefit of his readers back in England. He added helpful hints or cautions, too, for those who might attempt a similar trip: he had seen no signs of *banditti* in Italy, he assured them, but he found the Italian inns much less hospitable than the French. "There is either a fawning sleekness, which looks like design, or an insolence, which looks as if they had you in their power" (10:198).

At Parma the Hazlitts took "a very fine but faded apartment" at the Peacock Inn. The view from their windows was "exhilarating," "full of noise and bustle" from the carefree carnival crowds. They enjoyed the luxury of a carpet—the first they had seen so far on their trip; unfortunately, though, it "stuck to the tiled floor with dirt and age" (10:201). Hazlitt was disappointed in the neglected Correggios in the Archduchess Maria Louisa's new gallery, but pleased with the architecture of the Farnese Theatre.

Bologna appealed to him even more; "its long arcades, its porticos, and silent walks," he wrote, "are a perpetual feast to the eye and the imagination" (10:205). In the Marchese Zampieri's collection he found "not a single picture worth seeing, except some old and curious ones of Giotto and Ghirlandaio," of which he observed rather patronizingly: "One cannot look at these performances (imperfect as they are, with nothing but the high endeavour, the fixed purpose stamped on them, like the attempts of a de-formed person at grace) with sufficient veneration, when one considers what they must have cost their authors, or what they have enabled others to do" (10:205–6). But he reveled in the Raphaels, Carraccis, Domenichinos, and Guidos at the academy and "left this Gallery, once more reconciled to my favourite art" (10:207).

Next came a hazardous trip over the Apennines, with the coach pulled part of the time by a yoke of oxen, through sleet and wind, along a perilous stretch of icy road, but ending at last in a dazzling view of Florence—"a city planted in a garden" (10:211). They took "apartments fitted up in the English fashion, for ten piastres (two guineas) a month" (10:217) and settled down to absorb the beauty of the place and its reflections of the past.

At first Hazlitt found it rather tiresome. The carnival was still in pro-gress, and the masked crowds and the "noise and jangling of bells" grew monotonous. Then Lent brought a "fishy fume" to the streets, and prompt-ed in him some strictures on "Popish religion." He concluded, however, that Catholicism was, after all, eminently adapted to the essential nature of man:

This religion suits the pride and weakness of man's intellect, the indolence of his will, the cowardliness of his fears, the vanity of his hopes, his disposition to reap the profits of a good thing and leave the trouble to others, the magnificence of his pre-tensions with the meanness of his performance, the pampering of his passions, the stifling of his remorse, the making sure of this world and the next, the saving of his soul and the comforting of his body. It is adapted equally to kings and people—to those who love power or dread it—who look up to others as Gods, or who would trample them under their feet as reptiles—to the devotees of show and sound, or the visionary and gloomy recluse—to the hypocrite and bigot—to saints or sinners—to fools or knaves—to men, women, and children. (10:215)

He saw a good deal of Leigh Hunt, whom he found in a sorry state; the failure of *The Liberal* and the death of Shelley and Byron had disheartened him, and he was stranded far from home, without the means to take his wife and children back to England. Hazlitt later told Haydon that Hunt was "moulting"—"dull as a hen under a pent-house on a rainy day." [17] When Hazlitt invited him to travel as his guest to Venice or Rimini, he refused flatly. Nothing could rouse him from his depression. One day when the Hazlitts were at his house, he told Mrs. Hazlitt that he had written something about her husband, adding: "I will not let him see it till after dinner, as it might spoil his appetite." Mrs. Hazlitt, however, insisted that he see it at once; "it will do him good," she said. Hazlitt read it then and observed: "By God, sir, there's a good deal of truth in it." [18] For once he accepted criticism graciously—probably because he did not want to quarrel with Hunt when he was in such distress.

Gradually Florence induced a genial mood in Hazlitt. Hunt wrote in later years that he "beheld the scene around us with the admiration natural to a lover of old folios and great names, and confessed, in the language of Burns, that it was a sight to enrich the eyes." [19] He was enchanted by the view from Hunt's house: ". . . you see at one view the village of Setiniano, belonging to Michael Angelo's family, the house in which Machiavel lived, that where Boccaccio wrote, two ruined castles . . .; and not far from this is the *Valley of Ladies* (the scene of *The Decameron*) and Fesole, with the mountains of Perugia beyond" (10:211). "Florence is like a town that has survived itself," he wrote. "It is left where it was three hundred years ago. Its history does not seem brought down to the present period" (10:212).

He was astonished to see the "colossal statues, bleached in the open air" in front of the Palazzo Vecchio. He did not always approve of them. Michelangelo's *David* looked to him "like an awkward overgrown actor at one of our minor theatres, without his clothes: the head is too big for the body, and it has a helpless expression of distress" (10:220). There was "something petty and forced" about Cellini's *Perseus;* "it smells of the goldsmith's and silversmith's shop" (10:220). The Venus de' Medici seemed to

17. Stoddard, p. 224.
18. *Memoirs*, 2:304. As Howe observes (17:422), the passage may have been the "article" which was later deleted from Hunt's *Lord Byron and Some of His Contemporaries.*
19. Hunt, *Autobiography*, p. 372.

him not "a poetical and abstract personification of certain qualities" (10:223), but "a little too much like an exquisite marble doll" (10:222). As for the Apollo Belvedere, it was "positively bad, a theatrical coxcomb, and ill made" (10:222). Yet he was delighted by the antique busts in the Medici Gallery; they gave "life and body" to history. And he apologized for his failure to respond to some of the works he had seen:

> Nothing more casts one down than to find an utter disproportion between the reality and one's previous conceptions in a case of this kind, when one has been brooding all one's life over an idea of greatness. If one could sneak off with one's disappointment in one's pocket, and say nothing about it, or whisper it to the reeds, or bury it in a hole, or throw it into the river (Arno), where no one would fish it up, it would not signify; but to be obliged to note it in one's common-place book, and publish it to all the world, 'tis villainous! (10:220–21)

When he came to describe the paintings at the Pitti Palace, he was transported: "the walls are dark with beauty, and breathe an air of the highest art from them" (10:225), he wrote, noting that the collection could "boast names in the highest ranks of art, and many of their best works" (10:225). He rejoiced at seeing Titian's *Ippolito de' Medici* and others of his favorites from the Louvre. And he described lovingly the hosts of Raphaels, Rubenses, Correggios, Giorgiones, and Andrea del Sartos that surrounded him. "Those who come in search of high Italian art will here find it in perfection," he declared; "and if they do not feel this, they may turn back at once" (10:226).

Hazlitt was eager to meet another distinguished English visitor in Florence: Walter Savage Landor. Scorning any letter of introduction, he appeared one morning at the Palazzo Medici, where Landor was staying, wearing "a dress-coat and nankeen trousers halfway up his legs, leaving his stocking well visible over his shoes." [20] He was embarrassed at first because of his unfavorable critique of *Imaginary Conversations* in the *Edinburgh Review*. It was written, he explained, "for knaves and fools." But Landor bore him no ill will. "A funny fellow he was," Landor said later. "He used to say to me, 'Mr. Landor, I like you, sir—I like you very much, sir— you're an honest man, sir; but I don't approve, sir, of a great deal that you have written, sir. You must reform some of your opinions, sir.'" Landor was especially pleased when Hazlitt attempted to describe Wordsworth.

20. The words are Mrs. Landor's, quoted in R. S. Super's *Walter Savage Landor* (New York: New York University Press, 1954), p. 177. Super has provided the most complete account of the association of Hazlitt and Landor, drawn from several sources, including John Forster's biography of Landor.

"You have seen a horse, I suppose," he said; and when Landor only smiled, "Well, sir, if you have seen a horse, sir, I mean his head, sir, you have seen Wordsworth."

Soon the two men were fast friends, forming the nucleus of a group which included Leigh Hunt, the artist Seymour Kirkup, Keats's friend Charles Armitage Brown, and Lord Dillon, an Irish gentleman-poet who loved to read his own effusions. Hazlitt enlivened one of their meetings with his account of how he had provided the evidence needed for his divorce.[21] And when it came time for him to move on to Rome, he left copies of the Paris edition of *Table-Talk* and *The Spirit of the Age* behind as farewell gifts to his new friend. Landor countered by writing an appreciative comment on *Table-Talk* and sending it off to his friend Reverend J. C. Hare, asking him to insert it in the second edition of *Imaginary Conversations*.[22]

Hazlitt seems to have found time during his stay in Florence to write the article "On Reading New Books" which first appeared in print in the July, 1827, *Monthly Magazine*. He rambled from one argument to another in the course of the essay, first wondering why there should be such a rage for reading new books when so many old ones went unread, then acknowledging that there is a real satisfaction in opening a new book "teeming hot from the press, which we shall be the first to read, criticize, and pass an opinion on" (17:200–201). Throughout the essay he balanced the merits of new and old against each other, but generally favored the old, which he felt had been undervalued in recent years. He concluded that the "diffusion of knowledge" had, in many ways, proved harmful; critical judgments had fallen into the hands of those least able to wield them. And in conclusion he called on "Learning" to resume its "robe pontifical," to clothe itself "in pride and purple," and "draw a bandage over the eyes of the ignorant and unlettered" (17:221)— with more of the same kind. It all sounds at times as if he had been listening rather deferentially to the patrician theories of Savage Landor.

21. See above, p. 320 n.

22. Because Hare disapproved of Hazlitt, he persuaded Landor to modify his statement before it was published. In the meantime Landor had broken off his connection with Taylor and Hessey, publishers of the first edition of *Imaginary Conversations*, probably in part because Hunt and Hazlitt had convinced him that he could get a more favorable contract from another publisher (see Super, *Walter Savage Landor*, pp. 181–84). The second edition was published by Colburn. Later in life Landor told John Forster: "Hazlitt's books are delightful to read, pleasant always, often eloquent and affecting in the extreme. But I don't get much valuable criticism out of them. Coleridge was worth fifty of him in that respect. A point may be very sharp, and yet not go very deep; and the deficiency of penetrating may be the result of its fineness" (Forster, *Walter Savage Landor*, p. 424).

In the middle of March, Hazlitt and his wife left Florence for the six-day trip to Rome—a distance of 193 miles; price seven louis for two people, he told his *Morning Chronicle* readers. At Sienna he made no comment on the exotic striped *duomo*, but described the city as "a fine old town, but more like a receptacle of the dead than the residence of the living" (10:228). As they went south, he remarked on the "stately remains of the ancient Etruscan cities, cresting the heights" (10:228) and on the rugged fort at Radicofani, "a majestic shadow of the mighty past, suspended in another region, belonging to another age" (10:229). And soon they were crossing the "flat, hazy plain" with the dome of St. Peter's looming up ahead (10:231).

They took lodgings in a house once occupied by Salvator Rosa at 33 Via Gregoriana, where they could "feast the eye" on the view of the city stretched out beneath and "indulge in sentiment, without being poisoned by bad air" (10:231). At closer quarters, however, Rome proved to be less than a feast; "instead of standing on seven hills," Hazlitt complained, "it is situated in a low valley: the golden Tiber is a muddy stream," and "St. Peter's is not equal to St. Paul's" (10:232). Moreover, "in Rome you are for the most part lost in a mass of tawdry, fulsome *common-places*. . . . A dunghill, an outhouse, the weeds growing under an imperial arch offend me not; but what has a green grocer's stall, a stupid English china warehouse, a putrid *trattoria*, a barber's sign, an old clothes or picture shop or a Gothic palace, with two or three lacqueys in modern liveries lounging at the gate, to do with ancient Rome?" (10:232). The imperial city, he decided, was "great only in ruins: the Coliseum, the Pantheon, the Arch of Constantine fully answered my expectations; and an air breathes round her stately avenues, serene, blissful, like the mingled breath of spring and winter, betwixt life and death, betwixt hope and despair" (10:232–33).

He was irked by constant reminders of the power of Catholicism: the location of the Protestant chapel outside the walls, the defacement of the English cemetery, the ghetto just beyond a church where all Jews must listen each Good Friday to a sermon "in behalf of the truth of the Christian religion" (10:233). And he was outraged when he happened upon "a tablet stuck up in St. Peter's . . . to the memory of the three last of the Stuarts" (10:244); he considered it a mockery of the English love of liberty. Yet he admitted, with some surprise, that the priests whom he encountered displayed "a perfect propriety, decorum, and humanity, from the highest to the lowest" and offered "not the slightest look or gesture to remind you that you were foreigners or heretics" (10:261).

On Easter Sunday he went to St. Peter's and saw the pope, who seemed to him a "harmless, infirm, fretful old man." The hosts of healthy-looking country people gathered to celebrate the holiday cheered him momentarily, but he was downcast at the sight of "a dirty, disgusting set [of pilgrims], with a look of sturdy hypocrisy about them" (10:237). And although he was dazzled when he saw the great dome of the cathedral illuminated, he was moved to comment: "Now and then a life or so is lost in lighting up the huge fabric, but what is this to the glory of the church and the salvation of souls, to which it no doubt tends?" (10:235). The ruins of old Melrose Abbey in Scotland were, he concluded, more to his taste than this ornate edifice. "I am," he wrote, "no admirer of Pontificals, but . . . a slave to the picturesque" (10:236).

All in all, Hazlitt seems to have been too long away from the comforts of home. Even the picture galleries at the Vatican, which he had so longed to see, proved a disappointment, and in his articles for the *Morning Chronicle* he disposed of them and five other galleries in a passage of two thousand words. "I shall not dwell long upon them," he explained, "for they gave me little pleasure" (10:237). The figures of Adam and Jeremiah on the ceiling of the Sistine Chapel helped restore his good opinion of Michelangelo, but he was distressed that he could not get close enough to make out the expressions on most of the faces in either *The Creation* or *The Last Judgment*.[23]

His discontent was no empty pose, adopted to amuse his English readers. On April 9, after three weeks in Rome, he wrote to Landor: "Rome hardly answers your expectations; the ruins do not prevail enough over the modern buildings, which are commonplace things. . . . I have got pleasant lodgings, but find everything very bad and dear." He added that he had "done what I was obliged to write for the Papers"[24]—that is, he had written two more articles for the *Morning Chronicle*, bringing the series up to his arrival in Italy—and he was thinking of spending a month at Albano, where he hoped Landor would join him.

He abandoned that idea, however, and after a visit to Tivoli, which he described as "a fairy spot . . . light and fanciful, yet steeped in classic recollections" (10:257), he and his wife returned to Florence. He dismissed the hill towns along the way with a few words in his *Chronicle* articles, but

23. In 1827, in his essay "The Vatican," a dialogue between "L" and "H," he made much the same points and devoted most of his time to a comparison of the works of Raphael and Michelangelo. When L asked, "Was there nothing else worth mentioning after Raphael and Michael Angelo?" H replied, "So much, that it has slipped from my memory" (17:150). Hazlitt did not usually have reason to complain about his memory!

24. *Four Generations*, 1:183-84.

dwelt rather on accounts of Italian bandits which he had heard or the rudeness of Italian drivers and innkeepers. Even Florence, when he reached it,
pleased him less than it had before; the "sultry heat" was oppressive, and the
people "looked exceedingly plain and hard-featured"—like Scotsmen, in
fact, "only fiercer and more ill-tempered" (10:263).

Soon they set out again for Venice, and when they reached the plains of
Lombardy, "the Garden of Italy, or of the World" (10:264), his spirits
revived. Ferrara delighted him; it had not been spoiled by modern innova-
tions. "Nothing is to be seen of Ferrara," he wrote, "but the remains,
graceful and romantic, of what it was"; of all the places he had visited in
Italy, "it is the one by far I should most covet to live in" (10:265).

They went on then through Padua and beside the "sluggish, slimy
waves" of the Brenta. And soon they were crossing by boat from Fusina
with Venice "rising from the sea" ahead of them.

Venice, he wrote, has a "magical, dazzling, perplexing" effect; "you feel
at first a little giddy" (10:267). It was all too fanciful and lavish, obviously,
and yet here somehow it seemed right. "The want of simplicity and severity
in Venetian taste," he decided, "seems owing to this, that all here is factitious
and the work of art: redundancy again is an attribute of commerce, whose
eye is gross and large, and does not admit of the *too much;* and as to irregu-
larity and want of fixed principles, we may account by analogy at least for
these, from that element of which Venice is the nominal bride, to which she
owes her all, and the very essence of which is caprice, uncertainty, and
vicissitude" (10:268). He proceeded, then, to enjoy the city wholeheartedly, marveling at the palaces, "massy, elegant, well-proportioned,
costly in materials, profuse of ornament" (10:269), visiting Titian's studio
—"an event of one's life" (10:270), and glutting himself with the paintings
by all the Venetian masters. He was overjoyed to see his old favorite,
Titian's *St. Peter Martyr,* again and to find that it was, as he remembered
it, "most probably, as a picture, . . . the finest in the world" (10:272).

From Venice the Hazlitts headed back through the lush plain country
(where the fine-looking people seemed to serve as a rebuke to the theories
of Malthus), stopped briefly at Verona to see the landmarks associated with
Romeo and Juliet, and arrived at Milan in the midst of festivities honoring
the visiting emperor of Austria. Hazlitt went to a mediocre opera at La
Scala, but did not go out of his way to see *The Last Supper.*

They stopped only briefly at Como, but lingered several days at Baveno,
on Lake Maggiore, and even thought of spending the summer there or at
Intra, where they could have rented an apartment with garden for a guinea

per month. But they decided to continue on to Switzerland, and they drove through fog and sleet over the Simplon Pass—less impressive, Hazlitt decided, though more picturesque, than the Mont Cenis route—to the village of Brig.

After a week at Brig they continued on toward Lake Leman through more mountains—"a gloomy succession of cliffs," Hazlitt now called them. And he apologized to *Morning Chronicle* readers for his failure to provide more details, saying, "the fault of mountain scenery in general is, that it is too barren and naked, and that the whole is exposed in enormous and un-varying masses to the view at once. The clothing of trees is no less wanted as an ornament than partially to conceal objects, and thus present occasional new points of view" (10:281–82). Thomas Medwin claimed later that Hazlitt told him he was "sick of alps and glaciers. . . . One range of alps is like another range of alps, one valley is like another valley; the eye can scarce distinguish the difference, so nearly alike are their features." [25] They reached the lake at last and followed the north shore to Vevey, drawn to the place because of its associations with *La Nouvelle Héloïse.*

They took lodgings at a farmhouse called Gelamont, "so 'lapped in luxury,' so retired, so reasonable, and in every respect convenient, that we remained here for the rest of the summer, and felt no small regret at leaving it" (10:284). The view from the house was not remarkable; in fact the whole area around Vevey consisted of a series of vineyards sloping down to the lake, with the mountain ranges stretched out beyond it. But Gelamont was delightfully secluded—"so entirely embosomed in trees and 'upland swells,' that it might be called, in poetical phrase, 'the peasant's nest.'" "Here every thing was perfectly clean and commodious," he wrote. "The *fermier* or vineyard-keeper, with his family, lived below, and we had six or seven rooms on a floor (furnished with every article or convenience that a London lodging affords) for thirty Napoleons for four months, or about thirty shillings a week" (10:285).

They settled into a quiet routine:

> Days, weeks, months, and even years might have passed on much in the same manner with "but the season's difference." We breakfasted at the same hour, and the tea-kettle was always boiling (an excellent thing in housewifery)—a *lounge* in the orchard for an hour or two, and twice a week we could see the steam-boat creeping like a spider over the surface of the lake ; a volume of the Scotch novels (to be had in every library on the Continent, in English, French, German, or Italian, as the reader pleases),

25. Thomas Medwin, "Hazlitt in Switzerland: A Conversation," *Fraser's Magazine* 19 (1839):278.

or M. Galignani's Paris and London *Observer*, amused us till dinner time; then tea and a walk till the moon unveiled itself, "apparent queen of the night," or the brook, swoln with a transient shower, was heard more distinctly in the darkness, mingling with the soft, rustling breeze; and the next morning the song of peasants broke upon refreshing sleep, as the sun glanced among the clustering vine-leaves, or the shadowy hills, as the mists retired from the summits, looked in at our windows. (10:287)

The routine was broken at least twice by visits from Captain Thomas Medwin, a distant cousin of Shelley's, who had lately married a Swedish countess and settled near Vevey. Medwin later described Gelamont as "on the banks of a small and rapid stream that falls into the lake at the entrance of the town. The house lies very low, so that it possesses no other view from the windows than a green paddock, overshadowed by some enormous walnut-trees. Behind, and across the rivulet, rises a hill of vines, sufficiently elevated to screen out the western sun. The spot is lovely and secluded." He was struck at once by Hazlitt's mournful appearance: "The lines of his countenance are regular, but bear evident marks of late and intense application; and there was an habitual melancholy in the expression, as though he had been chewing the cud of past miseries, or brooding on bitter anticipations of the future. His figure was emaciated; and it is evident his mind has preyed upon and consumed much of the vital energies of his frame; and this last, as was said of Shelley, seemed only a tenement for spirit." [26]

The first time Medwin called, the talk centered on Byron. Hazlitt inveighed against his avarice, his jealousy, his vanity, and his cavalier attitude toward poetry. He praised *Don Juan*, damned Byron's plays as undramatic, and complained of the gloom of his serious poems. "They are most of them the reflections of his own mind," he charged, "and that not an enviable one." [27] The second day it was Scott's turn. Hazlitt branded him as "the high priest of legitimacy"; by means of his beguiling pictures of the past he had "done more to put back the age than any writer of the day, the political economists and Malthus only excepted." [28] Soon he was launched on a half-hour diatribe against *Blackwood's* and reviewers in general, so "painful and distressing" that Medwin left hurriedly.

There were other, less upsetting interruptions to the quiet routine at Vevey. Hazlitt met an elderly physician named Le Vade who had known Rousseau. He reread *La Nouvelle Héloïse* and visited Clarens, Julie's supposed birthplace, and the Castle of Chillon down the lake at Montreux. He also brought his travels up to date in eleven articles that he sent back to

26. Ibid.　　27. Ibid., p. 281.　　28. Ibid., p. 282.

the *Morning Chronicle*. And he found time to write an essay or two in addition.

One of these, "Merry England," which appeared in the December *New Monthly Magazine*, showed Hazlitt in an unusually cheerful frame of mind. He remarked, in fact, in the course of the essay: "As I write this, I am sitting in the open air in a beautiful valley, near Vevey; Clarens is on my left, the Dent de Jamant is behind me, the rocks of Meillerie opposite: under my feet is a green bank, enamelled with white and purple flowers, in which a dew-drop here and there still glitters with pearly light. . . . Intent upon the scene and upon the thoughts that stir within me, I conjure up the cheerful passages of my life, and a crowd of happy images appear before me" (17:161–62). The essay was an analysis of English mirth, indeed a defense of it—a reply to those, especially the French, who believe that the English have no fun in them. Hazlitt admitted that his countrymen were a naturally gloomy people whose gaiety was "intermittent, fitful, irregular" (17:152–53). Yet he insisted:

> No people ever laugh heartily who can give a reason for their doing so: and I believe the English in general are not yet in this predicament. They are not metaphysical, but very much in a state of nature; and this is one main ground why I give them credit for being merry, notwithstanding appearances. Their mirth is not the mirth of vice or desperation, but of innocence and a native wildness. They do not cavil or boggle at niceties, and not merely come to the edge of a joke, but break their necks over it with a wanton "Here goes," where others make a *pirouette* and stand upon decorum. (17:160)

"We seem duller and sadder than we are" (17:161), he declared, citing himself as a case in point. Though he is momentarily at ease with the world, soothed by his lovely surroundings and cheerful thoughts, "no one would see it in my looks" (17:162). The Englishman's "cloud has at least its rainbow tints; ours is not one long polar night of cold and dulness, but we have the gleaming lights of fancy and genius to amuse us, the household fires of truth and genius to warm us" (17:161). Not such a bad people after all, the English—at least when viewed from the vantage point of Lake Leman.

Quite different in tone was the other essay which Hazlitt probably wrote at Vevey, "On the Jealousy and the Spleen of Party," which first appeared in *The Plain Speaker*. It began as a reply to Thomas Moore, who had "taken an opportunity, in his 'Rhymes on the Road,' of abusing Madame Warens, Rousseau, and men of genius in general" (12:365). "I am not absolutely blind," Hazlitt wrote, "to the weak sides of authors, poets, and

philosophers (for "'tis my vice to spy into abuses') but that they are not generally in earnest in what they write, that they are not the dupes of their own
imaginations and feelings, before they turn the heads of the world at large,
is what I must utterly deny" (12:369). And, thinking certainly of himself,
he went on:

> An author, I grant, may be deficient in dress or address, may neglect his person, and
> his fortune— . . . he may be full of inconsistencies elsewhere, but he is himself in
> his books: he may be ignorant of the world we live in, but that he is not at home and
> enchanted with that fairy-world which hangs upon his pen, that he does not reign
> and revel in the creations of his own fancy, or tread with awe and delight the stately
> domes and empyrean palaces of eternal truth, the portals of which he opens to us, is
> what I cannot take Mr. Moore's word for. (12:370–71)

And suddenly his old resentment welled up again. He deplored the timidity
of Whigs like Moore who had proved faithless to the cause of liberty; he
charged Moore and John Cam Hobhouse with having persuaded Byron to
withdraw from *The Liberal*. He recalled that Moore seemed to lose interest
in Hazlitt himself after *Blackwood's* unleashed its attacks on him.[29] And soon
he was raging at all liberals who had failed to stand behind him: "The
Whigs never stomached the account of the 'Characters of Shakespear's
Plays' in the *Quarterly:* the Reformers never forgave me for writing them
at all, or for being suspected of an inclination to the *belles-lettres*. 'The
Gods,' they feared, 'had made me poetical'; and poetry with them is 'not
a true thing'" (12:381). He concluded:

> One is hard-bested in times like these, and between such opposite factions, when
> almost every one seems to pull his own way, and to make his principles a stalking-
> horse to some private end; when you offend some without conciliating others; when
> you incur most blame, where you expected most favour; when a universal outcry is
> raised against you on one side, which is answered by as dead a silence on the other;
> when none but those who have the worst designs appear to know their own meaning
> or to be held together by any mutual tie, and when the only assurance you can obtain
> that your intentions have been upright, or in any degree carried into effect, is that
> you are the object of *their* unremitting obloquy and ill-will. If you look for any other
> testimony to it, you will look in vain. The Tories know their enemies: the People
> do not know their friends. The frown and the lightning glance of power is upon you,
> and points out the path of honour and of duty: but you can hope to receive no note
> of encouragement or approbation from the painted booths of Whig Aristocracy, or
> the sordid styles of Reform! (12:382)

29. On May 23–24, 1826, Haydon reported that he had seen Moore and Hazlitt at
Lord Stafford's house and that Hazlitt "came up & whispered to me, 'I hope he won't
challenge me'" (*Haydon Diary*, 3:101).

Obviously Hazlitt's feelings about England were ambivalent. He longed to be back among his own people, yet recoiled at the thought of submitting himself again to partisan clashes. He had several times considered settling permanently on the Continent, yet the pull of his own country was strong. Still, he kept postponing his return. In a letter to his son, whom he addressed as "Baby," although the boy was now almost fourteen years old, he said he expected to leave Vevey late in August.[30] But instead he crossed the lake to Saint-Gingolph soon after the middle of the month, then walked to Martigny, and from there began the rugged climb—which he eased by clinging to a mule's tail—to the Col de Peaume. There he had a breathtaking view of Mont Blanc, "the King of Mountains, stretching away to the left, with clouds circling round its sides, and snows forever resting on its head. It was an image of immensity and eternity" (10:291). The party descended then through the vale of Chamouni past glaciers which "gleamed like gigantic shrouds" in the moonlight. Then on to Geneva, which Hazlitt described as "a very neat and picturesque town, not equal to some others we had seen, but very well for a Calvinistic capital" (10:294). There he visited the house where Rousseau had lived—and there he happened upon a copy of the April issue of the *Edinburgh Review* containing Francis Jeffrey's critique of *The Spirit of the Age*.

It was a shock. In 1827 he wrote: "When I told J[effrey] that I had composed a work in which I had 'in some sort handled' about a score of leading characters, he said, 'Then you will have one man against you, and the remaining nineteen for you!' I have not found it so" (17:300). He had certainly not expected to have Jeffrey against him—Jeffrey, whom he had praised in the book as an impartial and percipient critic, a master of lucid style, and "the best-natured of men" (11:133). But Jeffrey subjected *The Spirit of the Age* to close scrutiny, singled out its faults as he saw them, and stated frankly:

> His writing is often powerful, and his ideas are generally original—sometimes valuable, not seldom brilliant. But a perpetual hunting after originality, and a determination to say every thing in a strange manner, lead him into paradox, error, and extravagance; and give a tinge of affectation to his style, which is far from captivating. His besetting sin is self-sufficiency, and this in all its branches, whereof dogmatism is among the most prevailing. Whatever he writes is likely to be read, and either praised or censured beyond its deserts. But it is his own fault that he does not write much better than he ever has done. Let him only be somewhat more humble and diffident. Let him reflect, that fine writing really cannot exist without good sense,

30. *Four Generations*, 1:185–86.

and an earnest pursuit of "whatsoever things are just, and whatsoever things are true;" let him be assured, that the first object with every rational writer is to be in the right, rather than to strike by novelty; and that no degree of brilliancy will ever make up for want of sense and nature; and with his talents, nay with far less than his talents, far more valuable books will be produced.

Back in Vevey Hazlitt wrote the only piece of verse which survives from his pen. It was not long or eloquent, but it was deeply felt:

> The rock I'm told on which I split
> Is bad economy of wit—
> An affectation to be thought
> That which I am and yet am not,
> Deep, brilliant, new, and all the rest:
> Help, help, thou great economist
> Of what thou ne'er thyself possest,
> Of financiers the ruthless Moloch
> Dry, plodding, husky, stiff Maculloch!
> Or to avoid the consequences
> I may incur from corporate dunces,
> I'll write as Allen writes the livelong day;
> Whate'er his Lordship says, I'll say—
> (To hint what ne'er was said before
> Is but to be set down a *bore*
> By all the learned Whigs and Dames
> Who fear you should out-write Sir James)—
> I'll swear that every strutting elf
> Is just what he conceives himself,
> Or draw his picture to the life
> As all the world would—and *his wife!*
> From Mackintosh I'll nature learn,
> From Sidney Smith false glitter spurn;
> Lend me, oh! Brougham, thy modesty,
> Thou, Thomas Moore, simplicity;
> Mill, scorn of juggling politics;
> Thy soul of candour, Chenevix;
> And last, to make my measure full,
> Teach me, great J——y, to be dull! (20:393) [31]

When he sent it off to John Black, editor of the *Morning Chronicle*, he headed it "The Damned Author's Address to his Reviewers." But Black did not see fit to print it.

Regardless of what the reviewers said of him, it was time now for Hazlitt

31. McCulloch, Allen, Sir James [Mackintosh], etc., were, of course, all contributors to the *Edinburgh*.

to return to headquarters and resume his trade. On September 20 he and his wife left Vevey and traveled by *char-à-banc* to Basel. It was, at first, "like an aërial voyage" (10:295). For miles they could see the Alps, especially Mont Blanc, whenever they looked back. But Hazlitt spared his readers any full description. "The combinations of language . . . answer but ill to the varieties of nature," he wrote, "and by repeating these descriptions so often, I am afraid of becoming tiresome" (10:295). In fact, he made short work of the journey to Basel and from there by diligence along the Rhine to Amsterdam. "I begin to tire of these details," he explained, "and will hasten to the end of my journey, touching only on a few detached points and places" (10:298).

Neuchâtel caught his eye; it seemed like an ideal spot for quiet retirement, a retreat. "The *golden mean*," he wrote wryly, "is, indeed, an exact description of the mode of life I should like to lead—of the style I should like to write; but alas! I am afraid I shall never succeed in either object of my ambition" (10:297). Holland looked neat, prosperous, and monotonous—"lumpish"—"perhaps, the only country which you gain nothing by seeing" (10:301). "What," he asked, "is the use of seeing a hundred wind-mills, a hundred barges, a hundred willow-trees, or a hundred herds of cattle at once?" (10:300). Amsterdam struck him as "a kind of paltry, rubbishly Venice" (10:300); its Rembrandts he considered inferior to those he had seen in England. The Hague looked like "Hampton-Court turned into a large town" (10:301).

Soon he was at Calais, taking offense at the conduct of an impertinent waiter (11:194). He was disgruntled again when he reached Dover: "The beef-steak which you order . . . with patriotic tender yearnings for its reputation," he complained,

is accordingly filled with cinders—the mutton is done to a rag—the soup not eatable —the porter sour—the bread gritty—the butter rancid. Game, poultry, grapes, wine it is in vain to think of; and as you may be mortified at the privation, they punish you for your unreasonable dissatisfaction by giving you cause for it in the misman- agement of what remains. In the midst of all this ill fare you meet with equally bad treatment. While you are trying to digest a tough beef-steak, a fellow comes in and peremptorily demands your fare. (10:286–87)

It was hardly a happy homecoming.

Even London failed to buoy him up; it looked to him "like a long, straggling, dirty country-town" (10:302). "I am not sorry, however, that I have got back," he told his readers. "There is an old saying, *Home is home, be it never so homely.* However delightful or striking the objects may be abroad, they do not take the same hold of you, nor can you identify yourself with them as at home" (10:302).

Hazlitt and his wife settled again at their lodgings at 10 Down Street in Piccadilly, and he set to work to finish his series of articles for the *Morning Chronicle* and to prepare the whole series for publication in book form. He had another project in hand as well: writing the last of the essays which would appear in his next volume of miscellaneous pieces, *The Plain Speaker,* in the following May. One of these, "Hot and Cold," was suggested by his travels; it turned on the nice question, why are people in the South less clean than those in the North? Hazlitt worried away at the problem, admitting that the Southerner's laziness had something to do with it, but that his tendency to accept life as it is had more. Basically, he believed, it related to religion and morals: "Those of the Catholic Communion are willing to take it for granted that every thing is right; the professors of the Reformed religion have a pleasure in believing that every thing is wrong, in order that they may have to set it right" (12:178). He had, at least, some novel ideas to show for his travels.

During the last months of the year he published no new articles in the periodicals; he needed to re-establish his contacts, perhaps also to sound out prevailing attitudes. In one of his last essays in the *Morning Chronicle* he wrote: "We travel into foreign parts to get the start of those who stay behind us; we return home to hear what has been said of us in our absence" (10:284). On the whole, the signs were encouraging; temporary retreat had proved strategic. *Blackwood's* had wasted little ammunition on him while he was out of range, and Haydon had forgotten his grudge. Hazlitt called on him on November 10, and the two spent three hours "with great delight," as Haydon wrote to Miss Mitford that day. "Hazlitt looks ill," he added; "but his jaunt has done him great good. . . . I like Hazlitt, in spite of all; everybody must." [32] And a month later, on December 12, an especially gloomy day, Haydon "called on Hazlitt, as being all in character with the day, and had a regular groan." [33]

But Hazlitt's gloom was chronic; so too was his poor health. He told readers of his *Chronicle* articles that he had lately gone on a diet of "brown bread, beef, and tea" to counteract "the systematic conspiracy carried on against weak digestions" (10:286 n.). He was wearing his graying hair cropped close to his head, so that he looked more than usually gaunt. Still, Haydon was convinced that his jaunt had done him great good.

32. Stoddard, p. 225.   33. *Haydon Diary,* 3:70.

Hazlitt himself might well have disagreed. In 1828, in an essay "Travelling Abroad," he declared that he was "one of those who do not think that much is to be gained in point either of temper or understanding by travelling abroad" (17:332). He had not, certainly, solved any personal problems in the course of his trip, though he had gained a welcome respite from many of them. But he had gained in other ways: he had seen paintings that he had long yearned to see; he had studied Frenchmen and Italians and Swiss and Dutchmen, all in their native habitat; he had gained a knowledge of European cities and villages. Henceforth he could qualify as a citizen of the world, a cosmopolitan. And incidentally he had stored up a body of materials which he would draw on in his writing as long as he lived.

CHAPTER XV

Superannuated Man
(1826–1828)

Hazlitt had a major project in mind when he returned from the Continent: a biography of Napoleon designed to counterbalance the effect of the unsympathetic *Life of Napoleon* which Sir Walter Scott was writing. It was the most ambitious task Hazlitt had ever undertaken, and he confidently hoped it would outlast all his work for the periodicals. However, it would demand a good deal of time, travel, and research, and he must rely on the magazines for support in the meantime.

His first published article after his return was the nostalgic "Persons One Would Wish to Have Seen" in the January *New Monthly*, recalling the stimulating conversations at the Lambs' rooms at 16 Mitre Court Buildings one evening twenty years earlier.[1] In February he wrote a more serious essay, "The New School of Reform," which was not published until his *Plain Speaker* appeared later in the year. It was a leisurely, readable dialogue between "Rationalist" and "Sentimentalist" on the merits of utilitarianism. The Sentimentalist (obviously Hazlitt himself) deplored the heartlessness of this system directed by "these new ferrets and inspectors of a Police-Philosophy" (12:181). "Believe me," he warned, "their theories and their mode of enforcing them stand in the way of reform: their philosophy is as little addressed to the head as to the heart—it is fit neither for man nor beast" (12:184). He deplored, too, their scorn for the products of the imagination—notably "my *Sentimentalities*," as Hazlitt wrote, borrowing a word applied by the *Westminster Review* to his *Lectures on the Dramatic Literature of the Age of Elizabeth*. "The *imaginary*," he declared, "is what

1. See discussion above, pp. 93–94.

we conceive it to be; it is reality that tantalizes us and turns out a fiction—
that is the false Florimel!" (12:193). And presently: "I place the heart in
the centre of my moral system, and the senses and the understanding are
its two extremities" (12:193).

Hazlitt struck out at heartless theorizing again in "Queries Addressed to
Political Economists" in the April 9 issue of the *Examiner*. This was a
series of twelve specific, hard-hitting paragraphs questioning the theory that
people are not impoverished by taxation since the amount of capital in their
nation remains constant. In a final note Hazlitt replied to David Ricardo's
contention that war and taxes are necessary evils, like famine or "diminished
fertility." "It is thus," he wrote, "our Whig philosophers and reformists try
to cover a particular grievance by a general law—(too big for it)—and to
approximate the acts of Government (which they find they cannot controul)
to dispensations of Providence" (19:281). Much as he longed for reform
in government, he could not approve the theories of this new school.

For the April *New Monthly* he wrote another informal essay "On the
Conversation of Lords," claiming that noblemen's advantages of experience
and education are bound to render them more brilliant conversationalists
than mere authors can ever hope to be. Gradually, however, he worked
toward a discussion of the drawbacks of authors, who are specialists in one
subject, ill equipped to engage in general banter. Modern men of letters,
he observed, fall into three classes—the bookworm, the hack, and the man of
genius. "This last personage (if he acts up to his supposed character) has too
much to do to lend himself to a variety of pursuits, or to lay himself out
to please in all companies. He has a task in hand, a vow to perform; and he
cannot be diverted from it by incidental or collateral objects. All the time
that he does not devote to this paramount duty, he should have to himself, to
repose, to lie fallow, to gather strength and recruit himself" (17:171).

Hazlitt himself was hardly lying fallow during the early months of 1826.
He was busy writing essays to be included in the forthcoming *Plain Speaker*,
then seeing it and the account of his travels in Europe through the press.
Yet he managed to renew contact with several of his old friends. He saw a
good deal of Leigh Hunt, who had returned from Florence in October.
The new Mrs. Hazlitt proved to be a gracious hostess—so much so that
Hunt wrote Hazlitt on June 20 from Highgate: "I know but one thing
that would take me to town sooner than the pleasure of passing an evening
with your masculine discourse on one side the table and 'the calm of pleasant
womankind' which you have on the other. Pray forgive my saying this, and
let Mrs. Hazlitt forgive me, but I am more at ease with you in your own house

than anywhere else, and have felt so comfortable there both in Florence and in Down Street, that I trust to please you by saying what I do, and think you should be pleased because it is true."[2] Patmore also visited the Hazlitts at the Down Street house and met Charles and Mary Lamb there.[3] Hazlitt saw Godwin too; on April 9 Godwin asked Colburn to send Hazlitt a copy of his new *History of the English Commonwealth*, and soon afterwards the two men and Mary Shelley attended the theater together (16:444; 11:188). He probably saw most, though, of old James Northcote, as readers of the *New Monthly* were soon to realize. Yet there were some old friends from whom he was estranged. Francis Jeffrey, probably unaware that Hazlitt had taken offense at his review of *The Spirit of the Age*, wrote to Barry Cornwall in May: "Can you tell me anything of our ancient ally Hazlitt?"[4] Cornwall may or may not have relayed the query to Hazlitt. If so, it prompted no reply: Jeffrey was not to hear directly from Hazlitt for more than four years.

In May, Henry Leigh Hunt and his new partner, Charles Cowden Clarke, brought out Hazlitt's *Notes of a Journey through France and Italy* essentially as the series had originally appeared in the *Morning Chronicle*. Hazlitt changed the order of a few of the essays, and he made occasional minor textual changes.[5] Yet the single volume had obvious advantages over the original series published at irregular intervals over a fourteen-month period. Readers might be more aware of Hazlitt's chronic impatience with a task—his tendency to hurry over and slight the final chapters. But they could better appreciate the rapid narrative, share in the rigors and rewards of contemporary travel, and enjoy Hazlitt's keen observations and his spontaneous reactions. And even as they relished his informal, frequently discursive, treatment, they might welcome the unusual unity and coherence imposed by the chronological narrative.

Reflecting as it did Hazlitt's complex personality and varied interests, the book should have had wide appeal. There were passages for those who wished to vibrate to the splendors of romantic landscapes, others for those whose tastes ran to the old masters, and always a surprising amount of information

2. Howe, p. 352.

3. Patmore (1:3) dates the meeting in 1824, but as Howe (p. 350) points out, his reference to his recently published *Rejected Articles* indicates that it took place in 1826.

4. Howe, p. 351.

5. Howe records Hazlitt's alterations of the original essays in his notes to *Complete Works*, volume 10. The most remarkable change is the omission of a long footnote belaboring John Taylor for his apologetic reply in the October, 1824, *London Magazine*, to the *Blackwood's* article "Profligacy of the London Periodical Press" (see 10:325–26).

about mileages, living costs, and the like. Unfortunately, however, too many travelers had written accounts of their travels in Europe, and Hazlitt's had not been extraordinary. "Adventures, there are none," the reviewer in the October *Monthly Magazine* complained; "novelty of object, there is none: he has an eye mainly for pictures—picture after picture is inflicted upon us, without measure or mercy—but a reflection for any thing and every thing." He acknowledged that "the book is full of remarks, more or less lively, sometimes sagacious, but oftener fantastic—in the writer's usual rambling, but still agreeable manner—governed by no law of association that ever was heard of before, though never forgetting his contempt for Sir W. Scott, his abhorrence of Croker and the Quarterly, or a smile at the charlatannerie of our classical Foreign Minister. Let nobody be repulsed by the introductory letter, full of *niaiseries* as it is; they will find compensation for a little perseverance." The August *Monthly Review* was much more severe. "There is no distress more ludicrous than that of a man of thorough mediocrity employed on a subject essentially requiring taste, intelligence, and knowledge," the critic began. He concluded: ". . . whether as a collection of views of foreign manners, or of intelligence of the arts, habits, and knowledge of France and Italy, it is *puerile*."

The Plain Speaker: Opinions on Men, Books and Things, published by Colburn in two sizable octavo volumes, also came out in May. It contained nineteen essays published over the course of the preceding seven years and thirteen new ones written at London, Renton, Winterslow, Paris, and probably Vevey.[6] Of the three essays which cannot be specifically dated (and which may well have been written early in 1826) one, "Reason and Imagination," continued Hazlitt's campaign against the rationalists.[7] This time he scorned all who think in general terms, all who ignore personal feeling. "Logic," he maintained, "should enrich and invigorate its decisions by the use of imagination. . . . Neither, I apprehend, is sufficient alone. . . . Men act from individual impressions; and to know mankind, we should be acquainted with nature. Men act from passion; and we can only judge of

6. Of the previously published essays nine had appeared in the *New Monthly Magazine* between 1823 and 1825; nine—including some of the earlier Table Talk essays—in the *London Magazine* in 1820 and 1821; and one in the *Edinburgh Magazine* in 1818. All these have been discussed in previous chapters. The ten additional papers which can be definitely dated have likewise been discussed in the pages above.

7. This in itself would suggest that the essay was written early in 1826, were it not for the sentence "Lord Byron has launched several of these ventures lately . . . and may continue in the same strain as long as he pleases" (12:53). Hazlitt would hardly have expressed himself so after Byron's death.

passion by sympathy" (12:45). He launched then into an attack on the cold reasoning of Bentham and, similarly, on contemporary dramatists' (especially Byron's) fondness for *grandes pensées* rather than reflections of individual feeling. Too many of the men of his time, he believed, were interested in "maps, not pictures of the world we live in: as much as to say that a bird's-eye view of things contains the truth, the whole truth, and nothing but the truth" (12:44).

"On Envy (A Dialogue)," another new essay, was a purported conversation between "H" and "N"—in effect the first of Hazlitt's published conversations with James Northcote. H begins this one by remarking, "I had a theory about Envy at one time, which I have partly given up of late —which was, that there was no such feeling, or that what is usually considered as envy or dislike of real merit is, more properly speaking, jealousy of false pretensions to it" (12:97). N retorts: "That which you describe is not envy. Envy is when you hate and would destroy all excellence that you do not yourself possess" (12:98). The two then develop their points through allusions to contemporary poets, statesmen, and artists. But the essay is interesting primarily because Hazlitt talks about himself too. He remarks, for example, that he feels very little envy because he is "tenacious" only of his reputation as a metaphysician. Yet when he lets loose a tirade against Sir Walter Scott's "*misalliance* between first-rate intellect and want of principle," N tells him: "You start off with an idea as usual, and torture the plain state of the case into a paradox" (12:99). The truth of the matter, N charges, is that H envies Sir Walter Scott because he has made a fortune from his writing. "Why," he asks, "do you so constantly let your temper get the better of your reason?" (12:101). Hazlitt may have been reporting Northcote's words, or he may have been putting words into the artist's mouth; in either case he showed unusual candor. And he was so pleased with the dialogue that he wrote up several more for future publication.

The third of the new *Plain Speaker* essays, "On Depth and Superficiality," was an exercise in definition and analysis. "I wish to make this Essay a study of the meaning of several words, which have at different times a good deal puzzled me" (12:346), Hazlitt announced frankly at the outset. And he proceeded to wrestle with *wickedness*, "the words *false* and *true*, as applied to moral feelings" (12:352) as well as *depth* and *superficiality*. In the process he introduced some noteworthy passages of self-analysis, not all of them truly relevant. One of them is baldly stated:

> I have often been reproached with extravagance for considering things only in their abstract principles, and with heat and ill-temper, for getting into a passion about

what no ways concerned me. . . . I am not, in the ordinary acceptation of the term, *a good-natured man;* that is, many things annoy me besides what interferes with my own ease and interest. I hate a lie; a piece of injustice wounds me to the quick, though nothing but the report of it reach me. Therefore I have made many enemies and few friends. . . . The craniologists give me the *organ of local memory,* of which faculty I have not a particle, though they may say that my frequent allusions to conversations that occurred many years ago prove the contrary. . . . The only faculty I do possess, is that of a certain morbid interest in things, which makes me equally remember or anticipate by nervous analogy whatever touches it. . . . It vexes me beyond all bearing to see children kill flies for sport; for the principle is the same as in the most deliberate and profligate acts of cruelty they can afterwards exercise upon their fellow-creatures. And yet I let moths burn themselves to death in the candle, for it makes me mad; and I say it is in vain to prevent fools from rushing upon destruction. (12:347–48)

Another is thinly disguised:

Suppose a man to labour under an habitual indigestion. Does it not oppress the very sun in the sky, beat down all his powers of enjoyment, and imprison all his faculties in a living tomb? Yet he perhaps long laboured under this disease, and felt its wither-ing effects, before he was aware of the cause. It was not the less real on this account; nor did it interfere the less with the sincerity of his other pleasures, tarnish the face of nature, and throw a gloom over every thing. . . . Let any one feel the force of disappointed affection, and he may forget and scorn his error, laugh and be gay to all outward appearance, but the heart is not the less seared and blighted ever after. . . . Again, in travelling abroad, the mind acquires a restless and vagabond habit. There is more of hurry and novelty, but less of sincerity and certainty in our pursuits than at home. We snatch hasty glances of a great variety of things, but want some central point of view. After making the grand tour, and seeing the finest sights in the world, we are glad to come back at last to our native place and our own fireside. (12:354–55)

Throughout most of the essay Hazlitt seems to be thinking aloud. And the passages are especially revealing because he is trying not to justify his nature but only to observe it.

Not all the essays in *The Plain Speaker* were so searching; their subject matter and Hazlitt's approach to them varied widely. Psychological studies predominate, but literature, art, acting—even "craniology"—all take their turns. Hazlitt muses on dreams, on sitting for a portrait, on the conversation of authors, on English mirth, on worldly success—anything from the nature of genius to dirt in Europe. He may be reminiscent or analytical, conversa-tional or hortatory, anecdotal or "technical" (as in the essay on Spurzheim's theories). He displays his usual fondness for paradox; he recurs again and again in the essays written during his stay in Europe, to the differences between Frenchmen and Englishmen; and he commonly develops his ideas through references to literature, to art, and to himself. There is little that can be said by way of summary: the essays are as miscellaneous as the subtitle of the book implies. Hazlitt seems to have gathered together whatever pieces he could easily lay hands on—including some of the earliest Table Talk essays which had been excluded from the published *Table-Talk* volumes. Yet for reasons of his own he omitted some of his finest, more recent essays like "My First Acquaintance with Poets" and "On Persons One Would Wish to Have Seen."

Like the *Notes of a Journey*, *The Plain Speaker* attracted little attention. Although the editors of the *Monthly Review* accorded it their leading article in June, the critic found fault with Hazlitt's egotism, his misanthropy, his defense of Napoleon, and his wordiness. "We shall not disgust our readers by any extracts from this wild and unsparing effusion of egotism," he wrote, "and shall only say, in the words of the author, that 'having got to the end of the volume, we hope never to look into it again.'" The August *Monthly Magazine* was at first severe: "Plain speaking is not enough. Truth is not enough, though unadulterated as an infant's prattle—though eliciting esteem for the author, and ensuring pleasure to the reader. Truth, indeed, stript of all low accompaniments, is no other than the purified offspring of genius— the elaborated production of patient thought; but it must be intenser truth, or newer truth, or far more embellished truth, than the usual flow of Mr. H.'s thoughts, to carry his name down to posterity." But presently the reviewer relented: "We have said, perhaps, more than we meant; if what we have said seems severe, it *is* more then we mean. We seize his books with delight, sure of enjoying over the pages which he pens a calming, enlivening, inspiring pleasure. We forget them, indeed, but we can read them again and again; and this is, perhaps, the next best glory to that of printing imperishable thoughts upon us." But most of the periodicals ignored the new volumes,[8] and *The Plain Speaker* never went past this first edition. Hazlitt must have wondered if both editors and public had forgotten about him during his stay on the Continent. But he could always reassure himself with the thought that his next book, the biography of Napoleon, would command their attention.

Soon after the two new books were published, Hazlitt and his wife left London again for Paris so that he could have access to materials for his biography. On August 7 he wrote to Patmore that he had rented a house at

---

8. Leigh Hunt tried to rouse interest in *The Plain Speaker* by reviewing it at length in his *Companion* in 1828. And in 1841 he called attention to it again, describing it as "a book, like all Mr. Hazlitt's other works, not half enough known" (*Leigh Hunt's Literary Criticism*, pp. 243–67, 339).

58 Rue Mont-Blanc—and, because he had failed to receive two remittances due him, he desperately needed to borrow twenty pounds, for which he promised to send over manuscripts of equal value (13:354). G. Huntly Gordon, a slight acquaintance of Mrs. Hazlitt's, wrote in 1866 the only record that survives of this second stay in Paris:

> I found her out when I was passing a few weeks there, being very desirous of re-newing my acquaintance with my former flame of one day, and to see Mr. Hazlitt, many of whose works I had read with much delight. She told me she never saw him take such a fancy, a fancy for any one as he did for me. I suppose this was because he found me a capital listener. . . . Once when I dined with them, and he drank three or four basins of Tea, he dissertated most charmingly from six o'clock till two in the morning, and was my cicerone in the Louvre one day from ten till four. His conversation on that day I thought better than any book I had ever read on the art pictorial. He was more striking and eloquent even than his printed pages.[9]

Inevitably Hazlitt devoted much of his time and energy in Paris to work on his *Life of Napoleon*. It was a new sort of project for him. He was used to relying on his memory for material stored up from past reading and experiences; now he must gather and digest a mass of factual material—he must exercise industry rather than ingenuity. He probably found relief from his work in enjoying the sights of Paris as he had done during his last visit—strolling through the streets, studying the people, visiting the theaters and galleries. And he tried, as an experiment, copying Titian's *Man in Black* to see how much of his skill as a painter he still retained.

He found the job much more difficult than when he had first copied the painting back in 1802; he seemed to have lost the knack. "I failed, and floundered on for some days, as might be expected," he wrote in September, 1827. "My sky was suddenly overcast. Every thing seemed of the colour of the paints I used. Nature in my eyes became dark and gloomy" (17:219). Yet when he stopped to reflect that he now had in literature a means of self-expression formerly lacking to him, he took heart. "The copy went on better afterwards," he declared, "and the affair ended less tragically than I had apprehended." In fact he finished the copy, carried it back to London with him, and found "considerable satisfaction in occasionally looking at it" (17:220).

Soon after his arrival in France "Boswell Redivivus," a new series of articles written before his departure from London, began appearing in the *New Monthly*. The August, 1826, issue contained the first article, which was prefaced by an explanatory note signed "JBR":

9. Howe, pp. 353–54.

I differ from my great original and predecessor (James Boswell, Esq., of Auchinleck), in this, that whereas he is supposed to have invented nothing, I have feigned whatever I pleased. I have forgotten, mistaken, mis-stated, altered, transposed a number of things. All that can be relied upon for certain is a striking anecdote or a sterling remark or two in each page. These belong as a matter of right to my principal speaker: the rest I have made for him by interpolating or paraphrasing what he said. My object was to catch the tone and manner, rather than to repeat the exact expressions, or even opinions. . . . Sometimes I have allowed an acute or a severe remark to stand without the accompanying softenings or explanations, for the sake of effect; and at other times added whole passages without any foundation, to fill up space. . . . My friend Mr. N——is a determined Whig. I have, however, generally taken him as my lay-figure or model, and worked upon it, *selon mon gré*, by fancying how he would express himself on any occasion, and making up a conversation according to this preconception in my mind. I have also introduced little incidental details that never happened; thus, by lying, giving a greater air of truth to the scene—an art understood by most historians! In a word, Mr. N. —— is only answerable for the wit, sense, and spirit there may be in these papers: I take all the dulness, impertinence, and malice upon myself. (11:350)[10]

Then followed the first of what were later to be known as Hazlitt's "Conversations with Northcote."

Few people would have cared to cultivate James Northcote's company. His quarters on Argyll Street were so dirty as to have become almost legendary, and his irascible disposition had prompted Peter Pindar to label him "that walking thumb-bottle of *aqua fortis*." But Hazlitt was used to both dirt and irascibility, and he was quite willing to put up with both for the sake of good talk. In an article published in December, 1827, he asked himself, "What, do you still praise that little old withered wasp?" and replied at once, "Yes: spleen before everything but truth; but truth before everything" (20:151). The two men had a good deal in common: both had been reared in Unitarian families, both were lovers of literature and art—especially the art of Titian. Moreover, Northcote had a wealth of anecdotes about the good old days of Reynolds and his circle to purvey, and he was, Hazlitt had proclaimed in his essay "On the Conversation of Authors," "the best converser I know," and "the best listener" (12:39)—and later: "the person, whose doors I enter with most pleasure, and quit with most regret" (12:85). He could hardly have found a more congenial way to underwrite his stay in Paris than listening to Northcote's talk and editing it for the enjoyment of the public.

10. How much editing Hazlitt actually did is anyone's guess. He may have been seeking in his preface to protect Northcote. But see below, pp. 461–62 and n.

The first installment of the series was typical of the papers that were to follow: odds and ends of miscellaneous observations and gossip set down in terse style with little attempt at transition or climax, as if recorded at the moment of delivery. Hazlitt did not try to be discreet; when, for example, in discussing Lord Byron's character, H reported what "G.'s daughter" told him one evening at the theater, N exclaimed, "What, the beauty-daughter?" And when H asked, "Do you think her a beauty then?" N countered, "Why no, she rather thinks herself one, and yet there is something about her that would pass for such. Girls generally find out where to place themselves." H went on then to repeat the lady's alleged opinion that "nothing could be meaner than [Byron] was," that "F—— was hardly a fair judge" of Byron's character, and that "Mr. S——could only just endure Lord Byron's company" (11:188). From other hints along the way a reader needed no extraordinary knowledge of English literary society to identify "G.'s daughter" as Mary Shelley, "F——" as Leigh Hunt, and "Mr. S——" as Shelley. The conversation veered off presently to safer ground with a discussion of Hobbes and Locke. But the indiscreet passage went uncensored.

When Leigh Hunt read the article, he was outraged on both his own account and Mary Shelley's. Hazlitt, with whom he had recently been on cordial terms, had betrayed him again—and was in Paris, out of reach. He protested immediately to Thomas Campbell, editor of the *New Monthly*, and Campbell replied on August 11:

> For this detestable passage in Hazlitt's paper I am, as I deserve to be, visited with much regret; but in as far as *you* are concerned, I have not the least consciousness of being to blame. There was, I must say, a culpable negligence in my not rejecting what relates to Mr. S., although I declare that, to the best of my remembrance, my offence was no more than oversight; for I could not have deliberately admitted anything so against him, so meanly impertinent, if I had been thinking of what I was suffering to go to press. I know not what I was thinking about, but I suppose I was stupefied by the fatigue of looking over a long roll of articles. The oversight, nevertheless, I repeat, was blameable, and I am justly punished for it by finding myself made the cat's paw of Hazlitt's calumny.
>
> As to you, my dear Hunt, I am truly indignant at being made the means of annoying you. . . . If I can say or write anything that can make you a shadow of satisfaction, I am willing to do so; but I suppose you will despise this devil's aspersions.[11]

The series continued, however, although Campbell probably censored the papers more carefully. And Northcote and Hazlitt carried on their public dialogue on whatever happened to be uppermost in their minds. In

11. *Correspondence of Leigh Hunt*, 1:251–52.

the September installment the main topics were expression in painting, the acting of the onetime prodigy Master Betty, and the value of advice from "a man of sense" (11:193–98). In October the conversation began with criticism of Reynolds and other painters, shifted to Northcote's recollections of his stay in Rome and of Burke and Goldsmith, touched on the respect paid to royalty and to literary men, and concluded with a discussion of nicknames (11:198–206). Some remarks about Haydon's egotism, however, were struck out, probably by the watchful Campbell.[12] In November the topics discussed were the actor Michael Kelly's singing voice, imitations of the antique, Ireland's Shakespeare forgeries, the unchanging nature of the world, Quakers' objections to color, monasticism, a letter which Northcote had written to a young lady admirer, and the ability "to look beyond ourselves" (11:206–13).

Obviously the series made no great demands on Hazlitt's talents. Patmore claimed that he would inquire of his friends whether Northcote was "in talking cue" before he called on him and that he had a faculty for bringing Northcote out. Yet the old man, according to Patmore, "often dreaded, and therefore hated him," and on one occasion declared: "I think, Mister Hazlitt, you yourself are the most perfect specimen of the Cockney School that I ever met with" and proceeded to give "satisfying reasons" for the charge.[13] None the less Hazlitt persisted in his visits; he was willing to submit to a bit of abuse for the sake of lively copy.

Before the close of the year 1826 he published one more article, another contribution to his campaign against the reformers, this one entitled "Hints on Political Economy." It appeared in the *Examiner* for December 24 and was probably written in Paris. In it he dealt with "one or two logical fallacies or oversights in Mr. Ricardo's definitions and arguments" (19:281). Specifically, he denied that political economy could be considered a science, he rejected Ricardo's theories that the value of a product depends on the

12. See 20:391–92, 447.

13. Patmore, 1:130 n.; 2:335–39. In the course of a long conversation with Haydon on August 3, 1826, Northcote damned Hazlitt as a disappointed artist and a vengeful critic, declaring that he tolerated him only because he feared him (*Haydon Diary*, 3:129–33). The trouble seems to have been that Northcote welcomed the publicity Hazlitt gave him but quailed when the "Conversations" had unpleasant repercussions. On such occasions he insisted that Hazlitt had put words into his mouth, as Hazlitt had admitted doing in his prefatory note to the series. Haydon complained that "if you accuse Northcote, he swears Hazlitt has put down what he [did] not say, and if you go to Hazlitt, he says, 'Am I answerable for what Northcote says?'" (ibid., 3:464). In the Mudge affair (discussed below, p. 437), Northcote played the hypocrite, insisting that he would have no more to do with Hazlitt even while he was continuing to see him regularly.

amount of labor involved in it and that rent is "the difference between the product of the best and the worst land in cultivation" (19:285). And he stated emphatically: "Abstract principles of political economy or anything else are only good when acted upon generally" (19:287). As always, Hazlitt was concerned with the individual case, the human being; and he stated his arguments bluntly in terms within the grasp of any reader.

His first periodical contribution for the year 1827 was "On the Want of Money," which appeared in the *Monthly Magazine* for January. He acknowledged wryly that "this essay is not a fanciful speculation" (17:176). Yet he seemed to be in an unusually genial frame of mind as he detailed the inconveniences of going without breakfast or dinner, of being unable to pay a reckoning, of having a dunning creditor, and the like. He managed, indeed, to spin a delightful fabric out of very tenuous substance. Coming immediately after "Hints on Political Economy," the essay—especially the five-hundred-word sentence (17:186–87) summing up the disadvantages of poverty—strikingly illustrated Hazlitt's stylistic versatility.

The February and March issues of the *New Monthly* contained two new installments of "Boswell Redivivus." No. 5, in February, wandered characteristically from the suicide of the artist Thomas Foster to the relative importance of public recognition and personal dedication in an artist's career, then on to women and their talents, ending in "a character drawn of his deceased wife by a Dissenting Minister (a Mr. Fox of Plymouth)" (11:218). The topics of no. 6, in March, ranged from Edmund Burke's shortcomings to the need for apparent spontaneity in art; unfortunately the conversation lingered too long over the affairs of another Plymouth clergyman, the Reverend Zachariah Mudge, who had "run away from the Academy where he was brought up, because Moll Faux, the housemaid, would not have him" and had "left the Dissenters to go over to the church, because the former would not give him some situation that he wanted" (11:357–58). Inevitably a copy of the article reached the gentleman's family, and they lodged strenuous protests. Northcote, who had been enjoying the publicity given him by the conversations, now took alarm. In an irate letter to Thomas Campbell he branded the series as "despicable and worthless trash" and Hazlitt as "a wretch who has betrayed me, and who is gone to France to escape the vengeance of those he has injured." Campbell assured Northcote in reply that "the *infernal* Hazlitt shall never more be permitted to write for the 'New Monthly.'"[14] So ended the series.

14. Stuart C. Wilcox, "Hazlitt and Northcote," *ELH* 7 (1940):325–32. Howe (11:357–59) reprints the passages which were omitted from the *Conversations* as published in 1830.

For the time being Hazlitt, in Paris, was probably unaware of his proscription. Fortunately he retained his tie with the *Monthly Magazine*, which published in its March issue his essay "On the Feeling of Immortality in Youth," a lyrical piece abounding in reflections on life and death, on the freshness of youth, the decay of age, and the suddenness of death. It contained Hazlitt's nostalgic comment:

> For my part, I set out in life with the French Revolution, and that event had considerable influence on my early feelings, as on those of others. Youth was then doubly such. It was the dawn of a new era, a new impulse had been given to men's minds, and the sun of Liberty rose upon the sun of Life in the same day, and both were proud to run their race together. Little did I dream, while my first hopes and wishes went hand in hand with those of the human race, that long before my eyes should close, that dawn would be overcast, and set once more in the night of despotism— "total eclipse!" (17:196–97)

It also contained a long and wholly irrelevant footnote (17:192 n.) belittling Lady Mary Wortley Montagu's snobbish critical attitudes. Artistic unity meant little to Hazlitt when he felt the urge to register a grievance.

This essay was the last of the periodical contributions published during his long stay in Paris. He was still there, apparently, on August 9, when Lamb wrote to Stoddart (now Sir John): "Hazlitt is resident at Paris, whence he pours his lampoons in safety at his friends in England." He added: "He has his boy with him." [15]

Presently Hazlitt and his son returned to London alone; and either just before or just after their return he learned that his wife had decided to leave him—that she was going to Switzerland at once with her sister. According to Hazlitt's grandson, young William started the trouble when he complained that his father had treated his first wife badly—and the second Mrs. Hazlitt decided that she could not hope to live comfortably with the boy in her household. [16] Probably she had more than one reason for her decision: she might have realized that because her marriage was bigamous by English law, she had placed herself in an impossible social situation; she might have suspected that her husband had been attracted to her primarily by her annuity, or that he would always cling to his memories of Sally Walker; or, again, she might simply have found him impossible to live with, as many before had done.

15. *Lamb Letters*, 3:115. Actually Hazlitt had sent no "lampoons" back to London. Lamb was perhaps referring to the first "Boswell Redivivus" article.
16. *Memoirs*, 2:196.

If so, he would doubtless have agreed with her; in fact the August issue of the *Monthly Magazine* contained an essay by him "On Disagreeable People" which spelled out at least some of his shortcomings as a husband. "I do not here mean to speak of persons who offend intentionally, or are obnoxious to dislike from some palpable defect of mind or body, ugliness, pride, ill-humour, &c.," he explained, "—but those who are disagreeable in spite of themselves, and, as it might appear, with almost every qualification to recommend them to others" (17:227). He singled out and described several disagreeable types: *"friendly grievances,"* as he called those who neither give nor inspire sympathy; chronic complainers; intellectual bullies; Scotsmen; *"bores* (mostly German ones)"; *"croakers,"* among others. Then, near the end of the essay, he ventured "a word, if I durst, of love": "Gallantry to women (the sure road to their favour) is nothing but the appearance of extreme devotion to all their wants and wishes—a delight in their satisfaction, and a confidence in yourself, as being able to contribute towards it. The slightest indifference with regard to them, or distrust of yourself, are equally fatal" (17:236).

The separation was hardly a staggering blow to Hazlitt. His marriage had almost certainly been one of convenience; his writings suggest that his attitude toward his second wife was almost entirely negative. And the separation was probably, in large measure, only an inconvenience. It meant, of course, that he could no longer count on her yearly income to supplement his own, and perhaps for this reason he settled in rooms at 40 Half-Moon Street rather than at the Down Street house which had been their headquarters. However, he had hopes of receiving a substantial windfall soon, for he had nearly completed the manuscript of the first two volumes of his *Life of Napoleon Buonaparte*, and the firm of Hunt and Clarke had promised to pay him four hundred pounds for the completed work.

Still he needed to keep up his work for the periodicals, and for the September *Monthly Magazine* he wrote an essay "On Means and Ends." In it he attempted to interpret the national characteristics of Frenchmen and Englishmen by comparing their distinctive approaches to art. The English artist, he decided, is impatient: he is forever *"jumping at a conclusion"* (17:214); the French is deliberate: *"He looks before he leaps"* (17:215). Later in the essay he cited characteristic differences in their reactions to failure: "Even should a French artist fail, he is not disconcerted—there is something else he excels in"; but "if an Englishman (God help the mark!) fails in one thing, it is all over with him" (17:218). He added: "It is the same with us in love and literature. An Englishman makes love without thinking of the chances of success, his own disadvantages, or the character of his mistress—that is, without the adaptation of means to ends, consulting only his own humour or fancy" (17:221).

In October he resumed his contributions to the *New Monthly* with two articles, both based on recollections of his stay in Italy. "English Students at Rome" maintained that "Rome is of all places the worst to study in" (17:138) because it offers too many distractions, and "the having the works of the great masters of former times always before us is enough to discourage and defeat all ordinary attempts" (17:138). "On a Sun-Dial" tells of a sundial which he saw near Venice with the inscription "Horas non numero nisi serenas," which "in an instant restored me to myself" (17:238). Then, after some evocative reflections on the relative merits of sundials, hourglasses, clocks, watches, bells in general, or the want of timepieces altogether, he wrote: "For myself, I have never had a watch nor any other mode of keeping time in my possession, nor ever wish to learn how time goes. It is a sign I have had little to do, few avocations, few engagements" (17:245). And he announced mournfully: "I confess, nothing at present interests me but what has been—the recollection of the impressions of my early life, or events long past, of which only the dim traces remain in a smouldering ruin or half-obsolete custom" (17:242). He was slipping back into his old mournful, subjective strains, finding consolation only in the past.

In November he found a new outlet for his writing in the *London Weekly Review*, which David Lester Richardson had founded early in the year and which Colburn was publishing. For the November 17 issue he wrote "Queries and Answers; or the Rule of Contrary," a series of three paradoxical aphorisms with a cynical tinge:

> 1. Why is the word *comfort* so continually in the mouths of the English?—Because the English are the most uncomfortable of all people. . . .
> 2. Why are the English so fond of clubs, corporate bodies, joint stock companies, and large associations of all kinds?—Because they are the most unsociable set of people in the world. . . .
> 3. Why are the English a credulous nation, and the eager dupes of all sorts of quacks and impostors?—Because they are a dry, plodding, *matter-of-fact* people, and having, in general, no idea of the possibility of telling lies, think all they hear or read must be true, and are left at the mercy of every empiric or knavish pretender, who will take the trouble to impose on them. . . . (20:149–50)

The following day the *Examiner* contained Hazlitt's article "The Dandy School," an attack on the shallow snobbishness of Benjamin Disraeli's

Vivian Gray and Theodore Hook's *Sayings and Doings* (20:143–49). He contributed two articles to the November *New Monthly*, neither of them very remarkable. One, "The Vatican," was a dialogue between "L" and "H" which largely repeated the points made about Michelangelo and Raphael in his *Notes of a Journey* (17:144–51). The other, "Why the Heroes of Romance Are Insipid," argued that the heroes of modern novels fail to hold our interest because they are too highly idealized to be convincing, and their eventual success is too inevitable (17:246–54). Hazlitt was pushing himself hard, turning out more than his usual quota of words. But he was not maintaining his usual standard of excellence.

At the same time he was finishing off the first two volumes of his *Napoleon*, and it was causing him a good deal of worry. Burglars tried to break into his rooms, and he feared for his own safety and that of his manuscript. He told a friend that the thieves would never have believed that he had neither watch nor money—"and, by God, sir, they'd have cut my throat." [17] The next day he carried his manuscript to a publisher's office and asked him to keep it until it went to press. He himself took refuge at Winterslow.

There he encountered more serious trouble. On December 7 he wrote to Charles Cowden Clarke: "I got a violent spasm by walking fifteen miles in the mud, and getting into a coach with an old lady who would have the window open. Delicacy, moderation, complaisance, the *suaviter in modo*, whisper it about, my dear Clarke, these are my faults and have been my ruin." Though he made light of his illness, it had apparently been serious. "I have been nearly in the other world," he told Clarke. "My regret was 'to die and leave the world "rough" copy.' Otherwise I had thought of an epitaph and a good end. *Hic jacent reliquiae mortales Guglielmi Hazlitt, auctoris non intelligibilis: natus Maidstoniae in comi[ta]tu Cantiae*, Apr. 10, 1778. Obiit Winterslowe, Dec. 1827. I think of writing an epistle to C. Lamb, Esq. to say that I have passed near the shadowy world, and have had new impressions of the vanity of this, with hopes of a better. Don't you think this would be good policy?"

He was less playful in treating the matter which was uppermost in his mind: he was annoyed by Hunt and Clarke's objections to the preface which he had prepared for his *Napoleon*. "I thought all the world agreed with me at present that Buonaparte was better than the Bourbons," he wrote,

or that a tyrant was better than tyranny. In my opinion, no one of an understanding above the rank of a lady's waiting-maid could ever have doubted this, though I

17. Ibid., pp. 232–33.

alone said it ten years ago. It might be impolicy then and now for what I know, for the world stick to an opinion in appearance long after they have given it up in reality. I should like to know whether the preface is thought impolitic by some one who agrees with me in the main point, or by some one who differs with me and makes this excuse not to have his opinion contradicted ? In Paris (jubes regina renovare dolorem) the preface was thought a masterpiece, the best and only possible defence of Buonaparte, and quite new *there!* It would be an impertinence in me to write a Life of Buonaparte after Sir W. [Scott] without some object as that expressed in the preface.

He was resolved to print his "defence," whether or not it appeared in the preface. "After all," he wrote, "I do not care a *damn* about the preface. It will get me on four pages somewhere else." In a postscript he added: "I can't go to work before Sunday or Monday. By then the doctor says he shall have made a new man of me."[18]

The several articles which he wrote for publication in December had subjective, often defensive, overtones. In the essay "On Knowledge of the World," which appeared in three installments in the *London Weekly Review* for December 1, 8, and 15, he declared at the outset that knowledge of the world is instinctive in men rather than acquired through experience and observation, then went on to argue that "there may be said to be two classes of people in the world, which remain for ever distinct: those who consider things in the abstract, or with a reference to the truth, and those who consider them only with a reference to themselves, or to the *main chance*" (17:290). Of course he numbered himself among the former group, and he took the opportunity to review some of his impartial judgments of the past—on Tom Paine, on Anglicans and Methodists, on Tories and Whigs and Reformers, on the prose-writings of poets, on Wordsworth and Moore—which had been unpopular and brought him disfavor, even though most people would now agree that he was right. The passage sounds like a sequel to his letter to Clarke. He concluded the essay cynically: "No: the way to get on in the world is to be neither more nor less wise, neither better nor worse than your neighbors, neither to be a 'reformer nor a house-breaker,' neither to advance before the age nor lag behind it, but to be as like it as possible, to reflect its image and superscription at every turn, and then you will be its darling and its delight, and it will dandle you and fondle you, and make much of you, as a monkey doats upon its young!" (17:303).

"Grave Imposture," a brief article which appeared in the *Weekly Review* for December 29, was in much the same strain. Here Hazlitt was incensed

18. Ibid., pp. 217–18.

that Robert Peel should be a candidate for presidency of the Royal Society although he did not truly qualify for membership in the society. This absurd situation confirmed Hazlitt's beliefs about worldly success: "The superiority which is confidently assumed, is even better than that which is proved, for it amounts to a self-evident proposition" (20:151).

For the December *New Monthly* he wrote another related essay, "The Shyness of Scholars," this one reverting to an old complaint: why bookish men like himself are seldom at ease in society. Some, he pointed out, have resorted to solitude; others, to ignoble company for solace. Momentarily he seemed resigned rather than resentful. "Every thing has its own limits, a little centre of its own, round which it moves," he declared; "so that our true wisdom lies in keeping to our own walk in life, however humble or obscure, and being satisfied if we can succeed in it" (17:264).

But though he might be resigned to cultivating his own garden, he knew that he must cultivate it assiduously. He still had high hopes for the success of his *Napoleon*, and he wanted it to be widely reviewed. In an undated letter to Cowden Clarke late in December he wrote: "Do you think it would be amiss to give [James Silk] Buckingham the first vol. for next week's *Athenaeum*, though Hunt, etc., do not write in it? The public are to be won like a widow 'With brisk attacks and urging, / Not slow approaches, like a virgin.'"[19] At the same time he was seeking new outlets for his articles. His first piece published in 1828 appeared in the January 5 issue of the *Sphynx*, another paper just established by Buckingham. It was entitled "Illustrations of Toryism—from the Writings of Sir Walter Scott," and it consisted of five examples of "nick-names" or slanted writing designed, Hazlitt charged, to prejudice readers of volume 4 of Scott's *Life of Napoleon* in favor of the official Tory point of view (19:288–91). It was, however, Hazlitt's only contribution to the *Sphynx*. Although he had momentarily regarded Buckingham as "the Editor of editors,"[20] he soon changed his mind. On January 18 he wrote to Henry Hunt: "I am not surprised at what you tell me; but drowning men catch at Buckinghams," adding in a

19. *Four Generations,* 1:191. Both the *Athenaeum* and the *London Weekly Review* contained advance notices of the *Napoleon* during the first week in January.

20. In an undated letter to Clarke from Winterslow he asked Clarke to forward "the enclosed hare and Wiltshire bacon to the most agreeable of biographers at Highgate [i.e., Leigh Hunt]; & the other thumper & the article to the Editor of editors, J. S. Buckingham, Esq." (*Lamb and Hazlitt,* p. 144). His good will toward Buckingham may have been directly due to the advance notice of his *Life of Napoleon* in the *Athenaeum* (see above, n. 19).

postscript: "I won't send any more to B. unless he *remits*, which he does not seem inclined to do."[21]

Hazlitt was growing desperate, and he began casting about for editors who would accept his articles and remit promptly. In reply to a letter from David Constable of Edinburgh, who had succeeded his father, Archibald, as editor of the *Edinburgh Magazine*, he wrote on January 10:

> It has come into my head that I could make a little volume of outlines or elements of the following subjects. 1. Of Law. 2. Of Morals. 3. Of the Human Mind. 4. Of Taste. 5. Of Political Economy. 6. Of English Grammar. On all these but the fifth, I have something new to offer. Do you think you could print such a work (I would leave the price to you) or that it might possibly do for the Miscellany? . . . If you want to see how dry I can be in the way of elementary analysis, Ritchie has a book of mine *On Human Action* which no one can charge with being florid or *ad captandum vulgus*.

In a postscript he inserted an afterthought: "If I should go to Paris in the spring, could you find any use for a series of papers on French plays and players? I am a great admirer of their theatre—as much so as I abominate their style of art."[22]

In his January 18 letter to Henry Hunt he thanked him for a remittance of two pounds and suggested corrections for the manuscript of the *Life of Napoleon*. "Is the Preface to go?" he asked. "You'll see I can bear it out, and perhaps play the devil with some people." He suggested that the publishers place an advance notice of the book in the *Examiner* to "give us a kind of prepossession of the ground."[23] And when they demurred, he wrote earnestly to Clarke on February 1:

> "To you Duke Humphrey must unfold his grief" in the following queries.
> 1. Is it unworthy of our dignity and injurious to our interest to have the Life noticed favourably in a journal that is not the pink of classical elegance?
> 2. Are we to do nothing to secure (beforehand) a favourable hearing to it, lest we should be suspected or charged with being accomplices in the success of our own work by the Charing Cross Gang who would ruin you and me out of their sheer dogmatism and malignity?
> 3. Must we wait for Mr. Southern to give his opinion, before we dare come before the public even in an extract? Or be first hung up by our enemies, in order to be cut down by our zealous Whig and Reform friends?
> 4. When the house is beset by robbers, are we to leave the doors open, to shew our innocence and immaculateness of intention?

21. *Four Generations*, 1:188–89.   22. Howe, pp. 360–61.
23. *Four Generations*, 1:188–89.

5. Were you not pleased to see the extracts from Hunt's book in the *Athenaeum?* and do you not think they were of service? Why then judge differently of mine?

And after other, similar questions he concluded: "Do not suppose I am vexed; I am only frightened."[24]

Meanwhile he continued to turn out articles for the periodicals. The *London Weekly Review* for January 19 contained an essay by him "On Public Opinion," stressing the power of public opinion and the average man's helplessness to withstand it. In his distressed frame of mind he resurrected an old grievance:

> Suppose an individual of whom it has been repeatedly asserted that he has warts on his nose, were to enter the reading-room aforesaid in the Rue de la Paix—is there a single red-faced country squire who would not be surprised at not finding this part of the story true—would not persuade himself five minutes after that he could not have been seen correctly, or that some art had been used to conceal the defect, or would be led to doubt, from this instance, Mr. Blackwood's general candour and veracity? On the contrary, the gentleman would be obliged to disbelieve his senses rather than give Mr. Blackwood the lie, who is read and believed by the whole world. He would have a host of witnesses against him: there is not a reader of Blackwood who would not swear to the fact. Seeing is believing, it is said. Lying is believing, say I. (17:307–8)

The essay which he wrote for the January *Monthly Magazine,* "On Personal Identity," took a more positive attitude, but was still tinged with resignation. Though men may bewail their fate, Hazlitt argued, no one really wants to sacrifice his identity; men may envy others, but they would not willingly change places with anyone. Then, after speculating on a number of related points, he came to his own plight: although he has been advised "to settle down into some respectable profession for life," he is "'in no haste to be venerable!'" (17:272). Nor, it would seem, was he in haste to be known as a disciplined writer. His final paragraph began: "I have run myself out of materials for this Essay, and want a well-turned sentence or two to conclude with." And he chose, in his conclusion, to brood, quite irrelevantly, on another old grievance: "I believe there is one character that all the world would be glad to change with—which is that of a favoured rival. Even hatred gives way to envy. We would be any thing—a toad in a dungeon—to live upon her smile, which is our all of earthly hope and happiness; nor can we, in our infatuation, conceive that there is any difference of

24. Ibid., pp. 189–90. Henry Southern was the scholarly editor of the esoteric *Retrospective Review* who served also as coeditor, with Sir John Bowring, of the *Westminster Review.*

feeling on the subject, or that the pressure of her hand is not in itself divine, making those to whom such bliss is deigned like the Immortal Gods!" (17:274–75). Hazlitt was not only frightened; he was growing morbid.

At last, sometime before the end of January, the first two volumes of *The Life of Napoleon Buonaparte* were published by Hunt and Clarke. It was a momentous event for Hazlitt, and he was rightly apprehensive. He was offering the reading public what would eventually be a four-volume biography designed to challenge Sir Walter Scott's nine-volume *Life of Napoleon*. And he must have known from past experience that a large proportion of the English reading public would hesitate even to sample an apology for Napoleon written by William Hazlitt.

The new biography was just that. Hazlitt made no attempt to disguise his sympathies; he had long been convinced that Napoleon was the greatest man of his era, the apostle of freedom, a born leader of men in the old heroic mold: he had thrilled to his triumphs over "legitimacy" and suffered real anguish at his downfall. He sought now to counteract the prejudiced interpretations of Scott's biography and to awaken Englishmen to the real truth as it must be manifest to anyone who considered the facts of history impartially. Over and over again he pointed out that the excesses of the French Revolution had sprung directly from the excesses of the *ancien régime*. Over and over again he insisted that, despite his dictatorial policies, Napoleon had benefited (even liberated) France herself and the nations which he had conquered. Over and over again he attacked the policies of Pitt and other English leaders. He was positive, always, that he was an unbiased student of history, that he was reporting the true facts about Napoleon and his foes.

But the preface which he had prepared for volume 1 (and which appeared, in the event, at the beginning of volume 3) tipped his hand. It stated clearly and emphatically his cherished convictions, and it serves, as well as any passage in the book, to illustrate the force and passion which mark the finest "speculative episodes" (as Lamb was to call them) scattered throughout the book:

Of my object in writing the LIFE here offered to the public, and of the general tone that pervades it, it may be proper that I should render some account in order to prevent mistakes and false applications. It is true, I admired the man; but what chiefly attached me to him, was his being, as he had been long ago designated, "the child and champion of the Revolution." Of this character he could not divest himself, even though he wished it. He was nothing, he could be nothing but what he owed to himself and to his triumphs over those who claimed mankind as their inheritance by a divine right; and as long as he was *a thorn in the side of kings*, and kept them at bay, his cause rose out of the ruins and defeat of their pride and hopes of revenge. He stood (and he alone stood) between them and their natural prey. He kept off that last indignity and wrong offered to a whole people (and through them to the rest of the world) of being handed over, like a herd of cattle, to a particular family, and chained to the foot of a legitimate throne. This was the chief point at issue—this was the great question, compared with which all others were tame and insignificant—Whether mankind were, from the beginning to the end of time, born slaves or not? As long as he remained, his acts, his very existence gave a proud and full answer to this question. As long as he interposed a barrier, a gauntlet, an arm of steel between us and them who alone could set up the plea of old, indefeasible right over us, no increase of power could be too great that tended to shatter this claim to pieces: even his abuse of power and aping the style and title of the imaginary Gods of the earth only laughed their pretensions the more to scorn. He did many things wrong and foolish; but they were individual acts, and recoiled upon the head of the doer. . . . In fact, Buonaparte was not strictly a free agent. He could hardly do otherwise than he did, ambition apart, and merely to preserve himself and the country he ruled. . . . Who then shall blame Buonaparte for having taken the reins of government and held them with a tight hand? The English, who having set the example of liberty to the world, did all they could to stifle it? Or the Continental Sovereigns, who were only acquainted with its principles by their fear and hatred of them? Or the Emigrants, traitors to the name of men as well as Frenchmen? Or the Jacobins, who made the tree of liberty spout nothing but blood? Or its *paper* advocates, who reduced it to a harmless theory? Or its true friends, who would sacrifice all for its sake? The last, who alone have the right to call him to a severe account, will not; for they know that, being but a handful or scattered, they had not the power to effect themselves what they might have recommended to him; and that there was but one alternative between him and that slavery, which kills both the bodies and the souls of men! There were two other feelings that influenced me on this subject; a love of glory, when it did not interfere with other things, and the wish to see personal merit prevail over external rank and circumstance. I felt pride (not envy) to think that there was one reputation in modern times equal to the ancients, and at seeing one man greater than the throne he sat upon. (13:ix–x)

Yet the passage, fine as it is, reveals the shortcomings of the book: great histories may be written by men who express themselves as forcefully as Hazlitt does, but not by those who have reached their conclusions before they begin their research. And the verdict of Hazlitt's contemporaries and of later critics has been that, as Howe delicately phrased it, the *Life of Napoleon* should be approached "as a work by Hazlitt and not as a history of Napoleon" (13:356).

The reviewers lined up as might be expected. The *Literary Gazette* for November 8 discussed only the first ten pages of the first volume, then broke off with:

But it is not worth while to pursue such wild-goose foolery as this any farther. In ten pages we have found as much sheer nonsense as might suffice for a whole fashionable novel: and wherever we have taken the trouble to dip, the same jejune abstractions, the same want of reasoning powers, the same ludicrous attempts at paradox and effect, the same turgidness of language, blotted with every kind of misconstruction, and (to generalise the matter) the same rubbish, has offended grammar, taste, sense, feeling, and judgment. It is in principle a worthless, without being in execution a clever, book.

The *New Monthly Magazine* was disposed to be generous toward Hazlitt as one of their regular contributors, but their reviewer acknowledged in the April issue that "this kind of historical and lofty detail, this epic in writing we do not think Mr. Hazlitt's forte. He is a clever man, but on a different scale, and Teniers or Wilkie might as well attempt the style of the cartoons of Raphael." He concluded that "the history of Napoleon and his times yet remains to be written." The *Monthly Magazine* for June deferred "any thing like examination till the whole is before us," yet they declared that "the work is full of vigorous thinking; and at every page, directly or indirectly, the reader will find materials for sweet or bitter reflection. There is no insipidity in Mr. H. He cowers before no difficulty—is deterred by no peril—and compromises none of his convictions; but sets boldly to work, and sweeps before him the filth and rubbish of prejudice, with much the same sort of resolute and dogged spirit, as that with which Hercules turned the Achelous to cleanse the accumulations of the Augean stable."

A few men of open minds and liberal opinions, like Charles Lamb, admired the "speculative episodes," but even Lamb admitted that he "skip[ped] the battles." [25]

It remained for a twentieth-century scholar to disclose why the narrative passages were so dull—to reveal, in truth, some very damning facts about the book. After examining Hazlitt's sources Robert E. Robinson reported in 1959, with abundant documentation, that, of the 1049 pages in the Howe edition, "about 310 are verbatim or almost verbatim translation or transcription, or a shortened form of the original in which condensation is accomplished mainly by omissions; about 435 pages are made up of summary, paraphrase, and reorganization of the source materials" and that "Hazlitt's transitional, interpretive, and analytical passages, including his 'characters' of a number of important personages, fill about 240 pages" [26]—little more

25. *Lamb Letters*, 3:151–52.

26. Robert E. Robinson, *William Hazlitt's "Life of Napoleon Buonaparte," Its Sources and Characteristics* (Geneva and Paris: E. Droz, 1959), pp. 14–15. Robinson points out

than a fifth of the completed four volumes. Moreover, although much of his borrowing was translated from French sources, he sometimes worked directly from—and followed closely—English translations when they were available. Usually, of course, he relied on sources which favored Napoleon; yet at times he borrowed from authors whom he elsewhere branded as unreliable—most shockingly from Scott's *Napoleon*, which he followed closely in fifty-two of his pages.[27] When he drew on anti-Napoleonic writers, he frequently altered phrases or sentences or interpolated passages to slant the material his own way. When, for example, he encountered the phrase "un grand air de majesté" applied to Marie Antoinette in François Mignet's *Histoire de la Révolution Française*, he translated it as "an air at once dignified and forbidding"; and he sometimes rendered the *heroism* of his sources as *obstinacy*.[28]

The only defense of Hazlitt's practice is that literary property was less sacrosanct in 1828 than it is at present. Still, a man of his talents cannot be excused for making so little effort to improve on the flat style of most of his sources. The contrast between the factual passages and Hazlitt's original insertions is striking.[29] His failure to fuse his sources is less surprising: organization had never been one of his strong points. He had never before attempted a historical survey, and he was ignorant of the distinction between reporting fact and writing history. The most charitable explanation is that he was a broken man, too harried by illness and financial pressure to do justice to the ambitious task he had shouldered.

Yet the book has some merit; there are fine passages in Hazlitt's best and most original style. Chapter 3 shows what he still could do when he relied on recollection rather than the sources immediately before him. So do the "characters"—of Robespierre (13:153–54, 165) or Fox and Pitt (14:273–75)—which sketch the important figures of the narrative briefly and incisively. Hazlitt also wrote passages of splendid rhetoric quite in the manner of his literary idol, Burke, as well as of seasoned (if highly subjective—and often biased) reflections on the facts of history. But he reached his greatest heights when inspired by his passionate devotion to the cause of freedom.

---

that there are also ten pages of long acknowledged quotations in the book and another fifty-four, including the much admired third chapter, which he has not traced to their sources. The third chapter, "French Revolution—Preliminary Remarks," was doubtless composed from Hazlitt's general knowledge, gained over a long period of time.

27. Ibid., pp. 19–21.   28. Ibid., pp. 23–25.

29. Ironically, the reviewer for the *New Monthly* remarked, "The campaigns too, and this is what could hardly have been expected, are related with remarkable clearness."

For example:

> I have nowhere in any thing I may have written declared myself to be a Republican; nor should I think it worth while to be a martyr and a confessor to any form or mode of government. But what I have staked health and wealth, name and fame upon, and am ready to do so again and to the last gasp, is this, that there is a power in the people to change its government and its governors. That is, I am a Revolutionist: for otherwise I must allow that mankind are but a herd of slaves, the property of thrones, that no tyranny or insult can lawfully goad them to a resistance to a particular family, or impair in any possible degree the sacred and inalienable right of insolent, unmitigated controul over them;—and it is not in the power of mortal man to bring me to that acknowledgement on the part of myself and my fellows. This is the only remedy mankind have against oppression: if this is not enough, yet I am contented with it. While this right remains in force, not written indeed in the preambles of acts of parliament but engraved in a nation's history, proved in the heraldry of its kings, a country may call itself free. (14:236–37)

But the fine passages only heighten the pathos of Hazlitt's dismal failure.

While he waited for the verdicts of the reviewers, he continued to grind out articles at the rapid rate which he had maintained since his return from Paris. The *Weekly Review* for February 2 contained "Brummelliana," a series of anecdotes about Beau Brummell to illustrate that he was "the greatest of small wits," whose "*bons mots* turn upon a single circumstance, the exaggerating of the merest trifles into matters of importance, or treating everything else with the utmost *nonchalance* and indifference" (20:152). Then for the issue of February 16 he wrote "On the Causes of Popular Opinion," arguing that "in all cases . . . where disputes commonly arise, inclination, habit, and example have a powerful share in throwing in the casting-weight to our opinions; and that he who is only tolerably free from these, and not their regular dupe or slave, is indeed 'a man of ten thousand'" (17:309). And again he hearkened back to old grievances and self-justification: after the failure of his *Principles of Human Action* he decided "never to appear abroad but in an embroidered dress." Then:

> Having got my clue, I had no difficulty in stringing pearls upon it; and the more recondite the point, the more I laboured to bring it out and set it off by a variety of ornaments and allusions. This puzzled the court-scribes, whose business it was to crush me. They could not see the meaning: they would not see the colouring, for it hurt their eyes. Oh, had I been but one of them, I might even have dined with Mr. Murray! One cried out, it was dull; another, that it was too fine by half: my friends took up this last alternative as the most favourable; and since then it has been agreed that I am a florid writer, somewhat flighty and paradoxical. . . . The person-

alities I have fallen into have never been gratuitous. If I have sacrificed my friends, it has always been to a theory. I have been found fault with for repeating myself, and for a narrow range of ideas. To a want of general reading, I plead guilty and am sorry for it; but perhaps if I had read more, I might have thought less. As to my barrenness of invention, I have at least glanced over a number of subjects—painting, poetry, prose, plays, politics, parliamentary speakers, metaphysical lore, books, men, and things. There is some point, some fancy, some feeling, some taste shown in treating of these. Which of my conclusions has been reversed? Is it what I said ten years ago of the Bourbons that has raised the war-whoop against me? Surely all the world are of that opinion now. I have, then, given proofs of some talent, and of more honesty: if there is haste or want of method, there is no common-place, nor a line that licks the dust; and if I do not appear to more advantage, I at least appear such as I am. (17:312–13)

He managed to rise above his personal problems to something approaching his old philosophical attitudes in the essay "The Main-Chance" in the February *New Monthly*. "I am one of those," he began, "who do not think that mankind are exactly governed by reason or a cool calculation of consequences. I rather believe that habit, imagination, sense, passion, prejudice, words make a strong and frequent diversion from the right line of prudence and wisdom" (17:275). And he considered how men's avarice and extravagance, their approaches to love and marriage all reveal that they "form their opinions much more from prejudice than reason" (17:285); that is, their actions are not governed by "the main-chance."

On February 20 he wrote the essay "Recollections," which appeared in the *Weekly Review* for March 29 and was later published by his son as "A Farewell to Essay-Writing." He dated it from Winterslow, where he was enjoying "food, warmth, sleep, and a book . . . —the *ultima thule* of my wandering desires" (17:313). He needs no friend or mistress ("Beautiful mask, I know thee!") to keep him company; his desires are few and simple. Leigh Hunt, he says, has professed himself "puzzled to reconcile the shyness of my pretensions with the inveteracy and sturdiness of my principles" (17:317).[30] But there is nothing enigmatic about his nature: ". . . any one knows where to have me. What I have once made up my mind to, I abide by to the end of the chapter. . . . I have not sought to make partisans, still less did I dream of making enemies; and have therefore kept my opinions to myself, whether they were currently adopted or not" (17:318–19). He

30. Hazlitt wrote: "I have only seen by accident a page of the unpublished Manuscript relating to the present subject" (17:318). He was, presumably, alluding to the passage which Hunt showed him while he was in Florence (see discussion above, p. 411).

recalls the pleasures he has known in the past at Winterslow: reading "The Flower and the Leaf," walking across the fields with Charles and Mary Lamb. And he concludes:

> It is in looking back to such scenes that I draw my best consolation for the future. Later impressions come and go, and serve to fill up the intervals; but these are my standing resource, my true classics. If I have had few real pleasures or advantages, my ideas, from their sinewy texture, have been to me in the nature of realities; and if I should not be able to add to the stock, I can live by husbanding the interest. As to my speculations, there is little to admire in them but my admirations of others; and whether they have an echo in time to come or not, I have learned to set a grateful value on the past, and am content to wind up the account of what is personal only to myself and the immediate circle of objects in which I have moved, with an act of easy oblivion,
> "And curtain close such scene from every future view." (17:320)

The note of resignation is strong—and poignant, almost valedictory.

But Hazlitt could not long indulge himself in idle musing. He was probably already at work on the series of "outlines" which he had offered to David Constable, several of which were found among his papers after his death. Although he had told Constable that he had something new to offer on all but one of these topics, they contained little that he had not already expressed in print. "Outlines of Morals" (20:376–86), which he seems never to have finished, restated the thesis of his *Essay on the Principles of Human Action*. "Outlines of the Human Mind" (20:442–47), which was clearly unfinished, disputed Hobbes's theory that ideas are never complex or abstract.[31] "Outlines of Political Economy" (19:294–302), also unfinished, revived his recent charges against this new school of thought. "Outlines of Taste" (20:386–91) brought together several points: that taste depends on the pleasure derived by the best-informed minds from the contemplation of nature or an imitation of nature; that details do not determine the excellence of a painting, but that they should not be slighted; that beauty depends on harmony as well as association of ideas; that each artist must follow his original bent. The most interesting of the papers is one entitled "Project for a New Theory of Civil and Criminal Legislation," which probably developed from the "Outlines of Law" which Hazlitt had offered to write for Constable. In it he returned to the thesis which he had tried to develop for his tutor, Mr. Corrie, while he was still a student at Hackney College. He told

31. Howe (20:442) points out the similarity between "Outlines of the Human Mind" and Hazlitt's earlier letters (the third and fourth) on Madame de Staël's *Account of German Philosophy* and "Mr. Locke a Great Plagiarist" (see 20:22–36, 69–83).

of its origin in the conversation about the Test Acts with the old lady at Wem, recalled how he had struggled over it at Hackney, then tried once again to resolve it. A right he defined as "the duty which each man owes to himself"; a law, as "something to abridge, or, more properly speaking, to ascertain, the bounds of the original right, and to coerce the will of individuals in the community" (19:305). Then he applied these definitions to specific cases like the divine right of kings and the theories of political economy—with results which could easily have been anticipated. He may never have started the "Outlines of Grammar," since no trace of it survived him. Probably he intended to draw largely on the *New and Improved Grammar of the English Tongue* which he had written back in 1809. Hazlitt had been reduced to ransacking the dusty attics of his mind.

By the middle of March he was back in London. For the *Weekly Review* of March 15 he wrote an amusing trifle, "Civilization of Africa," arguing that those who sought to raise the level of culture in Africa should educate the female savages rather than the males, who naturally conform to the standards set by their women (20:154–55). And the following day he resumed his old position as dramatic critic for the *Examiner*.

He must have found it humiliating to return to the situation which he had abandoned, supposedly for better things, back in 1817. Yet there were compensations: he could take some comfort in playing the part of the seasoned veteran, sharing his opinion of a play with less experienced critics and then seeing his ideas reflected in their reviews.[32] He could bask, too, in the admiration of young disciples like Charles and Mary Cowden Clarke, who considered it "a treat to sit beside him, when he talked delightfully" or to be invited back to his rooms to see his first portrait, that of the old woman in the bonnet, and his copy of Titian's *Ippolito de' Medici*.[33] Usually, though, he finished off the evening among old friends at the Southampton Coffee House.[34]

There were several anecdotes repeated by the Hazlitt family in later years about his cavalier behavior at the theater: of the red-lined cloak which he sported in defiance of conventional notions of proper dress at the theater; of the favorite seat which he had reserved next to the private boxes, so that he could lean back comfortably against the partition. When he took friends to the theater, he often reserved the "looking-glass box"; and one evening

32. According to W. C. Hazlitt (*The Hazlitts*, p. 137), Payne Collier and P. G. Patmore were especially prone to depend on Hazlitt for advice.

33. See Cowden Clarke, *Recollections of Writers*, pp. 60–62, and Mary Cowden Clarke, *My Long Life* (London, 1896), pp. 83–84.

34. *The Hazlitts*, p. 138.

when he found it already occupied, he frightened "Old Pantaloon," the keeper of the boxes, into ousting the intruders. Another time when young Catherine Reynell was his guest, he paused as usual at the top of the stairs to sign the free-admission book and embarrassed Catherine by holding up a long line of people. He seemed totally unaware that he was causing a delay—in fact, looked up calmly as he was signing his name and asked the attendant, "What sort of a house is there to-night, sir?" 35

He no longer wrote the routine sort of review that he had done earlier for the *Examiner*: he contrived, usually, to subordinate the review proper to a more general essay on matters related to the theater. In his first article, on March 16, he praised Kean's playing of Shylock, but added strictures on the fickle public's delight in demolishing its idols (18:374–77). On March 23 and 30 he reviewed the French actor Adrien Perlet's playing of Molière, yet worked in a discussion of French acting generally, including remarks on performances that he had seen in Paris—and on French manners *versus* English (18:377–84). On April 6 he discussed the wisdom of closing the theaters during Passion Week (18:384–87); on the thirteenth, reviewing young Charles Kean's performance in Mrs. Inchbald's *Lovers' Vows*, he sympathized with a young man who strives to equal his father's successes and, reverting to an old theory, discounted the notion that young Kean might hope to improve in the future (18:387–91). On the twenty-seventh he apologized for his failure to review the performances of Miss Stephens, Charles Kemble, and Madame Vestris in familiar parts because he had nothing to offer that he had not already written. And since he had been unable to see Kean in *Othello* because the theater was so fully booked, he reprinted "the criticism (or eulogy, for it is the same thing)" (18:393) which he had originally written for the *Times* in October, 1817, and had already included in an article for the *London Magazine* in March, 1820.

He could not generate much enthusiasm for new developments in the London theater. On May 4 he deplored the behavior of audiences at the opera, contrasting them with French audiences and declaring that fashionable society in England was the most vulgar in all Europe (18:394–98). On the eleventh he found fault with a revival of *The Beggar's Opera* at Covent Garden: it had been abridged, the actors had failed to catch the proper raffish tone, and the sparse audience had obviously considered the play too "low" for their refined tastes—and meanwhile George Colman's sentimental *Poor Gentleman* was playing to full houses! "In a word," Hazlitt mourned,

35. *Memoirs*, 1:205-6.

"the French Revolution has spoiled all, like a great stone thrown into a well 'with hollow and rueful rumble,' and left no two ideas in the public mind but those of high and low. The jealousy of gentility, the horror of being thought vulgar, has put an end to the harmless *double-entendre* of wit and humour; and the glancing light and shades of life (nothing without each other) are sunk into the dull night of insipidity and affectation" (18:400).

On May 18, reviewing *The Taming of the Shrew*, he devoted a good part of his article to recollections of Liston's and Joseph Munden's interpretations of the character Christopher Sly—which had been omitted from this new production. "This digression is too long," he admitted, explaining that "without sometimes going out of our way, we should hardly get to the end of our task" (18:403–4). He devoted his next article, on May 25, to nostalgic recollections of the playing of Mrs. Siddons, Kean, and Madame Pasta. He went on, then, to complaints about the elaborateness of English productions which distract from the play itself and cut its profits. The French, he declared, managed much better with their smaller theaters and, thanks to the unity of place, their simple settings (18:406–10).

On June 1 he mocked attempts to make the theater in England more genteel (18:410–14). And shortly afterwards he resigned from his position and went once more to Paris, probably for further work on his *Napoleon*. But the change of scene did not improve his temper. He sent back an article on Kean, whose appearances in France had been less than successful. And now the French came under fire: they did not value originality; they had never cared for Shakespeare; naturally they would not appreciate Kean's acting (18:414–17).

Hazlitt's contributions to other periodicals fell off sharply during his term as critic for the *Examiner*. For the *London Weekly Review* he wrote three ephemeral articles. The first, "Byron and Wordsworth," in the issue for April 5, pointed up Byron's fondness for the exotic as against Wordsworth's, Rousseau's, and Scott's interest in the familiar and simple (20:155–57). The second, on May 17, was "The Modern Gradus ad Parnassum, No. 1," a dialogue between "H" and "S" defending Leigh Hunt's description of his sea journey to Italy, which had been ridiculed in a long review of *Lord Byron and Some of His Contemporaries* in the May *Blackwood's* (20:157–62). Then he wrote no other articles for the *Weekly Review* until June 14, when he reviewed the third volume of Landor's *Imaginary Conversations*. "Since his two former volumes," he announced, "Mr. Landor has not retrograded nor stood still" (19:104). Of course he did not let his friendship with Landor influence his criticism; he still found "no medium in his writing or opinions; not a passage to which we do not ascribe our hearty assent, or from which we do not absolutely revolt" (19:105).

In the meantime he wrote two more essays for the *New Monthly Magazine*. "The Influence of Books on the Progress of Manners," in the May issue, argued that "books are the scale in which right and wrong are fairly tried" (17:326), that they have been primarily responsible for the decline in warfare and "legitimacy" in modern times. Moreover, books teach people to broaden their outlook and to sympathize with their fellows; they serve, as the *Spectator* and *Rambler* prove, as " 'a discipline of humanity,' a kind of public monitor, a written conscience, from which nothing is hid: the councils of princes, 'the secrets of the grave,' are brought before it, arraigned and made to stand or fall by their own merits" (17:328). He closed with an appeal for intelligent men to resist the forces of reaction and work for progress. "We cannot go back to what we were," he wrote. "We can never be ourselves again, as long as the world lasts—let us try to be something better" (17:330). He still retained some hope for the future of mankind, if not for his own.

For the June *New Monthly* he sent back from Paris the essay "Travelling Abroad," a companion piece to "The Influence of Books" in that it considered the value of another means of broadening men's outlooks. But Hazlitt was less sanguine here: he was, he wrote at the outset, "one of those who do not think that much is to be gained in point either of temper or understanding by travelling abroad" (17:332). Soon he was analyzing the character of the French once again, and he described the plight of "an acquaintance of mine" who is "settled in a French boarding-house":

> What scenes we have (fit to make us die with laughter) in going over the messes and manners of the place! How we exult in the *soup-maigre!* How we triumph in *bouillé*, as hard as a bullet! If a single thing were good, it would ruin us for the evening. Then the knives will not cut—and what a thing to set down a single fowl before six people, who seem all ready to fall upon it and tear it in pieces! What meanness and wretched economy! Why don't they get a good substantial joint of meat, in which there would be *cut and come again?* If they had common sense they would. And then the lamentable want of decency and propriety is another never-failing and delightful topic. The child is unswaddled before company, and the dirty clothes for the next week's wash are left stewing in the window all dinner-time. The master is such a Goth too, a true Frenchman! When carving he flourishes his knife about in such a manner as to endanger those who sit near him, and stops in the middle with the wing of a duck suspended on the point of his fork, to spout a speech out of some play. Dinner is no sooner over than he watches his opportunity, collects all the bottles and glasses on the table, beer, wine, porter, empties them into his own, heaps his plate with the remnants of fricasees, gravy, vegetables, mustard, melted butter, and

sops them all up with a large piece of bread, wipes his plate clean as if a dog had licked it, dips his bread in some other dish that in his hurry had escaped him, and finishes off by picking his teeth with a sharp-pointed knife. He then, having satisfied his most urgent wants, amuses himself during the desert by putting salt in the governess's fruit, and giving a pinch of snuff to a cat which is seated in his lap with a string of beads round its neck. (17:336)

The details are specific and vivid; Hazlitt was almost certainly writing from firsthand experience during this, his fourth stay in Paris.[36] He could no longer afford the comforts of the Hôtel des Étrangers; he no longer had a wife to set up a household for him. He was a footloose old relict of fifty, a superannuated author, staying at a third-rate *pension*, supporting himself by writing odds and ends of reviews and articles. He had, he felt, a mission to vindicate the name of the man whom he regarded as the greatest hero of his era. In the process he might even salvage his own reputation.

36. Later in the essay he refers to "the house here in the Rue Chantereine" where he was staying (17:342).

CHAPTER XVI

Denouement
(1828–1830)

Sometime in the late summer or early autumn of 1828 Hazlitt returned from Paris and went down to Winterslow to write the final chapters of his *Life of Napoleon*. He had apparently fallen out with the landlady at The Hut, and he stayed this time at a house in the secluded village on the wooded hill above the high road. He was in a captious frame of mind; on October 6 he wrote to the postmaster at Salisbury:

> Each letter or newspaper I receive (brought out from Salisbury) is charged 4d. additional, which I understand is too much. This imposition is accompanied with impertinence and collusion, which make it worse. I sent a man down last night for a newspaper, which I was particularly anxious to see, and it was refused to be given up, because the messenger had not brought the 2d., though the landlady has in her possession 2d. of mine that had been left as change out of a letter paid for yesterday. This happens whenever the landlady at the Hut (Mrs. Hine) is in the humour, and the object is to keep the 2d. for the letter-carrier the next day. Nor is this all. The letters received in so unpleasant a manner do not reach Winterslow till the morning or middle of the next day after they arrive in Salisbury. They are brought out by the Guard at night, and sent up to the village at their leisure the next morning. For the additional 4d. many persons would be glad to fetch them out from Salisbury the same day, so that they would be received here two hours after they reach Salisbury, which would be a great convenience, and in some cases an object of importance.[1]

He needed to keep in close touch with his London contacts because he was still depending on the magazines to keep him solvent.

For the October *New Monthly* he wrote a curious essay, "Self-Love and

1. *Four Generations*, 1:195.

Benevolence," reporting a supposed conversation between "A" (probably William Ayrton) and "B" (certainly Hazlitt himself)[2] on the merits of the philosophy of Helvétius. A accepts the theory that man is motivated by self-interest; B disputes it. In effect, Hazlitt manages to restate the tenets of his *Principles of Human Action*, but to make them more readable by putting them into dialogue form.[3] A, of course, plays the foil; he advances the usual arguments in defense of Helvétius's theory and listens patiently while B strikes them down. At one point A objects: "I must give you fair warning, that in this last *tirade* you have more than once gone beyond my comprehension. Your distinctions are too fine-drawn, and there is a want of relief in the expression. Are you not getting back to what you describe as your *first manner?* Your present style is more amusing. See if you cannot throw a few high lights into that last argument!" (20:167). Hazlitt seems to have been trying consciously to blend his two "manners": to present a philosophical principle in a popular style.

He continued the dialogue in the December issue of the *New Monthly*. When "D" (Lamb) enters the discussion, he brightens it up considerably. Like A, he is skeptical of the theory of human disinterestedness, and both remain unconvinced at the end of the essay. In the meantime Hazlitt has despaired of making all his points by means of dialogue, and he finishes off his argument by letting D's brother John (i.e., John Lamb) quote a long passage on imagination from *Principles of Human Action*. Hazlitt then rounds out the essay cleverly by means of a couple of lines borrowed from *Henry IV*, *Part I:*

> J.D. "This is the strangest tale that e'er I heard."
> C.D. "It is the strangest fellow, brother John."
>
> (20:186)

In November Hazlitt resumed his regular writing for the *London Weekly Review*. "A Stuffed Man," in the issue for the twenty-second, was another dialogue, this one between "Artist" and "Philosopher"—probably a fragment of one of the conversations with Northcote. It was brief and inconsequential: the Artist declared that he disliked tight clothing; the Philosopher explained that people who "live on [their] ideas" prefer loose

2. As Howe points out (20:419), Hazlitt used the letters "A" and "H" in the manuscript of the essay.

3. Howe (20:441) suggests that Hazlitt may have left his "Outline of Morals" (see above, p. 452) unfinished because he had decided to present his ideas in more readable form in this essay.

clothing, while those "who live by eating and drinking alone" wish "to have a double sense of their own gross existence" (20:186). More ambitious was the essay "On Cant and Hypocrisy," which appeared in two installments in the *Weekly Review* for December 6 and 13. Hazlitt rambled about a good deal while reflecting on the mixture of good and evil, belief and disbelief, in human nature. But he proved in his conclusion that he could still, on occasion, turn out a penetrating analysis of human nature:

> Thus, though I think there is very little downright hypocrisy in the world, I do think there is a great deal of *cant*—"cant religious, cant political, cant literary," &c. as Lord Byron said. Though few people have the face to set up for the very thing they in their hearts despise, we almost all want to be thought better than we are, and affect a greater admiration or abhorrence of certain things than we really feel. . . . As our interest in anything wears out with time and habit, we exaggerate the outward symptoms of zeal as mechanical helps to devotion, dwell the longer on our words as they are less felt, and hence the very origin of the term, *cant*. The cant of sentimentality has succeeded to that of religion. There is a cant of humanity, of patriotism and loyalty—not that people do not feel these emotions, but they make too great a *fuss* about them, and drawl out the expression of them till they tire themselves and others. There is a cant about Shakespear. There is a cant about *Political Economy* just now. In short, there is and must be a cant about everything that excites a considerable degree of attention and interest, and that people would be thought to know and care rather more about than they actually do. Cant is the voluntary overcharging or prolongation of a real sentiment; hypocrisy is the setting up a pretension to a feeling you never had and have no wish for. (17:353–54)

However, such analytical writing was exceptional for Hazlitt; he was content, usually, to work at a much less ambitious level in the articles which he now began to write regularly for the weekly *Atlas*. The editors had apparently given him a free hand to write a brief "column" on whatever happened to catch his fancy, and the results were varied. His first contribution, in the *Atlas* for December 21, was "Mr. Cobbett and the Quakers," a biting attack on Cobbett, who had branded Quakers as blackguards in his *Political Register* and demanded that they be forced to conform to the laws of the land. Hazlitt countered with the charge that Cobbett resembled the Quakers in everything but his bitterness—that he was resentful because he could find no real basis for criticizing them (20:187–89). The second article, in the December 28 issue, was "Mr. Jeffrey and Mr. Owen," an amusing account, supposedly in Jeffrey's own words, of Robert Owen's absurd attempts to gain notice in the *Edinburgh Review* (20:189–90).

During the months of January and February, 1829, Hazlitt continued to write regularly for the *Atlas*. For the January 4 number he wrote "The

First Meeting between Fox and Grattan," merely relaying an anecdote which he had apparently heard from Henry Grattan himself (20:190–91). For the January 18 issue he wrote two quite different articles. One, "The Late Murders," analyzed public reaction to the trial of an Edinburgh man and woman charged with murdering people to provide cadavers for medical research (20:191–94); the other, "The Ruling Passion," was a comment, presumably by Northcote, on an unsympathetic biography of the sculptor Nollekens by John Thomas Smith (20:194–96). On January 25, in "Richesse de la Langue," Hazlitt warned against careless use of synonyms by citing thirty-five ways to "convey by a single word an expression of face which having risen from some strong passion, uneasiness, or emotion, is converted into an habitual character, and remains without any immediate object to excite it" (20:196).

Throughout February he continued to turn out similar brief essays for the *Atlas*—and nothing for any of the other periodicals. His topics were still varied: "Pope Benedict" on the first (20:197), "Butts of Different Sorts" on the eighth (20:197–200), "Burke and the Edinburgh Phrenologists" (mocking Dr. George Combe's phrenological analysis of one of the Edinburgh murderers) on the fifteenth (20:200–204), and "Common Fame" on the twenty-second (20:204–5). For the March 1 issue he managed to work up three pieces. "Lord North" began with the old nobleman's tendency to fall asleep on all occasions—and concluded with observations on proficiency in Latin among Eton graduates (20:205–6). "Old Cloaks" attacked the "Jew-women" who rented out fine clothes to young girls and then loitered around the theaters to collect their fees; such practices, Hazlitt declared, would not be tolerated "except in this shop-keeping and slop-selling country" (20:208). The third article, "Odds and Ends," was well named; it contained random thoughts about various actresses whom he had seen or wished that he might have seen (20:208–9). He could have found little satisfaction in purveying these literary scraps; he must have realized that he had descended to penny-a-line journalism.

On March 7 he introduced a new series, "Real Conversations," in the *London Weekly Review*. The first paper was preceded by a note:

> The Conversations here presented to the reader are *real*, not "Imaginary." How we came possessed of them, it is not necessary to disclose. Suffice it that they are set down almost exactly as they passed from the lips of the speakers; and that those speakers are living persons, sufficiently distinguished from the crowd by their name, talents, and acquirements, to render whatever they may have to say worthy attention, on whatever topic their talk may turn. We will only add, that the Conversations

here reported were entirely unpremeditated, and consequently spoken without the remotest view to anything but their immediate effect on the person addressed. (11:363)[4]

The article began: "As soon as I went in to-day A. asked me if that was *my* character of Shakspeare, which had been quoted in a newspaper the day before?" (11:248). The speaker replied that it was, rather, a passage from Edward Augustus Kendall's *Letters on Ireland*, and that, though he had "expressed nearly the same idea in print," he chose to be flattered, not angry. A footnote contained the passage in question, which argued that Shakespeare was unconscious of his extraordinary powers. The conversation moved next to "an answer in a newspaper to Canning's assertion, that 'Slavery was not inconsistent with the spirit of Christianity'" (11:249). Then came a discussion of "the inefficacy of the pictures in Protestant churches" and finally a chance remark by Charles Kemble. The whole article was quite in the manner of Hazlitt's "Boswell Redivivus" papers; in fact it was a continuation of the series. Both Kendall's book and Canning's remark dated from 1826, and so did the conversation; it had been lying, presumably, in Colburn's office ever since Campbell stopped the series in the *New Monthly*. The only apparent change was the substitution of "Mr. A." for "Mr. N.," but it was still, obviously, old Northcote who was providing copy. Colburn had decided to use in his *London Weekly* what Campbell had outlawed from the *New Monthly* two years earlier.

The second number of the series, in the *Weekly Review* for March 14, centered at first around authors: their lack of discrimination in choosing their associates, the public's prejudices against them, and the discrepancy between their conduct and their writings. But it soon took up other matters —among them the choice of a school for the present author's son, who, actually, had finished his schooling two years earlier (11:234–38). The third and fourth papers of the series (April 11 and 18) rambled on in the same style, considering whatever happened to arrest the attention of the two principals: literature, painting, religion, Queen Caroline, and human hair (11:238–42, 251–56). They bore no evidence of having been brought up to date; probably Hazlitt let the editors print them up from the manuscripts written in 1826.

He continued to do his weekly stint for the *Atlas*. The article "Poetry" in the March 8 issue must have surprised readers of the paper; it hymned

4. Note that this statement contradicts the preface to the *New Monthly* series. If Hazlitt wrote this one, he was perhaps attempting to counter Northcote's denial of responsibility for remarks attributed to him in the "Conversations."

the beauties of suggestive, as opposed to purely descriptive poetry, citing Perdita's description of flowers in *The Winter's Tale*—"one out of a thousand" in Shakespeare (20:209). There was more than a touch of Hazlitt's old gusto in his statement that "a literal description goes for nothing in poetry, a pure fiction is of little worth; but it is the extreme beauty and power of an impression with all its accompaniments, or the very intensity and truth of feeling, that pushes the poet over the verge of matter-of-fact, and justifies him in resorting to the license of fiction to express what without his 'winged words' must have remained for ever untold" (20:211). But he brought his readers back to earth on March 15 in "English Grammar," a critique of the definitions commonly used by grammarians (20:212–15).[5] And for the March 22 issue he wrote three trivial articles. One was "Memorabilia of Mr. Coleridge," a loose collection of remarks made by Coleridge, some of which had already appeared in "My First Acquaintance with Poets" (20:215–18). Another, entitled "Coquets," also drew on Hazlitt's memories of the past, for he discussed how helpless a man is in the hands of a seemingly modest woman who makes advances to him (20:218–20). The third piece consisted of a single sentence: "The science of Political Economy means the *divine right* of landlords" (19:291).

The dreary work went on and on. He resorted to an old standby on March 29, when he placed in the *Examiner* an article entitled "The Reverend Edward Irving: An Hypothesis," which ventured the opinion that Irving was guilty of supposing that God was as intolerant as he himself was (20:223–25). The *Atlas* for the same day contained "Manners Make the Man," an attack on the bad manners of his countrymen which took as its text "*Ill manners make the Englishman*" (20:220). It was followed by "Peter Pindar," an affectionate portrait of the elderly satirist (20:226–27) on April 5 and "Logic," a critique of the limitations of formal logic (20:227–30), on the twelfth.

The same issue of the *Atlas* carried a review of the recent two-volume *History of Napoleon Buonaparte* which had been brought out anonymously by Hazlitt's old *Blackwood's* foe, John Gibson Lockhart. The reviewer observed that a popular biography of Napoleon was much needed, adding that Hazlitt's book was "'dogmatical' in method, 'a subtle memoir of causes and effects—a philosophical statement of men and things—a connected series of essays, sometimes true, sometimes fantastic, and always

5. The essay may well have been all or part of the "Outlines on Grammar" which Hazlitt offered to prepare for David Constable (see above, p. 453)—the only one of the "outlines" which failed to survive in manuscript.

stamped with the impress of the individual mind'" (13:355). Hazlitt was naturally incensed that his book should be slightingly noticed in a paper to which he was a regular contributor. He undoubtedly wrote the letter, signed "Philalethes," which appeared in the April 19 *Atlas* protesting this judgment and pointing out that "all the three anecdotes you have quoted as characteristic of [Lockhart's] peculiarly popular style, I had read before in both the works [i.e., Scott's and Hazlitt's] you condemn as too much filled with irrelevant matter to leave room for such trifles" (13:355). The letter concluded: "With respect to Mr. Hazlitt's frequent and lengthened 'reflections,' it is to be remembered that he had to contend with strong prejudice on the other side, on which he could hope to make no impression without giving his reasons at length. If he had been disposed to be 'dogmatic,' he might have been shorter" (13:356). Turning out scraps for the newspapers —being forced to defend one's cherished masterpiece—were these the rewards for years of service in the cause of literature?

The April 19 *Atlas* also contained the first article of a new series, "Conversations as Good as Real," a dialogue between "J" and "T," which was obviously a continuation of the Northcote conversations. The *London Weekly Review* had failed, and Hazlitt had transferred his series to the *Atlas*, sparing himself the trouble of composing an essay on a new topic each week.

In the first article Northcote ("J") made some pertinent observations on the character of Hazlitt ("T"). He began abruptly: "That is your diffidence, which I can't help thinking you carry too far. For any one of real strength, you are the humblest person I ever knew"—to which Hazlitt replied, "It is owing to pride." Northcote continued: "You deny you have invention too. But it is want of practice. Your ideas run on before your executive power. It is a common case" (11:274). Soon they were discussing Scott's merits as compared to those of "the famous people of the last age, Johnson, Burke, &c.," and when Northcote accused Hazlitt of prejudice against Scott, Hazlitt responded, "Nay, it rather shows my liberality, if I am a devoted enthusiast, notwithstanding." But Northcote insisted that "whenever politics are concerned, your passions run away with your understanding" (11:276, 378).

"Conversations as Good as Real, No. 2," in the *Atlas* for April 26, continued the discussion of Scott, comparing him with Cobbett and later with Rousseau and Byron (11:276–80). And the series continued throughout the month of May, with Conversations nos. 3, 4, 5, and 6 appearing in the issues for the third, tenth, twenty-fourth, and thirty-first of the month

(11:281–89). They were considerably shorter than the earlier conversations published in the *New Monthly* and the *Weekly Review* and more likely to be confined to a single subject. Hazlitt may have used only portions of conversations which he had written earlier, sometimes adding matters of more recent interest, or he may have been writing new ones.[6] In either case they served to discharge his commitment to the *Atlas* for the month of May. After the brief "Late Mr. Curran," a genial portrait of John Philpot Curran in the April 26 number (20:230–31), he produced nothing, apart from the conversations, until June.

He had more pressing matters on his mind during the month, for it was sometime in May that the firm of Hunt and Clarke failed. Volumes 3 and 4 of the *Life of Napoleon*, which were about to be published, were withheld, and Hazlitt was left with a promissory note for a substantial sum which seemed likely to prove worthless.[7] He was in poor health, too, and he had no major works in progress. He moved from his lodgings in Half-Moon Street to rooms on the first floor at 3 Bouverie Street—from Westminster to the neighborhood of Fleet Street, probably in order to cut down expenses. He was living, as usual, an indolent kind of existence. According to P. G. Patmore, he "usually rose at from one to two o'clock in the day—scarcely ever before twelve; and if he had no work in hand, he would sit over his breakfast (of excessively strong black tea and a toasted French roll) till four or five in the afternoon—silent, motionless, and self-absorbed, as a Turk over his opium pouch; for tea served him precisely in this capacity. It was the only stimulant he ever took, and at the same time the only luxury."[8] When fire threatened the house, he scolded his son for not acting at once to rescue his paintings; yet he himself did nothing to save them.[9] Young William, who was living with him, was courting Catherine Reynell—and Hazlitt often went with him rather than to the houses of old friends like Hunt or the Lambs.[10]

6. When Hazlitt prepared the conversations for publication in book form in 1830, he combined these shorter articles into longer units. If the *Atlas* papers were taken from papers originally written for Colburn, Hazlitt at least subjected them to some minor revisions; for example, he referred, in the first paper of the series, to a portrait of Sir Walter Scott which Northcote painted in 1828.

7. The amount of the note has been variously reported. Lamb said it was for £100 (*Lamb Letters*, 3:238); Talfourd, £150 (Vera Watson, "Thomas Noon Talfourd and His Friends," *TLS*, 27 April, 1956, p. 260); and Hazlitt himself, £200 (*Athenaeum*, 15 August, 1819, p. 743).

8. Patmore, 2:312–18.

9. *Memoirs*, 2:233.

10. Lamb was unwell in mid-1829 and felt unable to receive visitors. He wrote to both

He had not learned any real prudence as a result of his troubles. In later years Catherine Reynell Hazlitt recalled his telling her one day that he had dined on pheasant—at a time when pheasants were selling at ten shillings apiece. "'Don't you think it was a good deal to give?' she asked. 'Well, I don't know but what it was, Kitty,' he replied, opening his eyes in his way, and tucking his chin into his shirt collar." Another time, when she met him in Piccadilly, he seemed especially downcast, and she asked what was troubling him. "Well, you know," he explained, "I've been having some hot boiled beef for my dinner, Kitty—a most *uncomfortable* dish." [11] He managed to retain a grim sort of humor, yet his mind was not at ease, and he bought a brace of pistols for his son to carry for protection when they went out the Oxford Road to visit the Reynells. Soon, however, he discarded them, having decided that he was "more afraid of the weapons than of the footpads." [12]

During the early summer of 1829 he resumed his brief essays for the *Atlas*. On June 7, in "The Waverley Notes," he defended Sir Walter Scott's practice of supplying the sources of his information in footnotes to his novels (20:231–33). In the same issue "The Court Journal," a brief conversation, with Northcote disguised as "M" and himself as "G," dissected the new *Court Journal* which Colburn had established as successor to the *London Weekly Review* and which Hazlitt's friend Patmore was editing (20:233–36). Then on June 14 he presented another portrait, "The Late Dr. Priestley" (20:236–39), and on the twenty-first, in "Mr. Jeffrey's Resignation of the Editorship of the *Edinburgh Review*," he praised Jeffrey, but added that he must be relieved to escape from the *Edinburgh*, which had grown repetitious and dull (20:243–46). For the June 28 issue he wrote two articles: "Autographs" (20:246–47) and a Northcote conversation entitled "A Discursive Dialogue on Arts and Sciences" (11:289–93); for the July 5 issue he turned out three: a conversation headed "Fashion" (11:293–94) and two articles, "Phrenological Fallacies" (20:248–51) and "English Characteristics" (20:247–48). In the latter he berated his countrymen again for their bad manners; they are, he declared, "the only people to whom the term *blackguard* is peculiarly applicable" (20:247). And for the benefit of readers who might complain that the *Atlas* could

---

Sarah Hazlitt and her son apologizing for his inability to see them (*Lamb Letters*, 3:222–23).

11. *The Hazlitts*, p. 147.

12. W. C. Hazlitt, *The Hazlitts, Part the Second* (Edinburgh: Ballantyne, Hanson and Co., 1912), p. 64.

hardly afford to fault the *Edinburgh* on the score of repetitiousness, he added: "If this subject be harping on a grievance, at least it is not an imaginary one" (20:248).

To repay Northcote for his share in the conversations Hazlitt had agreed to revise the *One Hundred Fables, Original and Selected* which the old artist was preparing for publication. It was a tedious job—merely reducing North-cote's little stories to appropriately simple style—and he made slow progress. When William Bewick, just back from Italy, met him one day near Trafalgar Square,

> he rushed up to me and caught me by both hands, exclaiming in amazement, "My dear fellow, where have you come from? where have you been? I have lost sight of you for an age." I replied, "I have been in the sunny clime, and am just on my way to Northcote to show him my [copy of Michelangelo's] 'Jeremiah.'" "Ah! I am so glad you are just come as my redeeming star,—my credit is at this time very low with him; you must know I am editing his Fables—I may say writing them—and he is just now very peevish and impatient at my not sending him some 'copy.' I shall be ready to-morrow. Now if you see him to-day and put him into a good humour, which you will do by showing him your 'Jeremiah'—you must speak of me, tell him you have just seen me, and that I shall see him tomorrow with more 'copy,' and then you can tell me how his pulse beats," &c.[13]

All Hazlitt's literary projects now seemed like chores that he must force himself to carry out.

However, early in July he received an unexpected promise of relief from the tiresome grind of the past months. Through Thomas Norton Longman, proprietor of the *Edinburgh Review*, he heard that Macvey Napier, who had succeeded Jeffrey as editor, would be interested in having him resume work as a regular contributor. Ignoring his complaints about the *Edinburgh* three weeks earlier, he replied on July 13: "I need not say that I shall be happy if you will lay your commands upon me to do any thing that lies in my power." He offered to review a new life of Locke and Southey's *Dialogues of Sir Thomas More*, signing himself "very respectfully, your obliged humble servant." [14]

Meanwhile, for the *Atlas* of July 12 he had written a continuation of his "Phrenological Fallacies" (20:251–53) and the seventh of his "Conversations as Good as Real" (11:297–99). And for the issue of the nineteenth he prepared two more articles: "The Champions of Phrenology," replying to a letter signed "Justitia" criticizing his earlier articles on the subject

13. Landseer, 2:122.
14. *Athenaeum*, 15 August, 1919, pp. 742–43.

(20:254–55), and "The Utilitarian Controversy—the *Edinburgh* and *Westminster Reviews*," warmly espousing the side of the *Edinburgh* in a quarrel about the nature of the *useful* and the *agreeable* (20:255–60).

On July 21 he wrote again to Macvey Napier, who had suggested that he review the American William Ellery Channing's *Sermons and Tracts* rather than the life of Locke or the *Dialogues of More*. He would indeed undertake the Channing review, he said, adding: "In case this and the others should fail, let me suggest another subject, the forthcoming *Life and Writings of Defoe*, in which I should be somewhat *au fait* and could treat *con amore*. I should be·sorry to do an indifferent article for a commencement." [15] And since he could not review Southey's *Dialogues of More* for the *Edinburgh*, he aired his impressions of them in "Conversations as Good as Real (1)" in the *Atlas* for the twenty-sixth, citing especially the author's egotism and his reactionary thinking. However, he was in a penitential mood, and he prefaced his criticism with the statement: "I would not be thought to bear him malice, for I owe him obligations" (20:260). In passing he took issue with Lamb's recent praise of the *Dialogues*—Lamb, who had spoken out so bravely in his "Letter to Robert Southey" just three years ago—but he added quickly that Lamb was "both a genius and a wit" and quoted one of his better quips to prove it. Another article in the July 26 *Atlas*, "The Exclusionists in Taste," censured critics who temper their praise of a piece of writing by comparing it with a work which they consider superior; and again he singled out Lamb, who had compared Scott unfavorably with Shakespeare and Milton (20:262–63).

In the meantime Hazlitt had re-established contact with the *Monthly Magazine*, and for its July issue he wrote "The Prose Album: Maxims on Mankind," a collection of thirteen maxims on literature, art, love, and life. The first four, which concern love, hint that, along with the other worries vexing him these days, he was still haunted by memories of his failure in love. For example:

> I. No person who is in love can ever be entirely persuaded that the passion is not reciprocal; as no one who does not feel it ever believes that it is sincere in others.

> III. Some have described love to be an exaggerated sense of excellence in another, without the chance or hope of making itself understood—a teazing pursuit of difficulty—a "hunting of the wind, and worshipping a statue." This is, at most, a definition of unsuccessful love. It has been made a question, whether any woman would be proof against the real language of the heart, had it words to express itself; or would not be won, were she assured of all that her despairing lover undergoes for her sake?

15. Ibid., p. 743.

But the lover, from the strength of his own attachment, almost always believes that there is a secret sympathy between them; that she knows what passes in his breast as well as in her own; and that she holds out only from caprice; and that she must at length yield. (20:239)

Maxim No. 6 was charged with personal feeling of another kind: "Someone absurdly expressed a wish to be young again, *if he could carry his experience back with him to the outset of life*. But the worst old age is that of the mind" (20:240). There was a tartness, too, in "Sects and Parties," in the August 2 *Atlas*. "We from our souls sincerely hate all cabals and coteries" (20:264), he began; and he went on to complain that reformers like Bentham and the rational Dissenters are prone to become as bigoted as those whose theories they would replace.

In the weeks that followed he presented more "Conversations as Good as Real," all of them short pieces which concentrated on a single subject: anecdotes of the Hanoverian line (11:299, 373), the delicacy of Guido Reni's nudes (11:294–97), Allan Cunningham's debt to Northcote in his recent short biography of Sir Joshua Reynolds (11:302–6). These were certainly not among the conversations originally written for the *New Monthly*; by now Hazlitt had adopted the dialogue form as a convenient device for informal presentation of whatever topic he wished to discuss in the *Atlas*.

A remark of Northcote's in Conversation no. 12 (August 30) prompted a series of papers on the subject of Hogarth. "Hogarth and Fielding—Mr. Northcote's Opinions" in the *Atlas* for September 6 contained a letter from Hazlitt signed "Your constant reader" objecting to Northcote's estimate of Hogarth in his last conversation (20:267–69; 11:302); and nos. 13 and 14, in the September 13 and 20 issues, continued the discussion. In the course of the controversy Hazlitt managed to restate his belief that Hogarth was a great comic genius, but did not deserve to be ranked among ideal or universal geniuses. Incidentally in "Conversations as Good as Real (2)," he accorded high praise to Lamb's essay on Hogarth (11:306–9; 20:272–77).

By August 26 he had finished his review of Channing's *Sermons and Tracts* for the *Edinburgh*, and he sent it off apologetically to Napier. "If you think the article I have sent will do," he wrote, "I would beg for a small advance upon it. I would not thus early appear in *forma pauperis*, but the loss of 200£ on my life of Napoleon through the failure of Messrs. Hunt & Clarke has driven me to great straits at the present moment." [16]

16. Ibid.

He was still under heavy pressure, and distress clouded the seventeen maxims which he wrote for the *Atlas* for September 27 and October 4— ironically entitled "Trifles Light as Air." It is a tired old man who is speaking; he resents the changing tastes in contemporary literature, questions notions of human progress. His fourteenth maxim reads:

> The human mind seems to improve, because it is continually in progress. But as it moves forward to new acquisitions and trophies, it loses its hold on those which formerly were its chief boast and employment. Men are better chemists than they were, but worse divines; they read the newspapers, it is true, but neglect the classics. Everything has its turn. Neither is error extirpated so much as it takes a new form and puts on a more artful disguise. Folly shifts its ground, but finds its level: absurdity is never left without a subterfuge. The dupes of dreams and omens of former times, are now the converts to graver and more solemn pieces of quackery. The race of the sanguine, the visionary, and the credulous, of those who believe what they wish, or what excites their wonder, in preference to what they know, or can have rationally explained, will never wear out; and they only transfer their innate love of the marvellous from old and exploded chimeras to fashionable theories, and the *terra incognita* of modern science. (20:284)

An eighteenth maxim, which was withheld from publication, showed even deeper skepticism:

> The French Revolutionists in the "Reign of Terror," with Robespierre at their head, made one grand mistake. They really thought that by getting rid of the patrons and abettors of the ancient *régime* they should put an end to the breed of tyrants and slaves; whereas in order to do this it would be necessary to put an end to the whole human race. (20:432)

"Inconveniences of Rank," Hazlitt's contribution to the *Atlas* for September 27, appeared in the published *Conversations of Northcote* as a long monologue by the artist; it certainly did not represent Hazlitt's thinking at this point in his life. The speaker considers the discomforts suffered by men in high position and those in humble life and concludes, in the best tradition of eighteenth-century popular philosophy, that people in middle circumstances "have little reason to be dissatisfied with our own situation in life," that "every thing has its place and due subordination" (11:314). Certainly Hazlitt himself, at this point, was less than ever in a mood to declare that whatever is, is right.

During the month of October he wrote regularly for the *Atlas*, but most of his contributions were inconsequential. Two, "Covent Garden Theatre" on the fourth and "Our National Theatres" on the eleventh, complained of contemporary conditions in the theater, though both echoed his enduring love of it (20:283–88). "A Newspaper Sketch," on the eighteenth, attacked John Black of the *Morning Chronicle* for his vacillating opinions (20:293–94), and "Conversations as Good as Real, No. 15" (erroneously headed "No. 13"), on the twenty-fifth, rambled from the difficulty of catching a true likeness in a portrait to "Cicero's account of the cardinal virtues" (11:316). But in a second article in the October 11 issue, "Common Sense," Hazlitt gave readers of the *Atlas* heavier fare than usual. He defined common sense as "a kind of mental instinct, that feels the air of truth and propriety as the fingers feel objects of touch"; it is "a rare and enviable quality" unfortunately lacking from some of the ablest men (20:289). Scots have very little of the precious quality, he added; women and the common people have much. And all men need it because, as Hazlitt admits with a hint of regret: "No one can have arrived at years of discretion without knowing or feeling that he cannot take a single step without some compromise with existing circumstances; that the path of life is intercepted with innumerable turnpike-gates, at which he must pay down the toll of his own convictions and of strict justice; that he cannot walk the streets but by tacit allowance" (20:290).

But Hazlitt's major publication for October—his most ambitious work in months—appeared in two articles in the *Edinburgh Review:* the critique of Channing's *Sermons and Tracts* which he had submitted in August and another, of John Flaxman's *Lectures on Sculpture*, which he had written later.

The Channing article was more than a review of *Sermons and Tracts*. Entitled "American Literature—Dr. Channing," it attempted a general estimate of American literature to date, with judicious comments on the work of Washington Irving, Charles Brockden Brown, and James Fenimore Cooper as well as brief notices of Franklin, Crèvecoeur, and Jonathan Edwards. When he dealt with Channing, he made some perceptive observations *à propos* of the "guarded" nature of *Sermons and Tracts:*

And here we will state a suspicion, into which we have been led by more than one Amercian writer, that the establishment of civil and religious liberty is not quite so favourable to the independent formation, and free circulation of opinion, as might be expected. Where there is a perfect toleration—where there is neither Censorship of the press nor Inquisition, the public take upon themselves the task of *surveillance*, and exercise the functions of a literary police, like so many familiars of the *Holy Office*. In a monarchy, or mixed government, there is an appeal open from the government to the people; there is a natural opposition, as it were, between prejudice, or authority, and reason : but when the community take the power into their own hands, and there is but one body of opinion, and one voice to express it, there can be no *reaction* against it ; and to remonstrate or resist, is not only a public outrage, but sounds like a personal insult to every individual in the community. It is differing from the company ; you become a *black sheep in the flock.* There is no excuse or mercy for it. (16 : 325)[17]

On the whole he could not say a great deal in Channing's favor: his conception of human piety and benevolence was unrealistic, his literary criticism was imitative, and his "Analysis of the Character of Napoleon Bonaparte" was based on inaccuracies and failed to recognize either Napoleon's political genius or his intellectual power.

"Flaxman's Lectures on Sculpture" was even less favorable. Hazlitt acknowledged that Flaxman was well grounded in his subject, but lamented his failure to express his ideas in readable form. He was at his best, Hazlitt maintained, when treating the history of sculpture rather than its theory; when he attempted to theorize, he dealt in rules rather than principles and usually erred when he departed from conventional thinking. In short, Flaxman treated sculpture as a science rather than an art; his "tone . . . is dogmatical rather than philosophical" (16 : 339). Not so William Hazlitt; he believed that the development of sculpture owed much to the aspiration of "some village Michael Angelo" who thrilled to the discovery of his power to create a "speaking statue" or a "stately pile" from stone (16 : 344). Again he praised the Elgin marbles, especially the statue of Theseus, observing that by contrast more "finished" pieces like the Apollo Belvedere "fall into an inferior class or style of art" (16 : 353). And he rejected Flaxman's theories of "the ideal" in sculpture and appended some new and pertinent remarks about painted statues.[18]

Hazlitt had reason to be proud of these two articles. He had proved that, given the opportunity, he could still turn out first-rate critical essays. However, Francis Jeffrey, playing the part of elder statesman, was not impressed, and on November 23 he cautioned Napier: "Your American reviewer

17. Hazlitt's disillusionment is reflected in another statement about America in "Trifles Light as Air," no. 17, in the *Atlas:* "I am by education and conviction inclined to republicanism and puritanism. In America they have both ; but I confess I feel a little staggered in the practical efficacy and saving grace of *first principles,* when I ask myself, 'Can they throughout the United States, from Boston to Baltimore, produce a single head like one of Titian's Venetian nobles, nurtured in all the pride of aristocracy and all the blindness of popery ?'" (20 : 283).

18. W. C. Hazlitt (*The Hazlitts,* pp. 189–91) prints the marginal comments which Hazlitt made in his copy of Flaxman's book.

[i.e., the author of the article on American literature] is not a first-rate man —a clever writer enough—but not deep or judicious—or even very fair. I have no notion who he is. If he is young, he may come to good, but he should be trained to a more modest opinion of himself, and to take a little more pains, and go more patiently and thoroughly into his subject." [19] Fortunately for Hazlitt, Napier had already assigned him another major book to review; on November 7 Hazlitt had written: "I am about the Defoe, and shall attend to your advice. The only reason why I presume to think that my articles may do for the Edinburgh (not in the sense in which some people would pretend) is that they make perhaps a variety. If not so good, they are different from others, and so far, are the better for being worse. There are licenses in criticism, as well as in poetry." [20] Though cautious still, he was encouraged.

On November 1 the *Atlas* contained "Conversations as Good as Real (3)," a brief paper in which Northcote, in a testy mood, charged Hazlitt with laying "too much stress on these speculative opinions and abstruse distinctions. . . . You fancy it is the love of truth," he added: "it is quite as much the pride of understanding" (20:295). Then, on November 15, came "Conversations as Good as Real, the Last—Mutual Confessions and Explanations." "I ought to cross myself like the Catholics, when I see you," Northcote began; and, alluding to some remarks about Sir Walter Scott: "You terrify me by repeating what I say" (11:316). Before long he was charging: "You turn your back on the world, and fancy that they turn their backs on you. This is a very dangerous principle. You become reckless of consequences. It leads to an abandonment of character." Hazlitt was immediately on the defensive:

> What you have stated is the best excuse I could make for my own faults or blunders. When one is found fault with for nothing, or for doing one's best, one is apt to give the world their revenge. All the former part of my life I was treated as a cipher; and since I have got into notice, I have been set upon as a wild beast. When this is the case, and you can expect as little justice as candour, you naturally in self-defence take refuge in a sort of misanthropy and cynical contempt for mankind. One is disposed to humour them, and to furnish them with some ground for their idle and malevolent censures. (11:318)

19. *Correspondence of the Late Macvey Napier*, pp. 69–70. It is difficult to believe that Jeffrey, who had read carefully (and revised) so many of Hazlitt's articles, would have had "no idea" who had written the review of Channing. He may well have been trying to warn Napier against accepting Hazlitt as a regular staff member.

20. *Athenaeum*, 15 August, 1919, p. 743.

But his mood soon changed to one of insouciance. "Taking one thing with another," he acknowledged,

> I have no great cause to complain. If I had been a merchant, a bookseller, or the proprietor of a newspaper, instead of what I am, I might have had more money or possessed a town and country-house, instead of lodging in a first or second floor, as it may happen. But what then? I see how the man of business and fortune passes his time. He is up and in the city by eight, swallows his breakfast in haste, attends a meeting of creditors, must read Lloyd's lists, consult the price of consols, study the markets, look into his accounts, pay his workmen, and superintend his clerks: he has hardly a minute in the day to himself, and perhaps in the four-and-twenty hours does not do a single thing that he would do if he could help it. . . . But how am I entitled to make my fortune (which cannot be done without all this anxiety and drudgery) who do hardly any thing at all, and never any thing but what I like to do? I rise when I please, breakfast *at length*, write what comes into my head, and after taking a mutton-chop and dish of strong tea, go to the play, and thus my time passes. (11:319)

And he proceeded to demonstrate his independence by making no further contributions to the *Atlas* during the remaining six weeks of the year.

He may have spent those six weeks in any of several ways: recuperating from another bout of his chronic illness, working on his review of Wilson's *Defoe* for the *Edinburgh* or the revision which he undertook now of North-cote's two-volume *Life of Titian*—or merely taking advantage of his recent payment from Macvey Napier to give himself a respite from weekly dead-lines—possibly spending the Christmas holidays at Winterslow. Lamb was again in touch with him: on November 15 he wrote Walter Wilson that Hazlitt had agreed "to make your book a basis for a review of Defoe's Novels in the 'Edinbro.'"[21] And on December 8 he told Bernard Barton that "Hazlitt has just been defrauded of £100 by his Bookseller-friend's breaking."[22]

Soon after the beginning of the year 1830 he moved from his Bouverie Street lodgings to rooms at 6 Frith Street in Soho.[23] And he began the new year by initiating in the *Atlas* a series entitled "Specimens of a Dictionary of Definitions." These were in the manner of his earlier essay "Common Sense": penetrating investigations of abstract terms seldom enlivened by anecdotes or heightened by his usual graces of style. He seemed determined to prove to the public and the critics how "dry" a writer he could be.

21. *Lamb Letters*, 3:233.
22. Ibid., p. 238.
23. The house is now marked by a plaque set up by the London County Council.

The first essay in the series, "Originality," in the January 3 *Atlas*, grappled at once with some knotty distinctions:

> Originality is any conception of things, taken immediately from nature, and neither borrowed from, nor common to, others. To deserve this appelation, the copy must be both true and new. But herein lies the difficulty of reconciling a seeming contradiction in the terms of the explanation. For as any thing to be *natural* must be referable to a consistent principle, and as the face of things is open and familiar to all, how can any imitation be new and striking, without being liable to the charge of extravagance, distortion, and singularity? And, on the other hand, if it has no such peculiar and distinguishing characteristics to set it off, it cannot possibly rise above the level of the trite and commonplace. This objection would indeed hold good and be unanswerable, if nature were one thing, or if the eye or mind comprehended the whole of it at a single glance; in which case, if an object had been once seen and copied in the most cursory and mechanical way, there could be no farther addition to, or variation from, this idea, without obliquity and affectation; but nature presents an endless variety of aspects, of which the mind seldom takes in more than a part or than one view at a time; and it is in seizing on this unexplored variety, and giving some one of these new but easily recognizable features, in its characteristic essence, and according to the peculiar bent and force of the artist's genius, that true originality consists. (20:296–97)

The rest of the essay was as terse and tightly packed. Hazlitt reiterated his theories that "the greatest works of genius are the earliest," that "the first productions of men of genius are often their best"; he outlined the original characteristics of a dozen painters and authors; he distinguished between originality and singularity; he maintained that "the value of any work of art or science depends chiefly on the quantity of originality contained in it" (20:302)—all in two paragraphs. Readers of the *Atlas* must have been left gasping.

Six days later, on January 9, Hazlitt made his first appearance in Colburn's *Court Journal*, which he and Northcote had dissected six months earlier. Ironically, his first contribution was "Conversations with an Eminent Living Artist, No. 1," a revival of the old series which had supposedly concluded in the *Atlas* for November 15. Northcote appeared again as "N," as he had in the original *New Monthly* papers, and the conversation touched on death, the nature of true beauty, the story of Jack the Giant Killer, the natural grace of children, and so on, in the manner of the first conversations. It was, in fact, almost certainly one of the articles which Campbell had failed to print in 1826 and which either Colburn or Hazlitt had preserved. In it Hazlitt asked the artist's permission to record their conversations, and

Northcote consented, provided Hazlitt "can keep clear of personalities" (11:228).

The following day, January 10, "Specimens of a Dictionary of Definitions, No. 2: The Ideal," appeared in the *Atlas*. This was again a complex subject for summary treatment, but Hazlitt tackled it manfully. "That amalgamation, then," he wrote, "of a number of different impressions into one, which in some sense is felt to constitute the *ideal*, is not to be sought in the dry and desert spaces or the endless void of metaphysical abstraction, or by taking a number of things and *muddling* them all together, but by singling out some one thing or leading quality of an object, and making it the pervading and regulating principle of all the rest, so as to produce the greatest strength and harmony of effect" (20:303-4). Yet his thoughts apparently turned inward again, and he concluded with a hint of ruefulness:

> Self-possession is the *ideal* in ordinary behaviour. A low or vulgar character seizes on every trifling or painful circumstance that occurs, from *irritability* and want of imagination to look beyond the moment; while a person of more refinement and capacity, or with a stronger predisposition of the mind to good, and a greater good sense and pleasurable feeling to second it, despises these idle provocations, and preserves an unruffled composure and serenity of temper. This internal character, being permanent, communicates itself to the outward expression in proportionable sweetness, delicacy, and unity of effect, which it requires all the same characteristics of the mind to feel and convey to others. (20:306)

By January 15 he had finished his review of Wilson's *Defoe*, and he sent it off to Napier, again with an apology and an appeal: "I have done as well as I could. I hope it will do. I hope you will let me know soon. If it is inserted, I shall be glad of a remittance for it as soon as convenient: but though I have put some strength & truth into it, I fear there is very little discretion." [24]

The *Court Journal* for January 30 contained "Conversations with an Eminent Living Artist, No. 2," another rambling dialogue, probably one of those written originally for the *New Monthly Magazine*. It was confined largely to opinions and anecdotes presented by Northcote, among them one which might have had repercussions: "Godwin called here with his daughter. I asked her about Lord Byron; she said his temper was so bad that nobody could live with him. The only way to pass the day tolerably well was to contradict him the first thing in the morning" (11:245). The remark, however, seems to have prompted no response from Hunt or Mary Shelley. They had perhaps decided that Hazlitt was incorrigible.

The next day, January 31, the *Atlas* included the third "Specimens of a

24. *Athenaeum*, 15 August, 1919, p. 743.

Dictionary of Definitions," this one entitled "The Spirit of Controversy."
Again Hazlitt compressed many ideas into few words; while recognizing
the dangers implicit in controversy, he stressed its benefits: keeping men's
minds alert, providing a safe outlet for their innate need for conflict, strength-
ening their beliefs, and the like. "Controversy, therefore," he declared,
"is a necessary evil or good (call it which you will) till all differences of
opinion or interest are reconciled, and absolute certainty or perfect indifference alike takes away the possibility or the temptation to litigation and
quarrels" (20:311).

His article "Wilson's Life and Times of Defoe," in the January *Edinburgh Review*, was, as Lamb had told Wilson, a critique of Defoe's works as
well as of the new biography. The latter Hazlitt pronounced "a very good
book, but spun out to too great a length" (16:364); he complained also that
Wilson was prone to overemphasize Whig principles and that he sometimes
lost sight of Defoe in his attempts to recount the history of his era. Hazlitt
himself focused his attention on Defoe the fighter for freedom rather than
Defoe the novelist, and he warmly defended him as an advocate of liberal
principles—one whose contribution to society had been grossly undervalued. "If an individual differs from you in common with others," he
wrote, "you do not so much mind it—it is the act of a body, and implies no
particular assumption of superior wisdom or virtue; but if he not only differs
from you, but from his own *side* too, you then can endure the scandal no
longer; but join to hunt him down as a prodigy of unheard-of insolence and
presumption, and to get rid of him and his boasted honesty and independence
together" (16:368). Hence Hazlitt's fears that he had shown "very little
discretion" in his review: he had found in Defoe a kindred spirit.

For the February 7 *Atlas* he wrote two short articles of the type that he
had contributed regularly during the previous year. One, "New President
of the Royal Academy," was a tribute to Martin Archer Shee, written up,
according to Charles Cowden Clarke, in a matter of ten or fifteen minutes
(18:184–85).[25] The other, "The Tithes," was a deft reply to the political
economists' claim that farmers would be no better off if tithes were abandoned. Hazlitt summed up his argument in a homely analogy: "There are
two persons sitting down to a roast pullet with greens and bacon; a knock is
heard at the door, it is the clergyman of the place; they deny themselves to
the new and uninvited guest, and finish their repast amicably, though the
squire may be helped to the breast and wings, and the farmer be contented
with the legs and *parson's nose*. Had the rector been in, there would have

25. See 18:442.

been enough for none of the party. This is all the political economy concerned in the case" (19:293–94).

The following week Hazlitt returned to his "Specimens of a Dictionary of Definitions" with no. 4 "Envy" in the *Atlas* for February 14. Again he examined his subject from many angles and presented some shrewd conclusions: that men envy only those who are working (and therefore competing) in their own field; that they are unwilling to credit anyone with excellence in more than a single field ("'but,'" he says, is "the favourite monosyllable of envy and self-love"); that men do not envy the dead or the greatest of their contemporaries; that they envy genius, which is innate, more than learning, which they persuade themselves they might acquire if they were so minded. He even succeeded in finding some good in envy: it has "some connexion with a sense of justice—is a defence against imposture and quackery" (20:314). His powers of analysis had seldom been keener.

Yet for the next six weeks he wrote nothing for the *Atlas;* in fact, except for "Conversations with an Eminent Living Artist, No. 3," in the *Court Journal* for February 20 (11:269–73), he published nothing in any of the periodicals. He had fallen into serious difficulties. "Poor Hazlitt has been arrested on one of those detestable Bills of that detestable firm of Hunt & Clarke for £150, all honestly earned by him, & is at a Lock-up-House," Talfourd wrote to Miss Mitford on February 18; "but I have endeavoured with the aid of Procter [i.e., Barry Cornwall], who is a good fellow in spite of his verses, to induce Basil Montague to procure Bail for him, & I hope I have succeeded."[26] Exactly what happened is not clear: Hazlitt's grandson later stated that "the pecuniary crisis . . . was accelerated by a knavish accountant, introduced to him (in ignorance of his real character, doubtless) by Mr. Hone."[27] Perhaps the knavish accountant induced Hazlitt to endorse the note to a creditor, who discovered its true value.

Montagu or someone else came to the rescue, and Hazlitt was soon released. But he was evidently in no mood—or physical condition—for writing. By March 19, however, he had rallied his energies and was asking Napier for further assignments. "I have looked at [Godwin's new novel] Cloudesley," he wrote, "and think I may make an article of it whether as a failure or successful, if you will give a certain latitude, I do not mean of space but style. I have a design upon Jefferson's Memoirs, if you please, & promise to do it well." Again he was humble and apprehensive: he was not sorry, he told Napier, that someone else had been assigned to review Southey's *Dialogues of Sir Thomas More* "as it is so ably done." And he

26. *TLS,* 27 April, 1956, p. 260. 27. *Memoirs,* 2:235.

added: "I received your remittance and am thankful for that, and still more for your approbation of my last. Pray tell me if there is any hurry: I hope to send you in a fortnight, if I am not prevented by accidents."[28] He chose not to reveal why he was especially grateful for a remittance just now or what accidents had recently befallen him.

Early in April he resumed his contributions to the *Court Journal* and the *Atlas*. The *Journal* for April 3 contained "Conversations with an Eminent Living Artist, No. 4" (11:228–34), which proved to be his last work for that periodical and the last of the conversations to be published. For the *Atlas* of the following day he wrote "An Analysis of Prejudice," which was continued in "Further Thoughts on Prejudice" in the April 18 issue. A similar article, "Party Spirit," appeared in the *Atlas* for April 25. All three essays offered the kind of close analysis that *Atlas* readers had grown accustomed to, the same close-packed succession of ideas set down in a style that recalls Bacon rather than Montaigne or Burke. They abound in aphoristic statements, many of which might stand by themselves or serve as the text of an essay. For example:

> Prejudice in short is egotism: we see a part and substitute it for the whole.... (20:319)

> The most dangerous enemies to established opinions are those who, by always defending them, call attention to their weak sides. (20:319)

> A conformity in sentiment strengthens our party and opinion; but those who have a similarity of pursuit are rivals in interest.... (20:324)

In the meantime Napier had agreed to let Hazlitt review *Cloudesley*, and his article "Mr. Godwin" appeared in the April *Edinburgh*. Again he did not confine himself to the one book but attempted a general estimate of Godwin's achievements. He compared *Cloudesley* unfavorably with Godwin's earlier novels *Caleb Williams* and *St. Leon*; his style, he acknowledged, had improved, but "the spirit of the execution is lost in the inertness of the subject-matter" (16:395). "In a word," he wrote, "the fault of this and some other of the author's productions is, that the critical and didactic part overlays the narrative and dramatic part" (16:401). He offered warm praise, however, of *Political Justice*, remarking again that Godwin was "the first *whole-length* broacher of the doctrine of Utility" (16:404) and that his theories would be admirable "if the author, in a word, could establish as the foundation, what he assumes as the result of his system, namely, the

28. *Athenaeum*, 15 August, 1919, pp. 743–44. The review of Southey's book was written by young Thomas Babington Macaulay.

omnipotence of mind over matter, and the triumph of truth over every warped and partial bias of the heart" (16:405). Incidentally, while considering the falling off in Godwin's work, he made some sympathetic remarks on the plight of the "author by profession":

> He cannot let well done alone. He cannot take his stand on what he has already achieved, and say, Let it be a durable monument to me and mine, and a covenant between me and the world for ever! He is called upon for perpetual new exertions, and urged forward by ever-craving necessities. The *wolf* must be kept from the door: the *printer's devil* must not go empty-handed away. He makes a second attempt, and though equal perhaps to the first, because it does not excite the same surprise, it falls tame and flat on the public mind. If he pursues the real bent of his genius, he is thought to grow dull and monotonous; or if he varies his style, and tries to cater for the capricious appetite of the town, he either escapes by miracle or breaks down that way, amidst the shout of the multitude and the condolence of friends, to see the idol of the moment pushed from its pedestal, and reduced to its proper level. (16:396)

And he closed with an ingenuous statement which might stand as an apology for all his criticism of his contemporaries: "We cannot tell whether Mr. Godwin will have reason to be pleased with our opinion of him; at least, he may depend on our sincerity, and will know what it is" (16:408).

During May and June Hazlitt published no work in any of the periodicals. He may again have been ill or perhaps preparing his *Conversations with Northcote* for publication or revising Northcote's *Life of Titian*. It was probably now too that he wrote the essay "Emancipation of the Jews," which Leigh Hunt published in the *Tatler* in March, 1831, and which Isaac Lyon Goldsmid (later the first Jewish baronet) brought out as a pamphlet. Parliament was considering the first Jewish disabilities bill, introduced in the House of Commons on May 23, 1830, and Hazlitt made use of the occasion to speak once more in behalf of human freedom. His argument was simple: he disposed of the evidence that had been presented against emancipation, insisting that England should have outgrown "Gothic" prejudices. And he summed up his thesis in a few cogent words: ". . . it is the test of reason and refinement to be able to subsist without bugbears" (19:324).

Yet though his mind was still keen, his body was failing. He fell seriously ill and put himself under the care of a physician named Sannier. He was probably more than usually irritable. When his son decided that he would like to study for a career as a singer, he consulted his mother as to how best to broach the idea to his father, and she in turn consulted his friends. Martin Burney seems to have refused to have any part in the scheme, and Sarah asked Lamb whether he or Ayrton would undertake it. Lamb wrote to her on June 3: "I named your thought about William to his father, who expressed such horror and aversion to the idea of his singing in public, that I cannot meddle in it directly or indirectly. Ayrton is a kind fellow, and if you chuse to consult him by Letter, or otherwise, he will give you the best advice, I am sure, very readily. *I have no doubt that M. Burney's objection to interfering was the same with mine.*" [29] Hazlitt had forgotten that only seven years earlier he had written sensibly: "If a boy shows no inclination for the Latin tongue, it is a sign he has not a turn for learning languages. Yet he dances well. Give up the thought of making a scholar of him, and bring him up to be a dancing-master!" (12:66 n.).[30]

He could still, on occasion, revive his old enthusiasm, and he turned out a diverting essay, "The Free Admission," for the July *New Monthly,* celebrating the free admission as "the *lotos* of the mind . . . an antidote for half the ills of life" (17:365) and recalling the delight he had known during his years of theatergoing. The essay amounts to a paean in praise of the theater and the escape from care which it offers—"a relief, a craving, a necessity—one cannot do without it" (17:369–70). He hymns the joys of the play itself, of the spirit of the eager audience, of the great actors whom he has watched. He even declares that he has seen G. H. B. Rodwell's farce *Teddy the Tiler* and Richard John Raymond's opera *Robert the Devil,* both first presented during the preceding February, "thirty times at least . . . and could sit them out thirty times more" (17:370). Through it all echoes his undying love of life; for in the theater, he observes, one "views the pageant of the world played before him; melts down years to moments; sees human life, like a gaudy shadow, glance across the stage; and here tastes of all earth's bliss, the sweet without the bitter, the honey without the sting, and plucks ambrosial fruits and amaranthine flowers (placed by the enchantress Fancy within his reach,) without having to pay a tax for it at the time, or repenting of it afterwards" (17:366). If only William Hazlitt could have looked on at the great spectacle of human life from a comfortable seat in the shadows!

By mid-July his *Conversations with Northcote* was ready for publication. He had assembled the various conversations from the *New Monthly,* the *London Weekly Review,* the *Atlas,* and the *Court Journal,* had added two new ones (nos. 13 and 14), and had made some judicious alterations in the text.[31] Then, without warning, he received from Northcote a panicky letter

29. *Lamb Letters,* 3:281–82.

30. In the previous year, however, he admitted in "On the Conduct of Life" that he had "somehow a prejudice against men-singers" (17:99).

31. Howe records the changes in the notes to volume 11 of *Complete Works.*

enclosing a note from Richard Rosdew, of the Mudge family in Plymouth, threatening to bring suit and to publish Northcote's letter to Campbell "descriptive of the character of your visitor" (i.e., Hazlitt) if the published *Conversations* contained "any of the *false* and *libellous* accounts of the Mudge family" which had appeared earlier.[32] Hazlitt was exasperated. On July 29 he replied to Northcote: "The subject of complaint . . . is entirely & sedulously removed in the forth-coming work. What cause of alarm there is from the evil of passages that are struck out, I can not well comprehend. If there is to be the same outcry about these obnoxious expressions after they have been cancelled as before, they might as well have remained to afford some rational ground for your fears & reproaches. At present, the first appear to me as entirely gratuitous as the others are (in what concerns the papers in their corrected state) unmerited on my part." He could not resist adding: "I cannot pretend to say what the character you have drawn of me is in your letter to Mr Campbell . . . ," and he signed himself "with much respect and some little disappointment."[33] Northcote insisted, however, on canceling six pages of the book, and publication was delayed.[34]

He found some consolation for his personal troubles in the Revolution of Three Days, which ended on the very day when he wrote to Northcote. He had said once that he hoped to live to see the downfall of the Bourbons, and with Charles X's abdication from the throne of France it seemed, once again, to have been accomplished. In an essay which he wrote in August, later published as "Personal Politics," he drew a moral: Charles X was, he acknowledged, a good-natured man—but like all kings, he was jealous of his supposed prerogatives and unwilling to accept constitutional restrictions on them. In a concluding footnote he added: "The Revolution of the Three Days was like a resurrection from the dead, and showed plainly that liberty too has a spirit of life in it; and the hatred of oppression is 'the unquenchable flame, the worm that dies not'" (19:334 n.). Yet when Charles Reynell congratulated him on this latest triumph of the liberal cause, he said only, "Ah, I am afraid, Charles, things will go back again."[35]

32. *ELH* 7 (1940): 326. Some remarks about "old Dr. M——" in "Conversations with an Eminent living Artist," no. 3, in the *Court Journal* for February 20, 1830, had brought objections from Bartholomew Dunsterville, a friend of the Mudge family (see Herschel M. Sikes, "'The Infernal Hazlitt,' *The New Monthly Magazine,* and the *Conversations of James Northcote, R.A.,*" in *Essays in History and Literature Presented by Fellows of the Newberry Library to Stanley Pargellis,* ed. Heinz Blum [Chicago, 1965], pp. 179–91).

33. Baker, pp. 465–66.   34. See Keynes, pp. 100–102.

35. *Four Generations,* 1:197.

Gradually his health declined. Yet he turned even his illness to account in an essay "The Sick Chamber" in the August *New Monthly*. "What a difference between this subject and my last—'a Free Admission!'" he began. "Yet from the crowded theatre to the sick chamber, from the noise, the glare, the keen delight, to the loneliness, the darkness, the dulness, and the pain, there is but one step" (17:371). Then he described vividly the anguish of illness—and, just as vividly, the ease with which the patient forgets it all when health returns. None the less "the machine has received a shock, and it moves more tremulously than before, and not all at once in the beaten track. . . . A cricket chirps on the hearth, and we are reminded of Christmas gambols long ago. The very cries in the street seem to be of a former date; and the dry toast eats very much as it did—twenty years ago . . . . But a book is the secret and sure charm to bring all these implied associations to a focus" (17:375–76). And he decided at last that "if the stage shows us the masks of men and the pageant of the world, books let us into their souls and lay open to us the secrets of our own. They are the first and last, the most home-felt, the most heart-felt of all our enjoyments" (17:376).

On September 6 he asked his son to send off a message to Thomas Norton Longman apologizing for his failure to return some borrowed books:

> Mr. Hazlitt is very sorry that he has been obliged to keep the Pelham, &c. [of Bulwer], but he was not quite sure as to whether he had to write an article respecting them. He has been some time confined to his bed, dangerously, and is consequently unable to take them himself or to see about sending another with them. If Messrs. Longman would direct any of their persons passing in this neighbourhood to call for them, Mr. Hazlitt would feel much obliged: he is already so for the use of them. (17:429)[36]

Yet he continued to work. "The second vol. of the Titian is at p. 304," he wrote to Basil Montagu, "& I will be done this week." He asked: "Could you in the course of today let me have 15£ on account to prevent law expences, which I dread?"[37]

Montagu called Dr. George Darling in on the case. But Hazlitt's health and spirits gradually sank. "Dear Sir, I am dying," he wrote to Francis Jeffrey: "can you send me £10, and so consummate your many kindnesses

36. Patmore (3:155–56) claims that after Hazlitt read Bulwer's *Paul Clifford* he offered to write a critique of all Bulwer's novels for the *Edinburgh*, of which Longman was proprietor.

37. Baker, p. 468.

to me?"[38] According to the actor Macready, he appealed also to Kean for a loan—of fifty pounds—but was refused.[39]

Soon he was "fast failing." He rallied at times; his son wrote hopefully to Catherine Reynell, now living with her family in Le Havre: "My father is much better, and ate a chicken for dinner, but he was disappointed, as he had ordered a fowl, chickens being injurious to him."[40] But when Charles Cowden Clarke visited him, Hazlitt was so weak that he begged his caller to "go into the next room and sit there for a time, as quiet as is your nature, for I cannot bear talking at present."[41] Another friend described later how he "lay, ghastly, shrunk, and helpless, on the bed from which he never afterwards arose. His mind seemed to have weathered all the dangers of extreme sickness, and to be safe and strong as ever. But the physical portion had endured sad decay. He could not lift his hand from the coverlid; and his voice was changed and diminished to a hoarse whistle, resembling the faint scream that I have heard from birds. I never was so sensible of the power of Death before."[42]

Some thought Hazlitt's mind was troubled. On Wednesday, September 15, J. A. Hessey wrote to the poet John Clare: "Poor Hazlitt is very ill indeed—I fear on his death bed—I saw him twice on Monday, but yesterday he was too ill to see me. I fear his mind is quite as ill at ease as his body."[43] And W. H. Reynell wrote to his sister at Le Havre: ". . . on Friday William told me that he was much better . . . but that he had *something in his mind*, which would kill him if he did not dispel it."[44]

38. Carlyle, *Reminiscences*, 2:38–39. Carlyle states that Jeffrey sent Hazlitt a check for fifty pounds, "and poor Hazlitt died in peace, from duns at least." But Talfourd (2:177–78) claims that the check arrived after Hazlitt's death.

39. *Diaries of William Charles Macready*, ed. William Toynbee, 2 vols. (New York: G. P. Putnam's Sons, 1912), 1:90.

40. *The Hazlitts*, p. 358.

41. Cowden Clarke, *Recollections of Writers*, pp. 62–3.

42. *New Monthly Magazine* 29 (1830), pt. 2, p. 478. When reading this and other accounts of Hazlitt's last days, it is perhaps well to bear in mind the words of Richard D. Altick: "The deathbed was . . . the one obligatory scene in nineteenth-century biography, particularly in the earlier decades when biography was most valued as a means of religious and ethical inspiration" (*Lives and Letters* [New York: Alfred A. Knopf, 1965], p. 210). The article "Hazlitt's Deathbed" (apparently by Thomas Holcroft the Younger) in the *Monthly Magazine* for March, 1833, is certainly not to be trusted, although it was widely quoted at the time. William Hazlitt, Jr., objected strenuously to it in a letter to the editor of the *True Sun* dated March 9 and preserved in the collection of the British Museum (Add. MS 38898, fols. 5–6).

43. Edmund Blunden, "New Sidelights on Keats, Lamb, and Others," *London Mercury* 4 (1921): 149.

44. *Memoirs*, 2:238.

In later years the family cherished several details about Hazlitt's last hours: that he asked to see his mother, but she could not make the trip from Crediton—that he told Lamb he was pleased at his son's engagement to Kitty Reynell—that young William distrusted Dr. Darling's method of treatment. There was also the tradition, which has persisted, that his last words were "Well, I've had a happy life."[45] It persisted because, on the surface, the words seemed so very ironical. But there was a world of meaning in that *well*.

There were four men present in Hazlitt's chamber on Saturday afternoon, September 18: his son, the publisher Hessey, Lamb's friend Edward White, and Charles Lamb himself—the friend who, over the years, had proved most loyal, most patient—who, seven years before, had proclaimed to all the world what he firmly believed: that William Hazlitt was "one of the wisest and finest spirits breathing." He might have added: "—and one of the stormiest."

Yet death came to him quietly—so quietly that, for a few moments, even those closest to him did not realize that he had stopped breathing forever.

45. Ibid., pp. 237–38. Thomas Carlyle later claimed that his brother John, a physician, saw Hazlitt during his fatal illness and that "the new doctor people" who were consulted believed that Darling had "fatally mistreated" his patient by submitting him to "a course of purgatives and blue pill, which irrecoverably wasted his last remnants of strength" (*Reminiscences*, 2:38–39).

CHAPTER XVII

Post Mortem

There was no state funeral for William Hazlitt, no burial in the Abbey. Charles Lamb took charge of the arrangements for the committal, which took place in the little churchyard of St. Anne's, Soho, late Thursday afternoon, September 23. Only Hazlitt's son and a handful of friends attended,[1] but others who had admired the dead man paid tribute in other ways. One, Richard Hengist Horne, had a death mask made[2] and cut two locks of hair from Hazlitt's head. Another, probably Charles Jeremiah Wells, set up a marker over the grave with a lengthy inscription hailing Hazlitt as "the unconquered Champion of Truth, Liberty, and Humanity" and describing himself as "one whose heart is with him, in his grave." [3]

The press was disposed to be generous. Leigh Hunt wrote warmly of his old friend in the September 20 *Tatler:* "Mr. Hazlitt was one of the profoundest writers of the day, an admirable reasoner (no one got better or sooner at the heart of a question than he did), the best general critic, the greatest critic on art that ever appeared (his writings on that subject cast a light like a painted window), exquisite in his relish of poetry, an untameable lover of liberty, and with all his humour and irritability (of which no man

1. Talfourd (2:178) stated that "Lamb joined a few friends in attending his funeral," but Patmore wrote in his copy of Talfourd's book: "Not 'a few'—only *one*—myself" (*TLS*, 19 June, 1953, p. 397). See also Patmore, 1:80, 95.

2. The mask is preserved in the Maidstone Museum. Joseph Durham used it in modeling four busts of Hazlitt, one of which was broken.

3. The complete epitaph is reprinted in Howe, pp. 386–87, as is also the much briefer inscription on the marker substituted for the earlier one in 1870. The Church of St. Anne was destroyed during the second World War, and the churchyard has been made into a park. A few of the old markers, including Hazlitt's, survived the destruction and have been left standing.

had more), a sincere friend and a generous enemy." [4] Even *Blackwood's,* willing at last to let bygones be bygones, [5] described Hazlitt in a brief notice in its November issue as "the ingenious author of numerous works, and an extensive contributor to the periodical literature of the day." [6] And the *Literary Gazette,* reviewing *Conversations with Northcote* on September 25, conceded that "though differing widely from their author on most of his opinions, as well as disliking the Cockney dogmatism he so often displayed, we must allow that he produced much that did credit to his abilities."

Hazlitt's sometime friends of the Lakes were less tolerant. Wordsworth, writing to William Rowan Hamilton on September 26, described Hazlitt as "a person for whom I never had any love, but with whom I had for a short time a good deal of intimacy," adding: "He was a man of extraordinary acuteness, but perverse as Lord Byron himself." [7] Coleridge composed a bitter epitaph for his former protege:

> Beneath this stone does William Hazlitt lie,
> Thankless of all that God or man could give.
> He lived like one who never thought to die,
> He died like one who dared not hope to live.

To it he adjoined the comment: "With a sadness at heart, and an earnest hope grounded on his misanthropic sadness, when I first knew him in

---

4. *Leigh Hunt's Literary Criticism,* pp. 658–69. Howe (pp. 368–70, 385) reprints obituaries from the *Atlas* and the *Athenaeum* which he suspects were written by Charles Cowden Clarke and R. H. Horne respectively. The *Gentleman's Magazine* for October contained a long notice made up of a summary of Hazlitt's career and excerpts from the *Atlas* obituary. The *New Monthly* for October contained a perceptive estimate (see below, p. 493–94), and the November issue included an article "Recollections of the Late William Hazlitt" signed "JB" [John Black?].

5. During the last four years of Hazlitt's life *Blackwood's* confined its criticism of him to occasional thrusts in the "Noctes Ambrosianae" series. See, for example, "Noctes" nos. 29 (November, 1826), 32 (April, 1827), and 40 (December, 1828).

6. William Maginn, who had gone on to become editor of the new *Fraser's Magazine,* remained adamant. In a sketch accompanying Daniel Maclise's portrait of Coleridge in *Fraser's* for July, 1833, he damned Hazlitt as "one of the most conspicuous thieves" of Coleridge. "There was," he charged, "not an observation—not a line—in all Hazlitt's critical works, which was worth reading, or remembering, that did not emanate directly from our old friend the Platonist." The charge, which has been too often repeated, is of course groundless; as René Wellek has observed (*A History of Modern Criticism: 1750–1950,* 5 vols. [New Haven: Yale University Press, 1955], 2:188): "Hazlitt's critical thought is based on philosophical assumptions very different from those of Coleridge. What is more important, the critical methods and procedures of the two are utterly different."

7. *Letters of William and Dorothy Wordsworth: The Later Years,* 1:511.

his twentieth or twenty-first year, that a something existed in his bodily organism that in the sight of the All-Merciful lessened his responsibility, and the moral imputation of his acts and feelings." [8]

Hazlitt himself was not silenced by death: though poor in pounds and shillings, he left a sizable body of unpublished material behind him. Colburn and Bentley published his delayed *Conversations with Northcote* within a day or two of his death.[9] Volumes 3 and 4 of the *Life of Napoleon Buonaparte* followed soon afterwards, having been taken over by the firms of Effingham Wilson and Chapman and Hall.[10] And before the end of the year Northcote's two-volume *Life of Titian*, revised by Hazlitt, came out with an appended translation of Stefano Ticozzi's biography of the painter in which both Hazlitt and his son had a share.

Meanwhile, during the last few months of the year, Hazlitt went on speaking his mind in contributions to the periodicals. Most of them had a valedictory air, as if he were seizing his last chance to restate some cherished convictions. "On Footmen," in the September *New Monthly*, was an ironic account of the aimless existence lived by footmen, who serve primarily to bolster their employers' vanity. It ended with a blast against "the lowest class" of the lot, "*literary footmen*," who "without a single grain of knowledge, taste, or feeling, put on the livery of learning, mimic its phrases by rote, and are retained in its service by dint of quackery and assurance alone" (17:359).

The *Monthly Magazine* for October contained Hazlitt's "Paragraphs on Prejudice," a defense of "true prejudice." "It is not always possible," he wrote, "to assign a 'reason for the faith that is in us,' not even if we take time and summon up all our strength; but it does not therefore follow that our faith is hollow and unfounded" (20:324). And once again he expressed his confidence in feeling, in "common sense" and nature, rather than reason: ". . . the greatest, the most solemn, and mischievous absurdities that mankind have been the dupes of, they have imbibed from the dogmatism and vanity or hypocrisy of the self-styled wise and learned, who have imposed profitable fictions upon them for self-evident truths, and contrived to enlarge their power with their pretensions to knowledge." And he declared that "in the

8. *Complete Poetical Works of Samuel Taylor Coleridge*, ed. E. H. Coleridge, 2 vols. (Oxford: Clarendon Press, 1912), 2:962.

9. The *Literary Gazette* reviewer stated that his copy of the book reached the *Gazette* office on Saturday, the eighteenth, the day Hazlitt died.

10. The two volumes may actually have been published before Hazlitt died. As Keynes points out (pp. 96–98), the four volumes were reviewed in the May 2 *Atlas*. However, surviving copies contain a preface and an index written after Hazlitt's death.

little world of our own knowledge and experience, we can hardly do better than attend to the 'still, small voice' of our own hearts and feelings, instead of being browbeat by the effrontery, or puzzled by the sneers and cavils of pedants and sophists, of whatever school or description" (20:328).

The October *Monthly* also contained the first of six installments of "Aphorisms on Man," which appeared in several issues of the magazine between then and the following June. There were seventy in all, many of them even more cynical in tone than Hazlitt's earlier maxims. No. 45, for example, reads:

> A man should never marry beneath his own rank in life—*for love*. It shews good-ness of heart, but want of consideration; and the very generosity of purpose will defeat itself. She may please him and be every way qualified to make him happy: but what will others think? Can he with equal certainty of the issue introduce her to his friends and family? If not, nothing is done; for marriage is an artificial institution, and a wife a part of the machinery of society. We are not in a state of nature, to be quite free and unshackled to follow our spontaneous impulses. Nothing can recon-cile the difficulty but a woman's being a paragon of wit or beauty; but every man fancies his Dulcinea a paragon of wit or beauty. Without this, he will only (with the best intentions in the world) have entailed chagrin and mortification both on himself and her; and she will be as much excluded from society as if he had made her his mistress instead of his wife. She must either mope at home, or tie him to her apron-string; and he will drag a clod and a load through life, if he be not saddled with a scold and a tyrant to boot. (20:342–43)

Immediately following in order, and perhaps in Hazlitt's train of thought, was the acid statement: "I believe in the theoretical benevolence, and prac-tical malignity of man."

There was bitterness, too, in the very title of "Hints to Persons in Busi-ness and Men of the World, the Properly Attending to Which May Save them from Losing Hundreds and Thousands," which remained in manu-script for a century until P. P. Howe published it in his *Complete Works*. There were only ten "hints" in all, but they hit hard. No. 5, for example, reads:

> If you find a person tells lies, believe him—if he is plain and straightforward, turn a deaf ear to what he says, as there is neither interest to amuse nor impudence to browbeat. There is all the difference that there is between poetry and prose, which is just as great in business as it is in books. (20:351)

Compare No. 10:

> If there is a prejudice against any one, believe it and act upon it as if it were true, though you know it to be false. If he is weak and dispirited, depress him still more:

if he is in danger of ruin (through the fault of others or even your own), stretch out your hand, not to save him but to push him over, and then say it was impossible to help him. (20:352)

And so on. Hazlitt seems, in these posthumous articles, to be allowing himself one final lash at a hostile world. He may, of course, have written some of them considerably earlier, and withheld them out of discretion. Or cautious editors may have had misgivings.

If so, he had his revenge in "A Chapter on Editors," which appeared in the November *New Monthly Magazine*. There he rehearsed all the faults of editors that he could think of, but concentrated on their timidity. "If an article has nothing to recommend it, is one of no mark or likelihood, it goes in," he averred; "there is no offence in it. If it is likely to strike, to draw attention, to make a noise, then every syllable is scanned, every objection weighed: if grave, it is too grave; if witty, it is too witty. One way or other, it might be better; and while this nice point is pending, it gives place, as a matter of course, to something that there is no question about" (17:361).

However, the last of his periodical essays, "The Letter-Bell," in the *New Monthly* for the following March, was a pleasant essay in Hazlitt's best genial, reminiscent strain. "Complaints are frequently made of the vanity and shortness of human life," he began, "when, if we examine its smallest details, they present a world by themselves" (17:376). Then he dilated on his enjoyment of the little things in life, wandering from the postman's passing bell to mail-coaches to the new telegraph. He spoke of the revival of his hopes for human freedom since the Revolution of Three Days; he speculated on Wordsworth's reaction to the event, and Coleridge's. And he proudly reaffirmed his own steadfast support of the noble cause: ". . . I have never given the lie to my own soul. If I have felt any impression once, I feel it more strongly a second time; and I have no wish to revile or discard my best thoughts. There is at least a thorough *keeping* in what I write—not a line that betrays a principle or disguises a feeling" (17:378).[11] He had at least the consolation of his own integrity to sustain him.

His son had doubtless overseen the publication of this and the other posthumous pieces. Young William had continued to pay court to Catherine Reynell, and during the early summer of 1831, having some prospects of a

11. W. C. Hazlitt (*The Hazlitts*, pp. 408–9) reprints a notice from the *Atlas* announcing that "A New Theory of Civil and Criminal Legislation" would appear serially in its columns beginning with the issue for January 1, 1832. This was the essay which Hazlitt had begun when he was a student at Hackney and which has been discussed above, pp. 452–53.

position on the staff of the *Morning Chronicle*, he wrote to his mother to announce his engagement. Sarah, who was staying at Crediton with old Mrs. Hazlitt and Peggy, wrote back approvingly (and with abundant advice) on July 10. She asked, incidentally if "Proctor" had written any more recollections and if Patmore had "receded from the assistance he professed affording you in literary matters (which I very much suspect)."[12]

Having published all his father's salable manuscripts, William was preparing a collection of "literary remains" to be prefaced by a biographical essay written by himself and essays of appreciation by some of his father's distinguished friends. On September 13, 1831, Lamb had written him: "I have turned & twisted what you ask'd me to do in my head, & am obliged to say I can not undertake it—but as a composition [compensation?] for declining it, will you accept some verses which I meditate to be addrest to you on your father, & prefixable to your Life? Write me a word that I may have 'em ready against I see you some 10 days hence." In a postscript he added: "Not a line is yet written—so say, if I shall do 'em."[13]

The project moved slowly. Two years later, when Catherine Reynell and William were married on September 8, 1833, the promised volumes still had not appeared. In a letter to John Stuart Mill dated November 19, 1832, Thomas Carlyle had prophesied that "Poor Hazlitt" would "pass away without Biography."[14] But by November 19, 1834, Edward Lytton Bulwer was having "a long and agreeable chat" with Crabb Robinson on the subject of Hazlitt, presumably to aid him in preparing an essay for the projected volumes.[15] And in 1836 they were published by the firm of Saunders and Otley.

Literary Remains of the Late William Hazlitt, in two volumes, opened with a biographical essay by William Hazlitt, Jr., and contained "Some Thoughts on the Genius of William Hazlitt" by Bulwer, "Thoughts upon

12. *Journals*, pp. 261–64. By "Proctor" Sarah meant Bryan Waller Procter ["Barry Cornwall"]. For information about the later history of the Hazlitt family, see Moyne, pp. 14–24, 167. Sarah, who remained on good terms with her husband's family, died in London on November 1, 1840, at the age of sixty-six. Mrs. Grace (Loftus) Hazlitt died at Crediton on June 10, 1837, aged ninety. Her daughter Peggy then went to live with the Reverend Mr. and Mrs. John Johns in Liverpool, where she died on September 19, 1841, at the age of seventy. John Hazlitt came to a melancholy end: he drank to excess, lost his reputation as a painter, was separated from his wife and children, and died at Stockport on May 16, 1837, also at the age of seventy.

13. *Lamb Letters*, 3:323.

14. *Letters of Thomas Carlyle to John Stuart Mill, John Sterling, and Robert Browning*, ed. Alexander Carlyle (New York: Frederick A. Stokes Co., 1923), pp. 28–29.

15. Robinson, 1:449.

the Intellectual Character of the Late William Hazlitt" by Talfourd, Sheridan Knowles's sonnet on Bewick's portrait of Hazlitt, and six other sonnets "by a Lady." By this time Lamb had died, apparently without writing the promised verses; but he was represented by the tribute which he had paid his friend in the *Letter to Robert Southey*.

Of the essays included in the volumes, only two had not been published earlier. One of these, "Definition of Wit," probably intended for the "Specimens of a Dictionary of Definitions" in the *Atlas* for 1830, was an involved analysis of the subject, stressing its complexity, citing the importance of incongruity and absurdity in true wit, and concluding with the candid admission: "I protest (if required) against having a grain of wit" (20:363). The other essay, "Belief, Whether Voluntary," advanced once more Hazlitt's theory that "passion and inclination," rather than reason, determine men's opinions. "In short," he wrote, "we believe just as little or as much as we please of those things in which our will can be supposed to interfere; and it is only by setting aside our own interests and inclinations on more general questions that we stand any chance of arriving at a fair and rational judgment. Those who have the largest hearts have the soundest understandings; and he is the truest philosopher who can forget himself" (20:369).

In this same year, 1836, William Hazlitt, Jr., brought out a new edition of his father's old "metaphysical choke-pear," the *Principles of Human Action*, and an unpublished essay, "The Spirit of Philosophy," appeared in Samuel Carter Hall's annual, *The Amulet*. The latter warned against mistaking prejudices for reasoning, but insisted that "common sense or a certain tact may be said to be the foundation of truest philosophy" (20:371). Ironically, Hazlitt quoted "The Tables Turned"—supposedly Wordsworth's rebuke to him for his preoccupation with metaphysics in 1798—to summarize "the temper and spirit of a true and improved method of philosophizing" (20:374). He worked in also some strictures on the utilitarians for overemphasizing rationalism and on the associationists for carrying a valid theory too far. Hazlitt had indeed "no wish to revile or discard" his best thoughts.

In the course of the next twenty-two years William Hazlitt, Jr., made virtually a secondary profession of bringing out new editions of his father's works. By the time he was forty-seven years old and settled as registrar of the London court of bankruptcy he had issued a dozen volumes of essays, lectures, criticism—even the unfortunate *Life of Napoleon*. He stopped then, but ten years later his son William Carew Hazlitt took up the good work, bringing out new editions of practically all the collections issued by his father and supplementing his career as an editor of literary oddities like the *Elizabethan Jest-Books* by telling and retelling the story of his distinguished forebears in *Memoirs of William Hazlitt* (1867), *Four Generations of a Literary Family* (1897), *Lamb and Hazlitt* (1900), and *The Hazlitts*, parts 1 and 2 (1911–12). Seldom has a penniless man left his heirs so substantial a legacy as William Hazlitt; if it did not make them rich, it at least kept them occupied—for the better part of a century.[16]

Carlyle's fears that Hazlitt would be forgotten proved groundless. His was a character that men could not easily forget, and practically all his distinguished acquaintances—Cornwall, Medwin, Patmore, Haydon, Bewick, DeQuincey, Carlyle, Cyrus Redding, John Clare—included him in their reminiscences. They found him enigmatic, fascinating; they noted his frosty manner as contrasted with his essential warmth and kindliness, his outbursts of anger as opposed to his taciturnity, his harsh treatment of others and his tender sensibilities. Most of them spoke of his eyes—those piercing, snapping eyes. In the fashion of the time they took pages usually to describe him, but Benjamin Haydon, a painter rather than a writer by trade, spoke for them all when he said tersely, "What a singular compound this man was of malice, candour, cowardice, genius, purity, vice, democracy and conceit." [17]

He baffled even his closest friends. They could describe the contradictions in his nature, but they could not explain them. The author of his obituary in the October, 1830, *New Monthly Magazine* understood him better than most. "In general he was not a man of violent temper," he wrote. "He was . . . apt to conceive strong and rooted prejudices against individuals on very slight grounds. But he was a good-hearted man, and ready to render services to individuals who differed materially with him in opinion." Moreover, "it might sometimes have been said to him, 'Perhaps it was right to

16. William Hazlitt, Jr., and his son were undoubtedly motivated in part by a desire to keep Hazlitt's fame alive. Yet they were probably interested in personal profit as well. In fact, after Coventry Patmore discovered some unpublished letters from Hazlitt among his father's papers and sent them to William Hazlitt, Jr., to be destroyed, he was outraged to learn that they had been offered for sale—and he wrote a letter to the *Times* to say so (see J. C. Reid, *The Mind and Art of Coventry Patmore* [London: Routledge and Kegan Paul, 1957], p. 17). Later W. Carew Hazlitt aided Richard Le Gallienne in bringing out Hazlitt's letters to Patmore in a "privately printed" edition of *Liber Amoris*, but he discreetly withheld his name from the title page.

17. Elwin, p. 200. On September 30, 1827, Haydon had recorded that he and Talfourd "talked of Hazlitt, & agreed that we felt inclined to overlook in him every thing villainous, treacherous, mean, dirty, & contemptible, from the apparent candour of his nature" (*Haydon Diary*, 3:225).

dissemble your love, but why did you kick us downstairs?'" Yet he insisted
that Hazlitt was never "deliberately malignant":

> Those who sometimes writhed under the lash of his pen might, perhaps, think him
> malignant; but in his private intercourse, kindly feeling and goodness of heart
> might be recognized. . . . There is a phrase in a modern comedy, of a 'good-natured
> man turned inside out,' and this might have been frequently applied to Mr. Hazlitt.
> He was undoubtedly good-natured, pleasant in conversation, and well disposed,
> frequently enlivening a company by telling comical stories, or amusing anecdotes,
> but sometimes (to use another well-known phrase) he flew off in a tangent.

He explained, also, that "private circumstances . . . contributed to sour his
temper, and to produce a peculiar excitement, which too frequently held
its sway over him."

The last was only too true: ill health, debts, the fall of Napoleon had all
contributed. But the souring of his temper had begun much earlier. His
frequent moves as a child—from Maidstone to Bandon to Philadelphia to
Boston to Wem—had given him no opportunity to form lasting friendships;
his only close ties had been with his parents and his older brother and sister.
He had learned to echo their grown-up talk, to court their approval, to
accept their narrow standards. Yet rebellion was in his blood, and once his
reading had exposed him to the world beyond his father's parsonage, he
rebelled—rebelled at home and even more at the New College at Hackney.
Unfortunately he could not do so without offending his parents—wounding
them—and wounding himself even more. Then came his frustrating
attempts to prove himself, first as a philosopher, later as a painter—and the
humiliation that followed his foolish conduct with the girl at Keswick.

Again he tried to perfect his art and to finish his metaphysical essay. He
married Sarah Stoddart probably less for love than for a meager security
while he strove to develop his talents. But his paintings were still rejected,
and his essay, when finally published, was ignored. As a writer for the magazines he enjoyed some success. Soon, though, he was refusing, like his father
before him, to exercise discretion—stubbornly flaying those who disagreed
with him and, inevitably, exposing himself to painful reprisals. As he wrote
in 1829, he had at first been "treated as a cipher," later "set upon as a wild
beast" (11:318). But it had been his "misfortune (perhaps) to be bred up
among Dissenters, who look with too jaundiced an eye on others, and set
too high a value on their own peculiar pretensions" (17:88). And his defense
was to "take refuge in a sort of misanthropy and cynical contempt for mankind" (11:318).

He turned for a while to lecturing, fleeing periodically to Winterslow, where he solaced himself with the thought that, as a scholar and philosopher, he was ill fitted to cope with a crass world. Then he met Sally Walker, and for a while he believed that he had found happiness at last. But instead he suffered the bitterest disillusionment of all. "I want a hand to guide me," he cried, "an eye to cheer me, a bosom to repose on; all which I shall never have, but shall stagger into my grave, old before my time, unloved and un-lovely" (9:115). He found some temporary relief in his second marriage, his travels on the Continent, and his plans for the *Life of Napoleon* which was to be his masterpiece. But by the time the first two volumes of the book appeared in 1828, he was, at the age of fifty, a disillusioned old man grinding out copy for the newspapers, finding what pleasure he could in books and plays and friendship, striving to temper his cynicism with an air of quiet resignation.

"The *golden mean* is, indeed, an exact description of the mode of life I should like to lead—of the style I should like to write," he declared in 1825; "but alas! I am afraid I shall never succeed in either object of my ambition" (10:297). He certainly never attained it in his life; he was a creature of extremes, often paradoxical extremes: a man of keen intellect and stormy passions, of sagacity and naïveté, of harshness and sensitivity—above all, of pride and humility. When Northcote in one of their conversations remarked, "For any one of real strength, you are the humblest person I ever knew," Hazlitt told him, "It is owing to pride" (11:274).

Certainly he was a proud man. His pride bred even more contradictions in his behavior. He boasted of his self-sufficiency, and his friend Patmore asserted that he "never met with any other man who so little needed society."[18] Yet he had no real self-confidence; he longed for attention—liked, as he admitted, "to be pointed out in the street, or to hear people ask in Mr. Powell's [fives] court, *which is Mr. H——?*" (8:288). He was, in fact, painfully self-conscious, with an odd propensity for studying himself in mirrors. Both Bewick and Haydon tell of finding him seated before a mirror, once practicing his coming lecture, the other time trying to decide how he should wear his hair.[19] He himself wrote in a letter to Patmore: "Looking in the glass to see why I am so hated, I think I see FREEDOM written on my brow."[20] Even more surprising was his remark, during his stay in Edinburgh in 1822, that there were no mirrors "in the best furnished rooms" there (18:167). Evidently he was used to looking for them.

18. Patmore, 2:319.   19. Landseer, 1:145; Elwin, p. 200.
20. *Liber Amoris*, p. 235.

Pride also accounted for his soaring ambitions; he was driven by a longing to distinguish himself as a philosopher or painter or writer—or rackets player. He said in 1820 that he had "a much greater ambition to be the best racket-player, than the best prose-writer of the age" (12:409). Yet in truth he yearned to excel in everything. "A prose-writer would be a fine tennis player," he remarked four years later, "and is thrown into despair because he is not one, without considering that it requires a whole life devoted to the game to excel in it; and that, even if he could dispense with this apprenticeship, he would still be just as much bound to excel in rope-dancing, or horsemanship, or playing at cup and ball like the Indian jugglers, all which is impossible" (12:168). He was fascinated by the myth of Endymion and his longing for the unattainable (6:199); he longed to paint Jacob's dream and could imagine how Rembrandt rose above all concern with self or technique as he strove to master the subject (12:120).

But when he himself tried to paint the scene, he failed; he seemed doomed always to fail. Then came humiliation, which was indeed "owing to pride." He told William Bewick that he could do nothing well—"'Damn it, nothing, Sir'; and when he missed a ball at rackets he shouted in despair, 'Sheer incapacity, by G——.'"[21] Patmore reported that he would "literally dash his head" against the wall when he flubbed a stroke.[22] "In trying to throw a hat or a book upon a table, I miss it," he complained; "it just reaches the edge and falls back again, and instead of doing what I mean to perform, I do what I intend to avoid" (8:101). He was, he virtually admitted, a "self-tormentor . . . never satisfied, come what will." "Let him succeed to his heart's content in all that is reasonable or important," he explained, "yet if there is any one thing (and *that* he is sure to find out) in which he does not get on, this embitters all the rest" (12:238). In the depths of humiliation, after his rejection by Sally, he went so far as to describe himself as a "poor, tortured worm"[23] or "a worm by the way-side, crushed, bleeding, lifeless" (17:107).

A proud man humiliated by repeated failures is bound to feel frustrated, and Hazlitt's sense of frustration went deep. He who had written, "We are not hypocrites in our sleep. The curb is taken off from our passions, and our imagination wanders at will," surely understood the significance of his bouts of sleepwalking, when he would "get up and go towards the window, and make violent efforts to throw it open" (12:19). There was evidence of

21. Landseer, 2:153.
22. Patmore, 3:130.
23. *Journals,* p. 272.

litt's love of mankind and his sympathetic imagination also underlay
icism of art and literature. The pattern can be clearly discerned in his
n of art—even better, in his own work as a painter. He was by choice
aitist: though he tried his hand at landscapes, he seems to have
—or at least saved—none of them. On one occasion he remarked
hat "landscape painting is the obvious resource of misanthropy"
). And William Hazlitt, even in his blackest moments, was never a
santhrope.

irst paintings were strictly realistic. When he painted the portrait of
woman in the bonnet, he strove to reproduce each vein, to catch
dow—to copy what he saw. At the Louvre, however, he lost much
ste for the painstaking Flemish painters and developed a new en-
for Titian and Raphael. These men, he believed, sought not a copy
e but an imitation, as he was later to call it. They were interested
ression"—"giving the soul of nature" (10:130). He decided that
ion is the great test and measure of a genius for painting, and the
" (12:290). It proved to be a test which he himself could not pass.
art critic, however, he sought such expression always in others'
le admired Titian's *Ippolito de' Medici* because the young man
ot to be sitting for a portrait but to have been caught unawares—in
ay would be called a "candid shot." By means of his sympathetic
on Titian had identified with his young sitter, caught the essence
racter, and conveyed it to the viewer. He provided not a mere copy
nitation, not dead nature but nature in action. He worked with
d passion—with *gusto*, which leaves a sting in the mind.
never presented his theories of art in a systematic treatise. Most of
sm concerns specific paintings or collections.[27] He comes closest to
tic discussion in his analysis of Reynolds's *Discourses*, where, as C.
has pointed out, the six "errors" he treats can be reduced to two:
ius or invention consists chiefly in borrowing the ideas of others"
the great style depends on leaving out the details."[28] Hazlitt
oth: for him genius is, above all, original; it is spontaneous, not
or "progressive"; no one can learn by imitating others how to

judicious estimate of Hazlitt's contributions to art criticism, viewed in the
s times, see J. D. O'Hara, "Hazlitt and Romantic Criticism of the Fine Arts,"
esthetics and Art Criticism 27 (1968): 72–85.
First English Romantic Art Critics," *Cambridge Review* 78 (1956): 671–73.
uctory discussion of Reynolds's character Hazlitt complained that the painter
high imagination [and] those strong feelings, without which no painter can
et in his art" (18:58).

ingrained frustration also in his admission: "I hate to be near the sea, and
to hear it roaring and raging like a wild beast in its den" (20:132).

"I want to know why everyone has such a dislike to me," he wrote
plaintively to Leigh Hunt in 1821. Yet he knew well enough; he acknowledged that "those people who are uncomfortable in themselves are disagreeable to others" (17:227)—that "those who are at war with others, are not
at peace with themselves" (16:288). He confessed that he was not "in the
ordinary acceptation of the term, *a good-natured man*" (12:347). Sometimes
he seemed apologetic, claiming that "it is impossible for those who are naturally disagreeable ever to become otherwise" (17:237). More often he was
defensive, calling good nature "the most selfish of all the virtues" (4:100–
101), bragging that he was a good hater, and stating defiantly:

> My standing upright, speaking loud, entering a room gracefully, proves nothing;
> therefore I neglect these ordinary means of recommending myself to the good graces
> and admiration of strangers.... Why? Because I have other resources, or, at least,
> am absorbed in other studies and pursuits. (17:317)

Self-tormentor indeed.

Yet this was the man whose last recorded words were "Well, I've had a
happy life." The qualifying *well* should not be overlooked; Hazlitt had not
forgotten the irritations and frustrations which had soured so much of his
life. But there had been carefree hours too, gained from books and plays
and paintings or from the company of loyal friends, among them his cronies
at the Southampton Coffee House like Martin Burney and William Ayrton
and Joseph Hume. With such men he could relax; in their company, Patmore reported, Hazlitt "tried *not* to shine, but, on the contrary, to be and to
seem not a whit superior to those about him."[24] Unfortunately they left
no account of their impressions of him. But his more literate friends did, and
their reminiscences show that the sparkling conversation at favorite haunts
like the Lambs' house or Haydon's or Hunt's often loosened his tongue, and
he forgot himself and his tribulations. Moreover, he found happiness apart
from superficial pleasures; he had indeed "other studies and pursuits." In
his essay "On the Love of Life" he wrote: "The love of life is, in general,
the effect not of our enjoyments, but of our passions" (4:1). And Hazlitt
was a man of intense passions. Even his amorous passions brought him great
happiness as well as intense pain. But his strongest and longest-lasting
passion, his passion for studying human nature, brought him his truest
happiness.

24. Patmore, 3:74–75.

He was a good lover as well as a good hater—a lover of art and philosophy, of poetry and drama, of nature and pre-eminently of man. "More than all, I like to study man," he told Thomas Medwin.[25] Much as he quarreled with individuals, he was always fascinated by the human spectacle. He loved to observe human nature directly and as he found it reflected in art and literature. His father had taught him a respect for man in the abstract, a zealous desire for religious and political emancipation. But novel-reading had awakened him to the richness and variety of life, and his studies at Hackney had shown him the complexity of human nature. Thereafter he would be interested in Catholics and Protestants, in Anglicans and Methodists, but not in religion itself—though he treated it always with the same respect that he paid to his father.[26] However, it was his conversion to Coleridge's "imaginative creed" and his "metaphysical discovery" of the importance of the sympathetic imagination that confirmed for all time his preoccupation with man and his works.

That discovery brought all his instinctive feelings into focus. He had always been sensitive to the plight of others. "When a boy I had my arm put out of joint," he wrote in *Principles of Human Action*, "and I feel a kind of nervous twitching in it to this day whenever I see any one with his arm bound up in consequence of a similar accident" (1:24). He described himself as one of those "disagreeable people" who "feel an interest in what does not concern them," who "have as much regard for others as they have for themselves," who are "general righters of wrongs and redressers of grievances," who "not only are annoyed by what they can help, by an act of inhumanity done in the next street, or in a neighbouring country, by their own countrymen . . . but a piece of injustice done three thousand years ago touches them to the quick" (4:101–2). And he summed up the creed which underlay his life's work when he wrote in 1821: "To be a hero, is . . . to lose the sense of our personal identity in some object dearer to us than ourselves" (20:104). The statesman, the artist, or the writer who had this power of sympathetic imagination, he who could truly *feel with* others, won Hazlitt's undying allegiance. He hoped to achieve a similar imaginative response in his own writing and to inspire it in his readers.

His political criticism, consequently, has distinct limitations. He was not deeply read in the history of English politics; he cared little for theories of

25. *Fraser's Magazine* 19 (1839): 278.

26. Haydon declared that he "never heard any sceptic but Hazlitt discuss [the validity of the Christian religion] with the gravity such a question demanded" (Elwin, p. 300). On at least one occasion he seemed more than merely respectful when he asked, "What proved Jesus Christ the Son of God hardly less than his miracles?" (19:66).

government, even for the abstract rights of m
observed in the preface to his *Political Essays:*
less can I be said to be a party-man: but I ha
contempt for its tools; and this feeling I have e>
ly as I could" (7:7). He was, he decided, "a
staked health and wealth, name and fame upo
and to the last gasp, is this, that there is a po
government and its governors" (14:236). A
'to be wise were to be obstinate,'" he wrote i
great a philosopher as the best of them; for
fixed and as incorrigible to proof as need
consequence of the pains, the anxiety, and t
me" (17:22). He had, as he said, "set out i
tion"; it had seemed like "the dawn of a
see "the night of despotism" return (17:1
commentary, accordingly, was nostalgic:
arguments for a new system, he lamented
sympathized with those of the lower order
from reactionary legislation. "The question
I and all mankind are born slaves or free'
beliefs, his statement of them can be stir
vince a nonbeliever. Hazlitt himself, h
accomplish more through feeling than thr

He was not ashamed of being a good h
its forms, reserving his most mordant ha
once admired but who had abandoned tl
sacrificed my friends," he stated candidly
(17:313)—he might have said "prejud
mently, he hated those like the utilitaria
supposing that they could solve the ills of
He wrote truly: "I place the heart in
(12:193).

He was a good lover too, after his fash
shared his unflagging loyalty to the cause
was one of those, and he revered him fo
There was always Napoleon too, and
But few readers agreed with his impas
and they survive today largely becau
some men will ever prize them for
glows through them.

27. For
context of
Journal of

28. "Th
In his intro
lacked "tha
become a p

exercise his sympathetic imagination. Moreover, he believed that an artist who sought some vague "ideal" or abstraction, "giving general appearances without individual details" (8:9), failed to reflect life truly. And that was basic: art must "anchor in nature" (12:334); he prized the Elgin marbles, which managed to fuse exact detail and grand design, far above the later, "idealized" Greco-Roman statues.[29]

Always he emphasized the subject of the painting—or, more properly, the feeling which it conveyed to the viewer. He had little to say of selection or composition, of line or coloring. "There is no rule for expression," he declared. "It is got at solely by feeling" (8:38). Yet though he disdained neoclassical rules, he was never a full-fledged Romantic. Originality and feeling and imagination were important to him, but so too was verisimilitude. He was a Romantic realist or a realistic Romantic—as little a "party man" in art as in politics.

His literary criticism sprang from the same roots; it too was an individual blend of realistic and Romantic, grounded in his interest in life and strengthened by his confidence in the sympathetic imagination.[30] He was never a critics' critic; he showed little interest in poetic technique. He protested that he did "not come to the task with a pair of compasses or a ruler in my pocket, to see whether a poem is round or square, or to measure its mechanical dimensions" (6:301). He sought "rather to direct attention to objects of taste, than to dictate to it" (10:222).

He was, truly, a readers' critic, a reviewer, one of the "tasters for the public," as he called them. He believed that poetry had much to offer the public—more than painting ever could because "painting gives the object itself; poetry what it implies" (5:10). Since it deals with "the flowing, not the fixed" (5:3), poetry comes closer to life; it can reach beyond the visual arts, can engage the sympathetic imagination, can enable readers to identify

29. See Stephen A. Larrabee, "Hazlitt's Criticism of Greek Sculpture," *Journal of the History of Ideas* 2 (1941): 77–94.

30. The philosophical basis of Hazlitt's criticism has been the subject of several monographs since J. M. Bullitt called attention to the tie between *Principles of Human Action* and Hazlitt's critical doctrines (see above, p. 85). Although their conclusions vary to some extent, all agree that Hazlitt was influenced by associational psychology as well as his theory of the sympathetic imagination. See, for example, J. C. Sallé, "Hazlitt the Associationist," *Review of English Studies*, 15 (1964):38–51; William P. Albrecht, *Hazlitt and the Creative Imagination* (Lawrence: University of Kansas Press, 1965), esp. chap. 1; J. D. O'Hara, "Hazlitt and the Functions of the Imagination," *PMLA* 81 (1966):552–62; and Albrecht and O'Hara, "More on Hazlitt and the Functions of the Imagination," *PMLA* 83 (1968): 151–54. For an earlier treatment of the subject, see Elisabeth Schneider, *The Aesthetics of William Hazlitt* (Philadelphia: University of Pennsylvania Press, 1933).

with others, lifting them above their own concerns, like true heroes. The poet thus imparts "informing principles" (5:11) which influence men's feelings and guide their conduct better than mere reason can; for always "those who have the largest hearts have the soundest understandings" (20:369).

Yet these "informing principles" must be more than a spontaneous overflow of subjective feeling. Hazlitt was most at ease when criticizing dramatic poetry; it was, he believed, the highest form of poetry because it offered a poet his best opportunity to achieve an objective view of life. By exercising his sympathetic imagination he could get inside the minds of his characters, see life as they see it, and formulate universal ideas of value to his readers. Always his emphasis was on the subject, its reflection of life, and its effect on the reader. He paid little attention to lyric poetry; or when he did, he concentrated on its concrete images, deploring "abstraction" when he encountered it, and often ignoring auditory appeal. He seldom mentioned sound effects, even when criticizing operas.

Shakespeare, "the least of an egotist that it was possible to be" (5:27), was, of course, his favorite. He could identify with character after character; he was "the Proteus of the human intellect" (8:42); chameleonlike he could take on the color of each of his characters. Hazlitt preferred the tragedies to the comedies because they engaged men's sympathetic imagination more, could give them "a high and permanent interest, beyond ourselves, in humanity as such" (4:200). By contrast comedy tends to "disconnect" our sympathies (6:23)—though elsewhere Hazlitt complained that Shakespeare's comic Muse was "too good-natured and magnanimous" because it failed to "take the highest pleasure in making human nature look as mean, as ridiculous, and contemptible as possible" (6:35). For him "the golden period of our comedy was just after the age of Charles II, when the town first became tainted with the affectation of the manners and conversation of fashionable life" (6:37) and the comic writer could ply his scalpel to expose "the difference between what things are, and what they ought to be" (6:5).

Always, however, Hazlitt favored tragedy, and he professed to see a steady decline in English literature after Shakespeare. Poetry of the imagination had given way to poetry of fancy in the reign of Charles I, then poetry of wit in the Restoration and the reign of Queen Anne, poetry of "mere common places, both in style and thought" in the late eighteenth century, and finally poetry of paradox since the French Revolution (5:82–83). Wordsworth, Byron, and Shelley were too egotistical to win his wholehearted approval; their poetry was hobbled by their own eccentric personalities and interests—they were subjective rather than truly original, and they failed to offer informing principles of universal value.

Obviously Hazlitt had limitations as a critic. Although he had immersed himself in Shakespeare and was well acquainted with recent English literature and philosophy, he was not well grounded in other literature. He confessed, on one occasion, to a "want of general reading" (17:313), but he was more likely to affect a scorn for "mere literary drudges" (8:71). His criticism suffered too from a similar scorn for system or thoroughness or sometimes even consistency. And in his eagerness to state the claims of the poetic imagination, he often overlooked the importance of poetic craftsmanship.

Yet he had great strength as a critic too. England had had systematic critics in the past; there was room for originals, men preoccupied with psychological effect rather than technique—above all, for men with open minds. And Hazlitt was such a man. He was not bound by convention, old or new; he was the first critic to take the novel seriously as literature, declaring that *Pilgrim's Progress, Robinson Crusoe* and Boccaccio's tales "come as near to poetry as possible without absolutely being so" (5:13); he could discern the merits of "masters of the artificial style of poetry" (5:68) like Dryden and Pope as few of his Romantic contemporaries could; and he praised the work of Wordsworth and Scott when he thought it deserved praise, even though he deplored their political principles.

His judgments have stood the test of time admirably. His theory of the sympathetic imagination helped break down the hard molds of neoclassical criticism; his insights into earlier writers, notably Shakespeare, still hold good; and his estimates of his contemporaries—especially those in *The Spirit of the Age*—have proved generally valid. As René Wellek has put it, he discerned "the best of his time remarkably well."[31] He remains a readers' critic, a *humane* critic, belonging to no one school but blending romantic and realistic as they are blended in normal human beings. He was his own man, convinced that literature should be a reflection of life, that the poetic genius should teach men to understand life, and that criticism should reveal what literature has to offer man. In his own criticism he strove always to hold men's attention, and it has retained that power. If at times his opinions seem to border on the obvious, it is because later critics have taken his conclusions as their premises. In his own time he was considered startlingly original— even "paradoxical."[32]

31. Wellek, *History of Modern Criticism*, 2:210.
32. In the later chapters of *Hazlitt and the Creative Imagination*, Albrecht presents a penetrating analysis of Hazlitt's criticism and his style.

Inevitably his interest in humanity shines most clearly in his familiar essays. Some of the best loved—"The Fight," "Persons One Would Wish to Have Seen," "My First Acquaintance with Poets," and the like—are vivid sketches of life itself, of human beings in action, viewed from Hazlitt's favorite stance as "a silent spectator in the mighty scene of things" (8:91). The more characteristic essays explore facets of human character: "The Love of Life," "The Fear of Death," "Why Distant Objects Please," "The Pleasure of Hating." These are often studded with gems of perception, "paradoxes" again, apparently new and original, yet, as Hazlitt himself said of Rembrandt's paintings, disclosing "what is before our eyes and under our feet, though we have had no suspicion of its existence, for want of sufficient strength of intuition, of determined grasp of mind to seize and retain it" (8:43).

In his essay "On the Causes of Popular Opinion" Hazlitt observed that his writings were "not, then, so properly the works of an author by profession, as the thoughts of a metaphysician expressed by a painter. . . . They are subtle and difficult problems translated into hieroglyphics," he explained. "I thought for several years on the hardest subjects, on Fate, Free Will, Foreknowledge absolute, without ever making use of words or images at all, and that has made them come in such throngs and confused heaps when I burst from that void of abstraction" (17:311–12). He was born with an inquisitive mind; he honed it by reading the philosophers and puzzling over his "metaphysical discovery." But his metaphysics had been largely confined to psychology, and he had developed his skills in character analysis during long sessions of quiet observing and listening to others. According to Patmore, he "never fairly *looked* at anybody; and yet, having once seen a person, he . . . could trace 'the mind's observance in the face' with a sagacity almost superhuman." "I am infallible in reading a face," he boasted.[33] And to Medwin: ". . . more than all, I like to study man."

He complained on occasion that he was "deficient in the faculty of imagination" (12:224). "The only faculty I do possess," he wrote elsewhere, "is that of a certain morbid interest in things, which makes me equally remember or anticipate by nervous analogy whatever touches it" (12:347). He had, in fact, a vivid memory for "things," especially for people and their actions.[34] And it was from his memory of his experiences and his reading that

33. Patmore, 3:123.

34. Although Hazlitt said that he had "not a particle" of "local memory" (12:347), Lamb (*Letters*, 2:124) and Patmore (3:63) testify to his remarkable memory for conversations and for details of paintings which he had not seen for years. Note also his extraordinary memory for quotations—which he obviously did not bother to check.

he drew the store of "hieroglyphics" or "images" that brighten the essays.

For a man of his era and class he had a rich lode of experience to mine. By the time he wrote his first essays he had lived in England, Ireland, America, and France; he knew the life of quiet farms, sleepy villages, bustling towns, and noisy cities. He had studied philosophy and theology, literature and painting; had spent hours in Parliament and the theater; had hobnobbed with clergymen and rackets players, poets and coffeehouse politicians, philosophers and streetwalkers. He had read widely too, if not systematically: he knew plays and novels galore—the kind of literature which presented people in action.

As time passed and troubles bore down on him, he drew more and more on his own character to illustrate his points. In the second volume of his *Table-Talk* his self-revelation often makes uncomfortable reading. Yet though subjective, he was never egotistical: he might be plaintive or defensive, but he never pontificated. He told all—most startlingly in *Liber Amoris*. As Lord David Cecil phrased it, "No one ever edited his personality for publication less." [35]

In truth Hazlitt did very little editing either before or after the fact. In writing, as in all else, he acted on impulse, often at the last possible moment. "How often have I put off writing a letter till it was too late!" he reflected in "The Letter-Bell." "How often had to run after the postman with it . . .! I do not recollect having ever repented giving a letter to the postman, or wishing to retrieve it after he had once deposited it in his bag. What I have once set my hands to, I take the consequences of, and have been always pretty much of the same humour in this respect" (17:379). When asked to write "an article on a difficult subject for an Encyclopedia and . . . advised to take time and give it a systematic and scientific form," he replied that he "had taken time to do all that I ever pretended to do, as I had thought incessantly on different matters for twenty years of my life" (8:47). He spent little time assembling or organizing his thoughts. "A practised writer ought never to hesitate for a sentence from the moment he sets pen to paper, or think about the course he is to take," he stated. "He must trust to his previous knowledge of the subject and to his immediate impulses, and he will get to the close of his task without accidents or loss of time" (12:61). And similarly: ". . . after I begin [these essays], I am only anxious to get to the end of them, which I am not sure I shall do, for I seldom see my way a page or even a sentence beforehand" (8:6). He began with an idea and

35. Lord David Cecil, *The Fine Art of Reading* (London: Constable and Co., Ltd., 1957), p. 247.

followed wherever it led him—followed swiftly, because he refused to believe that "rapidity of execution necessarily implies slovenliness or crudeness"— maintaining, rather, that "it is often productive both of sharpness and free-dom" (12:62). In effect Hazlitt's basic technique was the artless technique of fine conversation.

He was regarded as a taciturn man; yet Cornwall, Talfourd, and the Cowden Clarkes all testify that, when he was once jolted from his brooding silence, he could talk brilliantly. He may not have cultivated the effects of conversation when he first began writing for a popular audience. He was writing then under the pressure of rigid deadlines, turning out pages of copy at short order, and he could not afford to weigh each word. "Many of these articles . . . are unavoidably written over night, just as the paper is going to the press, without correction or previous preparation," he wrote in his *Edinburgh Review* essay "On the Periodical Press."

> Yet they will often stand a comparison with more laboured compositions. It is curious, that what is done at so short a notice should bear so few marks of haste. In fact, there is a kind of *extempore* writing, as well as *extempore* speaking. Both are the effect of necessity and habit. If a man has but words and ideas in his head, he can express himself in a longer or a shorter time (with little practice), just as he has a motive for doing it. Where there is the necessary stimulus for making the effort, what is given from a first impression, what is struck off at a blow, is in many respects better than what is produced on reflection, and at several heats. (16:222 n.)

Soon he was deliberately seeking for conversational effects; he liked the relaxed, meandering method, the spontaneous, extempore manner, and so did most of his readers. As he wrote in the advertisement to his Paris edition of *Table-Talk*, he felt that he could achieve "a greater variety and richness, and perhaps a greater sincerity, than could be attained by a more precise and scholastic method" (8:333). His confidence was borne out by others of his pet theories: that French painters marred their work by expending too many pains on it, that his own preliminary sketches were superior to his finished paintings, that practice in the arts does not make perfect, that the feeling conveyed by any work of art is more important than any prin-ciple of technique. He wrote rapidly and revised little; his friends marveled at his speed in composition and the few corrections he made, and his surviving manuscripts are singularly free of revisions. He himself wrote frankly: "I have . . . time on my hands to correct my opinions, and polish periods: but the one I cannot, and the other I will not do" (8:79).

Actually there were few "periods" in Hazlitt's writing. He eschewed the more studied forms of syntax: periodic or balanced sentences, inversions, rhetorical questions, and the like. His sentences varied greatly in length and complexity, but they adhered usually to the straightforward patterns of subject-verb-object. He adapted his tone and his rhythm to accord with his subject; now terse, now lyrical, he aimed to catch the "natural measure of prose in the feeling of the subject and the power of expression in the voice" (12:8). But he spurned mere decorative effects. "As an author," he wrote, "I endeavour to employ plain words and popular modes of construction, as were I a chapman and dealer, I should common weights and measures" (8:244). His preoccupation with feeling sometimes led him to lapse into sentimentality or rhapsody. But he was seldom false and never dull. Whatever his subject—even in his political essays—he speaks with the "ease, force, and perspicuity" (8:242) which he recommended in his essay "On Familiar Style." For him the essay was not an art form but a means to an end. As he modestly put it, "In seeking for truth I sometimes found beauty" (9:30).

In some ways Hazlitt's style has proved disadvantageous. In his own time even liberal critics bridled at his breezy manner, assuming that facility was a sure sign of superficiality; they failed to probe to the core of his critical principles. Moreover, his fame was and is confined largely to English-speaking countries, probably because translators have quailed at the challenge of approximating his style in another language. Twentieth-century readers, brought up in the Hemingway tradition, sometimes balk at his long sentences and his interminable paragraphs, at the quotations which tumbled from his retentive memory, and at his very intensity, which, undeniably, can prove exhausting. But professional writers continue to admire him; those who have struggled to keep their sentences natural and sparkling can only wonder at his success. He is, par excellence, the writers' writer. Stevenson was by no means the last to concede that, "though we are mighty fine fellows nowadays, we cannot write like Hazlitt." [36] Part of the trouble is that few writers have personalities as rich and varied as his, for with him style was indeed the man himself: masculine yet delicately perceptive, impulsive yet incisive, sometimes sentimental, often ill-tempered, yet unfailingly humane. It gives vitality and charm to discussions of political affairs and paintings and poems which would otherwise have been long since forgotten.

In his essay "On the Fear of Death," written probably in 1825, Hazlitt reflected: "I should like to see some prospect of good to mankind, such as my life began with. I should like to leave some sterling work behind me. I should like to have some friendly hand to consign me to the grave. On these

36. *Travels and Essays of Robert Louis Stevenson* (New York: Charles Scribner's Sons, 1909), p. 157.

conditions I am ready, if not willing, to depart. I could then write on my tomb—GRATEFUL AND CONTENTED!" (8:325–26).

By September of 1830 he had seen the downfall—once again—of the Bourbon dynasty as a possible fulfillment of his hopes of good for mankind. He had, too, faithful Charles Lamb to consign him to the grave—though surely his was not the hand that Hazlitt had had in mind in 1825. But he could hardly have believed that he was leaving any sterling work behind him. He knew, undoubtedly, that he had made no lasting contribution to philosophy, as he had hoped to do. Of his less ambitious works, many were still buried in the files of old newpapers and magazines, those that had been published had seldom reached a second edition, and his proposed masterpiece, the *Life of Napoleon*, had proved a dismal disappointment. He had no reason to suppose that future admirers would devote untiring efforts to ferreting out his forgotten writings, analyzing the complexities of his thinking, piecing together the fragmentary records of his life, and searching for the key to his paradoxical character.

But there was something about William Hazlitt and his work that the world would not willingly let die.

Index